NEURONAL DYNAMICS

What happens in our brain when we make a decision? What triggers a neuron to send out a signal? What is the neural code?

This textbook for advanced undergraduate and beginning graduate students provides a thorough and up-to-date introduction to the fields of computational and theoretical neuroscience. It covers classical topics, including the Hodgkin–Huxley equations and Hopfield model, as well as modern developments in the field such as Generalized Linear Models and decision theory. Concepts are introduced using clear step-by-step explanations suitable for readers with only a basic knowledge of differential equations and probabilities, and richly illustrated by figures and worked-out examples.

End-of-chapter summaries and classroom-tested exercises make the book ideal for courses or for self-study. The authors also give pointers to the literature and an extensive bibliography, which will prove invaluable to readers interested in further study.

WULFRAM GERSTNER is Director of the Laboratory of Computational Neuroscience and a Professor of Life Sciences and Computer Science at the École Polytechnique Fédérale de Lausanne (EPFL) in Switzerland. He studied physics in Tübingen and Munich and holds a PhD from the Technical University of Munich. His research in computational neuroscience concentrates on models of spiking neurons and synaptic plasticity. He teaches computational neuroscience to physicists, computer scientists, mathematicians, and life scientists. He is co-author of *Spiking Neuron Models* (Cambridge University Press, 2002).

WERNER M. KISTLER received a Master's and PhD in physics from the Technical University of Munich. He previously worked as Assistant Professor in Rotterdam for computational neuroscience and he is co-author of *Spiking Neuron Models*. He is now working in Munich as a patent attorney. His scientific contributions are related to spiking neuron models, synaptic plasticity, and network models of the cerebellum and the inferior olive.

RICHARD NAUD holds a PhD in computational neuroscience from the EPFL in Switzerland and a Bachelor's degree in Physics from McGill University, Canada. He has published several scientific articles and book chapters on the dynamics of neurons. He is now a post-doctoral researcher.

LIAM PANINSKI is a Professor in the statistics department at Columbia University and co-director of the Grossman Center for the Statistics of Mind. He is also a member of the Center for Theoretical Neuroscience, the Kavli Institute for Brain Science and the doctoral program in neurobiology and behavior. He holds a PhD in neuroscience from New York University and a Bachelor's from Brown University. His work focuses on neuron models, estimation methods, neural coding and neural decoding. He teaches courses on computational statistics, inference, and statistical analysis of neural data.

NEURONAL DYNAMICS

From Single Neurons to Networks and Models of Cognition

WULFRAM GERSTNER

WERNER M. KISTLER

RICHARD NAUD

LIAM PANINSKI

CAMBRIDGE
UNIVERSITY PRESS

CAMBRIDGE
UNIVERSITY PRESS

University Printing House, Cambridge CB2 8BS, United Kingdom

One Liberty Plaza, 20th Floor, New York, NY 10006, USA

477 Williamstown Road, Port Melbourne, VIC 3207, Australia

314-321, 3rd Floor, Plot 3, Splendor Forum, Jasola District Centre, New Delhi - 110025, India

79 Anson Road, #06-04/06, Singapore 079906

Cambridge University Press is part of the University of Cambridge.

It furthers the University's mission by disseminating knowledge in the pursuit of
education, learning and research at the highest international levels of excellence.

www.cambridge.org
Information on this title: www.cambridge.org/9781107635197

© Cambridge University Press 2014

First published 2014
Reprinted 2015

A catalogue record for this publication is available from the British Library

Library of Congress Cataloging in Publication data
Gerstner, Wulfram.
Neuronal dynamics : from single neurons to networks and models of cognition / Wulfram Gerstner,
Werner M. Kistler, Richard Naud, Liam Paninski.
pages cm
ISBN 978-1-107-06083-8 (Hardback : alk. paper)
ISBN 978-1-107-63519-7 (Paperback : alk. paper)
1. Neurobiology. 2. Neural networks (Neurobiology). 3. Cognitive neuroscience.
I. Kistler, Werner M., 1969– II. Naud, Richard. III. Paninski, Liam. IV. Title.
QP363.G474 2014
612.8–dc23 2013047693

ISBN 978-1-107-06083-8 Hardback
ISBN 978-1-107-63519-7 Paperback

Contents

Preface

This textbook for advanced undergraduate and beginning graduate students provides a systematic introduction into the fields of neuron modeling, neuronal dynamics, neural coding, and neural networks. It can be used as a text for introductory courses on Computational and Theoretical Neuroscience or as main text for a more focused course on Neural Dynamics and Neural Modeling at the graduate level. The book is also a useful resource for researchers and students who want to learn how different models of neurons and descriptions of neural activity are related to each other.

All mathematical concepts are introduced the pedestrian way: step by step. All chapters are richly illustrated by figures and worked examples. Each chapter closes with a short summary and a series of mathematical Exercises. On the authors' webpage Python source code is provided for numerical simulations that illustrate the main ideas and models of the chapter (http://lcn.epfl.ch/~gerstner/NeuronalDynamics.html).

The book is organized into four parts with a total of 20 chapters. Part I provides a general introduction to the foundations of computational neuroscience and its mathematical tools. It covers classic material such as the Hodgkin–Huxley model, ion channels and dendrites, or phase plane analysis of two-dimensional systems of differential equations. A special focus is put on the firing threshold for the generation of action potentials, in the Hodgkin–Huxley models, as well as in reduced two-dimensional neuron models such as the Morris–Lecar model.

Part II focuses on simplified models for the dynamics of a *single* neuron. It covers nonlinear integrate-and-fire models with and without adaptation, in particular the quadratic and exponential integrate-and-fire model, as well as the Izhikevich model and adaptive exponential integrate-and-fire model. The question of noise in the neural dynamics is posed and two classic descriptions of noise are presented. First, stochasticity arising from random spike arrival: this approach leads to a noise term in the differential equation of the voltage, and can be formulated as a Langevin equation. Second, intrinsic stochasticity of neurons leading to an "escape" across the firing threshold even when the neuron is in the subthreshold regime: this approach leads to the framework of a Generalized Linear Model which is systematically introduced and discussed in applications of neuronal coding and decoding. The relation between the neuron models of Part II and biological data is highlighted and systematic parameter optimization algorithms are presented.

Part III takes the simplified models derived in Part II and builds networks out of these. The collective properties of the network dynamics are described in terms of equations for the population activity also called the population firing rate. The conditions under which population activity can be described by a standard rate model are identified.

Part IV makes the link from dynamics to cognition. The population activity equations are used for an analysis of famous paradigms of computational and cognitive neuroscience, such as the neural activity during decision making or memory retrieval. In Part IV we also sketch the theory of learning in relation to synaptic plasticity. The book closes with a fascinating application of the principles of neuronal dynamics to help patients suffering from Parkinson's disease.

A small fraction of the text of the present book is based on *Spiking Neuron Models* (Cambridge University Press) which was first published in 2002 and has been reprinted several times since then. In the meantime, the field has changed and we felt that a simple update of *Spiking Neuron Models* for a second edition would not be enough to give credit to the developments that have occurred.

Scientifically, the scope of *Spiking Neuron Models* was limited in several respects. First, it mainly focused on *linear* integrate-and-fire models, and mentioned their nonlinear counterparts only in passing. In the present book, nonlinear integrate-and-fire models are treated in a full chapter. Second, adaptation was neglected in the treatment 10 years ago – mainly because population equations for adaptive neurons were not yet available. In the present book, adaptive integrate-and-fire models are covered at length in a separate chapter and the population activity equations for adaptive neurons are derived. Third, while the Spike Response Model with escape noise has always contained all the features of a Generalized Linear Model (GLM), by the year 2002 the theory of GLMs had not yet found its way into the field of neuroscience and was therefore simply absent from the original book. Given the phenomenal rise of GLMs in neuroscience, the theory of GLMs for fitting neuronal data is given a prominent role in this book. Finally, during teaching we always felt the need to show famous applications of the principles of neuronal dynamics, such as retrieval of contents from associative memories or decision dynamics and the neuroscience of free will. The present book covers these topics.

On a more general level, we felt that it would be useful to have a book that is, from the beginning, designed as a textbook rather than a monograph. Therefore, the present book makes the link to experimental data more visible, has more explanatory text, and, last but not least, provides a series of exercises that have already been tested in the classroom over several years.

We hope that this book will be useful for students and researchers alike.

Wulfram Gerstner, Werner Kistler, Richard Naud, Liam Paninski

Advice to the reader

Each chapter starts with a specific question and gives first intuitive answers in the first section. As the chapter proceeds, the material gets more advanced, and the presentation becomes more technical. For a first reading of the book, it is possible to read only the first section, or first two sections, of each chapter and just glance at the subsequent sections.

More specific advice depends on the background. For example, readers who are new to the field of computational neuroscience are advised to spend enough time with the classic material of Part I, before they move on to Parts II and IV. The expert reader may skip Part I completely and start directly with Part II.

In Part III, the main ideas are exposed in Chapters 12 and 15, which present the foundations for the rate models in Part IV. The more technical chapters and sections of Part III can be skipped at a first reading, but are necessary for a thorough understanding of the current developments in the field of computational neuroscience.

Part IV contains applications of neuronal dynamics to questions of cognition and can be read in any arbitrary order.

Sections marked by an asterisk ($*$) are mathematically more advanced and can be omitted during a first reading of the book.

Acknowledgements

We would like to thank our students, visitors, exchange students, and postdocs who carefully read and commented on at least two chapters each, some many more: Dane Corneil, Andrea De Antoni, Mortiz Deger, Mohammad Faraji, Nicolas Frémaux, Felipe Gerhard, Laureline Logiaco, Skander Mensi, Alexandre Payeur, Christian Pozzorini, Kerstin Preuschoff, Tilo Schwalger, Alex Seeholzer, Hesam Setareh, Carlos Stein, Tim Vogels, Friedemann Zenke, Lorric Ziegler.

The writing of the text was a joint work of the four authors. Werner Kistler and Wulfram Gerstner were the authors of *Spiking Neuron Models* from which several sections survived. Liam Paninski was mainly involved in writing Chapters 9–11 of the present book and gave valuable input to other chapters of Part II. Richard Naud contributed to writing Chapters 1–11 and 14 with a leading role in some of these, made valuable comments and suggestions for all other chapters, and was responsible for all the figures. Wulfram Gerstner wrote the first drafts of Parts III and IV and contributed text to all other chapters.

Wulfram Gerstner, Werner Kistler, Richard Naud, Liam Paninski

PART ONE
FOUNDATIONS OF NEURONAL DYNAMICS

1

Introduction: neurons and mathematics

The primary aim of this chapter is to introduce several elementary notions of neuroscience, in particular the concepts of action potentials, postsynaptic potentials, firing thresholds, refractoriness, and adaptation. Based on these notions a preliminary model of neuronal dynamics is built and this simple model (the leaky integrate-and-fire model) will be used as a starting point and reference for the generalized integrate-and-fire models, which are the main topic of the book, to be discussed in Parts II and III. Since the mathematics used for the simple model is essentially that of a one-dimensional linear differential equation, we take this first chapter as an opportunity to introduce some of the mathematical notation that will be used throughout the rest of the book.

Owing to the limitations of space, we cannot – and do not want to – give a comprehensive introduction to such a complex field as neurobiology. The presentation of the biological background in this chapter is therefore highly selective and focuses on those aspects needed to appreciate the biological background of the theoretical work presented in this book. For an in-depth discussion of neurobiology we refer the reader to the literature mentioned at the end of this chapter.

After the review of neuronal properties in Sections 1.1 and 1.2 we will turn, in Section 1.3, to our first mathematical neuron model. The last two sections are devoted to a discussion of the strengths and limitations of simplified models.

1.1 Elements of neuronal systems

Over the past hundred years, biological research has accumulated an enormous amount of detailed knowledge about the structure and function of the brain. The elementary processing units in the central nervous system are neurons, which are connected to each other in an intricate pattern. A tiny portion of such a network of neurons is sketched in Fig. 1.1, which shows a drawing by Ramón y Cajal, one of the pioneers of neuroscience around 1900. We can distinguish several neurons with triangular or circular cell bodies and long wire-like extensions. This picture can only give a glimpse of the network of neurons in the cortex. In reality, cortical neurons and their connections are packed into a dense network with more than 10^4 cell bodies and several kilometers of "wires" per cubic millimeter. Across areas of

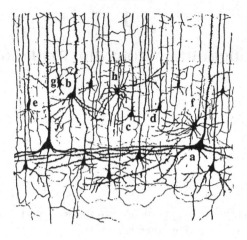

Fig. 1.1 This reproduction of a drawing of Ramón y Cajal shows a few neurons in the mammalian cortex that he observed under the microscope. Only a small portion of the neurons contained in the sample of cortical tissue have been made visible by the staining procedure; the density of neurons is in reality much higher. Cell b is a typical example of a pyramidal cell with a triangularly shaped cell body. Dendrites, which leave the cell laterally and upwards, can be recognized by their rough surface. The axons are recognizable as thin, smooth lines which extend downwards with a few branches to the left and right. From Ramòn y Cajal (1909).

the brain the wiring pattern may look different. In all areas, however, neurons of different sizes and shapes form the basic elements.

Still, the cortex does not consist exclusively of neurons. Beside the various types of neuron, there are a large number of "supporter" cells, so-called glia cells, that are required for energy supply and structural stabilization of brain tissue. Since glia cells are not directly involved in information processing, we will not discuss them any further. We will also neglect a few rare subtypes of neuron, such as non-spiking neurons in the mammalian retina. Throughout this book we concentrate on spiking neurons only.

1.1.1 The ideal spiking neuron

A typical neuron can be divided into three functionally distinct parts, called *dendrites*, the *soma*, and the *axon*; see Fig. 1.2. Roughly speaking, the dendrites play the role of the "input device" that collects signals from other neurons and transmits them to the soma. The soma is the "central processing unit" that performs an important nonlinear processing step: if the total input arriving at the soma exceeds a certain threshold, then an output signal is generated. The output signal is taken over by the "output device," the axon, which delivers the signal to other neurons.

The junction between two neurons is called a *synapse*. Let us suppose that a neuron sends a signal across a synapse. It is common to refer to the sending neuron as the *presynaptic cell* and to the receiving neuron as the *postsynaptic cell*. A single neuron in vertebrate

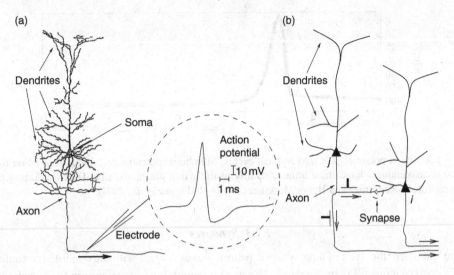

Fig. 1.2 (a) Single neuron in a drawing by Ramón y Cajal. Dendrites, soma, and axon can be clearly distinguished. The inset shows an example of a neuronal action potential (schematic). The action potential is a short voltage pulse of 1–2 ms duration and an amplitude of about 100 mV. (b) Signal transmission from a presynaptic neuron j to a postsynaptic neuron i. The synapse is marked by the dashed circle. The axons at the lower right end lead to other neurons. (Schematic figure.)

cortex often connects to more than 10^4 postsynaptic neurons. Many of its axonal branches end in the direct neighborhood of the neuron, but the axon can also stretch over several centimeters so as to reach neurons in other areas of the brain.

1.1.2 Spike trains

The neuronal signals consist of short electrical pulses and can be observed by placing a fine electrode either on the soma or close to the soma or axon of a neuron; see Fig. 1.2. The pulses, so-called action potentials or *spikes*, have an amplitude of about 100 mV and typically a duration of 1–2 ms. The form of the pulse does not change as the action potential propagates along the axon. A chain of action potentials emitted by a single neuron is called a *spike train* – a sequence of stereotyped events which occur at regular or irregular intervals; see Fig. 1.3. Since isolated spikes of a given neuron look alike, the form of the action potential does not carry any information. Rather, it is the number and the timing of spikes which matter. The action potential is the elementary unit of signal transmission.

Action potentials in a spike train are usually well separated. Even with very strong input, it is impossible to excite a second spike during or immediately after a first one. The minimal distance between two spikes defines the absolute refractory period of the neuron. The absolute refractory period is followed by a phase of relative refractoriness where it is difficult, but not impossible, to excite an action potential.

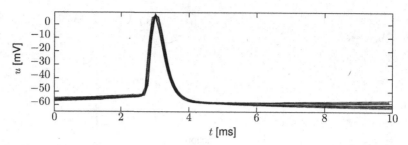

Fig. 1.3 Action potentials are stereotypical events. Membrane potential recordings aligned on the time of maximum voltage show little variability of the action potential shape. Data is courtesy of Maria Toledo-Rodriguez and Henry Markram (Toledo-Rodriguez *et al.*, 2004).

1.1.3 Synapses

The site where the axon of a presynaptic neuron makes contact with the dendrite (or soma) of a postsynaptic cell is the synapse. The most common type of synapse in the vertebrate brain is a chemical synapse. At a chemical synapse, the axon terminal comes very close to the postsynaptic neuron, leaving only a tiny gap between pre- and postsynaptic cell membrane. This is called the *synaptic cleft*. When an action potential arrives at a synapse, it triggers a complex chain of biochemical processing steps that lead to a release of neurotransmitter from the presynaptic terminal into the synaptic cleft. As soon as transmitter molecules have reached the postsynaptic side, they will be detected by specialized receptors in the postsynaptic cell membrane and lead (either directly or via a biochemical signaling chain) to an opening of specific channels causing ions from the extracellular fluid to flow into the cell. The ion influx, in turn, changes the membrane potential at the postsynaptic site so that, in the end, the chemical signal is translated into an electrical response. The voltage response of the postsynaptic neuron to a presynaptic spike is called the *postsynaptic potential*.

Apart from chemical synapses neurons can also be coupled by electrical synapses, sometimes called gap junctions. Specialized membrane proteins make a direct electrical connection between the two neurons. Not much is known about the functional aspects of gap junctions, but they are thought to be involved in the synchronization of neurons.

1.1.4 Neurons are part of a big system

Neurons are embedded in a network of billions of other neurons and glial cells that make up the brain tissue. The brain is organized into different regions and areas. The cortex can be thought of as a thin but extended sheet of neurons, folded over other brain structures. Some cortical areas are mainly involved in processing sensory input, other areas are involved in working memory or motor control.

Neurons in sensory cortices can be experimentally characterized by the stimuli to which they exhibit a strong response. For example, neurons in the primary visual cortex respond

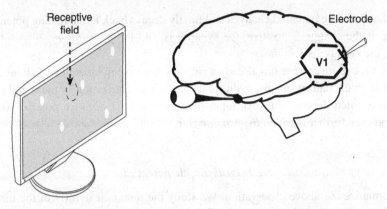

Fig. 1.4 Receptive fields in the visual cortex. An electrode probes the activity of a neuron while light dots are presented on a gray screen. The neuron responds whenever the stimulus falls into its receptive field, schematically indicated as an oval.

to dots of lights only within a small region of the visual space. The limited zone where a neuron is sensitive to stimuli is called the neuron's receptive field (Fig. 1.4).

The receptive field of so-called simple cells in the visual cortex is not homogeneous, but has typically two or three elongated subfields. When a light dot falls into one of the positive subfields, the neuron increases its activity, i.e., it emits more spikes than in the absence of a stimulus. When a light dot falls into a negative subfield, it decreases the activity compared to its spontaneous activity in the presence of a gray screen. A spot of light is in fact not the best stimulus. The neuron responds maximally to a moving light bar with an orientation aligned with the elongation of the positive subfield (Hubel and Wiesel, 1968).

A large body of the neuroscience literature consists in determining the receptive fields of neurons in sensory cortices. While neurons in the visual cortex respond to appropriate visual stimuli, neurons in the auditory cortex or somatosensory cortex respond to auditory or tactile stimuli. The concept of receptive field becomes less well defined if one moves away from the sensory cortex. For example, in the inferotemporal cortex, neurons respond to objects independently of their size and location; in working memory tasks, frontal cortex neurons are active during periods where no stimulus is present at all. In Parts II, III, and IV of this book we touch on aspects of receptive fields and memory of neuronal networks embedded in a big system. For the moment, we return to a simple, idealized neuron.

1.2 Elements of neuronal dynamics

The effect of a spike on the postsynaptic neuron can be recorded with an intracellular electrode which measures the potential difference $u(t)$ between the interior of the cell and its surroundings. This potential difference is called the *membrane potential*. Without any input, the neuron is at rest corresponding to a constant membrane potential u_{rest}. After the arrival of a spike, the potential changes and finally decays back to the resting potential; see Fig. 1.5a. If the change is positive, the synapse is said to be *excitatory*. If the change is negative, the synapse is *inhibitory*.

At rest, the cell membrane has already a strongly negative polarization of about −65 mV. An input at an excitatory synapse reduces the negative polarization of the membrane and is therefore called depolarizing. An input that increases the negative polarization of the membrane even further is called *hyperpolarizing*.

1.2.1 Postsynaptic potentials

Let us formalize the above observation. We study the time course $u_i(t)$ of the membrane potential of neuron i. Before the input spike has arrived, we have $u_i(t) = u_{\text{rest}}$. At $t = 0$ the presynaptic neuron j fires its spike. For $t > 0$, we see at the electrode a response of neuron i

$$u_i(t) - u_{\text{rest}} =: \varepsilon_{ij}(t). \tag{1.1}$$

The right-hand side of Eq. (1.1) defines the postsynaptic potential (PSP). If the voltage difference $u_i(t) - u_{\text{rest}}$ is positive (negative) we have an excitatory (inhibitory) postsynaptic potential or short EPSP (IPSP). In Fig. 1.5a we have sketched the EPSP caused by the arrival of a spike from neuron j at an excitatory synapse of neuron i.

1.2.2 Firing threshold and action potential

Consider two presynaptic neurons $j = 1, 2$, which both send spikes to the postsynaptic neuron i. Neuron $j = 1$ fires spikes at $t_1^{(1)}, t_1^{(2)}, \ldots$, similarly neuron $j = 2$ fires at $t_2^{(1)}, t_2^{(2)}, \ldots$. Each spike evokes a postsynaptic potential ε_{i1} or ε_{i2}, respectively. As long as there are only few input spikes, the total change of the potential is approximately the sum of the individual PSPs,

$$u_i(t) = \sum_j \sum_f \varepsilon_{ij}(t - t_j^f) + u_{\text{rest}}, \tag{1.2}$$

i.e., the membrane potential responds linearly to input spikes; see Fig. 1.5b.

On the other hand, linearity breaks down if too many input spikes arrive during a short interval. As soon as the membrane potential reaches a critical value ϑ, its trajectory shows a behavior that is quite different from a simple summation of PSPs: the membrane potential exhibits a pulse-like excursion with an amplitude of about 100 mV. This short voltage pulse will propagate along the axon of neuron i to the synapses with other neurons. After the pulse the membrane potential does not directly return to the resting potential, but passes, for many neuron types, through a phase of hyperpolarization below the resting value. This hyperpolarization is called "spike-afterpotential."

Single EPSPs have amplitudes in the range of 1 mV. The critical value for spike initiation is about 20 to 30 mV above the resting potential. In most neurons, four spikes – as shown

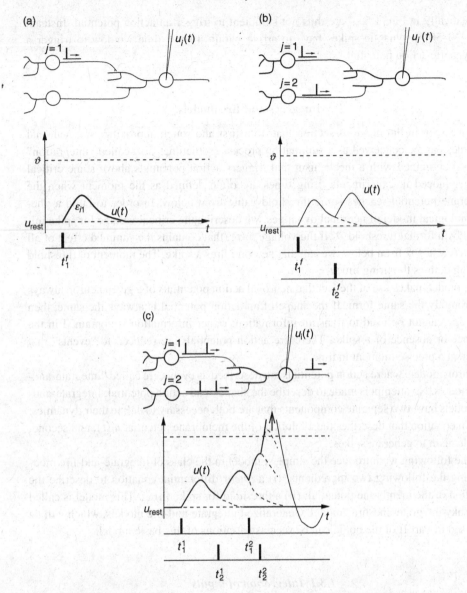

Fig. 1.5 A postsynaptic neuron i receives input from two presynaptic neurons $j = 1, 2$. (a) Each presynaptic spike evokes an excitatory postsynaptic potential (EPSP) that can be measured with an electrode as a potential difference $u_i(t) - u_{rest}$. The time course of the EPSP caused by the spike of neuron $j = 1$ is $\varepsilon_{i1}(t - t_1^f)$. (b) An input spike from a second presynaptic neuron $j = 2$ that arrives shortly after the spike from neuron $j = 1$ causes a second postsynaptic potential that adds to the first one. (c) If $u_i(t)$ reaches the threshold ϑ, an action potential is triggered. As a consequence, the membrane potential starts a large positive pulse-like excursion (arrow). On the voltage scale of the graph, the peak of the pulse is out of bounds. After the pulse the voltage returns to a value below the resting potential u_{rest}.

schematically in Fig. 1.5c – are thus not sufficient to trigger an action potential. Instead, about 20–50 presynaptic spikes have to arrive within a short time window to trigger a postsynaptic action potential.

1.3 Integrate-and-fire models

We have seen in the previous section that, to a first and rough approximation, neuronal dynamics can be conceived as a summation process (sometimes also called "integration" process) combined with a mechanism that triggers action potentials above some critical voltage. Indeed in experiments firing times are often defined as the moment when the membrane potential reaches some threshold value from below. In order to build a phenomenological model of neuronal dynamics, we describe the critical voltage for spike initiation by a formal threshold ϑ. If the voltage $u_i(t)$ (that contains the summed effect of all inputs) reaches ϑ from below, we say that neuron i fires a spike. The moment of threshold crossing defines the firing time t_i^f.

The model makes use of the fact that neuronal action potentials of a given neuron always have roughly the same form. If the shape of an action potential is always the same, then the shape cannot be used to transmit information: rather information is contained in the presence or absence of a spike. Therefore action potentials are reduced to "events" that happen at a precise moment in time.

Neuron models where action potentials are described as events are called "integrate-and-fire" models. No attempt is made to describe the shape of an action potential. Integrate-and-fire models have two separate components that are both necessary to define their dynamics: first, an equation that describes the evolution of the membrane potential $u_i(t)$; and second, a mechanism to generate spikes.

In the following we introduce the simplest model in the class of integrate-and-fire models using the following two ingredients: (i) a *linear* differential equation to describe the evolution of the membrane potential; (ii) a threshold for spike firing. This model is called the "leaky integrate-and-fire" model. Generalized integrate-and-fire models, which will be discussed in Part II of the book, can be seen as variations of this basic model.

1.3.1 Integration of inputs

The variable u_i describes the momentary value of the membrane potential of neuron i. In the absence of any input, the potential is at its resting value u_{rest}. If an experimenter injects a current $I(t)$ into the neuron, or if the neuron receives synaptic input from other neurons, the potential u_i will be deflected from its resting value.

In order to arrive at an equation that links the momentary voltage $u_i(t) - u_{\text{rest}}$ to the input current $I(t)$, we use elementary laws from the theory of electricity. A neuron is surrounded by a cell membrane, which is a rather good insulator. If a short current pulse $I(t)$ is injected into the neuron, the additional electrical charge $q = \int I(t')\mathrm{d}t'$ has to go somewhere: it will

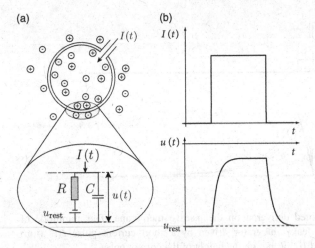

Fig. 1.6 Electrical properties of neurons: the passive membrane. (a) A neuron, which is enclosed by the cell membrane (big circle), receives a (positive) input current $I(t)$ which increases the electrical charge inside the cell. The cell membrane acts like a capacitor in parallel with a resistor which is in line with a battery of potential u_{rest} (zoomed inset). (b) The cell membrane reacts to a step current (top) with a smooth voltage trace (bottom).

charge the cell membrane (Fig. 1.6a). The cell membrane therefore acts like a capacitor of capacity C. Because the insulator is not perfect, the charge will, over time, slowly leak through the cell membrane. The cell membrane can therefore be characterized by a finite leak resistance R.

The basic electrical circuit representing a leaky integrate-and-fire model consists of a capacitor C in parallel with a resistor R driven by a current $I(t)$; see Fig. 1.6. If the driving current $I(t)$ vanishes, the voltage across the capacitor is given by the battery voltage u_{rest}. For a biological explanation of the battery we refer the reader to the next chapter. Here we have simply inserted the battery "by hand" into the circuit so as to account for the resting potential of the cell (Fig. 1.6a).

In order to analyze the circuit, we use the law of current conservation and split the driving current into two components,

$$I(t) = I_R + I_C. \tag{1.3}$$

The first component is the resistive current I_R which passes through the linear resistor R. It can be calculated from Ohm's law as $I_R = u_R/R$ where $u_R = u - u_{rest}$ is the voltage across the resistor. The second component I_C charges the capacitor C. From the definition of the capacity as $C = q/u$ (where q is the charge and u the voltage), we find a capacitive current $I_C = dq/dt = C du/dt$. Thus

$$I(t) = \frac{u(t) - u_{rest}}{R} + C\frac{du}{dt}. \tag{1.4}$$

We multiply Eq. (1.4) by R and introduce the time constant $\tau_m = RC$ of the "leaky integrator." This yields the standard form

$$\tau_m \frac{du}{dt} = -[u(t) - u_{rest}] + RI(t). \tag{1.5}$$

We refer to u as the membrane potential and to τ_m as the membrane time constant of the neuron.

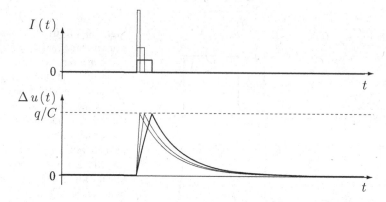

Fig. 1.7 Short pulses and total charged delivered on the passive membrane. The amplitude of the voltage response (bottom) of a leaky integrator driven by a short current pulse $I(t)$ (top) depends only on the total charge $q = \int I(t)\mathrm{d}t$, not on the height of the current pulse.

From a mathematical point of view, Eq. (1.5) is a linear differential equation. From the point of view of an electrical engineer, it is the equation of a leaky integrator or *RC*-circuit where resistor R and capacitor C are arranged in parallel. From the point of view of the neuroscientist, Eq. (1.5) is called the equation of a passive membrane.

What is the solution of Eq. (1.5)? We suppose that, for whatever reason, at time $t = 0$ the membrane potential takes a value $u_{\text{rest}} + \Delta u$. For $t > 0$ the input vanishes $I(t) = 0$. Intuitively we expect that, if we wait long enough, the membrane potential relaxes to its resting value u_{rest}. Indeed, the solution of the differential equation with initial condition $u(t_0) = u_{\text{rest}} + \Delta u$ is

$$u(t) - u_{\text{rest}} = \Delta u \exp\left(-\frac{t - t_0}{\tau_m}\right) \quad \text{for } t > t_0. \tag{1.6}$$

Thus, in the absence of input, the membrane potential decays exponentially to its resting value. The membrane time constant $\tau_m = RC$ is the characteristic time of the decay. For a typical neuron it is in the range of 10 ms, and hence rather long compared with the duration of a spike which is of the order of 1 ms.

The validity of the solution (1.6) can be checked by taking the derivative on both sides of the equation. Since it is the solution in the absence of input, it is sometimes called the "free" solution.

1.3.2 *Pulse input*

Before we continue with the definition of the integrate-and-fire model and its variants, let us study the dynamics of the passive membrane defined by Eq. (1.5) in a simple example. Suppose that the passive membrane is stimulated by a constant input current $I(t) = I_0$ which starts at $t = 0$ and ends at time $t = \Delta$. For the sake of simplicity we assume that the membrane potential at time $t = 0$ is at its resting value $u(0) = u_{\text{rest}}$.

As a first step, let us calculate the time course of the membrane potential. The trajectory of the membrane potential can be found by integrating (1.5) with the initial condition $u(0) = u_{\text{rest}}$. The solution for $0 < t < \Delta$ is

$$u(t) = u_{\text{rest}} + RI_0 \left[1 - \exp\left(-\frac{t}{\tau_m} \right) \right]. \tag{1.7}$$

If the input current never stopped, the membrane potential (1.7) would approach for $t \to \infty$ the asymptotic value $u(\infty) = u_{\text{rest}} + RI_0$. We can understand this result by looking at the electrical diagram of the RC-circuit in Fig. 1.6. Once a steady state is reached, the charge on the capacitor no longer changes. All input current must then flow through the resistor. The steady-state voltage at the resistor is therefore RI_0 so that the total membrane voltage is $u_{\text{rest}} + RI_0$.

Example: Short pulses and the Dirac δ-function

For short pulses the steady-state value is never reached. At the end of the pulse, the value of the membrane potential is given according to Eq. (1.7) by $u(\Delta) = u_{\text{rest}} + RI_0 \left[1 - \exp\left(-\frac{\Delta}{\tau_m} \right) \right]$. For pulse durations $\Delta \ll \tau_m$ (where $\ll$ means much smaller than) we can expand the exponential term into a Taylor series: $\exp(x) = 1 + x + x^2/2 + \cdots$. To first order in $x = -\frac{\Delta}{\tau_m}$ we find

$$u(\Delta) = u_{\text{rest}} + RI_0 \frac{\Delta}{\tau_m} \quad \text{for } \Delta \ll \tau_m. \tag{1.8}$$

Thus, the voltage deflection depends linearly on the amplitude and the duration of the pulse (Fig. 1.7, thick line).

We now make the duration Δ of the pulse shorter and shorter while increasing the amplitude of the current pulse to a value $I_0 = q/\Delta$, so that the integral $\int I(t) dt = q$ remains constant. In other words, the total charge q delivered by the current pulse is always the same. Interestingly, the voltage deflection at the end of the pulse calculated from Eq. (1.8) remains unaltered, however short we make the pulse. Indeed, from Eq. (1.8) we find $u(\Delta) - u_{\text{rest}} = qR/\tau_m = q/C$ where we have used $\tau_m = RC$. Thus we can consider the limit of an infinitely short pulse

$$I(t) = q\delta(t) = \lim_{\Delta \to 0} \frac{q}{\Delta} \quad \text{for } 0 < t < \Delta, \quad \text{and 0 otherwise.} \tag{1.9}$$

$\delta(t)$ is called the Dirac δ-function. It is defined by $\delta(x) = 0$ for $x \neq 0$ and $\int_{-\infty}^{\infty} \delta(x) dx = 1$.

Obviously, the Dirac δ-function is a mathematical abstraction since it is practically impossible to inject a current with an infinitely short and infinitely strong current pulse into a neuron. Whenever we encounter a δ-function, we should remember that, as a stand-alone object, it looks strange, but it becomes meaningful as soon as we integrate over it. Indeed the input current defined in Eq. (1.9) needs to be inserted into the differential equation (1.5) and integrated. The mathematical abstraction of the Dirac δ-function suddenly makes a lot of sense, because the voltage change induced by a short current pulse is always the same, whenever the duration of the pulse Δ is much

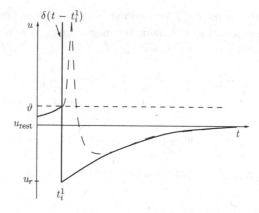

Fig. 1.8 In formal models of spiking neurons the shape of an action potential (dashed line) is usually replaced by a δ-pulse (vertical line). The negative overshoot (spike-afterpotential) after the pulse is replaced by a "reset" of the membrane potential to the value u_r. The pulse is triggered by the threshold crossing at t_i^1.

shorter than the time constant τ_m. Thus, the exact duration of the pulse is irrelevant, as long as it is short enough.

With the help of the δ-function, we no longer have to worry about the time course of the membrane potential *during* the application of the current pulse: the membrane potential simply jumps at time $t = 0$ by an amount q/C. Thus, it is as if we added instantaneously a charge q onto the capacitor of the RC circuit.

What happens for times $t > \Delta$? The membrane potential evolves from its new initial value $u_{\text{rest}} + q/C$ in the absence of any further input. Thus we can use the "free" solution from Eq. (1.6) with $t_0 = \Delta$ and $\Delta u = q/C$.

We can summarize the considerations of this section by the following statement. The solution of the linear differential equation with pulse input

$$\tau_m \frac{du}{dt} = -[u(t) - u_{\text{rest}}] + Rq\,\delta(t) \tag{1.10}$$

is $u(t) = u_{\text{rest}}$ for $t \leq 0$ and given by

$$u(t) - u_{\text{rest}} = q\,\frac{R}{\tau_m}\,\exp\left(-\frac{t}{\tau_m}\right) \quad \text{for } t > 0. \tag{1.11}$$

The right-hand side of the equation is called the impulse-response function or Green's function of the linear differential equation.

1.3.3 The threshold for spike firing

Throughout this book, the term "firing time" refers to the moment when a given neuron emits an action potential t^f. The firing time t^f in the leaky integrate-and-fire model is defined by a threshold criterion

$$t^f : \quad u(t^f) = \vartheta . \tag{1.12}$$

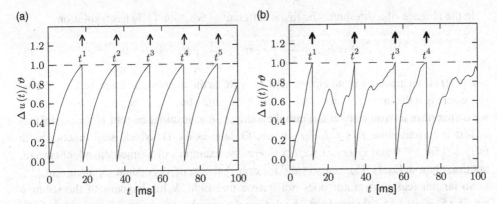

Fig. 1.9 Integrate-and-fire model. (a) Time course of the membrane potential of an integrate-and-fire neuron driven by constant input current $I_0 = 1.5$. The voltage $\Delta u(t) = u - u_{rest}$ is normalized by the value of the threshold ϑ. Units of input current are chosen so that $I_0 = 1$ corresponds to a trajectory that reaches the threshold for $t \to \infty$. After a spike, the potential is reset to $u_r = u_{rest}$. (b) Voltage response to a time-dependent input current.

The form of the spike is not described explicitly. Rather, the firing time is noted and immediately after t^f the potential is reset to a new value $u_r < \vartheta$,

$$\lim_{\delta \to 0; \delta > 0} u(t^f + \delta) = u_r. \tag{1.13}$$

For $t > t^f$ the dynamics is again given by (1.5) until the next threshold crossing occurs. The combination of leaky integration (1.5) and reset (1.13) defines the leaky integrate-and-fire model (Stein, 1967b). The voltage trajectory of a leaky integrate-and-fire model driven by a constant current I_0 is shown in Fig. 1.9.

For the firing times of neuron i we write t_i^f where $f = 1, 2, \ldots$ is the label of the spike. Formally, we may denote the spike train of a neuron i as the sequence of firing times

$$S_i(t) = \sum_f \delta(t - t_i^f) \tag{1.14}$$

where $\delta(x)$ is the Dirac δ-function introduced earlier, with $\delta(x) = 0$ for $x \neq 0$ and $\int_{-\infty}^{\infty} \delta(x) dx = 1$. Spikes are thus reduced to points in time (Fig. 1.8). We remind the reader that the δ-function is a mathematical object that needs to be inserted into an integral in order to give meaningful results.

1.3.4 Time-dependent input (*)[1]

We study a leaky integrate-and-fire model which is driven by an arbitrary time-dependent input current $I(t)$; see Fig. 1.9b. The firing threshold has a value ϑ and after firing the potential is reset to a value $u_r < \vartheta$.

---

[1] Sections marked by an asterisk are mathematically more advanced and can be omitted during a first reading of the book.

In the absence of a threshold, the linear differential equation (1.5) has a solution

$$u(t) = u_{rest} + \frac{R}{\tau_m} \int_0^\infty \exp\left(-\frac{s}{\tau_m}\right) I(t-s)\,ds, \tag{1.15}$$

where $I(t)$ is an arbitrary input current and $\tau_m = RC$ is the membrane time constant. We assume here that the input current is defined for a long time back into the past: $t \to -\infty$ so that we do not have to worry about the initial condition. A sinusoidal current $I(t) = I_0\sin(\omega t)$ or a step current pulse $I(t) = I_0\Theta(t)$, where Θ denotes the Heaviside step function with $\Theta(t) = 0$ for $t \le 0$ and $\Theta(t) = 1$ for $t > 0$, are two examples of a time-dependent current, but the solution, Eq. (1.15), is also valid for every other time-dependent input current.

So far our leaky integrator does not have a threshold. What happens to the solution Eq. (1.15) if we add a threshold ϑ? Each time the membrane potential hits the threshold, the variable u is reset from ϑ to u_r. In the electrical circuit diagram, the reset of the potential corresponds to removing a charge $q_r = C(\vartheta - u_r)$ from the capacitor (Fig. 1.6) or, equivalently, adding a negative charge $-q_r$ onto the capacitor. Therefore, the reset corresponds to a short current pulse $I_r = -q_r\,\delta(t-t^f)$ at the moment of the firing t^f. Indeed, it is not unusual to say that a neuron "discharges" instead of "fires." Since the reset happens each time the neuron fires, the reset current is

$$I_r = -q_r \sum_f \delta(t - t^f) = -C(\vartheta - u_r)S(t), \tag{1.16}$$

where $S(t)$ denotes the spike train, defined in Eq. (1.14).

The short current pulse corresponding to the "discharging" is treated mathematically just like any other time-dependent input current. The total current $I(t) + I_r(t)$, consisting of the stimulating current and the reset current, is inserted into the solution (1.15) to give the final result

$$u(t) = u_{rest} + \sum_f (u_r - \vartheta) \exp\left(-\frac{t-t^f}{\tau_m}\right) + \frac{R}{\tau_m} \int_0^\infty \exp\left(-\frac{s}{\tau_m}\right) I(t-s)\,ds, \tag{1.17}$$

where the firing times t^f are defined by the threshold condition

$$t^f = \{t \mid u(t) = \vartheta\}. \tag{1.18}$$

Note that with our definition of the Dirac δ-function in Eq. (1.9), the discharging reset follows immediately after the threshold crossing, so that the natural sequence of events – first firing, then reset – is respected.

Equation (1.17) looks rather complicated. It has, however, a simple explanation. In Section 1.3.2 we have seen that a short input pulse at time t' causes at time t a response of the membrane proportional to $\exp[-(t-t'/\tau_m)]$, sometimes called the impulse response function or Green's function; see Eq. (1.11). The second term on the right-hand side of Eq. (1.17) is the effect of the discharging current pulses at the moment of the reset.

In order to interpret the last term on the right-hand side, we think of a stimulating current $I(t)$ as consisting of a rapid sequence of discrete and short current pulses. In discrete time, there would be a different current pulse in each time step. Because of the linearity of the differential equation, the effect of all these short current pulses can be added. When we return from discrete time to continuous time, the sum of the impulse response functions turns into the integral on the right-hand side of Eq. (1.17).

1.3.5 Linear differential equation vs. linear filter: two equivalent pictures (*)

The leaky integrate-and-fire model is defined by the differential equation (1.5), i.e.,

$$\tau_m \frac{du}{dt} = -[u(t) - u_{\text{rest}}] + RI(t), \tag{1.19}$$

combined with the reset condition

$$\lim_{\delta \to 0; \delta > 0} u(t^f + \delta) = u_r, \tag{1.20}$$

where t^f are the firing times

$$t^f = \{t | u(t) = \vartheta\}. \tag{1.21}$$

As we have seen in the previous section, the linear equation can be integrated and yields the solution (1.17). It is convenient to rewrite the solution in the form

$$u(t) = \int_0^\infty \eta(s) S(t - s) ds + \int_0^\infty \kappa(s) I(t - s) ds, \tag{1.22}$$

where we have introduced filters $\eta(s) = (u_r - \vartheta) \exp\left(-\frac{s}{\tau_m}\right)$ and $\kappa(s) = \frac{1}{C} \exp\left(-\frac{s}{\tau_m}\right)$. Interestingly, Eq. (1.22) is much more general than the leaky integrate-and-fire model, because the filters do not need to be exponentials but could have any arbitrary shape. The filter η describes the reset of the membrane potential and, more generally, accounts for neuronal refractoriness. The filter κ summarizes the linear electrical properties of the membrane. Eq. (1.22) in combination with the threshold condition (1.21) is the basis of the Spike Response Model and Generalized Linear Models, which will be discussed in Part II.

1.3.6 Periodic drive and Fourier transform (*)

Formally, the complex Fourier transform of a real-valued function $f(t)$ with argument t on the real line is

$$\hat{f}(\omega) = \int_{-\infty}^{\infty} f(t) e^{-i\omega t} dt = |\hat{f}(\omega)| e^{i\phi_f(\omega)}, \tag{1.23}$$

where $|\hat{f}(\omega)|$ and $\phi_f(\omega)$ are called the amplitude and phase of the Fourier transform at frequency ω. The mathematical condition for a well-defined Fourier transform is that the function f be Lebesgue integrable with integral $\int_{-\infty}^{\infty} |f(t)| dt < \infty$. If f is a function of time, then $\hat{f}(\omega)$ is a function of frequency. An inverse Fourier transform leads back from frequency-space to the original space, i.e., time.

For a linear system, the above definition gives rise to several convenient rules for Fourier-transformed equations. For example, let us consider the system

$$u(t) = \int_{-\infty}^{\infty} \kappa(s) I(t-s) \, ds, \tag{1.24}$$

where $I(t)$ is a real-valued input (e.g., a current), $u(t)$ the real-valued system output (e.g., a voltage) and κ a linear response filter, or kernel, with $\kappa(s) = 0$ for $s < 0$ because of causality. The convolution on the right-hand side of Eq. (1.24) turns after Fourier transformation into a simple multiplication, as shown by the following calculation steps:

$$\begin{aligned} \hat{u}(\omega) &= \int_{-\infty}^{\infty} \left[\int_{-\infty}^{\infty} \kappa(s) I(t-s) \, ds \right] e^{-i\omega t} \, dt \\ &= \int_{-\infty}^{\infty} \int_{-\infty}^{\infty} \kappa(s) e^{-i\omega s} I(t-s) \, e^{-i\omega(t-s)} \, ds \, dt \\ &= \hat{\kappa}(\omega) \hat{I}(\omega), \end{aligned} \tag{1.25}$$

where we introduced in the last step the variable $t' = t - s$ and used the definition (1.23) of the Fourier transform.

Similarly, the derivative du/dt of a function $u(t)$ can be Fourier-transformed using the product rule of integration. The Fourier transform of the derivative of $u(t)$ is $i\omega\hat{u}(\omega)$.

While introduced here as a purely mathematical operation, it is often convenient to visualize the Fourier transform in the context of a physical system driven by a periodic input. Consider the linear system of Eq. (1.24) with an input

$$I(t) = I_0 \, e^{i\omega t}. \tag{1.26}$$

A short comment on the notation. If the input is a current, it should be real-valued, as opposed to a complex number. We therefore take I_0 as a real and positive number and focus on the *real part* of the complex equation (1.26) as our physical input. When we perform a calculation with complex numbers, we therefore implicitly assume that, at the very end, we take only the real part of solution. However, the calculation with complex numbers turns out to be convenient for the steps in between.

Inserting the periodic drive, Eq. (1.26), into Eq. (1.24) yields

$$u(t) = \int_{-\infty}^{\infty} \kappa(s) I_0 e^{i\omega(t-s)} \, ds = \left[\int_{-\infty}^{\infty} \kappa(s) e^{-i\omega s} \, ds \right] I_0 e^{i\omega t}. \tag{1.27}$$

Hence, if the input is periodic at frequency ω the output is too. The term in square brackets is the Fourier transform of the linear filter. We write $u(t) = u_0 e^{i\phi_\kappa(\omega)} e^{i\omega t}$. The ratio between the amplitude of the output and that of the input is

$$\frac{u_0}{I_0} = |\hat{\kappa}(\omega)|. \tag{1.28}$$

The phase $\phi_\kappa(\omega)$ of the Fourier-transformed linear filter κ corresponds to the phase shift between input and output or, to say it differently, a delay $\Delta = \phi_\kappa/\omega = \phi_\kappa T/2\pi$ where T is the period of the oscillation. Fourier transforms will play a role in the discussion of signal processing properties of connected networks of neurons in Part III of the book.

Example: Periodic drive of a passive membrane

We consider the differential equation of the passive membrane defined in Eq. (1.5) and choose voltage units such that $u_{\text{rest}} = 0$, i.e.,

$$\tau_m \frac{du}{dt} = -u(t) + RI(t).\tag{1.29}$$

The solution, given by Eq. (1.15), corresponds to the convolution of the input $I(t)$ with a causal linear filter $\kappa(s) = (1/C)\,e^{(-s/\tau_m)}$ for $s > 0$. In order to determine the response amplitude u_0 to a periodic drive $I(t) = I_0\,e^{i\omega t}$ we need to calculate the Fourier transform of κ:

$$|\hat{\kappa}(\omega)| = \left| \frac{1}{C} \int_0^\infty e^{\frac{-t}{\tau_m}}\, e^{-i\omega t}\, dt \right| = \frac{1}{C} \left| \frac{\tau_m}{1 + i\omega\tau_m} \right|.\tag{1.30}$$

For $\omega\tau_m \gg 1$ the right-hand side is proportional to ω^{-1}. Therefore the amplitude of the response to a periodic input decreases at high frequencies.

1.4 Limitations of the leaky integrate-and-fire model

The leaky integrate-and-fire model presented in Section 1.3 is highly simplified and neglects many aspects of neuronal dynamics. In particular, input, which may arise from presynaptic neurons or from current injection, is integrated linearly, independently of the state of the postsynaptic neuron:

$$\tau_m \frac{du}{dt} = -[u(t) - u_{\text{rest}}] + RI(t),\tag{1.31}$$

where $I(t)$ is the input current. Furthermore, after each output spike the membrane potential is reset,

$$\text{if } u(t) = \vartheta \text{ then } \lim_{\delta \to 0; \delta > 0} u(t + \delta) = u_r,\tag{1.32}$$

so that no memory of previous spikes is kept. Let us list the major limitations of the simplified model discussed so far. All of these limitations will be addressed in the extension of the leaky integrate-and-fire model presented in Part II of the book.

1.4.1 Adaptation, bursting, and inhibitory rebound

To study neuronal dynamics experimentally, neurons can be isolated and stimulated by current injection through an intracellular electrode. In a standard experimental protocol we could, for example, impose a stimulating current that is switched at time t_0 from a value I_1 to a new value I_2. Let us suppose that $I_1 = 0$ so that the neuron is quiescent for $t < t_0$. If the current I_2 is sufficiently large, it will evoke spikes for $t > t_0$. Most neurons will respond to the current step with a spike train where intervals between spikes increase

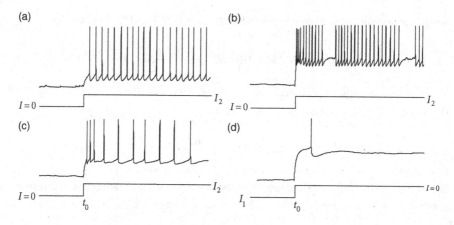

Fig. 1.10 Response to a current step. In (a)–(c), the current is switched on at $t = t_0$ to a value $I_2 > 0$. Fast-spiking neurons (a) have short interspike intervals without adaptation while regular-spiking neurons (c) exhibit adaptation, visible as an increase in the duration of interspike intervals. An example of a stuttering neuron is shown in (b). Many neurons emit an inhibitory rebound spike (d) after an inhibitory current $I_1 < 0$ is switched off. Data is courtesy of Henry Markram and Maria Toledo-Rodriguez (Markram *et al.*, 2004; Toledo-Rodriguez *et al.*, 2004).

successively until a steady state of periodic firing is reached; see Fig. 1.10c. Neurons that show this type of adaptation are called regularly firing neurons (Connors and Gutnick, 1990). Adaptation is a slow process that builds up over several spikes. Since the standard leaky integrate-and-fire model resets the voltage after each spike to the same value and restarts the integration process, no memory is kept beyond the most recent spike. Therefore, the leaky integrate-and-fire neuron cannot capture adaptation. Detailed neuron models, which will be discussed in Chapter 2, explicitly describe the slow processes that lead to adaptation. To mimic these processes in integrate-and-fire neurons, we need to add up the contributions to refractoriness of several spikes back in the past. As we shall see in Chapter 6, this can be done in the "filter" framework of Eq. (1.22) by using a filter η for refractoriness with a time constant much slower than that of the membrane potential, or by combining the differential equation of the leaky integrate-and-fire model with a second differential equation describing the evolution of a slow variable; see Chapter 6.

A second class of neurons are fast-spiking neurons. These neurons show no adaptation (see Fig. 1.10a) and can therefore be well approximated by non-adapting integrate-and-fire models. Many inhibitory neurons are fast-spiking neurons. Apart from regular-spiking and fast-spiking neurons, there are also bursting and stuttering neurons which form a separate group (Connors and Gutnick, 1990). These neurons respond to constant stimulation by a sequence of spikes that is periodically (bursting) or aperiodically (stuttering) interrupted by rather long intervals; see Fig. 1.10b. Again, a neuron model that has no memory beyond the most recent spike cannot describe bursting, but the framework in Eq. (1.22) with arbitrary "filters" is general enough to account for bursting as well.

Another frequently observed behavior is post-inhibitory rebound. Consider a step current with $I_1 < 0$ and $I_2 = 0$, i.e., an inhibitory input that is switched off at time t_0; see Fig. 1.10d.

Many neurons respond to such a change with one or more "rebound spikes"; even the release of inhibition can trigger action potentials. We will return to inhibitory rebound in Chapter 3.

1.4.2 Shunting inhibition and reversal potential

In the previous section we focused on an isolated neuron stimulated by an applied current. In reality, neurons are embedded into a large network and receive input from many other neurons. Suppose a spike from a presynaptic neuron j is sent at time t_j^f towards the synapse of a postsynaptic neuron i. When we introduced in Fig. 1.5 the postsynaptic potential that is generated after the arrival of the spike at the synapse, its shape and amplitude did not depend on the state of the postsynaptic neuron i. This is of course a simplification and reality is somewhat more complicated. In Chapter 3 we will discuss detailed neuron models that describe synaptic input as a change of the membrane conductance. Here we simply summarize the major phenomena.

In Fig. 1.11 we have sketched schematically an experiment where the neuron is driven by a constant current I_0. We assume that I_0 is too weak to evoke firing so that, after some relaxation time, the membrane potential settles at a constant value u_0. At $t = t^f$ one of the presynaptic neurons emits a spike so that shortly afterwards the action potential arrives at the synapse and provides additional stimulation of the postsynaptic neuron. More precisely, the spike generates a current pulse at the postsynaptic neuron (postsynaptic current, PSC) with amplitude

$$\text{PSC} \propto [u_0 - E_{\text{syn}}] \tag{1.33}$$

where u_0 is the membrane potential and E_{syn} is the "reversal potential" of the synapse. Since the amplitude of the current input depends on u_0, the response of the postsynaptic potential does so as well. Reversal potentials are systematically introduced in Chapter 2; models of synaptic input are discussed in Section 3.1.

Example: Shunting inhibition

The dependence of the postsynaptic response upon the momentary state of the neuron is most pronounced for inhibitory synapses. The reversal potential of inhibitory synapses E_{syn} is below, but usually close to the resting potential. Input spikes thus have hardly any effect on the membrane potential if the neuron is at rest; see Fig. 1.11a. However, if the membrane is depolarized, the very same input spikes evoke a larger inhibitory postsynaptic potential. If the membrane is already hyperpolarized, the input spike can even produce a depolarizing effect. There is an intermediate value $u_0 = E_{\text{syn}}$ – the reversal potential – where the response to inhibitory input "reverses" from hyperpolarizing to depolarizing.

Though inhibitory input usually has only a small impact on the membrane potential, the local conductivity of the cell membrane can be significantly increased. Inhibitory

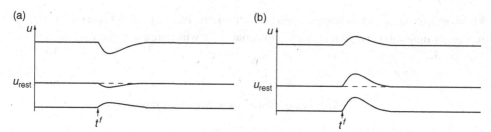

Fig. 1.11 The shape of postsynaptic potentials depends on the momentary level of depolarization. (a) A presynaptic spike that arrives at time t^f at an inhibitory synapse has hardly any effect on the membrane potential when the neuron is at rest, but a large effect if the membrane potential u is above the resting potential. If the membrane is hyperpolarized below the reversal potential of the inhibitory synapse, the response to the presynaptic input changes sign. (b) A spike at an excitatory synapse evokes a postsynaptic potential with an amplitude that depends only slightly on the momentary voltage u. For large depolarizations the amplitude saturates and becomes smaller. (Schematic figure.)

synapses are often located on the soma or on the shaft of the dendritic tree. Owing to their strategic position, a few inhibitory input spikes can "shunt" the whole input that is gathered by the dendritic tree from hundreds of excitatory synapses. This phenomenon is called "shunting inhibition."

The reversal potential for excitatory synapses is usually significantly above the resting potential. If the membrane is depolarized $u_0 \gg u_{rest}$ the amplitude of an excitatory postsynaptic potential is reduced, but the effect is not as pronounced as for inhibition. For very high levels of depolarization a saturation of the EPSPs can be observed; see Fig. 1.11b.

1.4.3 Conductance changes after a spike

The shape of the postsynaptic potentials depends not only on the level of depolarization but, more generally, on the internal state of the neuron, e.g., on the timing relative to previous action potentials.

Suppose that an action potential has occurred at time t_i^f and that a presynaptic spike arrives at a time $t_j^f > t_i^f$ at the synapse j. The form of the postsynaptic potential depends now on the time $t_j^f - t_i^f$; see Fig. 1.12. If the presynaptic spike arrives during or shortly after a postsynaptic action potential, it has little effect because some of the ion channels that were involved in firing the action potential are still open. If the input spike arrives much later, it generates a postsynaptic potential of the usual size. We will return to this effect in Chapter 2.

1.4.4 Spatial structure

The form of postsynaptic potentials also depends on the location of the synapse on the dendritic tree. Synapses that are located far away from the soma are expected to evoke a

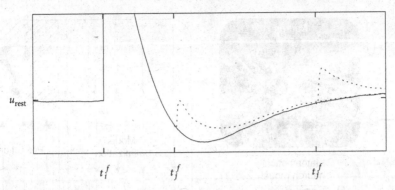

Fig. 1.12 The shape of postsynaptic potentials (dashed lines) depends on the time $t - t_i^f$ that has passed since the last output spike of neuron i. The postsynaptic spike has been triggered at time t_i^f. A presynaptic spike that arrives at time t_j^f shortly after the spike of the postsynaptic neuron has a smaller effect than a spike that arrives much later. Data is courtesy of Thomas Berger (Berger *et al.*, 2009).

smaller postsynaptic response at the soma than a synapse that is located directly on the soma; see Chapter 3. If several inputs occur on the same dendritic branch within a few milliseconds, the first input will cause local changes of the membrane potential that influence the amplitude of the response to the input spikes that arrive slightly later. This may lead to saturation or, in the case of so-called "active" currents, to an enhancement of the response. Such nonlinear interactions between different presynaptic spikes are neglected in the leaky integrate-and-fire model. Whereas a purely linear dendrite can be incorporated in the "filter" description of the model, as we shall see in Chapter 6, nonlinear interactions cannot. Small regions on the dendrite where a strong nonlinear boosting of synpatic currents occurs are sometimes called dendritic "hot spots." The boosting can lead to dendritic spikes which, in contrast to normal somatic action potentials last for tens of milliseconds (Larkum and Nevian, 2008).

1.5 What can we expect from integrate-and-fire models?

The leaky integrate-and-fire model is an extremely simplified neuron model. As we have seen in the previous section, it neglects many features that neuroscientists have observed when they study neurons in the living brain or in slices of brain tissue. Therefore the question arises: what should we expect from such a model? Clearly we cannot expect it to explain the complete biochemistry and biophysics of neurons. Nor do we expect it to account for highly nonlinear interactions that are caused by active currents in some "hot spots" on the dendritic tree. However, the integrate-and-fire model is surprisingly accurate when it comes to generating spikes, i.e., precisely timed events in time. Thus, it could potentially be a valid model of spike generation in neurons, or more precisely, in the soma.

It is reasonable to require from a model of spike generation that it should be able to predict the moments in time when a real neuron spikes. Let us look at the following schematic

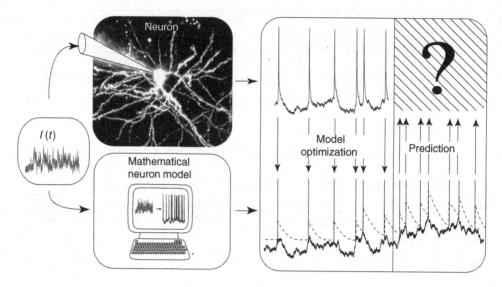

Fig. 1.13 The challenge of spike time prediction. A current $I(t)$ is experimentally injected into the soma of a real neuron *in vitro* through an electrode. The response of the neuron is recorded and half of the response is made available for model optimization while part of the response remains hidden. The challenge is then to use the input $I(t)$ to predict the spike times of the hidden response with a mathematical neuron model.

set-up (Fig. 1.13). An experimenter injects a time-dependent input current $I(t)$ into the soma of a cortical neuron using a first electrode. With an independent second electrode he or she measures the *voltage* at the soma of the neuron. Not surprisingly, the voltage trajectory contains from time to time sharp electrical pulses. These are the action potentials or spikes.

A befriended mathematical neuroscientist now takes the time course $I(t)$ of the input current that was used by the experimenter together with the time course of the membrane potential of the neuron and adjusts the parameters of a leaky integrate-and-fire model so that the model generates, for the very same input current, spikes at roughly the same moments in time as the real neuron. This needs some parameter tuning, but seems feasible. The relevant and much more difficult question, however, is whether the neuron model can now be used to predict the firing times of the real neuron for a novel time-dependent input current that was not used during parameter optimization (Fig. 1.13).

As discussed above, neurons not only show refractoriness after each spike but also exhibit adaptation which builds up over hundreds of milliseconds. A simple leaky integrate-and-fire model does not perform well at predicting the spike times of a real neuron. However, if adaptation (and refractoriness) is added to the neuron model, the prediction works surprisingly well. A straightforward way to add adaptation is to make the firing threshold of the neuron model dynamic: after each spike the threshold ϑ is increased by an amount θ, while during a quiescent period the threshold approaches its stationary value ϑ_0. We can

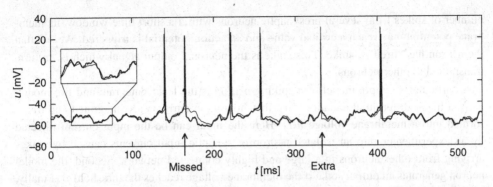

Fig. 1.14 Comparing a generalized integrate-and-fire model with experimental traces. A voltage trace (thick black trace) recorded in a real neuron driven by a fluctuating current is superposed on the voltage trace generated by a generalized integrate and fire model (thin line) driven by the same current. The subthreshold voltage fluctuations are accurately predicted (inset) and the spike timings are well predicted on average, apart from a few additional or missed spikes (arrows).

use the Dirac δ-function to express this idea

$$\tau_{\text{adapt}} \frac{\mathrm{d}}{\mathrm{d}t} \vartheta(t) = -[\vartheta(t) - \vartheta_0] + \theta \sum_f \delta(t - t^f) \tag{1.34}$$

where τ_{adapt} is the time constant of adaptation (a few hundred milliseconds) and $t^f = t^{(1)}, t^{(2)}, t^{(3)}, \ldots$ are the firing times of the neuron.

The predictions of an integrate-and-fire model with adaptive threshold agree nicely with the voltage trajectory of a real neuron, as can be seen from Fig. 1.14. The problem of how to construct practical, yet powerful, generalizations of the simple leaky integrate-and-fire model is the main topic of Part II of the book. Another question arising from this is how to quantify the performance of such neuron models (see Chapter 11).

Once we have identified good candidate neuron models, we will ask in Part III whether we can construct big populations of neurons with these models, and whether we can use them to understand the dynamic and computational principles as well as potential neural codes used by populations of neurons. Indeed, as we shall see, it is possible to make the transition from plausible single-neuron models to large and structured populations. This does not mean that we understand the full brain, but understanding the principles of large populations of neurons from well-tested simplified neuron models is a first and important step in this direction.

1.6 Summary

The neuronal signal consists of short voltage pulses called action potentials or spikes. These pulses travel along the axon and are distributed to several postsynaptic neurons where they evoke postsynaptic potentials. If a postsynaptic neuron receives a sufficient number of spikes from several presynaptic neurons within a short time window, its membrane potential may reach a critical value and an action potential is triggered. We say that the neuron has "fired" a spike. This spike is the neuronal output signal which is, in turn, transmitted to other neurons.

A particularly simple model of a spiking neuron is the leaky integrate-and-fire model. First, a linear differential equation describes how input currents are integrated and transformed into a membrane voltage $u(t)$. Here the input can be the input current injected by an experimenter into an isolated neuron or synaptic input currents caused by spikes arriving from other neurons in a large and highly connected network. Second, the model neuron generates an output spike if the membrane voltage reaches the threshold ϑ. Finally, after spike firing, the integration of the linear differential equation resumes from a reset value u_r.

The simple leaky integrate-and-fire model does not account for long-lasting refractoriness or adaptation. However, if the voltage dynamics of the leaky integrate-and-fire model is enhanced by mechanisms of adaptation, then it can be a powerful tool to accurately predict spike times of cortical neurons. Such generalized integrate-and-fire models are the main topic of Part II.

Literature

An elementary, non-technical introduction to neurons and synapses can be found in the book by Thompson (1993). At an intermediate level is the introductory textbook of Purves *et al.* (2008) while the *Principles of Neural Science* by Kandel *et al.* (2000) can be considered as a standard textbook on neuroscience covering a wealth of experimental results.

The use of mathematics to explain neuronal activity has a long tradition in theoretical neuroscience, over one hundred years. Phenomenological spiking neuron models similar to the leaky integrate-and-fire model were proposed in 1907 by Lapicque, who wanted to predict the first spike after stimulus onset (so that his model did not yet have the reset of the membrane potential after firing), and have been developed further in different variants by others (Lapicque, 1907; Hill, 1936; McCulloch and Pitts, 1943; Stein, 1965; Geisler and Goldberg, 1966; Weiss, 1966; Stein, 1967b). For the "filter" description of integrate-and-fire models see, for example, Gerstner *et al.* (1996b) and Pillow *et al.* (2008). The elegance and simplicity of integrate-and-fire models makes them a widely used tool to describe principles of neural information processing in neural networks of a broad range of sizes.

A different line of mathematical neuron models are biophysical models, first developed by Hodgkin and Huxley (1952); these biophysical models are the topic of the next chapter.

Exercises

1. **Synaptic current pulse**. *Synaptic inputs can be approximated by an exponential current* $I(t) = q \frac{1}{\tau_s} \exp[-\frac{t-t^f}{\tau_s}]$ *for* $t > t^f$ *where* t^f *is the moment when the spike arrives at the synapse.*

   (a) Use Eq. (1.5) to calculate the response of a passive membrane with time constant τ_m *to an input spike arriving at time* t^f.

   (b) In the solution resulting from (a), take the limit $\tau_s \to \tau_m$ *and show that in this limit the response is proportional to* $\propto [t - t^f] \exp[-\frac{t-t^f}{\tau_s}]$. *A function of this form is sometimes called an* α-*function.*

   (c) In the solution resulting from (a), take the limit $\tau_s \to 0$. *Can you relate your result to the discussion of the Dirac-*δ *function?*

2. **Time-dependent solution**. *Show that Eq. (1.15) is a solution of the differential equation Eq. (1.5) for time-dependent input* $I(t)$. *To do so, start by changing the variable in the integral from s to* $t' = t - s$. *Then take the derivative of Eq. (1.15) and compare the terms to those on both sides of the differential equation.*

3. **Chain of linear equations**. *Suppose that arrival of a spike at time* t^f *releases neurotransmitter into the synaptic cleft. The amount of available neurotransmitter at time t is* $\tau_x \frac{dx}{dt} = -x + \delta(t - t^f)$. *The neurotransmitter binds to the postsynaptic membrane and opens channels that enable a synaptic current* $\tau_s \frac{dI}{dt} = -I + I_0 x(t)$. *Finally, the current charges the postsynaptic membrane according to* $\tau_m \frac{du}{dt} = -u + RI(t)$. *Write the voltage response to a single current pulse as an integral.*

2

Ion channels and the Hodgkin–Huxley model

From a biophysical point of view, action potentials are the result of currents that pass through ion channels in the cell membrane. In an extensive series of experiments on the giant axon of the squid, Hodgkin and Huxley succeeded in measuring these currents and described their dynamics in terms of differential equations. Their paper published in 1952, which presents beautiful experiments combined with an elegant mathematical theory (Hodgkin and Huxley, 1952), was rapidly recognized as groundbreaking work and eventually led to the Nobel Prize for Hodgkin and Huxley in 1963. In this chapter, the Hodgkin–Huxley model is reviewed and its behavior illustrated by several examples.

The Hodgkin–Huxley model in its original form describes only three types of ion channel. However, as we shall see in Section 2.3 it can be extended to include many other ion channel types. The Hodgkin–Huxley equations are the basis for detailed neuron models which account for different types of synapse, and the spatial geometry of an individual neuron. Synaptic dynamics and the spatial structure of dendrites are the topics of Chapter 3. The Hodgkin–Huxley model is also the starting point for the derivation of simplified neuron models in Chapter 4 and will serve as a reference throughout the discussion of generalized integrate-and-fire models in Part II of the book.

Before we can turn to the Hodgkin–Huxley equations, we need to give some additional information on the equilibrium potential of ion channels.

2.1 Equilibrium potential

Neurons, just as other cells, are enclosed by a membrane which separates the interior of the cell from the extracellular space. Inside the cell the concentration of ions is different from that in the surrounding liquid. The difference in concentration generates an electrical potential which plays an important role in neuronal dynamics. In this section, we provide some background information and give an intuitive explanation of the equilibrium potential.

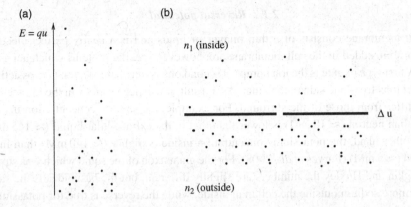

Fig. 2.1 (a) At thermal equilibrium, positive ions in an electric field will be distributed so that fewer ions are in a state of high energy and more at low energy. Thus a voltage difference generates a gradient in concentration. (b) Similarly, a difference in ion concentration generates an electrical potential. The concentration n_2 inside the neuron is different from the concentration n_1 of the surround. The resulting potential is called the Nernst potential. The solid line indicates the cell membrane. Ions can pass through the gap.

2.1.1 Nernst potential

From the theory of thermodynamics, it is known that the probability of a molecule taking a state of energy E is proportional to the Boltzmann factor, $p(E) \propto \exp(-E/kT)$, where k is the Boltzmann constant and T the temperature. Let us consider positive ions with charge q in a static electrical field. Their energy at location x is $E(x) = qu(x)$ where $u(x)$ is the potential at x. The probability of finding an ion in the region around x is therefore proportional to $\exp[-qu(x)/kT]$. Since the number of ions is huge, we may interpret the probability as an ion density. For ions with positive charge $q > 0$, the ion density is therefore higher in regions with low potential u. Let us write $n(x)$ for the ion density at point x. The relation between the density at point x_1 and point x_2 is

$$\frac{n(x_1)}{n(x_2)} = \exp\left[-\frac{qu(x_1) - qu(x_2)}{kT}\right]. \qquad (2.1)$$

A difference in the electrical potential $\Delta u = u(x_1) - u(x_2)$ generates therefore a difference in ion density; see Fig. 2.1.

Since this is a statement about an equilibrium state, the reverse must also be true. A difference in ion density generates a difference Δu in the electrical potential. We consider two regions of ions with concentration n_1 and n_2, respectively; see Fig. 2.1b. Solving (2.1) for Δu we find that, at equilibrium, the concentration difference generates a voltage

$$\Delta u = \frac{kT}{q} \ln \frac{n_2}{n_1} \qquad (2.2)$$

which is called the Nernst potential (Hille, 2001).

2.1.2 Reversal potential

The cell membrane consists of a thin bilayer of lipids and is a nearly perfect electrical insulator. Embedded in the cell membrane are, however, specific proteins which act as ion gates. A first type of gate is the ion pumps, a second one is ion channels. Ion pumps actively transport ions from one side to the other. As a result, ion concentrations in the intracellular liquid differ from those of the surround. For example, the sodium concentration inside a mammalian neuron (≈ 10 mM) is lower than that in the extracellular liquid (≈ 145 mM). On the other hand, the potassium concentration inside is higher (≈ 140 mM) than in the surround (≈ 5 mM) (Purves *et al.*, 2008). For the giant axon of the squid which was studied by Hodgkin and Huxley the numbers are slightly different, but the basic idea is the same: there is more sodium outside the cell than inside, while the reverse is true for potassium.

Let us focus for the moment on sodium ions. At equilibrium the difference in concentration causes a Nernst potential E_{Na} of about +67 mV. That is, at equilibrium the interior of the cell has a positive potential with respect to the surround. The interior of the cell and the surrounding liquid are in contact through ion channels where Na^+ ions can pass from one side of the membrane to the other. If the voltage difference Δu is smaller than the value of the Nernst potential E_{Na}, more Na^+ ions flow into the cell so as to decrease the concentration difference. If the voltage is larger than the Nernst potential ions would flow out the cell. Thus the direction of the current is reversed when the voltage Δu passes E_{Na}. For this reason, E_{Na} is called the reversal potential.

Example: Reversal potential for potassium

As mentioned above, the ion concentration of potassium is higher inside the cell (≈ 140 mM) than in the extracellular liquid (≈ 5 mM). Potassium ions have a single positive charge $q = 1.6 \times 10^{-19}$ C. Application of the Nernst formula, (2.2), with the Boltzmann constant $k = 1.4 \times 10^{-23}$ J/K yields $E_K \approx -83$ mV at room temperature. The reversal potential for K^+ ions is therefore negative.

Example: Resting potential

So far we have considered the presence of either sodium or potassium. In real cells, these and other ion types are simultaneously present and contribute to the voltage across the membrane. It is found experimentally that the resting potential of the membrane is about $u_{rest} \approx 65$ mV. Since $E_K < u_{rest} < E_{Na}$, potassium ions, at the resting potential, flow out of the cell while sodium ions flow into the cell. In the stationary state, the active ion pumps balance this flow and transport just as many ions back as pass through

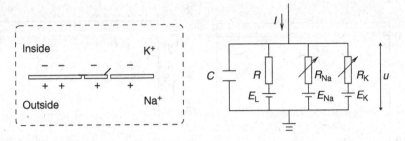

Fig. 2.2 Schematic diagram for the Hodgkin–Huxley model.

the channels. The value of u_{rest} is determined by the dynamic equilibrium between the ion flow through the channels (permeability of the membrane) and active ion transport (efficiency of the ion pump in maintaining the concentration difference).

2.2 Hodgkin–Huxley model

Hodgkin and Huxley (1952) performed experiments on the giant axon of the squid and found three different types of ion current, namely, sodium, potassium, and a leak current that consists mainly of Cl^- ions. Specific voltage-dependent ion channels, one for sodium and another one for potassium, control the flow of those ions through the cell membrane. The leak current takes care of other channel types which are not described explicitly.

2.2.1 Definition of the model

The Hodgkin–Huxley model can be understood with the help of Fig. 2.2. The semipermeable cell membrane separates the interior of the cell from the extracellular liquid and acts as a capacitor. If an input current $I(t)$ is injected into the cell, it may add further charge on the capacitor, or leak through the channels in the cell membrane. Each channel type is represented in Fig. 2.2 by a resistor. The unspecific channel has a leak resistance R, the sodium channel a resistance R_{Na} and the potassium channel a resistance R_K. The diagonal arrow across the diagram of the resistor indicates that the value of the resistance is not fixed, but changes depending on whether the ion channel is open or closed. Because of active ion transport through the cell membrane, the ion concentration inside the cell is different from that in the extracellular liquid. The Nernst potential generated by the difference in ion concentration is represented by a battery in Fig. 2.2. Since the Nernst potential is different for each ion type, there are separate batteries for sodium, potassium, and the unspecific third channel, with battery voltages E_{Na}, E_K and E_L, respectively.

Let us now translate the above schema of an electrical circuit into mathematical equations. The conservation of electric charge on a piece of membrane implies that the applied current $I(t)$ may be split into a capacitive current I_C which charges the capacitor C and

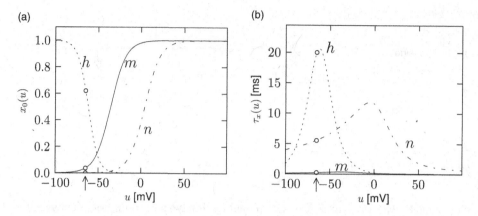

Fig. 2.3 The Hodgkin–Huxley model. (a) The equilibrium functions for the three variables m, n, h in the Hodgkin–Huxley model. (b) The voltage-dependent time constant. The resting potential is at $u = -65\,\mathrm{mV}$ (arrow) and parameters are those given in Table 2.1.

further components I_k which pass through the ion channels. Thus

$$I(t) = I_C(t) + \sum_k I_k(t), \tag{2.3}$$

where the sum runs over all ion channels. In the standard Hodgkin–Huxley model there are only three types of channel: a sodium channel with index Na, a potassium channel with index K and an unspecific leakage channel with resistance R; see Fig. 2.2. From the definition of a capacity $C = q/u$ where q is a charge and u the voltage across the capacitor, we find the charging current $I_C = C\,\mathrm{d}u/\mathrm{d}t$. Hence from (2.3)

$$C\frac{\mathrm{d}u}{\mathrm{d}t} = -\sum_k I_k(t) + I(t). \tag{2.4}$$

In biological terms, u is the voltage across the membrane and $\sum_k I_k$ is the sum of the ionic currents which pass through the cell membrane.

As mentioned above, the Hodgkin–Huxley model describes three types of channel. All channels may be characterized by their resistance or, equivalently, by their conductance. The leakage channel is described by a voltage-independent conductance $g_L = 1/R$. Since u is the total voltage across the cell membrane and E_L the voltage of the battery, the voltage at the leak resistor in Fig. 2.2 is $u - E_L$. Using Ohm's law, we get a leak current $I_L = g_L(u - E_L)$.

The mathematics of the other ion channels is analogous except that their conductance is voltage- and time-dependent. If all channels are open, they transmit currents with a maximum conductance g_{Na} or g_K, respectively. Normally, however, some of the channels are blocked. The breakthrough of Hodgkin and Huxley was that they succeeded in measuring how the effective resistance of a channel changes as a function of time and voltage. Moreover, they proposed a mathematical description of their observations. Specifically, they introduced additional "gating" variables m, n and h to model the probability that a

x	E_x [mV]	g_x [mS/cm^2]
Na	55	40
K	−77	35
L	−65	0.3

x	$\alpha_x(u/\text{mV})$ [ms^{-1}]	$\beta_x(u/\text{mV})$ [ms^{-1}]
n	$0.02(u-25)/[1-e^{-(u-25)/9}]$	$-0.002(u-25)/[1-e^{(u-25)/9}]$
m	$0.182(u+35)/[1-e^{-(u+35)/9}]$	$-0.124(u+35)/[1-e^{(u+35)/9}]$
h	$1/[1+e^{-(u+62)/6}]$	$4e^{(u+90)/12}/[1+e^{-(u+62)/6}]$

Table 2.1 *Parameters for the Hodgkin–Huxley equations fitted on pyramidal neurons of the cortex. The parameters for n and m were fitted by Zach Mainen (Mainen et al., 1995) on experiments reported by Huguenard et al. (1988) and the parameters for h by Richard Naud on the experiments reported in Hamill et al. (1991). Voltage is measured in mV and the membrane capacity is $C = 1\,\mu F/cm^2$.*

channel is open at a given moment in time. The combined action of m and h controls the Na$^+$ channels while the K$^+$ gates are controlled by n. For example, the effective conductance of sodium channels is modeled as $1/R_{Na} = g_{Na}\, m^3\, h$, where m describes the activation (opening) of the channel and h its inactivation (blocking). The conductance of potassium is $1/R_K = g_K\, n^4$, where n describes the activation of the channel.

In summary, Hodgkin and Huxley formulated the three ion currents on the right-hand-side of (2.4) as

$$\sum_k I_k = g_{Na}\, m^3 h\, (u - E_{Na}) + g_K\, n^4\, (u - E_K) + g_L\, (u - E_L). \tag{2.5}$$

The parameters E_{Na}, E_K, and E_L are the reversal potentials.

The three gating variables m, n, and h evolve according to differential equations of the form

$$\dot{x} = -\frac{1}{\tau_x(u)}[x - x_0(u)], \tag{2.6}$$

with $\dot{x} = dx/dt$, and where x stands for m, n, or h. The interpretation of (2.6) is simple: for a fixed voltage u, the variable x approaches the target value $x_0(u)$ with a time constant $\tau_x(u)$. The voltage dependence of the time constant and asymptotic value is illustrated in Fig. 2.3. The form of the functions plotted in Fig. 2.3, as well as the maximum conductances and reversal potentials in (2.5), were deduced by Hodgkin and Huxley from empirical measurements.

Example: Voltage step

Experimenters can hold the voltage across the cell membrane at a desired value by injecting an appropriate current into the cell. Suppose that the experimenter keeps the

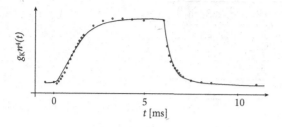

Fig. 2.4 Original data and fit of Hodgkin and Huxley (1952). The measured time course of the potassium conductance (circles) after application of a voltage step of 25 mV and after return to resting potential. The fit (solid line) is based on Eq. (2.8). Adapted from Hodgkin and Huxley (1952).

cell at resting potential $u_0 = -65$ mV for $t < t_0$ and switches the voltage at t_0 to a new value u_1. Integration of the differential equation (2.6) gives, for $t > t_0$, the dynamics

$$m(t) = m_0(u_1) + [m_0(u_0) - m_0(u_1)]\exp\left[\frac{-(t-t_0)}{\tau_m(u_1)}\right],$$

$$h(t) = h_0(u_1) + [h_0(u_0) - h_0(u_1)]\exp\left[\frac{-(t-t_0)}{\tau_h(u_1)}\right], \tag{2.7}$$

so that, based on the model with given functions for $m_0(u)$, $h_0(u)$, $\tau_m(u)$, $\tau_h(u)$, we can predict the sodium current $I_{Na}(t) = g_{Na}[m(t)^3]h(t)(u_1 - E_{Na})$ for $t > t_0$ generated by the voltage step at $t = t_0$.

Similarly, the potassium current caused by a voltage step is $I_K(t) = g_K[n(t)^4](u_1 - E_K)$ with

$$n(t) = n_0(u_1) + [n_0(u_0) - n_0(u_1)]\exp\left[\frac{-(t-t_0)}{\tau_n(u_1)}\right]. \tag{2.8}$$

Hodgkin and Huxley used Eqs. (2.7) and (2.8) to work the other way round. After blocking the sodium channel with appropriate pharmacological agents, they applied a voltage step and measured the time course of the potassium current. Dividing the recorded current through the driving potential $(u_1 - E_K)$ yields the time-dependent conductance $g_K[n(t)^4]$; see Fig. 2.4. Using (2.8), Hodgkin and Huxley deduced the value of $n_0(u_1)$ and $\tau_n(u_1)$ as well as the exponent of 4 in $n^4(t)$ for potassium. Repeating the experiments for different values u_1 gives the experimental curves for $n_0(u)$ and $\tau_n(u)$.

Example: Activation and de-inactivation

The variable m is called an activation variable. To understand this terminology, we note from Fig. 2.3 that the value of $m_0(u)$ at the neuronal resting potential of $u = -65$ mV is close to zero. Therefore, at rest, the sodium current $I_{Na} = g_{Na}m^3h(u - E_{Na})$ through the channel vanishes. In other words, the sodium channel is closed.

When the membrane potential increases significantly above the resting potential, the gating variable m increases to its new value $m_0(u)$. As long as h does not change, the

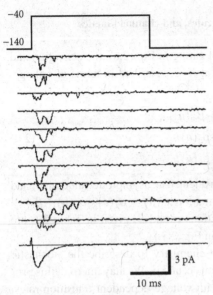

Fig. 2.5 Stochastic channel activation. The current flowing through a small patch of membrane after application of a voltage step (top row) shows step-like changes and is different in each trial (subsequent traces). Averaging over many trials yields the bottom trace. Adapted from Patlak and Ortiz (1985). ©1985 Rockefeller University Press. Originally published in *Journal of General Physiology*, **86**: 89–104.

sodium current increases and the gate opens. Therefore the variable m "activates" the channel. If, after a return of the voltage to rest, m decays back to zero, it is said to be "de-activating."

The terminology of the "inactivation" variable h is analogous. At rest, h has a large positive value. If the voltage increases to a value above $-40\,\mathrm{mV}$, h approaches a new value $h_0(u)$ which is close to rest. Therefore the channel "inactivates" (blocks) with a time constant that is given by $\tau_h(u)$. If the voltage returns to zero, h increases so that the channel undergoes "de-inactivation." This sounds like tricky vocabulary, but it turns out to be useful to distinguish between a deactivated channel (m close to zero and h close to 1) and an inactivated channel (h close to zero).

2.2.2 Stochastic channel opening

The number of ion channels in a patch of membrane is finite, and individual ion channels open and close stochastically. Thus, when an experimenter records the current flowing through a small patch of membrane, he does not find a smooth and reliable evolution of the measured variable over time but rather a highly fluctuating current, which looks different at each repetition of the experiment (Fig. 2.5).

The Hodgkin–Huxley equations, which describe the opening and closing of ion channels with deterministic equations for the variables m, h, and n, correspond to the current density through a hypothetical, extremely large patch of membrane containing an infinite number of channels or, alternatively, to the current through a small patch of membrane but averaged over many repetitions of the same experiment (Fig. 2.5). The stochastic aspects can be included by adding appropriate noise to the model.

Example: Time constants, transition rates, and channel kinetics

As an alternative to the formulation of channel gating in Eq. (2.6), the activation and inactivation dynamics of each channel type can also be described in terms of voltage-dependent transition rates α and β,

$$
\begin{aligned}
\dot{m} &= \alpha_m(u)(1-m) - \beta_m(u)m, \\
\dot{n} &= \alpha_n(u)(1-n) - \beta_n(u)n, \\
\dot{h} &= \alpha_h(u)(1-h) - \beta_h(u)h.
\end{aligned}
\tag{2.9}
$$

The two formulations Eqs. (2.6) and (2.9) are equivalent. The asymptotic value $x_0(u)$ and the time constant $\tau_x(u)$ are given by the transformation $x_0(u) = \alpha_x(u)/[\alpha_x(u) + \beta_x(u)]$ and $\tau_x(u) = [\alpha_x(u) + \beta_x(u)]^{-1}$. The various functions α and β, given in Table 2.1, are empirical functions of u that produce the curves in Fig. 2.3.

Equations (2.9) are typical equations used in chemistry to describe the stochastic dynamics of an activation process with rate constants α and β. We may interpret this process as a molecular switch between two states with voltage-dependent transition rates. For example, the activation variable n can be interpreted as the probability of finding a single potassium channel open. Therefore in a patch with K channels, $k \approx (1-n)K$ channels are expected to be closed. We may interpret $\alpha_n(u)\Delta t$ as the probability that in a short time interval Δt one of the momentarily closed channels switches to the open state.

2.2.3 Dynamics

In this section we study the dynamics of the Hodgkin–Huxley model for different types of input. Pulse input, constant input, step current input, and time-dependent input are considered in turn. These input scenarios have been chosen so as to provide an intuitive understanding of the dynamics of the Hodgkin–Huxley model.

The most important property of the Hodgkin–Huxley model is its ability to generate action potentials. In Fig. 2.6a an action potential has been initiated by a short current pulse of 1 ms duration applied at $t = 1$ ms. The spike has an amplitude of nearly 100 mV and a width at half maximum of about 2.5 ms. After the spike, the membrane potential falls below the resting potential and returns only slowly back to its resting value of -65 mV.

Ion channel dynamics during spike generation

In order to understand the biophysics underlying the generation of an action potential we return to Fig. 2.3a. We find that m_0 and n_0 increase with u whereas h_0 decreases. Thus, if some external input causes the membrane voltage to rise, the conductance of sodium channels increases due to increasing m. As a result, positive sodium ions flow into the cell and raise the membrane potential even further. If this positive feedback is large enough, an action potential is initiated. The explosive increase comes to a natural halt when the membrane potential approaches the reversal potential E_{Na} of the sodium current.

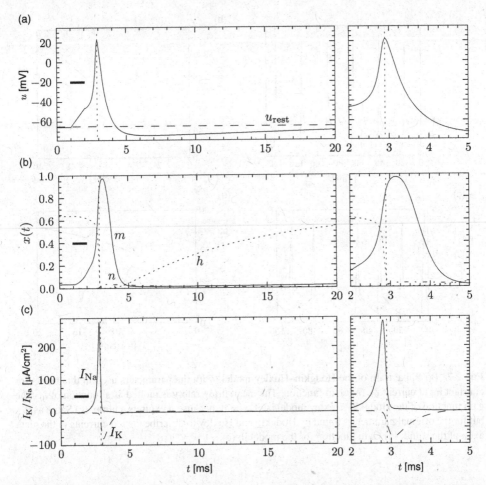

Fig. 2.6 (a) Action potential. The Hodgkin–Huxley model is stimulated by a short, but strong, current pulse between $t = 1$ ms and $t = 2$ ms. The time course of the membrane potential $u(t)$ for $t > 2$ ms shows the action potential (positive peak) followed by a relative refractory period where the potential is below the resting potential u_{rest} (dashed line). The right panel shows an expanded view of the action potential between $t = 2$ ms and $t = 5$ ms. (b) The dynamics of gating variables m, h, n illustrate how the action potential is mediated by sodium and potassium channels. (c) The sodium current I_{Na} which depends on the variables m and h has a sharp peak during the upswing of an action potential. The potassium current I_K is controlled by the variable n and starts with a delay compared with I_{Na}.

At high values of u the sodium conductance is slowly shut off due to the factor h. As indicated in Fig. 2.3b, the "time constant" τ_h is always larger than τ_m. Thus the variable h which inactivates the channels reacts more slowly to the voltage increase than the variable m which opens the channel. On a similar slow time scale, the potassium (K$^+$) current sets in Fig. 2.6c. Since it is a current in outward direction, it lowers the potential. The overall effect of the sodium and potassium currents is a short action potential followed by

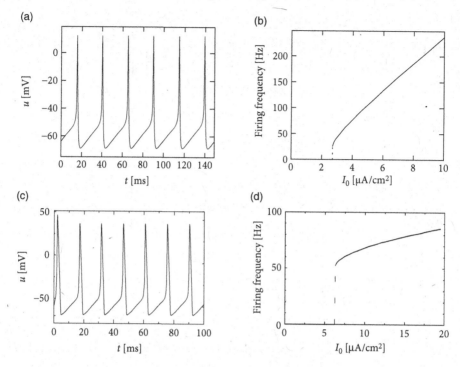

Fig. 2.7 (a) Spike train of the Hodgkin–Huxley model (with the parameters used in this book) for constant input current I_0. (b) Gain function. The mean firing rate v is plotted as a function of I_0. The gain function of the Hodgkin–Huxley model is of type II, because it exhibits a jump. (c) Same as (a), but for the original parameters found by Hodgkin and Huxley to describe the ion currents in the giant axon of the squid. (d) Gain function for the model in (c).

a negative overshoot; see Fig. 2.6a. The negative overshoot, called hyperpolarizing spike-afterpotential, is due to the slow de-inactivation of the sodium channel, caused by the h-variable.

Example: Mean firing rates and gain function

The Hodgkin–Huxley equations (2.4)–(2.9) may also be studied for constant input $I(t) = I_0$ for $t > 0$. (The input is zero for $t \leq 0$.) If the value I_0 is larger than a critical value $I_\theta \approx 2.7\,\mu\text{A/cm}^2$, we observe regular spiking; see Fig. 2.7a. We may define a firing rate $v = 1/T$ where T is the interspike interval.

The firing rate as a function of the constant input I_0, often called the "frequency–current" relation or "f–I plot," defines the gain function plotted in Fig. 2.7b. With the parameters given in Table 2.1, the gain function exhibits a jump at I_θ. Gain functions with a discontinuity are called "type II."

(a)

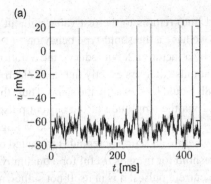

(b)

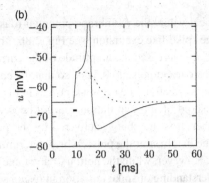

Fig. 2.8   (a) Spike train of the Hodgkin–Huxley model driven by a time-dependent input current. The action potentials occur irregularly. The figure shows the voltage u as a function of time. (b) Threshold effect. A short current pulse of 1 ms is applied which leads to a excursion of the membrane potential of a few millivolts (dashed line). A slight increase of the strength of the current pulse leads to the generation of an action potential (solid line) with an amplitude of about 100 mV above rest (out of bounds).

If we shift the curve of the inactivation variable h to more positive voltages, and keep the same parameters otherwise, the modified Hodgkin–Huxley model exhibits a smooth gain function; see Section 2.3.2 and Fig. 2.11. Neuron models or, more generally, "excitable membranes" are called "type I" or "class I" if they have a continuous frequency–current relation. The distinction between the excitability of type I and II can be traced back to Hodgkin (1948).

Example: Stimulation by time-dependent input

In order to explore a more realistic input scenario, we stimulate the Hodgkin–Huxley model by a time-dependent input current $I(t)$ that is generated by the following procedure. Every 2 ms, a random number is drawn from a Gaussian distribution with zero mean and standard deviation $\sigma = 34\ \mu\text{A/cm}^2$. To get a continuous input current, a linear interpolation was used between the target values. The resulting time-dependent input current was then applied to the Hodgkin–Huxley model (2.4)–(2.6). The response to the current is the voltage trace shown in Fig. 2.8a. Note that action potentials occur at irregular intervals.

Example: Firing threshold

In Fig. 2.8b an action potential (solid line) has been initiated by a short current pulse of 1 ms duration. If the amplitude of the stimulating current pulse is reduced below some critical value, the membrane potential (dashed line) returns to the rest value without a large spike-like excursion; see Fig. 2.8b. Thus we have a threshold-type behavior.

If we increased the amplitude of the current by a factor of 2, but reduced the duration of the current pulse to 0.5 ms, so that the current pulse delivers exactly the same electric charge as before, the response curves in Fig. 2.8b would look exactly the same. Thus, the threshold of spike initiation can *not* be defined via the amplitude of the current pulse. Rather, it is the charge delivered by the pulse or, equivalently, the membrane voltage immediately after the pulse, which determines whether an action potential is triggered or not. However, while the notion of a voltage threshold for firing is useful for a qualitative understanding of spike initiation in response to current pulses, it is in itself not sufficient to capture the dynamics of the Hodgkin–Huxley model; see the discussion in this and the next two chapters.

Example: Refractoriness

In order to study neuronal refractoriness, we stimulate the Hodgkin–Huxley model by a first current pulse that is sufficiently strong to excite a spike. A second current pulse of the *same* amplitude as the first one is used to probe the responsiveness of the neuron during the phase of hyperpolarization that follows the action potential. If the second stimulus is not sufficient to trigger another action potential, we have a clear signature of neuronal refractoriness. In the simulation shown in Fig. 2.9, a second spike is not emitted if the second stimulus is given less than 40 ms after the first one. It would, of course, be possible to trigger a second spike after a shorter interval, if a significantly stronger stimulation pulse was used; for classical experiments along those lines (see, e.g., Fuortes and Mantegazzini 1962).

If we look more closely at the voltage trajectory of Fig. 2.9, we see that neuronal refractoriness manifests itself in two different forms. First, owing to the hyperpolarizing spike-afterpotential, the voltage is lower. More stimulation is therefore needed to reach the firing threshold. Second, since a large portion of channels are open immediately after a spike, the resistance of the membrane is reduced compared with the situation at rest. The depolarizing effect of a stimulating current pulse therefore decays faster immediately after the spike than 10 ms later. An efficient description of refractoriness plays a major role in simplified neuron models discussed in Chapter 6.

Example: Damped oscillations and transient spiking

When stimulated with a small step-increase in current, the Hodgkin–Huxley model with parameters as in Table 2.1 exhibits a damped oscillation with a maximum of about

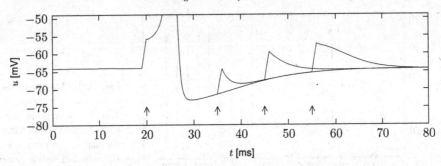

Fig. 2.9 Refractoriness of the Hodgkin–Huxley model. At $t = 20$ ms the model is stimulated by a short current pulse (left arrow) so as to trigger an action potential. A second current pulse of the same amplitude applied at $t = 35, 45,$ or 55 ms (subsequent arrows) is not sufficient to trigger a second action potential.

20 ms after the onset of the current step; see Fig. 2.10. If the step size is large enough, but not sufficient to cause sustained firing, a single spike can be generated. Note that in Fig. 2.10 the input current returns at 200 ms to the *same* value it had a hundred milliseconds before. While the neuron stays quiescent after the first step, it fires a transient spike the second time not because the total input is stronger but because the step *starts* from a strong negative value.

A spike which is elicited by a step current that starts from a strong negative value and then switches back to zero would be called a rebound spike. In other words, a rebound spike is triggered by release from inhibition. For example, the Hodgkin–Huxley model with the original parameters for the giant axon of the squid exhibits rebound spikes when a prolonged negative input current is stopped; the model with the set of parameters adopted in this book, however, does not.

The transient spike in Fig. 2.10 occurs about 20 ms after the start of the step. A simple explanation of the transient spike is that the peak of the membrane potential oscillation after the step reaches the voltage threshold for spike initiation, so that a single action potential is triggered. It is indeed the subthreshold oscillations that underly the transient spiking illustrated in Fig. 2.10.

Damped oscillations result from subthreshold inactivation of the sodium current. At rest the sodium currents are not activated ($m \approx 0$) but only partially inactivated ($h \approx 0.6$). Responding to the step stimulus, the membrane potential increases, which activates slightly and de-inactivates slowly the sodium channel. When the input is not strong enough for an action potential to be initiated, the de-inactivation of I_{Na} reduces the effective drive and thus the membrane potential. The system then relaxes to an equilibrium. If, on the other hand, the current was strong enough to elicit a spike, the equilibrium may be reached only after the spike. A further increase in the step current drives sustained firing (Fig. 2.10).

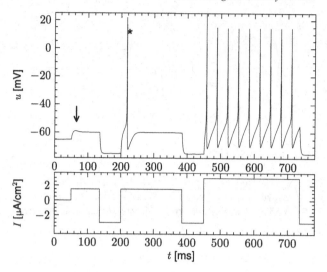

Fig. 2.10 Damped oscillations and a transient spike. Top. The voltage response to a step current shows a damped oscillation (arrow), a single rebound spike (asterisk) or repetitive firing. Bottom. Time course of the stimulating current.

2.3 The zoo of ion channels

Hodgkin and Huxley used their equations to describe the electrophysiological properties of the giant axon of the squid. These equations capture the essence of spike generation by sodium and potassium ion channels. The basic mechanism of generating action potentials is a short influx of sodium ions that is followed by an efflux of potassium ions. This mechanism of spike generation is essentially preserved in higher organisms, so that, with the choice of parameters given in Table 2.1, we already have a first approximate model of neurons in vertebrates. With a further change of parameters we could adapt the model equations to different temperatures to account for the fact that neurons at 37 degrees Celsius behave differently than neurons in a lab preparation held at a room temperature of 21 degrees Celsius.

However, in order to account for the rich biophysics observed in the neurons of the vertebrate nervous system, two types of ion channel are not enough. Neurons come in different types and exhibit different electrical properties which in turn correspond to a large variety of ion channels. Today, about 200 ion channels are known and many of these have been identified genetically (Ranjan *et al.*, 2011). In experimental laboratories where the biophysics and functional role of ion channels are investigated, specific ion channel types can be blocked through pharmacological manipulations. In order to make predictions of blocking results, it is important to develop models that incorporate multiple ion channels. As we shall see below (Section 2.3.1), the mathematical framework of the Hodgkin–Huxley model is well suited for such an endeavor.

For other scientific questions, we may be interested only in the firing pattern of neurons and not in the biophysical mechanisms that give rise to it. Later, in Part II of this book, we will show that generalized integrate-and-fire models can account for a large variety of neuronal firing patterns (Chapter 6) and predict spike timings of real neurons with high precision (Chapter 11). Therefore, in Parts III and IV of the book, where we focus on large networks of neurons, we mainly work with generalized integrate-and-fire rather than bio-physical models. Nevertheless, biophysical models, i.e., Hodgkin–Huxley equations with multiple ion channels, serve as an important reference.

2.3.1 Framework for biophysical neuron models

The formalism of the Hodgkin–Huxley equation is extremely powerful, because it enables researchers to incorporate known ion channel types into a given neuron model. Just as before, the electrical properties of a patch of neuronal membrane are described by the conservation of current

$$C\frac{du}{dt} = -\sum_k I_k(t) + I(t), \tag{2.10}$$

but in contrast to the simple Hodgkin–Huxley model discussed in the previous section, the right-hand side now contains all types of ion current found in a given neuron. For each ion channel type k, we introduce activation and inactivation variables

$$I_k(t) = g_k([Ca^{++}],...)m^{p_k}h^{q_k}(u - E_k), \tag{2.11}$$

where m and h describe activation and inactivation of the channel with equations analogous to (2.6), p_k and q_k are empirical parameters, E_k is the reversal potential, and g_k is the max-imum conductance which may depend on secondary variables such as the concentration of calcium, magnesium, dopamine or other substances. In principle, if the dynamics of each channel type (i.e., all parameters that go into Eqs. (2.11) and (2.6)) are available, then one needs only to know which channels are present in a given neuron in order to build a bio-physical neuron model. Studying the composition of messenger RNA in a drop of liquid extracted from a neuron gives a strong indication of which ion channels are present in a neuron, and which are not (Toledo-Rodriguez et al., 2004). The relative importance of ion channels is not fixed, but depends on the age of neuron as well as other factors. Indeed, a neuron can tune its spiking dynamics by regulating its ion channel composition via a modification of the gene expression profile.

Ion channels are complex transmembrane proteins which exist in many different forms. It is possible to classify an ion channel using (i) its genetic sequence; (ii) the ion type (sodium, potassium, calcium, ...) that can pass through the open channel; (iii) its voltage dependence; (iv) its sensitivity to second-messengers such as intracellular calcium; (v) its presumed functional role; (vi) its response to pharmacological drugs or to neuromodulators such as acetylcholine and dopamine.

Using a notation that mixes the classification schemes (i)–(iii), geneticists have dis-tinguished multiple families of voltage-gated ion channels on the basis of similarities in the amino acid sequences. The channels are labeled with the chemical symbol of the ion of their selectivity, one or two letters denoting a distinct characteristic and a number to determine the subfamily. For instance "Kv5" is the fifth subfamily of the voltage-sensitive potassium channel family "Kv". An additional number may be inserted to indicate the channel isoforms, for instance "Nav1.1" is the first isoform that was found within the first subfamily of voltage-dependent sodium channels. Sometimes a lower-case letter is used to point to the splice variants (e.g., "Nav1.1a"). Strictly speaking, these names apply to a single cloned gene which corresponds to a channel subunit, whereas the full ion channel is composed of several subunits usually from a given family but possibly from different subfamilies.

Traditionally, electrophysiologists have identified channels with subscripts that reflect a combination of the classification schemes (ii)–(vi). The index of the potassium "M-current" I_M points to its response to pharmacological stimulation of Muscarinic (M) acetylcholine receptors. Another potassium current, I_{AHP}, shapes the after-hyperpolarization (AHP) of the membrane potential after a spike. Thus the subscript corresponds to the presumed functional role of the channel. Sometimes the functionally characterized current can be related to the genetic classification; for instance I_{AHP} is a calcium-dependent potassium channel associated with the small-conductance "SK" family, but in other cases the link between an electrophysiologically characterized channel and its composition in terms of genetically identified subunits is still uncertain. Linking genetic expression with a functionally characterized ion current is a fast-expanding field of study (Ranjan *et al.*, 2011).

In this section we select a few examples from the zoo of ion channels and illustrate how ion channels can modify the spiking dynamics. The aim is not to quantitatively specify parameters of each ionic current as this depends heavily on the genetic expression of the subunits, cell type, temperature and neurotransmitters. Rather, we would like to explore qualitatively the influence of ion channel kinetics on neuronal properties. In other words, let us bring the zoo of ion channels to the circus and explore the stunning acts that can be achieved.

2.3.2 Sodium ion channels and the type-I regime

The parameters of the Hodgkin–Huxley model in Table 2.1 relate to only one type of sodium and potassium ion channel. There are more than 10 different types of sodium channels, each with a slightly different activation and inactivation profile. However, as we shall see, even a small change in the ion channel kinetics can profoundly affect the spiking characteristics of a neuron.

Let us consider a sodium ion channel which has its inactivation curve $h_0(u)$ (Fig. 2.3a) shifted to depolarized voltages by 20 mV compared with the parameters in Table 2.1. With maximal conductances $g_{Na} = 25$ nS/cm^2 and $g_K = 40$ nS/cm^2, the dynamics of a neuron with this modified sodium channel (Fig. 2.11) is qualitatively different from that of a neuron with the parameters as in Table 2.1 (Figs. 2.7 and 2.10).

(a)
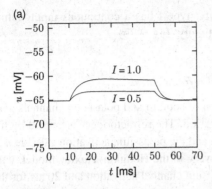

(b)
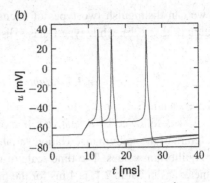

Fig. 2.11 A modification of sodium channel kinetics leads to different neuronal dynamics. (a) Response of a model with modified sodium channel to current steps of different amplitudes. (b) Delayed spike initiation. A short current pulse of 2 ms duration is applied at $t = 8$ ms. The action potential that is elicited in response to the current pulse is shown for decreasing pulse amplitudes ($I = 6.25, 5.90, 5.88 \, \mu A/cm^2$). Note that the action potential can occur more than 10 ms *after* the end of the current pulse.

(a)
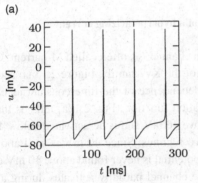

(b)
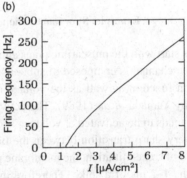

Fig. 2.12 Type-I regime with a modified sodium current. (a) Regular spiking response to constant input. (b) Firing frequency as a function of the constant current.

First, the neuron with the modified sodium dynamics shows no damped oscillations in response to a step input (Fig. 2.11a). Second, the neuron responds to a short current pulse which is just slightly above the firing threshold with a delayed action potential (Fig. 2.11b). Third, during regular spiking the shape of the action potential is slightly different in the model with the modified sodium channel (Fig. 2.12a). In particular, the membrane potential between the spikes exhibits an inflection point, unlike the spike train with the original set of parameters (Fig. 2.7a). Finally, the gain function (frequency–current plot) has no gap so that the neuron model can fire at arbitrarily small frequencies (Fig. 2.12b). If we compare this f–I plot with the gain function of the neuron with parameters from Table

2.1, we can distinguish two types of excitability: type I has a continuous input–output function (Fig. 2.12b), while type II has a discontinuity (Fig. 2.7b).

2.3.3 Adaptation and refractoriness

We have seen in Section 2.2 that the combination of sodium and potassium channels generates spikes followed by a relative refractory period. The refractoriness is caused by the slow return of the sodium inactivation variable h and the potassium activation variable n to their equilibrium values. The time scale of recovery in the Hodgkin–Huxley model, with parameters as in Table 2.1, is 4 ms for the potassium channel activation and 20 ms for the sodium channel inactivation. Other ion channel types, not present in the original Hodgkin–Huxley model, can affect the recovery process on much longer time scales and lead to spike-frequency adaptation: after stimulation with a step current, interspike intervals get successively longer. The basic mechanism of adaptation is the same as that of refractoriness: either a hyperpolarizing current is activated during a spike (and slowly de-activates thereafter) or a depolarizing current is inactivated during a spike and de-inactivates on a much slower time scale.

Example: Slow inactivation of a hyperpolarizing current

Let us start with the muscarinic potassium channel I_M, often called M-current. Genetically, the channel is composed of subunits of the Kv7 family. Figure 2.13a,b show the activation function as well as the voltage dependence of the time constant as characterized by Yamada *et al.* (1989). The activation function (Fig. 2.13a) tells us that this channel tends to be activated at voltages above 40 mV and is de-activated below 40 mV with a very sharp transition between the two regimes. Since 40 mV is well above the threshold of spike initiation, the membrane potential is never found above 40 mV except during the 1–2 ms of a spike. Therefore the channel partially activates during a spike and, after the end of the action potential, de-activates with a time constant of 40–60 ms (Fig. 2.13b). The slow deactivation of this potassium channel affects the time course of the membrane potential after a spike. Compared with the original Hodgkin–Huxley model, which has only the two currents specified in Table 2.1, a model with an additional I_M current exhibits a prolonged hyperpolarizing spike-afterpotential and therefore a longer relative refractory period (Fig. 2.13c–e).

In the regular firing regime, it is possible that the M-current caused by a previous spike is still partially activated when the next spike is emitted. The partial activation can therefore accumulate over successive spikes. By cumulating over spikes, the activation of I_M gradually forces the membrane potential away from the threshold, increasing the interspike interval. This results in a spiking response that appears to "adapt" to a step input, hence the name "spike-frequency adaptation" or simply "adaptation" (Fig. 2.13c–e).

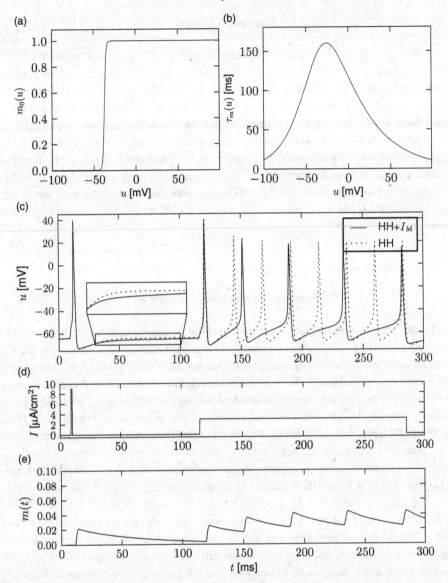

Fig. 2.13 Spike-frequency adaptation with I_M. (a) Voltage dependence of the stationary value of the activation variable m and (b) its time constants for the muscarinic potassium current $I_M = g_M m (u - E_k)$ extracted from experimental observations (Yamada *et al.*, 1989). (c) Voltage response to the current shown in (d) of the original Hodgkin–Huxley model with parameters from Table 2.1 (dashed line) and a model which also contains the I_M channel. The model with I_M exhibits adaptation. (e) Progressive activation of the potassium current I_M during the repetitive spiking period shown in (c).

Example: A-current

Another potassium ion channel with kinetics similar to I_M is I_A, but qualitatively different effects: I_A makes the relative refractory period longer and stronger without causing much adaptation. To see the distinction between I_A and I_M, we compare the activation kinetics of both channels (Figs. 2.13b and 2.14b). The time constant τ_m of activation is much faster for I_A than for I_M. This implies that the A-current increases rapidly during the short time of the spike and decays quickly afterward. In other words, the effect of I_A is short and strong whereas the effect of I_M is long and small. Because the effect of I_A does not last as long, it contributes to refractoriness, but only very little to spike frequency adaptation (Fig. 2.14c–e). Even though an inactivation process, with variable h, was reported for I_A, its time constant τ_h is so long (>150 ms) that it does not play a role in the above arguments.

Example: Slow extrusion of calcium

Multiple ion channel families contribute to spike-frequency adaptation. In contrast to the direct action of I_M, the calcium-dependent potassium channel $I_{K[Ca]}$ generates adaptation indirectly via its dependence on the intracellular calcium concentration. During each spike, calcium enters through the high-threshold calcium channel I_{HVA}. As calcium accumulates inside the cell, the calcium-dependent potassium channel $I_{K[Ca]}$ gradually opens, lowers the membrane potential, and makes further spike generation more difficult. Thus, the level of adaptation can be read out from the intracellular calcium concentration.

In order to understand the accumulation of calcium, we need to discuss the high-threshold calcium channel I_{HVA}. Since it activates above -40 mV to -30 mV, the channel opens during a spike. Its dynamics is therefore similar to that of the sodium current, but the direct effect of I_{HVA} on the shape of the spike is small. Its main role is to deliver a pulse of calcium ions into the neuron. The calcium ions have an important role as second-messengers; they can trigger various cascades of biophysical processes. Intracellular calcium is taken up by internal buffers, or slowly pumped out of the cell, leading to an intricate dynamics dependent on the properties of calcium buffers and calcium pumps. For small calcium transients, however, or when the calcium pump has high calcium affinity and slow extrusion rate, the intracellular calcium dynamics follow (Helmchen *et al.*, 2011)

$$\frac{d[Ca]}{dt} = \phi_{Ca} I_{Ca} + \tau_{Ca}^{-1} \left([Ca] - [Ca]_0\right), \tag{2.12}$$

where [Ca] denotes the intracellular calcium concentration, I_{Ca} is the sum of currents coming from all calcium ion channels, ϕ_{Ca} is a constant that scales the ionic current to changes in ionic concentration, $[Ca]_0$ is a baseline intracellular calcium concentration,

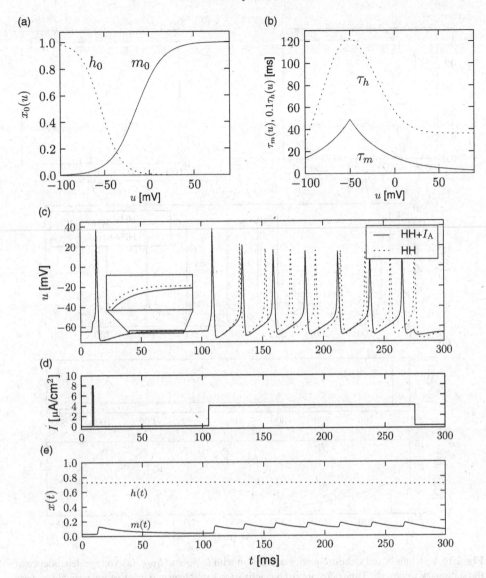

Fig. 2.14 I_A and the refractory period. (a) Voltage dependence of the stationary values and (b) time constants of the activation variable m and inactivation variable h for the A-type potassium current $I_A = g_A m h (u - E_K)$ extracted from experimental observations in pyramidal neurons of the cortex (Korngreen and Sakmann, 2000). (c) Voltage response to the current shown in (d), consisting of a single pulse and a step. (e) Progressive activation (solid line) and inactivation (dashed line) of the potassium current I_A during the stimulation shown in (c) and (d).

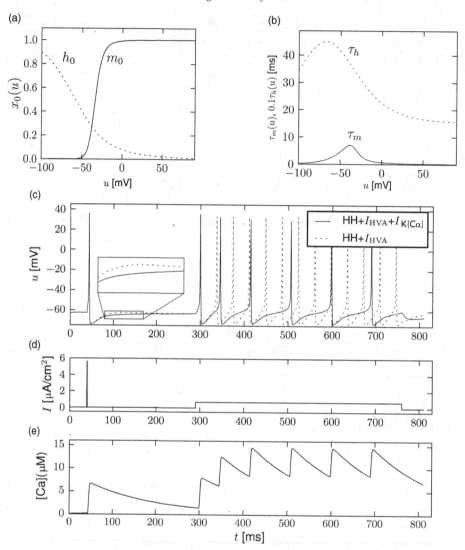

Fig. 2.15 Calcium-based spike-frequency adaptation with $I_{K[Ca]}$ and I_{HVA}. (a) Voltage dependence of the stationary values. (b) Time constants of the activation variable m and inactivation variable h of the high-threshold calcium current $I_{HVA} = g_L\,hm\,(u - E_{Ca})$ extracted from experiments (Reuveni *et al.*, 1993). (c) Voltage response of a Hodgkin–Huxley model with the calcium current I_{HVA} (dashed line) and a model that also contains a calcium-dependent potassium current $I_{K[Ca]}$. (d) External current used for the simulation in (c) and (e). (e) Progressive accumulation of intracellular calcium in the two models.

and τ_{Ca} is the effective time constant of calcium extrusion. In our simple example the sole source of incoming calcium ions is the high-threshold calcium channel hence $I_{Ca} = I_{HVA}$. Because of the short duration of the spike, each spike adds a fixed amount of intracellular calcium which afterward decays exponentially (Fig. 2.15e), as observed in many cell types (Helmchen *et al.*, 2011).

The calcium-dependent potassium channel $I_{K[Ca]} = g_{K[Ca]} n (u - E_K)$ is weakly sensitive to the membrane potential but highly sensitive to intra cellular calcium concentration. The dynamics of activation can be modeled with a calcium-dependent time constant (Destexhe *et al.*, 1994a) of the activation variable n

$$\tau_n([Ca]) = \frac{k_3}{1 + k_2 e^{k_1 [Ca]}} \tag{2.13}$$

and a stationary value (Destexhe *et al.*, 1994a)

$$n_0 = \frac{k_2 e^{k_1 [Ca]}}{1 + k_2 e^{k_1 [Ca]}} \tag{2.14}$$

where k_1, k_2, k_3, and $g_{K[Ca]}$ are constants.

Figure 2.15 shows the effect of the combined action of calcium channel and $I_{K[Ca]}$. A single spike generates a transient increase in intracellular calcium which in turn causes a transient increase in $I_{K[Ca]}$ activation which results in a hyperpolarization of the membrane potential compared with a model without $I_{K[Ca]}$. During sustained stimulation, calcium accumulates over several spikes, so that the effect of $I_{K[Ca]}$ becomes successively larger and interspike intervals increase. The time constant associated with adaptation is a combination of the calcium extrusion time constant and the potassium activation and de-activation time constant.

Example: Slow de-inactivation of a persistent sodium channel

The stationary values of activation and inactivation of the persistent sodium channel I_{NaP} (Fig. 2.16a) are very similar to that of the normal sodium channel of the Hodgkin–Huxley model. The main difference lies in the time constant. While activation of the channel is quick, it inactivates on a much slower time scale. Hence the name: the current "persists". The time constant of the inactivation variable h is of the order of a second.

During sustained stimulation, each spike contributes to the inactivation of the sodium channel and therefore reduces the excitability of the neuron. This special type of refractoriness is not visible in the spike-afterpotential, but can be illustrated as a relative increase in the effective spiking threshold (Fig. 2.16b). Since, after a first spike, the sodium channel is partially inactivated, it becomes more difficult to make the neuron fire a second time.

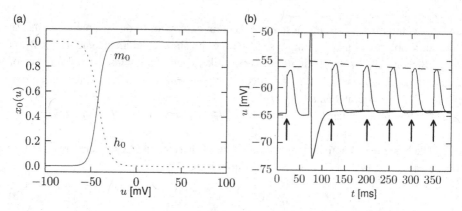

Fig. 2.16 The persistent sodium channel I_{NaP} increases the firing threshold. (a) Activation and inactivation profiles for $I_{NaP} = g_{NaP} m h (u - E_{Na})$. Activation is fast (a few ms) whereas inactivation is of the order of a second as measured in pyramidal neurons of the cortex (Aracri *et al.*, 2006). (b) Slow inactivation affects the effective threshold. In a Hodgkin–Huxley model with persistent sodium current, subthreshold current pulses are injected at different moments (arrows). At $t = 75$ ms (asterisk) only, a suprathreshold stimulation was applied. Tuning the strength of the other current pulses so that they are just below spike initiation reveals an effective voltage threshold (dashed line) that is higher immediately after the first spike.

2.3.4 Subthreshold effects

Some ion channels have an activation profile $m_0(u)$ which has a significant slope well below the spike initiation threshold. During subthreshold activation of the cell by background activity *in vivo*, or during injection of a fluctuating current, these currents partially activate and inactivate, following the time course of membrane potential fluctuations and shaping them in turn.

We describe two examples of subthreshold ion channel dynamics. The first one illustrates adaptation to a depolarized membrane potential by inactivation of a depolarizing current, which results in a subsequent reduction of the membrane potential. The second example illustrates the opposite behavior: in response to a depolarized membrane potential, a depolarizing current is triggered which increases the membrane potential even further. The two examples therefore correspond to subthreshold adaptation and subthreshold facilitation, respectively.

Example: Subthreshold adaptation by I_h

Subthreshold adaptation through a hyperpolarization-activated current I_h is present in many cell classes. As the name implies, the current is activated only at hyperpolarized voltages as can be seen in Fig. 2.17a. Thus, the voltage dependence of the activation variable is inverted compared with the normal case and has *negative* slope. Therefore, the activation variable looks more like an inactivation variable and this is why we choose h as the symbol for the variable. The channel is essentially closed for prolonged membrane

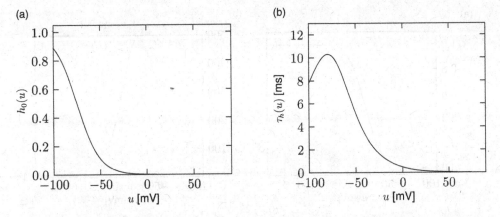

Fig. 2.17 Subthreshold adaptation with I_h. (a) Stationary values and (b) time constants of the variable h controlling the hyperpolarization-activated mixed current I_h as measured in pyramidal neurons of the hippocampus (Magee, 1998).

potential fluctuations above -30 mV. The I_h current is a non-specific cation current, meaning that sodium, potassium, and calcium can pass through the I_h channel when it is open. The reversal potential of this ion channel is usually around -45 mV so that the h-current $I_h = g_h h (u - E_h)$ is depolarizing at resting potential and over most of the subthreshold regime.

The presence of I_h causes the response to step changes in input current to exhibit damped oscillations. The interaction works as follows: suppose an external driving current depolarizes the cell. In the absence of ion channels this would lead to an exponential relaxation to a new value of the membrane potential of, say, -50 mV. Since I_h was mildly activated at rest, the membrane potential increase causes the channel to de-activate. The gradual closure of I_h removes the effective depolarizing drive and the membrane potential decreases, leading to a damped oscillation (as in Fig. 2.10). This principle can also lead to a rebound spike as seen in Fig. 2.10. Subthreshold adaptation and damped oscillations will be treated in more detail in Chapter 6.

Example: Subthreshold facilitation by I_{NaS}

The sodium ion channel I_{NaS} is slow to activate. Let us consider again stimulation with a step current using a model which contains both the fast sodium current of the Hodgkin–Huxley model and the slow sodium current I_{NaS}. If the strength of the current step is such that it does not activate the fast sodium channel but is strong enough to activate I_{NaS}, then the slow activation of this sodium current increases membrane potential gradually with the time constant of activation of the slow sodium current (Fig. 2.18b). The slow depolarization continues until the fast sodium current activates and an action potential

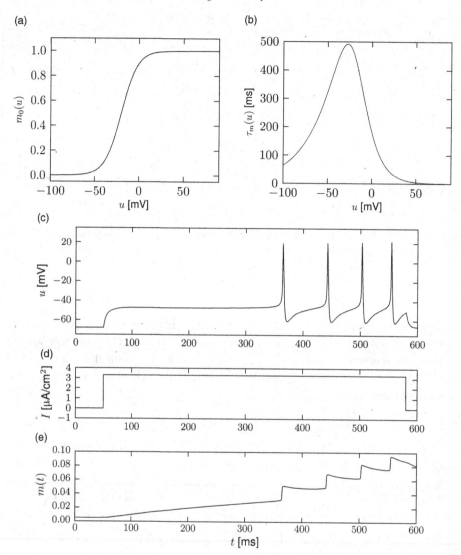

Fig. 2.18 Subthreshold facilitation with I_{NaS}. (a) Stationary values and (b) time constants of the activation variable m for the slow sodium current I_{NaS} similar to measurements done in pyramidal neurons of the hippocampus (Hoehn *et al.*, 1993). (c) Voltage response. (d) External current. (e) Slow sodium current activation, leading to delayed spike initiation and firing frequency facilitation.

is generated (Fig. 2.18c). Such delayed spike initiation has been observed in various types of interneurons of the cortex. If the amplitude of the step current is sufficient to immediately activate the fast sodium channels, the gradual activation of I_{NaS} increases the firing frequency leading to spike-frequency facilitation.

2.3.5 Calcium spikes and postinhibitory rebound

Postinhibitory rebound means that a hyperpolarizing current which is suddenly switched off results in an overshoot of the membrane potential or even in the triggering of one or more action potentials. Through this mechanism, action potentials can be triggered by *inhibitory* input. These action potentials, however, occur with a certain delay after the arrival of the inhibitory input, i.e., after the end of the IPSP (Aizenman and Linden, 1999).

Inactivating currents with a voltage threshold below the resting potential, such as the low-threshold calcium current, can give rise to a much stronger effect of inhibitory rebound than the one seen in the standard Hodgkin–Huxley model. Compared with the sodium current, the low-threshold calcium current I_T has activation and inactivation curves that are shifted significantly toward a hyperpolarized membrane potential so that the channel is

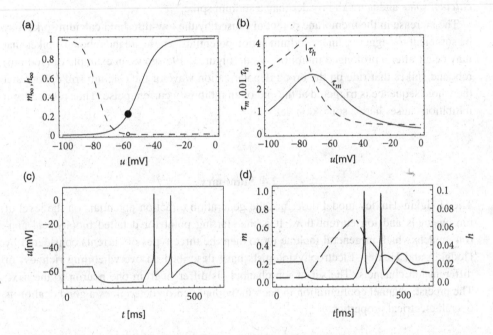

Fig. 2.19 Postinhibitory rebound through de-inactivation. (a) Activation $m_0(u)$ and inactivation $h_0(u)$ at equilibrium of the low-threshold calcium current I_T. Small circles indicate the equilibrium values of m and h at the resting potential. To de-inactivate the current, the membrane potential must be below rest. (b) The time constants of activation and inactivation. Note that different vertical scales have been used for τ_m and τ_h since the dynamics of the inactivation variable h is slower by a factor 10–100 than that of the activation variable m. Numerical values of parameters correspond to a model of neurons in the deep cerebellar nuclei (Kistler and van Hemmen, 2000). (c) Membrane potential as a function of time. Injection of a hyperpolarizing current pulse (100 pA during 200 ms from $t = 100$ ms to $t = 300$ ms) results, at the end of current injection, in a low-threshold calcium spike that in turn triggers two sodium action potentials. (d) Time course of activation (solid line, left scale) and inactivation (dashed line, right scale) variables of the I_T current that is responsible for this phenomenon.

completely *inactivated* $(h \approx 0)$ at the resting potential; see Fig. 2.19a and b. In order to open the low-threshold calcium channels it is first of all necessary to remove its inactivation by *hyperpolarizing* the membrane. The time constant of the inactivation variable h is rather high and it thus takes a while until h has reached a value sufficiently above zero; see Fig. 2.19b and d. But even if the channels have been successfully "de-inactivated" they remain in a closed state, because the activation variable m is zero as long as the membrane is hyperpolarized. However, the channels will be transiently opened if the membrane potential is rapidly relaxed from the hyperpolarized level to the resting potential, because activation is faster than inactivation and, thus, there is a short period when both m and h are nonzero. The current that passes through the channels is terminated ("inactivated") as soon as the inactivation variable h has dropped to zero again, but this takes a while because of the relatively slow time scale of τ_h. The resulting current pulse is called a *low-threshold calcium spike* and is much broader than a sodium spike.

The increase in the membrane potential caused by the low-threshold calcium spike may be sufficient to trigger ordinary sodium action potentials. These are the rebound spikes that may occur after a prolonged inhibitory input. Figure 2.19c shows an example of (sodium) rebound spikes that ride on the broad depolarization wave of the calcium spike; note that the whole sequence is triggered at the end of an inhibitory current pulse. Thus release from inhibition causes here a spike-doublet.

2.4 Summary

The Hodgkin–Huxley model describes the generation of action potentials on the level of ion channels and ion current flow. It is the starting point for detailed biophysical neuron models which in general include more than the three types of currents considered by Hodgkin and Huxley. Electrophysiologists have described an overwhelming richness of different ion channels. The set of ion channels is different from one neuron to the next. The precise channel configuration in each individual neuron determines a good deal of its overall electrical properties.

Literature

A nice review of the Hodgkin–Huxley model including some historical remarks can be found in Nelson and Rinzel (1995). A comprehensive and readable introduction to the biophysics of single neurons is provided by the book of Christof (1999). Even more detailed information on ion channels and nonlinear effects of the nervous membrane can be found in B. Hille's book of *Ionic Channels of Excitable Membranes* (Hille, 2001). The rapidly growing knowledge of the genetic description of ion channel families and associated phenotypes is condensed in Channelpedia (Ranjan *et al.*, 2011).

Exercises

1. **Nernst equation.** *Using the Nernst equation (Eq. 2.2) calculate the reversal potential of* Ca^{2+} *at room temperature (21 degrees Celsius), given an intracellular concentration of* 10^{-4} mM *and an extracellular concentration of* 1.5 mM.

2. **Reversal potential and stationary current–voltage relation.** *An experimenter studies an unknown ion channel by applying a constant voltage u while measuring the injected current I needed to balance the membrane current that passes through the ion channel.*

    (a) Sketch the current–voltage relationship (I as a function of u) assuming that the current follows $I_{ion} = g_{ion}mh\,(u - E_{rev})$ *with* $g_{ion} = 1$ nS *and* $E_{rev} = 0$ mV *where* $m = 0.1$ *and* $h = 1.0$ *are independent of the voltage.*

    (b) Sketch qualitatively the current–voltage relationship assuming that the current follows $I_{ion} = g_{ion}mh\,(u - E_{rev})$ *with* $g_{ion} = 1$ nS *and* $E_{rev} = 0$ mV *where* $m_0(u)$ *and* $h_0(u)$ *have the qualitative shape indicated in Fig. 2.15.*

3. **Activation time constant.** *An experimenter holds the channel from Fig. 2.15a and b at* $u = -50$ mV *for two seconds and then suddenly switches to* $u = 0$ mV. *Sketch the current passing through the ion channel as a function of time, assuming* $I_{ion} = g_{ion}mh\,(u - E_{rev})$ *with* $g_{ion} = 1$ nS *and* $E_{rev} = 0$ mV.

4. **The power of the exponent.** *An experimenter holds an unknown potassium ion channel with activation variable n with voltage dependence* $n_0(u)$ *and time constant* τ_n *at* $u = -50$ mV *for two seconds and then, at time* $t = 0$, *suddenly switches to* $u = 0$ mV.

    (a) Sketch the activation variable n, n^2, n^3 *as a function of time for times smaller than* τ_n.

    (b) Show mathematically that for $0 < t < \tau_n$ *the time course of the activation variable can be approximated* $n(t) = n_0(-50mV) + [n_0(0mV) - n_0(-50mV)]t/\tau_m$.

    (c) Do you agree with the statement that "the exponent p in the current formula $I_{ion} = g_{ion}n^p\,(u - E_{rev})$ *determines the "delay" of activation"? Justify your answer.*

5. **Hodgkin–Huxley parameter estimation.** *Design a set of experiments to constrain all the parameters of the two ion channels of the Hodgkin–Huxley model. Assume that the neuron has only the* I_{Na} *and* I_K *currents and that you can use tetrodotoxin (TTX) to block the sodium ion channel and tetraethylammonium (TEA) to block the potassium ion channel.*

    Hint: Use the results of the previous exercises.

6. **Simplified expression of the activation function.** *Show that with the voltage-dependent parameters* $\alpha_m(u) = 1/[1 - e^{-(u+a)/b}]$ *and* $\beta_m(u) = 1/[1 - e^{-(u+a)/b}]$ *(compare Table 2.1), the stationary value of the activation variable can be written as* $m_0(u) = 0.5[1 + \tanh[\beta\,(u - \theta_{act})]]$. *Determine the activation threshold* θ_{act} *and the activation slope* β.

    Hint: $\tanh(x) = [\exp(x) - \exp(-x)]/[\exp(x) + \exp(-x)]$.

3

Dendrites and synapses

Neurons have intricate morphologies: the central part of the cell is the soma, which contains the genetic information and a large fraction of the molecular machinery. At the soma originate long wire-like extensions which come in two different flavors. First, the dendrites form a multitude of smaller or larger branches on which synapses are located. The synapses are the contact points where information from other neurons (i.e., "presynaptic" cells) arrives. Second, also originating at the soma, is the axon, which the neuron uses to send action potentials to its target neurons. Traditionally, the transition region between soma and axon is thought to be the crucial region where the decision is taken whether a spike is sent out or not.

The Hodgkin–Huxley model, at least in the form presented in the previous chapter, disregards this spatial structure and reduces the neuron to a point-like spike generator – despite the fact that the precise spatial layout of a neuron could potentially be important for signal processing in the brain. In this chapter we will discuss how some of the spatial aspects can be taken into account by neuron models. In particular we focus on the properties of the synaptic contact points between neurons and on the electrical function of dendrites.

3.1 Synapses

In the previous chapter, we have encountered two classes of ion channels, namely *voltage*-activated and *calcium*-activated ion channels. The third type of ion channel we have to deal with are the *transmitter*-activated ion channels involved in synaptic transmission (see Fig. 3.1) and generally activated from outside the cell. Activation of a presynaptic neuron results in a release of neurotransmitters into the synaptic cleft. The transmitter molecules diffuse to the other side of the cleft and activate receptors that are located in the postsynaptic membrane. So-called *ionotropic receptors* have a direct influence on the state of an associated ion channel. *Metabotropic receptors* control the state of an ion channel by means of a biochemical cascade of G proteins and second-messengers. In both cases, the activation of the receptor results in the opening of certain ion channels and, thus, in an excitatory or inhibitory postsynaptic transmembrane current (EPSC or IPSC).

Instead of developing a mathematical model of the transmitter concentration in the synaptic cleft, we keep things simple and describe transmitter-activated ion channels as an explicitly time-dependent conductivity $g_{syn}(t)$ that will open whenever a presynaptic spike arrives. The current that passes through a synaptic channel depends, as before, on the difference between its reversal potential E_{syn} and the actual value of the membrane potential,

$$I_{syn}(t) = g_{syn}(t)(u(t) - E_{syn}). \qquad (3.1)$$

The parameter E_{syn} and the function $g_{syn}(t)$ can be used to describe different types of synapses. For inhibitory synapses E_{syn} is usually set to $-75\,\text{mV}$, whereas for excitatory synapses $E_{syn} \approx 0$.

Typically, a superposition of exponentials is used for $g_{syn}(t)$. A simple choice for the time course of the synaptic conductance in Eq. (3.1) is an exponential decay

$$g_{syn}(t) = \sum_f \bar{g}_{syn}\, e^{-(t-t^f)/\tau}\, \Theta(t-t^f), \qquad (3.2)$$

with a time constant of, e.g., $\tau = 5\,\text{ms}$ and an amplitude of $\bar{g}_{syn} = 40\,\text{pS}$. Here, t^f denotes the arrival time of a presynaptic action potential and $\Theta(x)$ is the Heaviside step function.

For some synapse types, a single exponential decay is not sufficient. Rather, the post-synaptic current is made up of two different components, a fast one with a decay time constant of a few milliseconds, and a second one that is often ten times slower. If we also take into account the smooth rise of the synaptic response, the postsynaptic conductance is of the form

$$g_{syn}(t) = \sum_f \bar{g}_{syn} \left[1 - e^{-(t-t^f)/\tau_{rise}}\right] \left[a\, e^{-(t-t^f)/\tau_{fast}} + (1-a)\, e^{-(t-t^f)/\tau_{slow}}\right] \Theta(t-t^f), \quad (3.3)$$

where a is the relative weight of the fast component. The time constant τ_{rise} characterizes the rise time of the synaptic conductance.

Example: A more detailed synapse model

Instead of considering a synapse with a fixed time course $g_{syn}(t)$, we can also make a model which has the flavor of a Hodgkin–Huxley channel. We describe the synaptic conductance $g_{syn}(t) = g_{max}\, R(t)$, by its maximal conductance g_{max} and a gating variable R, where $R(t)$ is the fraction of open synaptic channels. Channels open when neurotransmitter N binds to the synapse

$$\frac{dR}{dt} = \alpha N(1 - R) - \beta R, \qquad (3.4)$$

where α is the binding constant, β the unbinding constant and $(1 - R)$ the fraction of closed channels where binding of neurotransmitter can occur. Neurotransmitter N is released with each presynaptic spike so that the total amount of neurotransmitter at synapse j is

$$N(t) = \int_0^\infty \gamma(s)\, S_j(t - s)\, ds, \qquad (3.5)$$

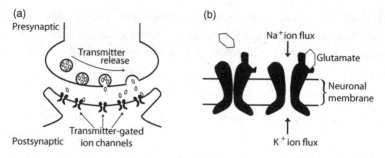

Fig. 3.1 (a) Schema of synaptic transmission. Upon arrival of a presynaptic spike, neurotransmitter spills into the synaptic cleft and is captured by postsynaptic receptors. (b) Schema of a postsynaptic AMPA[1] receptor of an excitatory synapse. When glutamate is bound to the receptor, sodium and potassium ions can flow through the membrane.

where $S_j = \sum_f \delta(t - t_j^f)$ is the presynaptic spike train (a sequence of δ-functions, see Chapter 1) and $\gamma(s)$ is the time course of the neurotransmitter density as measured at the site of the postsynaptic receptor. More advanced synaptic signaling schemes can be designed along the same line of argument (Destexhe *et al.*, 1994b).

3.1.1 Inhibitory synapses

The effect of fast inhibitory neurons in the central nervous system of higher vertebrates is almost exclusively conveyed by a neurotransmitter called γ-aminobutyric acid, or GABA for short. A characteristic feature of inhibitory synapses is that the reversal potential E_{syn} is in the range of -70 to -75 mV. Thus, if the neuronal membrane potential is above the reversal potential, presynaptic spike arrival leads to a hyperpolarization of the neuron, making action potential generation less likely. However, the same presynaptic spike would lead to a depolarization of the membrane if the neuron has its membrane potential at -80 mV or below.

There are many different types of inhibitory interneurons (Markram *et al.*, 2004; Klausberger and Somogyi, 2008). Biologists distinguish between two major types of inhibitory synapse, called $GABA_A$ and $GABA_B$. Both synapse types use GABA as the neurotransmitter. $GABA_A$ channels are ionotropic and open exclusively for chloride ions, whereas $GABA_B$ synapses have metabotropic receptors that trigger a comparatively slow signaling chain ultimately leading to the opening of K^+ channels. Consequently the value of the synaptic reversal potential E_{syn} depends for $GABA_A$ synapses on the concentration of chloride ions inside and outside the cell, while that of $GABA_B$ synapses depends on the potassium concentrations.

---

[1] AMPA is short for α-amino-3-hydroxy-5-methyl-4-isoxalone propionic acid.

Example: GABA$_A$ synapse model

GABA$_A$ synapses have a fast time course that can be approximated by a single term in Eq. (3.3) with $a = 1$, $\tau_{rise} \approx 1$ ms, and a time constant $\tau_{fast} \approx 6$ ms (Destexhe and Pare (1999); Fig. 3.2), which has also been deemed 3 times larger. More complex models are sometimes used (Destexhe *et al.*, 1994b).

Example: GABA$_B$ synapse model

This is a slow inhibitory synapse working via a second-messenger chain. Common models use Eq. (3.3) with a rise time of about 25–50 ms, a fast decay time in the range of 100–300 ms and a slow decay time of 500–1000 ms. The fast component accounts for about 80% of the amplitude of conductance ($a = 0.8$) (Destexhe *et al.*, 1994b; McCormick *et al.*, 1993), illustrated in Fig. 3.2.

3.1.2 Excitatory synapses

Most excitatory synapses in the vertebrate central nervous system rely on glutamate as their neurotransmitter. The postsynaptic receptors, however, can have very different pharmacological properties and different types of glutamate receptor units can be present in a single synapse. These receptors are classified using artificial drugs such as NMDA or AMPA that act as selective agonists. NMDA (N-methyl-D-aspartate) binds to channels with NMDA receptors, but not to other glutamate receptors. The most prominent among those glutamate receptors that do not respond to NMDA are the AMPA-receptors. AMPA is an artificial glutamate. Channels with AMPA-sensitive receptors are called "AMPA channels" because these channels react to AMPA, whereas channels with NMDA-sensitive receptors do not open upon application of AMPA. However, both NMDA and AMPA channels react to the natural form of glutamate that the nervous system uses as neurotransmitter.

AMPA receptors consist of four subunits, each with a glutamate binding site. Most AMPA receptors contain the subunit called GluR2. If an AMPA-receptor channel containing GluR2 is open, sodium and potassium ions can pass, but calcium ions cannot. Synaptic channels with AMPA-receptors are characterized by a fast response to presynaptic spikes and a quickly decaying postsynaptic current.

NMDA-receptor controlled channels are significantly slower and have additional interesting properties that are due to a voltage-dependent block by magnesium ions (Hille, 1992). In addition to sodium and potassium ions, also calcium ions can pass through open NMDA-channels.

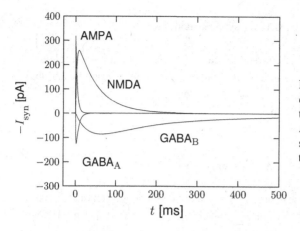

Fig. 3.2 Dynamics of postsynaptic current (3.1) after a single presynaptic spike at $t = 0$. $GABA_A$, $GABA_B$, AMPA, and NMDA without magnesium block are shown for a postsynaptic neuron at rest ($u = -65$mV).

Example: Conductance of glutamate channels with AMPA-receptors

The time course of the postsynaptic conductivity caused by an activation of AMPA-receptors at time $t = t^f$ is sometimes described by Eq. (3.2) with a decay time of about 2–5 ms (Gabbiani *et al.*, 1994; Destexhe *et al.*, 1994b).

Example: Conductance of glutamate channels with NMDA-receptors

NMDA-receptor controlled channels exhibit a rich repertoire of dynamic behavior because their state is controlled not only by the presence or absence of glutamate, but also by the membrane potential. At resting potential the NMDA channel is blocked by a common extracellular ion, Mg^{2+}, even if glutamate is present (Hille, 1992). Even in the presence of glutamate, the channel remains closed at the resting potential. If the membrane is depolarized beyond -50 mV, the Mg^{2+}-block is removed, the channel opens when glutamate binds to the receptor and, thereafter, stays open for 10–100 ms. A simple model of the voltage dependence of NMDA-receptor controlled channels is

$$g_{\text{NMDA}}(t) = \bar{g}_{\text{NMDA}} \cdot \left[1 - e^{-(t-t^f)/\tau_{\text{rise}}}\right] e^{-(t-t^f)/\tau_{\text{decay}}} g_\infty(u, [Mg^{2+}]_o) \,\Theta(t - t^f),$$

$$\text{with } g_\infty(u, [Mg^{2+}]_o) = \left(1 + \beta\, e^{\alpha u} [Mg^{2+}]_o\right)^{-1}, \quad (3.6)$$

with τ_{rise} in the range of 3 ms to 15 ms, τ_{decay} in the range of 40 ms to 100 ms, $\bar{g}_{\text{NMDA}} = 1.5$ nS, $\alpha = -0.062$ mV^{-1}, $\beta = 1/(3.57$mM$)$, and an extracellular magnesium concentration $[Mg^{2+}]_o = 1.2$ mM (McCormick *et al.*, 1993; Gabbiani *et al.*, 1994).

What is the potential functional role of NMDA receptors? First, their comparatively long time constant keeps a trace of presynaptic events and acts as a low-pass filter. Second, even though NMDA-receptor controlled ion channels are permeable to sodium and potassium ions, their permeability to Ca^{2+} is five or ten times larger. Calcium ions are known to play an important role in intracellular signalling and are probably involved in

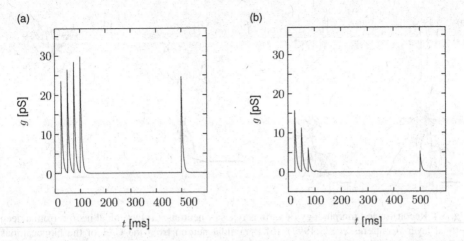

Fig. 3.3 Short-term plasticity. A synapse is activated by four presynaptic spikes and a fifth spike 400 ms later. (a) At a facilitating synapse, the effect of the second and third spike is larger than that of the first spike. The effect of a spike after a pause of 400 ms is approximately that of the first spike (time constant $\tau_P = 200$ ms). (b) At a depressing synapse, successive spikes in a periodic spike train have less and less effect: 400 ms later, the synapse has partially recovered, but is still significantly depressed ($\tau_P = 500$ ms).

long-term modifications of synaptic efficacy. Calcium influx through NMDA-controlled ion channels can occur if presynaptic spike arrival (leading to glutamate release from presynaptic sites) coincides with a depolarization of the postsynaptic membrane (leading to removal of the Mg^{2+}-block). Hence, NMDA-receptors operate as molecular coincidence detectors between pre- and postsynaptic events.

3.1.3 Rapid synaptic dynamics

Parameters of a synaptic contact point are not fixed, but can change as a function of the stimulation history. Some of these changes are long-lasting and are thought to represent the neuronal correlate of learning and memory formation. The description of these learning-related changes will be covered in Chapter 19. Here we concentrate on dynamic changes of the synapse that do not persist but decay back to their normal values within hundreds of milliseconds or a few seconds. These changes are called short-term synaptic plasticity.

Short-term synaptic plasticity can be measured if a presynaptic neuron is stimulated so as to generate a sequence of spikes. Synaptic facilitation means that the apparent amplitude of a postsynaptic current in response to the second spike is larger than that to the first spike. Synaptic depression is the opposite effect (Fig. 3.3).

As a simple model of synaptic facilitation and depression (Dayan and Abbott, 2001), we assume that the maximal synaptic conductance $\bar{g}_{syn}$ in Eq. (3.2) or (3.3) depends on the fraction P_{rel} of presynaptic sites releasing neurotransmitter. Facilitation and depression can both be modeled as presynaptic processes that modify P_{rel}. With each presynaptic spike, the number of available presynaptic release sites changes. Between spikes the value of P_{rel}

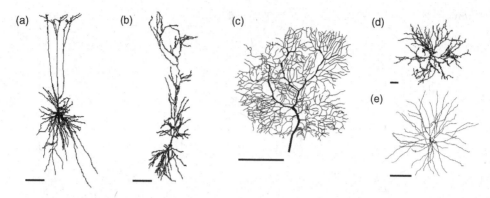

Fig. 3.4 Reconstructed morphology of various types of neurons. (a) Pyramidal neuron from a deep cortical layer (Contreras *et al.*, 1997). (b) Pyramidal neuron from the CA1 of the hippocampus (Golding *et al.*, 2005). (c) Purkinje cell from the cerebellum (Rapp *et al.*, 1994). (d) Motoneuron from the spinal cord (Cullheim *et al.*, 1987). (e) Stellate neuron from the neocortex (Mainen and Sejnowski, 1996). Reconstructed morphologies can be downloaded from http://NeuroMorpho.Org. Scale bars represent $100\,\mu$m.

returns exponentially to its resting value P_0. Thus,

$$\frac{dP_{\text{rel}}}{dt} = -\frac{P_{\text{rel}} - P_0}{\tau_P} + f_{\text{F}}(1 - P_{\text{rel}}) \sum_f \delta(t - t^f) \tag{3.7}$$

where τ_P is a time constant, f_{F} controls the degree of facilitation, and t^f denotes the times of presynaptic spike arrivals.

The model of a depressing synapse is completely analogous. The amount of neurotransmitter available for release develops according to the differential equation

$$\frac{dP_{\text{rel}}}{dt} = -\frac{P_{\text{rel}} - P_0}{\tau_P} - f_{\text{D}} P_{\text{rel}} \sum_f \delta(t - t^f) \tag{3.8}$$

where τ_P is a time constant and the parameter f_{D} with $0 < f_{\text{D}} < 1$ controls the amount of depression per spike.

The total effect of presynaptic spikes depends on the available neurotransmitter as well as the value g_0 of postsynaptic conductance if all synaptic ion channels are open, so that, for depressing or facilitating synapses, we can use Eq. (3.2) with a value $\bar{g}_{\text{syn}} = P_{\text{rel}} g_0$. This procedure has been used to generate Fig. 3.3.

3.2 Spatial structure: the dendritic tree

Neurons in the cortex and other areas of the brain often exhibit highly developed dendritic trees that may extend over several hundred microns (Fig. 3.4). Synaptic input to a neuron is mostly located on its dendritic tree. Disregarding NMDA- or calcium-based electrogenic "spikes," action potentials are generated at the soma near the axon hillock. Up to now we have discussed point neurons only, i.e., neurons without any spatial structure. What are the consequences of the spatial separation of input and output?

The electrical properties of point neurons have been described as a capacitor that is charged by synaptic currents and other *transversal* ion currents across the membrane. A non-uniform distribution of the membrane potential on the dendritic tree and the soma induces additional *longitudinal* current along the dendrite. We are now going to derive the cable equation that describes the membrane potential along a dendrite as a function of time *and* space. In Section 3.4 we shall see how geometric and electrophysiological properties can be integrated in a comprehensive biophysical model.

3.2.1 Derivation of the cable equation

Consider a piece of dendrite decomposed into short cylindric segments of length dx each. The schematic drawing in Fig. 3.5 shows the corresponding circuit diagram. Using Kirchhoff's laws we find equations that relate the voltage $u(x)$ across the membrane at location x with longitudinal and transversal currents. First, a longitudinal current $i(x)$ passing through the dendrite causes a voltage drop across the longitudinal resistor R_L according to Ohm's law,

$$u(t,x+dx) - u(t,x) = R_L\, i(t,x), \tag{3.9}$$

where $u(t,x+dx)$ is the membrane potential at the neighboring point $x+dx$. Second, the transversal current that passes through the RC-circuit is given by $C\,\partial u(t,x)/\partial t + \sum_{\text{ion}} I_{\text{ion}}$ where the sum runs over all ion channel types present in the dendrite. Kirchhoff's law regarding the conservation of current at each node leads to

$$i(t,x+dx) - i(t,x) = C\frac{\partial}{\partial t}u(t,x) + \sum_{\text{ion}} I_{\text{ion}} - I_{\text{ext}}(t,x). \tag{3.10}$$

The values of the longitudinal resistance R_L, the capacity C, the ionic currents as well as the externally applied current can be expressed in terms of specific quantities per unit length r_L, c, i_{ion} and i_{ext}, respectively, namely

$$R_L = r_L\, dx, \quad C = c\, dx, \quad I_{\text{ext}}(t,x) = i_{\text{ext}}(t,x)\, dx, \quad I_{\text{ion}}(t,x) = i_{\text{ion}}(t,x)\, dx. \tag{3.11}$$

These scaling relations express the fact that the longitudinal resistance and the capacity increases with the length of the cylinder. Similarly, the total amount of transversal current increases with the length dx simply because the surface through which the current can pass is increasing. Substituting these expressions in Eqs. (3.9) and (3.10), dividing by dx, and taking the limit $dx \to 0$ leads to

$$\frac{\partial}{\partial x}u(t,x) = r_L\, i(t,x) \tag{3.12a}$$

$$\frac{\partial}{\partial x}i(t,x) = c\frac{\partial}{\partial t}u(t,x) + \sum_{\text{ion}} i_{\text{ion}}(t,x) - i_{\text{ext}}(t,x). \tag{3.12b}$$

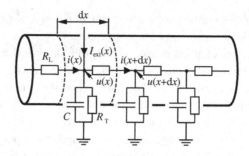

Fig. 3.5 Part of a dendrite and the corresponding circuit diagram. Longitudinal and transversal resistors are denoted by R_L and R_T, respectively. The electrical capacity of each small piece of dendrite is symbolized by capacitors C.

Taking the derivative of equation (3.12a) with respect to x and substituting the result into (3.12b) yields

$$\frac{\partial^2}{\partial x^2} u(t,x) = c\, r_L \frac{\partial}{\partial t} u(t,x) + r_L \sum_{\text{ion}} i_{\text{ion}}(t,x) - r_L\, i_{\text{ext}}(t,x). \tag{3.13}$$

Equation (3.13) is called the general cable equation.

Example: Cable equation for passive dendrite

The ionic currents $\sum_{\text{ion}} i_{\text{ion}}(t,x)$ in Eq. (3.13) can in principle comprise many different types of ion channel, as discussed in Section 2.3. For simplicity, the dendrite is sometimes considered as passive. This means that the current density follows Ohm's law $\sum_{\text{ion}} i_{\text{ion}}(t,x) = g_l(u - E_l)$ where $g_l = 1/r_T$ is the leak conductance per unit length and E_l is the leak reversal potential.

We introduce the characteristic length scale $\lambda^2 = r_T/r_L$ ("electrotonic length scale") and the membrane time constant $\tau = r_T c$. If we multiply Eq. (3.13) by λ^2 we get

$$\lambda^2 \frac{\partial^2}{\partial x^2} u(t,x) = \tau \frac{\partial}{\partial t} u(t,x) + [u(t,x) - E_l] - r_T\, i_{\text{ext}}(t,x). \tag{3.14}$$

After a transformation to unit-free coordinates,

$$x \to \hat{x} = x/\lambda, \quad t \to \hat{t} = t/\tau, \tag{3.15}$$

and a rescaling of the current and voltage variables,

$$i \to \hat{i} = \sqrt{r_T r_L}\, i, \quad i_{\text{ext}} \to \hat{i}_{\text{ext}} = r_T\, i_{\text{ext}}, \quad u \to \hat{u} = u - E_l, \tag{3.16}$$

we obtain the cable equation (where we have dropped the hats)

$$\frac{\partial}{\partial t} u(t,x) = \frac{\partial^2}{\partial x^2} u(t,x) - u(t,x) + i_{\text{ext}}(t,x), \tag{3.17}$$

in an elegant unit-free form.

The cable equation can be easily interpreted. The change in time of the voltage at location x is determined by three different contributions. The first term on the right-hand side of Eq. (3.17) is a diffusion term that is positive if the voltage is a convex function of x. The voltage at x thus tends to increase, if the values of u are higher in a neighborhood of x than at x itself. The second term on the right-hand side of Eq. (3.17) is a simple decay term that causes the voltage to decay exponentially towards zero. The third term, finally, is a source term that acts as an inhomogeneity in the otherwise autonomous differential equation. This source can be due to an externally applied current or to synaptic input arriving at location x.

Example: Stationary solutions of the cable equation

In order to get an intuitive understanding of the behavior of the cable equation of a passive dendrite we look for stationary solutions of Eq. (3.17), i.e., for solutions with $\partial u(t,x)/\partial t = 0$. In that case, the partial differential equation reduces to an ordinary differential equation in x, namely

$$\frac{\partial^2}{\partial x^2} u(t,x) - u(t,x) = -i_{\text{ext}}(t,x). \tag{3.18}$$

The general solution to the homogenous equation with $i_{\text{ext}}(t,x) \equiv 0$ is

$$u(t,x) = c_1 \sinh(x) + c_2 \cosh(x), \tag{3.19}$$

as can easily be checked by taking the second derivative with respect to x. Here, c_1 and c_2 are constants that are determined by the boundary conditions.

Solutions for non-vanishing input current can be found by standard techniques. For a stationary input current $i_{\text{ext}}(t,x) = \delta(x)$ localized at $x = 0$ and boundary conditions $u(\pm\infty) = 0$ we find

$$u(t,x) = \frac{1}{2} e^{-|x|}; \tag{3.20}$$

see Fig. 3.6. This solution is given in units of the intrinsic length scale $\lambda = (r_T/r_L)^{1/2}$. If we re-substitute the physical units, we see that λ is the length over which the stationary membrane potential drops by a factor $1/e$. In the literature λ is referred to as the electrotonic length scale (Rall, 1989). Typical values for the specific resistance of the intracellular medium and the cell membrane are $100\,\Omega\,\text{cm}$ and $30\text{k}\,\Omega\,\text{cm}^2$, respectively. In a dendrite with radius $\rho = 1\,\mu\text{m}$ this amounts to a longitudinal and a transversal resistance of $r_L = 100\Omega\text{cm}/(\pi\rho^2) = 3 \times 10^5\,\Omega\,\mu\text{m}^{-1}$ and $r_T = 30\text{k}\Omega\text{cm}^2/(2\pi\rho) = 5 \times 10^{11}\,\Omega\,\mu\text{m}$. The corresponding electrotonic length scale is $\lambda = 1.2\,\text{mm}$. Note that the electrotonic

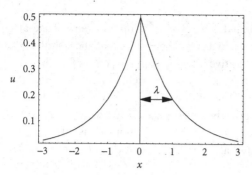

Fig. 3.6 Stationary solution of the cable equation with a constant current of unit strength being injected at $x = 0$, i.e., $i_{ext}(t,x) = \delta(x)$. The electrotonic length scale λ is the distance over which the membrane potential drops to $1/e$ of its initial value.

length can be significantly smaller if the transversal conductivity is increased, e.g., due to open ion channels.

For arbitrary stationary input current $i_{ext}(x)$ the solution of Eq. (3.17) can be found by a superposition of translated fundamental solutions (3.20), namely

$$u(t,x) = \int dx' \frac{1}{2} e^{-|x-x'|} i_{ext}(x'). \tag{3.21}$$

This is an example of the Green's function approach applied here to the stationary case. The general time-dependent case will be treated in the next section.

3.2.2 Green's function of the passive cable

In the following we will concentrate on the equation for the voltage and start our analysis by a discussion of the Green's function for a cable extending to infinity in both directions. The Green's function is defined as the solution of a linear equation such as Eq. (3.17) with a Dirac δ-pulse as its input. It can be seen as an elementary solution of the differential equation because – due to linearity – the solution for any given input can be constructed as a superposition of these Green's functions.

Suppose a short current pulse $i_{ext}(t,x)$ is injected at time $t = 0$ at location $x = 0$. As we will show below, the time course of the voltage at an arbitrary position x is given by

$$u(t,x) = \frac{\Theta(t)}{\sqrt{4\pi t}} \exp\left[-t - \frac{x^2}{4t}\right] \equiv G_\infty(t,x), \tag{3.22}$$

where $G_\infty(t,x)$ is the Green's function. Knowing the Green's function, the general solution for an infinitely long cable is given by

$$u(t,x) = \int_{-\infty}^{t} dt' \int_{-\infty}^{\infty} dx' \, G_\infty(t-t',x-x') i_{ext}(t',x'). \tag{3.23}$$

The Green's function is therefore a particularly elegant and useful mathematical tool: once you have solved the linear cable equation for a single short current pulse, you can write down the full solution to arbitrary input as an integral over (hypothetical) pulse-inputs at all places and all times.

Checking the Green's property (*)

We can check the validity of Eq. (3.22) by substituting $G_\infty(t,x)$ into Eq. (3.17). After a short calculation we find

$$\left[\frac{\partial}{\partial t} - \frac{\partial^2}{\partial x^2} + 1\right] G_\infty(t,x) = \frac{1}{\sqrt{4\pi t}} \exp\left(-t - \frac{x^2}{4t}\right) \delta(t), \qquad (3.24)$$

where we have used $\partial\Theta(t)/\partial t = \delta(t)$. As long as $t \neq 0$ the right-hand side of Eq. (3.24) vanishes, as required by Eq. (3.28). For $t \to 0$ we find

$$\lim_{t \to 0} \frac{1}{\sqrt{4\pi t}} \exp\left(-t - \frac{x^2}{4t}\right) = \delta(x), \qquad (3.25)$$

which proves that the right-hand side of Eq. (3.24) is indeed equivalent to the right-hand side of Eq. (3.28).

Having established that

$$\left[\frac{\partial}{\partial t} - \frac{\partial^2}{\partial x^2} + 1\right] G_\infty(t,x) = \delta(x)\,\delta(t), \qquad (3.26)$$

we can readily show that Eq. (3.23) is the general solution of the cable equation for arbitrary input currents $i_{\text{ext}}(t_0, x_0)$. We substitute Eq. (3.23) into the cable equation, exchange the order of integration and differentiation, and find

$$\left[\frac{\partial}{\partial t} - \frac{\partial^2}{\partial x^2} + 1\right] u(t,x)$$

$$= \int_{-\infty}^{t} dt' \int_{-\infty}^{\infty} dx' \left[\frac{\partial}{\partial t} - \frac{\partial^2}{\partial x^2} + 1\right] G_\infty(t - t', x - x')\, i_{\text{ext}}(t', x')$$

$$= \int_{-\infty}^{t} dt' \int_{-\infty}^{\infty} dx'\, \delta(x - x')\,\delta(t - t')\, i_{\text{ext}}(t', x') = i_{\text{ext}}(t,x). \qquad (3.27)$$

Derivation of the Green's function (*)

Previously, we have just "guessed" the Green's function and then shown that it is indeed a solution of the cable equation. However, it is also possible to derive the Green's function step by step. In order to find the Green's function for the cable equation we thus have to solve Eq. (3.17) with $i_{\text{ext}}(t,x)$ replaced by a δ-impulse at $x = 0$ and $t = 0$

$$\frac{\partial}{\partial t} u(t,x) - \frac{\partial^2}{\partial x^2} u(t,x) + u(t,x) = \delta(t)\,\delta(x). \qquad (3.28)$$

Fourier transformation with respect to the spatial variable yields

$$\frac{\partial}{\partial t} u(t,k) + k^2\, u(t,k) + u(t,k) = \delta(t)/\sqrt{2\pi}. \qquad (3.29)$$

This is an ordinary differential equation in t and has a solution of the form

$$u(t,k) = \exp\left[-\left(1 + k^2\right) t\right] / \sqrt{2\pi}\,\Theta(t), \qquad (3.30)$$

with $\Theta(t)$ denoting the Heaviside function. After an inverse Fourier transform we obtain the desired Green's function $G_\infty(t,x)$,

$$u(t,x) = \frac{\Theta(t)}{\sqrt{4\pi t}} \exp\left[-t - \frac{x^2}{4t}\right] \equiv G_\infty(t,x). \qquad (3.31)$$

Example: Finite cable

Real cables do not extend from $-\infty$ to $+\infty$ and we have to take extra care to correctly include boundary conditions at the ends. We consider a finite cable extending from $x = 0$ to $x = L$ with sealed ends, i.e., $i(t, x = 0) = i(t, x = L) = 0$ or, equivalently, $\frac{\partial}{\partial x}u(t, x = 0) = \frac{\partial}{\partial x}u(t, x = L) = 0$.

The Green's function $G_{0,L}$ for a cable with sealed ends can be constructed from G_∞ by applying a trick from electrostatics called "mirror charges" (Jackson, 1962). Similar techniques can also be applied to treat branching points in a dendritic tree (Abbott, 1991). The cable equation is linear and, therefore, a superposition of two solutions is also a solution. Consider a δ-current pulse at time t_0 and position x_0 somewhere along the cable. The boundary condition $\frac{\partial}{\partial x}u(t, x = 0) = 0$ can be satisfied if we add a second, virtual current pulse at a position $x = -x_0$ *outside* the interval $[0, L]$. Adding a current pulse outside the interval $[0, L]$ comes for free since the result is still a solution of the cable equation on that interval. Similarly, we can fulfill the boundary condition at $x = L$ by adding a mirror pulse at $x = 2L - x_0$. In order to account for both boundary conditions simultaneously, we have to compensate for the mirror pulse at $-x_0$ by adding another mirror pulse at $2L + x_0$ and for the mirror pulse at $x = 2L - x_0$ by adding a fourth pulse at $-2L + x_0$ and so forth. Altogether we have

$$G_{0,L}(t_0, x_0; t, x) = \sum_{n=-\infty}^{\infty} G_\infty(t - t_0, x - 2nL - x_0) + G_\infty(t - t_0, x - 2nL + x_0). \qquad (3.32)$$

We emphasize that in the above Green's function we have to specify both (t_0, x_0) and (t, x) because the setup is no longer translation invariant. The general solution on the interval $[0, L]$ is given by

$$u(t,x) = \int_{-\infty}^{t} dt_0 \int_0^L dx_0\, G_{0,L}(t_0, x_0; t, x)\, i_{\text{ext}}(t_0, x_0). \qquad (3.33)$$

An example for the spatial distribution of the membrane potential along the cable is shown in Fig. 3.7a, where a current pulse has been injected at location $x = 1$. In addition to Fig. 3.7a, Fig. 3.7b exhibits the *time course* of the membrane potential measured in various distances from the point of injection. It is clearly visible that the peak of the membrane potential measured at, say, $x = 3$ is more delayed than at, say, $x = 2$. Also the amplitude of the membrane potential decreases significantly with the distance from the injection point. This is a well-known phenomenon that is also present in neurons. In the absence of active amplification mechanisms, synaptic input at distal dendrites produces

(a)
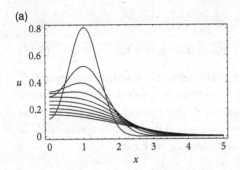

(b)
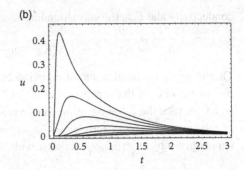

Fig. 3.7 Spatial distribution (a) and temporal evolution (b) of the membrane potential along a dendrite ($L = 5$) with sealed ends $\left(\frac{\partial}{\partial x} u \big|_{x \in \{0,L\}} = 0 \right)$ after injection of a unit current pulse at $x = 1$ and $t = 0$. The various traces in (a) show snapshots for time $t = 0.1, 0.2, \ldots, 1.0$, respectively (top to bottom). The traces in (b) give the membrane potential as a function of time for different locations $x = 1.5, 2.0, 2.5, \ldots, 5.0$ (top to bottom) along the cable.

broader and weaker response at the soma as compared to synaptic input at proximal dendrites.

3.2.3 Nonlinear extensions to the cable equation

In the context of a realistic modeling of "biological" neurons, two nonlinear extensions of the cable equation have to be discussed. The obvious one is the inclusion of nonlinear elements in the circuit diagram of Fig. 3.5 that account for specialized ion channels. As we have seen in the Hodgkin–Huxley model, ion channels can exhibit a complex dynamics that is in itself governed by a system of (ordinary) differential equations. The current through one of these channels is thus not simply a (nonlinear) function of the actual value of the membrane potential but may also depend on the time course of the membrane potential in the past. Using the symbolic notation $i_{\text{ion}}[u](t, x)$ for this functional dependence, the extended cable equation takes the form

$$\frac{\partial}{\partial t} u(t, x) = \frac{\partial^2}{\partial x^2} u(t, x) - u(t, x) - i_{\text{ion}}[u](t, x) + i_{\text{ext}}(t, x). \tag{3.34}$$

A more subtle complication arises from the fact that a synapse cannot be treated as an ideal current source. The effect of an incoming action potential is the opening of ion channels. The resulting current is proportional to the difference of the membrane potential and the corresponding ionic reversal potential. Hence, a time-dependent conductivity as in Eq. (3.1) provides a more realistic description of synaptic input than an ideal current source with a fixed time course.

If we replace in Eq. (3.17) the external input current $i_{\text{ext}}(t, x)$ by an appropriate synaptic input current $-i_{\text{syn}}(t, x) = -g_{\text{syn}}(t, x)[u(t, x) - E_{\text{syn}}]$ with g_{syn} being the synaptic conductivity and E_{syn} the corresponding reversal potential, we obtain[2]

$$\frac{\partial}{\partial t} u(t,x) = \frac{\partial^2}{\partial x^2} u(t,x) - u(t,x) - g_{\text{syn}}(t,x)[u(t,x) - E_{\text{syn}}]. \tag{3.35}$$

This is still a linear differential equation but its coefficients are now time-dependent. If the time course of the synaptic conductivity can be written as a solution of a differential equation, then the cable equation can be reformulated so that synaptic input reappears as an inhomogeneity to an autonomous equation. For example, if the synaptic conductivity is simply given by an exponential decay with time constant τ_{syn} we have

$$\frac{\partial}{\partial t} u(t,x) - \frac{\partial^2}{\partial x^2} u(t,x) + u(t,x) + g_{\text{syn}}(t,x)[u(t,x) - E_{\text{syn}}] = 0, \tag{3.36a}$$

$$\frac{\partial}{\partial t} g_{\text{syn}}(t,x) - \tau_{\text{syn}}^{-1} g_{\text{syn}}(t,x) = S(t,x). \tag{3.36b}$$

Here, $S(t,x)$ is a sum of Dirac δ-functions which describe the presynaptic spike train that arrives at a synapse located at position x. Note that this equation is *non*linear because it contains a product of g_{syn} and u which are both unknown functions of the differential equation. Consequently, the formalism based on Green's functions cannot be applied. We have reached the limit of what we can do with analytical analysis alone. To study the effect of ion channels distributed on the dendrites numerical approaches in compartmental models become invaluable (Section 3.4).

3.3 Spatial structure: axons

Any given neuron has a single axon that leaves the soma to make synaptic contacts. Like dendrites, axons have a range of different morphologies. Some axons project mainly to neurons close by. This is the case for neurons in the layer 2–3 of cortex; their axons branch out in all directions from the soma forming a star-shaped axonal arbor called a "daisy." Other neurons such as pyramidal neurons situated deeper in the cortex have axons that plunge in the white matter and may cross the whole brain to reach another brain area. There are even longer axons that leave the central nervous system and travel down the spinal cord to reach muscles at the tip of the foot.

In terms of propagation dynamics, we distinguish two types of axons: the myelinated and the unmyelinated axons. We will see that myelin is useful to increase propagation speed in far-reaching projections. This is the case for cortical projections passing through the white matter, or for axons crossing the spinal cord. Short projections on the other hand use axons devoid of myelin.

3.3.1 Unmyelinated axons

Mathematical description of the membrane potential in the axon is identical to that of dendrites with active ion channels. Unmyelinated axons contain sodium and potassium

---

[2] We want outward currents to be positive, hence the change in the sign of i_{ext} and i_{syn}.

channels uniformly distributed over their entire length. The classical example is the squid giant axon investigated by Hodgkin and Huxley. The Hodgkin–Huxley model described in Chapter 2 was developed for a small axon segment. The general equation for ion channels imbedded on a passive membrane is

$$c\, r_L \frac{\partial}{\partial t} u(t,x) = \frac{\partial^2}{\partial x^2} u(t,x) - r_L(u(t,x) - E_l) - r_L i_{\text{ion}}[u](t,x) \qquad (3.37)$$

where we have reverted to a variable u in units of mV from the equation of active dendrites seen in Section 3.2.3. For the giant squid axon, the ionic current are described by the Hodgkin–Huxley model

$$i_{\text{ion}}[u](t,x) = g_{\text{Na}}\, m^3(t,x) h(t,x)\, (u(t,x) - E_{\text{Na}}) + g_K\, n^4(t,x)\, (u(t,x) - E_K). \qquad (3.38)$$

In other systems, the axon may be covered with other types of sodium or potassium ion channels.

When an action potential is fired in the axon initial segment, the elevated membrane potential will depolarize the adjacent axonal segments. Sodium channels farther down the axon, which were previously closed, will start to open, thereby depolarizing the membrane further. The action potential propagates by activating sodium channels along the cable rather than by spreading the charges as in a passive dendrite. The properties of the ion channels strongly influence conduction velocity. In the unmyelinated axons of the hippocampus, the conduction velocity of the axons is 0.25 m/s.

The dynamics described by Eqs. (3.37)–(3.38) reproduces many properties of real axons. In particular, two spikes traveling in opposite direction will collide and annihilate each other. This is unlike waves propagating on water. Another property is reflection at branch points. When the impedance mismatch at the point where a single axon splits into two is significant, the action potential can reflect and start traveling in the direction it came from.

The solution of Eq. (3.37) with sodium and postassium ion channels as in Eq. (3.38) cannot be written in a closed form. Properties of axonal propagation are either studied numerically (see Section 3.4) or with reduced models of ion channels.

Example: Speed of propagation with simplified action potential dynamics

For the sake of studying propagation properties, we can replace the active properties of a small axonal segment by a bistable switch (FitzHugh, 1961; Nagumo *et al.*, 1962) . We can write the time- and space-dependent membrane potential as

$$c\, r_L \frac{\partial}{\partial t} u(t,x) = \frac{\partial^2}{\partial x^2} u(t,x) - \frac{r_L g}{1-a} u(t,x)(u(t,x) - 1)(u(t,x) - a), \qquad (3.39)$$

where $a < 1/2$ and g are parameters. The membrane potential is scaled such that it rests at zero but may be activated to $u = 1$. The reduced model can switch between $u = 0$ and $u = 1$ if it is pushed above $u = a$, but does not reproduce the full upswing followed by downswing of action potentials.

It turns out that Eq. (3.39) can also be interpreted as a model of flame front propagation. The solution of this equation follows (Zeldovich and Frank-Kamenetskii, 1938)

$$u(x,t) = \frac{1}{1 + \exp\left(\frac{x-vt}{\sqrt{2}\lambda^*}\right)} \tag{3.40}$$

with traveling speed

$$v = \frac{c(1-2a)}{\sqrt{2(1-a)r_L/g}}. \tag{3.41}$$

The propagation velocity depends on the capacitance per unit length c, the longitudinal resistance per unit length r_L, and the excitability parameters g and a.

How does the conduction velocity scale with axon size? Since r_L, c and g themselves depend on the diameter of the axon, we expect the velocity to reflect that relationship. The parameters c and g scale with the circumference of the cellular membrane and therefore scale linearly with the radius ρ. The cytoplasmic resistance per unit length, however, scales with the cross-sectional area, $r_L \propto \rho^2$. With these relations in mind, Eq. (3.41) shows that the conduction velocity is proportional to the square root of the diameter $v \propto \sqrt{\rho}$. Therefore, increasing the diameter improves propagation velocity. This is thought to be the reason why the unmyelinated axons that Hodgkin and Huxley studied were so large (up to $\rho = 500\,\mu\text{m}$).

3.3.2 Myelinated axons

Myelinated axons have sodium and potassium channels only in restricted segments called *nodes of Ranvier*. These nodes form only 0.2% of the axonal length, the rest is considered a passive membrane that is wrapped into a myelin sheath. Myelin mainly decreases the membrane capacitance C and increase the resistance R_T by a factor of up to 300 (Debanne *et al.*, 2011). Ions are trapped by myelin since it prevents them from either flowing outside the axon or accumulating on the membrane. Instead, ions flow in and out of the nodes such that an ion leaving a node of Ranvier forces another to enter the following node. Assuming that the nodes are equally separated by a myelinated segment of length L, we can model the evolution of the membrane potential at each node u_n. The dynamics of idealized myelinated axons follow Kirchoff's equation with a resistance $R_L = Lr_L$ replacing the myelinated segment

$$C\frac{du_n}{dt} = \frac{1}{Lr_L}(u_{n+1}(t) - 2u_n(t) + u_{n-1}(t)) - \sum_{\text{ion}} I_{\text{ion},n}(t) \tag{3.42}$$

where C is the total capacitance of the node. This equation was encountered in the derivation of the cable equation (Section 3.2.1). The conduction velocity is greatly increased by myelin such that some nerves reach 70–80 m/s (Debanne *et al.*, 2011).

Example: Propagation speed with simplified action potential dynamics

Using the simplification of the ion channel dynamics in Eq. (3.39) for each node

$$C\frac{du_n}{dt} = \frac{1}{Lr_L}(u_{n+1}(t) - 2u_n(t) + u_{n-1}(t)) - \frac{g}{1-a}u_n(t)(u_n(t) - 1)(u_n(t) - a) \quad (3.43)$$

where g and $a < 1/2$ are parameters regulating the excitability of the node. Unlike Eq. (3.39), the parameter g has units of conductance per node since the nodes of Ranvier are discrete segments. An activated node may fail to excite the adjacent nodes if the membrane potential does not reach $u = a$. In this model, the internodal distance must satisfy (Erneux and Nicolis, 1993)

$$L < L^* = \frac{1-a}{4a^2 r_L g} \quad (3.44)$$

for propagation to be sustained. When the internodal distance L is smaller than L^*, propagation will fail. When the internodal distance is larger, propagation will succeed.

The propagation velocity for small $L^* - L$ follows (Binczak *et al.*, 2001)

$$v \approx \frac{\pi g a}{(1-a)C}\sqrt{L(L^* - L)} \quad (3.45)$$

which is maximum at $L = L^*/2$. Since, in most myelinated axons, internodal distance scales linearly with their radius (Waxman, 1980), the velocity of myelinated axons also scales linearly with radius, $v \propto L \propto \rho$.

3.4 Compartmental models

We have seen that analytical solutions can be given for the voltage along a passive cable with uniform geometrical and electrical properties. If we want to apply the above results in order to describe the membrane potential along the dendritic tree of a neuron we face several problems. Even if we neglect "active" conductances formed by nonlinear ion channels, a dendritic tree is at most *locally* equivalent to a uniform cable. Numerous bifurcations and variations in diameter and electrical properties along the dendrite render it difficult to find a solution for the membrane potential analytically (Abbott *et al.*, 1991).

Numerical treatment of partial differential equations such as the cable equation requires a discretization of the spatial variable. Hence, all derivatives with respect to spatial variables are approximated by the corresponding quotient of differences. Essentially we are led back to the discretized model of Fig. 3.5 that has been used as the starting point for the derivation of the cable equation. After the discretization we have a large system of ordinary differential equations for the membrane potential at the chosen discretization points as a function of time. This system of ordinary differential equations can be treated by standard numerical methods.

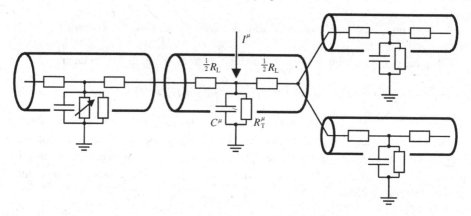

Fig. 3.8 Multi-compartment neuron model. Dendritic compartments with membrane capacitance C^μ and transversal resistance R_T^μ are coupled by a longitudinal resistance $r^{\mu\nu} = (R_L^\mu + R_L^\nu)/2$. External input to compartment μ is denoted by I^μ. Some or all compartments may also contain nonlinear ion channels (variable resistor in leftmost compartment).

In order to solve for the membrane potential of a complex dendritic tree numerically, compartmental models are used that are the result of the above mentioned discretization. The dendritic tree is divided into small cylindric compartments with an approximately uniform membrane potential. Each compartment is characterized by its capacity and transversal conductivity. Adjacent compartments are coupled by the longitudinal resistance determined by their geometrical properties (see Fig. 3.8).

Once numerical methods are used to solve for the membrane potential along the dendritic tree, some or all compartments can be equipped with nonlinear ion channels as well. In this way, effects of nonlinear integration of synaptic input can be studied. Apart from practical problems that arise from a growing complexity of the underlying differential equations, conceptual problems are related to a drastically increasing number of free parameters. To avoid these problems, all nonlinear ion channels responsible for generating spikes are usually lumped together at the soma and the dendritic tree is treated as a passive cable. For a review of the compartmental approach we refer the reader to Bower and Beeman (1995). In the following we illustrate the compartmental approach by a model of a pyramidal cell.

Example: A multi-compartment model of a deep-layer pyramidal cell

Software tools such as NEURON (Carnevale and Hines, 2006) or GENESIS (Bower and Beeman, 1995) enable researchers to construct detailed compartmental models of any type of neuron. The morphology of such a detailed model is constrained by the anatomical reconstruction of the corresponding "real" neuron. This is possible if length,

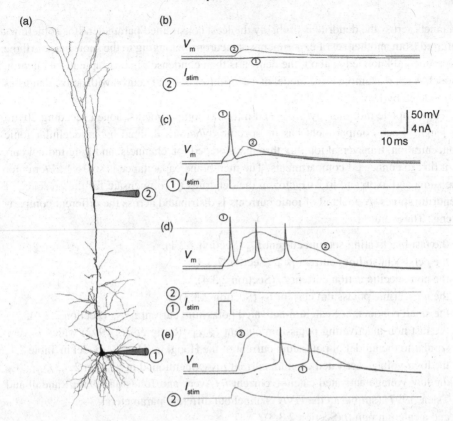

Fig. 3.9 Bursting in a computational model of a deep layer cortical neuron. (a) Reconstruction of the complete morphology indicating the location of injection and measurement sites marked "1" at the soma, and "2" at the dendrite. (b) A current is injected into the dendrite (lower trace, marked "2") mimicking an excitatatory postsynaptic current (EPSC). The model responds to the current injection in the dendrite with a voltage deflection at the dendrite (upper trace marked "2") but hardly any deflection at the soma ("1"). (c). A current pulse in the soma (lower trace, marked "1") causes an action potential at the soma (voltage trace marked "1") that back-propagates as a broader voltage pulse ("2") into the dendrite. (d) Coincidence of somatic current pulse and dendritic EPSC activates calcium currents in the dendrites and causes a burst of spikes in the soma. (e) A single, but large EPSC-shaped dendritic current can also activate calcium currents and leads to a delayed burst of spikes in the soma. Image modified from Hay *et al.* (2011).

size and orientation of each dendritic segment are measured under a microscope, after the neuron has been filled with a suitable dye. Before the anatomical reconstruction, the electrophysiological properties of the neuron can be characterized by stimulating the neuron with a time-dependent electric current. The presence of specific ion channel types can be inferred, with genetic methods, from the composition of the intracellular liquid, extracted from the neuron (Toledo-Rodriguez *et al.*, 2004). The distribution of ion channels across the dendrite is probably the least constrained parameter. It is sometimes inferred from another set of experiments on neurons belonging to the same class. All the experimental knowledge about the neuron is then condensed in a computational neuron model. A good example is the model of a deep-layer cortical neuron with active dendrites as modeled by Hay *et al.* (2011).

The complete morphology is divided into 200 compartments, none exceeding 20 μm in length. Each compartment has its specific dynamics defined by intracellular ionic concentration, transversal ion flux through modeled ion channels, and longitudinal current flux to connected compartments. The membrane capacitance is set to 1 μF/cm^2 for the soma and axon and to 2 μF/cm^2 in the dendrites to compensate for the presence of dendritic spines. A cocktail of ionic currents is distributed across the different compartments. These are:

- the fast inactivating sodium current I_{Na} (Section 2.2.1),
- the persistent sodium current I_{NaP} (Section 2.3.3),
- the non-specific cation current I_h (Section 2.3.4),
- the muscarinic potassium current I_M (Section 2.3.3),
- the small conductance calcium-activated potassium current $I_{K[Ca]}$ (Section 2.3.4),
- the fast non-inactivating potassium current $I_{Kv3.1}$ (Rettig *et al.*, 1992) which is very similar to the model of potassium current of the Hodgkin–Huxley model in Table 2.1,
- the high-voltage activated calcium current I_{HVA} (mentioned in Section 2.3.3),
- the low-voltage activated calcium current I_L(Avery and Johnston, 1996; Randall and Tsien, 1997) (similar to the HVA channel but different parameters),
- and a calcium pump (Section 2.3.3).

In addition, the model contains a slow and a fast inactivating potassium current I_{Kp}, I_{Kt}, respectively (Korngreen and Sakmann, 2000).

In the dendrites all these currents are modeled as uniformly distributed except I_h, I_{HVA} and I_L. The first one of these, I_h, is exponentially distributed along the main dendrite that ascends from the deep layers with low I_h concentration to the top layers with large I_h concentration (Kole *et al.*, 2006). The two calcium channels were distributed with a uniform distribution in all dendrites except for a single hotspot with a concentration 100 and 10 times higher for I_L and I_{HVA}, respectively. Finally, the strength of each ionic current was scaled by choosing the maximal conductance g_{ion} that best fit experimental data.

This detailed compartmental model can reproduce quantitatively some features of the deep-layer pyramidal neurons (Fig. 3.9). For example, a small dendritic current injection results in a transient increase of the dendritic voltage, but only a small effect in the soma (Fig. 3.9b). A sufficiently large current pulse in the soma initiates not only a spike at the soma but also a back-propagating action potential traveling into the dendrites (Fig. 3.9c). Note that it is the presence of sodium and potassium currents throughout the dendrites that support the back-propagation. In order to activate the dendritic calcium channels at the hotspot, either a large dendritic injection or a coincidence between the back-propagating action potential and a small dendritic injection is required (Fig. 3.9d, e). The activation of calcium channels in the hotspot introduces a large and long (around 40 ms) depolarizing current that propagates forward to the soma where it eventually causes a burst of action potentials.

3.5 Summary

"Real" neurons are complex biophysical and biochemical entities. Before designing a model it is therefore necessary to develop an intuition for what is important and what can be safely neglected. Synapses are usually modeled as specific ion channels that open for a certain time after presynaptic spike arrival. The geometry of the neuron can play an important role in the integration of incoming signals because the effect of synaptic input on the somatic membrane potential depends on the location of the synapses on the dendritic tree. Though some analytic results can be obtained for *passive* dendrites, it is usually necessary to resort to numerical methods and multi-compartment models in order to account for the complex geometry and presence of active ion channels on neuronal dendrites.

Literature

The book *Dendrites* (Stuart *et al.*, 2007) offers a comprehensive review of the role and importance of dendrites from multiple points of view. An extensive description of cable theory as applied to neuronal dendrites can be found in the collected works of Wilfrid Rall (Segev *et al.*, 1994). NEURON (Carnevale and Hines, 2006) and GENESIS (Bower and Beeman, 1995) are important tools to numerically solve the system of differential equations of compartmental neuron models. There are useful repositories of neuronal morphologies (see http://NeuroMorpho.Org for instance) and of published models on ModelDB (http://senselab.med.yale.edu/modeldb). The deep-layer cortical neuron discussed in this chapter is described in Hay *et al.* (2011). Potential computational consequences of nonlinear dendrites are described in Mel (1994).

Exercises

1. **Biophysical synapse model and its relation to other models**
   (a) *Consider Eq. (3.4) and discuss its relation to Eq. (3.2). Hint: (i) Assume that the time course $\gamma(t)$ can be described by a short pulse (duration of 1 ms) and that the unbinding is on a time scale $\beta^{-1} > 10$ ms. (ii) Assume that the interval between two presynaptic spike arrivals is much larger than β^{-1}.*
   (b) *Discuss the relation of the depressive synapse model in Eq. (3.8) with the biophysically model in Eq. (3.4). Hint: (i) Assume that the interval between two presynaptic spikes is of the same order β^{-1}. (ii) In Eq. (3.8) consider a variable $x = P_{rel}/P_0$.*

2. **Transmitter-gated ion channel**
   For each of the following statements state whether it is correct or wrong:
   (a) AMPA channels are activated by glutamate.
   (b) AMPA channels are activated by AMPA.
   (c) If the AMPA channel is open, AMPA can pass through the channel.
   (d) If the AMPA channel is open, glutamate can pass through the channel.
   (e) If the AMPA channel is open, potassium can pass through the channel.
3. **Cable equation**
   (a) Show that the passive cable equation for the current is

$$\frac{\partial}{\partial t} i(t,x) = \frac{\partial^2}{\partial x^2} i(t,x) - i(t,x) + \frac{\partial}{\partial x} i_{ext}(t,x). \tag{3.46}$$

   (b) Set the external current to zero and find the mapping to the heat equation

$$\frac{\partial}{\partial t} y(t,x) = \frac{\partial^2}{\partial x^2} y(t,x). \tag{3.47}$$

   Hint: Try $y(t,x) = f(t)i(t,x)$ with some function f.
   (c) Find the solution to the current equation in (a) for the infinite cable receiving a short current pulse at time $t = 0$ and show that the corresponding equation for y satisfies the heat equation in (b).
4. **Non-leaky cable**
   (a) Redo the derivation of the cable equation for the case of an infinite one-dimensional passive dendrite without transversal leak and show that the solution to the equation is of the form

$$u(x,t) = \int_{-\infty}^{t} dt' \int_{-\infty}^{\infty} dx' \, G_d(t-t', x-x') i_{ext}(t', x') \tag{3.48}$$

   where G_d is a Gaussian of the form

$$G_d(x,t) = \frac{1}{\sqrt{2\pi\sigma(t)}} \exp -\frac{x^2}{2\sigma^2(t)}. \tag{3.49}$$

   Determine $\sigma(t)$ and discuss the result.
   (b) Use the method of mirror charges to discuss how the solution changes if the cable is semi-infinite and extends from zero to infinity.
   (c) Take the integral over space of the elementary solution of the non-leaky cable equation and show that the value of the integral does not change over time. Give an interpretation of this result.
   (d) Take the integral over space of the elementary solution of the normal leaky cable equation of a passive dendrite and derive an expression for its temporal evolution. Give an interpretation of your result.
5. **Conduction velocity in unmyelinated axons**
   (a) Using the simplified ion channel dynamics of Eq. (3.39), transform x and t to dimensionless variables using effective time and electrotonic constants.
   (b) A traveling pulse solution will have the form $u(x,t) = \tilde{u}(x - vt)$ where v is the conduction velocity. Find the ordinary differential equation that rules $\tilde{u}$.
   (c) Show that $\tilde{u}(y) = \frac{1}{1+\exp(y)}$ with traveling speed $v = \frac{1-2a}{\sqrt{2}}$ is a solution.

4
Dimensionality reduction and phase plane analysis

The firing of action potentials has been successfully described by the Hodgkin–Huxley model, originally for the spikes in the giant axon of the squid but also, with appropriate modifications of the model, for other neuron types. The Hodgkin–Huxley model is defined by four nonlinear differential equations. The behavior of high-dimensional systems of nonlinear differential equations is difficult to visualize – and even more difficult to analyze. For an understanding of the firing behavior of the Hodgkin–Huxley model, we therefore need to turn to numerical simulations of the model. In Section 4.1 we show, as an example, some simulation results in search of the firing threshold of the Hodgkin–Huxley model. However, it remains to show whether we can get some deeper insights into the observed behavior of the model.

Four equations are in fact just two more than two: in Section 4.2 we exploit the temporal properties of the gating variables of the Hodgkin–Huxley model so as to approximate the four-dimensional differential equation by a two-dimensional one. Two-dimensional differential equations can be studied in a transparent manner by means of a technique known as "phase plane analysis." Section 4.3 is devoted to the phase plane analysis of generic neuron models consisting of two coupled differential equations, one for the membrane potential and the other for an auxiliary variable.

The mathematical tools of dimension reduction and phase plane analysis that are presented in Sections 4.2 and 4.3 will be repeatedly used throughout this book, in particular in Chapters 5, 6, 16 and 18. As a first application of phase plane analysis, we study in Section 4.4 the classification of neurons into type I and type II according to their frequency–current relation. As a second application of phase plane analysis, we return in Section 4.5 to some issues around the notion of a "firing threshold," which will be sketched now.

4.1 Threshold effects

Many introductory textbooks of neuroscience state that neurons fire an action potential if the membrane potential reaches a threshold. Since the onset of an action potential is characterized by a rapid rise of the voltage trace, the onset points can be detected in experiment recordings (Fig. 4.1a). Intuitively, the onset of an action potential occurs when the membrane potential crosses the firing threshold.

The firing threshold is not only a useful concept for experimental neuroscience, it is also at the heart of most integrate-and-fire models and therefore central to Parts II and III of this book. But does a firing threshold really exist?

Experimenters inject currents into a single neuron to probe its firing characteristics. There is a large choice of potential current wave forms, but only few of these are routinely used in many labs. In this section we use current pulses and steps in order to explore the threshold behavior of the Hodgkin–Huxley model.

4.1.1 Pulse input

A Hodgkin–Huxley model is stimulated by a short current pulse of 1 ms duration. If the stimulus is strong enough, it elicits a spike. In Fig. 4.1a,b the amplitude of the stimulating current is only slightly increased between the first and second current pulse. The membrane potential returns directly to the resting potential after the stimulus, while the neuron fires a spike in response to the second pulse. This seems to suggest that the voltage threshold for spike firing is just above the maximum voltage that is reached after the first current injection (upper horizontal dashed line in Fig. 4.1b).

Unfortunately, however, such an interpretation is incorrect. If we use a longer current pulse of 100 ms duration and apply the same argument as before, we would find a different voltage threshold, indicated by the lower horizontal dashed line in Fig. 4.1b.

Despite the fact that neuronal action potential firing is often treated as a threshold-like behavior, such a threshold is not well defined mathematically (Rinzel and Ermentrout, 1998; Koch *et al.*, 1995). For practical purposes, however, the transition can be treated as a threshold effect. However, the threshold we find depends on the stimulation protocol.

For a mathematical discussion of the threshold phenomenon, it is helpful to reduce the system of four differential equations to two equations; this is the topic of Section 4.2. We will return to pulse currents in Section 4.5.

Example: Short current pulse as voltage step

The above argument excludes a voltage threshold, but could there be a current threshold? Instead of injecting a current of 1 ms duration we can use a shorter pulse that lasts only half as long. Numerically, we find that the minimal current necessary to trigger an action potential of the Hodgkin–Huxley model is now twice as large as before. We conclude that, for short current pulses, it is not the amplitude of the current that sets the effective firing threshold, but rather the integral of the current pulse or the charge. Indeed, the more charge we put on the membrane the higher the voltage, simply because of the capacitance C of the membrane. For very short current pulses

(a)

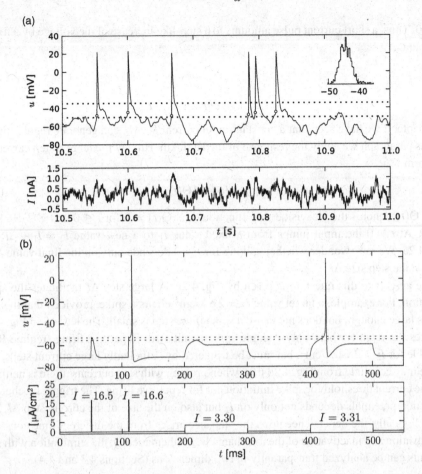

(b)

Fig. 4.1 Firing threshold. (a) Experimental recording of membrane voltage (top) during stimulation with a time-dependent current (bottom). The onset of spikes, defined as the moment when the voltage starts its upswing, is marked by open circles. The lowest and highest onset voltage during a recording of 20 s are marked by dotted horizontal lines. Inset: Histogram of onset voltages; adapted from Mensi *et al.* (2013). (b) Stimulation of the Hodgkin–Huxley model with pulse and step current. Voltage (top) in response to pulses and steps (bottom). The apparent voltage threshold is higher (dotted lines in top panel) for a pulse than for a step current. The critical currents are $16.6\ \mu\text{A/cm}^2$ for the 1 ms pulse and $3.31\ \mu\text{A/cm}^2$ for the step. Parameters of the Hodgkin–Huxley model as in Table 2.1.

$$I(t) = q\,\delta(t) = \lim_{\Delta \to 0} \frac{q}{\Delta} \quad \text{for } 0 < t < \Delta \quad \text{and } 0 \text{ otherwise.} \tag{4.1}$$

The voltage of the Hodgkin–Huxley model increases at the moment of current injection by an amount $\Delta u = q/C$ where q is the charge of the current pulse (see Section 1.3.2). If the model was at rest for $t < 0$, the new voltage $u = u_{\text{rest}} + \Delta u$ can be used as the initial condition for the numerical integration of the Hodgkin–Huxley model for times

$t > 0$. Thus, a short current pulse amounts to a step-like increase of the voltage by a fixed amount.

4.1.2 Step current input

In Chapter 2 we have seen that a constant input current $I_0 > I_\theta$ can generate regular firing. In this paragraph we study the response of the Hodgkin–Huxley model to a step current of the form

$$I(t) = I_1 + \Delta I \, \Theta(t). \tag{4.2}$$

Here $\Theta(t)$ denotes the Heaviside step function, i.e., $\Theta(t) = 0$ for $t \leq 0$ and $\Theta(t) = 1$ for $t > 0$. At $t = 0$ the input jumps from a fixed value I_1 to a new value $I_2 = I_1 + \Delta I$; see Fig. 4.2a. We may wonder whether spiking for $t > 0$ depends only on the final value I_2 or also on the step size ΔI.

The answer to this question is given by Fig. 4.2d. A large step ΔI facilitates the spike initiation. For example, a target value $I_2 = 2 \, \mu\text{A/cm}^2$ elicits a spike, provided that the step size is large enough, but does not cause a spike if the step is small. The letter S in Fig. 4.2d denotes the regime where only a single spike is initiated. Repetitive firing (regime R) is possible for $I_2 > 2.6 \, \mu\text{A/cm}^2$, but must be triggered by sufficiently large current steps.

We may conclude from Fig. 4.2d that, when probing with step currents, there is neither a unique current threshold for spike initiation nor for repetitive firing. The trigger mechanism for action potentials depends not only on I_2 but also on the size of the current step ΔI.

Biologically, the dependence upon the step size arises from the different time constants of activation and inactivation of the ion channels. Mathematically, the stimulation with step currents can be analyzed transparently in two dimensions (Sections 4.3 and 4.4).

4.2 Reduction to two dimensions

A system of four differential equations, such as the Hodgkin–Huxley model, is difficult to analyze, so that normally we are limited to numerical simulations. A mathematical analysis is, however, possible for a system of two differential equations.

In this section we perform a systematic reduction of the four-dimensional Hodgkin–Huxley model to two dimensions. To do so, we have to eliminate two of the four variables. The essential ideas of the reduction can also be applied to detailed neuron models that may contain many different ion channels. In these cases, more than two variables would have to be eliminated, but the procedure would be completely analogous (Kepler *et al.*, 1992).

4.2.1 General approach

We focus on the Hodgkin–Huxley model discussed in Chapter 2 and start with two qualitative observations. First, we see from Fig. 2.3b that the time scale of the dynamics of the

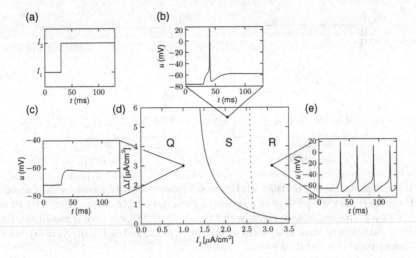

Fig. 4.2 Phase diagram for stimulation with a step current. (a) The input current $I(t)$ changes at $t = 0$ from I_1 to I_2. (b), (c), (e). Sample responses of the Hodgkin–Huxley model to step current input. (d) The outcome of the simulation experiment as a function of the final current I_2 and the step size $\Delta I = I_2 - I_1$. Three regimes denoted by S, R, and Q may be distinguished. In Q no action potential is initiated (quiet regime). In S, a single spike is initiated by the current step (single spike regime). In R, periodic spike trains are triggered by the current step (repetitive firing). Examples of voltage traces in the different regimes are presented in the smaller graphs (b, c, e) with stimulation parameters indicated by the filled circles in (d). Note that for the same final current I_2 (e.g., (d) 2.0 μA/cm^2), the neuron model emits a spike if the current step ΔI is large enough (regime S), or no spike if the step is too small. For a final current $I_2 = 3$ μA/cm^2, the model exhibits bistability between repetitive firing and quiescence.

gating variable m is much faster than that of the variables n and h. Moreover, the time scale of m is fast compared with the membrane time constant $\tau = C/g_L$ of a passive membrane, which characterizes the evolution of the voltage u when all channels are closed. The relatively rapid time scale of m suggests that we may treat m as an instantaneous variable. The variable m in the ion current equation (2.5) of the Hodgkin–Huxley model can therefore be replaced by its steady-state value, $m(t) \to m_0[u(t)]$. This is what we call a *quasi steady-state approximation* which is possible because of the "separation of time scales" between fast and slow variables.

Second, we see from Fig. 2.3b that the time constants $\tau_n(u)$ and $\tau_h(u)$ have similar dynamics over the voltage u. Moreover, the graphs of $n_0(u)$ and $1 - h_0(u)$ in Fig. 2.3a are also similar. This suggests that we may approximate the two variables n and $(1 - h)$ by a single effective variable w. To keep the formalism slightly more general we use a linear approximation $(b - h) \approx an$ with some constants a, b and set $w = b - h = an$. With $h = b - w$, $n = w/a$, and $m = m_0(u)$, Eqs. (2.4)–(2.5) become

$$C\frac{du}{dt} = -g_{Na}[m_0(u)]^3 (b - w)(u - E_{Na}) - g_K \left(\frac{w}{a}\right)^4 (u - E_K) - g_L(u - E_L) + I, \quad (4.3)$$

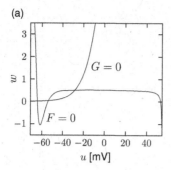
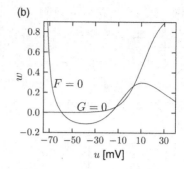

Fig. 4.3 Phase plane u, w of a Hodgkin–Huxley model reduced to two dimensions. (a) The reduction of the Hodgkin–Huxley model leads to a system of two equations, $\tau\, du/dt = F(u, w) + RI$ and $\tau_w\, dw/dt = G(u, w)$. The ensemble of points with $F(u, w) = 0$ and $G(u, w) = 0$ is shown as a function of voltage u and recovery variable w, based on Eqs. (4.3), (4.20) and (4.21). (b) As in (a), but for the Morris–Lecar model (see text for details).

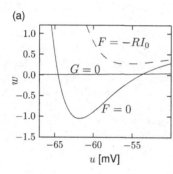
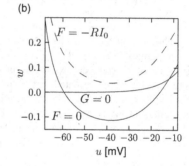

Fig. 4.4 Close-up of Fig. 4.3a and b. Solid lines: the sets of points with $F(u, w) = 0$ and $G(u, w) = 0$ are determined in the absence of stimulation ($I = 0$). Dashed line: in the presence of a constant current $I = I_0 > 0$, the set of points with $du/dt = 0$ is given $F(u, w) = -RI_0$. The curve $G(u, w) = 0$ characterizing the points with $dw/dt = 0$ starts (for $u \to -\infty$) nearly horizontally at $w = 0$ and does not change under stimulation.

or

$$\frac{du}{dt} = \frac{1}{\tau}\left[F(u, w) + RI\right], \tag{4.4}$$

with $R = g_L^{-1}$, $\tau = RC$ and some function F. We now turn to the three equations (2.9). The m equation has disappeared since m is treated as instantaneous. Instead of the two equations (2.9) for n and h, we are left with a single effective equation

$$\frac{dw}{dt} = \frac{1}{\tau_w} G(u, w), \tag{4.5}$$

where τ_w is a parameter and G a function that interpolates between dn/dt and dh/dt (see

Section 4.2.2). Equations (4.4) and (4.5) define a general two-dimensional neuron model. If we start with the Hodgkin–Huxley model and implement the above reduction steps we arrive at functions $F(u,w)$ and $G(u,w)$ which are illustrated in Figs. 4.3a and 4.4a. The mathematical details of the reduction of the four-dimensional Hodgkin–Huxley model to the two equations (4.4) and (4.5) are given below.

Before we go through the mathematical steps, we present two examples of two-dimensional neuron dynamics which are not directly derived from the Hodgkin–Huxley model, but are attractive because of their mathematical simplicity. We will return to these examples repeatedly throughout this chapter.

Example: Morris–Lecar model

Morris and Lecar (1981) proposed a simplified two-dimensional description of neuronal spike dynamics. A first equation describes the evolution of the membrane potential u, the second equation the evolution of a slow "recovery" variable $\hat{w}$. The Morris–Lecar equations read

$$C\frac{du}{dt} = -g_1\,\hat{m}_0(u)\,(u - V_1) - g_2\,\hat{w}\,(u - V_2) - g_L\,(u - V_L) + I, \qquad (4.6)$$

$$\frac{d\hat{w}}{dt} = -\frac{1}{\tau(u)}\,[\hat{w} - w_0(u)]\,. \qquad (4.7)$$

If we compare Eq. (4.6) with Eq. (4.3), we note that the first current term on the right-hand side of Eq. (4.3) has a factor $(b - w)$ which closes the channel for high voltage and which is absent in (4.6). Another difference is that neither $\hat{m}_0$ nor $\hat{w}$ in Eq. (4.6) have exponents. To clarify the relation between the two models, we could set $\hat{m}_0(u) = [m_0(u)]^3$ and $\hat{w} = (w/a)^4$. In the following we consider Eqs. (4.6) and (4.7) as a model in its own right and drop the hats over m_0 and w.

The equilibrium functions shown in Fig. 2.3a typically have a sigmoidal shape. It is reasonable to approximate the voltage dependence by

$$m_0(u) = \frac{1}{2}\left[1 + \tanh\left(\frac{u - u_1}{u_2}\right)\right], \qquad (4.8)$$

$$w_0(u) = \frac{1}{2}\left[1 + \tanh\left(\frac{u - u_3}{u_4}\right)\right], \qquad (4.9)$$

with parameters $u_1, \ldots, u_4$, and to approximate the time constant by

$$\tau(u) = \frac{\tau_w}{\cosh\left(\frac{u - u_3}{2u_4}\right)} \qquad (4.10)$$

with a further parameter τ_w. With the above assumptions, the zero-crossings of functions $F(u,w)$ and $G(u,w)$ of the Morris–Lecar model have the shape illustrated in Fig. 4.3b.

The Morris–Lecar model (4.6)–(4.10) gives a phenomenological description of action potentials. We shall see later on that the mathematical conditions for the firing of action potentials in the Morris–Lecar model can be discussed by phase plane analysis.

Example: FitzHugh–Nagumo model

FitzHugh and Nagumo where probably the first to propose that, for a discussion of action potential generation, the four equations of Hodgkin and Huxley can be replaced by two, i.e., Eqs. (4.4) and (4.5). They obtained sharp pulse-like oscillations reminiscent of trains of action potentials by defining the functions $F(u,w)$ and $G(u,w)$ as

$$F(u,w) = u - \frac{1}{3}u^3 - w,$$
$$G(u,w) = b_0 + b_1 u - w, \tag{4.11}$$

where u is the membrane voltage and w is a recovery variable (FitzHugh, 1961; Nagumo *et al.*, 1962). Note that both F and G are linear in w; the sole nonlinearity is the cubic term in u. The FitzHugh–Nagumo model is one of the simplest models with non-trivial behavior lending itself to a phase plane analysis, which will be discussed below in Sections 4.3–4.5.

4.2.2 Mathematical steps (*)

The reduction of the Hodgkin–Huxley model to Eqs. (4.4) and (4.5) presented in this section is inspired by the geometrical treatment of Rinzel (1985); see also the slightly more general method of Abbott and Kepler (1990) and Kepler *et al.* (1992).

The overall aim of the approach is to replace the variables n and h in the Hodgkin–Huxley model by a single effective variable w. At each moment of time, the values $(n(t), h(t))$ can be visualized as points in the two-dimensional plane spanned by n and h; see Fig. 4.5b. We have argued above that the time course of the scaled variable an is expected to be similar to that of $b - h$. If, at each time, $an(t)$ were equal to $b - h(t)$, then all possible points (n,h) would lie on the straight line $h = b - an$ which changes through $(0, b)$ and $(1, b - a)$. It would be unreasonable to expect that all points $(n(t), h(t))$ that occur during the temporal evolution of the Hodgkin–Huxley model fall exactly on that line. Indeed, during an action potential (Fig. 4.5a), the variables $n(t)$ and $h(t)$ stay close to a straight line, but are not perfectly on it (Fig. 4.5b). The reduction of the number of variables is achieved by a projection of those points onto the line. The position along the line $h = b - an$ gives the new variable w; see Fig. 4.6. The projection is the essential approximation during the reduction.

To perform the projection, we will proceed in three steps. A minimal condition for the projection is that the approximation introduces no error while the neuron is at rest. As a first step, we therefore shift the origin of the coordinate system to the rest state and introduce

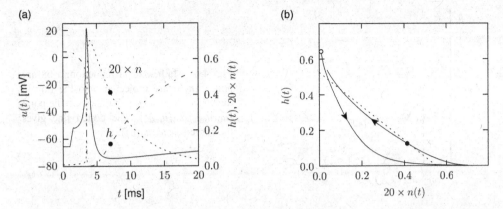

Fig. 4.5 Similarity of gating variables h and n. (a). After stimulation of the Hodgkin–Huxley model by a short current pulse, the membrane potential (solid line) exhibits an action potential. The time course of the variables n (dashed line) mirrors that of the variable h (dot-dashed). (b). During and after the action potential, the trajectory of the variables $n(t)$ and $h(t)$ (solid line) stays very close to the straight line $h = b - an$ (dashed) with slope a and offset b. The point $(n_0(u_{\text{rest}}), h_0(u_{\text{rest}}))$ is indicated with a circle.

new variables

$$x = n - n_0(u_{\text{rest}}), \tag{4.12}$$

$$y = h - h_0(u_{\text{rest}}). \tag{4.13}$$

At rest, we have $x = y = 0$.

Second, we turn the coordinate system by an angle α which is determined as follows. For a given constant voltage u, the dynamics of the gating variables n and h approaches the equilibrium values $(n_0(u), h_0(u))$. The points $(n_0(u), h_0(u))$ as a function of u define a curve in the two-dimensional plane. The slope of the curve at $u = u_{\text{rest}}$ yields the rotation angle α via

$$\tan \alpha = \frac{\frac{dh_0}{du}\big|_{u_{\text{rest}}}}{\frac{dn_0}{du}\big|_{u_{\text{rest}}}}. \tag{4.14}$$

Rotating the coordinate system by α turns the abscissa e_1 of the new coordinate system in a direction tangential to the curve. The coordinates (z_1, z_2) in the new system are

$$\begin{pmatrix} z_1 \\ z_2 \end{pmatrix} = \begin{pmatrix} \cos \alpha & \sin \alpha \\ -\sin \alpha & \cos \alpha \end{pmatrix} \begin{pmatrix} x \\ y \end{pmatrix}. \tag{4.15}$$

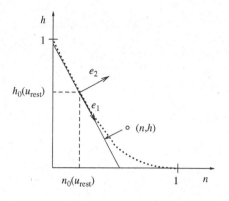

Fig. 4.6 Mathematical reduction: arbitrary points (n,h) are projected onto the line in direction of e_1 and passing through the point $(n_0(u_{rest}), h_0(u_{rest}))$. The dotted line gives the curve $(n_0(u), h_0(u))$.

Third, we set $z_2 = 0$ and retain only the coordinate z_1 along e_1. The inverse transform,

$$\begin{pmatrix} x \\ y \end{pmatrix} = \begin{pmatrix} \cos\alpha & -\sin\alpha \\ \sin\alpha & \cos\alpha \end{pmatrix} \begin{pmatrix} z_1 \\ z_2 \end{pmatrix}, \tag{4.16}$$

yields $x = z_1 \cos\alpha$ and $y = z_1 \sin\alpha$ since $z_2 = 0$. Hence, after the projection, the new values of the variables n and h are

$$n' = n_0(u_{rest}) + z_1 \cos\alpha, \tag{4.17}$$

$$h' = h_0(u_{rest}) + z_1 \sin\alpha. \tag{4.18}$$

In principle, z_1 can directly be used as the new effective variable. From (4.15) we find the differential equation

$$\frac{dz_1}{dt} = \cos\alpha \frac{dn}{dt} + \sin\alpha \frac{dh}{dt}. \tag{4.19}$$

We use Eq. (2.6) and replace, on the right-hand side, $n(t)$ and $h(t)$ by (4.17) and (4.18). The result is

$$\frac{dz_1}{dt} = -\cos\alpha \frac{z_1 \cos\alpha + n_0(u_{rest}) - n_0(u)}{\tau_n(u)} - \sin\alpha \frac{z_1 \sin\alpha + h_0(u_{rest}) - h_0(u)}{\tau_h(u)}, \tag{4.20}$$

which is of the form $dz_1/dt = G(u, z_1)$, as desired.

To see the relation to Eqs. (4.3) and (4.5), it is convenient to rescale z_1 and define

$$w = -\tan\alpha\, n_0(u_{rest}) - z_1 \sin\alpha. \tag{4.21}$$

If we introduce $a = -\tan\alpha$ and $b = a n_0(u_{rest}) + h_0(u_{rest})$, we find from Eq. (4.17) the variable $n' = w/a$ and from Eq. (4.18) $h' = b - w$, which are exactly the approximations that we used in (4.3). The differential equation for the variable w is of the desired form $dw/dt = G(u, w)$ and can be found from Eqs. (4.20) and (4.21). The resulting function $G(u, w)$ of the two-dimensional model is illustrated in Fig. 4.3a.

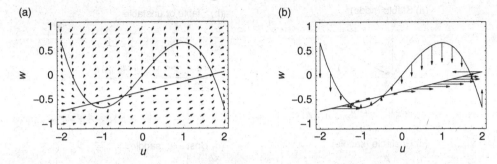

Fig. 4.7 (a) Phase portrait of the FitzHugh–Nagumo model. The u-nullcline (curved line) and the w-nullcline (straight line) intersect at the three fixed points. The direction of the arrows indicates the flow $(\dot{u},\dot{w})^T$. (b) Arrows on the u-nullcline point vertically upward or downward, while on the w-nullcline arrows are horizontal. In the neighborhood of the fixed points, arrows have a short length indicating slow movement. At the fixed point, the direction of the arrows change.

Example: Further simplification

We may further approximate the time constants τ_n and τ_h by a common function $\tau(u)$ so that the dynamics of w is

$$\frac{dw}{dt} = -\frac{1}{\tau(u)}[w - w_0(u)], \qquad (4.22)$$

with a new equilibrium function $w_0(u)$ that is a linear combination of the functions h_0 and n_0. From Eqs. (4.20) and (4.21) we find

$$w_0(u) = -\sin\alpha\,[\cos\alpha\,n_0(u) + \sin\alpha\,h_0(u) - b\sin\alpha]. \qquad (4.23)$$

In practice, $w_0(u)$ and $\tau(u)$ can be fitted by the expressions (4.9) and (4.10), respectively.

4.3 Phase plane analysis

In two-dimensional models, the temporal evolution of the variables $(u,w)^T$ can be visualized in the so-called phase plane. From a starting point $(u(t),w(t))^T$ the system will move in a time Δt to a new state $(u(t+\Delta t), w(t+\Delta t))^T$ which has to be determined by integration of the differential equations (4.4) and (4.5). For Δt sufficiently small, the displacement $(\Delta u, \Delta w)^T$ is in the direction of the flow $(\dot{u},\dot{w})^T$, i.e.,

$$\begin{pmatrix} \Delta u \\ \Delta w \end{pmatrix} = \begin{pmatrix} \dot{u} \\ \dot{w} \end{pmatrix} \Delta t, \qquad (4.24)$$

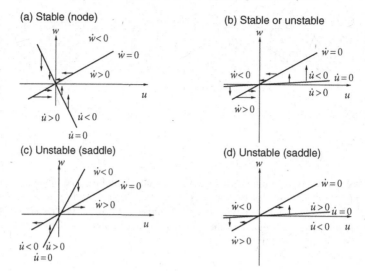

Fig. 4.8 Four examples of phase portraits around a fixed point. Case (a) is stable, cases (c) and (d) are unstable. Stability in case (b) cannot be decided with the information available from the picture alone. Cases (c) and (d) are saddle points.

which can be plotted as a vector field in the phase plane. Here $\dot{u} = du/dt$ is given by (4.4) and $\dot{w} = dw/dt$ by (4.5). The flow field is also called the phase portrait of the system. An important tool in the construction of the phase portrait is the nullcline, which is introduced now.

4.3.1 Nullclines

Let us consider the set of points with $\dot{u} = 0$, called the u-nullcline. The direction of flow on the u-nullcline is in the direction of $(0, \dot{w})^T$, since $\dot{u} = 0$. Hence arrows in the phase portrait are vertical on the u-nullcline. Similarly, the w-nullcline is defined by the condition $\dot{w} = 0$ and arrows are horizontal. The fixed points of the system, defined by $\dot{u} = \dot{w} = 0$ are given by the intersection of the u-nullcline and the w-nullcline. In Fig. 4.7 we have three fixed points.

So far we have argued that arrows on the u-nullcline are vertical, but we do not know yet whether they point up or down. To get the extra information needed, let us return to the w-nullcline. By definition, it separates the region with $\dot{w} > 0$ from the area with $\dot{w} < 0$. Suppose we evaluate $G(u,w)$ on the right-hand side of Eq. (4.5) at a single point, e.g., at $(0,-1)$. If $G(0,-1) > 0$, then the whole area on that side of the w-nullcline has $\dot{w} > 0$. Hence, all arrows along the u-nullcline that lie on the same side of the w-nullcline

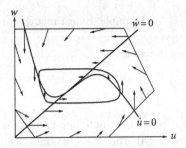

Fig. 4.9 Bounding surface around an unstable fixed point and the limit cycle (schematic figure).

as the point $(0, -1)$ point upward. The direction of arrows normally[1] changes where the nullclines intersect; see Fig. 4.7b.

4.3.2 Stability of Fixed Points

In Fig. 4.7 there are three fixed points, but which of these are stable? The local stability of a fixed point (u_{FP}, w_{FP}) is determined by linearization of the dynamics at the intersection. With $x = (u - u_{FP}, w - w_{FP})^T$, we have after the linearization

$$\frac{d}{dt}x = \begin{pmatrix} F_u & F_w \\ G_u & G_w \end{pmatrix} x, \tag{4.25}$$

where $F_u = \partial F / \partial u$, $F_w = \partial F / \partial w$, ..., are evaluated at the fixed point. To study the stability we set $x(t) = e \exp(\lambda t)$ and solve the resulting eigenvalue problem. There are two solutions with eigenvalues λ_+ and λ_- and eigenvectors e_+ and e_-, respectively. Stability of the fixed point $x = 0$ in Eq. (4.25) requires that the real part of both eigenvalues be negative. The solution of the eigenvalue problem yields $\lambda_+ + \lambda_- = F_u + G_w$ and $\lambda_+ \lambda_- = F_u G_w - F_w G_u$. The necessary and sufficient condition for stability is therefore

$$F_u + G_w < 0 \quad \text{and} \quad F_u G_w - F_w G_u > 0. \tag{4.26}$$

If $F_u G_w - F_w G_u < 0$, then the imaginary part of both eigenvalues vanishes. One of the eigenvalues is positive, the other one negative. The fixed point is then called a saddle point.

Eq. (4.25) is obtained by Taylor expansion of Eqs. (4.4) and (4.5) to first order in x. If the real part of one or both eigenvalues of the matrix in Eq. (4.25) vanishes, the complete characterization of the stability properties of the fixed point requires an extension of the Taylor expansion to higher order.

---

[1] Exceptions are the rare cases where the function F or G is degenerate: for example, $F(u, w) = w^2$.

Example: Linear model

Let us consider the linear dynamics

$$\dot{u} = au - w,$$
$$\dot{w} = \varepsilon(bu - w), \tag{4.27}$$

with positive constants $b, \varepsilon > 0$. The u-nullcline is $w = au$, the w-nullcline is $w = bu$. For the moment we assume $a < 0$. The phase diagram is that of Fig. 4.8a. Note that by decreasing the parameter ε, we may slow down the w-dynamics in Eq. (4.27) without changing the nullclines.

Because $F_u + G_w = a - \varepsilon < 0$ for $a < 0$ and $F_uG_w - F_wG_u = \varepsilon(b - a) > 0$, it follows from (4.26) that the fixed point is stable. Note that the phase portrait around the left fixed point in Fig. 4.7 has locally the same structure as the portrait in Fig. 4.8a. We conclude that the left fixed point in Fig. 4.7 is stable.

Let us now keep the w-nullcline fixed and turn the u-nullcline by increasing a to positive values; see Fig. 4.8b and c. Stability is lost if $a > \min\{\varepsilon, b\}$. Stability of the fixed point in Fig. 4.8b can therefore not be decided without knowing the value of ε. On the other hand, in Fig. 4.8c we have $a > b$ and hence $F_uG_w - F_wG_u = \varepsilon(b - a) < 0$. In this case one of the eigenvalues is positive ($\lambda_+ > 0$) and the other one negative ($\lambda_- < 0$), hence we have a saddle point. The imaginary parts of the eigenvalues vanish. The eigenvectors e_- and e_+ are therefore real and can be visualized in the phase space. A trajectory through the fixed point in the direction of e_- is attracted toward the fixed point. This is, however, the only direction by which a trajectory may reach the fixed point. Any small perturbation around the fixed point which is not strictly in the direction of e_2 will grow exponentially. A saddle point as in Fig. 4.8c plays an important role in so-called type I neuron models that will be introduced in Section 4.4.1.

For the sake of completeness we also study the linear system

$$\dot{u} = -au + w,$$
$$\dot{w} = \varepsilon(bu - w), \quad \text{with } 0 < a < b, \tag{4.28}$$

with positive constants a, b, and ε. This system is identical to Eq. (4.27) except that the sign of the first equation is flipped. As before we have nullclines $w = au$ and $w = bu$; see Fig. 4.8d. Note that the nullclines are identical to those in Fig. 4.8b, only the direction of the horizontal arrows on the w-nullcline has changed.

Since $F_uG_w - F_wG_u = \varepsilon(a - b)$, the fixed point is unstable if $a < b$. In this case, the imaginary part of the eigenvalues vanish and one of the eigenvalues is positive ($\lambda_+ > 0$) while the other one is negative ($\lambda_- < 0$). Thus the fixed point can be classified as a saddle point.

One of the attractive features of phase plane analysis is that there is a direct method to show the existence of limit cycles. The theorem of Poincaré–Bendixson (Hale and

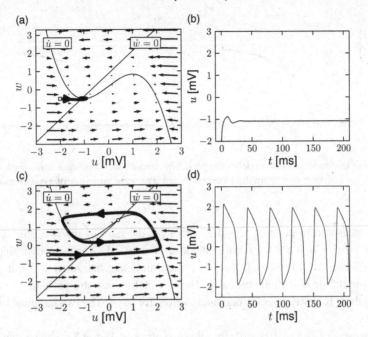

Fig. 4.10 (a) The nullclines of the FitzHugh–Nagumo model for zero input. The thin curved line is the u-nullcline; the w-nullcline is the straight line, $w = b_0 + b_1 u$, with $b_0 = 0.9, b_1 = 1.0$. The thick line is a trajectory that starts at $(-2, -0.5)$ (open square) and converges to the fixed point at $(-1.1, -0.5)$. (b) Time course of the membrane potential of the trajectory shown in (a). (c) Same as in (a) but with positive input $I = 2$ so that the fixed point in (a) is replaced by a limit cycle (thick line). (d) Voltage time course of the trajectory shown in (c). Trajectories are the result of numerical integration of Eqs. (4.29) and (4.30) with $\varepsilon = 1.25$.

Koçac, 1991) tells us that, if (i) we can construct a bounding surface around a fixed point so that all flux arrows on the surface are pointing toward the interior, and (ii) the fixed point in the interior is repulsive (real part of both eigenvalues positive), then there must exist a stable limit cycle around that fixed point.

The proof follows from the uniqueness of solutions of differential equations, which implies that trajectories cannot cross each other. If all trajectories are pushed away from the fixed point, but cannot leave the bounded surface, then they must finally settle on a limit cycle; see Fig. 4.9. Note that this argument holds only in two dimensions.

In dimensionless variables the FitzHugh–Nagumo model is

$$\frac{du}{dt} = u - \frac{1}{3}u^3 - w + I, \tag{4.29}$$

$$\frac{dw}{dt} = \varepsilon \left(b_0 + b_1 u - w\right). \tag{4.30}$$

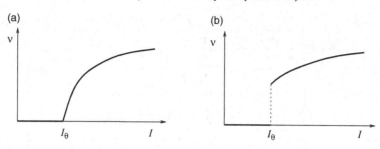

Fig. 4.11 (a) Gain function for models of type I. The frequency v during a limit cycle oscillation is a continuous function of the applied current I. (b) The gain function of type II models has a discontinuity.

Time is measured in units of τ, and $\varepsilon = \tau/\tau_w$ is the ratio of the two time scales. The u-nullcline is $w = u - u^3/3 + I$ with maxima at $u = \pm 1$. The maximal slope of the u-nullcline is $dw/du = 1$ at $u = 0$; for $I = 0$ the u-nullcline has zeros at 0 and $\pm\sqrt{3}$. For $I \neq 0$ the u-nullcline is shifted vertically. The w-nullcline is a straight line $w = b_0 + b_1 u$. For $b_1 > 1$, there is always exactly one intersection, for any I. The two nullclines are shown in Fig. 4.10.

A comparison of Fig. 4.10a with the phase portrait of Fig. 4.8a, shows that the fixed point is stable for $I = 0$. If we increase I the intersection of the nullclines moves to the right; see Fig. 4.10c. According to the calculation associated with Fig. 4.8b, the fixed point loses stability as soon as the slope of the u-nullcline becomes larger than ε. It is possible to construct a bounding surface around the unstable fixed point so that we know from the Poincaré–Bendixson theorem that a limit cycle must exist. Figures 4.10a and 4.10c show two trajectories, one for $I = 0$ converging to the fixed point and another one for $I = 2$ converging toward the limit cycle. The horizontal phases of the limit cycle correspond to a rapid change of the voltage, which results in voltage pulses similar to a train of action potentials; see Fig. 4.10d.

4.4 Type I and type II neuron models

We have already seen in Chapter 2 that neuron models fall into two classes: those with a continuous frequency–current curve are called type I whereas those with a discontinuous frequency–current curve are called type II. The characteristic curves for both model types are illustrated in Fig. 4.11. The onset of repetitive firing under constant current injection is characterized by a minimal current I_θ, also called the rheobase current.

For two-dimensional neuron models, the firing behavior of both neuron types can be understood by phase plane analysis. To do so we need to observe the changes in structure and stability of fixed points when the current passes from a value below I_θ to a value just above I_θ, where I_θ determines the onset of repetitive firing. Mathematically speaking, the point I_θ where the transition in the number or stability of fixed points occurs is called a bifurcation point and I is the bifurcation parameter.

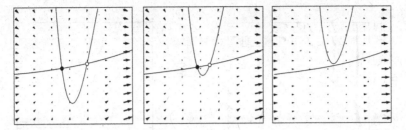

Fig. 4.12 Saddle-node bifurcation. The u-nullcline is represented as a parabola that moves upward as the current is increased (from left to right). The saddle point is shown as an open circle and the node as a filled circle. When the current is increased, the two fixed points, which are initially far apart (left), move closer together (middle) and finally annihilate (right).

Example: Number of fixed points changes at bifurcation

Let us recall that the fixed points of the system lie at the intersection of the u-nullcline with the w-nullcline. Fig. 4.3 shows examples of two-dimensional neuron models where the u-nullcline crosses the w-nullclines three times so that the models exhibit three fixed points. If the external driving current I is slowly increased, the u-nullcline shifts vertically upward.[2] If the driving current I becomes strong enough, the two left-most fixed points merge and disappear; see Fig. 4.4. The moment when the two fixed points disappear is the bifurcation point. At this point a qualitative change in the dynamics of the neuron model is observed, e.g., the transition from the resting state to periodic firing. These changes are discussed in the following subsections.

4.4.1 Type I models and saddle-node-onto-limit-cycle bifurcation

Neuron models with a continuous gain function are called type I. Mathematically, a saddle-node-onto-limit-cycle bifurcation generically gives rise to a type I behavior, as we will explain now.

For zero input and weakly positive input, we suppose that our neuron model has three fixed points in a configuration such as that in Fig. 4.13: a stable fixed point (node) to the left, a saddle point in the middle, and an unstable fixed point to the right. If I is increased, the u-nullcline moves upward and the stable fixed point merges with the saddle and disappears (Fig. 4.12). We are left with the unstable fixed point around which there must be a limit cycle provided the flux is bounded. If the limit cycle passes through the region where the saddle and node disappeared, the scenario is called a saddle-node-onto-limit-cycle bifurcation.

Can we say anything about the frequency of the limit cycle? Just before the transition point where the two fixed points merge, the system exhibits a stable fixed point which (locally) attracts trajectories. As a trajectory gets close to the stable fixed point, its velocity

---

[1] It may also undergo some changes in shape, but these are not relevant for the following discussion.

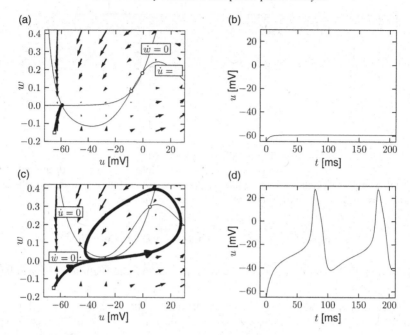

Fig. 4.13 (a) The nullclines of the Morris–Lecar model for zero input. The w-nullcline is flat at low u but increases monotonically above $u = -20$, the u-nullcline is the nonlinear curve crossing the w-nullcline in three points. (a) Trajectory starting at $(-65, -0.15)$ (open square) converges to the stable fixed point at (-59,0) (filled circle). (b) Time course of the membrane potential of the trajectory shown in (a). (c) Same as in (a) but with positive input $I = 45$. The stable fixed point in (a) has merged with the saddle (open circle in (a)) and disappeared leaving a limit cycle around the third, unstable, fixed point. (d) Voltage time course of the trajectory shown in (c). Trajectories are the results of numerical integration of Eqs. (4.6)–(4.10).

decreases until it finally stops at the fixed point. Let us now consider the situation where the driving current is a bit larger so that $I = I_\theta$. This is the transition point, where the two fixed points merge and a new limit cycle appears. At the transition point the limit cycle has zero frequency because it passes through the two merging fixed points where the velocity of the trajectory is zero. If I is increased a little, the limit cycle still "feels" the "ghost" of the disappeared fixed points in the sense that the velocity of the trajectory in that region is very low. While the fixed points have disappeared, the "ruins" of the fixed points are still present in the phase plane. Thus the onset of oscillation is continuous and occurs with zero frequency. Models which fall into this class are therefore of type I; see Fig. 4.11.

From the above discussion it should be clear that, if we increase I, we encounter a transition point where two fixed points disappear, namely, the saddle and the stable fixed point (node). At the same time a limit cycle appears. If we come from the other side, we have first a limit cycle which disappears at the moment when the saddle-node pair shows up. The transition is therefore called a saddle-node bifurcation on a limit cycle.

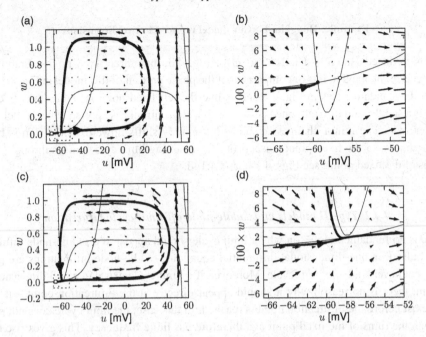

Fig. 4.14 Reduced Hodgkin–Huxley model with nullclines and dynamics of a type I model. (a) For weakly positive input, the u-nullcline has three intersections with the w-nullcline. (b) Zoom onto the two left-most fixed points. A trajectory (thick solid line) is attracted toward the left fixed point. (c) For input $I > I_\theta$, the u-nullcline is shifted vertically and only one fixed point remains which is unstable. The trajectory starting from the same initial condition as in (a) turns into a limit cycle. (d) Zoom onto the same region as in (b). The limit cycle passes through the region where the two fixed points have been before, but these fixed points have now disappeared. The nearly vanishing length of the arrows indicates that movement of the trajectory in this region is very slow giving rise to a near-zero firing frequency.

Example: Morris–Lecar model

Depending on the choice of parameters, the Morris–Lecar model is of either type I or type II. We consider a parameter set where the Morris–Lecar model has three fixed points located such that two of them lie in the unstable region where the u-nullcline has large positive slope as indicated schematically in Fig. 4.13. Comparison of the phase portrait of Fig. 4.13 with that of see Fig. 4.8 shows that the left fixed point is stable as in Fig. 4.8a, the middle one is a saddle point as in Fig. 4.8c, and the right one is unstable as in Fig. 4.8b provided that the slope of the u-nullcline is sufficiently positive. Thus we have the sequence of three fixed points necessary for a saddle-node-onto-limit-cycle bifurcation.

Example: Hodgkin–Huxley model reduced to two dimensions

The reduced Hodgkin–Huxley model of Fig. 4.3a has three fixed points. Stability analysis of the fixed points or comparison of the phase portrait of this model in Fig. 4.14a with the standard cases in Fig. 4.8 shows that the left fixed point is stable, the middle one is a saddle, and the right one is unstable. If a step current I is applied, the u-nullcline undergoes some minor changes in shape, but mainly shifts upward. If the step is big enough, two of the fixed points disappear. The resulting limit cycle passes through the ruins of the fixed point; see Figs. 4.14c and 4.14d.

4.4.2 Type II models and saddle-node-off-limit-cycle bifurcation

There is no fundamental reason why a limit cycle should appear at a saddle-node bifurcation. Indeed, in one-dimensional differential equations, saddle-node bifurcations are possible, but never lead to a limit cycle. Moreover, if a limit cycle exists in a two-dimensional system, there is no reason why it should appear directly at the bifurcation point – it can also exist before the bifurcation point is reached. In this case, the limit cycle does not pass through the ruins of the fixed point and therefore has finite frequency. This gives rise to a type II neuron model. The corresponding bifurcation can be classified as saddle-node-off-limit-cycle.

Example: Hodgkin–Huxley model reduced to two dimensions

Fig. 4.15 shows the same neuron model as Fig. 4.14 except for one single change in parameter: the time scale τ_w in Eq. (4.5) for the w-dynamics is slightly faster. While the position and shape of the nullclines is unchanged, the dynamics are different.

To understand the difference we focus on Fig. 4.15d. The limit cycle triggered by a current step does not touch the region where the ruins of the fixed points lie, but passes further to the right. Thus the bifurcation is of the type saddle-node-off-limit-cycle, the limit cycle has finite frequency, and the neuron model is of type II.

Example: Saddle-node without limit cycle

Not all saddle-node bifurcations lead to a limit cycle. If the slope of the w-nullcline of the FitzHugh–Nagumo model defined in Eqs. (4.29) and (4.30) is smaller than 1, it is possible to have three fixed points, one of them unstable and the other two stable; see Fig. 4.7. The system is therefore bistable. If a positive current $I > 0$ is applied the u-nullcline moves upward. Eventually the left stable fixed point and the saddle merge and disappear via a (simple) saddle-node bifurcation. Since the right fixed point remains stable, no oscillation occurs.

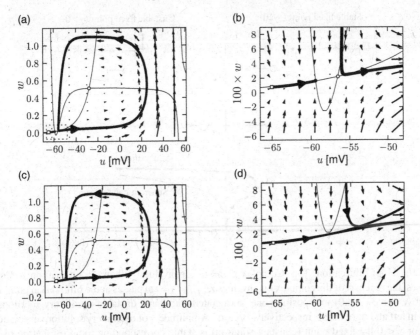

Fig. 4.15 Reduced Hodgkin–Huxley model with nullclines and dynamics of a type II model. (a) For weakly positive input, the u-nullcline (solid line) has three intersections with the w-nullcline (dashed line). (b) Zoom onto the two left-most fixed points. A trajectory (thick solid line) is attracted toward the left fixed point. (c) For input $I > I_\theta$, only one fixed point remains which is unstable. The trajectory starting from the same initial condition as in A turns into a limit cycle. (d) Zoom onto the same region as in (b). The limit cycle passes to the right of the region where the two fixed points have been in (b). Arrows along the limit cycle indicate finite speed of the trajectory, so that the limit cycle has a nonzero firing frequency.

4.4.3 Type II models and Hopf bifurcation

The typical jump from zero to a finite firing frequency, observed in the frequency–current curve of type II models can arise by different bifurcation types. One important example is a Hopf bifurcation.

Let us recall that the fixed points of the system lie at the intersection of the u-nullcline with the w-nullcline. In the FitzHugh–Nagumo model, with parameters as in Fig. 4.10, there is always a single fixed point whatever the (constant) driving current I. Nevertheless, while I is slowly increased, the behavior of the system changes qualitatively from a stable fixed point to a limit cycle; see Fig. 4.10. The transition occurs when the fixed point loses its stability.

From the solution of the stability problem in Eq. (4.25) we know that the eigenvalues $\lambda_{+/-}$ form a complex conjugate pair with a real part γ and a imaginary part $+/-\omega$

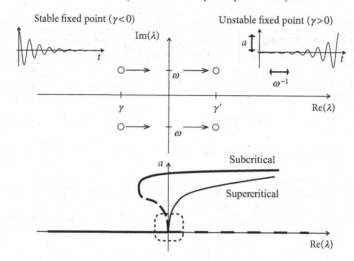

Fig. 4.16 Hopf bifurcation. Top: Complex plane of eigenvalues. When the bifurcation parameter increases, the real part of the complex eigenvalues $\lambda_{+/-} = \gamma \pm i\omega$ passes at the bifurcation point from a negative value ($\gamma < 0$) to a positive one. Associated stable and unstable oscillatory solutions are shown in left and right insets, respectively. Bottom: Amplitude a of oscillatory solutions as a function of γ. For $\gamma < 0$ the fixed point (constant solution) is stable corresponding to an oscillation of zero amplitude. At the bifurcation point, the constant solution loses its stability (dashed line) and a novel oscillatory solution appears. The amplitude of the oscillatory solution increases continuously. For a supercritical Hopf bifurcation the oscillatory solution is stable (solid line) whereas for a subcritical Hopf bifurcation, it is unstable close to the bifurcation point. The linear bifurcation analysis is valid only in the direct neighborhood of the bifurcation point (dashed box) and cannot predict the stable limit cycle (solid line) of the subcritical Hopf bifurcation.

(Fig. 4.16). The fixed point is stable if $\gamma < 0$. At the transition point, the real part vanishes and the eigenvalues are

$$\lambda_{\pm} = \pm i \sqrt{F_u G_w - G_u F_w}. \qquad (4.31)$$

These eigenvalues correspond to an oscillatory solution (of the linearized equation) with a frequency given by $\omega = \sqrt{F_u G_w - G_u F_w}$. The above scenario of stability loss in combination with an emerging oscillation is called a Hopf bifurcation.

Unfortunately, the discussion so far does not tell us anything about the stability of the oscillatory solution. If the new oscillatory solution, which appears at the Hopf bifurcation, is itself unstable (which is more difficult to show), the scenario is called a subcritical Hopf bifurcation (Fig. 4.16). This is the case in the FitzHugh–Nagumo model where, owing to the instability of the oscillatory solution in the neighborhood of the Hopf bifurcation, the system blows up and approaches another limit cycle of large amplitude; see Fig. 4.10. The stable large-amplitude limit cycle solution exists, in fact, slightly before I reaches the critical value of the Hopf bifurcation. Thus there is a small regime of bistability between the fixed point and the limit cycle.

In a supercritical Hopf bifurcation, on the other hand, the new periodic solution is stable. In this case, the limit cycle would have a small amplitude if I is just above the bifurcation point. The amplitude of the oscillation grows with the stimulation I (Fig. 4.16). Such periodic oscillations of small amplitude are not linked to neuronal firing, but must rather be interpreted as spontaneous subthreshold oscillations.

Whenever we have a Hopf bifurcation, be it subcritical or supercritical, the limit cycle starts with finite frequency. Thus if we plot the frequency of the oscillation in the limit cycle as a function of the (constant) input I, we find a discontinuity at the bifurcation point. However, only models with a subcritical Hopf bifurcation give rise to large-amplitude oscillations close to the bifurcation point. We conclude that models where the onset of oscillations occurs via a subcritical Hopf bifurcation exhibit a gain function of type II.

Example: FitzHugh–Nagumo model

The appearance of oscillations in the FitzHugh–Nagumo Model discussed above in Fig. 4.10 is of type II. If the slope of the w-nullcline is larger than 1, there is only one fixed point, whatever I. With increasing current I, the fixed point moves to the right. Eventually it loses stability via a Hopf bifurcation.

4.5 Threshold and excitability

We have seen in Section 4.1 that the Hodgkin–Huxley model does not have a clear-cut firing threshold. Nevertheless, there is a critical regime where the sensitivity to input current pulses is so high that it can be fairly well approximated by a threshold. For weak stimuli, the voltage trace returns more or less directly to the resting potentials. For stronger stimuli it makes a large detour, that is, the model emits a spike; see Fig. 4.1b. This property is characteristic for a large class of systems collectively termed *excitable systems*.

For two-dimensional models, excitability can be discussed in phase space in a transparent manner. We pose the following questions. What are the conditions for a threshold behavior? If there is no sharp threshold, what are the conditions for a regime of high (threshold-like) sensitivity? As we have seen in Section 4.1, the search for a threshold yields different results for step or pulsatile currents. We shall see now that, for stimulation with a short current pulse of variable amplitude, models with saddle-node bifurcation (on or off a limit cycle) indeed have a threshold, whereas models where firing arises via a Hopf bifurcation have not. On the other hand, even models with Hopf bifurcation can show threshold-like behavior for current pulses if the dynamics of w are considerably slower than that of u.

Throughout this section we use the following stimulation paradigm. We assume that the neuron is at rest (or in a known state) and apply a short current pulse $I(t) = q\,\delta(t)$

(a)

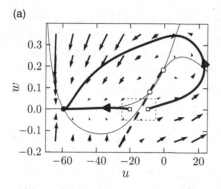

(b)

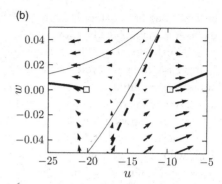

Fig. 4.17   Threshold in a type I model. (a) The stable manifold (thick dashed line) acts as a threshold. Trajectories (thick solid lines) that start to the right of the stable manifold cannot return directly to the stable fixed point (filled circle) but have to take a detour around the repulsive fixed point (circle at $(u, w) \approx (-1, 0.2)$). The result is a spike-like excursion of the u-variable. Thin lines are the nullclines. (b) Blow-up of the rectangular region in (a). The starting points of the two sample trajectories are marked by squares.

of amplitude $q > 0$. The input pulse influences the neuronal dynamics via Eq. (4.4). As a consequence, the voltage u jumps at $t = 0$ by an amount $\Delta u = qR/\tau$; see Eq. (4.4). With $\tau = RC$ the voltage jump can be written $\Delta u = q/C$ in agreement with the discussion in Section 4.1.1.

Since the current pulse does not act directly on the recovery variable w (see Eq. (4.5)), the time course of $w(t)$ is continuous. In the phase plane, the current pulse therefore shifts the value of state variables (u, w) of the system *horizontally* to a new value $(u + \Delta u, w)$. How does the system return to equilibrium? How does the behavior depend on the amplitude q of the current pulse?

We will see that the behavior can depend on the charge q of the current pulse in two qualitatively distinct ways. In type I models, the response to the input shows an "all-or-nothing" behavior and consists of either a significant pulse (that is, an action potential) or a simple decay back to rest. To this effect, type I models exhibit a threshold behavior. If the action potential occurs, it has always roughly the same amplitude, but occurs at different delays depending on the strength q of the stimulating current pulse. In models with a Hopf bifurcation, on the other hand, the amplitude of the response depends continuously on the amplitude q. Therefore, models with a Hopf bifurcation do not have a sharp threshold. Type II models with a saddle-node-off-limit-cycle bifurcation have a threshold behavior for pulse injection similar to that of type I models.

Example: Single current pulses versus multiple pulses

The discussion so far has been focused on an isolated current pulse of charge q. Note, however, that even in a model with threshold, a first input pulse that lifts the state of the system above the threshold can be counterbalanced by a second negative input which

(a)

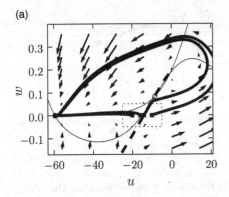

(b)

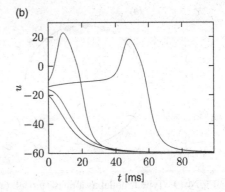

Fig. 4.18 Type I model and delayed spike initiation. (a) Trajectories in the phase starting with initial conditions (u_0, w_{rest}) where $u_0 = -20, -17, -14, -10$ are close to the threshold. (b) Projection of the trajectories on the voltage axis. Close to the threshold, spike initiation starts with a delay, but the amplitude of the action potential is always roughly the same.

pulls the state of the system back. Thus, even in models with a threshold, the threshold is only "seen" for the specific input scenario considered here, namely, one isolated short current pulse.

4.5.1 Type I models

As discussed above, type I models are characterized by a set of three fixed points, a stable one to the left, a saddle point in the middle, and an unstable one to the right. The linear stability analysis at the saddle point reveals, by definition of a saddle, one positive and one negative eigenvalue, λ_+ and λ_-, respectively. The imaginary parts of the eigenvalues vanish. Associated with λ_- is the (real) eigenvector e_-. A trajectory which approaches the saddle in the direction of e_- from either side will eventually converge toward the fixed point. There are two of these trajectories. The first one starts at infinity and approaches the saddle from below. In the case of a type I mode, the second one starts at the unstable fixed point and approaches the saddle from above. The two together define the stable manifold of the fixed point (Hale and Koçac, 1991). A perturbation around the fixed point that lies on the stable manifold returns to the fixed point. All other perturbations will grow exponentially.

The stable manifold plays an important role for the excitability of the system. Due to the uniqueness of solutions of differential equations, trajectories cannot cross. This implies that all trajectories with initial conditions to the right of the stable manifold must make a detour around the unstable fixed point before they can reach the stable fixed point. Trajectories with initial conditions to the left of the stable manifold return immediately toward the stable fixed point; see Fig. 4.17.

Let us now apply these considerations to neuron models driven by a short current pulse. At rest, the neuron model is at the stable fixed point. A short input current pulse moves the

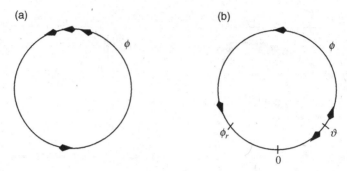

Fig. 4.19 Type I model as a phase model. (a) For $I > 0$, the system is on a limit cycle. The phase velocity $d\phi/dt$ is positive everywhere. (b) For $I < 0$, the phase has a stable fixed point at $\phi = \phi_r$ and an unstable fixed point at $\phi = \vartheta$.

state of the system to the right. If the current pulse is small, the new state of the system is to the left of the stable manifold. Hence the membrane potential u decays back to rest. If the current pulse is sufficiently strong, it will shift the state of the system to the right of the stable manifold. Since the resting point is the only stable fixed point, the neuron model will eventually return to the resting potential. To do so, it has, however, to take a large detour which is seen as a pulse in the voltage variable u. The stable manifold thus acts as a threshold for spike initiation, if the neuron model is probed with an isolated current pulse.

Example: Delayed spike initiation

We consider a sequence of current pulse of variable amplitude that cause a jump to initial values (u_0, w_{rest}) where u_0 is close to the firing threshold identified above. As u_0 approaches the firing threshold from above, action potentials are elicited with increasing delay; see Fig. 4.18b. The reason is that close to the firing threshold (i.e., the stable manifold of the saddle point) the trajectory is attracted toward the saddle point without reaching it. At the saddle point, the velocity of the trajectory would be zero. Close to the saddle point the velocity of the trajectory is nonzero, but extremely slow. The rapid rise of the action potential only starts after the trajectory has gained a minimal distance from the saddle point.

Example: Canonical type I model

We have seen in the previous example that, for various current amplitudes, the trajectory always takes nearly the same path on its detour in the two-dimensional phase plane. Let us therefore simplify further and just describe the position or "phase" on this standard path.

(a)
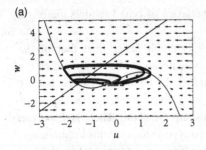

(b)
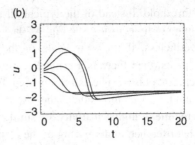

Fig. 4.20 Threshold behavior in a model with Hopf bifurcation. (a) Trajectories in the phase starting with initial conditions (u_0, w_{rest}) where $u_0 = -0.5, -0.25, -0.125, 0, 0.25$. (b) Projection of the trajectories on the voltage axis. For $u_0 \leq -0.25$, the trajectories return rapidly to rest. The trajectories with $u_0 \geq -0.125$ start with positive slope. Parameters were $b_0 = 2$, $b_1 = 1.5$, $\varepsilon = 0.1$ with $I = 0$.

Consider the one-dimensional model

$$\frac{d\phi}{dt} = q(1 - \cos \phi) + I(1 + \cos \phi) \qquad (4.32)$$

where $q > 0$ is a parameter and I is the applied current, with $0 < |I| < q$. The variable ϕ is the phase along the limit cycle trajectory. Formally, a spike is said to occur whenever $\phi = \pi$.

For $I < 0$ on the right-hand side of Eq. (4.32), the phase equation $d\phi/dt$ has two fixed points. The resting state is at the stable fixed point $\phi = \phi_r$. The unstable fixed point at $\phi = \vartheta$ acts as a threshold; see Fig. 4.19b. Let us now assume initial conditions slightly above threshold, namely, $\phi_0 = \vartheta + \delta \phi$. Since $d\phi/dt|_{\phi_0} > 0$ the system starts to fire an action potential but for $\delta \phi \ll 1$ the phase velocity is still close to zero and the maximum of the spike (corresponding to $\phi = \pi$) is reached only after a long delay. This delay depends critically on the initial condition.

For all currents $I > 0$, we have $d\phi/dt > 0$, so that the system is circling along the limit cycle; see Fig. 4.19a. The minimal velocity is $d\phi/dt = I$ for $\phi = 0$. The period of the limit cycle can be found by integration of (4.32) around a full cycle. Let us now reduce the amplitude of the applied current I. For $I \to 0$, the velocity along the trajectory around $\phi = 0$ tends to zero. The period of one cycle $T(I)$ therefore tends to infinity. In other words, for $I \to 0$, the frequency of the oscillation $\nu = 1/T(I)$ decreases (continuously) to zero, the characteristic feature of type I models.

The model (4.32) is a canonical model in the sense that all type I neuron models close to the point of a saddle-node-on-limit-cycle bifurcation can be mapped onto Eq. (4.32) (Ermentrout, 1996).

4.5.2 Hopf bifurcations

In contrast to models with saddle-node bifurcation, a neuron model with a Hopf bifurcation does not have a stable manifold and, hence, there is no "forbidden line" that acts as a sharp threshold. Instead of the typical all-or-nothing behavior of type I models there is a continuum of trajectories; see Fig. 4.20a.

Nevertheless, if the time scale of the u-dynamics is much faster than that of the w-dynamics, then there is a critical regime where the sensitivity to the amplitude of the input current pulse can be extremely high. If the amplitude of the input pulse is increased by a tiny amount, the amplitude of the response increases a lot. In practice, the consequences of the regime of high sensitivity are similar to that of a sharp threshold. There is, however, a subtle difference in the timing of the response between type I models with saddle-node-onto-limit-cycle bifurcation and type II models with Hopf bifurcation. In models with Hopf bifurcation, the peak of the response is always reached with roughly the same delay, independently of the size of the input pulse. It is the amplitude of the response that increases rapidly but continuously; see Fig. 4.20b.

This is to be contrasted with the behavior of models with a saddle-node-onto-limit cycle behavior. As discussed above, the amplitude of the response of type I models is rather stereotyped: either there is an action potential or not. For input currents which are just above threshold, the action potential occurs, however, with an extremely long delay.

4.6 Separation of time scales and reduction to one dimension

Consider the generic two-dimensional neuron model given by Eqs. (4.4) and (4.5). We measure time in units of τ and take $R = 1$. Equations (4.4) and (4.5) are then

$$\frac{du}{dt} = F(u,w) + I, \tag{4.33}$$

$$\frac{dw}{dt} = \varepsilon\, G(u,w), \tag{4.34}$$

where $\varepsilon = \tau/\tau_w$. If $\tau_w \gg \tau$, then $\varepsilon \ll 1$. In this situation the time scale that governs the evolution of u is much faster than that of w. This observation can be exploited for the analysis of the system. The general idea is that of a "separation of time scales;" in the mathematical literature the limit of $\varepsilon \to 0$ is called "singular perturbation." Oscillatory behavior for small ε is called a "relaxation oscillation."

What are the consequences of the large difference of time scales for the phase portrait of the system? Recall that the flow is in the direction of $(\dot{u}, \dot{w})$. In the limit of $\varepsilon \to 0$, all arrows in the flow field are therefore horizontal, except those in the neighborhood of the u-nullcline. On the u-nullcline, $\dot{u} = 0$ and arrows are vertical as usual. Their length, however, is only of order ε. Intuitively speaking, the horizontal arrows rapidly push the trajectory toward the u-nullcline. Only close to the u-nullcline are directions of movement other than horizontal possible. Therefore, trajectories slowly follow the u-nullcline, except at the knees of the nullcline where they jump to a different branch.

Excitability can now be discussed with the help of Fig. 4.21. A current pulse shifts the state of the system horizontally away from the stable fixed point. If the current pulse is small, the system returns immediately (i.e., on the fast time scale) to the stable fixed point. If the current pulse is large enough so as to put the system beyond the middle branch of

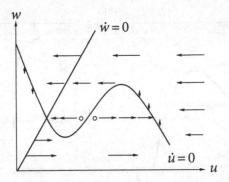

Fig. 4.21 Excitability in a type II model with separated time scales. The u-dynamics are much faster than the w-dynamics. The flux is therefore close to horizontal, except in the neighborhood of the u-nullcline (schematic figure). Initial conditions (circle) to the left of the middle branch of the u-nullcline return directly to the stable fixed point; a trajectory starting to the right of the middle branch develops a voltage pulse.

the u-nullcline, then the trajectory is pushed toward the right branch of the u nullcline. The trajectory follows the u-nullcline slowly upward until it jumps back (on the fast time scale) to the left branch of the u-nullcline. The "jump" between the branches of the null-cline corresponds to a rapid voltage change. In terms of neuronal modeling, the jump from the right to the left branch corresponds to the downstroke of the action potential. The middle branch of the u-nullcline (where $\dot{u} > 0$) acts as a threshold for spike initiation; see Fig. 4.22.

If we are not interested in the shape of an action potential, but only in the process of spike initiation, we can exploit the separation of time scales for a further reduction of the two-dimensional system of equations to a *single* variable. Without input, the neuron is at rest with variables $(u_{rest}, w_{rest})^T$. An input current $I(t)$ acts on the voltage dynamics, but has no direct influence on the variable w. Moreover, in the limit of $\varepsilon \ll 1$, the influence of the voltage u on the w-variable via Eq. (4.34) is negligible. Hence, we can set $w = w_{rest}$ and summarize the voltage dynamics of spike initiation by a singe equation

$$\frac{du}{dt} = F(u, w_{rest}) + I. \tag{4.35}$$

Equation (4.35) is the basis of the nonlinear integrate-and-fire models that we will discuss in Chapter 5.

In a two-dimensional neuron model with separation of time scales, the upswing of the spike corresponds to a rapid horizontal movement of the trajectory in the phase plane. The upswing is therefore correctly reproduced by Eq. (4.35). The recovery variable departs from its resting value w_{rest} only during the return of the system to rest, after the voltage has (nearly) reached its maximum (Fig. 4.22a). In the one-dimensional system, the downswing of the action potential is replaced by a simple reset of the voltage variable, as we shall see in the next chapter.

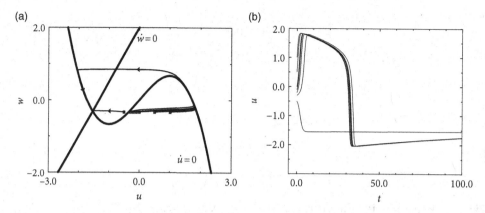

Fig. 4.22 FitzHugh–Nagumo model with separated time scales. All parameters are identical to those of Fig. 4.20 except for ε in Eq. (4.34) which has been reduced by a factor of 10. (a) A trajectory which starts to the left-hand side of the middle branch of the u-nullcline returns directly to the rest state; all other trajectories develop a pulse. (b) Owing to slow w-dynamics, pulses are much broader than in Fig. 4.20.

Example: Piecewise linear nullclines

Let us study the piecewise linear model shown in Fig. 4.23,

$$\frac{du}{dt} = f(u) - w + I, \tag{4.36}$$

$$\frac{dw}{dt} = \varepsilon (bu - w), \tag{4.37}$$

with $f(u) = au$ for $u < 0.5$, $f(u) = a(1-u)$ for $0.5 < u < 1.5$ and $f(u) = c_0 + c_1 u$ for $u > 1.5$ where $a, c_1 < 0$ are parameters and $c_0 = -0.5a - 1.5c_1$. Furthermore, $b > 0$ and $0 < \varepsilon \ll 1$.

The rest state is at $u = w = 0$. Suppose that the system is stimulated by a short current pulse that shifts the state of the system horizontally. As long as $u < 1$, we have $f(u) < 0$. According to (4.36), $\dot{u} < 0$ and u returns to the rest state. For $u < 0.5$ the relaxation to rest is exponential with $u(t) = \exp(at)$ in the limit of $\varepsilon \to 0$. Thus, the return to rest after a small perturbation is governed by the *fast* time scale.

If the current pulse moves u to a value larger than unity, we have $\dot{u} = f(u) > 0$. Hence the voltage u increases and a pulse is emitted. That is to say, $u = 1$ acts as a threshold. Hence, under the assumption of a strict separation of time scales, this neuron model does have a threshold when stimulated with pulse input. The threshold sits on the horizontal axis $w = 0$ at the point where $\dot{u} = 0$.

Let us now suppose that the neuron receives a weak and constant background current during our threshold-search experiments. A constant current shifts the u-nullcline vertically upward. Hence the point where $\dot{u} = 0$ shifts leftward and therefore the voltage

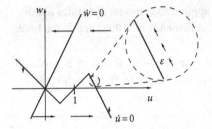

Fig. 4.23 Piecewise linear model with separation of time scale. The inset shows the trajectory (arrows) which follows the u-nullcline at a distance of order ε where $\varepsilon \ll 1$ is the ratio of the time scale of the u-dynamics and that of the w-dynamics in unit-free coordinates; see Eq. (4.37).

threshold for pulse stimulation sits now at a lower value. Again, we conclude that the threshold value we find depends on the stimulation protocol.

4.7 Summary

The four-dimensional model of Hodgkin–Huxley can be reduced to two dimensions under the assumption that the m-dynamics are fast compared with u, h, and n, and that the latter two evolve on the same time scale. Two-dimensional models can readily be visualized and studied in the phase plane.

As a first application of phase plane analysis, we asked whether neuron models have a firing threshold – and found that the answer is something like "No, but ... ." The answer is "No," because the threshold value depends on the stimulation paradigm. The voltage threshold derived with short current pulses is different from that found with constant current or slow ramps. In type II models the onset of repetitive firing at the rheobase current value starts with nonzero frequency. Type I models exhibit onset of repetitive firing with zero frequency. The transition to repetitive firing in type I models arises through a saddle-node-onto-limit-cycle bifurcation whereas several bifurcation types can give rise to a type II behavior.

The methods of phase plane analysis and dimension reduction are generic tools and will also play a role in several chapters of Parts II and IV of this book. In particular, the separation of time scales between the fast voltage variable and the slow recovery variable enables a further reduction of neuronal dynamics to a one-dimensional nonlinear integrate-and-fire model, a fact which we will exploit in the next chapter.

Literature

An in-depth introduction to dynamical systems, stability of fixed points, and (un)stable manifolds can be found, for example, in the book of Hale and Koçak (1991). The book by Strogatz (1994) presents the theory of dynamical systems in the context of various problems of physics, chemistry, biology, and engineering. A wealth of applications of dynamical systems to various (mostly non-neuronal) biological systems can be found in the comprehensive book by Murray (1993), which also contains a thorough discussion of the FitzHugh–Nagumo model. Phase plane methods applied to neuronal dynamics are discussed in the clearly written review paper of Rinzel and Ermentrout (1998) and in the book by Izhikevich (2007b).

The classification of neuron models as type I and type II can be found in Rinzel and Ermentrout (1998) and in Ermentrout (1996), and systematically in Izhikevich (2007b). The steps of dimensionality reduction are presented in Kepler *et al.* (1992).

Exercises

1. **Inhibitory rebound.**
   (a) *Draw on the phase plane a schematic representation of the nullclines and flow for the piecewise linear FitzHugh–Nagumo (Eqs. (4.36) and (4.37)) with parameters $a = c_1 = -1$ and $b = 2$, and mark the stable fixed point.*
   (b) *A hyperpolarizing current is introduced very slowly and increased up to a maximal value of $I = -2$. Calculate the new value of the stable fixed point. Draw the nullclines and flow for $I = -2$ on a different phase plane.*
   (c) *The hyperpolarizing current is suddenly removed. Use the phase planes in (a) and (b) to find out what will happen. Draw schematically the evolution of the neurons state as a membrane potential time-series and as a trajectory in the phase plane. Use $\varepsilon = 0.1$.*
      Hint: The resting state from b is the initial value of the trajectory in c.
2. **Separation of time scales and quasi-stationary assumption.**
   (a) *Consider the following differential equation:*

$$\tau \frac{dx}{dt} = -x + c, \tag{4.38}$$

   where c is a constant. Find the fixed point of this equation. Determine the stability of the fixed point and the solution for any initial condition.
   (b) *Suppose that c is now piecewise constant:*

$$c = c(t) = \begin{cases} 0 & \text{for } t < 0 \\ c_0 & \text{for } 0 \leq t \leq 1 \\ 0 & \text{for } t > 1. \end{cases} \tag{4.39}$$

   Calculate the solution $x(t)$ for the initial condition $x(t = -10) = 0$.
   (c) *Now consider the linear system:*

$$\begin{aligned} \frac{du}{dt} &= f(u) - m, \\ \varepsilon \frac{dm}{dt} &- m + c(u). \end{aligned} \tag{4.40}$$

   Exploit the fact that $\varepsilon \ll 1$ to reduce the system to one equation. Note the similarity with the equations in (a) and (b).
3. **Separation of time scale and relaxation oscillators.**
   (a) *Show that in the piecewise linear neuron model defined in Eqs. (4.36) and (4.37) the trajectory evolves parallel to the right branch of the u-nullcline, shifted upward by a distance of order ε (Fig. 4.23) or parallel to the lifted branch of the u-nullcline, shifted downward by a distance of order ε.*

   Hint: If the u-nullcline is given by the function $f(u)$, set $w(t) = f[u(t)] + \varepsilon x(t)$ where $x(t)$ is the momentary distance and study the evolution of du/dt and dw/dt according to the differential equations of u and w. At the same time, under the assumption of parallel movement, $x(t)$ is

a constant and the geometry of the problem in the two-dimensional phase space tells us that $dw/dt = (df/du)(du/dt)$. *Show that this leads to a consistent solution for the distance x.*
(b) What is the time course of the voltage u(t) while the trajectory follows the branch?

PART TWO

GENERALIZED INTEGRATE-AND-FIRE NEURONS

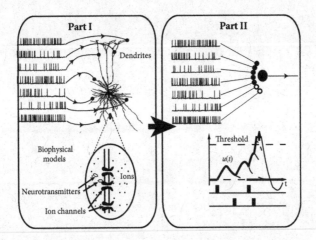

In Part II we exploit the mathematical and biophysical foundations that were laid in Part I in order to reduce the complexity of neuron models. Part II is focused on simplified phenomenological models in which spikes are generated by a threshold criterion, possibly in combination with a stochastic process. We start in Chapter 5 with a determinstic one-dimensional integrate-and-fire model. It turns out that such a model is not powerful enough to account for firing properties of real neurons so that we add adaptation variables (Chapter 6) and stochasticity (Chapters 7–9). These simplified neuron models, often called generalized integrate-and-fire models or generalized linear models, can be systematically fitted to experimental data (Chapter 10). Moreover they allow a transparent discussion of neuronal encoding in (and decoding of) stochastic spike trains (Chapter 11). The simplified neuron models of Part II will be the starting point of the analysis of large neuronal networks in Part III.

5

Nonlinear integrate-and-fire models

Detailed conductance-based neuron models can reproduce electrophysiological measurements to a high degree of accuracy, but because of their intrinsic complexity these models are difficult to analyze. For this reason, simple phenomenological spiking neuron models are highly popular for studies of neural coding, memory, and network dynamics. In this chapter we discuss formal threshold models of neuronal firing, also called integrate-and-fire models.

The shape of the action potential of a given neuron is rather stereotyped with very little change between one spike and the next. Thus, the shape of the action potential which travels along the axon to a postsynaptic neuron cannot be used to transmit information; rather, from the point of view of the receiving neuron, action potentials are "events" which are fully characterized by the arrival time of the spike at the synapse. Note that spikes from different neuron types can have different shapes and the duration and shape of the spike does influence neurotransmitter release; but the spikes that arrive at a given synapse all come from the same presynaptic neuron and – if we neglect effects of fatigue of ionic channels in the axon – we can assume that its time course is always the same. Therefore we make no effort to model the exact shape of an action potential. Rather, spikes are treated as events characterized by their firing time – and the task consists in finding a model so as to reliably predict spike timings.

In generalized integrate-and-fire models, spikes are generated whenever the membrane potential u crosses some threshold θ_{reset} from below. The moment of threshold crossing defines the firing time t^f,

$$t^f: \quad u(t^f) = \theta_{reset} \quad \text{and} \quad \left.\frac{du(t)}{dt}\right|_{t=t^f} > 0. \tag{5.1}$$

In contrast to the two-dimensional neuron models, encountered in Chapter 4, we don't have a relaxation variable that enables us to describe the return of the membrane potential to rest. In the integrate-and-fire models, discussed in this and the following chapters, the downswing of the action potential is replaced by an algorithmic reset of the membrane potential to a new value u_r each time the threshold θ_{reset} is reached. The duration of an action potential is sometimes, but not always, replaced by a dead-time Δ^{abs} after each spike, before the voltage dynamics restarts with $u = u_r$ as initial condition.

In this chapter, we focus on integrate-and-fire models with a single variable u which describes the time course of the membrane potential. In Chapter 6, we extend the models developed in this chapter so as to include adaptation of neuronal firing during extended strong stimulation. In Chapters 7–11 we consider questions of coding, noise, and reliability of spike-time prediction – using the generalized integrate-and-fire model which we introduce now.

5.1 Thresholds in a nonlinear integrate-and-fire model

In a general *nonlinear* integrate-and-fire model with a single variable u, the membrane potential evolves according to

$$\tau \frac{\mathrm{d}}{\mathrm{d}t} u = f(u) + R(u) I. \tag{5.2}$$

As mentioned above, the dynamics is stopped if u reaches the threshold θ_{reset}. In this case the firing time t^f is noted and integration of the membrane potential equation restarts at time $t^f + \Delta^{\text{abs}}$ with initial condition u_r. A typical example of the function $f(u)$ in Eq. (5.2) is shown in Fig. 5.1. If not specified otherwise, we always assume in the following a constant input resistance $R(u) = R$ independent of voltage.

A comparison of Eq. (5.2) with the equation of the standard leaky integrate-and-fire model

$$\tau \frac{\mathrm{d}}{\mathrm{d}t} u = -(u - u_{\text{rest}}) + RI, \tag{5.3}$$

which we encountered in Chapter 1, shows that the nonlinear function $R(u)$ can be interpreted as a voltage-dependent input resistance while $f(u)$ replaces the leak term $-(u - u_{\text{rest}})$. Some well-known examples of nonlinear integrate-and-fire models include the exponential integrate-and-fire model (Section 5.2) and the quadratic integrate-and-fire model (Section 5.3). Before we turn to these specific models, we discuss some general aspects of nonlinear integrate-and-fire models.

Example: Rescaling and standard forms (*)

It is always possible to rescale the variables in Eq. (5.2) so that the threshold and membrane time constant are equal to unity and the resting potential vanishes. Furthermore, there is no need to interpret the variable u as the membrane potential. For example, starting from the nonlinear integrate-and-fire model Eq. (5.2), we can introduce a new variable $\tilde{u}$ by the transformation

$$u(t) \longrightarrow \tilde{u}(t) = \tau \int_0^{u(t)} \frac{\mathrm{d}x}{R(x)}, \tag{5.4}$$

which is possible if $R(x) \neq 0$ for all x in the integration range. In terms of $\tilde{u}$ we have a

(a)

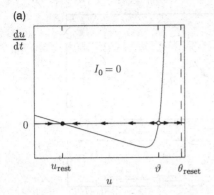

(b)

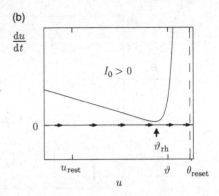

Fig. 5.1 Thresholds in a nonlinear integrate-and-fire model. The change du/dt of the voltage is plotted as a function $f(u)$ of the voltage u. (a) In the absence of stimulation $I_0 = 0$, the zero-crossings $du/dt = 0$ define the resting potential u_{rest} and the firing threshold ϑ of the nonlinear integrate-and-fire model. A positive change in the membrane potential $du/dt = f(u) > 0$ implies that the voltage increases (flow arrow to the right), while $du/dt < 0$ implies a decay of the voltage. The pattern of arrows indicates a stable fixed point at rest, but an unstable fixed point at ϑ. Whenever the voltage reaches the value θ_{reset} the voltage is reset to a lower value. (b) For a constant positive input $I_0 > 0$, the curve of du/dt is shifted vertically upward. The rheobase threshold ϑ_{rh} indicates the maximal voltage that can be reached with constant current injection before the neuron starts repetitive firing.

new nonlinear integrate-and-fire model of the form

$$\frac{d\tilde{u}}{dt} = d(\tilde{u}) + I(t) \tag{5.5}$$

with $d(\tilde{u}) = f(u)/R(u)$. In other words, a general integrate-and-fire model (5.2) can always be reduced to the standard form (5.5). By a completely analogous transformation, we could eliminate the voltage-dependence of the function f in Eq. (5.2) and move all the dependence into a new voltage-dependent $R(u)$ (Abbott and van Vreeswijk, 1993).

5.1.1 *Where is the firing threshold?*

In the standard leaky integrate-and-fire model, the linear equation Eq. (5.3) is combined with a numerical threshold θ_{reset}. We may interpret θ_{reset} as the firing threshold in the sense of the minimal voltage necessary to cause a spike, whatever stimulus we choose. In other words, if the voltage is currently marginally below θ_{reset} and no further stimulus is applied, the neuron inevitably returns to rest. If the voltage reaches θ_{reset}, the neuron fires. For nonlinear integrate-and-fire models, such a clear-cut picture of a firing threshold no longer holds.

The typical shape of a function $f(u)$ used in the nonlinear integrate-and-fire model defined in Eq. (5.2) is sketched in Fig. 5.1. Around the resting potential, the function f is linear and proportional to $(u - u_{rest})$. But in contrast to the leaky integrate-and-fire model

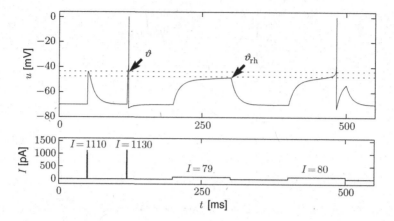

Fig. 5.2 Stimulation of a nonlinear integrate-and-fire model with pulses and step currents. Voltage as a function of time (top) in response to the currents indicated at the bottom. The firing threshold ϑ found with pulse stimuli and the threshold ϑ_{rh} for repetitive firing under prolonged current injection are indicated by the dashed horizontal lines.

of Eq. (5.3) where the voltage dependence is linear everywhere, the function $f(u)$ of the nonlinear model turns at some point sharply upwards.

If the nonlinear integrate-and-fire model is stimulated with currents of various shapes, we can identify, from the simulation of the model, the threshold for spike generation. We search for the maximal voltage which can be reached before the model fires a spike. Figure 5.2 shows that the voltage threshold ϑ determined with pulse-like input currents is different from the voltage threshold determined with prolonged step currents.

For an explanation, we return to Fig. 5.1a which shows du/dt as a function of u. There are two zero-crossings $du/dt = f(u) = 0$, which we denote as u_{rest} and ϑ, respectively. The first one, u_{rest}, is a stable fixed point of the dynamics, whereas ϑ is an unstable one.

A short current pulse $I(t) = q\delta(t - t_0)$ injected into Eq. (5.2) delivers at time t_0 a total charge q and causes a voltage step of size $\Delta u = Rq/\tau$ (see Section 1.3.2). The new voltage $u = u_{rest} + \Delta u$ serves as initial condition for the integration of the differential equation *after* the input pulse. For $u < \vartheta$ the membrane potential returns to the resting potential, while for $u > \vartheta$ the membrane potential increases further, until the increase is stopped at the numerical threshold θ_{reset}. Thus the unstable fixed point ϑ serves as a voltage threshold, if the neuron model is stimulated by a short current pulse.

Under the application of a constant current, the picture is different (Fig. 5.1b). Since we plot du/dt along the vertical axis, a constant current I_0 shifts the curve of du/dt shown in Fig. 5.1a vertically upward to a new value $f(u) + RI_0$; see Eq. (5.2). If the current is sufficiently large, both fixed points disappear so that du/dt is always positive. As a result, the voltage increases until it hits the numerical threshold θ_{reset}, at which point it is reset and the same picture repeats. In other words, the neuron model has entered the regime of repetitive firing.

The critical current for initiation of repetitive firing corresponds to the voltage where the stable fixed point disappears, or $\vartheta_{\rm rh} = I_c R$. In the experimental literature, the critical current $I_c = \vartheta_{\rm rh}/R$ is called the "rheobase" current. In the mathematical literature, it is called the bifurcation point. Note that a stationary voltage $u > \vartheta_{\rm rh}$ is not possible. On the other hand, for pulse inputs or time-dependent currents, voltage transients into the regime $\vartheta_{\rm rh} < u(t) < \vartheta$ routinely occur without initiating a spike.

5.1.2 Detour: Analysis of one-dimensional differential equations

For those readers who are not familiar with figures such as Fig. 5.1, we add a few mathematical details.

The momentary state of one-dimensional differential equations such as Eq. (5.2) is completely described by a single variable, called u in our case. This variable is plotted in Fig. 5.1 along the horizontal axis. An increase in voltage corresponds to a movement to the right, a decrease to a movement to the left. Thus, in contrast to the phase plane analysis of two-dimensional neuron models, encountered in Section 4.3, the momentary state of the system always lies on the horizontal axis.

Let us suppose that the momentary value of the voltage is $u(t_0)$. The value a short time afterwards is given by $u(t_0 + \Delta t) = u(t_0) + \dot{u} \Delta t$ where $\dot{u} = du/dt$ is given by the differential equation Eq. (5.2). The difference $u(t_0 + \Delta t) - u(t_0)$ is positive if $\dot{u} > 0$ and indicated by a flow arrow to the right; the arrow points leftwards if $\dot{u} < 0$.

A nice aspect of a plot such as in Fig. 5.1a is that, for each u, the vertical axis of the plot indicates $\dot{u} = f(u)$, i.e., we can directly read off the value of the flow without further calculation. If the value of the function $f(u)$ is above zero, the flow is to the right; if it is negative, the flow is to the left.

By definition, the flow du/dt vanishes at the fixed points. Thus fixed points are given by the zero-crossings $f(u) = 0$ of the curve. Moreover, the flow pattern directly indicates the stability of a fixed point. From the figure, we can read off that a fixed point at u_0 is stable (arrows pointing towards the fixed point) if the slope of the curve df/du evaluated at u_0 is negative.

The mathematical proof goes as follows. Suppose that the system is, at time t_0, slightly perturbed around the fixed point to a new value $u_0 + x(t_0)$. We focus on the evolution of the perturbation $x(t)$. The perturbation follows the differential equation $dx/dt = \dot{u} = f(u_0 + x)$. Taylor expansion of f around u_0 gives $dx/dt = f(u_0) + (df/du)_{u_0} x$. At the fixed point, $f(u_0) = 0$. The solution of the differential equation therefore is $x(t) = x(t_0) \exp[b(t - t_0)]$. If the slope $b = (df/du)_{u_0}$ is negative, the amplitude of the perturbation $x(t)$ decays back to zero, indicating stability. Therefore, negative slope $(df/du)_{u_0} < 0$ implies stability of the fixed point.

5.2 Exponential integrate-and-fire model

In the exponential integrate-and-fire model (Fourcaud-Trocme *et al.*, 2003), the differential equation for the membrane potential is given by

$$\tau \frac{d}{dt} u = -(u - u_{rest}) + \Delta_T \exp\left(\frac{u - \vartheta_{rh}}{\Delta_T}\right) + RI. \tag{5.6}$$

The first term on the right-hand side of Eq. (5.6) is identical to Eq. (5.3) and describes the leak of a passive membrane. The second term is an exponential nonlinearity with "sharpness" parameter Δ_T and "threshold" ϑ_{rh}.

The moment when the membrane potential reaches the numerical threshold θ_{reset} defines the firing time t^f. After firing, the membrane potential is reset to u_r and integration restarts at time $t^f + \Delta^{abs}$ where Δ^{abs} is an absolute refractory time, typically chosen in the range $0 < \Delta^{abs} < 5$ ms. If the numerical threshold is chosen sufficiently high, $\theta_{reset} \gg \vartheta + \Delta_T$, its exact value does not play any role. The reason is that the upswing of the action potential for $u \gg \vartheta + \Delta_T$ is so rapid that it goes to infinity in an incredibly short time (Touboul, 2009). The threshold θ_{reset} is introduced mainly for numerical convenience. For a formal mathematical analysis of the model, the threshold can be pushed to infinity.

Example: Rheobase threshold and interpretation of parameters

The exponential integrate-and-fire model is a special case of the general nonlinear model defined in Eq. (5.2) with a function

$$f(u) = -(u - u_{rest}) + \Delta_T \exp\left(\frac{u - \vartheta_{rh}}{\Delta_T}\right). \tag{5.7}$$

In the absence of external input ($I = 0$), the differential equation of the exponential integrate-and-fire model (5.6) has two fixed points, defined by the zero-crossings $f(u) = 0$; see Fig. 5.1a. We suppose that parameters are chosen such that $\vartheta_{rh} \gg u_{rest} + \Delta_T$. Then the stable fixed point is at $u \approx u_{rest}$ because the exponential term becomes negligibly small for $u \ll \vartheta_{rh} - \Delta_T$. The unstable fixed point which acts as a threshold for pulse input lies to the right-hand side of ϑ_{rh}.

If the external input increases slowly in a quasi-constant fashion, the two fixed points move closer together until they finally merge at the bifurcation point; see Fig. 5.1b. The voltage at the bifurcation point can be determined from the condition $df/du = 0$ to lie at $u = \vartheta_{rh}$. Thus ϑ_{rh} is the threshold found with constant (rheobase) current, which justifies its name.

Example: Relation to the leaky integrate-and-fire model

In the exponential integrate-and-fire model, the voltage threshold ϑ for pulse input is different from the rheobase threshold ϑ_{rh} for constant input (Fig. 5.1). However, in the limit $\Delta_T \to 0$, the sharpness of the exponential term increases and ϑ approaches ϑ_{rh}

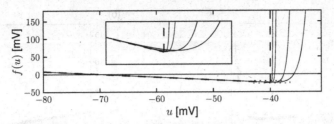

Fig. 5.3 Exponential and leaky integrate-and-fire model. The function $f(u)$ is plotted for different choices of the "sharpness" of the threshold ($\Delta_T = 1, 0.5, 0.25, 0.05$ mV). In the limit $\Delta_T \to 0$ the exponential integrate-and-fire model becomes equivalent to a leaky integrate-and-fire model (dashed line). The inset shows a zoom onto the threshold region (dotted box).

(Fig. 5.3). In the limit, $\Delta_T \to 0$, we can approximate the nonlinear function by the linear term

$$f(u) = -(u - u_{\text{rest}}) \quad \text{for } u < \vartheta_{\text{rh}} \tag{5.8}$$

and the model fires whenever u reaches $\vartheta_{\text{rh}} = \vartheta$. Thus, in the limit $\Delta_T \to 0$, we return to the leaky integrate-and-fire model.

5.2.1 Extracting the nonlinearity from data

Why should we choose an exponential nonlinearity rather than any other nonlinear dependence in the function $f(u)$ of the general nonlinear integrate-and-fire model? Can we use experimental data to determine the "correct" shape of $f(u)$ in Eq. (5.2)?

We can rewrite the differential equation (5.2) of the nonlinear integrate-and-fire model by moving the function $f(u)$ to the left-hand side and all other terms to the right-hand-side of the equation. After rescaling with the time constant τ, the nonlinearity $\tilde{f}(u) = f(u)/\tau$ is

$$\tilde{f}(u(t)) = \frac{1}{C}I(t) - \frac{\mathrm{d}}{\mathrm{d}t}u(t), \tag{5.9}$$

where $C = \tau/R$ can be interpreted as the capacity of the membrane.

In order to determine the function $\tilde{f}(u)$, an experimenter injects a time-dependent current $I(t)$ into the soma of a neuron while measuring with a second electrode the voltage $u(t)$. From the voltage time course, one finds the voltage derivative $\mathrm{d}u/\mathrm{d}t$.

A measurement at time t yields a value $u(t)$ (which we use as value along the x-axis of a plot) and a value $[(I(t)/C) - (\mathrm{d}u/\mathrm{d}t)]$ (which we plot along the y-axis). With a thousand or more time points per second, the plot fills up rapidly. For each voltage u there are many data points with different values along the y-axis. The best choice of the parameter C is the one that minimizes the width of this distribution. At the end, we average across all points at a given voltage u to find the empirical function (Badel et al., 2008a)

$$\tilde{f}(u(t)) = \left\langle \frac{1}{C}I(t) - \frac{\mathrm{d}}{\mathrm{d}t}u(t) \right\rangle, \tag{5.10}$$

(a)

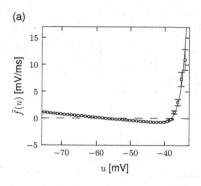

(b)

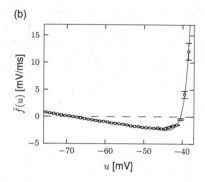

Fig. 5.4 Extracting nonlinear integrate-and-fire models from data. The function $f(u)$ characterizing the nonlinearity of an integrate-and-fire model according to Eq. (5.2) is derived from experimental data using random current injection into neurons. (a) Cortical pyramidal cells. Experimental data points (symbols) and fit by an exponential integrate-and-fire model. (b) As in (a), but for an inhibitory interneuron. Data courtesy of Laurent Badel and Sandrine Lefort (Badel *et al.*, 2008a),

where the angle brackets indicate averaging. This function is plotted in Fig. 5.4. We find that the empirical function extracted from experiments is well approximated by a combination of a linear and exponential term

$$\tilde{f}(u) = -\frac{u - u_{\text{rest}}}{\tau} + \frac{\Delta_T}{\tau} \exp\left(\frac{u - \vartheta_{\text{rh}}}{\Delta_T}\right), \tag{5.11}$$

which provides an empirical justification of the choice of nonlinearity in the exponential integrate-and-fire model.

We note that the slope of the curve at the resting potential is related to the membrane time constant τ while the threshold parameter ϑ_{rh} is the voltage at which the function $\tilde{f}$ goes through its minimum.

Example: Refractory exponential integrate-and-fire model

The above procedure for determining the nonlinearity can be repeated for a set of data points restricted to a few milliseconds *after* an action potential (Fig. 5.6). After a spike, the threshold ϑ_{rh} is slightly higher, which is one of the signs of refractoriness. Moreover, the location of the zero-crossing u_{rest} and the slope of the function $\tilde{f}$ at u_{rest} are different, which is to be expected since after a spike the sodium channel is inactivated while several other ion channels are open. All parameters return to the "normal" values within a few tens of milliseconds. An exponential integrate-and-fire model where the parameters depend on the time since the last spike has been called the "refractory exponential integrate-and-fire model" (Badel *et al.*, 2008a). The refractory exponential integrate-and-fire model predicts the voltage time course of a real neuron for novel time-dependent stimuli to a high degree of accuracy, if the input statistics is similar to the one used for parameter extraction (Fig. 5.5).

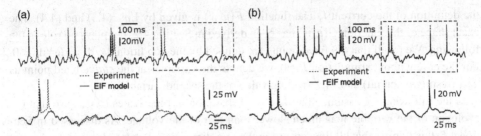

Fig. 5.5 Predicting the membrane voltage with an exponential integrate-and-fire model. (a) Comparison of membrane voltage in experiments (thick line) with the predictions of the exponential integrate-and-fire model (thin line). The fit is excellent, except during a short period after a spike. (b) Same as in (a), but in a model with refractoriness. Modified from Badel *et al.* (2008b).

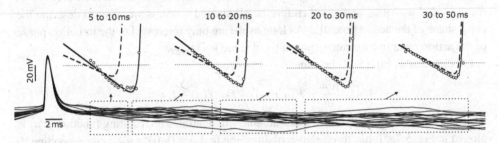

Fig. 5.6 Refractory effects in the exponential integrate-and-fire model. Top: Because of refractoriness immediately after a spike, the exponential integrate-and-fire model has a higher firing threshold and increased slope in the linear section. Data points and fit as in Fig. 5.4, but data points restricted to intervals 5–10 ms (far left), 10–20 ms (left), 20–30 ms (right), or 30–50 ms (far right) after a spike. As the time since the last spike increases, refractoriness decays and the parameters of the exponential integrate-and-fire model approach their standard values (dashed lines). Bottom: Sample voltage traces during and after a spike. From Badel *et al.* (2008b).

5.2.2 From Hodgkin–Huxley to exponential integrate-and-fire

In Section 4.2 we have already seen that the four-dimensional system of equations of Hodgkin and Huxley can be reduced to two equations. Here we show how to take a further step so as to arrive at a single nonlinear differential equation combined with a reset (Jolivet *et al.*, 2004).

After appropriate rescaling of all variables, the system of two equations that summarizes a Hodgkin–Huxley model reduced to two dimensions can be written as

$$\frac{du}{dt} = F(u,w) + I, \tag{5.12}$$

$$\frac{dw}{dt} = \varepsilon G(u,w), \tag{5.13}$$

which is just a copy of Eqs. (4.33) and (4.34) in Section 4.6; note that time is measured in units of the membrane time constant τ_m and that the resistance has been absorbed into the definition of the currrent I. The function $F(u, w)$ is given by Eqs. (4.3) and (4.4). The exact shape of the function $G(u, w)$ has been derived in Section 4.2, but plays no role in the following. We recall that the fixed points are defined by the condition $du/dt = dw/dt = 0$. For the case without stimulation $I = 0$, we denote the variables at the *stable* fixed point as u_{rest} (resting potential) and w_{rest} (resting value of the second variable).

In the following we assume that there is a separation of time scales ($\varepsilon \ll 1$) so that the evolution of the variable w is much slower than that of the voltage. As discussed in Section 4.6, this implies that all flow arrows in the two-dimensional phase plane are horizontal except those in the neighborhood of the u-nullcline. In particular, after a stimulation with short current pulses, the trajectories move horizontally back to the resting state (no spike elicited) or horizontally leftward (upswing of an action potential) until they hit one of the branches of the u-nullcline; see Fig. 4.22. In other words, the second variable stays at its resting value $w = w_{rest}$ and can therefore be eliminated – unless we want to describe the exact shape of the action potential. As long as we are only interested in the initiation phase of the action potential we can assume a fixed value $w = w_{rest}$.

For constant w, Eq. (5.12) becomes

$$\frac{du}{dt} = F(u, w_{rest}) + I = f(u) + I, \tag{5.14}$$

which has the form of a nonlinear integrate-and-fire neuron. The resulting function $f(u)$ is plotted in Fig. 5.7a. It has three zero-crossings: the first one (left) at u_{rest}, corresponding to a stable fixed point; a second one (middle) which acts as a threshold ϑ; and a third one to the right, which is again a stable fixed point and limits the upswing of the action potential. The value of the reset threshold $\theta_{reset} > \vartheta$ should be reached during the upswing of the spike and must therefore be chosen between the second and third fixed point. While in the two-dimensional model the variable w is necessary to describe the downswing of the action potential on a smooth trajectory back to rest, we replace the downswing in the nonlinear integrate-and-fire model by an artificial reset of the voltage variable to a value u_r whenever u hits θ_{reset}.

If we focus on the region $u < \theta_{reset}$, the function $f(u) = F(u, w_{rest})$ is very well approximated by the nonlinearity of the exponential integrate-and-fire model (Fig. 5.7b).

Example: Exponential activation of sodium channels

In the previous section, we followed a series of formal mathematical steps, from the two-dimensional version of the Hodgkin–Huxley model to a one-dimensional differential equation which looked like a combination of linear and exponential terms, i.e., an exponential integrate-and-fire model. For a more biophysical derivation and interpretation of the exponential integrate-and-fire model, it is, however, illustrative to start directly with the voltage equation of the Hodgkin–Huxley model, (2.4)–(2.5), and replace the variables h and n by their values at rest, h_{rest} and n_{rest}, respectively. Furthermore, we assume that m approaches instantaneously its equilibrium value $m_0(u)$.

(a)

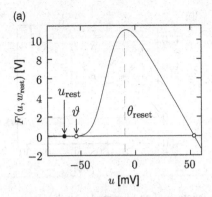

(b)

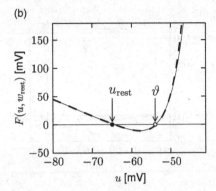

Fig. 5.7 Approximating Hodgkin–Huxley by an exponential integrate-and-fire model. (a) The value of the $F(u, w_{\text{rest}})$ for fixed value of the second variable $w = w_{\text{rest}}$ is plotted as a function of the voltage variable u. The choice of a reset threshold θ_{reset} is indicated. (b) Solid line as in A, restricted to $u < \theta_{\text{reset}}$. The dashed line shows the approximation by an exponential integrate-and-fire model.

This yields

$$C\frac{du}{dt} = -g_{\text{Na}}[m_0(u)]^3 h_{\text{rest}}(u - E_{\text{Na}}) - g_{\text{K}}(n_{\text{rest}})^4(u - E_{\text{K}}) - g_L(u - E_L) + I. \quad (5.15)$$

Potassium and leak currents can now be summed up to a new effective leak term $g^{\text{eff}}(u - E^{\text{eff}})$. In the voltage range close to the resting potential the driving force $(u - E_{\text{Na}})$ of the sodium current can be well approximated by $(u_{\text{rest}} - E_{\text{Na}})$. Then the only remaining nonlinearity on the right-hand side of Eq. (5.15) arises from $m_0(u)$. For voltages around rest, $m_0(u)$ has, however, an exponential shape. In summary, the right-hand side of Eq. (5.15) can be approximated by a linear and an exponential term – and this gives rise to the exponential integrate-and-fire model (Fourcaud-Trocme *et al.*, 2003).

5.3 Quadratic integrate and fire

A specific instance of a nonlinear integrate-and-fire model is the *quadratic* model (Latham *et al.*, 2000; Hansel and Mato, 2001),

$$\tau\frac{d}{dt}u = a_0(u - u_{\text{rest}})(u - u_c) + RI, \quad (5.16)$$

with parameters $a_0 > 0$ and $u_c > u_{\text{rest}}$; see Fig. 5.8a. For $I = 0$ and initial condition $u < u_c$, the voltage decays to the resting potential u_{rest}. For $u > u_c$ it increases so that an action potential is triggered. The parameter u_c can therefore be interpreted as the critical voltage for spike initiation by a short current pulse. We will see in the next subsection that the quadratic integrate-and-fire model is closely related to the so-called Θ-neuron, a canonical type-I neuron model (Ermentrout, 1996; Latham *et al.*, 2000).

For numerical implementation of the model, the integration of Eq. (5.16) is stopped if the voltage reaches a numerical threshold θ_{reset} and restarted with a reset value u_r as

(a)

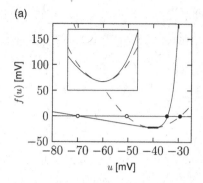

(b)

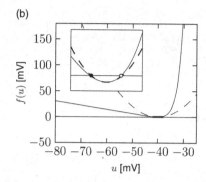

Fig. 5.8 Quadratic integrate-and-fire model. (a) The quadratic integrate-and-fire model (dashed line), compared with an exponential integrate-and-fire model (solid line). (b) The quadratic integrate-and-fire model can be seen as an approximation of an exponential integrate-and-fire model (or any other type I model) depolarized to a state close to repetitive firing. In (a) and (b), the value $f(u)$ and curvature $d^2 f/du^2$ are matched at $u = \vartheta_{\text{rh}}$. Note that the rise in the quadratic model is slower in the superthreshold regime $u > \vartheta_{\text{rh}}$.

new initial condition (Fig. 5.9b). For a mathematical analysis of the model, however, the standard assumption is $\theta_{\text{reset}} \to \infty$ and $u_r \to -\infty$.

We have seen in the previous section that experimental data suggests an exponential, rather than quadratic nonlinearity. However, close to the threshold for repetitive firing, the exponential integrate-and-fire model and the quadratic integrate-and-fire model become very similar (Fig. 5.8b). Therefore the question arises whether the choice between the two models is a matter of personal preference only.

For a mathematical analysis, the quadratic integrate-and-fire model is sometimes more handy than the exponential one. However, the fit to experimental data is much better with the exponential than with the quadratic integrate-and-fire model. For a prediction of spike times and voltage of real neurons (see Fig. 5.5), it is therefore advisable to work with the exponential rather than the quadratic integrate-and-fire model. Loosely speaking, the quadratic model is too nonlinear in the subthreshold regime and the upswing of a spike is not rapid enough once the voltage is above threshold. The approximation of the exponential integrate-and-fire model by a quadratic one only holds if the mean driving current is close to the rheobase current.

Example: Approximating the exponential integrate-and-fire

Let us suppose that an exponential integrate-and-fire model is driven by a depolarizing current that shifts its effective equilibrium potential u_r^{eff} close to the rheobase firing threshold ϑ_{rh}. The stable fixed points at $u = u_r^{\text{eff}}$ and the unstable fixed point at $u = \vartheta^{\text{eff}}$ corresponding to the effective firing threshold for pulse injection now lie symmetrically around ϑ_{rh} (Fig. 5.8b). In this region, the shape of the function $f(u)$ is well approximated

(a)

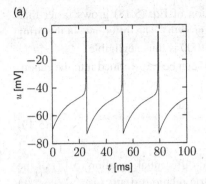

(b)

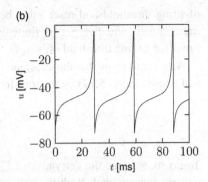

Fig. 5.9 Repetitive firing in nonlinear integrate-and-fire models. (a) Exponential integrate-and-fire model and (b) quadratic integrate-and-fire model receiving a constant current sufficient to elicit repetitive firing. Note the comparatively slow upswing of the action potential in the quadratic integrate-and-fire model. Numerical simulation with parameters of equivalent models as illustrated in Fig. 5.8.

by a quadratic function (dashed line). In other words, in this regime the exponential and quadratic integrate-and-fire neuron become identical.

If the constant input current is increased further, the stable and unstable fixed point move closer together and finally merge and disappear at the bifurcation point, corresponding to a critical current I_c. More generally, any type I neuron model close to the bifurcation point can be approximated by a quadratic integrate-and-fire model – and this is why it is sometimes called the "canonical" type I integrate-and-fire model (Ermentrout, 1996; Ermentrout and Kopell, 1986).

5.3.1 Canonical type I model (*)

In this section, we show that there is a one-to-one relation between the quadratic integrate-and-fire model (5.16) and the canonical type I phase model,

$$\frac{d\phi}{dt} = [1 - \cos\phi] + \Delta I[1 + \cos\phi], \tag{5.17}$$

defined in Chapter 4; see Section 4.4.1 (Ermentrout, 1996; Ermentrout and Kopell, 1986).

Let us denote by I_θ the minimal current necessary for repetitive firing of the quadratic integrate-and-fire neuron. With a suitable shift of the voltage scale and constant current $I = I_\theta + \Delta I$ the equation of the quadratic neuron model can then be cast into the form

$$\frac{du}{dt} = u^2 + \Delta I. \tag{5.18}$$

For $\Delta I > 0$ the voltage increases until it reaches the firing threshold $\vartheta \gg 1$ where it is reset to a value $u_r \ll -1$. Note that the firing times are insensitive to the actual values of firing threshold and reset value because the solution of Eq. (5.18) grows faster than exponentially and diverges for finite time (hyperbolic growth). The difference in the firing times for a finite threshold of, say, $\vartheta = 10$ and $\vartheta = 10000$ is thus negligible.

We want to show that the differential equation (5.18) can be transformed into the canonical phase model (5.17) by the transformation

$$u(t) = \tan\left(\frac{\phi(t)}{2}\right). \tag{5.19}$$

To do so, we take the derivative of (5.19) and use the differential equation (5.17) of the generic phase model. With the help of the trigonometric relations $d\tan x/dx = 1/\cos^2(x)$ and $1 + \cos x = 2\cos^2(x/2)$ we find

$$\frac{du}{dt} = \frac{1}{\cos^2(\phi/2)} \frac{1}{2} \frac{d\phi}{dt}$$
$$= \tan^2(\phi/2) + \Delta I = u^2 + \Delta I. \tag{5.20}$$

Thus Eq. (5.19) with $\phi(t)$ given by (5.17) is a solution to the differential equation of the quadratic integrate-and-fire neuron. The quadratic integrate-and-fire neuron is therefore (in the limit $\vartheta \to \infty$ and $u_r \to -\infty$) equivalent to the generic type I neuron (5.17).

5.4 Summary

The standard leaky integrate-and-fire model is rather limited in scope, since it has one universal voltage threshold. Nonlinear integrate-and-fire neurons, however, can account for the fact that in real neurons the effective voltage threshold for repetitive firing is different than the voltage threshold found with short current pulses. These two voltage thresholds, which are related to the minimum of the nonlinearity $f(u)$ and to the unstable fixed point, respectively, are *intrinsic* features of nonlinear integrate-and-fire models. Once the membrane potential is above the intrinsic threshold, the upswing of the membrane potential starts. The integration is stopped at a numerical threshold θ_{reset} which is much higher and conceptually very different than the intrinsic firing threshold of the model. In fact, the exact value of the numerical threshold does not matter, since, without such a threshold, the membrane potential would go to infinity in *finite* time.

In principle, many different forms of nonlinearity are imaginable. It turns out, however, that many neurons are well described by a linear term (the "leak" term) combined with an exponential term (the "activation" term); see Fig. 5.4. Therefore, the exponential integrate-and-fire model has the "correct" nonlinearity, whereas the quadratic integrate-and-fire model is too nonlinear in the subthreshold regime and too slow in the superthreshold regime.

Both the exponential and the quadratic integrate-and-fire model show a frequency–current curve of type I. Indeed, close to the bifurcation point the two models become identical and can be mapped onto the canonical type I model.

Literature

Nonlinear generalizations of the one-dimensional equation of the leaky integrate-and-fire model can be found in the paper by Abbott and van Vreeswijk (1993). While the form of the nonlinearity was left open at that time, analytical methods from bifurcation theory suggested that there was a canonical one-dimensional model which describes the saddle-node-onto-limit-cycle bifurcation of type I models. This is called the canonical type I model or Theta model or Ermentrout–Kopell model (Ermentrout and Kopell, 1986; Ermentrout, 1996). While the quadratic nonlinearity in the voltage appeared in many early papers on bifurcations and type I models (Ermentrout, 1996; Ermentrout and Kopell, 1986; Strogatz, 1994; Hoppensteadt and Izhikevich, 1997) the active use of the quadratic integrate-and-fire model for simulations seems to have been started by Latham et al. in 2000 and later popularized by Izhikevich (2007b).

Based on biophysical and mathematical arguments, the exponential integrate-and-fire model was introduced in 2003 by Fourcaud-Trocme, Hansel, Vreeswijk and Brunel. While the quadratic integrate-and-fire model is the canonically correct type I model close to the bifurcation point, i.e., at the transition to repetitive firing, there is no fundamental reason why the quadratic nonlinearity should also be correct further away from the threshold, and it was unclear at that time what the nonlinearity of real neurons would look like. The issue was settled by the work of Badel *et al.* (2008a,b) who designed an experimental method to measure the nonlinearity directly in experiments. The nonlinearity found in experiments is extremely well matched by the exponential integrate-and-fire model.

The link between ion channel activation or inactivation in conductance-based neuron models and the parameters of an exponential integrate-and-fire model with refractoriness (Badel *et al.*, 2008a,b) is discussed in the overview paper by Platkiewicz and Brette (2010).

We shall see in the next chapter that the single-variable exponential integrate-and-fire model as it stands is not sufficient to account for the wide variety of neuronal firing patterns, but needs to be complemented by a second variable to account for slow processes such as adaptation – and this leads eventually to the adaptive exponential integrate-and-fire model.

Exercises

1. **Quadratic vs. exponential integrate-and-fire**. *For a comparison of the two models, take a look at Fig. 5.8b and answer the following questions:*

    (a) Show for the exponential integrate-and-fire model that the minimum of the nonlinearity $f(u)$ occurs at $u = \vartheta_{\text{rh}}$. Calculate the curvature $d^2/du^2 f(u)$ at $u = \vartheta_{\text{rh}}$.

    (b) Find parameters of the quadratic integrate-and-fire model so that it matches the location and curvature of the exponential model in (a).

    (c) Suppose that the value of the numerical threshold is $\theta_{\text{reset}} = \vartheta_{\text{rh}} + 2\Delta_T$. When the threshold

is reached the membrane potential is reset to $u_r = \vartheta_{rh} - 2\Delta_T$. Sketch qualitatively the trajectory $u(t)$ for both neuron models in the repetitive firing regime. Pay particular attention to the following questions: (i) For $u > \vartheta_{rh}$ which of the two trajectories rises more rapidly towards the numerical threshold? (ii) For $u = \vartheta_{rh}$, do both trajectories have the same speed of rise du/dt or a different one? (iii) For $u < \vartheta_{rh}$, which of the two trajectories rises more rapidly? (iv) Should your drawing of the trajectories follow any symmetry rules? Compare your results with Fig. 5.9.

2. **Zero-curvature and rheobase threshold.** *Experimenters sometimes determine the threshold voltage for spike initiation by searching for the zero-curvature point in the voltage trajectory, just before the upswing of the action potential. Show for a general nonlinear integrate-and-fire model that the zero-curvature point is equivalent to the rheobase threshold ϑ_{rh}. Hints: (i) Minimal curvature means that the voltage trajectory passes through a point $d^2u/dt^2 = 0$. (ii) Note that the slope of the voltage trajectory du/dt is given by the function $f(u)$. (iii) Recall that the minimum of f is taken at $u = \vartheta_{rh}$.*

3. **Exponential integrate-and-fire and sodium activation.** *To derive the exponential integrate-and-fire model from a Hodgkin–Huxley model with multiple channels, follow the procedure indicated in Section 5.2.2 and perform the following steps.*

   (a) Show that N linear currents can always be rewritten as one effective leak current $\sum_k g_k (u - E_k) = g^{eff} (u - E^{eff})$. Determine the effective conductance g^{eff} and the effective reversal potential E^{eff}.

   (b) Assume that the sodium activation is rapid and approaches an equilibrium value $m_0(u) = 1/\{1 + \exp[-\beta (u - \theta_{act})]\} = 0.5\{1 + \tanh[-\beta (u - \theta_{act})/2]\}$ where θ_{act} is the activation threshold of the sodium channel and β the sharpness of the threshold. Using a Taylor expansion, show that for $u < \theta_{act} - \beta^{-1}$ the activation function can be approximated by an exponential $m_0(u) = \exp[\beta (u - \theta_{act})]$.

   (c) Assume that $u < \theta_{act} - \beta^{-1} < E_{Na}$ and show that the sodium current

$$I_{Na} = g_{Na}[m_0(u)]^3 h_{rest} (u - E_{Na}) \tag{5.21}$$

   gives rise to the exponential term.

   (d) Using the steps (a) – (c), map (5.15) to the exponential integrate-and-fire model

$$\frac{du}{dt} = \tilde{f}(u) = -\frac{u - u_{rest}}{\tau} + \frac{\Delta_T}{\tau} \exp\left(\frac{u - \vartheta_{rh}}{\Delta_T}\right). \tag{5.22}$$

   Determine the parameters u_{rest}, τ and Δ_T.

4. **Refractory exponential integrate-and-fire model and sodium *inactivation*.** *In the previous exercise, we have assumed that $h = h_{rest}$ is constant throughout the spiking process. Repeat the steps of the previous calculation, but set $h(t) = h_{rest} + x(t)$ and show that the sodium inactivation dynamics leads to an increase in the the firing threshold a few milliseconds after the spike.*

   Hints. (i) Linearize the dynamics of gating variable h in the Hodgkin–Huxley model around $h = h_{rest}$ so as to derive $dx/dt = -x/\tau_0$. (ii) Assume that during each spike, the inactivation variable h increases by a fixed amount Δh.

5. **Quadratic integrate-and-fire model.**
   Consider the dimensionless quadratic integrate-and-fire model

$$\frac{d}{dt}u = (u - u_{rest})(u - u_c) + I, \tag{5.23}$$

   with $u_{rest} = -1$ and $u_c = 1$ and $I = 0$.

   (a) Suppose that a trajectory starts at time $t = 0$ at $-\infty$. How long does it take to get close to the resting state and reach the value $u = -1 - \varepsilon$ where $\varepsilon \ll 1$?

   (b) Suppose that a trajectory is initialized at $u(0) = 1 + \varepsilon$, where $\varepsilon \ll 1$. How long does it take to reach $u = \infty$?

   (c) Initialize as in (b) but stop the integration at $u = \theta_{reset}$. How long does the trajectory take to reach the reset threshold? Is the difference between (b) and (c) important?

Hint: Use $\int dx/[1-x^2] = \text{arcoth}(x) = 0.5[\ln(x+1) - \ln(x-1)]$ and $\coth(x) = [e^x + e^{-x}]/[e^x - e^{-x}]$.

6. **Gain function of the quadratic integrate-and-fire model.**
   We consider a quadratic integrate-and-fire model in the superthreshold regime

   $$\frac{d}{dt}u = u^2 + I,$$ (5.24)

   with constant current $I > 0$.
   (a) Give a transformation of variables from Eq. (5.23) to (5.24).
   (b) Calculate the duration T of a trajectory which starts at time $t = 0$ at $u(0) = -\infty$ and ends at time T at $u(T) = +\infty$.
   Hint: Use $\int dx/[1+x^2] = \text{artan}(x)$.
   (c) Plot the frequency $\nu = 1/T$ as a function of I.

6

Adaptation and firing patterns

When an experimenter injects a strong step current into the soma of a neuron, the response consists of a series of spikes separated by long or short intervals. The stereotypical arrangement of short, long or very long interspike intervals defines the neuronal *firing pattern*. In Chapter 2 we have already encountered firing patterns such as tonic, adapting, or delayed spike firing. In addition to these, several variants of burst firing have also been observed in real neurons (see Fig. 6.1). This diversity of firing patterns can be explained, to a large extent, by adaptation mechanisms which in turn depend on the zoo of available ion channels (Chapter 2) and neuronal anatomy (Chapter 3).

In order to describe firing patterns, and in particular adaptation, in a transparent mathematical framework, we start in this chapter with the simplified model of spike initiation from Chapter 5 and include a phenomenological equation for subthreshold and spike-triggered adaptation. The resulting model is called the adaptive exponential integrate-and-fire (AdEx; Section 6.1). We then use this simple model to explain the main firing patterns (Section 6.2). In Section 6.3, we describe how the parameters of the subthreshold and spike-triggered adaptation reflect the contribution of various ion channels and of dendritic morphology. Finally, we introduce the Spike Response Model (SRM; Section 6.4) as a transparent framework to describe neuronal dynamics. The Spike Response Model will serve as a starting point for the Generalized Linear Models which we will discuss later, in Chapter 9.

6.1 Adaptive exponential integrate-and-fire

In the previous chapter we have explored nonlinear integrate-and-fire neurons where the dynamics of the membrane voltage is characterized by a function $f(u)$. A single equation is, however, not sufficient to describe the variety of firing patterns that neurons exhibit in response to a step current. We therefore couple the voltage equation to abstract current variables w_k, each described by a linear differential equation. The set of equations is

$$\tau_m \frac{du}{dt} = f(u) - R \sum_k w_k + RI(t), \tag{6.1}$$

$$\tau_k \frac{dw_k}{dt} = a_k (u - u_{\text{rest}}) - w_k + b_k \tau_k \sum_{t^f} \delta(t - t^f). \tag{6.2}$$

The coupling of voltage to the adaptation current w_k is implemented by the parameter a_k and evolves with time constant τ_k. The adaptation current is fed back to the voltage equation with resistance R. Just as in other integrate-and-fire models, the voltage variable u is reset if the membrane potential reaches the numerical threshold Θ_{reset}. The moment $u(t) = \Theta_{\text{reset}}$ defines the firing time $t^f = t$. After firing, integration of the voltage restarts at $u = u_r$. The δ-function in the w_k equations indicates that, during firing, the adaptation currents w_k are increased by an amount b_k. For example, a value $b_k = 10\,\text{pA}$ means that the adaptation current w_k is $10\,\text{pA}$ stronger after a spike than it was just before the spike. The parameters b_k are the "jump" of the spike-triggered adaptation. One possible biophysical interpretation of the increase is that during the action potential calcium enters the cell so that the amplitude of a calcium-dependent potassium current is increased. The biophysical origins of adaptation currents will be discussed in Section 6.3. Here we are interested in the dynamics and neuronal firing patterns generated by such adaptation currents. Various choices are possible for the nonlinearity $f(u)$ in the voltage equation. We have seen in the previous chapter (Section 5.2) that the experimental data suggests a nonlinearity consisting of a linear leak combined with an exponential activation term, $f(u) = -(u - u_{\text{rest}}) + \Delta_T \exp\left(\frac{u - \vartheta_{\text{rh}}}{\Delta_T}\right)$. The adaptive exponential integrate-and-fire model (AdEx) consists of such an exponential nonlinearity in the voltage equation coupled to a single adaptation variable w

$$\tau_m \frac{du}{dt} = -(u - u_{\text{rest}}) + \Delta_T \exp\left(\frac{u - \vartheta_{\text{rh}}}{\Delta_T}\right) - Rw + RI(t), \tag{6.3}$$

$$\tau_w \frac{dw}{dt} = a(u - u_{\text{rest}}) - w + b\tau_w \sum_{t^f} \delta(t - t^f). \tag{6.4}$$

At each threshold crossing the voltage is reset to $u = u_r$ and the adaptation variable w is increased by an amount b. Adaptation is characterized by two parameters: the parameter a is the source of subthreshold adaptation because it couples adaptation to the voltage. Spike-triggered adaptation is controlled by a combination of a and b. The choice of a and b largely determines the firing patterns of the neuron (Section 6.2) and can be related to the dynamics of ion channels (Section 6.3). Before exploring the AdEx model further, we discuss two other examples of adaptive integrate-and-fire models.

Example: Izhikevich model

While the AdEx model exhibits the nonlinearity of the exponential integrate-and-fire model, the Izhikevich model uses the quadratic integrate-and-fire model for the first

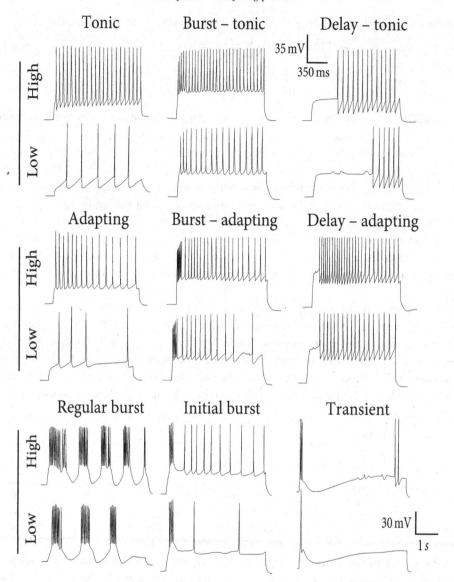

Fig. 6.1 Multiple firing patterns in cortical neurons. For each type, the neuron is stimulated with a step current with low or high amplitude. Modified from Markram *et al.* (2004).

equation

$$\tau_m \frac{du}{dt} = (u - u_{\text{rest}})(u - \vartheta) - Rw + RI(t), \qquad (6.5)$$

$$\tau_w \frac{dw}{dt} = a(u - u_{\text{rest}}) - w + b\tau_w \sum_{t^f} \delta(t - t^f). \qquad (6.6)$$

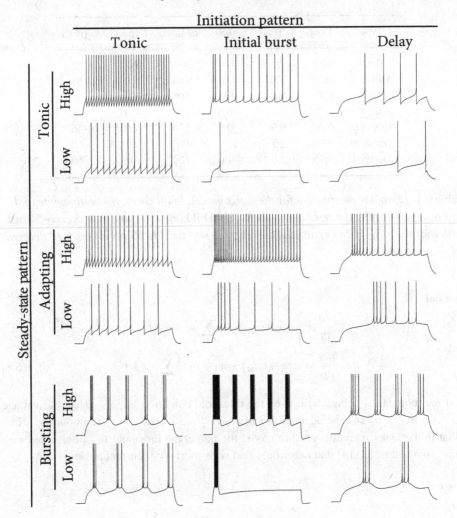

Fig. 6.2 Multiple firing patterns in the AdEx neuron model. For each set of parameters, the model is stimulated with a step current with low or high amplitude. The spiking response can be classified by the steady-state firing behavior (vertical axis: tonic, adapting, bursting) and by its transient initiation pattern as shown along the horizontal axis: tonic (i.e., no special transient behavior), initial burst, or delayed spike initiation.

If $u = \theta_{\text{reset}}$, the voltage is reset to $u = u_r$ and the adaptation variable w is increased by an amount b. Normally b is positive, but $b < 0$ is also possible.

Example: Leaky model with adaptation

Adaptation variables w_k can also be combined with a standard leaky integrate-and-fire

Type	Fig.	τ_m (ms)	a (nS)	τ_w (ms)	b (pA)	u_r (mV)
Tonic	6.3a	20	0.0	30.0	60	−55
Adapting	6.3b	200	0.0	100	5.0	−55
Init. burst	6.4a	5.0	0.5	100	7.0	−51
Bursting	6.4c	5.0	−0.5	100	7.0	−46
Irregular	6.5a	9.9	−0.5	100	7.0	−46
Transient	6.9a	10	1.0	100	10	−60
Delayed	6.9c	5.0	−1.0	100	10	−60

Table 6.1 *Exemplar parameters for the AdEx model. In all cases, the resting potential was $u_{rest} = -70$ mV, the resistance was $R = 500$ MΩ, the threshold was $\vartheta_{rh} = -50$ mV with sharpness $\Delta_T = 2$ mV, and the current step was fixed to 65 pA except for "delayed" where it was at 25 pA.*

model

$$\tau_m \frac{du}{dt} = -(u - u_{rest}) - R \sum_k w_k + RI(t), \tag{6.7}$$

$$\tau_k \frac{dw_k}{dt} = a(u - u_{rest}) - w_k + b_k \tau_k \sum_{t^f} \delta(t - t^f). \tag{6.8}$$

At the moment of firing, defined by the threshold condition $u(t^f) = \theta_{reset}$, the voltage is reset to $u = u_r$ and the adaptation variables w_k are increased by an amount b_k. Note that in the leaky integrate-and-fire model the numerical threshold θ_{reset} coincides with the voltage threshold ϑ that one would find with short input current pulses.

6.2 Firing patterns

The AdEx model is capable of reproducing a large variety of firing patterns that have been observed experimentally. In this section, we show some typical firing patterns, and show how the patterns can be understood mathematically, adapting the tools of phase plane analysis previously encountered in Chapter 4.

6.2.1 Classification of firing patterns

How are the firing patterns classified? Across the vast field of neuroscience and over more than a century of experimental work, different classification schemes have been proposed. For a rough qualitative classification (Fig. 6.2, exemplar parameters in Table 6.1), it is advisable to separate the steady-state pattern from the initial transient phase (Markram *et al.*, 2004). The initiation phase refers to the firing pattern right after the onset of the

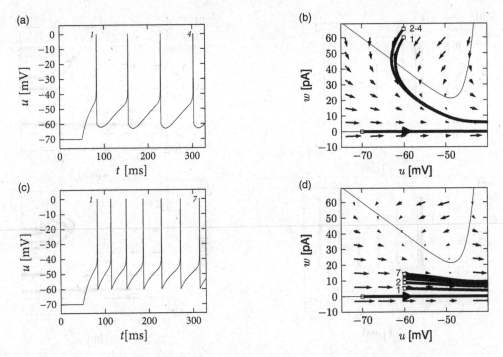

Fig. 6.3 Tonic and adapting firing patterns in the AdEx model. (a) Tonic spiking with a strong spike-triggered current ($b = 60\,\mathrm{pA}$) of short duration ($\tau_w = 30\,\mathrm{ms}$). (b) If the reset (empty squares) leads to a value above the u-nullcline, the trajectories make a detour to lower values of u. (c) Spike-frequency adaptation with a weak spike-triggered current ($b = 5\,\mathrm{pA}$) and slow decay ($\tau_w = 100\,\mathrm{ms}$). (d) If the reset lands below the u-nullcline, the membrane potential immediately increase towards the next spike. Parameters in Table 6.1.

current step. There are three main initiation patterns: the initiation cannot be distinguished from the rest of the spiking response (tonic); the neuron responds with a significantly greater spike frequency in the transient (initial burst) than in the steady state; the neuronal firing starts with a delay (delay).

After the initial transient, the neuron exhibits a steady-state pattern. Again there are three main types: regularly spaced spikes (tonic); gradually increasing interspike intervals (adapting); or regular alternations between short and long interspike intervals (bursting). Irregular firing patterns are also possible in the AdEx model, but their relation to irregular firing patterns in real neurons is less clear because of potential noise sources in biological cells (Chapter 7). The discussion in the next sections is restricted to deterministic models.

Example: Tonic, adapting and facilitating

When the subthreshold coupling a is small and the voltage reset is low ($u_r \approx u_{\mathrm{rest}}$),

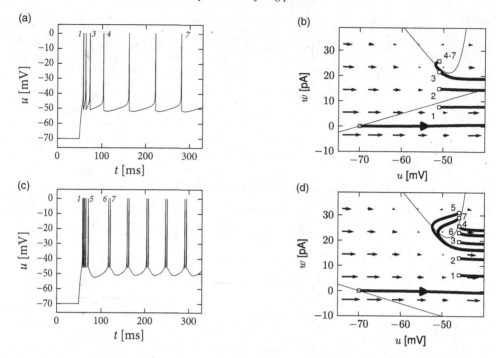

Fig. 6.4 Phase plane analysis of initial bursting and sustained bursting patterns. (a) Voltage trace of an AdEx model with parameters producing an initial burst. (b) In the phase plane, the initial burst is generated by a series of resets below the u-nullcline. Only the fourth reset arrives above the u-nullcline. (c) Voltage trace of an AdEx model exhibiting regular bursts. (d) The phase plane for regular bursting is similar to those of initial burst, except that the first reset above the u-nullcline yields a trajectory that travels below at least one of the previous resets. Hence, the neuron model alternates between direct and detour resets.

the AdEx response is either tonic or adapting. This depends on the two parameters regulating the spike-triggered current: the jump b and the time scale τ_w. A large jump with a small time scale creates evenly spaced spikes at low frequency (Fig. 6.3a). On the other hand, a small spike-triggered current decaying on a long time scale can accumulate strength over several spikes and therefore successively decreases the net driving current $I - w$ (Fig. 6.3b). In general, weak but long-lasting spike-triggered currents cause spike-frequency adaptation, while short but strong currents lead only to a prolongation of the refractory period. There is a continuum between purely tonic spiking and strongly adapting.

Similarly, when the spike-triggered current is depolarizing ($b < 0$) the interspike interval may gradually decrease, leading to spike-frequency facilitation.

6.2.2 *Phase plane analysis of nonlinear integrate-and-fire models in two dimensions*

Phase plane analysis, which has been a useful tool to understand the dynamics of the reduced Hodgkin–Huxley model (Chapter 4), is also helpful to illustrate the dynamics of the AdEx model. Let us plot the two state variables $u(t)$ and $w(t)$ in the plane and indicate the regions where $\dot{u} = 0$ (u-nullcline) and $\dot{w} = 0$ (w-nullcline) with solid lines.

In the AdEx model, the nullclines look similar to the one-dimensional figures of the exponential integrate-and-fire model in Chapter 5. The u-nullcline is again linear in the subthreshold regime and rises exponentially when u is close to ϑ. Upon current injection, the u-nullcline is shifted vertically by an amount proportional to the magnitude of the current I. The w-nullcline is a straight line with a slope tuned by the parameter a. If there is no coupling between the adaptation variable and the voltage in the subthreshold regime ($a = 0$), then the w-nullcline is horizontal. The fixed points are the points where the curved u-nullcline intersects with the straight w-nullcline. Solutions of the system of differential equations (6.3) and (6.4) appear as a trajectory in the (u, w)-plane.

In contrast to the two-dimensional models in Chapter 4, the AdEx model exhibits a reset which correspond to a jump of the trajectory. Each time the trajectory reaches $u = \theta_{\text{reset}}$, it will be reinitialized at a reset value $(u_r, w + b)$ indicated by an empty square (Fig. 6.3). We note that for the voltage variable the reinitialization occurs always at the same value $u = u_r$; for the adaptation variable, however, the reset involves a vertical shift upwards by an amount b compared with the value of w just before the reset. Thus, the reset maps w to a potentially new initial value after each firing.

There are three regions of the phase plane with qualitatively different ensuing dynamics. These regions are distinguished by whether the reset point is in a region where trajectories are attracted to the stable fixed point or not; and whether the reset is above or below the u-nullcline. Trajectories attracted to a fixed point will simply converge to it. Trajectories not attracted to a fixed point all go eventually to θ_{reset} but they can do so directly or with a detour. A detour is introduced whenever the reset falls above the u-nullcline, because in the area above the u-nullcline the derivative is $\dot{u} < 0$ so that the voltage $u(t)$ must first decrease before it can eventually increase again. Thus a "detour reset" corresponds to a downswing of the membrane potential after the end of the action potential. The distinction between detour and direct resets is helpful to understand how different firing patterns arise. Bursting, for instance, can be generated by a regular alternation between direct resets and detour resets.

Example: Bursting

Before considering regular bursting, we describe the dynamics of an initial burst. By definition, an initial burst means a neuron first fires a group of spikes at a considerably higher spiking frequency than the steady-state frequency (Fig. 6.4a). In the phase plane, initial bursting is caused by a series of one or more direct resets followed by detour resets (Fig. 6.4b). This firing pattern may appear very similar to strong adaptation where

(a)

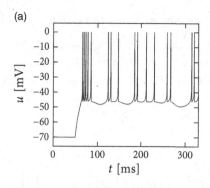

(b)

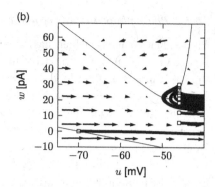

Fig. 6.5 Phase plane analysis of an irregular firing pattern. (a) Voltage trace of an AdEx model showing irregularly spaced spikes. (b) The evolution of trajectories in the phase plane during the simulation in (a) shows that the model switches irregularly between direct and detour resets.

the first spikes also have a larger frequency, but the shape of the voltage trajectory after the end of the action potential (downswing or not) can be used to distinguish between adapting (strictly detour or strictly direct resets) and initial bursting (first direct then detour resets).

Regular bursting can arise from a similar process, by alternation between direct and detour resets. In the phase plane, regular bursting is made possible by a reset u_r higher than the effective threshold ϑ. After a series of direct resets, the first reset that falls above the u-nullcline must make a large detour and is forced to pass under the u-nullcline. When this detour trajectory is mapped below at least one of the previous reset points, the neuron may burst again (Fig. 6.4b).

While the AdEx can generate a regular alternation between direct and detour resets, it can also produce an irregular alternation (Fig. 6.5). Such irregular firing patterns can occur in the AdEx model despite the fact that the equations are deterministic. The aperiodic mapping between the two types of reset is a manifestation of chaos in the discrete map (Naud *et al.*, 2008; Touboul and Brette, 2008). This firing pattern appears for a restricted set of parameters such that, unlike regular and initial bursting, it occupies a small and patchy volume in parameter space.

6.2.3 *Exploring the space of reset parameters*

The AdEx model in the form of Eqs. (6.3) and (6.4) has nine parameters. Some combinations of parameters lead to initial bursting, others to adaptation, yet others to delayed spike onset, and so on. As we change parameters, we find that each firing pattern occurs in a restricted region of the nine-dimensional parameter space – and this can be labeled by the corresponding firing pattern, e.g., bursting, initial bursting, or adaptive. While inside a given region the dynamics of the model can exhibit small quantitative changes; the big qualitative changes occur at the transition from one region of parameter space to the next.

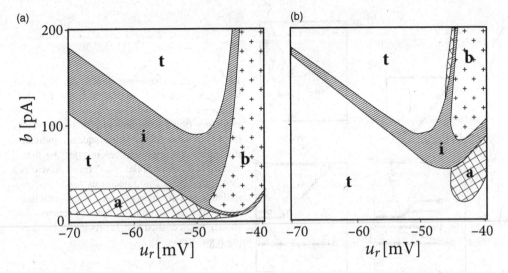

Fig. 6.6 Parameter space of the AdEx model. (a) Combinations of the voltage reset u_r and of the spike-triggered jump b of the adaptation current leading to a tonic (**t**), adapting (**a**), initial burst (**i**) and bursting (**b**) firing patterns for a long adaptation time constant ($\tau_w = 100$ ms) and small subthreshold coupling ($a = 0.001$ nS). (b) Same as (a) but for $\tau_w = 5$ ms. Current was switched from zero to twice the rheobase current and all other parameters are fixed at $\tau_m = 10$ ms, $R = 100$ MΩ, $u_{\text{rest}} = -70$ mV, $\vartheta_{\text{rh}} = -50$ mV and $\Delta_T = 2$ mV.

Thus, boundaries in the parameter space mark transitions between different types of firing pattern – which are often correlated with types of cells.

To illustrate the above concept of regions inside the parameter space, we apply a step current with an amplitude twice as large as the minimal current necessary to elicit a spike and study the dependence of the observed firing pattern on the reset parameters u_r and b (Fig. 6.6). All the other parameters are kept fixed. We find that the line separating initial bursting and tonic firing resembles the shape of the u-nullcline. This is not unexpected given that the location of the reset with respect to the u-nullcline plays an important role in determining whether the reset is "direct" or leads to a "detour." Regular bursting is possible, if the voltage reset u_r is located above the voltage threshold ϑ. Irregular firing patterns are found within the bursting region of the parameter space. Adapting firing patterns occur only over a restricted range of jump amplitudes b of the spike-triggered adaptation current.

Example: Piecewise-linear model (*)

In order to understand the location of the boundaries in parameter space we consider a piecewise-linear version of the AdEx model

$$f(u) = \begin{cases} -(u - u_{\text{rest}}) & \text{if } u \leq \vartheta_{\text{rh}}, \\ \Delta_T(u - u_p) & \text{otherwise}, \end{cases} \qquad (6.9)$$

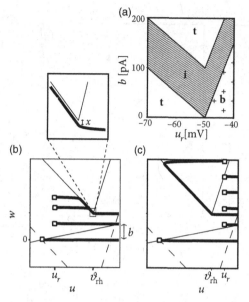

Fig. 6.7 Piecewise-linear model. (a) Parameter space analogous to Fig. 6.6 but for the piecewise-linear model. (b) Evolution of the trajectory (thick solid lines) in the phase plane during tonic spiking. Open squares indicate the initial condition and resets after the first, second, and third spike. Nullclines drawn as thin solid lines. The trajectories follow the u-nullcline at a distance x (inset). The u-nullcline before the application of the step current is shown with a dashed line. (c) As in (b), but during regular bursting.

with

$$u_p = \vartheta_{\text{rh}} + \frac{\vartheta_{\text{rh}} - u_{\text{rest}}}{\Delta_T}, \tag{6.10}$$

which we insert into the voltage equation $\tau_m \mathrm{d}u/\mathrm{d}t = f(u) + RI - Rw$; compare Eq. (6.1) with a single adaptation variable of the form (6.2). Note that the u-nullcline is given by $w = f(u)/R + I$ and takes at $u = \vartheta_{\text{rh}}$ its minimum value $w_{\text{min}} = f(\vartheta_{\text{rh}})/R + I$.

We assume separation of time scale ($\tau_m/\tau_w << 1$) and exploit the fact that the trajectories in the phase plane are nearly horizontal (w takes a constant value) – unless they approach the u-nullcline. In particular, all trajectories that start at a value $w_r < w_{\text{min}}$ stay horizontal and pass unperturbed below the u-nullcline.

To determine the firing pattern, we need to map the initial condition (u_r, w_r) after a first reset to the value w_e of the adaptation variable at the end of the trajectory: $w_e = M(u_r, w_r)$. The next reset starts then from $(u_r, w_e + b)$ and with the help of the mapping function M we can iterate the above procedure. We know already that all trajectories with $w_r < w_{\text{min}}$ remain horizontal, so that $w_e = w_r$.

The more interesting situation is $w_r > w_{\text{min}}$. We distinguish two possible cases. The first one corresponds to a voltage reset below the threshold, $u_r < \vartheta_{\text{rh}}$. A trajectory initiated at $u_r < \vartheta_{\text{rh}}$ evolves horizontally until it comes close to the left branch of the u-nullcline. It then follows the u-nullcline at a small distance $x(u)$ below it (see Section 4.6). This distance can be shown to be

$$x(u) = \frac{\tau_m}{\tau_w} \left[I - (a + R^{-1})(u - u_{\text{rest}}) \right], \tag{6.11}$$

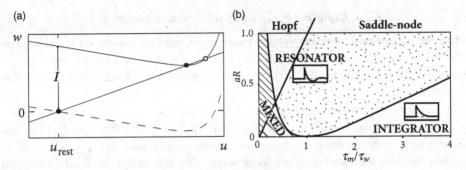

Fig. 6.8 Hopf bifurcation and space of subthreshold parameters. (a) Nullclines and fixed points (filled and open circles) during a Hopf bifurcation. A step current I shifts the u-nullcline upward (solid line). The stability of the stable fixed point (filled circle) is lost in a Hopf bifurcation before the two fixed points merge. If it is not lost before the merge then the bifurcation is saddle-node. (b) The ratio of time constants τ_m/τ_w (horizontal axis) and the factor aR which controls the coupling between voltage and adaptation. The straight diagonal line separates the region where the stationary state of the system loses stability through a Hopf bifurcation ($aR > \tau_m/\tau_w$) from the region of saddle-node bifurcation. The linear response of the subthreshold dynamics is characterized as resonator (dotted region), integrator (blank), or mixed (stripes).

which vanishes in the limit $\tau_m/\tau_w \to 0$. When the u-nullcline reaches its minimum, the trajectory is again free to evolve horizontally. Therefore the final w-value of the trajectory is the one it takes at the minimum of the u-nullcline, so that for $u_r < \vartheta_{\text{rh}}$

$$M(u_r, w_r) = \begin{cases} w_r & \text{if } w_r < f(\vartheta_{\text{rh}})/R + I, \\ f(\vartheta_{\text{rh}})/R + I & \text{otherwise.} \end{cases} \tag{6.12}$$

If $u_r > \vartheta_{\text{rh}}$ then we have a direct reset (i.e., movement starts to the right) if (u_r, w_r) lands below the right branch of the u-nullcline (Fig. 6.7c) and a detour reset otherwise

$$M(u_r, w_r) = \begin{cases} w_r & \text{if } w_r < f(u_r)/R + I, \\ f(\vartheta_{\text{rh}})/R + I & \text{otherwise.} \end{cases} \tag{6.13}$$

The map M uniquely defines the firing pattern. Regular bursting is possible only if $u_r > \vartheta_{\text{rh}}$ and $b < f(u_r) - f(\vartheta_{\text{rh}})$ so that at least one reset in each burst lands below the u-nullcline (Fig. 6.7a). For $u_r > \vartheta_{\text{rh}}$, we have tonic spiking with detour resets when $b > f(u_r) + I$ and initial bursting if $f(u_r) + I > b > f(u_r) - f(\vartheta_{\text{rh}}) + x(\vartheta_{\text{rh}})$.

If $u_r \le \vartheta$ we have tonic spiking with detour resets when $b > f(u_r) + I$, tonic spiking with direct reset when $b < f(u_r) - f(\vartheta_{\text{rh}})$ and initial bursting if $f(u_r) + I > b > f(u_r) - f(\vartheta_{\text{rh}})$. Note that the rough layout of the parameter regions in Fig. 6.7a, which we just calculated analytically, matches qualitatively the organization of the parameter space in the AdEx model (Fig. 6.6).

6.2.4 Exploring the space of subthreshold parameters

While the exponential integrate-and-fire model loses stability always via a saddle-node bifurcation, the AdEx can become unstable either via a Hopf or a saddle-node bifurcation. Thus, we see again that the addition of an adaptation variable leads to a much richer dynamics.

In the absence of external input, the AdEx has two fixed points, a stable one at u_{rest} and an unstable one at some value $u > \vartheta_{\text{rh}}$. We recall from Chapter 4 that a gradual increase of the driving current corresponds to a vertical shift of the u-nullcline (Fig. 6.8a), and to a slow change in the location of the fixed points. The stability of the fixed points, and hence the potential occurrence of a Hopf bifurcation, depends on the slope of the u- and w-nullclines. In the AdEx, an eigenvalue analysis shows that the stable fixed point loses stability via a Hopf bifurcation if $aR > \tau_m/\tau_w$. Otherwise, when the coupling from voltage to adaptation (parameter a) and back from adaptation to voltage (parameter R) are both weak ($aR < \tau_m/\tau_w$), an increase in the current causes the stable fixed point to merge with the unstable one, so that both disappear via a saddle-node bifurcation – just like in the normal exponential integrate-and-fire model. Note, however, that the type of bifurcation has no influence on the firing pattern (bursting, adapting, tonic), which depends mainly on the choice of reset parameters.

However, the subthreshold parameters do control the presence or absence of oscillations in response to a short current pulse. A model showing damped oscillations is often called a *resonator* while a model without is called an *integrator*. We have seen in Chapter 4 that Hopf bifurcations are associated with damped oscillations, but this statement is valid only close to the bifurcation point or rheobase-threshold. The properties can be very different far from the threshold. Indeed, the presence of damped oscillations depends nonlinearly on a/g_L and τ_m/τ_w as summarized in Fig. 6.8b. The frequency of the damped oscillation is given by

$$\omega = \frac{4}{\tau_w}\left[aR - \frac{2\tau_w}{\tau_m}\left(1 - \frac{\tau_m}{\tau_w}\right)^2\right]. \tag{6.14}$$

Example: Transient spiking

Upon the onset of a current step, some neurons may fire a small number of spikes and then remain silent, even if the stimulus is maintained for a very long time. An AdEx model with subthreshold coupling $a > 0$ can explain this phenomenon whereas pure spike-triggered adaptation ($a = 0; b > 0$) cannot account for it, because adaptation would eventually decay back to zero so that the neuron fires another spike.

To understand the role of subthreshold coupling, let us choose parameters a and τ_w such that the neuron is in the resonator regime. The voltage response to a step input then exhibits damped oscillations (Fig. 6.9a). Similar to the transient spiking in the Hodgkin–Huxley model, the AdEx can generate a transient spike if the peak of the (a)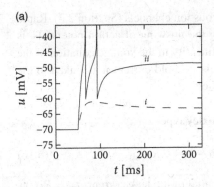

(b)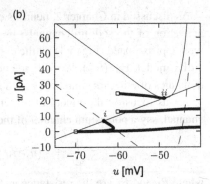

Fig. 6.9 Phase plane analysis of transient spiking in the AdEx model. (a) Voltage trace of an AdEx model with parameters producing transient spiking upon a strong step current input (solid line marked *ii*). A weaker step input generates damped oscillations (dashed line marked *i*). (b) Phase plane with nullclines after application of the strong (solid lines: u- and w-nullclines) or weak step current (dashed line: u-nullcline). Upon injection of the weak step, the stable fixed point is reached after a short transient. Upon injection of the strong current, a stable fixed point remains, but the initial state is outside the region where it would be attracted to the stable fixed point. Only after the second reset (open squares), does the trajectory converge to the fixed point.

oscillation is sufficient to reach the firing threshold. Phase plane analysis reveals that sometimes several resets are needed before the trajectory is attracted towards the fixed point (Fig. 6.9b). In Chapter 2, damped oscillations were due to sodium channel inactivation or I_h. Indeed, the subthreshold coupling can be seen as a simplification of I_h, but many other biophysical mechanisms can be responsible.

6.3 Biophysical origin of adaptation

We have introduced, in Section 6.1, formal adaptation variables w_k which evolve according to a linear differential equation (6.2). We now show that the variables w_k can be linked to the biophysics of ion channels and dendrites.

6.3.1 Subthreshold adaptation by a single slow channel

First we focus on one variable w at a time and study its *subthreshold* coupling to the voltage. In other words, the aim is to give a biophysical interpretation of the parameters a, τ_w, and the variable w that show up in the adaptation equation

$$\tau_w \frac{dw}{dt} = a(u - E_0) - w. \tag{6.15}$$

The biophysical components of *spike-triggered* adaptation (i.e., the interpretation of the reset parameter b) is deferred to Section 6.3.2. Here and in the following we write E_0 instead of u_{rest} in order to simplify notation and keep the treatment slightly more general.

As discussed in Chapter 2, neurons contain numerous ion channels (Section 2.3). Rapid activation of the sodium channels, important during the upswing of action potentials, is well approximated (Fig. 5.4) by the exponential nonlinearity in the voltage equation of the AdEx model, Eq. (6.3). We will see now that the subthreshold current w is linked to the dynamics of other ion channels with a slower dynamics.

Let us focus on the model of a membrane with a leak current and a single, slow, ion channel, say a potassium channel of the Hodgkin–Huxley type

$$\tau_m \frac{du}{dt} = -(u - E_L) - R_L g_K n^p (u - E_K) + R_L I_{ext}, \tag{6.16}$$

where R_L and E_L are the resistance and reversal potential of the leak current, $\tau_m = R_L C$ is the membrane time constant, g_K the maximal conductance of the open channel and n the gating variable (which appears with arbitrary power p) with dynamics

$$\frac{dn}{dt} = -\frac{n - n_0(u)}{\tau_n(u)}. \tag{6.17}$$

As long as the membrane potential stays below threshold, we can linearize the equations (6.16) and (6.17) around the resting voltage E_0, given by the fixed point condition

$$E_0 = \frac{E_L + (R_L g_K) n_0(E_0)^p E_K}{1 + (R_L g_K) n_0(E_0)^p}. \tag{6.18}$$

The resting potential is shifted with respect to the leak reversal potential if the channel is partially open at rest, $n_0(E_0) > 0$. We introduce a parameter $\beta = g_K p n_0(E_0)^{p-1} (E_0 - E_K)$ and expand $n_0(u) = n_0(E_0) + n_0'(u - E_0)$ where n_0' is the derivative dn_0/du evaluated at E_0.

The variable $w = \beta [n - n_0(E_0)]$ then follows the linear equation

$$\tau_n(E_0) \frac{dw}{dt} = a(u - E_0) - w. \tag{6.19}$$

We emphasize that the time constant of the variable w is given by the time constant of the channel at the resting potential. The parameter a is proportional to the sensitivity of the channel to a change in the membrane voltage, as measured by the slope dn_0/du at the equilibrium potential E_0.

The adaptation variable w is coupled into the voltage equation in the standard form

$$\tau_m^{eff} \frac{du}{dt} = -(u - E_0) - Rw + RI_{ext}. \tag{6.20}$$

Note that the membrane time constant and the resistance are rescaled by a factor $[1 + (R_L g_K) n_0(E_0)^p]^{-1}$ with respect to their values in the passive membrane equation, Eq. (6.16). In fact, both are smaller because of partial opening of the channel at rest.

In summary, each channel with nonzero slope dn_0/du at the equilibrium potential E_0 gives rise to an effective adaptation variable w. Since there are many channels, we can expect many variables w_k. Those with similar time constants can be summed and grouped into a single equation. But if time constants are different by an order of magnitude or more,

Type	Fig.	Act./inact.	τ_w (ms)	β (pA)	a (nS)	δ_x	b (pA)
I_{Na}	2.3	inact.	20	−120	5.0	−	−
I_M	2.13	act.	61	12	0.0	0.0085	0.1
I_A	2.14	act.	33	12	0.3	0.04	0.5
$I_{HVA} + I_{K[Ca]}$	2.15	act.	150	12	0	0.05	0.6
I_h	2.17	inact.	8.5	−48	0.8	−	−
I_{NaS}	2.18	act	200	−120	−0.08	0.0041	−0.48

Table 6.2 *Parameter values for ion channels presented in Chapter 2 for model linearized around −65 mV for $Rg_k = 1$. The action potential is assumed to consist of a pulse of 1 ms duration at 0 mV. The approximation to obtain δ_x and b is valid only when $\tau_x(0\,mV)$ is significantly larger than one millisecond.*

then several adaptation variables are needed, which leads to the model equations (6.1) and (6.2).

6.3.2 Spike-triggered adaptation arising from a biophysical ion channel

We have seen in Chapter 2 that some ion channels are partially open at the resting potential, while others react only when the membrane potential is well above the firing threshold. We now focus on the second group in order to give a biophysical interpretation of the jump amplitude b of a spike-triggered adaptation current.

Let us return to the example of a single ion channel of the Hodgkin and Huxley type such as the potassium current in Eq. (6.16). In contrast to the treatment earlier, we now study the change in the state of the ion channel induced during the large-amplitude excursion of the voltage trajectory during a spike. During the spike, the target $n_0(u)$ of the gating variable is close to 1; but since the time constant τ_n is long, the target is not reached during the short time that the voltage stays above the activation threshold. Nevertheless, the ion channel is partially activated by the spike. Unless the neuron is firing at a very large firing rate, each additional spike activates the channel further, always by the same amount Δ_n, which depends on the duration of the spike and the activation threshold of the current (Table 6.2). The spike-triggered jump in the adapting current w is then

$$b = \beta \Delta_n, \tag{6.21}$$

where $\beta = g_K \, p \, n_0 (E_0)^{p-1} (E_0 - E_K)$ has been defined before.

Again, real neurons with their large quantity of ion channels have many adaptation currents w_k, each with its own time constant τ_k, subthreshold coupling a_k and spike-triggered jump b_k. The effective parameter values depend on the properties of the ion channels (Table 6.2).

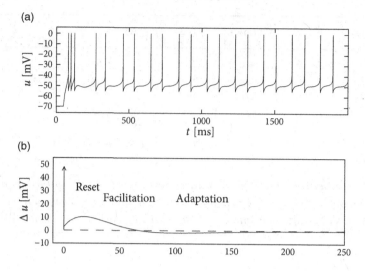

Fig. 6.10 Another type of bursting in a model with two spike-triggered currents. (a) Voltage trace of the neuron model Eqs. (6.3)–(6.4) with $u_{reset} = -55 \, mV$, $\vartheta_{rh} = -50 \, mV$, $b_1 = -12 \, pA$, $b_2 = 60 \, pA$, $\tau_1 = 20 \, ms$, $\tau_2 = 61 \, ms$, $a_1 = -3 \, nS$ and $a_2 = 0$. Parameters were chosen to correspond to a neuron coupled with a dendritic compartment and I_M. (b) Voltage deflection brought by an isolated spike. Each spike brings first refractoriness, then a facilitation and finally adaptation on a longer time scale.

Example: Calculating the jump b of the spike-triggered adaptation current

We consider a gating dynamics

$$\frac{dn}{dt} = -\frac{n - n_0(u)}{\tau_n(u)}, \tag{6.22}$$

with the steplike activation function $n_0(u) = \Theta(u - u_0^{act})$ where $u_0^{act} = -30$ mV and $\tau_n(u) = 100$ ms independent of u. Thus, the gating variable n approaches a target value of 1 whenever the voltage u is above the activation threshold u_0^{act}. Since the activation threshold of -30 mV is *above* the firing threshold (typically in the range of $-40 \, mV$) we can safely state that the neuron activation of the channel can only occur during an action potential. Assuming that during an action potential the voltage remains above u_0^{act} for $t = 1$ ms, we can integrate Eq. (6.22) and find that each spike causes an increase $\Delta_n = t/\tau_n$ where we have exploited that $t \ll \tau_n$. If we plug in the above numbers, we see that each spike causes an increase of n by a value of 0.01. If the duration of the spike were twice as long, the increase would be 0.02. After the spike the gating variable decays with the time constant τ_n back to zero. The increase Δ_n leads to a jump amplitude of the adaptation current given by Eq. (6.21).

6.3.3 Subthreshold adaptation caused by passive dendrites

While in the previous section, we have focused on the role of ion channels, here we show that a passive dendrite can also give rise to a subthreshold coupling of the form of Eq. (6.15).

We focus on a simple neuron model with two compartments, representing the soma and the dendrite, superscripts s and d respectively. The two compartments are both passive with membrane potential V^s, V^d, transversal resistance R_T^s, R_T^d, capacity C^s, C^d and resting potential u_r, E^d. The two compartments are linked by a longitudinal resistance R_L (see Chapter 3). If current is injected only in the soma, then the two-compartment model with passive dendrites corresponds to

$$\frac{d}{dt}V^s = \frac{1}{C^s}\left[-\frac{(V^s - u_{rest})}{R_T^s} - \frac{V^s - V^d}{R_L} + I(t)\right], \tag{6.23}$$

$$\frac{d}{dt}V^d = \frac{1}{C^d}\left[-\frac{(V^d - E^d)}{R_T^d} - \frac{V^d - V^s}{R_L}\right]. \tag{6.24}$$

Such a system of differential equations can be mapped to the form of Eq. (6.15) by considering that the variable w represents the current flowing from the dendrite into the soma. In order to keep the treatment transparent, we assume that $E^d = u_{rest} = E$. In this case the adaptation current is $w = -(V^d - u_{rest})/R_L$ and the two equations above reduce to

$$\tau^{eff}\frac{dV^s}{dt} = -(V^s - E) - R^{eff}w \tag{6.25}$$

$$\tau_w\frac{dw}{dt} = a(V^s - E) - w \tag{6.26}$$

with an effective input resistance $R^{eff} = R_T^s/[1 + (R_T^s/R_L)]$, an effective somatic time constant $\tau^{eff} = C^s R^{eff}$, an effective adaptation time constant $\tau_w = R_L C^d/[1 + (R_L/R_D)]$ and a coupling between somatic voltage and adaptation current $a = -[R_L + (R_L^2/R_D)]^{-1}$.

There are three conclusions we should draw from this mapping. First, a is always negative, which means that passive dendrites introduce a *facilitating* subthreshold coupling. Second, facilitation is particularly strong with a small longitudinal resistance. Third, the timescale of the facilitation τ_w is smaller than the dendritic time constant $R_T^d C^d$ – so that, compared with other "adaptation" currents, the dendritic current is a relatively fast one.

In addition to the subthreshold coupling discussed here, dendritic coupling can also lead to a spike-triggered current as we shall see in the next example.

Example: Bursting with a passive dendrite and I_M

Suppose that the action potential can be approximated by a 1 ms pulse at 0 mV. Then each spike brings an increase in the dendritic membrane potential. In terms of the current w, the increase is $b = -aE_0(1 - e^{1 \text{ ms}/\tau_w})$. Again, the spike-triggered jump is always negative, leading to spike-triggered facilitation. Figure 6.10 shows an example where we combined a dendritic compartment with the linearized effects of the M-current (Table 6.2) to result in regular bursting. The bursting is mediated by the dendritic facilitation which is counterbalanced by the adapting effects of I_M. The firing pattern looks different to the bursting in the AdEx (Fig. 6.4) as there is no alternation between detour and direct resets. Indeed, many different types of bursting are possible (see Izhikevich 2007a). This example (especially Fig. 6.10b) suggests that the dynamics of spike-triggered currents on multiple time scales can be understood in terms of their stereotypical effect on the membrane potential – and this insight is the starting point for the Spike Response Model in the next section.

6.4 Spike Response Model (SRM)

So far, we have described neuronal dynamics in terms of systems of differential equations. There is another approach that was introduced in Section 1.3.5 as the "filter picture." In this picture, the parameters of the model are replaced by (parametric) functions of time, generically called "filters." The neuron model is therefore interpreted in terms of a membrane filter as well as a function describing the shape of the spike (Fig. 6.11) and, potentially, also a function for the time course of the threshold. Together, these three functions establish the Spike Response Model (SRM).

The Spike Response Model is – just like the nonlinear integrate-and-fire models in Chapter 5 or the AdEx in Section 6.1 – a generalization of the leaky integrate-and-fire model. In contrast to nonlinear integrate-and-fire models, the SRM has no "intrinsic" firing threshold but only the sharp numerical threshold for reset. If the nonlinear function of the AdEx is fitted to experimental data, the transition between the linear subthreshold and superthreshold behavior is found to be rather abrupt, so that the nonlinear transition is, for most neurons, well approximated by a sharp threshold (see Fig. 5.3). Therefore, in the SRM, we work with a sharp threshold combined with a linear voltage equation.

While the SRM is therefore somewhat simpler than other models on the level of the spike generation mechanism, the subthreshold behavior of the SRM is richer than that of the integrate-and-fire model discussed so far and can account for various aspects of refractoriness and adaptation. In fact, the SRM combines the most general linear model with a sharp threshold.

It turns out that the integral formulation of the SRM is very useful for data fitting and also the starting point for the Generalized Linear Models in Chapter 9 and 10. Despite the apparent differences between integrate-and-fire models and the SRM, the leaky integrate-and-fire model, with or without adaptation variables, is a special case of the SRM. The relation of the SRM to integrate-and-fire models is the topic of Sections 6.4.3–6.4.4. We now start with a detailed explanation.

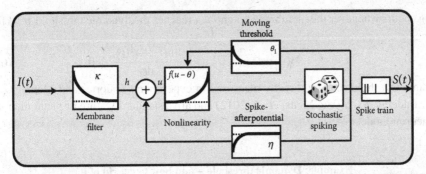

Fig. 6.11 Spike Response Model (SRM). Input current $I(t)$ is filtered with a filter $\kappa(s)$ and yields the input potential $h(t) = \int_0^\infty \kappa(s)I(t-s)ds$. Firing occurs if the membrane potential u reaches the threshold ϑ. Spikes $S(t) = \sum_f \delta(t-t^f)$ are fed back into the threshold process in two distinct ways. Each spike causes an increase θ_1 of the threshold: $\vartheta(t) = \vartheta_0 + \int_0^\infty \theta_1(s)S(t-s)ds$. Moreover, each spike generates a voltage contribution η to the membrane potential: $u(t) = h(t) + \int_0^\infty \eta(s)S(t-s)ds$, where η captures the time course of the action potential and the spike-afterpotential; schematic figure.

6.4.1 Definition of the SRM

In the framework of the Spike Response Model (SRM) the state of a neuron is described by a single variable u which we interpret as the membrane potential. In the absence of input, the variable u is at its resting value, u_{rest}. A short current pulse will perturb u and it takes some time before u returns to rest (Fig. 6.11). The function $\kappa(s)$ describes the time course of the voltage response to a short current pulse at time $s = 0$. Because the subthreshold behavior of the membrane potential is taken as linear, the voltage response h to an arbitrary time-dependent stimulating current $I^{\text{ext}}(t)$ is given by the integral $h(t) = \int_0^\infty \kappa(s)I^{\text{ext}}(t-s)\,ds$.

Spike firing is defined by a threshold process. If the membrane potential reaches the threshold ϑ, an output spike is triggered. The form of the action potential and the afterpotential is described by a function η. Let us suppose that the neuron has fired some earlier spikes at times $t^f < t$. The evolution of u is given by

$$u(t) = \sum_f \eta(t-t^f) + \int_0^\infty \kappa(s)I^{\text{ext}}(t-s)\,ds + u_{\text{rest}}. \tag{6.27}$$

The sum runs over all past firing times t^f with $f = 1, 2, 3, \ldots$ of the neuron under consideration. Introducing the spike train $S(t) = \sum_f \delta(t-t^f)$, Eq. (6.27) can be also written as a convolution

$$u(t) = \int_0^\infty \eta(s)S(t-s)ds + \int_0^\infty \kappa(s)I^{\text{ext}}(t-s)\,ds + u_{\text{rest}}. \tag{6.28}$$

In contrast to the leaky integrate-and-fire neuron discussed in Chapter 1 the threshold ϑ is not fixed, but time-dependent

$$\vartheta \quad \longrightarrow \quad \vartheta(t). \tag{6.29}$$

Firing occurs whenever the membrane potential u reaches the dynamic threshold $\vartheta(t)$ from below

$$t = t^f \quad \Leftrightarrow \quad u(t) = \vartheta(t) \text{ and } \frac{\mathrm{d}[u(t) - \vartheta(t)]}{\mathrm{d}t} > 0. \tag{6.30}$$

Dynamic thresholds can be directly measured in experiments (Fuortes and Mantegazzini, 1962; Badel *et al.*, 2008a; Mensi *et al.*, 2012) and are a standard feature of phenomenological neuron models.

Example: Dynamic threshold – and how to get rid of it

A standard model of the dynamic threshold is

$$\vartheta(t) = \vartheta_0 + \sum_f \theta_1(t - t^f) = \vartheta_0 + \int_0^\infty \theta_1(s)S(t - s)\mathrm{d}s, \tag{6.31}$$

where ϑ_0 is the "normal" threshold of neuron i in the absence of spiking. After each output spike, the firing threshold of the neuron is increased by an amount $\theta_1(t - t^f)$ where $t^f < t$ denote the firing times in the past. For example, during an absolute refractory period Δ^{abs}, we may set θ_1 for a few milliseconds to a large and positive value so as to avoid any firing and let it relax back to zero over the next few hundred milliseconds; see Fig. 6.12a.

From a formal point of view, there is no need to interpret the variable u as the membrane potential. It is, for example, often convenient to transform the variable u so as to remove the time dependence of the threshold. In fact, a general Spike Response Model with arbitrary time-dependent threshold as in Eq. (6.31) can always be transformed into a Spike Response Model with fixed threshold ϑ_0 by a change of variables

$$\eta(t - t^f) \longrightarrow \eta^{\mathrm{eff}}(t - t^f) = \eta(t - t^f) - \theta_1(t - t^f). \tag{6.32}$$

In other words, the dynamic threshold can be absorbed in the definition of the η kernel. Note, however, that in this case η can no longer be interpreted as the experimentally measured spike afterpotential, but must be interpreted as an "effective" spike afterpotential.

The argument can also be turned the other way round, so as to remove the spike afterpotential and only work with a dynamic threshold; see Fig. 6.12b. However, when an SRM is fitted to experimental data, it is convenient to separate the spike after-effects that are visible in the voltage trace (e.g., in the form of a hyperpolarizing spike-afterpotential, described by the kernel η), from the spike after-effects caused by an increase in the threshold which can be observed only *indirectly* via the absence of spike firing. Whereas the prediction of spike times is insensitive to the relative contribution of η and θ_1, the prediction of the subthreshold voltage time course is not. Therefore, it is useful to explicitly work with two distinct adapatation mechanisms in the SRM (Mensi *et al.*, 2012).

(a)

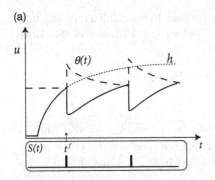

(b)

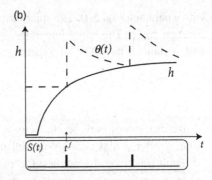

Fig. 6.12 Spike-afterpotential and dynamic threshold in the SRM. (a) At time t^f a spike occurs because the membrane potential hits the threshold $\vartheta(t)$. The threshold jumps to a higher value (dashed line) and, at the same time, a contribution $\eta(t - t^f)$ is added to the membrane potential, i.e., the spike and its spike-afterpotential are "pasted" into the picture. If no further spikes are triggered, the threshold decays back to its resting value and the spike-afterpotential decays back to zero. The total membrane potential (thick solid line) after a spike is $u(t) = h(t) + \sum_f \eta(t - t^f)$ where $h(t)$ is the input potential (thin dotted line). (b) If the model is used to predict spike times, but not the membrane potential, the spike-afterpotential η can be integrated into the dynamic threshold so that $u(t) = h(t)$. At the moment of spiking the value of the threshold is increased, but the membrane potential is not affected (either through reset or spike-afterpotential).

6.4.2 Interpretation of η and κ

So far Eq. (6.27) in combination with the threshold condition (6.30) defines a mathematical model. Can we give a biological interpretation of the terms?

The kernel $\kappa(s)$ is the *linear response* of the membrane potential to an input current. It describes the time course of a deviation of the membrane potential from its resting value that is caused by a short current pulse ("impulse response").

The kernel η describes the standard form of an action potential of neuron i including the negative overshoot which typically follows a spike (the spike-afterpotential). Graphically speaking, a contribution η is "pasted in" each time the membrane potential reaches the threshold ϑ (Fig. 6.12a). Since the form of the spike is always the same, the exact time course of the action potential carries no information. What matters is whether there is the event "spike" or not. The event is fully characterized by the firing time t^f.

In a simplified model, the *form* of the action potential may therefore be neglected as long as we keep track of the firing times t^f. The kernel η then describes simply the "reset" of the membrane potential to a lower value after the spike at t^f just as in the integrate-and-fire model

$$\eta(t - t^f) = -\eta_0 \exp\left(-\frac{t - t^f}{\tau_{\text{recov}}}\right), \tag{6.33}$$

with a parameter $\eta_0 > 0$. The spike-afterpotential decays back to zero with a recovery time constant τ_{recov}. The leaky integrate-and-fire model is in fact a special case of the SRM, with parameter $\eta_0 = (\vartheta - u_r)$ and $\tau_{\text{recov}} = \tau_m$.

Example: Refractoriness

Refractoriness may be characterized experimentally by the observation that immediately after a first action potential it is impossible (absolute refractoriness) or more difficult (relative refractoriness) to excite a second spike. In Fig. 5.5. we have already seen that refractoriness shows up as increased firing threshold and increased conductance immediately after a spike.

Absolute refractoriness can be incorporated in the SRM by setting the dynamic threshold during a time Δ^{abs} to an extremely high value that cannot be attained.

Relative refractoriness can be mimicked in various ways. First, after a spike the firing threshold returns only slowly back to its normal value (increase in firing threshold). Second, after the spike the membrane potential, and hence η, passes through a regime of hyperpolarization (spike-afterpotential) where the voltage is *below* the resting potential. During this phase, more stimulation than usual is needed to drive the membrane potential above threshold. In fact, this is equivalent to a transient increase of the firing threshold (see above).

Third, the responsiveness of the neuron is reduced immediately after a spike. In the SRM we can model the reduced responsiveness by making the shape of ε and κ depend on the time since the *last* spike timing $\hat{t}$.

We label output spikes such that the most recent one receives the label t^1 (i.e., $t > t^1 > t^2 > t^3 \ldots$). This means that, after each firing event, output spikes need to be relabeled. The advantage, however, is that the *last* output spike always keeps the label t^1. For simplicity, we often write $\hat{t}$ instead of t^1 to denote the most recent spike.

With this notation, a slightly more general version of the Spike Response Model is

$$u(t) = \sum_f \eta(t - t^f) + \int_0^\infty \kappa(t - \hat{t}, s)\, I^{\text{ext}}(t - s)\, \mathrm{d}s + u_{\text{rest}}. \tag{6.34}$$

6.4.3 Mapping the integrate-and-fire model to the SRM

In this section, we show that the leaky integrate-and-fire neuron with adaptation defined above in Eqs. (6.7) and (6.8) is a special case of the Spike Response Model. Let us recall that the leaky integrate-and-fire model follows the equation of a linear circuit with resistance R and capacity C

$$\tau_m \frac{\mathrm{d}u_i}{\mathrm{d}t} = -(u_i - E_0) - R \sum_k w_k + R I_i(t), \tag{6.35}$$

where $\tau_m = RC$ is the time constant, E_0 the leak reversal potential, w_k are adaptation variables, and I_i is the input current to neuron i. At each firing time

$$\{t_i^f\} \in \{t | u_i(t) = \vartheta\}, \tag{6.36}$$

the voltage is reset to a value u_r. At the same time, the adaptation variables are increased by an amount b_k

$$\tau_k \frac{dw_k}{dt} = a_k (u_i - E_0) - w_k + \tau_k b_k \sum_{t^f} \delta(t - t^f). \tag{6.37}$$

The equations of the adaptive leaky integrate-and-fire model, Eqs. (6.35) and (6.37), can be classified as *linear* differential equations. However, because of the reset of the membrane potential after firing, the integration is not completely trivial. In fact, there are two different ways of proceeding with the integration. The first method is to treat the reset after each firing as a new initial condition – this is the procedure typically chosen for a numerical integration of the model. Here we follow a different path and describe the reset as a current pulse. As we shall see, the result enables a mapping of the leaky integrate-and-fire model to the SRM.

Let us consider a short current pulse $I_i^{\text{out}} = -q\,\delta(t)$ applied to the RC circuit. It removes a charge q from the capacitor C and lowers the potential by an amount $\Delta u = -q/C$. Thus, a reset of the membrane potential from a value of $u = \vartheta$ to a new value $u = u_r$ corresponds to an "output" current pulse which removes a charge $q = C(\vartheta - u_r)$. The reset takes place every time when the neuron fires. The total reset current is therefore

$$I_i^{\text{out}}(t) = -C(\vartheta - u_r) \sum_f \delta(t - t_i^f), \tag{6.38}$$

where the sum runs over all firing times t_i^f. We add the output current (6.38) on the right-hand side of (6.35),

$$\tau_m \frac{du_i}{dt} = -(u_i - E_0) - R \sum_k w_k + R I_i(t) - RC(\vartheta - u_r) \sum_f \delta(t - t_i^f), \tag{6.39}$$

$$\tau_k \frac{dw_k}{dt} = a_k (u_i - E_0) - w_k + \tau_k b_k \sum_{t^f} \delta(t - t^f). \tag{6.40}$$

Since Eqs. (6.39) and (6.40) define a system of linear equations, we can integrate each term separately and superimpose the result at the end. To perform the integration, we proceed in three steps. First, we shift the voltage so as to set the equilibrium potential to zero. Second, we calculate the eigenvalues and eigenvectors of the "free" equations in the absence of input (and therefore no spikes). If there are K adaptation variables, we have a total of $K + 1$ eigenvalues which we label as $\lambda_1, \lambda_2, \ldots$ The associated eigenvectors are e_k with components $(e_{k0}, e_{k1}, \ldots, e_{kK})^T$. Third, we express the response to an impulse $\Delta u = 1$ in the voltage (no perturbation in the adaptation variables) in terms of the $K + 1$ eigenvectors: $(1, 0, 0, \ldots, 0)^T = \sum_{k=0}^{K} \beta_k e_k$. Finally, we express the pulse caused by a reset of

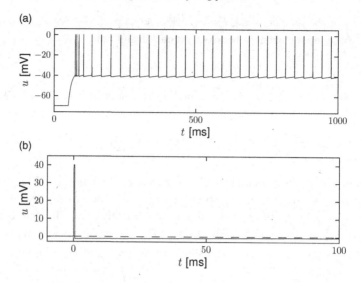

Fig. 6.13 SRM with a choice of η leading to adaptation. (a) The response of the neuron model to injection of a step current. (b) The spike-afterpotential η with adaptation time constant $\tau_w = 100$ ms. A short (0.5 ms) period at +40 mV replaces the stereotypical shape of the action potential.

voltage and adaptation variables in terms of the eigenvectors $(-\vartheta + u_r, b_1, b_2, \ldots, b_K)^T = \sum_{k=0}^{K} \gamma_k e_k$.

The response to the reset pulses yields the kernel η while the response to voltage pulses yields the filter $\kappa(s)$ of the SRM

$$u_i(t) = \sum_f \eta(t - t_i^f)$$

$$+ \int_0^\infty \kappa(s) I_i(t - s) \, ds, \tag{6.41}$$

with kernels

$$\eta(s) = \sum_{k=0}^{K} \gamma_k e_{k0} \exp(\lambda_k s) \Theta(s), \tag{6.42}$$

$$\kappa(s) = \sum_{k=0}^{K} \beta_k e_{k0} \exp(\lambda_k s) \Theta(s). \tag{6.43}$$

As usual, $\Theta(x)$ denotes the Heaviside step function.

Example: Adaptation and bursting

Let us first study a leaky integrate-and-fire model with a single slow adaptation variable $\tau_w \gg \tau_m$ which is coupled to the voltage in the subthreshold regime ($a > 0$) and increased during spiking by an amount b. In this case there are only two equations, one for the voltage and one for adaptation, so that the eigenvectors and eigenvalues can be calculated "by hand." With a parameter $\delta = \tau_m/\tau_w \ll 1$, the eigenvalues are $\lambda_1 = -\tau_w [1 - a\delta]$ and $\lambda_2 = -\tau_w \delta [1 + a]$, associated to eigenvectors $e_1 = (1, a\delta)^{\mathrm{T}}$ and $e_2 = (1, -1 + \delta + a\delta)^{\mathrm{T}}$. The resulting spike-afterpotential kernel $\eta(s)$ is shown in Fig. 6.13b. Because of the slow time constant $\tau_w \gg \tau_m$, the kernel η has a long hyperpolarizing tail. The neuron model responds to a step current with adaptation, because of accumulation of hyperpolarizing spike-afterpotentials over many spikes.

As a second example, we consider four adaptation currents with different time constants $\tau_1 < \tau_2 < \tau_3 < \tau_4$. We assume pure spike-triggered coupling ($a = 0$) so that the integration of the differential equations of w_k gives each an exponential current

$$w_k(t) = \sum_f b_k \exp\left(-\frac{t - t^f}{\tau_k}\right) \Theta(t - t^f). \tag{6.44}$$

We choose the time constant of the first current to be very short and $b_1 < 0$ (inward current) so as to model the upswing of the action potential (a candidate current would be sodium). A second current (e.g., a fast potassium channel) with a slightly longer time constant is outgoing ($b_2 > 0$) and leads to the downswing and rapid reset of the membrane potential. The third current, with a time constant of tens of milliseconds, is inward ($b_3 < 0$), while the slowest current is again hyperpolarizing ($b_4 > 0$). Integration of the voltage equation with all four currents generates the spike-afterpotential η shown Fig. 6.14b. Because of the depolarizing spike-afterpotential induced by the inward current w_3, the neuron model responds to a step current of appropriate amplitude with bursts. The bursts end because of the accumulation of the hyperpolarizing effect of the slowest current.

6.4.4 Multi-compartment integrate-and-fire model as an SRM (*)

The models discussed in this chapter are point neurons, i.e., models that do not take into account the spatial structure of a real neuron. In Chapter 3 we have already seen that the electrical properties of dendritic trees can be described by compartmental models. In this section, we want to show that neurons with a linear dendritic tree and a voltage threshold for spike firing at the soma can be mapped to the Spike Response Model.

We study an integrate-and-fire model with a passive dendritic tree described by n compartments. Membrane resistance, core resistance, and capacity of compartment μ are denoted by R_T^μ, R_L^μ, and C^μ, respectively. The longitudinal core resistance between compartment μ and a neighboring compartment ν is $r^{\mu\nu} = (R_L^\mu + R_L^\nu)/2$; see Fig. 3.8. Compartment $\mu = 1$ represents the soma and is equipped with a simple mechanism for spike generation, i.e., with a threshold criterion as in the standard integrate-and-fire model. The remaining dendritic compartments ($2 \le \mu \le n$) are passive.

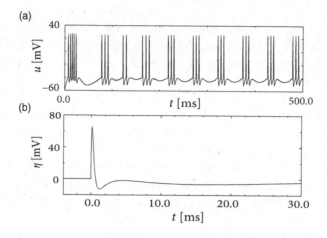

Fig. 6.14 SRM with choice of η leading to bursting. (a) The refractory kernel η of an integrate-and-fire model with four spike-triggered currents. (b) The voltage response to a step current exhibits bursting. Adapted from Gerstner *et al.* (1996b).

Each compartment $1 \leq \mu \leq n$ of neuron i may receive input $I_i^\mu(t)$ from presynaptic neurons. As a result of spike generation, there is an additional reset current $\Omega_i(t)$ at the soma. The membrane potential V_i^μ of compartment μ is given by

$$\frac{\mathrm{d}}{\mathrm{d}t} V_i^\mu = \frac{1}{C_i^\mu} \left[-\frac{V_i^\mu}{R_{\mathrm{T},i}^\mu} - \sum_\nu \frac{V_i^\mu - V_i^\nu}{r_i^{\mu\nu}} + I_i^\mu(t) - \delta^{\mu 1} \Omega_i(t) \right], \tag{6.45}$$

where the sum runs over all neighbors of compartment μ. The Kronecker symbol $\delta^{\mu\nu}$ equals unity if the upper indices are equal; otherwise, it is zero. The subscript i is the index of the neuron; the upper indices μ or ν refer to compartments. Below we will identify the somatic voltage V_i^1 with the potential u_i of the Spike Response Model.

Equation (6.45) is a system of linear differential equations if the external input current is independent of the membrane potential. The solution of Eq. (6.45) can thus be formulated by means of Green's functions $G_i^{\mu\nu}(s)$ that describe the impact of a current pulse injected in compartment ν on the membrane potential of compartment μ. The solution is of the form

$$V_i^\mu(t) = \sum_\nu \frac{1}{C_i^\nu} \int_0^\infty G_i^{\mu\nu}(s) \left[I_i^\nu(t-s) - \delta^{\nu 1} \Omega_i(t-s) \right] \mathrm{d}s. \tag{6.46}$$

Explicit expressions for the Green's function $G_i^{\mu\nu}(s)$ for arbitrary geometry have been derived by Abbott *et al.* (1991) and Bressloff and Taylor (1994).

We consider a network made up of a set of neurons described by Eq. (6.45) and a simple threshold criterion for generating spikes. We assume that each spike t_j^f of a presynaptic neuron j evokes, for $t > t_j^f$, a synaptic current pulse $\alpha(t - t_j^f)$ into the postsynaptic neuron i. The actual amplitude of the current pulse depends on the strength W_{ij} of the synapse that connects neuron j to neuron i. The total input to compartment μ of neuron i is thus

$$I_i^{\mu}(t) = \sum_{j \in \Gamma_i^{\mu}} W_{ij} \sum_f \alpha(t - t_j^f). \tag{6.47}$$

Here, Γ_i^{μ} denotes the set of all neurons that have a synapse with compartment μ of neuron i. The firing times of neuron j are denoted by t_j^f.

In the following we assume that spikes are generated at the soma in the manner of the integrate-and-fire model. That is to say, a spike is triggered as soon as the somatic membrane potential reaches the firing threshold, ϑ. After each spike the somatic membrane potential is reset to $V_i^1 = u_r < \vartheta$. This is equivalent to a current pulse

$$\gamma_i(s) = C_i^1 (\vartheta - u_r) \delta(s), \tag{6.48}$$

so that the overall current due to the firing of action potentials at the soma of neuron i amounts to

$$\Omega_i(t) = \sum_f \gamma_i(t - t_i^f). \tag{6.49}$$

We will refer to Eqs. (6.46)–(6.49) together with the threshold criterion for generating spikes as the multi-compartment integrate-and-fire model.

Using the above specializations for the synaptic input current and the somatic reset current the membrane potential (6.46) of compartment μ in neuron i can be rewritten as

$$V_i^{\mu}(t) = \sum_f \eta_i^{\mu}(t - t_i^f) + \sum_v \sum_{j \in \Gamma_i^v} W_{ij} \sum_f \varepsilon_i^{\mu v}(t - t_j^f), \tag{6.50}$$

with

$$\varepsilon_i^{\mu v}(s) = \frac{1}{C_i^v} \int_0^{\infty} G_i^{\mu v}(s') \alpha(s - s') \, ds', \tag{6.51}$$

$$\eta_i^{\mu}(s) = \frac{1}{C_i^1} \int_0^{\infty} G_i^{\mu 1}(s') \gamma_i(s - s') \, ds'. \tag{6.52}$$

The kernel $\varepsilon_i^{\mu v}(s)$ describes the effect of a presynaptic action potential arriving at compartment v on the membrane potential of compartment μ. Similarly, $\eta_i^{\mu}(s)$ describes the response of compartment μ to an action potential generated at the soma.

The triggering of action potentials depends on the *somatic* membrane potential only. We define $u_i = V_i^1$, $\eta_i(s) = \eta_i^1(s)$ and, for $j \in \Gamma_i^v$, we set $\varepsilon_{ij} = \varepsilon_i^{1v}$. This yields the equation of the SRM

$$u_i(t) = \sum_f \eta_i(t - t_i^f) + \sum_j W_{ij} \sum_f \varepsilon_{ij}(t - t_j^f). \tag{6.53}$$

Example: Two-compartment integrate-and-fire model

We illustrate the methodology by mapping a simple model with two compartments and a reset mechanism at the soma (Rospars and Lansky, 1993) to the Spike Response

(a)

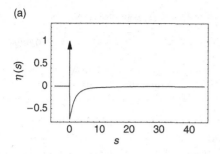

(b)

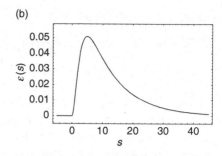

Fig. 6.15 Two-compartment integrate-and-fire model. (a) Response kernel $\eta_0(s)$ of a neuron with two compartments and a fire-and-reset threshold dynamics. The response kernel is a double exponential with time constants $\tau_{12} = 2$ ms and $\tau_0 = 10$ ms. The spike at $s = 0$ is indicated by a vertical arrow. (b) Response kernel $\varepsilon_0(s)$ for excitatory synaptic input at the dendritic compartment with a synaptic time constant $\tau_s = 1$ ms. The response kernel is a superposition of three exponentials and exhibits the typical time course of an excitatory postsynaptic potential.

Model. The two compartments are characterized by a somatic capacitance C^1 and a dendritic capacitance $C^2 = aC^1$. The membrane time constant is $\tau_0 = R^1 C^1 = R^2 C^2$ and the longitudinal time constant $\tau_{12} = r^{12} C^1 C^2 / (C^1 + C^2)$. The neuron fires if $V^1(t) = \vartheta$. After each firing the somatic potential is reset to u_r. This is equivalent to a current pulse

$$\gamma(s) = q\,\delta(s)\,, \tag{6.54}$$

where $q = C^1[\vartheta - u_r]$ is the charge lost during the spike. The dendrite receives spike trains from other neurons j and we assume that each spike evokes a current pulse with time course

$$\alpha(s) = \frac{1}{\tau_s} \exp\left(-\frac{s}{\tau_s}\right) \Theta(s)\,. \tag{6.55}$$

For the two-compartment model it is straightforward to integrate the equations and derive the Green's function. With the Green's function we can calculate the response kernels $\eta_0(s) = \eta_i^{(1)}$ and $\varepsilon_0(s) = \varepsilon_i^{12}$ as defined in Eqs. (6.51) and (6.52). We find

$$\eta_0(s) = -\frac{\vartheta - u_r}{(1+a)} \exp\left(-\frac{s}{\tau_0}\right)\left[1 + a \exp\left(-\frac{s}{\tau_{12}}\right)\right], \tag{6.56}$$

$$\varepsilon_0(s) = \frac{1}{(1+a)} \exp\left(-\frac{s}{\tau_0}\right)\left[\frac{1 - e^{-\delta_1 s}}{\tau_s \delta_1} - \exp\left(-\frac{s}{\tau_{12}}\right)\frac{1 - e^{-\delta_2 s}}{\tau_s \delta_2}\right],$$

with $\delta_1 = \tau_s^{-1} - \tau_0^{-1}$ and $\delta_2 = \tau_s^{-1} - \tau_0^{-1} - \tau_{12}^{-1}$. Figure 6.15 shows the two response kernels with parameters $\tau_0 = 10$ ms, $\tau_{12} = 2$ ms, and $a = 10$. The synaptic time constant is $\tau_s = 1$ ms. The kernel $\varepsilon_0(s)$ describes the voltage response of the soma to an input at the dendrite. It shows the typical time course of an excitatory or inhibitory postsynaptic potential. The time course of the kernel $\eta_0(s)$ is a double exponential and reflects the dynamics of the reset in a two-compartment model.

6.5 Summary

By adding one or several adaptation variables to integrate-and-fire models, a large variety of firing patterns found in real neurons, such as adaptation, bursting or initial bursting, can be explained. The dynamics of the adaptation variables has two components: (i) a coupling to the voltage u via a parameter a which provides subthreshold adaptation and, in nonlinear neuron models, also a contribution to spike-triggered adaptation; and (ii) an explicit spike-triggered adaptation via an increase of the adaptation current during each firing by an amount b. While positive values for a and b induce a hyperpolarization of the membrane and therefore lead to spike-frequency adaptation, negative values induce a depolarization and lead to delayed onset of spiking and spike frequency facilitation. Bursting is most easily achieved by a suitable combination of the reset parameters u_r and b.

The phenomenological adaptation variables w_k can be derived from the ionic currents flowing through different ion channels. Coupling of an integrate-and-fire model to a passive dendrite also yields effective adaptation variables which have, however, a facilitating influence.

The adaptation variables can be combined with a quadratic integrate-and-fire model which leads to the Izhikevich model; with an exponential integrate-and-fire model which leads to the AdEx model; or with a leaky integrate-and-fire model. In the latter case, the differential equations can be analytically integrated in the presence of an arbitrary number of adaptation variable. Integration leads to the Spike Response Model (SRM) which presents a general linear model combined with a sharp firing threshold. The Spike Response Model is the starting point for the Generalized Linear Models in the presence of noise which we will introduce in Chapter 9.

Literature

Formal neuron models where spikes are triggered by a threshold process were popular in the 1960s (Stein, 1965, 1967b; Geisler and Goldberg, 1966; Weiss, 1966), but the ideas can be traced back much earlier (Lapicque, 1907; Hill, 1936). It was recognized early that these models lend themselves for hardware implementations (French and Stein, 1970) and mathematical analysis (Stein, 1965, 1967a), and can be fitted to experimental data (Brillinger, 1988, 1992).

Dynamic thresholds that increase after each spike have been a standard feature of phenomenological neuron models for a long time (Fuortes and Mantegazzini, 1962; Geisler and Goldberg, 1966; Weiss, 1966) and so have the slow subthreshold processes of adaptation (Sabah and Leibovic, 1969; Mauro *et al.*, 1970; Fishman *et al.*, 1977; Sirovich and Knight, 1977). While the linear subthreshold coupling of voltage and adaptation currents via a coupling parameter a is nicely presented and analyzed in Richardson *et al.* (2003), the spike-triggered jump b of the adaptation current has been mainly popularized by Izhikevich (2003) – but can be found in earlier papers (e.g., Gerstner *et al.*, 1996b; Liu and Wang, 2001), and much earlier in the form of a spike-triggered increase in the threshold (Fuortes and Mantegazzini, 1962; Geisler and Goldberg, 1966; Weiss, 1966).

The phase plane analysis of the AdEx model presented in this chapter is based on Naud *et al.* (2008). The main difference between the AdEx model (Brette and Gerstner, 2005) and the highly influential model of Izhikevich (2003) is that the AdEx uses in the voltage equation an exponential nonlinearity (as suggested by experiments (Badel *et al.*, 2008a)) whereas the Izhikevich model uses a quadratic nonlinearity (as suggested by bifurcation analysis close to the bifurcation point (Ermentrout, 1996)).

The book by Izhikevich (2007a) as well as the Scholarpedia articles on the Spike Response Model (SRM) and the adaptive exponential integrate-and-fire (AdEx) model (Gerstner, 2008; Gerstner and Brette, 2009), present readable reviews of the model class discussed in this chapter.

The functions η, κ, and ε_{ij} are *response kernels* that describe the effect of spike emission and spike reception on the variable u_i. This interpretation has motivated the name "Spike Response Model." While the name and the specific formulation of the model equations (6.27)–(6.30) has been used since 1995 (Gerstner, 1995; Gerstner *et al.*, 1996b; Kistler *et al.*, 1997), closely related models can be found in earlier works; see, e.g., Hill (1936); Geisler and Goldberg (1966).

Exercises

1. **Time scale of firing rate decay.** *The characteristic feature of adaptation is that, after the onset of a superthreshold step current, interspike intervals become successively longer, or, equivalently, the momentary firing rate drops. The aim is to make a quantitative prediction of the decay of the firing rate of a leaky integrate-and-fire model with a single adaptation current.*
   (a) Show that the firing rate of Eqs. (6.7) and (6.8) with constant I, constant w and $a = 0$ is

$$f(I, w) = - \left[\tau_m \log \left(1 - \frac{\vartheta_{rh} - u_{reset}}{R(I - w)} \right) \right]^{-1}. \tag{6.57}$$

   (b) For each spike (i.e., once per interspike interval), w jumps by an amount b. Show that for I constant and w averaged over one interspike interval, Eq. (6.8) becomes:

$$\tau_w \frac{dw}{dt} = -w + b\tau_w f(I, w). \tag{6.58}$$

   (c) At time t_0, a strong current of amplitude I_0 is switched on that causes transiently a firing rate $f \gg \tau_w$. Afterward the firing rate decays. Find the effective time constant of the firing rate for the case of strong input current.
   Hint: Start from Eq. (6.58) and consider a Taylor expansion of $f(I, w)$.
2. **Subthreshold resonance.** *We study a leaky integrate-and-fire model with a single adaptation variable w.*
   (a) Assume $E_0 = u_{rest}$ and cast equation Eqs. (6.7) and (6.8) in the form of Eq. (6.27). Set

$\varepsilon = 0$ and calculate η and κ. Show that $\kappa(t)$ can be written as a linear combination $\kappa(t) = k_+ e^{\lambda_+ t} + k_- e^{\lambda_- t}$ with

$$\lambda_\pm = \frac{1}{2\tau_m \tau_w} \left(-(\tau_m + \tau_w) \pm \sqrt{\tau_m + \tau_w - 4\tau_m \tau_w (1 + aR)} \right) \tag{6.59}$$

and

$$k_\pm = \pm \frac{R(\lambda_\pm \tau_w + 1)}{\tau_m \tau_w (\lambda_+ - \lambda_-)}. \tag{6.60}$$

(b) What are the parameters of Eqs. (6.7)–(6.8) that lead to oscillations in $\kappa(t)$?

(c) What is the frequency of the oscillation?
  Hint: Section 4.4.3.

(d) Take the Fourier transform of Eqs. (6.7)–(6.8) and find the function $\hat{R}(\omega)$ that relates the current $\hat{I}(\omega)$ at frequency ω to the voltage $\hat{u}(\omega)$ at the same frequency, i.e., $\hat{u}(\omega) = \hat{R}(\omega)\hat{I}(\omega)$. Show that, in the case where κ has oscillations, the function $\hat{R}(\omega)$ has a global maximum. What is the frequency where this happens?

3. **Integrate-and-fire model with slow adaptation.**
The aim is to relate the leaky integrate-and-fire model with a single adaptation variable, defined in Eqs. (6.7) and (6.8), to the Spike Response Model in the form of Eq. (6.27). Adaptation is slow so that $\tau_m / \tau_w = \delta \ll 1$ and all calculations can be done to first order in δ.

(a) Show that the spike-afterpotential is given by

$$\eta(t) = \gamma_1 e^{\lambda_1 t} + \gamma_2 e^{\lambda_2 t}, \tag{6.61}$$
$$\gamma_1 = \Delta u (1 - \delta - \delta a) - b(1 + \delta), \tag{6.62}$$
$$\gamma_2 = \Delta u - \gamma_1. \tag{6.63}$$

(b) Derive the input response kernel $\kappa(s)$.
  Hint: Use the result from (a).

4. **Integrate-and-fire model with time-dependent time constant**. *Since many channels are open immediately after a spike, the effective membrane time constant after a spike is smaller than the time constant at rest. Consider an integrate-and-fire model with spike-time-dependent time constant, i.e., with a membrane time constant τ that is a function of the time since the last postsynaptic spike,*

$$\frac{du}{dt} = -\frac{u}{\tau(t - \hat{t})} + \frac{1}{C} I^{\text{ext}}(t); \tag{6.64}$$

see Wehmeier et al. (1989); Stevens and Zador (1998). As usual, $\hat{t}$ denotes the last firing time of the neuron. The neuron fires if $u(t)$ hits a fixed threshold ϑ and integration restarts with a reset value u_r.

  (a) Suppose that the time constant is $\tau(t - \hat{t}) = 2\,\text{ms}$ for $t - \hat{t} < 10\,\text{ms}$ and $\tau(t - \hat{t}) = 20\,\text{ms}$ for $t - \hat{t} \geq 10\,\text{ms}$. Set $u_r = -10\,\text{mV}$. Sketch the time course of the membrane potential for an input current $I(t) = q\,\delta(t - t')$ arriving at $t' = 5\,\text{ms}$ or $t' = 15\,\text{ms}$. What are the differences between the two cases?

  (b) Integrate Eq. (6.64) for arbitrary input with $u(\hat{t}) = u_r$ as initial condition and interpret the result.

5. **Spike-triggered adaptation currents.** *Consider a leaky integrate-and-fire model. A spike at time t^f generates several adaptation currents $dw_k/dt = -\frac{w_k}{\tau_k} + b_k \delta(t - t^f)$ with $k = 1, \dots, K$.*

  (a) Calculate the effect of the adaptation current on the voltage.

  (b) Construct a combination of spike-triggered currents that could generate slow adaptation.

  (c) Construct a combination of spike-triggered currents that could generate bursts.

7

Variability of spike trains and neural codes

The neuron models discussed in the previous chapters are deterministic and generate, for most choices of parameters, spike trains that look regular when driven by a constant stimulus. *In vivo* recordings of neuronal activity, however, are characterized by a high degree of irregularity. The spike train of an individual neuron is far from being periodic, and correlations between the spike timings of neighboring neurons are weak. If the electrical activity picked up by an extracellular electrode is made audible by a loudspeaker then what we basically hear is noise. The question whether this is indeed just noise or rather a highly efficient way of coding information cannot easily be answered. Indeed, listening to a computer modem or a fax machine might also leave the impression that this is just noise. Being able to decide whether we are witnessing the neuronal activity that is underlying the composition of a poem (or the electronic transmission of a love letter) and not just meaningless flicker is one of the most burning problems in neuroscience.

Several experiments have been undertaken to tackle this problem. It seems that a neuron *in vitro*, once it is isolated from the network, can react in a very reliable and reproducible manner to a fluctuating input current, and so can neurons in the sensory cortex *in vivo* when driven by a strong time-dependent signal. On the other hand, neurons produce irregular spike trains in the absence of any temporally structured stimuli. Irregular spontaneous activity, i.e., activity that is not related in any obvious way to external stimulation, and trial-to-trial variations in neuronal responses are often considered as noise.

The origin of this irregularity of neuronal dynamics *in vivo* is poorly understood. In integrate-and-fire models, noise is therefore often added explicitly to neuronal dynamics so as to mimic the unpredictability of neuronal recordings. How to add noise to neuron models is the topic of Chapters 8 and 9. The aim of the present chapter is a mere description and quantification of the variability of neuronal spike trains. We review in Section 7.1 some experimental evidence for noise in neurons and introduce in Sections 7.2–7.5 a statistical framework of spike-train analysis. In particular, we present the definitions of firing rate, interval distribution, power spectrum, and renewal statistics. In Section 7.6 we ask whether the firing rate, which is such a useful measure for quantification of spike trains, can also be considered as the code used by neurons in the brain.

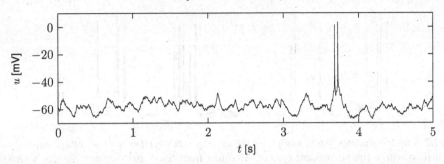

Fig. 7.1 Spontaneous activity *in vivo*. Sample of a voltage trace (whole-cell recording) of a cortical neuron when the animal receives no experimental stimulation. The neuron is from layer 2/3 of the C2 cortical column, a region of the cortex associated with whisker movement. The recording corresponds to a period of time where the mouse is awake and freely whisking. Data courtesy of Sylvain Crochet and Carl Petersen (Crochet *et al.*, 2011).

7.1 Spike-train variability

If neuron models such as the Hodgkin–Huxley or the integrate-and-fire model are driven by a sufficiently strong constant current, they generate a regular sequence of spikes. In neuronal models with adaptation currents[1] there might be a short transient phase at the beginning, but then all interspike intervals are constant. Spike trains of typical neurons *in vivo* show much more irregular behavior. Whether the irregularity is the sign of thermal noise, microscopic chaos, or rather the signature of an intricate neural code is at present an open question. In the first subsection we review some evidence for neuronal variability and spike-train irregularity. We then discuss potential sources of noise.

7.1.1 Are neurons noisy?

Many *in vivo* experiments show noisy behavior of cortical neurons. The activity of neurons from the visual cortex, for example, can be recorded while a slowly moving bar is presented on a screen within the visual field of the animal. As soon as the bar enters the neuron's receptive field the firing rate goes up. The spike train, however, varies considerably from trial to trial, if the same experiment is repeated several times. Similarly, neurons in a region of the sensory cortex of rats or mice respond systematically to whisker movements, but the response is somewhat different between one trial and the next. Furthermore, the very same neuron occasionally emits a spontaneous spike, even if no external stimulus is applied. During spontaneous activity, the voltage trajectory fluctuates considerably and intervals between one spike and the next exhibit a large degree of variability (Fig. 7.1).

Are these experiments convincing evidence for ubiquitous noise in the central nervous system? The above observations refer to experiments on the neural system as a whole. The cortical neuron that is recorded from receives input not only from the sensors, but

---

[1] We neglect here intrinsically bursting and chaotic neurons.

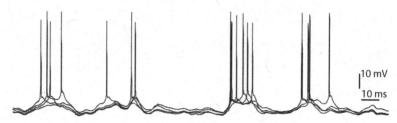

Fig. 7.2 Variability across four repetitions of the same stimulus *in vitro*. Sample voltage traces during stimulation with a time-dependent current. Modified from Naud and Gerstner (2012b) with kind permission from Springer Science and Business Media.

also from many other neurons in the brain. The effective input to this neuron is basically unknown. It is thus possible that there is a substantial fluctuation in the input current to cortical neurons, even though the external (e.g., visual or tactile) stimulus is always the same.

The advantage of experiments *in vitro* is that the stimulus injected into the neuron can be well controlled. If the stimulation consists of a known time-dependent current directly injected into the neuron, the neuronal response also varies from one trial to the next, even if the very same stimulation is repeated several times (Fig. 7.2). Is this an indication of "real" noise? The variability is visible only if the stimulating current is nearly constant (Fig. 7.3). In fact, when neurons are driven by a current with large-amplitude fluctuations of the input signal, neurons behave more or less deterministically (Bryant and Segundo, 1976; Mainen and Sejnowski, 1995).

Similarly, in the full and intact brain, neurons react much more reliably to a rapidly changing external stimulus than to constant or slowly moving stimuli. For example, spatially uniform random flicker of an image elicits more or less the same spike train in retinal ganglion cells if the same flicker sequence is presented again (Berry *et al.*, 1997). A similar behavior has been reported for motion-sensitive neurons of the visual system in flies (de Ruyter van Steveninck *et al.*, 1997) and monkey cortex (Bair and Koch, 1996); see Fig. 7.4 for an example of a cortical neuron. Whether a neuron behaves nearly deterministically or rather randomly thus depends, at least to a certain extent, on the stimulus.

In the following, we distinguish between intrinsic noise sources that generate stochastic behavior on the level of the *neuronal* dynamics and are present even in an isolated neuron *in vitro*; and extrinsic sources that arise from network effects and synaptic transmission naturally occurring *in vivo*.

7.1.2 Intrinsic noise sources

A source of noise which is literally omnipresent is thermal noise. Owing to the discrete nature of electric charge carriers, the voltage u across any electrical resistor R fluctuates at finite temperature (Johnson noise). The variance of the fluctuations at rest is $\langle \Delta u^2 \rangle \propto$

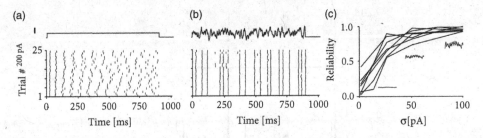

Fig. 7.3 Variability across repetitions of the same stimulus *in vitro*. (a) A constant stimulus leads to a large variability of spike timing between one trial and the next. (b) A stimulus with large-amplitude signal fluctuations generates reliable spike timing so that spike times vary across trials. (c) Reliability of spike timing (arbitrary units) as a function of the amplitude σ of signal fluctuations. Modified from Mainen and Sejnowski (1995) with permission from AAAS.

$RkTB$ where k is the Boltzmann constant, T the temperature and B the bandwidth of the system. Since neuronal dynamics is described by an equivalent electrical circuit containing resistors (see Chapter 2), the neuronal membrane potential fluctuates as well. Fluctuations due to Johnson noise are, however, of minor importance compared to other noise sources in neurons (Manwani and Koch, 1999).

Another source of noise that is specific to neuronal cells and present already in an isolated neuron arises from the finite number of ion channels in a patch of neuronal membrane. Most ion channels have only two states: they are either open or closed. The electrical conductivity of a patch of membrane for ion type i is proportional to the number of open ion channels. For a given constant membrane potential u, a fraction $P_i(u)$ of ion channel of type i is open *on average*. The actual number of open channels fluctuates around $N_i P_i(u)$ where N_i is the total number of ion channels of type i in that patch of membrane; see Fig. 2.5.

The formulation of the Hodgkin–Huxley equations in terms of ion channel conductivities (see Chapter 2) is implicitly based on the assumption of a large number of ion channels so that fluctuations can be neglected. Since, in reality, N_i is finite, the conductivity fluctuates and so does the potential. If the membrane potential is close to the threshold, channel noise can be critical for the generation of action potentials. Models that take the finite number of ion channels into account can reproduce the observed variability of real neurons with intracellular stimulation (Schneidman *et al.*, 1998; Chow and White, 1996). In particular, they show little spike jitter if the input current is rapidly changing, but are less reliable if the input current is constant.

7.1.3 Noise from the network

Apart from intrinsic noise sources at the level of an individual neuron there are also sources of noise that are due to signal transmission and network effects (extrinsic noise). Synaptic transmission failures, for instance, seem to impose a substantial limitation to signal transmission within a neuronal network. Experiments with double electrode recordings from

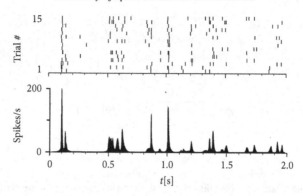

Fig. 7.4 Variability across repetitions of the same stimulus *in vivo*. Activity of a neuron in visual cortex (area MT) driven by a stimulus consisting of randomly moving dots. The same stimulus is repeated many times. Spikes in a single trial are shown as short vertical dashes along a horizontal line. Only 15 trials are shown. The peri-stimulus-time-histogram (accumulated over many more trials) is indicated at the bottom. Redrawn after Bair and Koch (1996), who show data from the Newsome lab (Newsome *et al.*, 1989).

two synaptically connected neurons suggest that only 10–30% of presynaptic spikes generate a postsynaptic response (Hessler *et al.*, 1993; Markram and Tsodyks, 1996).

Finally, an important part of the irregularity of neuronal spiking during spontaneous activity seems to be due to properties of the network – even if the network itself is completely deterministic. Model studies show that networks of excitatory and inhibitory neurons with fixed random connectivity can produce highly irregular spike trains – even in the absence of any source of noise. An example of variability in a deterministic network of leaky integrate-and-fire neurons with random excitatory and inhibitory interactions is shown in Fig. 7.5. We will discuss the underlying mechanisms in Part III of this book (see Sections 12.3.4 and 12.4.4). As a result of the network activity, each neuron receives as input an irregular spike sequence that can be described as stochastic spike arrival; see Chapter 8. The difference between the large variability of neurons *in vivo* compared to the variability during intracellular stimulation *in vitro* can therefore be, at least partially, attributed to network effects.

7.2 Mean firing rate

In the next few sections, we introduce some important concepts commonly used for the statistical description of neuronal spike trains. Central notions will be the interspike interval distribution (Section 7.3), the noise spectrum (Section 7.4), but most importantly the concept of "firing rate," which we discuss first.

A quick glance at the experimental literature reveals that there is no unique and well-defined concept of "mean firing rate." In fact, there are at least three different notions of rate, which are often confused and used simultaneously. The three definitions refer to three

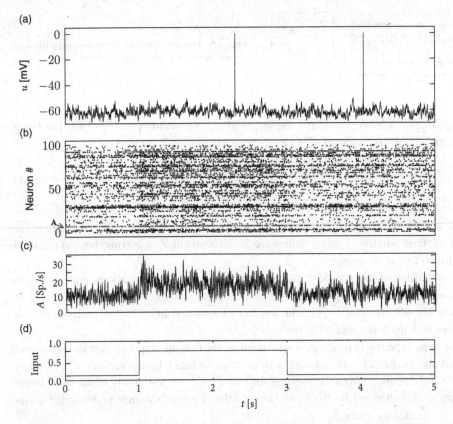

Fig. 7.5 Variability in a deterministic model network of 8000 excitatory and 2000 inhibitory neurons, both modeled as leaky integrate-and-fire neurons. (a) Voltage trace as a function of time for a single model neuron. Spikes (vertical lines) are generated whenever the membrane potential (solid line) hits the firing threshold. (b) Spike raster of 100 neurons in the network. Spike times (dots) of a single neuron appear along a horizontal line. (C) Population activity A as a function of time t, measured by averaging across the spikes of the subpopulation of 100 neurons shown in (b). From time $t = 1$ s to $t = 3$ s, all neurons in this population receive a nonzero input. (d) Input to the subpopulation of 100 neurons. Simulation results courtesy of F. Zenke and T. P. Vogels (Vogels *et al.*, 2011).

different averaging procedures: an average over time, or an average over several repetitions of the experiment, or an average over a population of neurons. The following three subsections will revisit in detail these three concepts.

7.2.1 *Rate as a spike count and Fano factor*

The first and most commonly used definition of a firing rate refers to a temporal average.

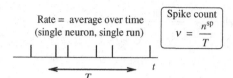

Rate = average over time
(single neuron, single run)

$v = \dfrac{n^{\text{sp}}}{T}$

Fig. 7.6 The spike count measure: definition of the mean firing rate by temporal average.

An experimenter observes in trial k the spikes of a given neuron (see Fig. 7.6). The firing rate in trial k is the spike count n_k^{sp} in an interval of duration T divided by T

$$v_k = \frac{n_k^{\text{sp}}}{T}. \tag{7.1}$$

The length T of the time window is set by the experimenter and depends on the type of neuron and the stimulus. In practice, to get sensible averages, several spikes should occur within the time window. Typical values are $T = 100\,\text{ms}$ or $T = 500\,\text{ms}$, but the duration may also be longer or shorter.

This definition of rate has been successfully used in many preparations, particularly in experiments on sensory or motor systems. A classical example is the stretch receptor in a muscle spindle (Adrian, 1926). The number of spikes emitted by the receptor neuron increases with the force applied to the muscle.

If the same experiment is repeated several times, the measured spike count varies between one trial and the next. Let us denote the spike count in trial k by the variable n_k^{sp}, its mean by $\langle n^{\text{sp}} \rangle$ and deviations from the mean as $\Delta n_k^{\text{sp}} = n_k^{\text{sp}} - \langle n^{\text{sp}} \rangle$. Variability of the spike count measure is characterized by the Fano factor, defined as the variance of the spike count $\langle (\Delta n^{\text{sp}})^2 \rangle$ divided by its mean

$$F = \frac{\langle (\Delta n^{\text{sp}})^2 \rangle}{\langle n^{\text{sp}} \rangle}. \tag{7.2}$$

In experiments, the mean and variance are estimated by averaging over K trials $\langle n^{\text{sp}} \rangle = (1/K)\sum_{k=1}^{K} n_k^{\text{sp}}$ and $\langle (\Delta n^{\text{sp}})^2 \rangle = (1/K)\sum_{k=1}^{K} (\Delta n_k^{\text{sp}})^2$.

If we find on average $\langle n^{\text{sp}} \rangle$ spikes in a long temporal window of duration T, the mean interval between two subsequent spikes is $T/\langle n^{\text{sp}} \rangle$. Indeed, using the notion of interspike-interval distribution to be introduced below (Section 7.3), we can make the following statement: the firing rate defined here as spike count divided by the measurement time T is identical to the inverse of the mean interspike interval. We will come back to interspike intervals in Section 7.3.

It is tempting, but misleading, to consider the inverse interspike interval as a "momentary firing rate:" if a first spike occurs at time t^k and the next one at time t^{k+1}, we could artificially assign a variable $\tilde{v}(t) = 1/(t^{k+1} - t^k)$ for all times $t^k < t \leq t^k$. However, the temporal average of $\tilde{v}(t)$ over a much longer time T is *not* the same as the mean rate v defined here as spike count divided by T, simply because $1/\langle x \rangle \neq \langle (1/x) \rangle$. A practical definition of "instantaneous firing rate" will be given below in Section 7.2.2.

Example: Homogeneous Poisson process

If the rate v is defined via a spike count over a time window of duration T, the exact firing time of a spike does not matter. It is therefore tempting to describe spiking as a Poisson process where spikes occur independently and stochastically with a constant rate v.

Let us divide the duration T (say 500 ms) into a large number of short segments Δt (say $\Delta t = 0.1$ ms). In a homogeneous Poisson process, the probability of finding a spike in a *short* segment of duration Δt is

$$P_F(t;t+\Delta t) = v\,\Delta t. \tag{7.3}$$

In other words, spike events are independent of each other and occur with a *constant* rate (also called stochastic intensity) defined as

$$v = \lim_{\Delta t \to 0} \frac{P_F(t;t+\Delta t)}{\Delta t}. \tag{7.4}$$

The expected number of spikes to occur in the measurement interval T is therefore

$$\langle n^{\mathrm{sp}} \rangle = v\,T, \tag{7.5}$$

so that the experimental procedure of (i) counting spikes over a time T and (ii) dividing by T gives an empirical estimate of the rate v of the Poisson process.

For a Poisson process, the Fano factor is exactly 1. Therefore, measuring the Fano factor is a powerful test so as to find out whether neuronal firing is Poisson-like; see the discussion in Rieke *et al.* (1997).

7.2.2 Rate as a spike density and the peri-stimulus-time histogram

An experimenter records from a neuron while stimulating with some input sequence. The same stimulation sequence is repeated several times and the neuronal response is reported in a peri-stimulus-time histogram (PSTH) with bin width Δt; see Fig. 7.7. The time t is measured with respect to the start of the stimulation sequence and Δt defines the time bin for generating the histogram, it is typically of the order of milliseconds.

The number of occurrences of spikes $n_K(t;t+\Delta t)$ summed over all repetitions of the experiment divided by the number K of repetitions is a measure of the typical activity of the neuron between time t and $t+\Delta t$. A further division by the interval length Δt yields the spike density

$$\rho(t) = \frac{1}{\Delta t}\frac{n_K(t;t+\Delta t)}{K}. \tag{7.6}$$

Sometimes the result is smoothed to get a continuous (time-dependent) rate variable, usually reported in units of hertz. As an experimental procedure, the PSTH measure is a useful method to evaluate neuronal activity, in particular in the case of time-dependent stimuli; see Fig. 7.4. We call it the time-dependent firing rate.

Rate = average over several runs
     (single neuron, repeated runs)

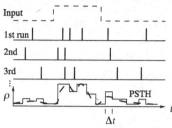

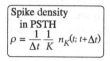

Fig. 7.7 The peri-stimulus-time histogram (PSTH) and the time-dependent firing rate as an average over several runs of the experiment.

In order to see the relation of Eq. (7.6) to a time-dependent firing rate, we recall that spikes are formal events characterized by their firing time t^f where f counts the spikes. In Chapter 1 we have defined (Eq. (1.14)) the spike train as a sum of δ-functions:

$$S(t) = \sum_f \delta(t - t^f). \tag{7.7}$$

If each stimulation can be considered as an independent sample from the identical stochastic process, we can define an *instantaneous firing rate* as an expectation over trials

$$v(t) = \langle S(t) \rangle. \tag{7.8}$$

An expectation value over δ-functions may look strange to the reader not used to seeing such mathematical objects. Let us therefore consider the experimental procedure to estimate the expectation value. First, in each trial k, we count the number of spikes that occur in a short time interval Δt by integrating the spike train over time, $n_k^{\text{sp}}(t) = \int_t^{t+\Delta t} S_k(t')dt'$ where the lower index k denotes the trial number. Note that integration removes the δ-function. Obviously, if the time bin Δt is small enough we will find at most one spike so that n_k^{sp} is either zero or 1. Second, we average over the K trials and divide by Δt in order to obtain the empirical estimate

$$v(t) = \frac{1}{K\Delta t} \sum_{k=1}^{K} n_k^{\text{sp}}(t). \tag{7.9}$$

The PSTH, defined as spike count per time bin averaged over several trials and divided by the bin length (the right-hand side of Eq. (7.9)), provides therefore an empirical estimate of the instantaneous firing rate (the left-hand side).

Example: Inhomogeneous Poisson process

An inhomogeneous Poisson process can be used to describe the spike density measured in a PSTH. In an inhomogeneous Poisson process, spike events are independent of each other and occur with an instantaneous firing rate

$$v(t) = \lim_{\Delta t \to 0} \frac{P_F(t; t + \Delta t)}{\Delta t}. \tag{7.10}$$

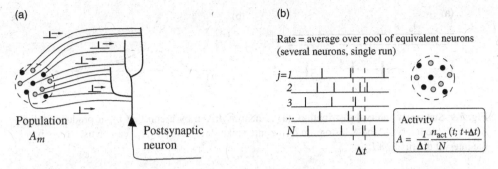

Fig. 7.8 (a) A postsynaptic neuron receives spike input from the population m with activity A_m. (b) The population activity is defined as the fraction of neurons that are active in a short interval $[t, t + \Delta t]$ divided by Δt.

Therefore, the probability of finding a spike in a *short* segment of duration Δt, say, a time bin of 1 ms, is $P_F(t; t + \Delta t) = v(t) \Delta t$. More generally, the expected number of spikes in an interval of finite duration T is $\langle n^{\mathrm{sp}} \rangle = \int_0^T v(t) \, dt$ and the Fano factor is 1, as was the case for the homogeneous Poisson process.

Once we have measured a PSTH, we can always find an inhomogeneous Poisson process which reproduces the PSTH. However, this does not imply that neuronal firing is Poisson-like. A Poisson process has, for example, the tendency to generate spikes with very short interspike intervals, which cannot occur for real neurons because of refractoriness.

7.2.3 *Rate as a population activity (average over several neurons)*

The number of neurons in the brain is huge. Often many neurons have similar properties and respond to the same stimuli. For example, neurons in the primary visual cortex of cats and monkeys are arranged in columns of cells with similar properties (Hubel and Wiesel, 1962). Let us idealize the situation and consider a population of neurons with identical properties. In particular, all neurons in the population should have the same pattern of input and output connections. The spikes of the neurons in a population m are sent off to another population n. In our idealized picture, each neuron in population n receives input from all neurons in population m. The relevant quantity, from the point of view of the receiving neuron, is the proportion of active neurons in the presynaptic population m; see Fig. 7.8a. Formally, we define the population activity

$$A(t) = \frac{1}{\Delta t} \frac{n_{\mathrm{act}}(t; t + \Delta t)}{N} = \frac{1}{\Delta t} \frac{\int_t^{t + \Delta t} \sum_j \sum_f \delta(t - t_j^f) \, dt}{N}, \qquad (7.11)$$

where N is the size of the population, $n_{\mathrm{act}}(t; t + \Delta t)$ is the number of spikes (summed over all neurons in the population) that occur between t and $t + \Delta t$, where Δt is a small time

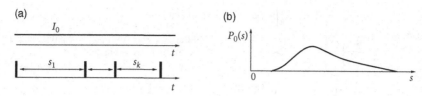

Fig. 7.9 Stationary interval distribution. (a) A neuron driven by a constant input produces spikes with variable intervals. (b) A histogram of the interspike intervals $s_1, s_2, \ldots$ can be used to estimate the interval distribution $P_0(s)$.

interval; see Fig. 7.8. Eq. (7.11) defines a variable with units inverse time – in other words, a rate.

As we can see from Fig. 7.5c, the population activity may vary rapidly and can reflect changes in the stimulus conditions nearly instantaneously. Before we discuss the problem of neural coding (Section 7.6), let us first study further statistical measures of spike train statistics.

7.3 Interval distribution and coefficient of variation

The estimation of interspike-interval (ISI) distributions from experimental data is a common method to study neuronal variability given a certain *stationary* input. In a typical experiment, the spike train of a single neuron (e.g., a neuron in the visual cortex) is recorded while driven by a constant stimulus. The stimulus might be an external input applied to the system (e.g., a visual contrast grating moving at constant speed); or it may be an intracellularly applied constant driving current. The spike train is analyzed and the distribution of intervals s_k between two subsequent spikes is plotted in a histogram. For a sufficiently long spike train, the histogram provides a good estimate of the ISI distribution, which we denote as $P_0(s)$; see Fig. 7.9. The interval distribution can be interpreted as a conditional probability density

$$P_0(s) = P(t^f + s | t^f),\tag{7.12}$$

where $\int_t^{t+\Delta t} P(t'|t^f) \, dt'$ is the probability that the next spike occurs in the interval $[t, t+\Delta t]$ given that the last spike occurred at time t^f.

In order to extract the mean firing rate from a stationary interval distribution $P_0(s)$, we start with the definition of the mean interval,

$$\langle s \rangle = \int_0^\infty s P_0(s) \, ds.\tag{7.13}$$

The mean firing rate is the inverse of the mean interval

$$\nu = \frac{1}{\langle s \rangle} = \left[\int_0^\infty s P_0(s) \, ds \right]^{-1}.\tag{7.14}$$

7.3.1 Coefficient of variation C_V

Interspike-interval distributions $P_0(s)$ derived from a spike train under stationary conditions can be broad or sharply peaked. To quantify the width of the interval distribution, neuroscientists often evaluate the coefficient of variation, C_V, defined as the ratio of the standard deviation and the mean. Therefore the square of the C_V is

$$C_V^2 = \frac{\langle \Delta s^2 \rangle}{\langle s \rangle^2}, \tag{7.15}$$

where $\langle s \rangle = \int_0^\infty s P_0(s)\, ds$ and $\langle \Delta s^2 \rangle = \int_0^\infty s^2 P_0(s)\, ds - \langle s \rangle^2$. A Poisson process produces distributions with $C_V = 1$. A value of $C_V > 1$ implies that a given spike train is less regular than a Poisson process with the same firing rate. If $C_V < 1$, then the spike train is more regular. Most deterministic integrate-and-fire neurons fire periodically when driven by a constant stimulus and therefore have $C_V = 0$. Intrinsically bursting neurons, however, can have $C_V > 1$.

Example: Poisson process with absolute refractoriness

We study a Poisson neuron with absolute refractory period Δ^{abs}. For times since the last spike larger than Δ^{abs}, the neuron is supposed to fire stochastically with rate r. The interval distribution of a Poisson process with absolute refractoriness (Fig. 7.10a) is given by

$$P_0(s) = \begin{cases} 0 & \text{for} \quad s < \Delta^{\text{abs}}, \\ r \exp\left[-r(s - \Delta^{\text{abs}})\right] & \text{for} \quad s > \Delta^{\text{abs}}, \end{cases} \tag{7.16}$$

and has a mean $\langle s \rangle = \Delta^{\text{abs}} + 1/r$ and variance $\langle \Delta s^2 \rangle = 1/r^2$. The coefficient of variation is therefore

$$C_V = 1 - \frac{\Delta^{\text{abs}}}{\langle s \rangle}. \tag{7.17}$$

Let us compare the C_V of Eq. (7.17) with that of a homogeneous Poisson process of the same mean rate $v = \langle s \rangle^{-1}$. As we have seen, a Poisson process has $C_V = 1$. A refractory period $\Delta^{\text{abs}} > 0$ lowers the C_V, because a neuron with absolute refractoriness fires more regularly than a Poisson neuron. If we increase Δ^{abs}, we must increase the instantaneous rate r in order to keep the same mean rate v. In the limit of $\Delta^{\text{abs}} \to \langle s \rangle$, the C_V approaches zero, since the only possible spike train is regular firing with period $\langle s \rangle$.

7.4 Autocorrelation function and noise spectrum

Suppose that, during a stationary input scenario, we observe a neuron i firing a first spike at time t. While the interval distribution $P_0(s)$ describes the probability that the *next* spike occurs at time $t + s$, the autocorrelation function $C(s)$ focuses on the probability of finding *another* spike at time $t+s$ – independent of whether this is the next spike of the neuron or not.

In order to make the notion of an autocorrelation function more precise, let us consider a spike train $S_i(t) = \sum_f \delta(t - t_i^f)$ of length T. The firing times t_i^f might have been measured in an experiment or else generated by a neuron model. We suppose that T is sufficiently long so that we can formally consider the limit $T \to \infty$. The autocorrelation function $C_{ii}(s)$ of the spike train is a measure for the probability of finding two spikes at a time interval s, i.e.,

$$C_{ii}(s) = \langle S_i(t) S_i(t+s) \rangle_t , \tag{7.18}$$

where $\langle \cdot \rangle_t$ denotes an average over time t,

$$\langle f(t) \rangle_t = \lim_{T \to \infty} \frac{1}{T} \int_{-T/2}^{T/2} f(t) \, dt . \tag{7.19}$$

We note that the right-hand side of Eq. (7.18) is symmetric so that $C_{ii}(-s) = C_{ii}(s)$ holds. The calculation of the autocorrelation function for a stationary renewal process is the topic of Section 7.5.2.

It turns out that the autocorrelation function is intimately linked to the power spectrum of a neuronal spike train, also called the noise spectrum. The power spectrum (or power spectral density) of a spike train is defined as $\mathscr{P}(\omega) = \lim_{T \to \infty} \mathscr{P}_T(\omega)$, where $\mathscr{P}_T$ is the power of a segment of length T of the spike train,

$$\mathscr{P}_T(\omega) = \frac{1}{T} \left| \int_{-T/2}^{T/2} S_i(t) e^{-i\omega t} \, dt \right|^2 . \tag{7.20}$$

The power spectrum $\mathscr{P}(\omega)$ of a spike train is equal to the Fourier transform $\hat{C}_{ii}(\omega)$ of its autocorrelation function (Wiener–Khinchin theorem). To see this, we use the definition of the autocorrelation function

$$\hat{C}_{ii}(\omega) = \int_{-\infty}^{\infty} \langle S_i(t) S_i(t+s) \rangle e^{-i\omega s} \, ds$$

$$= \lim_{T \to \infty} \frac{1}{T} \int_{-T/2}^{T/2} S_i(t) \int_{-\infty}^{\infty} S_i(t+s) e^{-i\omega s} \, ds \, dt$$

$$= \lim_{T \to \infty} \frac{1}{T} \int_{-T/2}^{T/2} S_i(t) e^{+i\omega t} \, dt \int_{-\infty}^{\infty} S_i(s') e^{-i\omega s'} \, ds'$$

$$= \lim_{T \to \infty} \frac{1}{T} \left| \int_{-T/2}^{T/2} S_i(t) e^{-i\omega t} \, dt \right|^2 . \tag{7.21}$$

In the limit of $T \to \infty$, Eq. (7.20) becomes identical to (7.21) so that the assertion follows. The power spectral density of a spike train during spontaneous activity is called the noise spectrum of the neuron. Noise is a limiting factor to all forms of information transmission and in particular to information transmission by neurons. An important concept of the theory of signal transmission is the signal-to-noise ratio. A signal that is transmitted at a certain frequency ω should be stronger than (or at least of the same order of magnitude as) the noise at the same frequency. For this reason, the noise spectrum $\mathscr{P}(\omega)$ of the transmission channel is of interest. As we shall see in the next section, the noise spectrum of a stationary renewal process is intimately related to the interval distribution $P_0(s)$.

7.5 Renewal statistics

Poisson processes do not account for neuronal refractoriness and cannot be used to describe realistic interspike-interval distributions. In order to account for neuronal refractoriness in the stochastic description of spike trains, we need to switch from a Poisson processes to a renewal process. Renewal processes keep a memory of the last event (last firing time) $\hat{t}$, but not of any earlier events. More precisely, spikes are generated in a renewal process, with a stochastic intensity (or "hazard")

$$\rho(t|\hat{t}) = \rho_0(t - \hat{t}) \tag{7.22}$$

which depends on the time since the last spike. One of the simplest example of a renewal system is a Poisson process with absolute refractoriness which we have already encountered in the previous section; see Eq. (7.16).

Renewal processes are a class of stochastic point processes that describe a sequence of events in time (Cox, 1962; Papoulis, 1991). Renewal systems in the *narrow* sense (stationary renewal processes), presuppose stationary input and are defined by the fact that the state of the system, and hence the probability of generating the next event, depends only on the "age" $t - \hat{t}$ of the system, i.e., the time that has passed since the last event (last spike). The central assumption of renewal theory is that the state does not depend on earlier events (i.e., earlier spikes of the same neuron). The aim of renewal theory is to predict the probability of the next event given the age of the system. In other words, renewal theory allows us to calculate the interval distribution

$$P_0(s) = P(t^f + s|t^f), \tag{7.23}$$

i.e., the probability density that the next event occurs at time $t^f + s$ given that the last event was observed at time t^f.

While for a Poisson process all events occur independently, in a renewal process generation of events (spikes) depends on the previous event, so that events are *not* independent. However, since the dependence is restricted to the most recent event, *intervals between subsequent events are independent*. Therefore, an efficient way of generating a spike train of a renewal system is to draw interspike intervals from the distribution $P_0(s)$.

Example: Light bulb failure as a renewal system

A generic example of a renewal system is a light bulb. The event is the failure of the bulb and its subsequent exchange. Obviously, the state of the system only depends on the age of the current bulb, and not on that of any previous bulb that has already been exchanged. If the usage pattern of the bulbs is stationary (e.g., the bulb is switched on for 10 hours each night) then we have a stationary renewal process. The aim of renewal theory is to calculate the probability of the next failure given the age of the bulb.

7.5.1 Survivor function and hazard

The interval distribution $P(t|\hat{t})$ as defined above is a probability *density*. Thus, integration of $P(t|\hat{t})$ over time yields a probability. For example, $\int_{\hat{t}}^{t} P(t'|\hat{t}) \, dt'$ is the probability that a neuron which has emitted a spike at $\hat{t}$ fires the next action potential between $\hat{t}$ and t. Thus

$$S(t|\hat{t}) = 1 - \int_{\hat{t}}^{t} P(t'|\hat{t}) \, dt' \tag{7.24}$$

is the probability that the neuron stays quiescent between $\hat{t}$ and t. $S(t|\hat{t})$ is called the *survivor function*: it gives the probability that the neuron "survives" from $\hat{t}$ to t without firing.

The survivor function $S(t|\hat{t})$ has an initial value $S(\hat{t}|\hat{t}) = 1$ and decreases to zero for $t \to \infty$. The rate of decay of $S(t|\hat{t})$ will be denoted by $\rho(t|\hat{t})$ and is defined by

$$\rho(t|\hat{t}) = -\frac{\frac{d}{dt} S(t|\hat{t})}{S(t|\hat{t})} = \frac{P(t|\hat{t})}{1 - \int_{\hat{t}}^{t} P(t'|\hat{t}) \, dt'}. \tag{7.25}$$

In the language of renewal theory, $\rho(t|\hat{t})$ is called the "age-dependent death rate" or "hazard" (Cox, 1962; Cox and Lewis, 1966).

Integration of the differential equation $dS/dt = -\rho S$ [see the first identity in Eq. (7.25)] yields the survivor function

$$S(t|\hat{t}) = \exp\left[-\int_{\hat{t}}^{t} \rho(t'|\hat{t}) \, dt'\right]. \tag{7.26}$$

According to the definition of the survivor function in Eq. (7.24), the interval distribution is given by

$$P(t|\hat{t}) = -\frac{d}{dt} S(t|\hat{t}) = \rho(t|\hat{t}) S(t|\hat{t}), \tag{7.27}$$

which has a nice intuitive interpretation: In order to emit its *next* spike at t, the neuron has to survive the interval $(\hat{t}, t)$ without firing and then fire at t. The survival probability is $S(t|\hat{t})$ and the hazard of firing a spike at time t is $\rho(t|\hat{t})$. Multiplication of the survivor function S with the momentary hazard ρ gives the two factors on the right-hand side of Eq. (7.27). Inserting Eq. (7.26) in (7.27), we obtain an explicit expression for the interval distribution in terms of the hazard:

$$P(t|\hat{t}) = \rho(t|\hat{t}) \exp\left[-\int_{\hat{t}}^{t} \rho(t'|\hat{t}) \, dt'\right]. \tag{7.28}$$

On the other hand, given the interval distribution we can derive the hazard from Eq. (7.25). Thus, each of the three quantities $\rho(t|\hat{t})$, $P(t|\hat{t})$, and $S(t|\hat{t})$ is sufficient to describe the

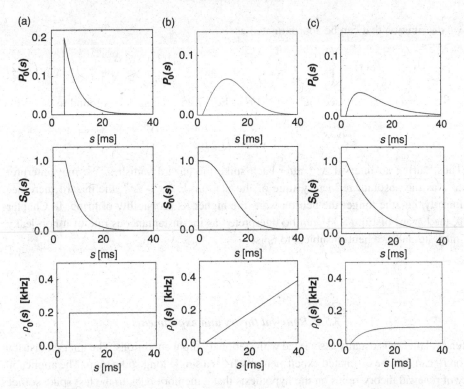

Fig. 7.10 Interval distribution $P_0(s)$ (top), survivor function $S_0(s)$ (middle) for three different hazard functions (bottom). (a) Hazard function corresponds to a Poisson neuron with absolute refractoriness of 5 ms. (b) Hazard function defined by $\rho_0(s) = a_0\,(s - \Delta^{abs})\,\Theta(s - \Delta^{abs})$ with $a_0 = 0.01\,\mathrm{ms}^{-2}$ and $\Delta^{abs} = 2\,\mathrm{ms}$. (c) Hazard function defined by $\rho_0(s) = v\{1 - \exp[-\lambda\,(s - \Delta^{abs})]\}\,\Theta(s - \Delta^{abs})$ with $v = 0.1\,\mathrm{kHz}$, $\lambda = 0.2\,\mathrm{kHz}$, and $\Delta^{abs} = 2\,\mathrm{ms}$.

statistical properties of a renewal system. Since we focus on stationary renewal systems, the notation can be simplified and Eqs. (7.24)–(7.28) hold with the replacement

$$P(t|\hat{t}) = P_0(t - \hat{t}), \tag{7.29}$$

$$S(t|\hat{t}) = S_0(t - \hat{t}), \tag{7.30}$$

$$\rho(t|\hat{t}) = \rho_0(t - \hat{t}). \tag{7.31}$$

Eqs. (7.24)–(7.28) are standard results of renewal theory. The notation that we have chosen in Eqs. (7.24)–(7.28) will turn out to be useful in later chapters and highlights the fact that these quantities are conditional probabilities, probability densities, or rates.

Example: From interval distribution to hazard function

Let us suppose that we have found under stationary experimental conditions an interval distribution that can be approximated as

$$P_0(s) = \begin{cases} 0 & \text{for } s \leq \Delta^{\text{abs}}, \\ a_0\,(s - \Delta^{\text{abs}})\,, e^{-\frac{a_0}{2}(s - \Delta^{\text{abs}})^2} & \text{for } s > \Delta^{\text{abs}}, \end{cases} \tag{7.32}$$

with a constant $a_0 > 0$; see Fig. 7.10b. From Eq. (7.25), the hazard is found to be

$$\rho_0(s) = \begin{cases} 0 & \text{for } s \leq \Delta^{\text{abs}}, \\ a_0\,(s - \Delta^{\text{abs}}) & \text{for } s > \Delta^{\text{abs}}. \end{cases} \tag{7.33}$$

Thus, during an interval Δ^{abs} after each spike the hazard vanishes. We may interpret Δ^{abs} as the absolute refractory time of the neuron. For $s > \Delta^{\text{abs}}$ the hazard increases linearly, i.e., the longer the neuron waits the higher its probability of firing. In Chapter 9, the hazard of Eq. (7.33) can be interpreted as the instantaneous rate of a non-leaky integrate-and-fire neuron subject to noise.

7.5.2 Renewal theory and experiments

Renewal theory is usually associated with stationary input conditions. The interval distribution P_0 can then be estimated experimentally from a single long spike train. The applicability of renewal theory relies on the hypothesis that a memory back to the last spike suffices to describe the spike statistics. In particular, there should be no correlation between one interval and the next. In experiments, the renewal hypothesis can be tested by measuring the correlation between subsequent intervals. Under some experimental conditions, correlations are small, indicating that a description of spiking as a stationary renewal process is a good approximation (Goldberg *et al.*, 1964); however, under experimental conditions where neuronal adaptation is strong, intervals are *not* independent (Fig. 7.11). Given a time series of events with variable intervals s_j, a common measure of memory effects is the serial correlation coefficients

$$c_k = \frac{\langle s_{j+k}s_j \rangle_j - \langle s_j \rangle_j^2}{\langle s_j^2 \rangle - \langle s_j \rangle^2}. \tag{7.34}$$

Spike-frequency adaptation causes a negative correlation between subsequent intervals ($c_1 < 0$). Long intervals are most likely followed by short ones, and vice versa, so that the assumption of renewal theory does not hold (Schwalger *et al.*, 2010; Ratnam and Nelson, 2000; Chacron *et al.*, 2000).

The notion of stationary input conditions is a mathematical concept that cannot be easily translated into experiments. With intracellular recordings under *in vitro* conditions, constant input current can be imposed and thus the renewal hypothesis can be tested directly. Under *in vivo* conditions, the assumption that the input current to a neuron embedded in a large neural system is constant (or has stationary statistics) is questionable; see (Perkel

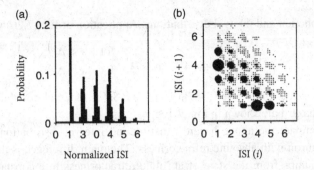

Fig. 7.11 Limitations of the renewal assumption. (a) The interval distribution $P_0(s)$ of an afferent sensory fiber in the weakly electric fish exhibits periodic peaks, which are associated to the background oscillation normalized to period $T = 1$. The most likely interval is exactly one period, but longer intervals are possible. (b) Testing for renewal in a plot of the joint density of the interval i (horizontal axis) and the next interval $i+1$ (vertical axis). Size of symbol indicates probability of occurrence. The most likely sequence is that an interval of length 4 is followed by an interval of length 1; moreover, a short interval of length 1 is most likely followed by a long interval of length 4. Modified from Ratnam and Nelson (2000).

et al., 1967a,b) for a discussion. While the externally controlled stimulus can be made stationary (e.g., a grating drifting at constant speed), the input to an individual neuron is out of control.

Let us suppose that, for a given experiment, we have checked that the renewal hypothesis holds to a reasonable degree of accuracy. From the experimental interval distribution P_0 we can then calculate the survivor function S_0 and the hazard ρ_0 via Eqs. (7.24) and (7.25). If some additional assumptions regarding the nature of the noise are made, the form of the hazard $\rho_0(t|\hat{t})$ can be interpreted in terms of neuronal dynamics. In particular, a reduced hazard immediately after a spike is a signature of neuronal refractoriness (Goldberg *et al.*, 1964; Berry and Meister, 1998).

> ### Example: Plausible hazard function and interval distributions
>
> Interval distributions and hazard functions have been measured in many experiments. For example, in auditory neurons of the cat driven by stationary stimuli, the hazard function $\rho_0(t - \hat{t})$ increases, after an absolute refractory time, to a constant level (Goldberg *et al.*, 1964). We approximate the time course of the hazard function as
>
> $$\rho_0(s) = \begin{cases} 0 & \text{for } s \leq \Delta^{\text{abs}}, \\ v\left[1 - e^{-\lambda(s-\Delta^{\text{abs}})}\right] & \text{for } s > \Delta^{\text{abs}}, \end{cases} \quad (7.35)$$
>
> with parameters $\Delta^{\text{abs}}, \lambda$, and v; Fig. 7.10c. In Chapter 9 we shall see how the hazard (7.35) can be related to neuronal dynamics. Given the hazard function, we can calculate

the survivor function and interval distributions. Application of Eq. (7.26) yields

$$
S_0(s) = \begin{cases} 1 & \text{for } s < \Delta^{\text{abs}}, \\ e^{-\nu(s-\Delta^{\text{abs}})} e^{\rho_0(s)/\lambda} & \text{for } s > \Delta^{\text{abs}}. \end{cases} \tag{7.36}
$$

The interval distribution is given by $P_0(s) = \rho_0(s) S_0(s)$. Interval distribution, survivor function, and hazard are shown in Fig. 7.10c.

We may compare the above hazard function and interval distribution with that of the Poisson neuron with absolute refractoriness. The main difference is that the hazard in Eq. (7.16) jumps from the state of absolute refractoriness to a constant firing rate, whereas in Eq. (7.35) the transition is smooth.

7.5.3 *Autocorrelation and noise spectrum of a renewal process* (*)

In case of a stationary renewal process, the interval distribution P_0 contains *all* the statistical information so that the autocorrelation function and noise spectrum can be derived. In this section we calculate the noise spectrum of a stationary renewal process. As we have seen above, the noise spectrum of a neuron is directly related to the autocorrelation function of its spike train. Both noise spectrum and autocorrelation function are experimentally accessible.

Let $v_i = \langle S_i \rangle$ denote the mean firing rate (expected number of spikes per unit time) of the spike train. Thus the probability of finding a spike in a short segment $[t, t + \Delta t]$ of the spike train is $v \Delta t$. For large intervals s, firing at time $t + s$ is independent of whether or not there was a spike at time t. Therefore, the expectation of finding a spike at t and another spike at $t + s$ approaches for $s \to \infty$ a limiting value $\lim_{s \to \infty} \langle S_i(t) S_i(t + s) \rangle = \lim_{s \to \infty} C_{ii}(s) = v_i^2$. It is convenient to subtract this baseline value and introduce a "normalized" autocorrelation,

$$
C_{ii}^0(s) = C_{ii}(s) - v_i^2, \tag{7.37}
$$

with $\lim_{s \to \infty} C_{ii}^0(s) = 0$. The Fourier transform of Eq. (7.37) yields

$$
\hat{C}_{ii}(\omega) = \hat{C}_{ii}^0(\omega) + 2\pi v_i^2 \delta(\omega). \tag{7.38}
$$

Thus $\hat{C}_{ii}(\omega)$ diverges at $\omega = 0$; the divergence is removed by switching to the normalized autocorrelation. In the following we will calculate the noise spectrum $\hat{C}_{ii}(\omega)$ for $\omega \neq 0$.

In the case of a stationary renewal process, the autocorrelation function is closely related to the interval distribution $P_0(s)$. This relation will now be derived. Let us suppose that we have found a first spike at t. To calculate the autocorrelation we need the probability density for a spike at $t + s$. Let us construct an expression for $C_{ii}(s)$ for $s > 0$. The correlation function for positive s will be denoted by $v_i C_+(s)$ or

$$
C_+(s) = \frac{1}{v_i} C_{ii}(s) \Theta(s). \tag{7.39}
$$

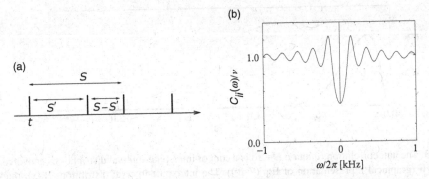

Fig. 7.12 (a) The autocorrelation of a spike train describes the chance to find two spikes at a distance s, independent of the number of spikes that occur in between. (b) Fourier transform of the autocorrelation function C_{ii} of a Poisson neuron with absolute refractoriness ($\Delta^{ax} = 5\,\mathrm{ms}$) and constant stimulation ($\nu = 100\,\mathrm{Hz}$).

The factor ν_i in Eq. (7.39) takes care of the fact that we expect a first spike at t with rate ν_i; $C_+(s)$ gives the *conditional* probability density that, given a spike at t, we will find another spike at $t + s > t$. The spike at $t + s$ can be the first spike after t, or the second one, or the nth one; see Fig. 7.12. Thus for $s > 0$

$$C_+(s) = P_0(s) + \int_0^\infty P_0(s') P_0(s - s') \, ds'$$
$$+ \int_0^\infty \int_0^\infty P_0(s') P_0(s'') P_0(s - s' - s'') \, ds' \, ds'' + \cdots \qquad (7.40)$$

or

$$C_+(s) = P_0(s) + \int_0^\infty P_0(s') C_+(s - s') \, ds' \qquad (7.41)$$

as can be seen by inserting Eq. (7.40) on the right-hand side of (7.41); see Fig. 7.13.

Owing to the symmetry of C_{ii}, we have $C_{ii}(s) = \nu C_+(-s)$ for $s < 0$. Finally, for $s = 0$, the autocorrelation has a δ peak reflecting the trivial autocorrelation of each spike with itself. Hence,

$$C_{ii}(s) = \nu_i \left[\delta(s) + C_+(s) + C_+(-s) \right]. \qquad (7.42)$$

In order to solve Eq. (7.41) for C_+ we take the Fourier transform of Eq. (7.41) and find

$$\hat{C}_+(\omega) = \frac{\hat{P}_0(\omega)}{1 - \hat{P}_0(\omega)}. \qquad (7.43)$$

Together with the Fourier transform of Eq. (7.42), $\hat{C}_{ii} = \nu_i[1 + 2\,\mathrm{Re}\{\hat{C}_+(\omega)\}]$, we obtain

$$\hat{C}_{ii}(\omega) = \nu_i \, \mathrm{Re}\left\{ \frac{1 + \hat{P}_0(\omega)}{1 - \hat{P}_0(\omega)} \right\} \quad \text{for} \quad \omega \neq 0. \qquad (7.44)$$

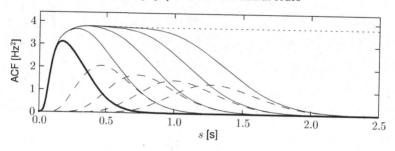

Fig. 7.13 The autocorrelation function (ACF) is a sum of interspike-interval distributions convolved with itself (graphical representation of Eq. (7.40)). The interspike-interval distribtion ($P_0(s)$, thick line) is added sequentially to self-convolutions such as $\int_0^\infty P_0(s')P_0(s-s')ds'$ (dashed lines). The partial sums (solid lines) gradually converge to the autocorrelation function ($C_+(s)$, dotted line).

For $\omega = 0$, the Fourier integral over the right-hand side of Eq. (7.40) diverges, since $\int_0^\infty P_0(s)ds = 1$. If we add the diverging term from Eq. (7.38), we arrive at

$$\hat{C}_{ii}(\omega) = v_i \,\mathrm{Re}\left\{\frac{1+\hat{P}_0(\omega)}{1-\hat{P}_0(\omega)}\right\} + 2\pi v_i^2 \delta(\omega). \tag{7.45}$$

This is a standard result of stationary renewal theory (Cox and Lewis, 1966) which has been repeatedly applied to neuronal spike trains (Edwards and Wakefield, 1993; Bair *et al.*, 1994).

Example: Stationary Poisson process

In Sections 7.2.1 and 7.5 we have already discussed the Poisson neuron from the perspective of mean firing rate and renewal theory, respectively. The autocorrelation of a Poisson process is

$$C_{ii}(s) = v\,\delta(s) + v^2. \tag{7.46}$$

We want to show that Eq. (7.46) follows from Eq. (7.40).

Since the interval distribution of a Poisson process is exponential [see Eq. (7.16) with $\Delta^{\mathrm{abs}} = 0$], we can evaluate the integrals on the right-hand side of Eq. (7.40) in a straightforward manner. The result is

$$C_+(s) = v\,e^{-vs}\left[1 + vs + \frac{1}{2}(vs)^2 + \cdots\right] = v. \tag{7.47}$$

Hence, with Eq. (7.42), we obtain the autocorrelation function (7.46) of a homogeneous Poisson process. The Fourier transform of Eq. (7.46) yields a flat spectrum with a δ peak at zero:

$$\hat{C}_{ii}(\omega) = v + 2\pi v^2 \delta(\omega). \tag{7.48}$$

The result could have also been obtained by evaluating Eq. (7.45).

Example: Poisson process with absolute refractoriness

We return to the Poisson process with absolute refractoriness defined in Eq. (7.16). Apart from an absolute refractory time Δ^{abs}, the neuron fires with rate r. For $\omega \neq 0$, Eq. (7.45) yields the noise spectrum

$$\hat{C}_{ii}(\omega) = v \left\{ 1 + 2\frac{v^2}{\omega^2}[1 - \cos(\omega \Delta^{\text{abs}})] + 2\frac{v}{\omega}\sin(\omega \Delta^{\text{abs}}) \right\}^{-1}; \qquad (7.49)$$

see Fig. 7.12b. In contrast to the stationary Poisson process Eq. (7.46), the noise spectrum of a neuron with absolute refractoriness $\Delta^{\text{abs}} > 0$ is no longer flat. In particular, for $\omega \to 0$, the noise spectrum is *decreased* by a factor $[1 + 2(v\Delta^{\text{abs}}) + (v\Delta^{\text{abs}})^2]^{-1}$. Eq. (7.49) and generalizations thereof have been used to fit the power spectrum of, e.g., auditory neurons (Edwards and Wakefield, 1993) and MT (middle temporal) neurons (Bair *et al.*, 1994).

Can we understand the decrease in the noise spectrum for $\omega \to 0$? The mean interval of a Poisson neuron with absolute refractoriness is $\langle s \rangle = \Delta^{\text{abs}} + r^{-1}$. Hence the mean firing rate is

$$v = \frac{r}{1 + \Delta^{\text{abs}} r}. \qquad (7.50)$$

For $\Delta^{\text{abs}} = 0$ we retrieve the stationary Poisson process Eq. (7.3) with $v = r$. For finite Δ^{abs} the firing is more regular than that of a Poisson process with the same mean rate v. We note that, for finite $\Delta^{\text{abs}} > 0$, the mean firing rate remains bounded even if $r \to \infty$. The neuron then fires regularly with period Δ^{abs}. Because the spike train of a neuron with refractoriness is more regular than that of a Poisson neuron with the same mean rate, the spike count over a long interval, and hence the spectrum for $\omega \to 0$, is less noisy. This means that Poisson neurons with absolute refractoriness can transmit slow signals more reliably than a simple Poisson process.

7.5.4 Input-dependent renewal theory (*)

It is possible to use the renewal concept in a broader sense and define a renewal process as a system where the state at time t (and hence the probability of generating an event at t), depends both on the time that has passed since the last event (i.e., the firing time $\hat{t}$) *and* the input $I(t')$, $\hat{t} < t' < t$, that the system received since the last event. Input-dependent renewal systems are also called modulated renewal processes (Reich *et al.*, 1998), non-stationary renewal systems (Gerstner, 1995, 2000), or inhomogeneous Markov interval processes (Kass and Ventura, 2001). The aim of a theory of input-dependent renewal systems is to predict the probability density

$$P_I(t|\hat{t}) \qquad (7.51)$$

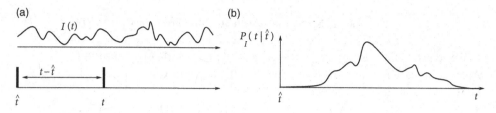

Fig. 7.14 Input-dependent interval distribution. (a) A neuron, stimulated by the current $I(t)$ has emitted a first spike at $\hat{t}$. (b) The interval distribution $P_I(t|\hat{t})$ gives the probability density that the next spike occurs after an interval $t - \hat{t}$.

of the next event to occur at time t, given the timing $\hat{t}$ of the last event *and* the input $I(t')$ for $\hat{t} < t' < t$; see Fig. 7.14. The relation between hazard, survivor function, and interval distribution for the input-dependent case is the same as the one given in Eqs. (7.25)–(7.28). The generalization to a time-dependent renewal theory will be useful later on, in Chapter 9.

The lower index I of $P_I(t|\hat{t})$ is intended to remind the reader that the probability density $P_I(t|\hat{t})$ depends on the time course of the input $I(t')$ for $t' < t$. Since $P_I(t|\hat{t})$ is conditioned on the spike at $\hat{t}$, it can be called a spike-triggered spike density. We interpret $P_I(t|\hat{t})$ as the distribution of interspike intervals in the presence of an input current I or as the *input-dependent interval distribution*. For stationary input, $P_I(t|\hat{t})$ reduces to $P_0(t - \hat{t})$.

7.6 The problem of neural coding

We have discussed in the preceding sections measures to quantify neural spike train data. This includes measures of interval distribution, autocorrelation, noise spectrum, but also simple measures such as the firing rate. All of these measures are useful tools for an experimenter who plans to study a neural system. A completely different question, however, is whether neurons transmit information by using any of these quantities as a neural code.

In this section we critically review the notion of rate codes, and contrast rate coding schemes with spike codes.

7.6.1 Limits of rate codes

The successful application of rate concepts to neural data does not necessarily imply that the neuron itself uses a rate code. Let us look at the limitations of the spike count measure and the PSTH.

Limitations of the spike count code

An experimenter as an external observer can evaluate and classify neuronal firing by a spike count measure – but is this really the code used by neurons in the brain? In other words, is a cortical neuron which receives signals from a sensory neuron only looking at and reacting to the number of spikes it receives in a time window of, say, 500 ms? We will approach this question from a modeling point of view later on in the book. Here we discuss some critical experimental evidence.

From behavioral experiments it is known that reaction times are often rather short. A fly can react to new stimuli and change the direction of flight within 30–40 ms; see the discussion in (Rieke *et al.*, 1997). This is not long enough for counting spikes and averaging over some long time window. The fly has to respond after a postsynaptic neuron has received one or two spikes. Humans can recognize visual scenes in just a few hundred milliseconds (Thorpe *et al.*, 1996), even though recognition is believed to involve several processing steps. Again, this does not leave enough time to perform temporal averages on each level.

From the point of view of rate coding, spikes are just a convenient way to transmit the analog output variable v over long distances. In fact, the best coding scheme to transmit the value of the rate v would be by a regular spike train with intervals $1/v$. In this case, the rate could be reliably measured after only two spikes. From the point of view of rate coding, the irregularities encountered in real spike trains of neurons in the cortex must therefore be considered as noise. In order to get rid of the noise and arrive at a reliable estimate of the rate, the experimenter has to average over a larger number of spikes.

Temporal averaging can work well in cases where the stimulus is constant or slowly varying and does not require a fast reaction of the organism – and this is the situation encountered in many experimental protocols. Real-world input, however, is rarely stationary, but often changing on a fast time scale. For example, even when viewing a static image, humans perform saccades, rapid changes of the direction of gaze. The image projected onto the retinal photo receptors changes therefore every few hundred milliseconds – and with each new image the retinal photo receptors change the response (Fig. 7.16c). Since, in a changing environment, a postsynaptic neuron does not have the time to perform a temporal average over many (noisy) spikes, we consider next whether the PSTH could be used by a neuron to estimate a time-dependent firing rate.

Limitations of the PSTH

The obvious problem with the PSTH is that it needs several trials to build up. Therefore it cannot be the decoding scheme used by neurons in the brain. Consider, for example, a frog that wants to catch a fly. It cannot wait for the insect to fly repeatedly along exactly the same trajectory. The frog has to base its decision on a single run – each fly and each trajectory is different.

Nevertheless, the PSTH measure of the instantaneous firing rate can make sense if there are large populations of similar neurons that receive the same stimulus. Instead of recording from a population of N neurons in a single run, it is experimentally easier to record from a single neuron and average over N repeated runs. Thus, a neural code based on the PSTH relies on the implicit assumption that there are always populations of neurons with similar properties.

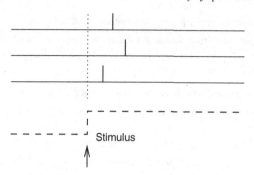

Fig. 7.15 Time-to-first-spike. The spike train of three neurons are shown. The third neuron from the top is the first one to fire a spike after the stimulus onset (arrow). The dashed line indicates the time course of the stimulus.

Limitations of rate as a population average

A potential difficulty with the definition (7.11) of the firing rate as an average over a population of neurons is that we have formally required a homogeneous population of neurons with identical connections, which is hardly realistic. Real populations will always have a certain degree of heterogeneity both in their internal parameters and in their connectivity pattern. Nevertheless, rate as a population activity (of suitably defined pools of neurons) may be a useful coding principle in many areas of the brain.

For inhomogeneous populations, the definition (7.11) may be replaced by a weighted average over the population. To give an example of a weighted average in an inhomogeneous population, we suppose that we are studying a population of neurons which respond to a stimulus x. We may think of x as the location of the stimulus in input space. Neuron i responds best to stimulus x_i, another neuron j responds best to stimulus x_j. In other words, we may say that the spikes of a neuron i "represent" an input vector x_i and those of j an input vector x_j. In a large population, many neurons will be active simultaneously when a new stimulus x is represented. The location of this stimulus can then be estimated from the weighted population average

$$x^{\text{est}}(t) = \frac{\int_t^{t+\Delta t} \sum_j \sum_f x_j \, \delta(t - t_j^f) \, dt}{\int_t^{t+\Delta t} \sum_j \sum_f \delta(t - t_j^f) \, dt}.$$ (7.52)

Both numerator and denominator are closely related to the population activity (7.11). The estimate (7.52) has been successfully used for an interpretation of neuronal activity in primate motor cortex (Georgopoulos *et al.*, 1986) and hippocampus (Wilson and McNaughton, 1993). It is, however, not completely clear whether postsynaptic neurons really evaluate the fraction (7.52) – a potential problem for a neuronal coding and decoding scheme lies in the normalization by division.

7.6.2 Candidate temporal codes

Rate coding in the sense of a population average is one of many candidate coding schemes that could be implemented and used by neurons in the brain. In this section, we introduce some potential coding strategies based on spike timing.

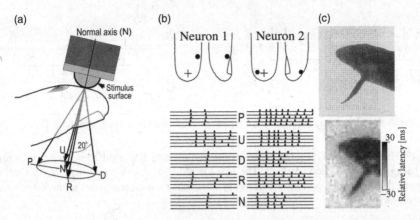

Fig. 7.16 Time-to-first-spike. (a) Touching the finger tip with a sharp object can be quantified by a force vector with total strength in the normal direction (N), possibly superimposed with a tangential component in one of four possible directions (P, U, D, R). (b) Spike response to onset of touch force in the five possible direction (P, U, D, R, N). Different stimuli yield different spike latencies which are consistent across the five repetitions. Different neurons have different response patterns (two selected neurons are shown). The location where stimulation yields maximal response is shown with a filled circle. (c) (Top) Presentation of an image on the retina. The grid of recording electrodes is indicated by dots. (Bottom) The latency of the first spike detected at each electrode reflects the original image. Each pixel corresponds to one recorded neuron. (a) and (b) modified from Johansson and Birznieks (2004), (c) is modified from Gollisch and Meister (2008) with permission from AAAS.

Time-to-first-spike: latency code

Let us study a neuron which abruptly receives a new constant input at time t_0. For example, a neuron might be driven by an external stimulus which is suddenly switched on at time t_0. This seems to be somewhat artificial, but even in a realistic situation abrupt changes in the input are quite common. When we look at a picture, our gaze jumps from one point to the next. After each saccade, the photo receptors in the retina receive a new visual input. Information about the onset of a saccades should easily be available in the brain and could serve as an internal reference signal. We can then imagine a code where for each neuron the timing of the *first* spike after the reference signal contains all information about the new stimulus. A neuron which fires shortly after the reference signal is interpreted as a strong stimulation of this neuron, whereas firing somewhat later would signal a weaker stimulation; see Fig. 7.15.

In a pure version of this coding scheme, each neuron needs to fire only a single spike to transmit information. If it emits several spikes, only the first spike after the reference signal counts. All following spikes would be irrelevant. To implement a clean version of such a coding scheme, we imagine that each neuron is shut off by inhibition as soon as it has fired a spike. Inhibition ends with the onset of the next stimulus (e.g., after the next saccade). After the release from inhibition the neuron is ready to emit its next spike, which now transmits information about the new stimulus. Since each neuron in such a scenario

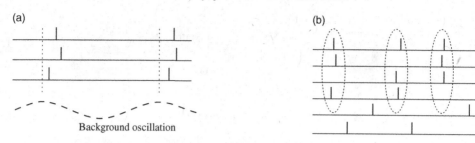

Fig. 7.17 Phase and synchrony. (a) Phase coding: the neurons fire at different phases with respect to the background oscillation (dashed). The phase could code relevant information. (b) Coding by synchrony: the upper four neurons are nearly synchronous: two other neurons at the bottom are not synchronized with the others.

transmits exactly one spike per stimulus, it is clear that only the timing conveys information and not the number of spikes.

Experimental evidence indicates that a coding scheme based on the latency of the first spike transmit a large amount of information. For example, touch sensors in the finger tip encode the strength and direction of the touch in the timing of the first spike emitted by each neuron (Fig. 7.16). Similarly, the relative latency of first spikes of retinal neurons encode the image projected on the retina (Fig. 7.16c). In a slightly different context coding by first spikes has been discussed by Thorpe *et al.* (1996). Thorpe argues that the brain does not have time to evaluate more than one spike from each neuron per processing step. Therefore the first spike should contain most of the relevant information, which is read out by neurons further down the processing chain. Using information-theoretic measures on their experimental data, several groups have shown that most of the information about a new stimulus is indeed conveyed during the first 20 or 50 milliseconds after the onset of the neuronal response (Optican and Richmond, 1987; Tovee and Rolls, 1995).

Phase

We can apply a code by "time to first spike" also in the situation where the reference signal is not a single event, but a periodic signal. In the hippocampus, in the olfactory system, and also in other areas of the brain, oscillations of some global variable (for example the population activity) are quite common. These oscillations could serve as an internal reference signal. Neuronal spike trains could then encode information in the phase of a pulse with respect to the background oscillation. If the input does not change between one cycle and the next, then the same pattern of phases repeats periodically; see Fig. 7.17a.

The concept of coding by phases has been studied by several different groups. There is, for example, evidence that the phase of a spike during an oscillation in the hippocampus of the rat conveys information on the spatial location of the animal which is not fully accounted for by the firing rate of the neuron (O'Keefe and Recce, 1993).

Correlations and synchrony

We can also use spikes from other neurons as the reference signal for a spike code. For example, synchrony of a pair or of many neurons could signify special events and convey information which is not contained in the firing rate of the neurons; see Fig. 7.17b. One famous idea is that synchrony could mean "belonging together." Consider, for example, a complex scene consisting of several objects. It is represented in the brain by the activity of a large number of neurons. Neurons that represent the same object could be "labeled" by the fact that they fire synchronously (von der Malsburg, 1981; Eckhorn *et al.*, 1988; Gray and Singer, 1989).

More generally, not only synchrony but any precise spatio-temporal pulse pattern could be a meaningful event. For example, a spike pattern of three neurons, where neuron 1 fires at some arbitrary time t_1 followed by neuron 2 at time $t_1 + \delta_{12}$ and by neuron 3 at $t_1 + \delta_{13}$, might represent a certain stimulus condition. The same three neurons firing with different relative delays might signify a different stimulus. The relevance of precise spatio-temporal spike patterns has been studied intensively by Abeles (1991). Similarly, but on a somewhat coarse time scale, correlations of auditory and visual neurons are found to be stimulus dependent and might convey information beyond that contained in the firing rate alone (deCharms and Merzenich, 1996; Steinmetz *et al.*, 2000).

Stimulus reconstruction and reverse correlation

Let us consider a neuron which is driven by a time-dependent stimulus $s(t)$. Every time a spike occurs, we note the time course of the stimulus in a time window of about 100 ms immediately before the spike. Averaging the results over several spikes yields the typical time course of the stimulus just before a spike (de Boer and Kuyper, 1968). Such a procedure is called a "reverse correlation" approach; see Fig. 7.18. In contrast to the PSTH experiment sketched in Section 7.2.2 where the experimenter averages the neuron's response over several trials with the same stimulus, reverse correlation means that the experimenter averages the input under the condition of an identical response, i.e., a spike. In other words, it is a spike-triggered average (see, e.g., de Ruyter van Stevenhick and Bialek 1988; Rieke *et al.* 1997). The results of the reverse correlation, i.e., the typical time course of the stimulus that has triggered a spike, can be interpreted as the "meaning" of a single spike. Reverse correlation techniques have made it possible to measure, for example, the spatio-temporal characteristics of neurons in the visual cortex (Eckhorn *et al.*, 1993; DeAngelis *et al.*, 1995).

With a somewhat more elaborate version of this approach, W. Bialek and his coworkers have been able to "read" the neural code of the H1 neuron in the fly and to reconstruct a time-dependent stimulus (Bialek *et al.*, 1991; Rieke *et al.*, 1997). Here we give a simplified version of their argument.

Results from reverse correlation analysis suggest that each spike signifies the time course of the stimulus preceding the spike. If this is correct, a reconstruction of the complete time course of the stimulus $s(t)$ from the set of firing times $\mathcal{F} = \{t^{(1)}, \dots t^{(n)}\}$ should be

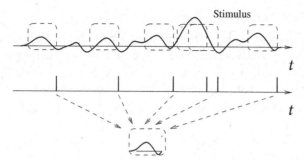

Stimulus

t

t

Fig. 7.18 Reverse correlation technique (schematic). The stimulus in the top trace has caused the spike train shown immediately below. The time course of the stimulus just before the spikes (dashed boxes) has been averaged to yield the typical time course (bottom).

possible; see Fig. 7.19. As a simple test of this hypothesis, Bialek and coworkers have studied a linear reconstruction. A spike at time t^f gives a contribution $\kappa(t - t^f)$ to the estimation $s^{\text{est}}(t)$ of the time course of the stimulus. Here, $t^f \in \mathcal{F}$ is one of the firing times and $\kappa(t - t^f)$ is a kernel which is nonzero during some time before and around t^f; see Fig. 7.19b. A linear estimate of the stimulus is

$$s^{\text{est}}(t) = \sum_{f=1}^{n} \kappa(t - t^f). \tag{7.53}$$

The form of the kernel κ was determined through optimization so that the average reconstruction error $\int dt [s(t) - s^{\text{est}}(t)]^2$ was minimal. The quality of the reconstruction was then tested on additional data which was not used for the optimization. Surprisingly enough, the simple linear reconstruction (7.53) gave a fair estimate of the time course of the stimulus even though the stimulus varied on a time scale comparable to the typical interspike interval (Bialek *et al.*, 1991; Rieke *et al.*, 1997). This reconstruction method shows nicely that information about a time-dependent input can indeed be conveyed by spike timing. Chapter 11 will revisit the spike train decoding in the presence of refractoriness and adaptation.

Rate versus temporal codes (*)

The dividing line between spike codes and firing rates is not always as clearly drawn as it may seem at first sight. Some codes which were first proposed as pure examples of pulse codes have later been interpreted as variations of rate codes. For example, the stimulus reconstruction (7.53) with kernels seems to be a clear example of a spike code. Nevertheless, it is also not so far from a rate code based on spike counts (Abbott, 1994; Theunissen and Miller, 1995). To see this, consider a spike count measure with a running time window $K(.)$. We can estimate the rate v at time t by

$$v(t) = \frac{\int K(\tau) S(t - \tau) d\tau}{\int K(\tau) d\tau}, \tag{7.54}$$

where $S(t) = \sum_{f=1}^{n} \delta(t - t^f)$ is the spike train under consideration. The integrals run from minus to plus infinity. For a rectangular time window $K(\tau) = 1$ for $-T/2 < \tau < T/2$ and zero otherwise, (7.54) reduces exactly to our definition of a rate as a spike count measure in Eq. (7.1).

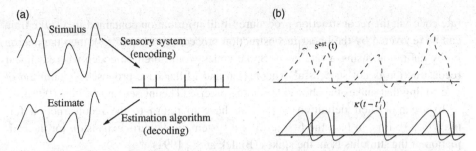

Fig. 7.19 Reconstruction of a stimulus (schematic). (a) A stimulus evokes a spike train of a neuron. The time course of the stimulus may be estimated from the spike train; redrawn after Rieke et al., (1996). (b) In the framework of linear stimulus reconstruction, the estimation $s^{est}(t)$ (dashed) is the sum of the contributions κ (solid lines) of all spikes.

The time window in (7.54) can be made rather short so that at most a few spikes fall into the interval T. Furthermore, there is no need for the window $K(.)$ to be symmetric and rectangular. We might just as well take an asymmetric time window with smooth borders. Moreover, we can perform the integration over the δ-function, which yields

$$v(t) = c \sum_{f=1}^{n} K(t - t^f), \tag{7.55}$$

where $c = [\int K(s)ds]^{-1}$ is a constant. Except for the constant c (which sets the overall scale to units of 1 over time), the generalized rate formula (7.55) is now identical to the reconstruction formula (7.53). In other words, the linear reconstruction is just the firing rate measured with a cleverly optimized time window.

Similarly, a code based on the "time-to-first-spike" is also consistent with rate coding. If, for example, the mean firing rate of a neuron is high for a given stimulus, then the first spike is expected to occur early. If the rate is low, the first spike is expected to occur later. Thus the timing of the first spike contains a lot of information about the underlying rate.

The discussion of whether or not to call a given code a rate code is still ongoing. What is important, in our opinion, is to have a coding scheme which allows neurons to quickly respond to stimulus changes. A naïve spike count code with a long time window is unable to do this, but a code based on population activities introduced above and many of the other codes are. The name of such a code, whether it is deemed a rate code or not is of minor importance.

Example: Towards a definition of rate codes

We have seen above in Eq. (7.55) that stimulus reconstruction with a linear kernel can be seen as a special instance of a rate code. This suggests a formal definition of a rate code via the reconstruction procedure: if all information contained in a spike train can be recovered by the linear reconstruction procedure of Eq. (7.53), then the neuron is, by definition, using a rate code. Spike codes would then be codes where a linear reconstruction is not successful. Theunissen and Miller have proposed a definition of rate coding that makes the above ideas more precise (Theunissen and Miller, 1995).

To see how their definition works, we have to return to the reconstruction formula (7.53). It is, in fact, the first term of a systematic Volterra expansion for the estimation of the stimulus from the spikes (Bialek *et al.*, 1991)

$$s^{\text{est}}(t) = \sum_f \kappa_1(t - t^f) + \sum_{f,f'} \kappa_2(t - t^f, t - t^{f'}) + \cdots. \tag{7.56}$$

For a specific neuron, inclusion of higher-order terms $\kappa_2, \kappa_3, \ldots$ may or may not improve the quality of the estimation. For most neurons where the reconstruction has been carried through, it seems that the higher-order terms do not contribute a large amount of information (Rieke *et al.*, 1997). The neurons would then be classified as rate coding.

Let us now suppose that the reconstruction procedure indicates a significant contribution of the second-order term. Does this exclude rate coding? Unfortunately this is not the case. We have to exclude two other possibilities. Firstly, we might have chosen a suboptimal stimulus. A neuron might, for example, encode the variable x by a rate code, so that a nearly perfect linear reconstruction of x would be possible,

$$x(t) \approx x^{\text{est}} = \sum_{f=1}^n \kappa_1(t - t^f). \tag{7.57}$$

But if we chose a stimulus $s = x^2$ instead of x, then the reconstruction for s^{est} would involve second-order terms, even though the neuron is really using rate code.

Secondly, according to Theunissen and Miller (1995) a spike code should show a temporal structure that is more precise than the temporal structure of the stimulus. The fact that neurons show precise and reliable spike timing as such is, for them, not sufficient to classify the neuron as a temporal encoder, since the neuronal precision could just be the image of precise temporal input. For a more quantitative treatment, let us consider a stimulus with cut-off frequency ω. In order to exclude the possibility that the timing is induced by the stimulus, Theunissen and Miller propose to consider the Fourier spectrum of the higher-order reconstruction kernels. If the Fourier transform of the higher-order kernels contains frequencies less than ω only, then the code is a rate code. If higher-order kernels are significant and contain frequencies above ω, then the information is encoded temporally. A positive example of a spike code (or of "temporal encoding") according to this definition would be the code by correlation and synchrony introduced above. Another example would be the phase code, in particular if the number of spikes per cycle is independent of the stimulus strength.

7.7 Summary

Variability of spike timing is a common phenomenon in biological neurons. Variability can be quantified by the C_V value of interval distributions, by the Fano factor of the spike count, or by the repeatability of spike timings between one trial and the next. Whether the variability represents noise or uncontrolled components of a signal which is not well characterized is a topic of debate. Experiments show that a neuron *in vitro*, or in one of the sensory areas *in vivo*, shows highly reliable spike timings if driven by a strong stimulus with large-amplitude fluctuations of the signal. Spontaneous activity *in vivo*, however, is unreliable and exhibits large variability of interspike intervals and spike counts.

The simplest stochastic description of neuronal firing is a Poisson process. However, since each spike firing in a Poisson process is independent of earlier spikes, Poisson firing cannot account for refractoriness. In renewal processes, the probability of firing depends on the time since the last spike. Therefore refractoriness is taken care of. The independent events are the interspike intervals which are drawn from an interval distribution $P_0(s)$. Knowledge of $P_0(s)$ is equivalent to knowing the survivor function $S_0(s)$ or the hazard $\rho_0(s)$. In neurons showing strong adaptation, interspike intervals are *not* independent so that renewal theory is not sufficient. Moreover, standard renewal theory is limited to stationary stimuli, whereas real-world stimuli have a strong temporal component – the solution is then a time-dependent generalization of renewal theory which we will encounter in Chapter 14.

A description of neuronal spike trains in terms of firing rates or interval distributions does not imply that neurons use the firing rate (or interval distribution) to transmit signals. In fact, neither the spike count (averaging over time) nor the time-dependent rate of the PSTH (averaging over trials) can be the neural code of sensory processing because they are too slow given known reaction times. A firing rate in the sense of a population activity, defined as the instantaneous average of spikes across a population of neurons with similar properties, is, however, a candidate neural code. Other candidate codes, with some experimental support are a latency code (time-to-first-spike), or a phase code.

In models, noise is usually added ad hoc to account for the observed variability of neural spike trains: two standard ways of adding noise to neuron models will be presented in the next two chapters. But even without explicit noise source, neural activity may look noisy if the neuron is embedded in a large deterministic network with fixed random connectivity. The analysis of such networks will be the topic of Part III.

Literature

A review of noise in the nervous system with a focus on internal noise sources can be found in Faisal *et al.* (2008). Analysis of spike trains in terms of stochastic point processes has a long tradition (Perkel *et al.*, 1967a; Gerstein and Perkel, 1972) and often involves concepts from renewal theory (Cox and Lewis, 1966). Some principles of spike-train analysis with an emphasis on modern results have been reviewed by Gabbiani and Koch (1998) and Rieke *et al.* (1997). For a discussion of the variability of interspike intervals see the debate of Shadlen and Newsome (1994), Softky (1995), and Bair and Koch (1996); these papers also give a critical discussion of the concept of temporal averaging. An accessible mathematical treatment of the inhomogeneous Poisson model in the context of neuronal signals is given in Rieke *et al.* (1997). The same book can also be recommended for its excellent discussion of rate codes, and their limits, as well as the method of stimulus reconstruction (Rieke *et al.*, 1997).

Exercises

1. **Poisson process in discrete and continuous time**. *We consider a Poisson neuron model in discrete time. In every small time interval Δt, the probability that the neuron fires is given by $v \Delta t$. Firing in different time intervals is independent. The limit $\Delta t \to 0$ will be taken only at the end.*
   (a) What is the probability that the neuron does not fire during a time of arbitrarily large length $t = N \Delta t$?
   Hint: Consider first the probability of not firing during a single short interval Δt, and then extend your reasoning to N time steps.
   (b) Suppose that the neuron has fired at time $t = 0$. Calculate the distribution of intervals $P(t)$, i.e., the probability density that the neuron fires its next spike at a time $t = N \Delta t$.
   (c) Start from your results in (a) and (b) and take the limit $N \to \infty$, $\Delta t \to 0$, while keeping t fixed. What is the resulting survivor function $S_0(t)$ and the interval distribution $P_0(s)$ in continuous time?
   (d) Suppose that the neuron is driven by some input. For $t < t_0$, the input is weak, so that its firing rate is $v = 2\,\text{Hz}$. For $t_0 < t < t_1 = t_0 + 100$ ms, the input is strong and the neuron fires at $v = 20\,\text{Hz}$. Unfortunately, however, the onset time t_0 of the strong input is unknown; can an observer, who is looking at the neurons output, detect the period of strong input? How reliably?
   Hint: Calculate the interval distributions for weak and strong stimuli. What is the probability of having a burst consisting of two intervals of less than 20 ms each if the input is weak/strong?

2. **Autocorrelation of a Poisson process in discrete time**. *The autocorrelation*

$$C_{ii}(s) = \langle S_i(t) S_i(t+s) \rangle_t \tag{7.58}$$

   *is defined as the joint probability density of finding a spike at time t **and** a spike at time $t+s$. In Eq. (7.46) we have stated the autocorrelation of the homogeneous Poisson process in continuous time. Derive this result by starting with a Poisson process in discrete time where the probability of firing in a small time interval Δt is given by $v \Delta t$. To do so, take the following steps:*
   (a) What is the joint probability of finding a spike in the bin $[t, t+\Delta t]$ AND in the bin $[t', t'+\Delta t]$ where $t \neq t'$?
   (b) What is the joint probability of finding a spike in the bin $[t, t+\Delta t]$ AND in the bin $[t', t'+\Delta t]$ where $t = t'$?
   (c) What is the probability of finding two spikes in the bin $[t, t+\Delta t]$? Why can this term be neglected in the limit $\Delta t \to 0$?
   (d) Take the limit $\Delta t \to 0$ while keeping t and t' fixed so as to find the autocorrelation function $C_0(s)$ in continuous time.

3. **Repeatability and random coincidences**. *Suppose that a Poisson neuron with a constant rate of 20 Hz emits, in a trial of 5-second duration, 100 spikes at times $t^{(1)}; t^{(2)}; \ldots t^{(100)}$. Afterward, the experiment is repeated and a second spike train with a duration of 5 seconds is observed. How many spikes in the first trial can be expected to coincide with a spike in the second trial? More generally, what percentage of spikes coincide between two trials of a Poisson neuron with arbitrary rate v_0 under the assumption that trials are sufficiently long?*

4. **Spike count and Fano factor.** *A homogeneous Poisson process has a probability to fire in a very small interval Δt equal to $\nu\,\Delta t$.*
   (a) Show that the probability of observing exactly k spikes in the time interval $T = N\Delta t$ is $P_k(T) = [1/k!]\,(\nu T)^k \exp(-\nu T)$.
   Hint: Start in discrete time and write the probability of observing k events in N slots using the binomial distribution: $P(k;N) = [N!/k!(N-k)!]\,p^k\,(1-p)^{N-k}$ where p is the probability of firing in a time bin of duration Δt. Take the continuous time limit with Stirling's formula $N! \approx (N/e)^N$.
   (b) Repeat the above argument for an inhomogeneous Poisson process.
   (c) Show for the inhomogeneous Poisson process that the mean spike count in an interval of duration T is $\langle k \rangle = \int_0^T \nu(t)\,dt$.
   (d) Calculate the variance of the spike count and the Fano factor for the inhomogeneous Poisson process.

5. **From interval distribution to hazard.** *During stimulation with a stationary stimulus, interspike intervals in a long spike train are found to be independent and given by the distribution*

$$P(t|t') = \frac{(t-t')}{\tau^2} \exp\left(-\frac{t-t'}{\tau}\right) \tag{7.59}$$

   for $t > t'$.
   (a) Calculate the survivor function $S(t|t')$, i.e., the probability that the neuron survives from time t' to t without firing.
   Hint: You can use $\int_0^y x e^{ax}\,dx = e^{ay}[ay-1]/a^2$.
   (b) Calculate the hazard function $\rho(t|t')$, i.e., the stochastic intensity that the neuron fires, given that its last spike was at t' and interpret the result: what are the signs of refractoriness?
   (c) A spike train starts at time 0 and we have observed a first spike at time t_1. We are interested in the probability that the nth spike occurs around time $t_n = t_1 + s$. With this definition of spike labels, calculate the probability density $P(t_3|t_1)$ that the third spike occurs around time t_3.

6. **Gamma distribution.** *Stationary interval distributions can often be fitted by a Gamma distribution (for $s > 0$)*

$$P(s) = \frac{1}{(k-1)!} \frac{s^{k-1}}{\tau^k} e^{-s/\tau}, \tag{7.60}$$

   where k is a positive natural number. We consider in the following $k=1$.
   (a) Calculate the mean interval $\langle s \rangle$ and the mean firing rate.
   (b) Assume that intervals are independent and calculate the power spectrum.
   Hint: Use Eq. (7.45).

7. **C_V value of Gamma distribution.** *Stationary interval distributions can often be fitted by a Gamma distribution*

$$P(s) = \frac{1}{(k-1)!} \frac{s^{k-1}}{\tau^k} e^{-s/\tau}, \tag{7.61}$$

   where k is a positive natural number.
   Calculate the coefficient of variation C_V for $k = 1, 2, 3$. Interpret your result.

8. **Poisson with dead time as a renewal process.** *Consider a process where spikes are generated with rate ρ_0, but after each spike there is a dead time of duration Δ^{abs}. More precisely, we have a renewal process*

$$\rho(t|\hat{t}) = \rho_0 \quad \text{for } t > \hat{t} + \Delta^{abs}, \tag{7.62}$$

   and zero otherwise.
   (a) Calculate the interval distribution, using Eqs. ((7.26)) and ((7.27)).
   (b) Calculate the Fano factor.
   (c) If a first spike occurred at time $t = 0$, what is the probability that a further spike (there could be other spikes in between) occurs at $t = x\Delta^{abs}$ where $x = 0.5, 1.5, 2.5$.

8

Noisy input models: barrage of spike arrivals

Neurons in the brain receive input from thousands of other, presynaptic neurons, which emit action potentials and send their spikes to their postsynaptic targets. From the perspective of a postsynaptic neuron receiving a barrage of spikes, spike arrival times may look completely random, even under the assumption that presynaptic neurons generate their spikes by a deterministic process. Indeed, as we have seen in the preceding chapter, internal noise sources of a cell, such as spontaneous opening of ion channels, do not account for all the variability of spike-trains encountered in freely behaving animals *in vivo*. Rather, it is likely that a large fraction of the apparent variability is generated by the network. Modeling studies confirm that networks with fixed random connectivity can lead to chaos on the microscopic level, so that spike arrival times appear to be random even if generated by a deterministic network.

In this chapter, we discuss the consequences of stochastic spike arrivals for modeling. The "noise" generated by the network is often described by a noise term in the differential equation of the membrane voltage (Section 8.1). Such a noise term, typically modeled as white noise or colored noise, can be derived in a framework of stochastic spike arrival, as shown in Section 8.2. Stochastic spike arrival leads to fluctuations of the membrane potential which will be discussed in the case of a passive membrane (Section 8.2.1) – or, more generally, for neuron models in the subthreshold regime. In Section 8.3 we discuss the differences between subthreshold and superthreshold stimulation and explain its consequences for spike-train variability. We close the discussion of stochastic spike arrival models in Section 8.4 with a more mathematically oriented exposition of the diffusion limit and the Fokker–Planck equation.

8.1 Noise input

Neurons are driven by an input current $I(t)$ which summarizes the effect of synaptic input from other neurons in the network *in vivo* or the current injected by an experimenter into a cell *in vitro*. Modeling the noisiness of the input amounts to splitting the input current into two components, a deterministic and a stochastic one

$$I(t) = I^{\text{det}}(t) + I^{\text{noise}}(t), \tag{8.1}$$

(a)

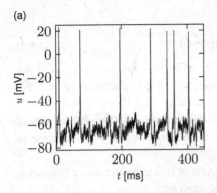

(b)

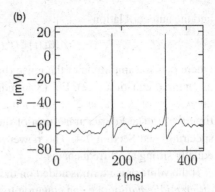

Fig. 8.1 Noisy input. (a). A Hodgkin–Huxley model with parameters as in Chapter 2 driven with white-noise input. (b). The same model driven with colored noise with time constant $\tau_s = 50$ ms. Note that the fluctuations of the membrane potential are slower.

where the deterministic term I^{det} summarizes the part of the current which is known, or at least predictable, while the stochastic term I^{noise} is the unpredictable, or noisy, part of the current.

For example, during an *in vitro* study with intracellular current injection, I^{det} would be the current that is set on the switchboard of the current generator, but the actual current fluctuates around the preset value because of finite temperature. In a neural recording during a visual psychophysics experiment *in vivo*, the part of the input current that does not change across trials with the same visual stimulus would be summarized as I^{det}, while all the remaining inputs to the neuron, which vary from one trial to the next, are treated as noise and summarized as I^{noise}.

For modeling, the noise term is simply added on the right-hand side of the differential equation of the voltage. For example, a nonlinear integrate-and-fire model with noisy input has the voltage equation

$$\tau_m \frac{\mathrm{d}}{\mathrm{d}t} u = f(u) + R I^{\text{det}}(t) + R I^{\text{noise}}(t). \tag{8.2}$$

If u reaches the threshold θ_{reset}, the integration is stopped and the membrane potential reset to u_r. The procedure of adding input noise is completely analogous for biophysical models of the Hodgkin–Huxley type or integrate-and-fire models with adaptation; see Fig. 8.1.

8.1.1 *White noise*

The standard procedure of implementing the noise term $R I^{\text{noise}}$ in the differential equation of the membrane voltage is to formulate it as a "white noise," $R I^{\text{noise}}(t) = \xi(t)$. White noise ξ is a stochastic process characterized by its expectation value,

$$\langle \xi(t) \rangle = 0, \tag{8.3}$$

and the autocorrelation

$$\langle \xi(t)\,\xi(t') \rangle = \sigma^2\,\tau_m\,\delta(t-t')\,, \qquad (8.4)$$

where σ is the amplitude of the noise (in units of voltage) and τ_m the time constant of the differential equation (8.2). Eq. (8.4) indicates that the process ξ is uncorrelated in time: knowledge of the value ξ at time t does not enable us to predict its value at any other time $t' \neq t$. The Fourier transform of the autocorrelation function (8.4) yields the power spectrum; see Section 7.4. The power spectrum of white noise is flat, i.e., the noise is equally strong at all frequencies.

If the white noise term is added on the right-hand side of (8.2), we arrive at a *stochastic differential equation*, i.e., an equation for a stochastic process,

$$\tau_m \frac{\mathrm{d}}{\mathrm{d}t} u(t) = f(u(t)) + R I^{\mathrm{det}}(t) + \xi(t)\,, \qquad (8.5)$$

also called Langevin equation. In Section 8.2 we will indicate how the noise term $\xi(t)$ can be derived from a model of stochastic spike arrival.

In the mathematical literature, instead of a "noise term" $\xi(t)$, a different style of writing the Langevin equation dominates. To arrive at this alternative formulation we first divide both sides of Eq. (8.5) by τ_m and then multiply by the short time step $\mathrm{d}t$,

$$\mathrm{d}u = f(u)\,\frac{\mathrm{d}t}{\tau_m} + R I^{\mathrm{det}}(t)\,\frac{\mathrm{d}t}{\tau_m} + \sigma\mathrm{d}W_t\,, \qquad (8.6)$$

where $\mathrm{d}W_t$ are the increments of the Wiener process in a short time $\mathrm{d}t$, i.e., $\mathrm{d}W_t$ are random variables drawn from a Gaussian distribution with zero mean and variance proportional to the step size $\mathrm{d}t$. This formulation therefore has the advantage that it can be directly used for simulations of the model in discrete time. White noise which is Gaussian distributed is called Gaussian white noise. Note for a numerical implementation of Eq. (8.6) that it is the *variance* of the Gaussian which is proportional to the step size; therefore its standard deviation is proportional to $\sqrt{\mathrm{d}t}$.

Example: Leaky integrate-and-fire model with white noise input

In the case of the leaky integrate-and-fire model (with voltage scale chosen such that the resting potential is at zero), the stochastic differential equation is

$$\tau_m \frac{\mathrm{d}}{\mathrm{d}t} u(t) = -u(t) + R I^{\mathrm{det}}(t) + \xi(t)\,, \qquad (8.7)$$

which is called the Ornstein–Uhlenbeck process (Uhlenbeck and Ornstein, 1930; van Kampen, 1992).

We note that the white noise term on the right-hand side is integrated by a time constant τ_m to yield the membrane potential. Therefore fluctuations of the membrane potential have an autocorrelation with characteristic time τ_m. We will refer to Eq. (8.7) as the Langevin equation of the noisy integrate-and-fire model.

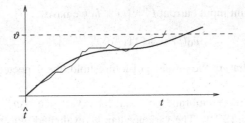

Fig. 8.2 Noisy integration. A stochastic contribution in the input current of an integrate-and-fire neuron causes the membrane potential to drift away from the reference trajectory (thick solid line). The neuron fires if the noisy trajectory (thin line) hits the threshold ϑ.

A realization of a trajectory of the noisy integrate-and-fire model defined by Eq. (8.7) is implemented in discrete time by the iterative update

$$du = (-u + RI^{\text{det}})\frac{dt}{\tau_m} + \sigma\sqrt{dt}\,y, \qquad (8.8)$$

where y is a random number drawn from a zero-mean Gaussian distribution of unit variance (i.e., $dW = \sqrt{dt}\,y$ has variance proportional to dt). Note that for small step size dt and finite current amplitude I^{det}, the voltage steps du are small as well so that, despite the noise, the trajectory becomes smooth in the limit of $dt \to 0$.

A noisy integrate-and-fire neuron is said to fire an action potential whenever the membrane potential u updated via (8.8) reaches the threshold ϑ; see Fig. 8.2. The analysis of Eq. (8.7) in the presence of the threshold ϑ is one of the major topics of this chapter. Before turning to the problem with threshold, we determine now the amplitude of membrane potential fluctuations in the absence of a threshold.

8.1.2 Noisy versus noiseless membrane potential

The Langevin equation of the leaky integrate-and-fire model with white noise input is particularly suitable to compare the membrane potential trajectory of a noisy neuron model with that of a noiseless one.

Let us consider Eq. (8.7) for constant σ. At $t = \hat{t}$ the membrane potential starts at a value $u = u_r = 0$. Since (8.7) is a linear equation, its solution for $t > \hat{t}$ is

$$u(t) = \frac{R}{\tau_m}\int_0^{t-\hat{t}} e^{-s/\tau_m} I^{(\text{det})}(t-s)\,ds + \frac{1}{\tau_m}\int_0^{t-\hat{t}} e^{-s/\tau_m}\xi(t-s)\,ds. \qquad (8.9)$$

Since $\langle \xi(t) \rangle = 0$, the expected trajectory of the membrane potential is

$$u_0(t) = \langle u(t|\hat{t}) \rangle = \frac{R}{\tau_m}\int_0^{t-\hat{t}} e^{-s/\tau_m} I^{(\text{det})}(t-s)\,ds. \qquad (8.10)$$

In particular, for constant input current $I^{(\mathrm{det})}(t) \equiv I_0$ we have

$$u_0(t) = u_\infty \left[1 - e^{-(t-\hat{t})/\tau_m} \right] \tag{8.11}$$

with $u_\infty = R I_0$. Note that, in the absence of a threshold, the expected trajectory is that of the noiseless model.

The fluctuations of the membrane potential have variance $\langle \Delta u^2 \rangle = \langle [u(t|\hat{t}) - u_0(t)]^2 \rangle$ with $u_0(t)$ given by Eq. (8.10). The variance can be evaluated with the help of Eq. (8.9), i.e.,

$$\langle \Delta u^2(t) \rangle = \frac{1}{\tau_m^2} \int_0^{t-\hat{t}} ds \int_0^{t-\hat{t}} ds'\, e^{-s/\tau_m} e^{-s'/\tau_m} \langle \xi(t-s)\,\xi(t-s') \rangle. \tag{8.12}$$

We use $\langle \xi(t-s)\,\xi(t-s') \rangle = \sigma^2\,\tau_m\,\delta(s-s')$ and perform the integration. The result is

$$\langle \Delta u^2(t) \rangle = \frac{1}{2}\sigma^2 \left[1 - e^{-2(t-\hat{t})/\tau_m} \right]. \tag{8.13}$$

Hence, noise causes the actual membrane trajectory to drift away from the noiseless reference trajectory $u_0(t)$. If the threshold is high enough so that firing is a rare event, the typical distance between the actual trajectory and the mean trajectory approaches with time constant $\tau_m/2$ a limiting value

$$\sqrt{\langle \Delta u_\infty^2 \rangle} = \frac{1}{\sqrt{2}}\sigma. \tag{8.14}$$

In proximity to the firing threshold the above arguments break down; however, in the subthreshold regime the mean and the variance of the membrane potential are well approximated by formulas (8.11) and (8.13), respectively. The mean trajectory and the standard deviation of the fluctuations can also be estimated in simulations, as shown in Fig. 8.3 for the leaky and the exponential integrate-and-fire models.

8.1.3 Colored noise

A noise term with a power spectrum which is not flat is called colored noise. Colored noise $I^{\mathrm{noise}}(t)$ can be generated from white noise by suitable filtering. For example, low-pass filtering

$$\tau_s \frac{dI^{\mathrm{noise}}(t)}{dt} = -I^{\mathrm{noise}}(t) + \xi(t), \tag{8.15}$$

where $\xi(t)$ is the white noise process defined above, yields colored noise with reduced power at frequencies above $1/\tau_s$. Eq. (8.15) is another example of an Ornstein–Uhlenbeck process.

To calculate the power spectrum of the colored noise defined in Eq. (8.15), we proceed in two steps. First we integrate (8.15) so as to arrive at

$$I^{\mathrm{noise}}(t) = \int_0^\infty \kappa(s)\,\xi(t-s)\,ds, \tag{8.16}$$

(a)

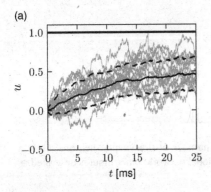

(b)

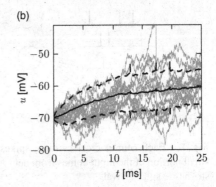

Fig. 8.3 Mean trajectory and fluctuations for (a) the leaky integrate-and-fire model and (b) the exponential integrate-and-fire model driven by white noise superimposed on a constant input that drives the neuron half-way between resting potential and firing threshold. Integration starts at $u = u_r$ and is repeated for 15 trials (gray lines). The solid line indicates mean trajectories and dashed lines indicate one standard deviation around the mean. Both models have a time constant of 10 ms. The threshold is at 1 for the leaky integrate-and-fire neuron (a) and at -50 mV for the exponential integrate-and-fire neuron (b). The numerical threshold is set at $\theta_{\text{reset}} = -30$ mV.

where $\kappa(s)$ is an exponential low-pass filter with time constant τ_s. The autocorrelation function is therefore

$$\langle I^{\text{noise}}(t) I^{\text{noise}}(t') \rangle = \int_0^\infty \int_0^\infty \kappa(s)\,\kappa(s')\,\langle \xi(t-s)\,\xi(t'-s') \rangle \, ds' ds. \tag{8.17}$$

Second, we exploit the definition of the white noise correlation function in (8.4), and find

$$\langle I^{\text{noise}}(t) I^{\text{noise}}(t') \rangle = a \exp\left(-\frac{|t-t'|}{\tau_s} \right) \tag{8.18}$$

with an amplitude factor a. Therefore, knowledge of the input current at time t gives us a hint about the input current shortly afterward, as long as $|t'-t| \ll \tau_s$.

The noise spectrum is the Fourier transform of (8.18). It is flat for frequencies $\omega \ll 1/\tau_s$ and falls off for $\omega > 1/\tau_s$. Sometimes $1/\tau_s$ is called the cut-off frequency.

The colored noise defined in (8.15) is a suitable noise model for synaptic input, if spikes arrive stochastically and synapses have a finite time constant τ_s. The relation of input noise to stochastic spike arrival is the topic of the next section.

8.2 Stochastic spike arrival

A typical neuron, for example, a pyramidal cell in the vertebrate cortex, receives input spikes from thousands of other neurons, which in turn receive input from their presynaptic neurons and so forth; see Fig. 8.4. While it is not impossible to incorporate millions of integrate-and-fire neurons into a huge network model, it is often reasonable to focus the modeling efforts on a specific subset of neurons, for example, a column in the visual cortex, and describe input from other parts of the brain as a stochastic background activity.

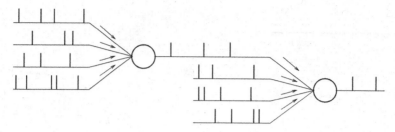

Fig. 8.4 Each neuron receives input spikes from a large number of presynaptic neurons. Only a small portion of the input comes from neurons within the model network; other input is described as stochastic spike arrival.

Let us consider a nonlinear integrate-and-fire neuron with index i that is part of a large network. Its input consists of (i) an external input $I_i^{\text{ext}}(t)$; (ii) input spikes t_j^f from other neurons j of the network; and (iii) stochastic spike arrival t_k^f due to the background activity in other parts of the brain. The membrane potential u_i evolves according to

$$\frac{d}{dt}u_i = \frac{f(u_i)}{\tau_m} + \frac{1}{C}I^{\text{ext}}(t) + \sum_j \sum_{t_j^f} w_{ij}\,\delta(t-t_j^f) + \sum_k \sum_{t_k^f} w_{ik}\,\delta(t-t_k^f), \qquad (8.19)$$

where δ is the Dirac δ-function and w_{ij} is the coupling strength from a presynaptic neuron j in the network to neuron i. Input from background neurons is weighted by the factor w_{ik}. While the firing times t_j^f are generated by the threshold crossings of presynaptic integrate-and-fire neurons, the firing times t_k^f of a background neuron k are generated by a Poisson process with mean rate ν_k.

To simplify the following discussions we adopt three simplifications. First, we focus on a leaky integrate-and-fire neuron and shift the voltage so that the resting potential is at zero. Hence we can set $f(u) = -u$. Second, we concentrate on a *single* neuron receiving stochastic input from background neurons. Hence we can drop the sum over j which represents input from the network and also drop the index i of our specific neuron. We therefore arrive at

$$\frac{d}{dt}u = -\frac{u}{\tau_m} + \frac{1}{C}I^{\text{ext}}(t) + \sum_k \sum_{t_k^f} w_k\,\delta(t-t_k^f). \qquad (8.20)$$

The membrane potential is reset to u_r whenever it reaches the threshold ϑ. Eq. (8.20) is called Stein's model (Stein, 1965, 1967b).

In Stein's model, each input spike generates a postsynaptic potential $\Delta u(t) = w_k \varepsilon(t - t_k^{(f)})$ with $\varepsilon(s) = e^{-s/\tau_m}\Theta(s)$, i.e., the potential jumps upon spike arrival by an amount w_k and decays exponentially thereafter. Integration of Eq. (8.20) yields

$$u(t|\hat{t}) = u_r \exp\left(-\frac{t-\hat{t}}{\tau_m}\right) + \frac{1}{C}\int_0^{t-\hat{t}} \exp\left(-\frac{s}{\tau_m}\right) I(t-s)\,ds + \sum_{k=1}^{N}\sum_{t_k^f} w_k \varepsilon(t-t_k^f) \qquad (8.21)$$

for $t > \hat{t}$ where $\hat{t}$ is the last firing time of the neuron. It is straightforward to generalize the model so as to include a synaptic time constant and work with arbitrary postsynaptic potentials $\varepsilon(s)$ that are generated by stochastic spike arrival; see Fig. 8.5a.

8.2.1 Membrane potential fluctuations caused by spike arrivals

To calculate the fluctuations of the membrane potential caused by stochastic spike arrival, we assume that the firing threshold is relatively high and the input weak so that the neuron does not reach its firing threshold. Hence, we can safely neglect both threshold and reset. The leaky integrate-and-fire model of Stein (Eq. (8.21)) is then equivalent to a model of a passive membrane driven by stochastic spike arrival.

We assume that each input spike evokes a postsynaptic potential $w_0\,\varepsilon(s)$ of the same amplitude and shape, independent of k. The input statistics is assumed to be Poisson, i.e., firing times are independent. Thus, the total input spike train (summed across all synapses)

$$S(t) = \sum_{k=1}^{N} \sum_{t_k^f} \delta(t - t_k^f) \tag{8.22}$$

that arrives at neuron i is a random process with expectation

$$\langle S(t) \rangle = \nu_0 \tag{8.23}$$

and autocorrelation

$$\langle S(t)\,S(t') \rangle - \nu_0^2 = \nu_0\,\delta(t - t'); \tag{8.24}$$

see Eq. (7.46).

Suppose that we start the integration of the passive membrane equation at $t = -\infty$ with initial condition $u_r = 0$. We rewrite Eq. (8.21) using the definition of the spike train in Eq. (8.22)

$$u(t) = \frac{1}{C} \int_0^\infty \exp\left(-\frac{s}{\tau_m}\right) I(t - s)\,\mathrm{d}s + w_0 \int_0^\infty \varepsilon(s)\,S(t - s)\,\mathrm{d}s. \tag{8.25}$$

Obviously, the integration over the δ-function in the last term on the right-hand side is possible and would lead back to the more compact representation $w_0 \sum_{t_k^f} \varepsilon(t - t_k^f)$. The advantage of having the spike train $S(t)$ appear explicitly is that we can exploit the definition of the random process S, in particular, its mean and variance.

We are interested in the mean potential $u_0(t) = \langle u(t) \rangle$ and the variance $\langle \Delta u^2 \rangle = \langle [u(t) - u_0(t)]^2 \rangle$. Using Eqs. (8.23) and (8.24) we find

$$u_0(t) = \frac{1}{C} \int_0^\infty \exp\left(-\frac{s}{\tau_m}\right) I(t - s)\,\mathrm{d}s + w_0\,\nu_0 \int_0^\infty \varepsilon(s)\,\mathrm{d}s \tag{8.26}$$

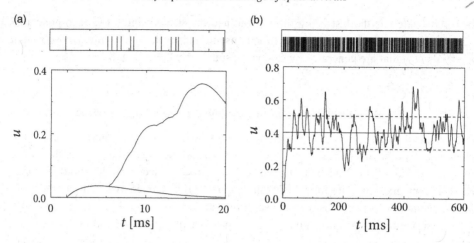

Fig. 8.5 Input spikes arrive stochastically (upper panel) at a mean rate of 1 kHz. (a). Each input spike evokes an excitatory postsynaptic potential (EPSP) $\varepsilon(s) \propto s\exp(-s/\tau)$ with $\tau = 4\,\mathrm{ms}$. The first EPSP (the one generated by the spike at $t = 0$) is plotted. The EPSPs of all spikes sum up and result in a fluctuating membrane potential $u(t)$. (b). Continuation of the simulation shown in (a). The horizontal lines indicate the mean (solid line) and the standard deviation (dashed lines) of the membrane potential.

and

$$\langle \Delta u^2 \rangle = w_0^2 \int_0^\infty \int_0^\infty \varepsilon_0(s)\,\varepsilon_0(s')\,\langle S(t)\,S(t') \rangle \, ds\, ds' - u_0^2$$

$$= w_0^2 v_0 \int_0^\infty \varepsilon^2(s)\, ds. \tag{8.27}$$

In Fig. 8.5 we have simulated a neuron which receives input from $N = 100$ background neurons with rate $v_0 = 10$ Hz. The total spike arrival rate is therefore $v_0 = 1$ kHz. Each spike evokes an EPSP $w_0\,\varepsilon(s) = 0.1\,(s/\tau)\exp(-s/\tau)$ with $\tau = 4$ ms. The evaluation of Eqs. (8.26) and (8.27) for constant input $I = 0$ yields $u_0 = 0.4$ and $\sqrt{\langle \Delta u^2 \rangle} = 0.1$.

Example: Stein's model with step current input

In Stein's model each background spike evokes an EPSP $\varepsilon(s) = e^{-s/\tau_m}$. In addition, we assume a step current input which switches at $t = 0$ from zero to I_0 ($I_0 < 0$).

Mean and fluctuations for Stein's model can be derived by evaluation of Eqs. (8.26) and (8.27) with $\varepsilon(s) = e^{-s/\tau_m}$. The result is

$$u_0 = I_0\left[1 - \exp(-t/\tau_m)\right] + w_0\, v_0\, \tau_m, \tag{8.28}$$

$$\langle \Delta u^2 \rangle = 0.5\, w_0^2\, v_0\, \tau_m. \tag{8.29}$$

Note that with stochastic spike arrival at excitatory synapses, as considered here, mean and variance cannot be changed independently. As we shall see in the next subsection, a

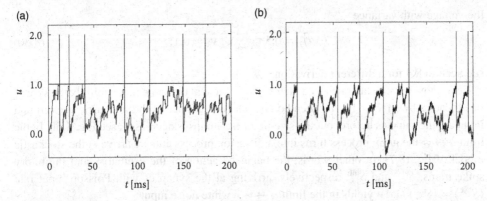

Fig. 8.6 (a). Voltage trajectory of an integrate-and-fire neuron ($\tau_m = 10\,\text{ms}$, $u_r = 0$) driven by stochastic excitatory and inhibitory spike input at $\nu_+ = \nu_- = 1\,\text{kHz}$. Each input spike causes a jump of the membrane potential by $w_\pm = \pm 0.1$. The neuron is biased by a constant current $I_0 = 0.8$ which drives the membrane potential to a value just below the threshold of $\vartheta = 1$ (horizontal line). Spikes are marked by vertical lines. (b). Similar plot as in (a) except that the jumps are smaller ($w_\pm = \pm 0.025$) while rates are higher ($\nu_\pm = 16\,\text{kHz}$).

combination of excitation and inhibition allows us to increase the variance while keeping the mean of the potential fixed.

8.2.2 Balanced excitation and inhibition

Let us suppose that an integrate-and-fire neuron defined by Eq. (8.20) with $\tau_m = 10\,\text{ms}$ receives input from 100 excitatory neurons ($w_k = +0.1$) and 100 inhibitory neurons ($w_k = -0.1$). Each background neuron k fires at a rate of $\nu_k = 10\,\text{Hz}$. Thus, in each millisecond, the neuron receives on average one excitatory and one inhibitory input spike. Each spike leads to a jump of the membrane potential of ± 0.1. The trajectory of the membrane potential is therefore similar to that of a random walk subject to a return force caused by the leak term that drives the membrane potential always back to zero; see Fig. 8.6a.

If, in addition, a constant stimulus $I^{\text{ext}} = I_0 > 0$ is applied so that the mean membrane potential (in the absence of the background spikes) is just below threshold, then the presence of random background spikes may drive u toward the firing threshold. Whenever $u \geq \vartheta$, the membrane potential is reset to $u_r = 0$.

Since firing is driven by the fluctuations of the membrane potential, the interspike intervals vary considerably; see Fig. 8.6. Balanced excitatory and inhibitory spike input could thus contribute to the large variability of interspike intervals in cortical neurons; see Section 8.3.

With the above set of parameters, the mean of the stochastic background input vanishes since $\sum_k w_k \nu_k = 0$. Using the same arguments as in the previous example, we can convince ourselves that the stochastic arrival of background spikes generates fluctuations of the voltage with variance

$$\langle \Delta u^2 \rangle = 0.5 \, \tau_m \sum_k w_k^2 \, v_k = 0.1; \tag{8.30}$$

see Section 8.4 for a different derivation.

Let us now increase all rates by a factor of $a > 1$ and at the same time multiply the synaptic efficacies by a factor $1/\sqrt{a}$. Then both mean and variance of the stochastic background input are the same as before, but the size w_k of the jumps is decreased; see Fig. 8.6b. In the limit $a \to \infty$ the jump process turns into a diffusion process and we arrive at the stochastic model of Eq. (8.7). In other words, the balanced action of the excitatory and inhibitory spike trains, S^{exc} and S^{inh} respectively, arriving at the synapses with Poisson input rate $\langle S^{\mathrm{exc}} \rangle = \langle S^{\mathrm{inh}} \rangle = a v$ yields in the limit $a \to \infty$ a white noise input

$$\frac{w}{\sqrt{a}} S^{\mathrm{exc}} - \frac{w}{\sqrt{a}} S^{\mathrm{inh}} \longrightarrow \xi(t). \tag{8.31}$$

The above transition is called the diffusion limit and will be systematically discussed in Section 8.4. Intuitively, the limit process implies that in each short time interval Δt a large number of excitatory and inhibitory input spikes arrive, each one causing the membrane potential to jump by a tiny amount upward or downward.

Example: Synaptic time constants and colored noise

In contrast to the previous discussion of balanced input, we now assume that each spike arrival generated a current pulse $\alpha(s)$ of finite duration so that the total synaptic input current is

$$RI(t) = w^{\mathrm{exc}} \int_0^\infty \alpha(s) S^{\mathrm{exc}}(t-s) \mathrm{d}s - w^{\mathrm{inh}} \int_0^\infty \alpha(s) S^{\mathrm{inh}}(t-s) \mathrm{d}s. \tag{8.32}$$

If the spike arrival is Poisson with rates $\langle S^{\mathrm{exc}} \rangle = \langle S^{\mathrm{inh}} \rangle = a v$ and the synaptic weights are $w^{\mathrm{exc}} = w^{\mathrm{inh}} = w/\sqrt{a}$, then we can take the limit $a \to \infty$ with no change of mean or variance. The result is colored noise.

An instructive case is $\alpha(s) = (1/\tau_s) \exp(-s/\tau_s)\Theta(s)$ with synaptic time constant τ_s. In the limit $\tau_s \to 0$ we are back to white noise.

8.3 Subthreshold vs. superthreshold regime

One of the aims of noisy neuron models is to mimic the large variability of interspike intervals found, for example, in vertebrate cortex. To arrive at broad interval distributions, it is not just sufficient to introduce noise into a neuron model. Apart from the noise level, other neuronal parameters such as the firing threshold or a bias current have to be tuned so as to make the neuron sensitive to noise. In this section we introduce a distinction between super- and subthreshold stimulation (Abeles, 1991; Shadlen and Newsome, 1994; König *et al.*, 1996; Troyer and Miller, 1997; Bugmann *et al.*, 1997).

An arbitrary time-dependent stimulus $I(t)$ is called subthreshold if it generates a membrane potential that stays – in the absence of noise – below the firing threshold. Owing to noise, however, even subthreshold stimuli can induce action potentials. Stimuli that induce spikes even in a noise-free neuron are called superthreshold.

The distinction between sub- and superthreshold stimuli has important consequences for the firing behavior of neurons in the presence of noise. To see why, let us consider a leaky integrate-and-fire neuron with constant input I_0 for $t > 0$. Starting from $u(t = 0) = u_r$, the trajectory of the membrane potential is

$$u_0(t) = u_\infty \left[1 - e^{-t/\tau_m}\right] + u_r e^{-t/\tau_m}. \tag{8.33}$$

In the absence of a threshold, the membrane potential approaches the value $u_\infty = RI_0$ for $t \to \infty$. If we take the threshold ϑ into account, two cases may be distinguished. First, if $u_\infty < \vartheta$ (subthreshold stimulation), the neuron does not fire at all. Second, if $u_\infty > \vartheta$ (superthreshold stimulation), the neuron fires regularly. The interspike interval is s_0 derived from $u_0(s_0) = \vartheta$. Thus

$$s_0 = \tau \ln \frac{u_\infty - u_r}{u_\infty - \vartheta}. \tag{8.34}$$

We now add diffusive noise. In the superthreshold regime, noise has little influence, except that it broadens the interspike interval distribution. Thus, in the superthreshold regime, the spike train in the presence of diffusive noise is simply a noisy version of the regular spike train of the noise-free neuron.

On the other hand, in the subthreshold regime, the spike train changes qualitatively if noise is switched on; see König *et al.* (1996) for a review. Stochastic background input turns the quiescent neuron into a spiking one. In the subthreshold regime, spikes are generated by the *fluctuations* of the membrane potential, rather than by its mean (Abeles, 1991; Shadlen and Newsome, 1994; Troyer and Miller, 1997; Bugmann *et al.*, 1997; Feng, 2001). The interspike interval distribution is therefore broad; see Fig. 8.7.

Example: Interval distribution in the superthreshold regime

For small noise amplitude $0 < \sigma \ll u_\infty - \vartheta$, and superthreshold stimulation, the interval distribution is centered at the deterministic interspike interval s_0. Its width can be estimated from the width of the fluctuations $\langle \Delta u_\infty^2 \rangle$ of the free membrane potential; see Eq. (8.13). After the reset, the variance of the distribution of membrane potentials is zero and increases slowly thereafter. As long as the mean trajectory is far away from the threshold, the distribution of membrane potentials has a Gaussian shape.

As time goes on, the distribution of membrane potentials is pushed across the threshold. Since the membrane potential crosses the threshold with slope u_0', there is a scaling factor $u_0' = du_0(t)/dt$ evaluated at $t = s_0$ between the (approximately) Gaussian distribution of membrane potential and the interval distribution; see Fig. 8.8. The interval

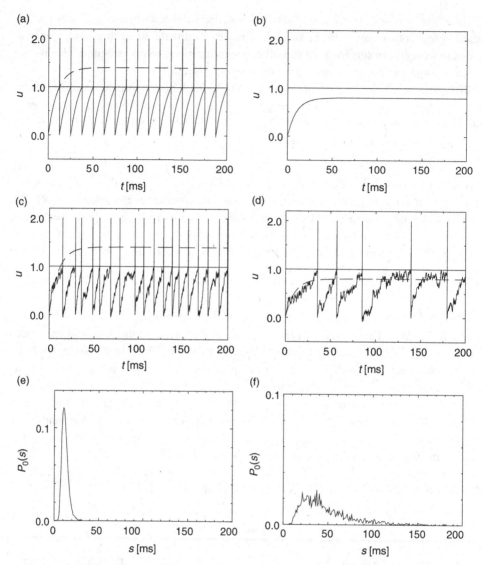

Fig. 8.7 Integrate-and-fire neuron ($\tau_m = 10$ ms) with superthreshold (left column) and subthreshold (right column) stimulation. (a). Without noise, a neuron with superthreshold stimulus I_a fires regularly. Spikes are marked by vertical lines. The threshold is indicated by a horizontal line. The dashed line shows the evolution of the membrane potential in the absence of the threshold. (b). The same neuron with subthreshold stimulation I_b does not fire. (c). If we add stochastic excitatory and inhibitory spike input ($w_\pm = 0.05$ at $\nu_\pm = 1.6$ kHz) to the constant input I_a, the membrane potential drifts away from the noise-free reference trajectory, but firing remains fairly regular. (d). The same sequence of input spikes added to the subthreshold current I_b generates irregular spiking. (e) and (f) Histogram of interspike intervals in (c) and (d), respectively, as an estimator of the interval distribution $P_0(s)$ in the super- and subthreshold regime. The mean interval $\langle s \rangle$ is 12 ms (e) and 50 ms (f); the C_V values are 0.30 and 0.63, respectively.

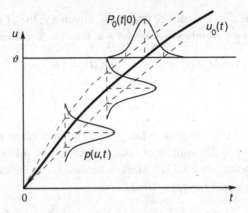

Fig. 8.8 Interval distribution $P_0(t|0)$ for superthreshold stimuli. The membrane potential distribution $p(u,t)$ is shifted across the threshold and generates an interval distribution $P_0(t|0)$ (schematic figure).

distribution is therefore also approximately given by a Gaussian with mean s_0 and width $\sigma/\sqrt{2}u_0'$ (Tuckwell, 1988), i.e.,

$$P_0(t|0) = \frac{1}{\sqrt{\pi}} \frac{u_0'}{\sigma} \exp\left[-\frac{(u_0')^2 (t - s_0)^2}{\sigma^2}\right]. \tag{8.35}$$

8.4 Diffusion limit and Fokker–Planck equation (*)

In this section we analyze the model of stochastic spike arrival defined in Eq. (8.20) and show how to map it to the diffusion model defined in Eq. (8.7) (Gluss, 1967; Johannesma, 1968; Capocelli and Ricciardi, 1971). Suppose that the neuron has fired its last spike at time $\hat{t}$. Immediately after the firing the membrane potential was reset to u_r. Because of the stochastic spike arrival, we cannot predict the membrane potential for $t > \hat{t}$, but we can calculate its probability density, $p(u,t)$. The evolution of the probability density as a function of time is described, in the diffusion limit, by the Fokker–Planck equation which we derive here in the context of a *single* neuron subject to noisy input. In Part III (Section 13.1.1) the Fokker–Planck equation will be introduced systematically in the context of populations of neurons.

For the sake of simplicity, we set for the time being $I^{\text{ext}} = 0$ in Eq. (8.20). The input spikes at synapse k are generated by a Poisson process and arrive stochastically with rate $\nu_k(t)$. The probability that no spike arrives in a short time interval Δt is therefore

$$\text{Prob}\{\text{no spike in } [t, t + \Delta t]\} = 1 - \sum_k \nu_k(t)\Delta t. \tag{8.36}$$

If no spike arrives in $[t, t + \Delta t]$, the membrane potential changes from $u(t) = u'$ to $u(t + \Delta t) = u' \exp(-\Delta t/\tau_m)$. On the other hand, if a spike arrives at synapse k, the membrane potential changes from u' to $u' \exp(-\Delta t / \tau_m) + w_k$. Given a value of u' at time t, the probability density of finding a membrane potential u at time $t + \Delta t$ is therefore given by

$$P^{\text{trans}}(u, t + \Delta t | u', t) = \left[1 - \Delta t \sum_k v_k(t) \right] \delta \left(u - u' e^{-\Delta t / \tau_m} \right)$$

$$+ \Delta t \sum_k v_k(t) \delta \left(u - u' e^{-\Delta t / \tau_m} - w_k \right). \qquad (8.37)$$

We will refer to P^{trans} as the transition law. Since the membrane potential is given by the differential equation (8.20) with input spikes generated by a Poisson distribution, the evolution of the membrane potential is a Markov Process (i.e., a process without memory) and can be described by (van Kampen, 1992)

$$p(u, t + \Delta t) = \int P^{\text{trans}}(u, t + \Delta t | u', t) \, p(u', t) \, du'. \qquad (8.38)$$

We insert Eq. (8.37) in Eq. (8.38). To perform the integration, we have to recall the rules for δ-functions, namely, $\delta(au) = a^{-1} \delta(u)$. The result of the integration is

$$p(u, t + \Delta t) = \left[1 - \Delta t \sum_k v_k(t) \right] e^{\Delta t / \tau_m} p \left(e^{\Delta t / \tau_m} u, t \right)$$

$$+ \Delta t \sum_k v_k(t) e^{\Delta t / \tau_m} p \left(e^{\Delta t / \tau_m} u - w_k, t \right). \qquad (8.39)$$

Since Δt is assumed to be small, we expand Eq. (8.39) about $\Delta t = 0$ and find to first order in Δt

$$\frac{p(u, t + \Delta t) - p(u, t)}{\Delta t} = \frac{1}{\tau_m} p(u, t) + \frac{1}{\tau_m} u \frac{\partial}{\partial u} p(u, t)$$

$$+ \sum_k v_k(t) \left[p(u - w_k, t) - p(u, t) \right]. \qquad (8.40)$$

For $\Delta t \to 0$, the left-hand side of Eq. (8.40) turns into a partial derivative $\partial p(u, t) / \partial t$. Furthermore, if the jump amplitudes w_k are small, we can expand the right-hand side of Eq. (8.40) with respect to u about $p(u, t)$:

$$\tau_m \frac{\partial}{\partial t} p(u, t) = -\frac{\partial}{\partial u} \left[-u + \tau_m \sum_k v_k(t) w_k \right] p(u, t)$$

$$+ \frac{1}{2} \left[\tau_m \sum_k v_k(t) w_k^2 \right] \frac{\partial^2}{\partial u^2} p(u, t), \qquad (8.41)$$

where we have neglected terms of order w_k^3 and higher. The expansion in w_k is called the Kramers–Moyal expansion. Eq. (8.41) is an example of a Fokker–Planck equation (van Kampen, 1992), i.e., a partial differential equation that describes the temporal evolution of a probability distribution. The right-hand side of Eq. (8.41) has a clear interpretation: the first term in rectangular brackets describes the systematic drift of the membrane potential due to leakage ($\propto -u$) and *mean* background input ($\propto \sum_k v_k(t) w_k$). The second term in rectangular brackets corresponds to a "diffusion constant" and accounts for the fluctuations of the membrane potential. The Fokker–Planck equation (8.41) is equivalent to the Langevin equation (8.7) with $RI(t) = \tau_m \sum_k v_k(t) w_k$ and time-dependent noise amplitude

$$\sigma^2(t) = \tau_m \sum_k v_k(t) w_k^2. \tag{8.42}$$

The specific process generated by the Langevin equation (8.7) with *constant* noise amplitude σ is called the Ornstein–Uhlenbeck process (Uhlenbeck and Ornstein, 1930), but Eq. (8.42) indicates that, in the context of neuroscience, the effective noise amplitude generated by stochastic spike arrival is in general time-dependent. We will return to the Fokker–Planck equation in Chapter 13.

For the transition from Eq. (8.40) to (8.41) we have suppressed higher-order terms in the expansion. The missing terms are

$$\sum_{n=3}^{\infty} \frac{(-1)^n}{n!} A_n(t) \frac{\partial^n}{\partial u^n} p(u,t) \tag{8.43}$$

with $A_n = \tau_m \sum_k v_k(t) w_k^n$. What are the conditions that these terms vanish? As in the example of Fig. 8.6a and b, we consider a sequence of models where the size of the weights w_k decreases so that $A_n \to 0$ for $n \geq 3$ while the mean $\sum_k v_k(t) w_k$ and the second moment $\sum_k v_k(t) w_k^2$ remain constant. It turns out, that, given both excitatory and inhibitory input, it is always possible to find an appropriate sequence of models (Lansky, 1984, 1997). For $w_k \to 0$, the diffusion limit is attained and Eq. (8.41) is exact. For excitatory input alone, however, such a sequence of models does not exist (Plesser, 1999).

8.4.1 Threshold and firing

The Fokker–Planck equation (8.41) and the Langevin equation (8.7) are equivalent descriptions of drift and diffusion of the membrane potential. Neither of these describe spike firing. To turn the Langevin equation (8.7) into a sensible neuron model, we have to incorporate a threshold condition. In the Fokker–Planck equation (8.41), the firing threshold is incorporated as a boundary condition

$$p(\vartheta,t) \equiv 0 \quad \text{for all } t. \tag{8.44}$$

The boundary condition reflects the fact that, under a white noise model, in each short interval Δt many excitatory and inhibitory input spikes arrive which each cause a tiny jump of size $\pm\delta$ of the membrane potential. Any finite density $p(u,t)$ at a value $\vartheta - \delta < u \leq \vartheta$ would be rapidly removed, because one of the many excitatory spikes which arrive at each moment would push the membrane potential above threshold. The white noise limit corresponds to infinite spike arrival rate and jump size $\delta \to 0$, as discussed above. As a consequence there are, in each short interval Δt infinitely many "attempts" to push the membrane potential above threshold. Hence the density at $u = \vartheta$ must vanish. The above argument also shows that for colored noise the density at threshold is finite, because the effective frequency of "attempts" is limited by the cut-off frequency of the noise.

Before we continue the discussion of the diffusion model in the presence of a threshold, let us study the solution of Eq. (8.41) without threshold.

Example: Free distribution

The solution of the Fokker–Planck equation (8.41) with initial condition $p(u,\hat{t}) = \delta(u - u_r)$ is a Gaussian with mean $u_0(t)$ and variance $\langle \Delta u^2(t) \rangle$, i.e.,

$$p(u,t) = \frac{1}{\sqrt{2\pi \langle \Delta u^2(t) \rangle}} \exp \left\{ -\frac{[u(t|\hat{t}) - u_0(t)]^2}{2 \langle \Delta u^2(t) \rangle} \right\}, \tag{8.45}$$

as can be verified by inserting Eq. (8.45) into (8.41). In particular, the stationary distribution that is approached in the limit of $t \to \infty$ for constant input I_0 is

$$p(u,\infty) = \frac{1}{\sqrt{\pi}} \frac{1}{\sigma} \exp \left\{ \frac{[u - R I_0]^2}{\sigma^2} \right\}, \tag{8.46}$$

which describes a Gaussian distribution with mean $u_\infty = R I_0$ and variance $\sigma/\sqrt{2}$.

8.4.2 Interval distribution for the diffusive noise model

Let us consider a leaky integrate-and-fire neuron that starts at time $\hat{t}$ with a membrane potential u_r and is driven for $t > \hat{t}$ by a known input $I(t)$. Because of the diffusive noise generated by stochastic spike arrival, we cannot predict the exact value of the neuronal membrane potential $u(t)$ at a later time $t > \hat{t}$, only the probability that the membrane potential is in a certain interval $[u_0, u_1]$. Specifically, we have

$$\text{Prob}\{u_0 < u(t) < u_1 \mid u(\hat{t}) = u_r\} = \int_{u_0}^{u_1} p(u,t)\,du, \tag{8.47}$$

where $p(u,t)$ is the probability density of the membrane potential at time t. In the diffusion limit, $p(u,t)$ can be found by solution of the Fokker–Planck equation (8.41) with initial condition $p(u,\hat{t}) = \delta(u - u_r)$ and boundary condition $p(\vartheta,t) = 0$.

The boundary is absorbing. In other words, in a simulation of a single realizations of the stochastic process, the simulation is stopped when the trajectory passes the threshold for the first time. To be concrete, imagine that we run 100 simulation trials, i.e., 100 realizations of a leaky integrate-and-fire model with diffusive noise. Each trial starts at the same value $u(\hat{t}) = u_r$ and uses the same input current $I(t')$ for $t' > \hat{t}$. Some of the trials will exhibit trajectories that reach the threshold at some point $t' < t$. Others stay below threshold for the whole period $\hat{t} < t' < t$. The expected fraction of simulations that have not yet reached the threshold and therefore still "survive" up to time t is given by the survivor function,

$$S_I(t|\hat{t}) = \int_{-\infty}^{\vartheta} p(u,t)\,du. \tag{8.48}$$

In other words, the survivor function in the diffusive noise model is equal to the probability that the membrane potential has not yet reached the threshold between $\hat{t}$ and t.

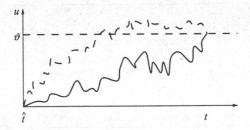

Fig. 8.9 Without a threshold, several trajectories can reach at time t the same value $u = \vartheta$ from above or below.

In view of Eq. (7.24), the input-dependent interval distribution is therefore

$$P_I(t|\hat{t}) = -\frac{d}{dt} \int_{-\infty}^{\vartheta} p(u,t)\,du. \tag{8.49}$$

We recall that $P_I(t|\hat{t})\,\Delta t$ for $\Delta t \to 0$ is the probability that a neuron fires its next spike between t and $t+\Delta t$ given a spike at $\hat{t}$ and input I. In the context of noisy integrate-and-fire neurons $P_I(t|\hat{t})$ is called the distribution of "first passage times." The name is motivated by the fact, that firing occurs when the membrane potential crosses ϑ for the first time. Unfortunately, no general solution is known for the first passage time problem of the Ornstein–Uhlenbeck process. For constant input $I(t) = I_0$, however, it is at least possible to give a moment expansion of the first passage time distribution. In particular, the mean of the first passage time can be calculated in closed form.

Example: Numerical evaluation of $P_I(t|\hat{t})$

We have seen that, in the absence of a threshold, the Fokker–Planck equation (8.41) can be solved; see Eq. (8.45). The transition probability from an arbitrary starting value u' at time t' to a new value u at time t is

$$P^{\text{trans}}(u,t|u',t') = \frac{1}{\sqrt{2\pi\,\langle \Delta u^2(t)\rangle}}\,\exp\left\{-\frac{[u-u_0(t)]^2}{2\,\langle \Delta u^2(t)\rangle}\right\} \tag{8.50}$$

with

$$u_0(t) = u'\,e^{-(t-t')/\tau_m} + \int_0^{t-t'} e^{-s'/\tau_m}\,I(t-s')\,ds', \tag{8.51}$$

$$\langle \Delta u^2(t)\rangle = \frac{\sigma^2}{2}\left[1 - e^{-2(t-s)/\tau_m}\right]. \tag{8.52}$$

A method due to Schrödinger uses the solution of the unbounded problem in order to calculate the input-dependent interval distribution $P_I(t|\hat{t})$ of the diffusion model with threshold (Schrödinger, 1915; Plesser and Tanaka, 1997; Burkitt and Clark, 1999). The

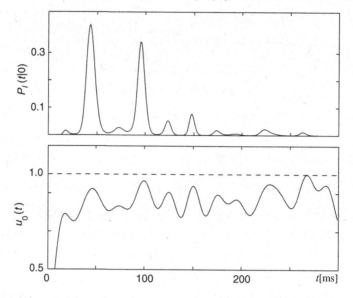

Fig. 8.10 A time-dependent input current $I(t)$ generates a noise-free membrane potential $u_0(t)$ shown in the lower part of the figure. In the presence of diffusive noise, spikes can be triggered although the reference trajectory stays below the threshold (dashed line). This gives rise to an input-dependent interval distribution $P_I(t|0)$ shown in the upper panel. Taken from Plesser and Gerstner (2000).

idea of the solution method is illustrated in Fig. 8.9. Because of the Markov property, the probability density of crossing the threshold (not necessarily for the first time) at a time t is equal to the probability of crossing it for the first time at $t' < t$ and returning back to ϑ at time t, i.e.,

$$P^{\text{trans}}(\vartheta, t | u_r, \hat{t}) = \int_{\hat{t}}^{t} P_I(t' | \hat{t}) P^{\text{trans}}(\vartheta, t | \vartheta, t') \, dt'. \qquad (8.53)$$

This integral equation can be solved numerically for the distribution $P_I(t' | \hat{t})$ for arbitrary input current $I(t)$ (Plesser, 2000). An example is shown in Fig. 8.10. The probability of emitting a spike is high whenever the noise-free trajectory is close to the firing threshold. Very long intervals are unlikely, if the noise-free membrane potential was already several times close to the threshold before, so that the neuron has had ample opportunity to fire earlier.

8.4.3 *Mean interval and mean firing rate (diffusive noise)*

For constant input I_0 the mean interspike interval is $\langle s \rangle = \int_0^\infty s P_{I_0}(s|0) \, ds = \int_0^\infty s P_0(s) \, ds$; see Eq. (7.13). For the diffusion model Eq. (8.7) with threshold ϑ, reset potential u_r, and

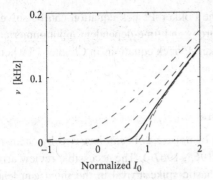

Fig. 8.11 Mean firing rate of a leaky integrate-and-fire model as a function of constant input evaluated for different levels of diffusive noise, using the Siegert formula, Eq. (8.54). From top to bottom: $\sigma = 1.0$, $\sigma = 0.5$, $\sigma = 0.2$ (solid line), $\sigma = 0.1$, $\sigma = 0.0$.

membrane time constant τ_m, the mean interval is

$$\langle s \rangle = \tau_m \sqrt{\pi} \int_{\frac{u_r - h_0}{\sigma}}^{\frac{\vartheta - h_0}{\sigma}} du \exp\left(u^2\right) \left[1 + \mathrm{erf}(u)\right], \tag{8.54}$$

where $h_0 = RI_0$ is the input potential caused by the constant current I_0 (Siegert, 1951; Johannesma, 1968). Here "erf" denotes the error function $\mathrm{erf}(x) = \frac{2}{\sqrt{\pi}} \int_0^x \exp(-u^2) du$. This expression, sometimes called the Siegert formula, can be derived by several methods; for reviews see, for example, van Kampen (1992). The inverse of the mean interval is the mean firing rate. Hence, Eq. (8.54) enables us to the express the mean firing rate of a leaky integrate-and-fire model with diffusive noise as a function of a (constant) input I_0 (Fig. 8.11). We will derive Eq. (8.54) in Chapter 13 in the context of populations of spiking neurons.

8.5 Summary

Each spike arrival at a synapse causes an excursion of the membrane potential of the post-synaptic neuron. If spikes arrive stochastically the membrane potential exhibits fluctuations around a mean trajectory. If the fluctuations stay in the subthreshold regime where the membrane properties can be approximated by a linear equation, the mean and the standard deviation of the trajectory can be calculated analytically, given the parameters of the stochastic process that characterize spike arrivals. In the presence of a firing threshold, the fluctuations in the membrane potential caused by stochastic spike arrivals can make the neuron fire even if the mean trajectory would never reach the firing threshold.

In the limit that the rate of spike arrival at excitatory and inhibitory synapses is high while each spike causes only a small jump of the membrane potential, synaptic bombardment can be approximated by the sum of two terms: a mean input current and a Gaussian white noise input. The white noise leads to a "diffusion" of the membrane potential trajectory around the mean trajectory. The evolution of the probability distribution $p(u,t)$ of the membrane potential over time is described by a Fokker–Planck equation. For the leaky integrate-and-fire model and stationary input, the Fokker–Planck equation can be solved analytically. For nonlinear integrate-and-fire neurons and time-dependent input numerical solutions are possible. We will return to the Fokker–Planck equations in Chapter 13 where further results will be derived.

Literature

Stochastic spike arrival as an important source of noise has been discussed by Stein in the context of integrate-and-fire models (Stein, 1965, 1967b). The accessible review article of König *et al.* (1996) highlights how stochastic spike arrival in the input can lead to a broad interspike interval distribution in the output of a neuron. The close relation between stochastic spike arrival and diffusive noise has been known for a long time (Gluss, 1967; Johannesma, 1968). The leaky integrate-and-fire model with diffusive noise is equivalent to the Ornstein–Uhlenbeck process (Uhlenbeck and Ornstein, 1930) with an absorbing boundary. Mathematical results for integrate-and-fire models with diffusive noise are reviewed in Tuckwell (1989). An in-depth treatment of the mathematical theory of stochastic processes and Fokker–Planck equations can be found in van Kampen (1992).

Exercises

1. **Colored noise.**
   (a) *Calculate the noise spectrum of the colored noise defined by Eq. (8.15) which we repeat here:*

$$\tau_s \frac{dI^{\text{noise}}(t)}{dt} = -I^{\text{noise}}(t) + \xi(t), \tag{8.55}$$

where $\xi(t)$ is white noise with mean zero and variance

$$\langle \xi(t)\,\xi(t') \rangle = \sigma^2\,\tau_s\,\delta(t - t'). \tag{8.56}$$

   (b) *Calculate the membrane potential fluctuations $\langle (\Delta u(t))^2 \rangle$ caused by the colored noise in Eq. (8.55), using the differential equation*

$$\tau_m \frac{d}{dt} u(t) = -u(t) + R I^{\text{det}}(t) + R I^{\text{noise}}(t). \tag{8.57}$$

   (c) *Show that the limit process of balanced excitatory and inhibitory input with synaptic time constant τ_s leads to colored noise.*

2. **Autocorrelation of the membrane potential.** *Determine the autocorrelation $\langle u(t) u(t') \rangle$ of the Langevin equation (8.7) where $\xi(t)$ is white noise.*

3. **Membrane potential fluctuations and balance condition.** *Assume that each spike arrival at an excitatory synapse causes an EPSP with weight $w^{\text{exc}} = +w$ and time course $\varepsilon^{\text{exc}}(t) = (t^2/\tau_{\text{exc}}^3)$ $\exp(-t/\tau_{\text{exc}})$ for $t > 0$. Spike arrival at an inhibitory synapse causes an IPSP with weight $-b\,w^{\text{exc}}$ and, for $t > 0$, a time course $\varepsilon^{\text{inh}}(t) = (t/\tau_{\text{inh}}^2) \exp(-t/\tau_{\text{inh}})$ where $\tau_{\text{inh}} > \tau_{\text{exc}}$ and $b > 1$.*
   The membrane potential is

$$u(t) = w^{\text{exc}} \sum_{t^f} \varepsilon^{\text{exc}}(t - t^f) - b\,w^{\text{inh}} \sum_{t^f} \varepsilon^{\text{inh}}(t - t^f). \tag{8.58}$$

Excitatory and inhibitory spike arrival are generated by Poisson processes rate $v^{exc} = v_1$ and $v^{inh} = \beta v_1$, respectively.

(a) Determine the mean membrane potential.

(b) Calculate the variance of the fluctuations of the membrane potential.

(c) You want to increase the rate v_1 without changing the mean or the variance of the membrane potential. Does this limit exist for all combinations of parameters b and β or do you have to impose a specific relation $b = f(\beta)$? Interpret your result.

9
Noisy output: escape rate and soft threshold

There are various ways to introduce noise in formal spiking neuron models. In the previous chapter we focused on input noise in the form of stochastic spike arrival. In this chapter we assume that the input is known or can be estimated. Stochasticity arises at the level of the neuronal spike generation, i.e., at the moment of the output. The noisy output can be interpreted as arising from a "soft" threshold that enables an "escape" of the membrane potential across the threshold even before the threshold is reached. Models with a noisy threshold or escape noise are the basis of Generalized Linear Models which will be used in Chapters 10 and 11 as a powerful statistical tool for modeling spike-train data.

In Section 9.1, the notion of escape noise is introduced. In Section 9.2 we determine the likelihood that a specific spike train is generated by a neuron model with escape noise. In Section 9.3 we apply the escape noise formalism to the Spike Response Model already encountered in Chapter 6 and show an interesting link to the renewal statistics encountered in Chapter 7. The escape rate formalism gives rise to an efficient description of noise processes, independently of their biophysical nature, be it channel noise or stochastic spike arrival. Indeed, as shown in Section 9.4, noisy input models and noisy output models can behave rather similarly.

9.1 Escape noise

In the escape noise model, we imagine that an integrate-and-fire neuron with threshold ϑ can fire even though the formal threshold ϑ has not been reached, or may stay quiescent even though the formal threshold has transiently been passed. To do this consistently, we introduce an "escape rate" or "firing intensity" which depends on the momentary state of the neuron.

9.1.1 Escape rate

Given the input $I(t')$ for $t' < t$ and the past firing times $t^f < t$, the membrane potential of a generalized integrate-and-fire model (e.g., the adaptive leaky integrate-and-fire model) or a Spike Response Model (SRM) can be calculated from Eq. (6.7) or Eq. (6.27) respectively;

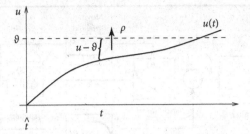

Fig. 9.1 Noisy threshold. A neuron can fire at time t with probability density $\rho(t) = f[u(t) - \vartheta]$ even though the membrane potential u has not yet reached the threshold ϑ. In other words, the sharp threshold of the deterministic neuron is replaced by a "soft" threshold.

see Chapter 6. For example, the value of the membrane potential of an SRM can be expressed as

$$u(t) = \sum_f \eta(t - t^f) + \int_0^\infty \kappa(s) I^{\text{det}}(t - s) \, ds + u_{\text{rest}}, \tag{9.1}$$

where I^{det} is the known driving current (the superscript "det" stands for deterministic) and κ and η are filters that describe the response of the membrane to an incoming pulse or an outgoing spike; see Chapter 6. In the deterministic model the next spike occurs when u reaches the threshold ϑ. In order to introduce some variability into the neuronal spike generator, we replace the strict threshold by a stochastic firing criterion. In the noisy threshold model, spikes can occur at any time with a probability density

$$\rho(t) = f(u(t) - \vartheta) \tag{9.2}$$

that depends on the momentary distance between the (noiseless) membrane potential and the threshold; see Fig. 9.1. We can think of f as an escape rate similar to the one encountered in models of chemical reactions (van Kampen, 1992). In the mathematical theory of point processes, the quantity ρ is called a "stochastic intensity." Since we use ρ in the context of neuron models we will refer to it as a firing intensity.

The choice of the escape function f in Eq. (9.2) is arbitrary. A reasonable condition is to require $f \to 0$ for $u \to -\infty$ so that the neuron does not fire if the membrane potential is far below threshold. A common choice is the exponential,

$$f(u - \vartheta) = \frac{1}{\tau_0} \exp[\beta(u - \vartheta)], \tag{9.3}$$

where β and τ_0 are parameters. For $\beta \to \infty$, the soft threshold turns into a sharp one so that we return to the noiseless model. Below we discuss some further choices of the escape function in Eq. (9.2).

The SRM of Eq. (9.1) together with the exponential escape rate of Eq. (9.3) is an example of a Generalized Linear Model. Applying the theory of Generalized Linear Mod-

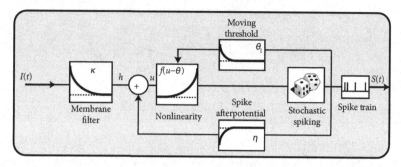

Fig. 9.2 Flow diagram for a Spike Response Model (SRM) with escape noise. The stochasticity at the noisy threshold is indicated by the dice; see Fig. 6.11. The noisy SRM (Gerstner and van Hemmen, 1992; Gerstner and Kistler, 2002) is an example of a Generalized Linear Model (GLM) (Truccolo *et al.*, 2005; Pillow *et al.*, 2008).

els (see Chapter 10) to the SRM with escape noise enables a rapid extraction of model parameters from experimental data.

In slice experiments it was found (Jolivet *et al.*, 2006) that the exponential escape rate of Eq. (9.3) provides an excellent fit to the spiking intensity of real neurons (Fig. 9.3). Moreover, the firing times of an AdEx model driven by a deterministic fluctuating current $I^{\text{det}}(t)$ and a unknown white noise current $\xi(t)$ can also be well fitted by the Spike Response Model of Eq. (9.1) combined with an exponential escape rate as we shall see below in Section 9.4.

Nevertheless, we may wonder whether Eq. (9.2) is a sufficiently general noise model. We have seen in Chapter 2 that the concept of a pure voltage threshold is questionable. More generally, the spike trigger process could, for example also depend on the slope $\dot{u} = du/dt$ with which the "threshold" is approached. In the noisy threshold model, we may therefore also consider an escape rate (or hazard) which depends not only on u but also on its derivative $\dot{u}$

$$\rho(t) = f[u(t) - \vartheta, \dot{u}(t)]. \tag{9.4}$$

We will return to Eq. (9.4) in Section 9.4.

Note that the time dependence of the firing intensity $\rho(t)$ on the right-hand side of Eq. (9.4) arises *implicitly* via the membrane potential $u(t)$. In an even more general model, we could in addition include an *explicit* time dependence, for example, to account for a reduced spiking probability immediately after a spike at t^f. Instead of an explicit dependence, a slightly more convenient way to implement an additional time dependence is via a time-dependent threshold $\vartheta \longrightarrow \vartheta(t)$ which we have already encountered in Eq. (6.31). An even more general escape rate model therefore is

$$\rho(t) = f[u(t) - \vartheta(t), \dot{u}(t)]. \tag{9.5}$$

In Chapter 11 we shall see that a Spike Response Model with escape noise and dynamic threshold can explain neuronal firing with a high degree of accuracy.

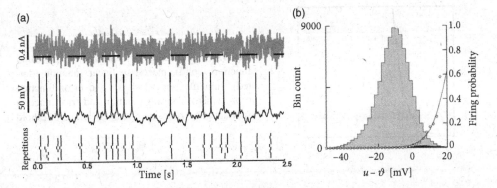

Fig. 9.3 The instantaneous firing intensity extracted from experiments can be fitted by an exponential escape rate. (a) A real neuron is driven by a time-dependent input current (top) generating a fluctuating voltage with occasional spikes (middle), which are repeated with high precision, but not perfectly, across several trials (bottom). (b) The black histogram (very small) shows the number of times (bin count, vertical axis) that the model voltage calculated from Eq. (9.1) falls in the bin $u - \vartheta$ (horizontal axis) *and* the real neuron fires. The gray histogram indicates distribution of voltage when the real neuron does not fire. The ratio (black/black plus gray) in each bin gives the firing probability $P_F(u - \vartheta)$ (open circles, probability scale on the right) which can be fitted by Eq. (9.8) using an exponential escape rate (solid line), $f(u - \vartheta) = \frac{1}{\tau_0} \exp[\beta(u - \vartheta)]$ with a steepness of $\beta = (4\,\text{mV})^{-1}$ and a mean latency at threshold of $\tau_0 = 19$ ms. From Jolivet *et al.* (2006) with kind permission from Springer Science and Business Media.

Example: Bounded versus unbounded escape rate

A stochastic intensity which diverges for $u \gg \vartheta$, such as the exponential escape rate of Eq. (9.3), may seem surprising at a first glance, but it is in fact a necessary requirement for the transition from a soft to a sharp threshold process. Since the escape model has been introduced as a noisy threshold, there should be a limit of low noise that leads us back to the sharp threshold. In order to explore the relation between noisy and deterministic threshold models, we consider as a first step a bounded escape function f defined as

$$f(u - \vartheta) = \begin{cases} 0 & \text{for } u < \vartheta, \\ \Delta^{-1} & \text{for } u \geq \vartheta. \end{cases} \qquad (9.6)$$

Thus, the neuron never fires if the voltage is below the threshold. If $u > \vartheta$, the neuron fires stochastically with a rate Δ^{-1}. Therefore, the mean latency, or expected delay, of a spike is Δ. This implies that the neuron responds slowly and imprecisely, even when the membrane potential is significantly above threshold – and this result looks rather odd. Only in the limit where the parameter Δ goes to zero would the neuron fire immediately and reliably as soon as the membrane potential crosses the threshold. Thus, a rapid response requires the escape to diverge.

The argument here was based on a step function for the escape rate. A simple choice

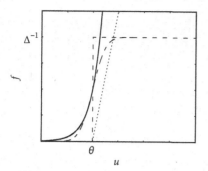

Fig. 9.4 Soft threshold escape rates. Exponential function (solid), piecewise linear function (dotted), step function (dashed), and error function (dot-dashed). The step function and error function saturate at a maximum rate of Δ^{-1}. The threshold is ϑ.

for a soft threshold which enables a rapid response is a piecewise linear escape rate,

$$f(u - \vartheta) = \alpha\,[u - \vartheta]_+ = \begin{cases} 0 & \text{for } u < \vartheta, \\ \alpha\,(u - \vartheta) & \text{for } u \geq \vartheta, \end{cases} \tag{9.7}$$

with slope α for $u > \vartheta$. For $u > \vartheta$, the firing intensity is proportional to $u - \vartheta$; see Fig. 9.4. This corresponds to the intuitive idea that instantaneous firing rates increase with the membrane potential. Variants of the linear escape–rate model are commonly used to describe spike generation in, for example, auditory nerve fibers (Siebert and Gray, 1963; Miller and Mark, 1992).

9.1.2 Transition from continuous time to discrete time

In discrete time, we consider the probability $P_F(u)$ of firing in a finite time step given that the neuron has membrane potential u. It is bounded from above by 1 – despite the fact that the escape rate can be arbitrarily large. We start from a model in continuous time and discretize time as is often done in simulations. In a straightforward discretization scheme, we would calculate the probability of firing during a time step Δt as $\int_t^{t+\Delta t} \rho(t')\mathrm{d}t' \approx \rho(t)\,\Delta t$. However, for $u \gg \vartheta$, the hazard $\rho(t) = f(u(t) - \vartheta)$ can take large values; see, for example, Eq. (9.3). Thus Δt must be taken extremely short so as to guarantee $\rho(t)\,\Delta t < 1$.

To arrive at an improved discretization scheme, we calculate the probability that a neuron does *not* fire in a time step Δt. The probability $S(t)$ of surviving for a time t without firing decays according to $\mathrm{d}S/\mathrm{d}t = -\rho(t)\,S(t)$. Integration of the differential equation over a *finite* time Δt yields an exponential factor $S(t) = \exp[-\int_0^t \rho(t')\,\mathrm{d}t']$; compare the discussion of the survivor function in Chapter 7 (Section 7.5). If the neuron does not survive, it must have fired. Therefore we arrive at a firing probability

$$P_F(u) = \text{Prob}\,\{\text{spike in } [t, t+\Delta t]\,|\,u(t)\} \approx 1 - \exp\{-\Delta t\, f(u(t) - \vartheta)\}\,. \tag{9.8}$$

Even if f diverges for $u \to \infty$, the probability of firing remains bounded between zero and 1. Also, we see that, for small Δt, the probability P_F scales as $f\Delta t$. We see from Fig. 9.5a that, for an exponential escape rate, an increase in the discretization Δt mainly shifts the

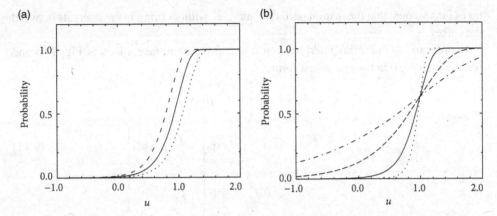

Fig. 9.5 The unbounded exponential escape rate yields a bounded firing probability in a discrete time step. (a) Probability of firing in a discrete time interval Δt as a function of the membrane potential u for different discretizations $\Delta t = 0.5$ ms (dashed line), $\Delta t = 1$ ms (solid line), and $\Delta t = 2$ ms (dotted line) with $\beta = 5$. (b) Similar plot as in A but for different noise levels $\beta = 10$ (dotted line), $\beta = 5$ (solid line), $\beta = 2$ (dashed line), and $\beta = 1$ (dot-dashed line) with $\Delta t = 1$ ms. The escape rate is given by (9.3) with parameters $\vartheta = 1$ and $\tau_0 = 1$ ms.

firing curve to the left while the form remains roughly the same. An increase of the noise level makes the curve flatter; see Fig. 9.5b.

Note that, because of refractoriness, it is impossible for integrate-and-fire models (and for real neurons) to fire more than one spike in a short time bin Δt. Refractoriness is implemented in the model of Eq. (9.1) by a significant reset of the membrane potential via the refractory kernel η.

9.2 Likelihood of a spike train

In the previous subsection, we calculated the probability of firing in a short time step Δt from the continuous-time firing intensity $\rho(t)$. Here we ask a similar question, not on the level of a single spike, but on that of a full spike train.

Suppose we know that a spike train has been generated by an escape noise process

$$\rho(t) = f(u(t) - \vartheta) \tag{9.9}$$

as in Eq. (9.2), where the membrane potential $u(t)$ arises from the dynamics of one of the generalized integrate-and-fire models such as the SRM.

The likelihood L^n that spikes occur at the times $t^1, \ldots, t^f, \ldots, t^n$ is (Brillinger, 1988)

$$L^n(\{t^1, t^2, \ldots, t^n\}) = \rho(t^1) \cdot \rho(t^2) \cdot \ldots \rho(t^n) \exp\left[-\int_0^T \rho(s) \, ds\right], \tag{9.10}$$

where $[0, T]$ is the observation interval. The product on the right-hand side contains the momentary firing intensity $\rho(t^f)$ at the firing times $t^1, t^2, \ldots, t^n$. The exponential factor takes into account that the neuron needs to "survive" without firing in the intervals between the spikes.

In order to highlight this interpretation it is convenient to take a look at Fig. 9.6a and rewrite Eq. (9.10) in the equivalent form

$$L^n(\{t^1, t^2, \ldots, t^n\}) = \exp\left[-\int_0^{t^1} \rho(s)\mathrm{d}s\right]$$

$$\cdot \rho(t^1) \quad \exp\left[-\int_{t^1}^{t^2} \rho(s)\mathrm{d}s\right] \tag{9.11}$$

$$\cdot \rho(t^2) \quad \exp\left[-\int_{t^2}^{t^3} \rho(s)\mathrm{d}s\right]$$

$$\cdots \rho(t^n) \quad \exp\left[-\int_{t^n}^{T} \rho(s)\mathrm{d}s\right].$$

Intuitively speaking, the likelihood of finding n spikes at times t^f depends on the instantaneous rate at the time of the spikes and the probability of surviving the intervals in between without firing; see the survivor function introduced in Chapter 7, Eq. (7.26).

Instead of the likelihood, it is sometimes more convenient to work with the logarithm of the likelihood, called the log-likelihood

$$\log L^n(\{t^1, \ldots, t^f, \ldots, t^n\}) = -\int_0^T \rho(s)\mathrm{d}s + \sum_{f=1}^n \log\rho(t^f). \tag{9.12}$$

The three formulations Eqs. (9.10)–(9.12) are equivalent and it is a matter of taste if one is preferred over the others.

Example: Discrete-time version of likelihood and generative model

In a discrete-time simulation of an SRM or generalized integrate-and-fire model with escape noise, we divide the simulation interval $[0, T]$ into N time steps $\Delta t = T/N$; see Fig. 9.6b. In each time step, we first calculate the membrane potential $u(t)$ and then generate a spike with probability $P_t = P_F(u(t))$ given by Eq. (9.8). To do so, we generate on the computer a random number r_t between zero and unity. If $P_t > r_t$, a spike is generated, i.e., the spike count number in this time bin is $n_t = 1$. The probability of finding an empty time bin (spike count $n_t = 0$) is

$$\text{Prob}\{\text{silent in } [t, t+\Delta t]\} = 1 - P_t = \exp\{-\Delta t\,\rho(t)\}, \tag{9.13}$$

where we have assumed that time bins are short enough so that the membrane potential does not change a lot from one time step to the next. The spike train can be summarized as a binary sequence $\{0, 0, 1, 0, 0, 0, 1, 0, \ldots\}$ of N numbers $n_t \in \{0, 1\}$. We emphasize that, with the above discrete-time spike generation model, it is impossible to have two spikes in a time bin Δt. This reflects the fact that, because of neuronal refractoriness, neurons cannot emit two spikes in a time bin shorter than, say, half the duration of an action potential.

Since we generate an independent random number in each time bin, a specific spike train occurs with a probability given by the product of the probabilities per bin:

$$P_{\text{total}} = \Pi_{\text{bins with spike}}[P_t] \cdot \Pi_{\text{empty bins}}[1 - P_t] \tag{9.14}$$

$$= \Pi_t \left\{ [P_t]^{n_t} \cdot [1 - P_t]^{1-n_t} \right\}, \tag{9.15}$$

where the product runs over all time bins and $n_t \in \{0,1\}$ is the spike count number in each bin.

We now switch our perspective and study an *observed* spike train in continuous time with spike firings at times t^f with $0 < t^1, t^2, \ldots, t^n < T$. The spike train was generated by a real neuron in a slice experiment under current injection with a known current $I(t)$. We now ask the following question: What is the probability that the observed spike train *could have been generated* by our model? Thus, we consider our discrete-time model with escape noise as a *generative* model of the spike train. To do so, we calculate the voltage using a discrete-time version of Eq. (9.1). Given the (known) injected input $I(t)$ and the (observed) spike times t^f, we can calculate the voltage $u(t)$ of our model and therefore the probability of firing in each time step.

The observed spike train has n spikes at times $0 < t^1, t^2, \ldots, t^n < T$. Let us denote time bins containing a spike by t_k with index k (i.e., $t_1 < t^1 \le t_1 + \Delta t$; $t_2 < t^2 \le t_2 + \Delta t$; ...) and empty bins by $t_{k'}$ with a dummy index k'. Using Eq. (9.14), the probability that the observed spike train could have been generated by our model is

$$P_{\text{total}} = \Pi_{k=1}^n [P_{t_k}] \cdot \Pi_{k', t_{k'} \neq t_k} [1 - P_{t_{k'}}]. \tag{9.16}$$

Eq. (9.16) is the starting point for finding optimal parameters of neuron models (Chapter 10).

We can gain some additional insights, if we rearrange the terms on the right-hand side of Eq. (9.16) differently. All time bins that fall into the interval *between* two spikes can be regrouped as follows

$$\Pi_{\{k' | t_k < t_{k'} \le t_{k+1}\}} [1 - P_{t_{k'}}] = \Pi_{\{k' | t_k < t_{k'} \le t_{k+1}\}} \exp\left\{ -\Delta t\, \rho(t_{k'}) \right\}$$

$$= \exp\left\{ -\sum_{t_k < t_{k'} < t_{k+1}} \Delta t\, \rho(t_{k'}) \right\}. \tag{9.17}$$

Ideally, a spike train in continuous time should be described by a model in continuous time. We therefore ask whether the discretization of time is critical or whether we can get rid of it. The transition to continuous time corresponds to the limit of $N \to \infty$ while T is kept fixed. The Riemann sum on the right-hand side of Eq. (9.17) then turns into an integral. In the same limit, the contribution of the bins containing a spike to Eq. (9.16) can be written as $P_{t_k} = \rho(t_k)\Delta t$. We are led back from the discrete-time generative model

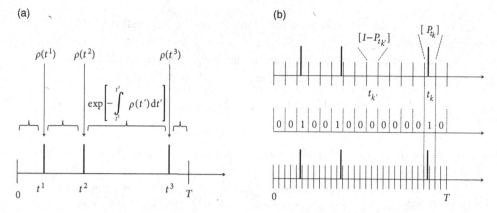

Fig. 9.6 Likelihood of a spike train. Three spikes (thick vertical lines) have been observed in the interval $[0,T]$. (a) The instantaneous firing rates at the moment of the spikes are $\rho(t^1), \rho(t^2), \rho(t^3)$, respectively. The intervals without spike firing are indicated by horizontal braces. The probability of staying quiescent during these intervals decays exponentially with the time-dependent rate $\rho(t')$. (b) Likelihood of a spike train in discrete time. Top: The probability that a time bin $t_{k'}$ contains no spike is $1 - P_{t_{k'}}$ whereas the probability that a spike occurs in bin t_k is P_{t_k}. Middle: The spike count numbers $n_t \in \{0,1\}$ in each time bin. Bottom: The same spike train can also be described using a finer time discretization.

to Eq. (9.11) in continuous time with the replacement

$$P_{\text{total}} = L^n(\{t^1, t^2, \ldots t^n\})(\Delta t)^n, \tag{9.18}$$

i.e., the continuum limit exists. In other words, once the time steps Δt are short enough, the exact discretization scheme does not play a role. Alternative, more efficient, sampling schemes exist that avoid discretization (Brown *et al.*, 2002); see Section 10.3.3.

9.3 Renewal approximation of the Spike Response Model

We focus on a Spike Response Model with escape noise; see Eqs. (9.1)–(9.3). If the firing rate is low, so that the interspike interval is much longer than the decay time of the refractory kernel η, then we can truncate the sum over past firing times and keep track only of the effect of the most recent spike (Gerstner, 1995)

$$u(t) = \eta(t - \hat{t}) + \int_0^\infty \kappa(s) I^{\text{det}}(t - s) \, ds + u_{\text{rest}}, \tag{9.19}$$

where $\hat{t}$ denotes the *last* firing time $t^f < t$.

Eq. (9.19) is called the "short-term memory" approximation of the SRM and abbreviated as SRM$_0$. This model can be efficiently fitted to neural data (Kass and Ventura, 2001) and will play an important role in Chapter 14. In order to emphasize that the value of the membrane potential depends only on the most recent spike, in what follows we write $u(t|\hat{t})$

(a)

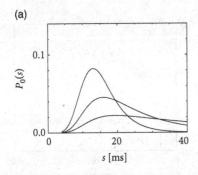

(b)

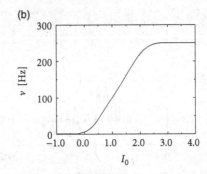

Fig. 9.7 (a) Interval distribution $P_0(s)$ for an SRM$_0$ neuron with absolute refractory period $\Delta^{abs} = 4$ ms followed by an exponentially decreasing afterpotential as in Eq. (9.24) with $\eta_0 = 1$ and $\tau = 4$ ms. The model neuron is stimulated by a constant current $I_0 = 0.7, 0.5, 0.3$ (from top to bottom). (b) Output rate ν as a function of I_0 (gain function). The escape rate is given by Eq. (9.3) with $\vartheta = 1$, $\beta = 5$, and $\tau_0 = 1$ ms.

instead of $u(t)$. Let us summarize the total effect of the input by introducing the "input potential"

$$h(t) = \int_0^\infty \kappa(s) I^{\text{det}}(t - s) \, ds, \tag{9.20}$$

which allows us to rewrite Eq. (9.19) as

$$u(t|\hat{t}) = \eta(t - \hat{t}) + h(t) + u_{\text{rest}}. \tag{9.21}$$

The escape rate

$$\rho(t|\hat{t}) = f(u(t|\hat{t})) \tag{9.22}$$

depends on the time since the last spike and, implicitly, on the stimulating current $I_{\text{det}}(t)$. Hence $\rho(t|\hat{t})$ is similar to the hazard variable of stationary renewal theory. The arguments of Chapter 7 can be generalized to the case of time-dependent input $I^{\text{det}}(t)$ which gives rise to a time-dependent input potential $h(t)$. Given that the neuron has fired its last spike at time $\hat{t}$ and that we know the input $I^{\text{det}}(t')$ for $t' < t$ we can calculate the probability density that the next spike occurs at time $t > \hat{t}$

$$P_I(t|\hat{t}) = \rho(t|\hat{t}) \exp\left[-\int_{\hat{t}}^t \rho(t'|\hat{t}) \, dt'\right]. \tag{9.23}$$

Eq. (9.23) generalizes renewal theory to the time-dependent case. Time-dependent renewal theory will play an important role in Chapter 14.

Compared to the standard stationary renewal theory discussed in Chapter 7, there are two important differences. First, the Spike Response Model with escape noise provides a direct path from stationary to time-dependent renewal theory. Second, interval distributions can be linked to refractoriness and vice versa. More precisely, a reduced firing intensity $\rho(t|\hat{t})$ immediately after a spike is an indication that the distance between the membrane

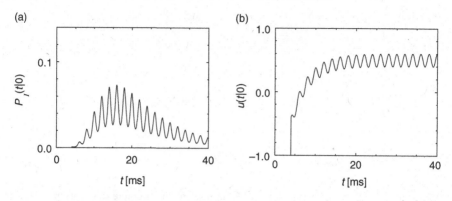

Fig. 9.8 (a) Input-dependent interval distribution $P_I(t|0)$ for an SRM_0 neuron as in Fig. 9.7 stimulated by a periodically modulated input field $h(t) = h_0 + h_1 \cos(2\pi f t)$ with $h_0 = 0.5$, $h_1 = 0.1$, and frequency $f = 500\,\text{Hz}$. (b) The membrane potential $u(t|0) = \eta(t) + h(t)$ during stimulation as in (a).

potential $u(t|\hat{t})$ and the threshold is increased. The reason can be either a hyperpolarizing spike-afterpotential $\eta(t)$ or an increase in the firing threshold $\vartheta(t|\hat{t})$ immediately after a spike

Example: Interval distribution with exponential escape noise

We study a model SRM_0 with membrane potential $u(t|\hat{t}) = \eta(t - \hat{t}) + h(t)$ and choose a refractory kernel with absolute and relative refractoriness defined as

$$\eta(s) = \begin{cases} -\infty & \text{for } s < \Delta^{\text{abs}}, \\ -\eta_0 \exp\left(-\frac{s - \Delta^{\text{abs}}}{\tau}\right) & \text{for } s > \Delta^{\text{abs}}. \end{cases} \qquad (9.24)$$

We adopt the exponential escape rate (9.3).

Fig. 9.7 shows the interval distribution for constant input current I_0 as a function of $s = t - \hat{t}$. With the normalization $\int_0^\infty \kappa(s)\,ds = 1$, we have $h_0 = I_0$. Owing to the refractory term η, extremely short intervals are impossible and the maximum of the interval distribution occurs at some finite value of s. If I_0 is increased, the maximum is shifted to the left. The interval distributions of Fig. 9.7a have qualitatively the same shape as those found for cortical neurons. The gain function $v = g(I_0)$ of a noisy SRM_0 neuron is shown in Fig. 9.7b.

We now study the same model with periodic input $I^{\text{det}}(t) = I_0 + I_1 \cos(\Omega t)$. This leads to an input potential $h(t) = h_0 + h_1 \cos(\Omega t + \varphi_1)$ with bias $h_0 = I_0$ and a periodic component with a certain amplitude h_1 and phase φ_1.

Suppose that a spike has occurred at $\hat{t} = 0$. The probability density that the next spike occurs at time t is given by $P_I(t|\hat{t})$ and can be calculated from Eq. (9.23). The result is shown in Fig. 9.8a.

We note that the periodic component of the input is well represented in the response of the neuron. This example illustrates how neurons in the auditory system can transmit stimuli of frequencies higher than the mean firing rate of the neuron. We emphasize that the threshold in Fig. 9.8b is at $\vartheta = 1$. Without noise there would be no output spike. On the other hand, at very high noise levels, the modulation of the interval distribution would be much weaker. Thus a certain amount of noise is beneficial for signal transmission. The existence of an optimal noise level is a phenomenon called stochastic resonance and will be discussed below in Section 9.4.2.

9.4 From noisy inputs to escape noise

The total input current $I(t)$ which drives a neuron can often be separated into a deterministic component I^{det}, which is known and repeats between one trial and the next; and a stochastic component ξ which is unknown and potentially changes between trials:

$$I(t) = I^{\text{det}}(t) + \xi(t).\tag{9.25}$$

In this section we show that the noisy, unknown part in the input can be approximated to a high degree of accuracy by an appropriately chosen escape function.

Example: Adaptive exponential integrate-and-fire model with noisy input

Suppose that the AdEx model which we encountered in Chapter 6 (see Eqs. (6.3) and (6.4)) is driven by an input as in Eq. (9.25) containing a rapidly moving deterministic signal $I^{\text{det}}(t)$ as well as a white noise component $\xi(t)$. This model generates spikes with a millisecond precision and a high degree of reliability from one trial to the next (Fig. 9.9). We now approximate the voltage of the AdEx model by a linear model

$$u(t) = \sum_f \eta(t - t_i^f) + \int_0^\infty \kappa(s) I^{\text{det}}(t - s)\, ds + u_{\text{rest}}.\tag{9.26}$$

In the subthreshold regime $u < \vartheta - \Delta_T$, the filters κ and η can be calculated analytically using the methods discussed in Chapter 6. The voltage equation (9.26) is then combined with the exponential escape rate

$$f(u - \vartheta) = \frac{1}{\tau_0} \exp[\beta\,(u - \vartheta)].\tag{9.27}$$

The resulting SRM with escape noise (i.e., a linear model with exponential soft-threshold noise in the output) describes the activity of the AdEx with noisy input (i.e., an exponential neuron model with additive white noise in the input) surprisingly well (Fig. 9.9). In other words, in the presence of an input noise $\xi(t)$ the exponential term in the voltage equation of the AdEx model can be replaced by an exponential escape rate (Mensi et al., 2011).

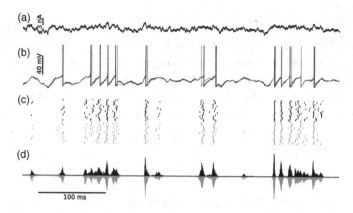

Fig. 9.9 From input noise to output noise. (a) An AdEx model neuron is driven by a fluctuating current containing a deterministic part which is the same during each trial and a stochastic white noise part. (b) Voltage trace of the AdEx model (black) and the SRM with exponential escape rate (gray) during a single trial. The SRM is driven by the deterministic part of the input current. (c) Spike times during 20 trials with the same deterministic current for the AdEx model (black) and SRM with exponential escape noise (gray). For the AdEx the stochasticity arises from white noise in the input whereas for the SRM it arises from escape noise in the output. (d) Comparison of the PSTH of the AdEx model (black) with that of the SRM (gray). Adapted from Mensi *et al.* (2011).

9.4.1 Leaky integrate-and-fire model with noisy input

In the subthreshold regime, the leaky integrate-and-fire model with stochastic input (white noise) can be mapped approximately onto an escape noise model with a certain escape rate f (Plesser and Gerstner, 2000). In this section, we motivate the mapping and the choice of f.

In the absence of a threshold, the membrane potential of an integrate-and-fire model has a Gaussian probability distribution around the noise-free reference trajectory $u_0(t)$. If we take the threshold into account, the probability density at $u = \vartheta$ of the exact solution vanishes, since the threshold acts as an absorbing boundary; see Eq. (8.44). Nevertheless, in a phenomenological model, we can approximate the probability density near $u = \vartheta$ by the "free" distribution (i.e., without the threshold)

$$\text{Prob}\{u \text{ reaches } \vartheta \text{ in } [t, t + \Delta t]\} \propto \Delta t \exp\left\{-\frac{[u_0(t) - \vartheta]^2}{2\langle \Delta u^2(t)\rangle}\right\}, \qquad (9.28)$$

where $u_0(t)$ is the noise-free reference trajectory. The idea is illustrated in Fig. 9.10. We note that in a leaky integrate-and-fire model with colored noise (as opposed to white noise) in the input the density at threshold is *not* zero.

We have seen in Eq. (8.13) that the variance $\langle \Delta u^2(t)\rangle$ of the free distribution rapidly approaches a constant value $\sigma^2/2$ where σ scales with the strength of the diffusive input. We therefore replace the time-dependent variance $2\langle \Delta u(t)^2\rangle$ by its stationary value σ^2. The

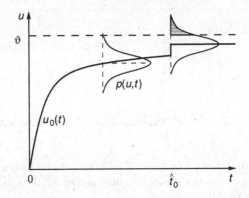

Fig. 9.10 The distribution of the membrane potential around the noise-free reference trajectory $u_0(t)$ is given by $p(u,t)$. At $t = t_0$, where the reference trajectory has a discontinuity, the distribution of the membrane potential is shifted instantaneously across the threshold. The probability of firing at t_0 is given by the shaded surface under the distribution.

right-hand side of Eq. (9.28) is then a function of the noise-free reference trajectory only. To transform the left-hand side of Eq. (9.28) into an escape rate, we divide both sides by Δt. The firing intensity is thus

$$f(u_0 - \vartheta) = \frac{c_1}{\tau_m} \exp\left\{-\frac{[u_0(t) - \vartheta]^2}{\sigma^2}\right\}. \tag{9.29}$$

The factor in front of the exponential has been split into a constant parameter $c_1 > 0$ and the time constant τ_m of the neuron in order to show that the escape rate has units of 1 over time. Equation (9.29) is the well-known Arrhenius formula for escape across a barrier of height $(\vartheta - u_0)^2$ in the presence of thermal energy σ^2 (van Kampen, 1992).

Let us now suppose that the neuron receives, at $t = t_0$, an input current pulse which causes a jump of the membrane trajectory by an amount $\Delta u > 0$; see Fig. 9.10. In this case the Gaussian distribution of membrane potentials is shifted *instantaneously* across the threshold so that there is a nonzero probability that the neuron fires exactly at t_0. In other words, the firing intensity $\rho(t) = f[u_0(t) - \vartheta]$ has a δ peak at $t = t_0$. The escape rate of Eq. (9.29), however, cannot reproduce this δ peak. More generally, whenever the noise-free reference trajectory increases with slope $\dot{u}_0 > 0$, we expect an increase of the instantaneous rate proportional to $\dot{u}_0$, because the tail of the Gaussian distribution drifts across the threshold; see Eq. (8.35). In order to take the drift into account, we generalize Eq. (9.29) and study

$$f(u_0, \dot{u}_0) = \left(\frac{c_1}{\tau_m} + \frac{c_2}{\sigma}[\dot{u}_0]_+\right) \exp\left\{-\frac{[u_0(t) - \vartheta]^2}{\sigma^2}\right\}, \tag{9.30}$$

where $\dot{u}_0 = du_0/dt$ and $[x]_+ = x$ for $x > 0$ and zero otherwise. We call Eq. (9.30) the Arrhenius&Current model (Plesser and Gerstner, 2000).

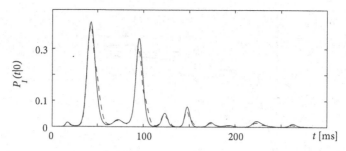

Fig. 9.11 The interval distributions $P_I(t|0)$ for diffusive noise (solid line) and Arrhenius&Current escape noise (dashed line) are nearly identical. The input potential is the same as in Fig. 8.10. Taken from Plesser and Gerstner (2000).

We emphasize that the right-hand side of Eq. (9.30) depends only on the dimensionless variable

$$x(t) = \frac{u_0(t) - \vartheta}{\sigma} \tag{9.31}$$

and its derivative $\dot{x}$. Thus the amplitude of the fluctuations σ define a "natural" voltage scale. The only relevant variable is the momentary distance of the noise-free trajectory from the threshold in units of the noise amplitude σ. A value of $x = -1$ implies that the membrane potential is one σ below threshold. A distance of $u - \vartheta = -10\,\text{mV}$ at high noise (e.g., $\sigma = 10\,\text{mV}$) is as effective in firing a cell as a distance of $1\,\text{mV}$ at low noise ($\sigma = 1\,\text{mV}$).

Example: Comparison of diffusion model and Arrhenius&Current escape rate

To check the validity of the arguments that led to Eq. (9.30), let us compare the interval distribution generated by the diffusion model with that generated by the Arrhenius&Current escape model. We use the same input potential $u_0(t)$ as in Fig. 8.10. We find that the interval distribution for the diffusive white noise model (derived from stochastic spike arrival; see Chapter 8) and that for the Arrhenius&Current escape model are nearly identical; see Fig. 9.11. Thus the Arrhenius&Current escape model yields an excellent approximation to the diffusive noise model.

Even though the Arrhenius&Current model has been designed for subthreshold stimuli, it also works remarkably well for superthreshold stimuli. An obvious shortcoming of the escape rate (9.30) is that the instantaneous rate decreases with u for $u > \vartheta$. The superthreshold behavior can be corrected if we replace the Gaussian $\exp(-x^2)$ by $2\exp(-x^2)/[1 + \text{erf}(-x)]$ (Herrmann and Gerstner, 2001). The subthreshold behavior remains unchanged compared to Eq. (9.30) but the superthreshold behavior of the escape rate f becomes linear.

9.4.2 *Stochastic resonance*

Noise can – under certain circumstances – improve the signal transmission properties of neuronal systems. In most cases there is an optimum for the noise amplitude which has motivated the name *stochastic resonance* for this rather counterintuitive phenomenon. In this section we discuss stochastic resonance in the context of noisy spiking neurons.

We study the relation between an input $I(t)$ to a neuron and the corresponding output spike train $S(t) = \sum_f \delta(t - t^f)$. In the absence of noise, a subthreshold stimulus $I(t)$ does not generate action potentials so that no information on the temporal structure of the stimulus can be transmitted. In the presence of noise, however, spikes do occur. As we have seen in Eq. (9.30), spike firing is most likely at moments when the normalized distance $|x| = |(u - \vartheta)/\sigma|$ between the membrane potential and the threshold is small. Since the escape rate in Eq. (9.30) depends exponentially on x^2, any variation in the membrane potential $u_0(t)$ that is generated by the temporal structure of the input is enhanced; see Fig. 9.8. On the other hand, for very large noise ($\sigma \to \infty$), we have $x^2 \to 0$, and spike firing occurs at a constant rate, irrespective of the temporal structure of the input. We conclude that there is some intermediate noise level where signal transmission is optimal.

The optimal noise level can be found by plotting the signal-to-noise ratio as a function of noise. Even though stochastic resonance does not require periodicity (see, e.g., Collins *et al.*, 1996), it is typically studied with a periodic input signal such as

$$I^{\text{det}}(t) = I_0 + I_1 \cos(\Omega t). \tag{9.32}$$

For $t - \hat{t} \gg \tau_m$, the membrane potential of the noise-free reference trajectory has the form

$$u_0(t) = u_\infty + u_1 \cos(\Omega t + \varphi_1), \tag{9.33}$$

where u_1 and φ_1 are the amplitude and phase of its periodic component. To quantify the signal transmission properties, a long spike train is studied and the signal-to-noise ratio (SNR) is computed. The signal $\mathscr{S}$ is measured as the amplitude of the power spectral density of the spike train evaluated at frequency Ω, i.e., $\mathscr{S} = \mathscr{P}(\Omega)$. The noise level $\mathscr{N}$ is usually estimated from the noise power $\mathscr{P}_{\text{Poisson}}$ of a Poisson process with the same number of spikes as the measured spike train, i.e., $\mathscr{N} = \mathscr{P}_{\text{Poisson}}$. Figure 9.12 shows the signal-to-noise ratio $\mathscr{S}/\mathscr{N}$ of a periodically stimulated integrate-and-fire neuron as a function of the noise level σ. Two models are shown, namely, diffusive noise (solid line) and escape noise with the Arrhenius&Current escape rate (dashed line). The two curves are rather similar and exhibit a peak at

$$\sigma^{\text{opt}} \approx \frac{2}{3} (\vartheta - u_\infty). \tag{9.34}$$

Since $\sigma^2 = 2\langle \Delta u^2 \rangle$ and $\sqrt{2} \cdot 2/3 \approx 1$, signal transmission is optimal if the stochastic fluctuations of the membrane potential have an amplitude

$$2\sqrt{\langle \Delta u^2 \rangle} \approx \vartheta - u_\infty. \tag{9.35}$$

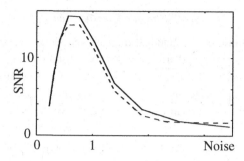

Fig. 9.12 Signal-to-noise ratio (SNR) for the transmission of a periodic signal as a function of the noise level $\sigma/(\vartheta - u_0)$. Solid line: Diffusion model. Dashed line: Arrhenius&Current escape model. Taken from Plesser and Gerstner (2000).

An optimality condition similar to (9.34) holds over a wide variety of stimulation parameters (Plesser, 1999). We will come back to the signal transmission properties of noisy spiking neurons in Chapter 15.

Example: Extracting oscillations

The optimality condition (9.34) can be fulfilled by adapting either the left-hand side or the right-hand side of the equation. Even though it cannot be excluded that a neuron changes its noise level so as to optimize the left-hand side of Eq. (9.34) this does not seem very likely. On the other hand, it is easy to imagine a mechanism that optimizes the right-hand side of Eq. (9.34). For example, an adaptation current could change the value of ϑ, or synaptic weights could be increased or decreased so that the mean potential u_∞ is in the appropriate regime.

We apply the idea of an optimal threshold to a problem of neural coding. More specifically, we study the question of whether an integrate-and-fire neuron or an SRM neuron is sensitive only to the total number of spikes that arrive in some time window T, or also to the relative timing of the input spikes. To do so, we compare two different scenarios of stimulation. In the first scenario, input spikes arrive with a periodically modulated rate,

$$v^{\text{in}}(t) = v_0 + v_1 \cos(\Omega t) \tag{9.36}$$

with $0 < v_1 < v_0$. Thus, even though input spikes arrive stochastically, they have some inherent temporal structure, since they are generated by an *inhomogeneous* Poisson process. In the second scenario, input spikes are generated by a homogeneous (that is, stationary) Poisson process with constant rate v_0. In a large interval $T \gg \Omega^{-1}$, however, we expect in both cases a total number of $v_0 T$ input spikes.

Stochastic spike arrival leads to a fluctuating membrane potential with variance $\Delta^2 = \langle \Delta u^2 \rangle$. If the membrane potential hits the threshold an output spike is emitted. If stimulus

1 is applied during the time T, the neuron emits a certain number of action potentials, say $n^{(1)}$. If stimulus 2 is applied it emits $n^{(2)}$ spikes. It is found that the spike count numbers $n^{(1)}$ and $n^{(2)}$ are significantly different if the threshold is in the range

$$u_\infty + \sqrt{\langle \Delta u^2 \rangle} < \vartheta < u_\infty + 3\sqrt{\langle \Delta u^2 \rangle}. \tag{9.37}$$

We conclude that a neuron in the subthreshold regime is capable of transforming a temporal code (amplitude v_1 of the variations in the input) into a spike count code (Kempter et al., 1998). Such a transformation plays an important role in the auditory pathway (Miller and Mark, 1992; Konishi, 1993; Kempter et al., 1999b).

9.5 Summary

Neuronal noise in the output can be described as a stochastic firing intensity, or escape rate, which depends on the momentary distance of the membrane potential from the threshold. The concept of escape rate can be applied to a large class of generalized integrate-and-fire models. An SRM with exponential escape rate is particularly attractive for several reasons. First, experimental data suggest an exponential escape rate (Fig. 9.3). Second, a wide spectrum of subthreshold effects can be captured by the linear filters of the SRM (Chapter 6). Third, when driven with a noisy input, nonlinear neuron models such as the AdEx can be well approximated by the SRM with exponential escape noise (Fig. 9.9). Fourth, the explicit formulas for the likelihood of an observed spike train (Section 9.2) enable a rapid fit of the neuron model to experimental data, using the concept of Generalized Linear Models to be discussed in the next chapter.

Escape noise gives rise to variability in spike firing even if the input is perfectly known. It can therefore be linked to intrinsic noise sources such as channel noise. However, more generally, any unknown component of the input which may, for example, arise from stochastic spike arrival can also be approximated by an appropriate escape rate function (Section 9.4). Thus the escape rate provides a phenomenological noise model that summarizes effects of biophysical channel noise as well as stochastic input.

Literature

The Spike Response Model with exponential escape noise was introduced in Gerstner and van Hemmen (1992) and Gerstner (1995), but closely related models had already been applied to neuronal data by Brillinger (1988) and have an obvious link to Generalized Linear Models, which were used in statistics as early as the 1970s (Nelder and Wederburn, 1972) and have been repeatedly applied to neuronal data (Truccolo et al., 2005; Pillow et al., 2008). The choice of an exponential escape rate for experimental data has been demonstrated by Jolivet et al. (2006).

The term escape noise has been chosen in analogy to the Arrhenius formula which describes the escape of a particle (or a chemical process) across an energy barrier in the presence of thermal energy (van Kampen, 1992).

The relation of diffusive noise in the input to escape noise has been studied by Plesser and Gerstner (2000), Herrmann and Gerstner (2001) and Mensi *et al.* (2011). Stochastic resonance has been a popular topic of research for many years, starting in 1989 (McNamara and Wiesenfeld, 1989; Douglass *et al.*, 1993; Longtin, 1993; Collins *et al.*, 1996). A nice review on stochastic resonance can be found in Gammaitoni *et al.* (1998).

Exercises

1. **Integrate-and-fire model with linear escape rates.** *Consider a leaky integrate-and-fire neuron with linear escape rate,*

$$\rho_I(t|\hat{t}) = \beta \, [u(t|\hat{t}) - \vartheta]_+. \tag{9.38}$$

   (a) Start with the non-leaky integrate-and-fire model by considering the limit of $\tau_m \to \infty$. The membrane potential of the model is then

$$u(t|\hat{t}) = u_r + \frac{1}{C} \int_{\hat{t}}^{t} I(t')dt' . \tag{9.39}$$

   Assume constant input, set $u_r = 0$ and calculate the hazard and the interval distribution.

   (b) Consider the leaky integrate-and-fire model with time constant τ and constant input I_0. Determine the membrane potential, the hazard, and the interval distribution.

2. **Likelihood of a spike train.** *In an in-vitro experiment, a time-dependent current $I(t)$ was injected into a neuron for a time $0 < t < T$ and four spikes were observed at times $0 < t^1 < t^2 < t^3 < t^4 < T$.*

   (a) What is the likelihood that this spike train could have been generated by a leaky integrate-and-fire model with linear escape rate defined in Eq. (9.38)?

   (b) Rewrite the likelihood in terms of the interval distribution and hazard of time-dependent renewal theory.

10

Estimating parameters of probabilistic
neuron models

It is helpful to break neural data analysis into two basic problems. The "encoding" problem concerns how information is encoded in neural spike trains: can we predict the spike trains of a neuron (or population of neurons), given an arbitrary synaptic input, current injection, or sensory stimulus? Conversely, the "decoding" problem concerns how much we can learn from the observation of a sequence of spikes: in particular, how well can we estimate the stimulus that gave rise to the spike train?

The problems of encoding and decoding are difficult both because neural responses are stochastic and because we want to identify these response properties given any possible stimulus in some very large set (e.g., all images that might occur in the world), and there are typically many more such stimuli than we can hope to sample by brute force. Thus the neural coding problem is fundamentally *statistical*: given a finite number of samples of noisy physiological data, how do we estimate, in a global sense, the neural codebook?

This basic question has taken on a new urgency as neurophysiological recordings allow us to peer into the brain with ever greater facility: with the development of fast computers, inexpensive memory, and large-scale multineuronal recording and high-resolution imaging techniques, it has become feasible to directly observe and analyze neural activity at a level of detail that was impossible in the twentieth century. Experimenter now routinely record from hundreds of neurons simultaneously, providing great challenges for data analysis by computational neuroscientists and statisticians. Indeed, it has become clear that sophisticated statistical techniques are necessary to understand the neural code: many of the key questions cannot be answered without powerful statistical tools.

This chapter describes statistical model-based techniques that provide a unified approach to both encoding and decoding. These *statistical* models can capture stimulus dependencies as well as spike history and interneuronal interaction effects in population of spike trains, and are intimately related to the generalized integrate-and-fire models discussed in previous chapters.

In Section 10.1, we establish the notation that enables us to identify relevant model parameters and introduce the concept of parameter optimization in a linear model. We then leave the realm of linear models and turn to the models that we have discussed in preceding chapters (e.g., the Spike Response Model with escape noise in Chapter 9) where spike generation is stochastic and nonlinear.

In Section 10.2, we describe the same neuron models of spike trains in the slightly more abstract language of statistics. The likelihood of a spike train given the stimulus plays a central role in statistical models of encoding. As we have seen in Chapter 9, the stochasticity introduced by "escape noise" in the Spike Response Model (SRM) or other generalized integrate-and-fire models enables us to write down the likelihood that an observed spike train could have been generated by the neuron model. Likelihood-based optimization methods for fitting these neuron models to data allow us to predict neuronal spike timing for future, unknown stimuli. Thus, the SRM and other generalized integrate-and-fire models can be viewed as *encoding* models. In Chapter 11 we shall see that the same models can also be used to perform optimal decoding.

The emphasis of this chapter is on likelihood-based methods for model optimization. The likelihood-based optimization methods are computationally tractable, due to a key concavity property of the model likelihood (Paninski, 2004). However, likelihood is just one of several quantities that can be chosen to compare spike trains, and other measures to quantify the performance of models can also be used. In Section 10.3 we review different performance measures for the "goodness-of-fit" of a model. In particular, we present the notion of "spike train similarity" and the "time rescaling theorem" (Brown *et al.*, 2002).

Finally, in Section 10.4 we apply the ideas developed in this chapter to adaptively choose the optimal stimuli for characterizing the response function.

10.1 Parameter optimization in linear and nonlinear models

Before we turn to the statistical formulation of models of encoding and decoding, we need to introduce the language of statistics into neuron modeling. In particular, we will define what is meant by convex problems, optimal solutions, *linear* models and *generalized linear* models.

When choosing a neuron model for which we want to estimate the parameters from data, we must satisfy three competing desiderata:

(i) The model must be flexible and powerful enough to fit the observed data. For example, a linear model might be easy to fit, but not powerful enough to account for the data.

(ii) The model must be tractable: we need to be able to fit the model given the modest amount of data available in a physiological recording (preferably using modest computational resources as well); moreover, the model should not be so complex that we cannot assign an intuitive functional role to the inferred parameters.

(iii) The model must respect what is already known about the underlying physiology and anatomy of the system; ideally, we should be able to interpret the model parameters and predictions not only in statistical terms (e.g., confidence intervals, significance tests) but also in biophysical terms (membrane noise, dendritic filtering, etc.). For example, with a purely statistical "black box" model we might be able to make predictions and test their significance, but we will not be able to make links to the biophysics of neurons.

While in general there are many varieties of encoding models that could conceivably

(a)

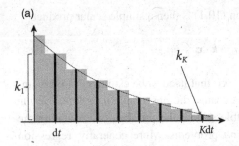

(b)

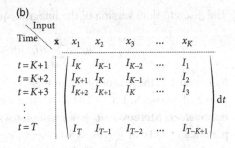

Fig. 10.1 Measurement of membrane filter. (a) Schematic of the linear membrane filter κ in discrete time. (b) Matrix of temporal inputs (schematic). At each moment in time, the last K time steps of the input current I_t serve as an input vector. Rows of the matrix correspond to different input samples.

satisfy these three conditions, in this chapter we will mainly focus on the SRM with escape noise (Chapter 9). In a more general setting (see Chapter 11), the linear filter can be interpreted not just as local biophysical processes within the neuron, but as a summary of the whole signal processing chain from sensory inputs to the neuron under consideration. In such a general setting, the SRM may also be seen as an example of a "generalized linear" model (GLM) (Paninski, 2004; Truccolo *et al.*, 2005). In the following two subsections, we review linear and Generalized Linear Models from the point of view of neuronal dynamics: how is a stimulus $I(t)$ encoded by the neuron?

10.1.1 *Linear models*

Let us suppose that an experimenter injects, with a first electrode, a time-dependent current $I(t)$ in an interval $0 < t \le T$ while recording with a second electrode the membrane voltage $u^{\text{exp}}(t)$. The maximal amplitude of the input current has been chosen small enough for the neuron to stay in the subthreshold regime. We may therefore assume that the voltage is well described by our linear model

$$u(t) = \int_0^\infty \kappa(s)I(t-s)\,\mathrm{d}s + u_{\text{rest}}; \tag{10.1}$$

see Section 1.3.5. In order to determine the filter κ that describes the linear properties of the experimental neuron, we discretize time in steps of $\mathrm{d}t$ and denote the voltage measurement and injected current at time t by u_t^{exp} and I_t, respectively. Here the time subscript $t \in \mathbb{Z}$ is an integer time step counter. We set $K = s^{\text{max}}/\mathrm{d}t$ where $\max(s) \in \mathbb{N}$ and introduce a vector

$$k = (\kappa(\mathrm{d}t), \kappa(2\mathrm{d}t), \dots, \kappa(K\mathrm{d}t)) \tag{10.2}$$

which describes the time course κ in discrete time; see Fig. 10.1a. Similarly, the input current I during the last K time steps is given by the vector

$$x_t = (I_{t-1}, I_{t-2}, \dots, I_{t-K})\,\mathrm{d}t. \tag{10.3}$$

The discrete-time version of the integral equation (10.1) is then a simple scalar product

$$u_t = \sum_{l=1}^{K} k_l I_{t-l} dt + u_{\text{rest}} = \boldsymbol{k} \cdot \boldsymbol{x}_t + u_{\text{rest}}. \tag{10.4}$$

Note that $\boldsymbol{k}$ is the vector of parameters $k_1, k_2, \ldots, k_K$ that need to be estimated. In the language of statistics, Eq. (10.4) is a linear model because the observable u_t is *linear in the parameters*. Moreover, u_t is a continuous variable so that the problem of estimating the parameters falls in the class of *linear regression* problems. More generally, regression problems refer to the prediction or modeling of continuous variables whereas classification problems refer to the modeling or prediction of discrete variables.

To find a good choice of parameters $\boldsymbol{k}$, we compare the prediction u_t of the model equation (10.4) with the experimental measurement u_t^{exp}. In a least-square error approach, the components of the vector $\boldsymbol{k}$ will be chosen such that the squared difference between model voltage and experimental voltage

$$E(\boldsymbol{k}) = \sum_{t=K+1}^{T} \left(u_t^{\text{exp}} - u_t\right)^2 \tag{10.5}$$

is minimal. An important insight is the following. For any model that is linear in the parameters, the function E in Eq. (10.5) is *quadratic and convex* in the parameters $\boldsymbol{k}$ of the model. Therefore

(i) the function E has no non-global local minima as a function of the parameter vector $\boldsymbol{k}$ (in fact, the set of minimizers of E forms a linear subspace in this case, and simple conditions are available to verify that E has a single global minimum, as discussed below);

(ii) the minimum can be found either numerically by gradient descent or analytically by matrix inversion.

While the explicit solution is only possible for linear models, the numerical gradient descent is possible for all kinds of error functions E and yields a unique solution if the error has a *unique* minimum. In particular, for all error functions which are convex, gradient descent converges to the optimal solution (Fig. 10.2) – and this is what we will exploit in Section 10.2.

Example: Analytical solution

For the analytical solution of the least-square optimization problem, defined by Eqs. (10.4) and (10.5), it is convenient to collect all time points u_t, $K+1 < t < T$ into a single vector $u = (u_{K+1}, u_{K+2}, \ldots, u_T)$ which describes the membrane voltage of the model. Similarly, the observed voltage in the experiment is summarized by the vector $u^{\text{exp}} = (u_{K+1}^{\text{exp}}, \ldots, u_T^{\text{exp}})$. Furthermore, let us align the observed input vectors $\boldsymbol{x}$ into a matrix X. More precisely, the matrix has $T - K$ rows consisting of the vector $\boldsymbol{x}_t$; see Fig. 10.1b. With this notation, Eq. (10.4) can be written as a matrix equation

$$u = X \boldsymbol{k}^{\text{T}} + u_{\text{rest}}, \tag{10.6}$$

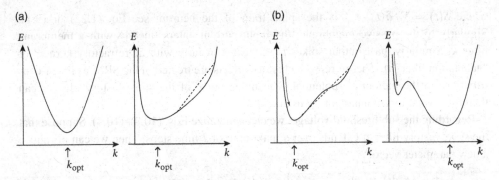

Fig. 10.2 Convex function and global minimum. (a) A quadratic function (left) and an arbitrary convex function (right). A convex function is curved upward so that any straight line (dashed) connecting two points on the curve stays above the curve. A convex function cannot have a non-global minimum. (b) A non-convex function without (left) and with (right) a non-global minimum. Gradient descent refers to a change of the parameter k that leads to a downward move (arrow) on the error surface. In the case on the right, a gradient-descent method can get stuck in the local minimum.

where u_{rest} is a vector with all components equal to u_{rest}. We suppose that the value of u_{rest} has already been determined in an earlier experiment.

We search for the minimum of Eq. (10.5), defined by $\nabla_k E = 0$ (where $\nabla_k E$ denotes the gradient of E with respect to k), which gives rise a single linear equation for each component of the parameter vector k, i.e., a set of K linear equations. With our matrix notation, the error function is a scalar product

$$E(k) = [u^{\text{exp}} - Xk - u_{\text{rest}}]^{\text{T}} \cdot [u^{\text{exp}} - Xk - u_{\text{rest}}] \tag{10.7}$$

and the unique solution of the set of linear equations is the parameter vector

$$\hat{k}_{\text{LS}} = (X^{\text{T}}X)^{-1} X^{\text{T}} (u^{\text{exp}} - u_{\text{rest}}), \tag{10.8}$$

assuming the matrix $(X^{\text{T}}X)$ is invertible. (If this matrix is non-invertible, then a unique minimum does not exist.) The subscript highlights that the parameter $\hat{k}_{\text{LS}}$ has been determined by least-square optimization.

10.1.2 Generalized Linear Models

The above linearity arguments not only work in the subthreshold regime, but can be extended to the case of spiking neurons. In the deterministic formulation of the Spike Response Model, the membrane voltage is given as

$$u(t) = \int_0^\infty \eta(s)S(t-s)\,ds + \int_0^\infty \kappa(s)I(t-s)\,ds + u_{\text{rest}}, \tag{10.9}$$

where $S(t) = \sum_f \delta(t - t^f)$ is the spike train of the neuron; see Eq. (1.22) or (9.1). Similarly to the passive membrane, the input current enters linearly with a membrane filter κ. Similarly, past output spikes $t^f < t$ enter linearly with a "refractory kernel" or "adaptation filter" η. Therefore, spike history effects are treated in the SRM as linear contributions to the membrane potential. The time course of the spike history filter η can therefore be estimated analogously to that of κ.

Regarding the subthreshold voltage, we can generalize Eqs. (10.2)–(10.4). Suppose that the spike history filter η extends over a maximum of J time steps. Then we can introduce a new parameter vector

$$k = (\kappa(dt), \kappa(2dt), \ldots, \kappa(Kdt), \eta(dt), \eta(2dt), \ldots, \eta(Jdt), u_{\text{rest}}) \qquad (10.10)$$

which includes both the membrane filter κ and the spike history filter η. The spike train in the last J time steps is represented by the spike count sequence $n_{t-1}, n_{t-2}, \ldots, n_{t-J}$, where $n_t \in \{0, 1\}$, and included into the "input" vector

$$x_t = (I_{t-1}dt, I_{t-2}dt, \ldots, I_{t-K}dt, n_{t-1}, n_{t-2}, \ldots, n_{t-J}, 1). \qquad (10.11)$$

The discrete-time version of the voltage equation in the SRM is then again a simple scalar product

$$u_t = \sum_{j=1}^{J} k_{K+j} n_{t-j} + \sum_{k=1}^{K} k_k I_{t-k} dt + u_{\text{rest}} = k \cdot x_t. \qquad (10.12)$$

Thus, the membrane voltage during the interspike intervals is a linear regression problem that can be solved as before by minimizing the mean square error.

Spiking itself, however, is a *nonlinear* process. In the SRM with escape rate, the firing intensity is

$$\rho(t) = f(u(t) - \vartheta) = f(k \cdot x_t - \vartheta). \qquad (10.13)$$

We have assumed that the firing threshold is constant, but this is no limitation since, in terms of spiking, any dynamic threshold can be included into the spike-history filter η.

We emphasize that the firing intensity in Eq. (10.13) is a *nonlinear* function of the parameters k and b that we need to estimate. Nevertheless, rapid parameter estimation is still possible if the function f has properties that we will identify in Section 10.2. The reason is that in each time step firing is stochastic with an instantaneous firing intensity f that only depends on the momentary value of the membrane potential – where the membrane potential can be written as a *linear* function of the parameters. This insight leads to the notion of Generalized Linear Models (GLM). For an SRM with exponential escape noise $\rho(t) = f(u(t) - \vartheta) = \rho_0 \exp(u(t) - \vartheta)$ the likelihood of a spike train

$$L^n(\{t^{(1)}, t^{(2)}, \ldots, t^{(n)}\}) = \rho(t^{(1)}) \cdot \rho(t^{(2)}) \cdot \ldots \cdot \rho(t^{(n)}) \exp\left[-\int_0^T \rho(s)ds\right], \qquad (10.14)$$

which we have already defined in Eq. (9.10), is a log-concave function of the parameters (Paninski, 2004); i.e., the loglikelihood is a concave function. We will discuss this result in

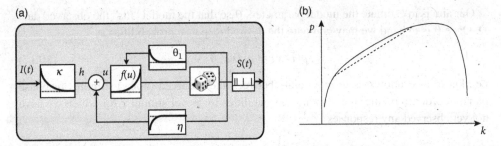

Fig. 10.3 SRM revisited. (a) The SRM takes as input a time-dependent current $I(t)$ and generates a spike train $S(t)$ at the output. The parameters of the model control the shape of the filters κ, θ_1 and η. (b) If the escape rate $f(u - \vartheta)$ is exponential and the parameters k enter linearly into the voltage equation u and the threshold ϑ, then the likelihood p that a specific spike train is generated by the model is a concave (i.e., downward curving) function of the parameters (Paninski, 2004).

the next section as it is the fundamental reason why parameter optimization for the SRM is computationally efficient (Fig. 10.3).

GLMs are fundamental tools in statistics for which a great deal of theory and computational methods are available. In what follows we exploit the elegant mathematical properties of GLMs.

10.2 Statistical formulation of encoding models

Let us denote the observed spike train data by D. In general, D could represent measurements from a population of neurons. To keep the arguments simple, we focus for the moment on a single neuron, but at the end of the section we will extend the approach to a population of interacting neurons. If the time bins are chosen smaller than the absolute refractory period, the discretized spike train is described by a sequence of scalar variables n_t in an interval $0 < t \leq T$

$$D = \{n_1, n_2, \ldots, n_T\} \tag{10.15}$$

see Fig. 9.6. If time bins are large, spike counts can take values larger than 1.

A neural "encoding model" is a model that assigns a conditional probability, $p(D|x)$, to any possible neural response D given a stimulus x. The vector x_t can include the momentary stimulus presented at time t, or more generally the concatenated spatio-temporal stimulus history up to time t. Examples have been given in Section 10.1.

As emphasized in the introduction to this chapter, it is not feasible to directly measure this probability $p(D|x)$ for all stimulus-response pairs (x, D), simply because there are infinitely many potential stimuli. We therefore hypothesize some encoding model,

$$p(D|x, \theta). \tag{10.16}$$

Here θ is a short-hand notation for the set of all model parameters. In the examples of the previous section, the model parameters are $\theta = \{k, b\}$.

Our aim is to estimate the model parameters θ so that the model "fits" the observed data D. Once θ is in hand we may compute the desired response probabilities as

$$p(D|x) \approx p(D|x, \theta),\tag{10.17}$$

i.e., knowing θ allows us to interpolate between the observed (noisy) stimulus-response pairs, in order to predict the response probabilities for novel stimuli x for which we have not yet observed any responses.

10.2.1 Parameter estimation

How do we find a good estimate for the parameters θ for a chosen model class? The general recipe is as follows. The first step is to introduce a model that makes sense biophysically, and incorporates our prior knowledge in a tractable manner. Next we write down the likelihood of the observed data given the model parameters, along with a prior distribution that encodes our prior beliefs about the model parameters. Finally, we compute the posterior distribution of the model parameters given the observed data, using Bayes' rule, which states that

$$p(\theta|D) \propto p(D|\theta)p(\theta);\tag{10.18}$$

the left-hand side is the desired posterior distribution, while the right-hand side is just the product of the likelihood and the prior.

In the current setting, we need to write down the likelihood $p(D|X, k)$ of the observed spike data D given the model parameter k and the observed set of stimuli summarized in the matrix X, and then we may employ standard likelihood optimization methods to obtain the maximum likelihood (ML) or maximum a posteriori (MAP) solutions for k, defined by

$$\text{ML}: \quad \hat{k}_{\text{ML}} = \text{argmax}_k\{p(D|X, k)\},\tag{10.19}$$

$$\text{MAP}: \quad \hat{k}_{\text{MAP}} = \text{argmax}_k\{p(D|X, k)\, p(k)\},\tag{10.20}$$

where the maximization runs over all possible parameter choices.

We assume that spike counts per bin follow a conditional Poisson distribution, given $\rho(t)$:

$$n_t \sim \text{Poiss}[\rho(t)dt];\tag{10.21}$$

see text and exercises of Chapter 7. For example, with the rate parameter of the Poisson distribution given by a GLM or SRM model $\rho(t) = f(k \cdot x_t)$, we have

$$p(D|X, k) = \prod_t \left\{ \frac{[f(k \cdot x_t)dt]^{n_t}}{(n_t)!} \exp[-f(x_t \cdot k)dt] \right\}.\tag{10.22}$$

Here $\prod_t$ denotes the product over all time steps. We recall that, by definition, $n_t! = 1$ for $n_t = 0$.

Our aim is to optimize the parameter k. For a given observed spike train, the spike count numbers n_t are fixed. In this case, $(dt)^{n_t}/(n_t)!$ is a constant which is irrelevant for the parameter optimization. If we work with a fixed time step dt and drop all units, we can therefore reshuffle the terms and consider the logarithm of the above likelihood

$$\log p(D|X,k) = c_0 + \sum_t (n_t \log f(k \cdot x_t) - f(x_t \cdot k) dt) .$$ (10.23)

If we choose the time step dt shorter than the half-width of an action potential, say 1 ms, the spike count variable n_t can only take the values zero or 1. For small dt, the likelihood of Eq. (10.22) is then identical to that of the SRM with escape noise, defined in Chapter 9; see Eqs. (9.10) and (9.15)–(9.17).

We don't have an analytical expression for the maximum of the likelihood defined in Eq. (10.22), but nonetheless we can numerically optimize this function quite easily if we are willing to make two assumptions about the nonlinear function $f(.)$. More precisely, if we assume that

(i) $f(u)$ is a convex (upward-curving) function of its scalar argument u, and

(ii) $\log f(u)$ is concave (downward-curving) in u,

then the log likelihood above is guaranteed to be a concave function of the parameter k, since in this case the log-likelihood is just a sum of concave functions of k (Paninski, 2004).

This implies that the likelihood has no non-global maximum (also called local maximum). Therefore the maximum likelihood parameter $\hat{k}_{ML}$ may be found by numerical ascent techniques; see Fig. 10.2. Functions $f(.)$ satisfying these two constraints are easy to think of: for example, the standard linear rectifier and the exponential function both work.

Fitting model parameters proceeds as follows: we form the (augmented) matrix X where each row is now

$$x_t = (1, I_{t-1} dt, I_{t-2} dt, \ldots, I_{t-K} dt, n_{t-1}, n_{t-2}, \ldots, n_{t-J}) .$$ (10.24)

Similarly, the parameter vector is in analogy to Eq. (10.10)

$$k = (b, \kappa(dt), \kappa(2dt), \ldots, \kappa(Kdt), \eta(dt), \eta(2dt), \ldots, \eta(Jdt));$$ (10.25)

here $b = u_{rest} - \vartheta$ is a constant offset term which we want to optimize.

We then calculate the log-likelihood

$$\log p(D|X,k) = \sum_t (n_t \log f(X_t \cdot k) - f(X_t \cdot k) dt)$$ (10.26)

and compute the ML or maximum *a posteriori* (MAP) solution for the model parameters k by a concave optimization algorithm. Note that, while we still assume that the conditional spike count n_t within a given short time bin is drawn from a one-dimensional Poiss ($\rho(t) dt$) distribution given $\rho(t)$, the resulting model displays strong history effects (since $\rho(t)$ depends on the past spike trains) and therefore the output of the model, considered as a vector of counts $D = \{n_t\}$, is no longer a Poisson process, unless $\eta = 0$. Importantly, because of the refractory effects incorporated by a strong negative η at small times, the spike count variable n_t cannot take a value larger than 1 if dt is in the range of one or a few milliseconds. Therefore, we can expect that interspike intervals are correctly reproduced in the model; see Fig. 10.5 for an example application.

Finally, we may expand the definition of X to include observations of other spike trains, and therefore develop GLMs not just of single spike trains, but network models of how populations of neurons encode information jointly (Chornoboy *et al.*, 1988; Paninski *et al.*, 2004; Truccolo *et al.*, 2005; Pillow *et al.*, 2008). The resulting model is summarized as follows: Spike counts are conditionally Poisson distributed given $\rho_i(t)$ $n_{i,t} \sim \text{Poiss}(\rho_i(t)dt)$ with a firing rate

$$\rho_i(t) = f\left(k_i \cdot x_t + \sum_{i' \neq i,j} \varepsilon_{i',j} n_{i',t-j}\right). \tag{10.27}$$

Here, $\rho_i(t)$ denotes the instantaneous firing rate of the ith cell at time t and k_i is the cell's linear receptive field including spike-history effects; see Eq. (10.25). The net effect of a spike of neuron i' onto the membrane potential of neuron i is summarized by $\varepsilon_{i',j}$; these terms are summed over all past spike activity $n_{i',t-j}$ in the population of cells from which we are recording simultaneously. In the special case that we record from all neurons in the population, $\varepsilon_{i',j}$ can be interpreted as the excitatory or inhibitory postsynaptic potential caused by a spike of neuron i' a time $j\,dt$ earlier.

Example: Linear regression and voltage estimation

It may be helpful to draw an analogy to linear regression here. We want to show that the standard procedure of least-square minimization can be linked to statistical parameter estimation under the assumption of Gaussian noise.

We consider the linear voltage model of Eq. (10.1). We are interested in the temporal filter properties of the neuron when it is driven by a time-dependent input $I(t)$. Let us set $x_t = (I_t, I_{t-1}, \ldots, I_{t-K})\,dt$ and $k = (\kappa(dt), \ldots, \kappa(K\,dt))$. If we assume that the discrete-time voltage measurements have a Gaussian distribution around the mean predicted by the model of Eq. (10.4), then we need to maximize the likelihood

$$\log p(D|X,k) = c_1 - c_2 \sum_t (u_t - (k \cdot x_t))^2, \tag{10.28}$$

where $X = (x_1, x_2, \ldots, x_T)$ is the matrix of observed stimuli, c_1, c_2 are constants that do not depend on the parameter k, and the sum in t is over all observed time bins. Maximization yields $k_{\text{opt}} = (X^T X)^{-1} \left(\sum_t u_t x_t / dt\right)$ which determines the time course of the filter $\kappa(s)$ that characterizes the passive membrane properties. The result is identical to Eq. (10.8):

$$\hat{k}_{\text{opt}} = \hat{k}_{\text{LS}}. \tag{10.29}$$

10.2.2 Regularization: maximum penalized likelihood

In the linear regression case it is well known that estimates of the components of the parameter vector k can be quite noisy when the dimension of k is large. The noisiness of the estimate $\hat{k}_{\text{ML}}$ is roughly proportional to the dimensionality of k (the number of parameters

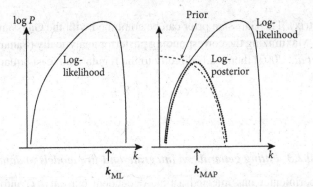

Fig. 10.4 Regularization. Because of the concavity, there is only a single global maximum of the log-likelihood which defines the optimal parameter choice k_{ML}. Right: Example of regularization by a prior (dashed line) that favors a smaller value for k_{MAP}.

in k that we need to estimate from data) divided by the total number of observed samples (Paninski, 2003). The same "overfitting" phenomenon (estimator variability increasing with number of parameters) occurs in the GLM context. A variety of methods have been introduced to "regularize" the estimated k, to incorporate prior knowledge about the shape and/or magnitude of the true k to reduce the noise in $\hat{k}_{\mathrm{ML}}$. One basic idea is to restrict k to lie within a lower-dimensional subspace; we then employ the same fitting procedure to estimate the coefficients of k within this lower-dimensional basis (model selection procedures may be employed to choose the dimensionality of this subspace (Truccolo *et al.*, 2005)).

A slightly less restrictive approach is to maximize the posterior

$$p(k|X,D) \propto p(D|X,k)p(k) \tag{10.30}$$

(with k allowed to take values in the full original basis), instead of the likelihood $p(D|X,k)$; here $p(k)$ encodes our *a priori* beliefs about the true underlying k.

It is easy to incorporate this maxima *a posteriori* idea in the GLM context (Paninski, 2004): we simply maximize

$$\log p(k|X,D) = c + \log p(k) + \log p(D|X,k) \tag{10.31}$$
$$= c + \log p(k) + \sum_t \left(n_t \log f(x_t \cdot k) - f(x_t \cdot k) dt \right). \tag{10.32}$$

Whenever $\log p(k)$ is a concave function of k, this "penalized" likelihood (where $\log p(k)$ acts to penalize improbable values of k) is a concave function of k, and ascent-based maximization may proceed (with no local maximum) as before; see Fig. 10.4.

Example: Linear regression and Gaussian prior

In the linear regression case, the computationally simplest prior is a zero-mean Gaussian, $\log p(k) = c - k^{\mathrm{T}} A k / 2$, where A is a positive definite matrix (the inverse covariance matrix). The Gaussian prior can be combined with the Gaussian noise model of Eq. (10.28). Maximizing the corresponding posterior analytically (Sahani and Linden, 2003; Smyth *et al.*, 2003) then leads directly to the regularized least-square estimator

$$\hat{k}_{\text{RLS}} = (X^{\mathsf{T}}X + A)^{-1} \left(\sum_t u_t x_t / \mathrm{d}t \right). \tag{10.33}$$

10.2.3 Fitting generalized integrate-and-fire models to data

Suppose an experimenter has injected a time-dependent current $I(t)$ into a neuron and has recorded with a second electrode the voltage $u^{\text{exp}}(t)$ of the same neuron. The voltage trajectory contains spikes $S(t) = \sum_f \delta(t - t^f)$ with firing times $t^{(1)}, t^{(2)}, ..., t^{(N)}$. The natural approach would be to write down the joint likelihood of observing both the spike times and the subthreshold membrane potential (Paninski *et al.*, 2005). A simpler approach would be to maximize the likelihood of observing the spike separately from the likelihood of observing the membrane potential.

Given the input $I(t)$ and the spike train $S(t)$, the voltage of an SRM is given by Eq. (10.9) and we can adjust the parameters of the filter κ and η so as to minimize the squared error Eq. (10.5). We now fix the parameters for the membrane potential and maximize the likelihood of observing the spike times given our model voltage trajectory $u(t)$. We insert $u(t)$ into the escape rate function $\rho(t) = f(u(t) - \vartheta(t))$ which contains the parameters of the threshold

$$\vartheta(t) = \vartheta_0 + \int_0^\infty \theta_1(s) S(t - s) \mathrm{d}s. \tag{10.34}$$

We then calculate the log-likelihood

$$\log p(D|X, k) = c + \sum_t \left(n_t \log f(X_t \cdot k) - f(X_t \cdot k) \mathrm{d}t \right) \tag{10.35}$$

and compute the ML or maximum *a posteriori* (MAP) solution for the model parameters k (which are the parameters of the threshold – the subthreshold voltage parameters are already fixed) by an optimization algorithm for concave functions.

Fig. 10.5 shows an example application. Both voltage in the subthreshold regime and spike times are nicely reproduced. Therefore, we can expect that interspike intervals are correctly reproduced as well. In order to quantify the performance of neuron models, we need to develop criteria of "goodness-of-fit" for subthreshold membrane potential, spike timings, and possibly higher-order spike-train statistics. This is the topic of Section 10.3; we will return to similar applications in the next chapter.

10.2.4 Extensions (*)

The GLM encoding framework described here can be extended in a number of important directions. We briefly describe two such directions here.

First, as we have described the GLM above, it may appear that the model is restricted to including only linear dependencies on the stimulus x_t, through the $k \cdot x_t$ term. However, if we modify our input matrix X once again, to include nonlinear transformations $\mathscr{F}_j(x)$ of the stimulus x, we may fit nonlinear models of the form

$$\rho(t) = f\left(\sum_j a_j \mathscr{F}_j(x)\right) \tag{10.36}$$

efficiently by maximizing the log-likelihood $\log p(D|X, a)$ with respect to the weight parameter a (Wu *et al.*, 2006; Ahrens *et al.*, 2008). Mathematically, the nonlinearities $\mathscr{F}_j(x)$ may take essentially arbitrary form; physiologically speaking, it is clearly wise to choose $\mathscr{F}_j(x)$ to reflect known facts about the anatomy and physiology of the system (e.g., $\mathscr{F}_j(x)$ might model inputs from a presynaptic layer whose responses are better-characterized than are those of the neuron of interest (Rust *et al.*, 2006)).

Second, in many cases it is reasonable to include terms in X that we may not be able to observe or calculate directly (e.g., intracellular noise, or the dynamical state of the network); fitting the model parameters in this case requires that we properly account for these "latent," unobserved variables in our likelihood. While inference in the presence of these hidden parameters is beyond the scope of this chapter, it is worth noting that this type of model may fit tractably using generalizations of the methods described here, at the cost of increased computational complexity, but the benefit of enhanced model flexibility and realism (Smith and Brown, 2003; Yu *et al.*, 2009; Vidne *et al.*, 2012).

Example: Estimating spike triggered currents and dynamic threshold

In Fig. 10.1a, we have suggested estimating the filter $\kappa(s)$ by extracting its values $k_j = \kappa(j dt)$ at discrete equally spaced time steps: the integral $\int_0^\infty \kappa(s) I(t-s) ds = \sum_{j=1}^K k_l I_{t-j} dt$ is linear in the K parameters.

However, the observables remain *linear in the parameters* (k_j) if we set $\kappa(s) = \sum_{j=1}^4 k_j \exp(-s/\tau_j)$ with fixed time constants, e.g., $\tau_j = 10^j$ ms. Again, the integral $\int_0^\infty \kappa(s) I(t-s) ds = \sum_{j=1}^4 k_j \int_0^\infty \exp(-s/\tau_j) I(t-s) ds$ is linear in the parameters. The exponentials play the role of "basis functions" F_j.

Similarly, the threshold filter $\vartheta_1(s)$ or the spike-afterpotential $\eta(s)$ can be expressed with basis functions. A common choice is to take rectangular basis functions F_j which take a value of unity on a finite interval $[t_j, t_{j+1}]$. Exponential spacing $t_j = 2^{j-1}$ ms of time points allows us to cover a large time span with a small number of parameters. Regular spacing leads back to the naive discretization scheme.

10.3 Evaluating goodness-of-fit

No single method provides a complete assessment of goodness-of-fit; rather, model fitting should always be seen as a loop, in which we start by fitting a model, then examine the

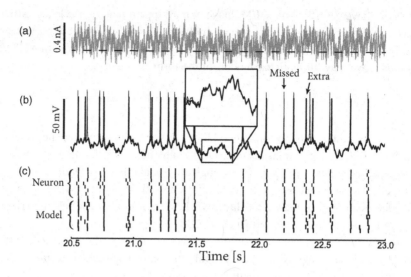

Fig. 10.5 Comparing models with intracellular recordings. (a) A noisy time-dependent current is used to stimulate the neurons experimentally (dashed line corresponds to zero current). (b) Recording from the neuron (thin black line) shows membrane potential fluctuations and action potentials. Simulating an SRM (thick black line) with the same current and using parameters previously optimized on a different dataset shows similar membrane potential fluctuations (inset) and action potentials. Some of the spikes are missed, some are added, but most coincide with the recorded ones. (c) Multiple repeated stimulations with the same current shows the intrinsic variability of neural responses (the first nine rows are recorded action potentials indicated by thick black ticks). The variability is matched by the model (the last nine rows are model action potentials). Data and models from Mensi *et al.* (2012).

results, attempt to diagnose any model failures, and then improve our model accordingly. In the following, we describe different methods for assessing the goodness-of-fit.

Before beginning with specific examples of these methods, we note that it is very important to evaluate the goodness-of-fit on data that was not used for fitting. The part of the data used for fitting model parameters is called the *training set* and the part of the data reserved to evaluate the goodness-of-fit is called the *test set*. Data in the test set is said to be *predicted* by the model, while it is simply *reproduced* in the training set. By simply adding parameters to the model, the quality of the fit on the training set increases. Given a sufficient number of parameters, the model might be able to reproduce the training set perfectly, but that does not mean that data in the test set is well predicted. In fact it is usually the opposite: overly complicated models that are "overfit" on the training data (i.e., which fit not only the reproducible signal in the training set but also the noise) will often do a bad job generalizing and predicting new data in the test set. Thus in the following we assume that the goodness-of-fit quantities are computed using "cross-validation": parameters are estimated using the training set, and then the goodness-of-fit quantification is performed on the test set.

10.3.1 Comparing spiking membrane potential recordings

Given a spiking membrane potential recording, we can use traditional measures such as the squared error between model and recorded voltage to evaluate the goodness-of-fit. This approach, however, implicitly assumes that the remaining error has a Gaussian distribution (recall the close relationship between Gaussian noise and the squared error, discussed above). Under diffusive noise, we have seen (Chapter 8) that membrane potential distributions are Gaussian only when all trajectories started at the same point and none have reached threshold. Also, a small jitter in the firing time of the action potential implies a large error in the membrane potential, much larger than the typical subthreshold membrane potential variations. For these two reasons, the goodness-of-fit in terms of subthreshold membrane potential away from spikes is considered separately from the goodness-of-fit in terms of the spike times only.

To evaluate how the model predicts subthreshold membrane potential we must compare the average error with the intrinsic variability. To estimate the first of these two quantities, we compute the squared error between the recorded membrane potential $u_t^{\exp}$ and model membrane potential $u_t^{\mod}$ with forced spikes at the times of the observed ones. Since spike times in the model are made synchronous with the experimental recordings, all voltage traces start at the same point. A Gaussian assumption thus justified, we can average the squared error over all recorded times t that are not too close to an action potential:

$$\text{RMSE}_{\text{nm}} = \sqrt{\frac{1}{T_{\Omega_1} N_{\text{rep}}} \sum_{i=1}^{N_{\text{rep}}} \int_{\Omega_1} \left(u_i^{\exp}(t) - u_i^{\mod}(t) \right)^2 \mathrm{d}t}, \qquad (10.37)$$

where Ω_1 refers to the ensemble of time bins at least 5 ms before or after any spikes and T_{Ω_1} is the total number of time bins in Ω_1. RMSE_{nm} has index n for "neuron" and index m for "model." It estimates the error between the real neuron and the model.

To evaluate the second quantity, we compare recorded membrane potential from multiple repeated stimulations having the same stimulus. Despite the variability in spike timings, it is usually possible to find times which are sufficiently away from a spike in any repetition and compute the averaged squared error

$$\text{RMSE}_{\text{nn}} = \sqrt{\frac{2}{T_{\Omega_2} N_{\text{rep}}(N_{\text{rep}} - 1)} \sum_{i=1}^{N_{\text{rep}}} \sum_{j=1}^{i-1} \int_{\Omega_2} \left(u_j^{\exp}(t) - u_i^{\exp}(t) \right)^2 \mathrm{d}t}, \qquad (10.38)$$

where Ω_2 refers to the ensemble of time bins far from the spike times in any repetition and T_{Ω_2} is the total number of time bins in Ω_2. Typically, 20 ms before and 200 ms after the spike is considered sufficiently far. Note that with this approach we implicitly assume that spike-afterpotentials have vanished 200 ms after a spike. However, as we shall see in Chapter 11, the spike-afterpotentials can extend for more than one second, so that the above assumption is a rather bad approximation. Because the earlier spiking history will affect the membrane potential, the RMSE_{nn} calculated in Eq. (10.38) is an overestimate.

To quantify the predictive power of the model, we finally compute the model error with the intrinsic error by taking the ratio

$$\text{RMSER} = \frac{\text{RMSE}_{nn}}{\text{RMSE}_{nm}}. \tag{10.39}$$

The root-mean-squared-error ratio (RMSER) reaches 1 if the model precision is matched with intrinsic error. When smaller than 1, the RMSER indicates that the model could be improved. Values larger than 1 are possible because RMSE_{nn} is an overestimate of the true intrinsic error.

10.3.2 Spike train likelihood

The likelihood is the probability of generating the observed set of spike times $S(t)$ with the current set of parameters in our stochastic neuron model. It was defined in Eq. (9.10), which we reproduce here

$$L^n(S|\theta) = \prod_{t^{(i)} \in S} \rho(t^{(i)}|S, \theta) \exp\left[-\int_0^T \rho(s|S, \theta)ds\right], \tag{10.40}$$

where we use $\rho(t^{(i)}|S, \theta)$ to emphasize that the firing intensity of a spike at $t^{(i)}$ depends on both the stimulus and spike history as well as the model parameters θ.

The likelihood L^n is a conditional probability density and has units of inverse time to the power of n (where n is the number of observed spikes). To arrive at a more interpretable measure, it is common to compare L^n with the likelihood of a homogeneous Poisson model with a constant firing intensity $\rho_0 = n/T$, i.e., a Poisson process which is expected to generate the same number of spikes in the observation interval T. The difference in log-likelihood between the Poisson model and the neuron model is finally divided by the total number n of observed spikes in order to obtain a quantity with units of "bits per spike":

$$\frac{1}{n} \log_2 \frac{L^n(S|\theta)}{\rho_0^n e^{-\rho T}}. \tag{10.41}$$

This quantity can be interpreted as an instantaneous mutual information between the spike count in a single time bin and the stimulus given the parameters. Hence, it is interpreted as a gain in predictability produced by the set of model parameters θ. One advantage of using the log-likelihood of the conditional firing intensity is that it does not require multiple stimulus repetitions. It is especially useful to compare on a given dataset the performances of different models: better models achieve higher cross-validated likelihood scores.

10.3.3 Time-rescaling theorem

For a spike train with spikes at $t^1 < t^2 < ... < t^n$ and with firing intensity $\rho(t|S, \theta)$, the time-rescaling transformation $t \to \Lambda(t)$ is defined as

$$\Lambda(t) = \int_0^t \rho(x|S, \theta)dx. \tag{10.42}$$

(a)
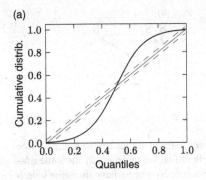

(b)
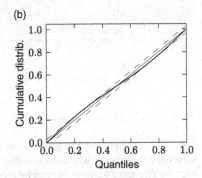

Fig. 10.6 Time-rescaling theorem as a goodness-of-fit. Illustrating the K–S test by plotting the cumulative probability of z_k as a function of quantiles. (a) Rescaling time using an inadequate model does not result in a uniform distribution of z_k as can be seen by comparing the empirical distribution (thick black line) with the diagonal. Dashed lines illustrate 95% confidence bounds. (b) As in (a) but with a better rescaling of time. The empirical distribution follows the cumulative of the uniform distribution within the confidence bounds.

It is a useful and somewhat surprising result that $\Lambda(t^k)$ (evaluated at the measured firing times) is a Poisson process with unit rate (Brown *et al.*, 2002). A correlate of this time-rescaling theorem is that the time intervals

$$\Lambda(t^k) - \Lambda(t^{k-1}) \tag{10.43}$$

are independent random variables with an exponential distribution (see Chapter 7). Rescaling again the time axis with the transformation

$$z_k = 1 - \exp\left[-\left(\Lambda(t^k) - \Lambda(t^{k-1})\right)\right] \tag{10.44}$$

forms independent uniform random variables on the interval zero to 1.

Therefore, if the model $\rho(t|S,\theta)$ is a valid description of the spike train $S(t)$, then the resulting z_k should have the statistics of a sequence of independent uniformly distributed random variables. As a first step, one can verify that the z_ks are independent by looking at the serial correlation of the interspike intervals or by using a scatter plot of z_{k+1} against z_k. Testing whether the z_ks are uniformly distributed can be done with a Kolmogorov–Smirnov (K–S) test. The K–S statistic evaluates the distance between the empirical cumulative distribution function of z_k, $P(z)$, and the cumulative distribution of the reference function. In our case, the reference function is the uniform distribution, so that its cumulative is simply z. Thus,

$$D = \sup_z |P(z) - z|. \tag{10.45}$$

The K–S statistic converges to zero as the empirical probability $P(z)$ converges to the reference. The K–S test then compares D with the critical values of the Kolmogorov distribution. Figure 10.6 illustrates two examples: one where the empirical distribution was

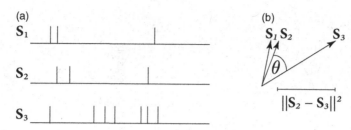

Fig. 10.7 Distance and angular separation between spike trains seen as vectors. (a) Three schematic spike trains where the first two have the same number of spikes and roughly the same timing. (b) The spike trains in (a) can be represented as vectors where S_1 and S_2 have the same length but a slightly different orientation due to small differences in spike timing. The third spike train S_3 is much longer due to the larger number of spikes. It is at a squared distance $D_{23} = ||S_2 - S_3||^2$ from S_2 and at angle θ.

far from a uniform distribution and the other where the model rescaled time correctly. See (Gerhard *et al.*, 2011) for a multivariate version of this idea that is applicable to the case of coupled neurons. To summarize, the time-rescaling theorem along with the K–S test provide a useful goodness-of-fit measure for spike train data with confidence intervals that does not require multiple repetitions.

10.3.4 Spike-train metric

Evaluating the goodness-of-fit in terms of log-likelihood or the time-rescaling theorem requires that we know the conditional firing intensity $\rho(t|S, \theta)$ accurately. For biophysical models as seen in Chapter 2 but complemented with a source of variability, the firing intensity is unavailable analytically. The intensity can be estimated numerically by simulating the model with different realizations of noise, or by solving a Fokker–Planck equation, but this is sometimes impractical.

Another approach for comparing spike trains involves defining a metric between spike trains. Multiple spike timing metrics have been proposed, with different interpretations. A popular metric was proposed by Victor and Purpura (1996). Here, we describe an alternative framework for the comparison of spike trains that makes use of vector space ideas, rather than more general metric spaces.

Let us consider spike trains as vectors in an abstract vector space, with these vectors denoted with boldface: S. A vector space is said to have an inner (or scalar) product if for each vector pair S_i and S_j there exists a unique real number (S_i, S_j) satisfying the following axioms: commutativity, distributivity, associativity, and positivity. There are multiple candidate inner products satisfying the above axioms. The choice of inner product will be related to the type of metric being considered. For now, consider the general form

$$(S_i, S_j) = \int_0^T \int_{-\infty}^{\infty} \int_{-\infty}^{\infty} K_\Delta(s, s') S_i(t - s) S_j(t - s') ds ds' dt, \tag{10.46}$$

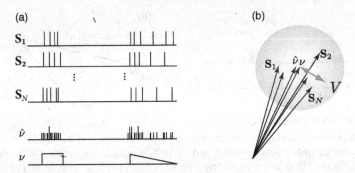

Fig. 10.8 The spike density vector. (a) A set of N spike trains $(\mathbf{S}_1, \mathbf{S}_2, ..., \mathbf{S}_N)$ is combined to yield an estimate of the spike density $\hat{v}$. At the limit $N \to \infty$ the spike density converges to the instantaneous firing rate v. (b) Schematic representation of the quantities in (a). The variability V measures the scatter of the individual spike trains around their mean $\hat{v}_X$.

where K_Δ is a two-dimensional coincidence kernel with a scaling parameter Δ, and T is the maximum length of the spike trains. Here K_Δ is required to be a non-negative function with a global maximum at $s = s' = 0$. Moreover, $K_\Delta(s, s')$ should fall off rapidly so that $K_\Delta(s, s') \approx 0$ for all $s, s' > \Delta$. Examples of kernels include $K_\Delta(s, s') = k_1(s)k_2(s')$. For instance, $k_1(s) = k_2(s) = \frac{1}{\Delta} e^{-s/\Delta}\Theta(s)$ is a kernel that was used by van Rossum (2001). The scaling parameter Δ must be small, much smaller than the length T of the spike train.

For a comparison of spike trains seen as vectors the notions of angular separation, distance, and norm of spike trains are particularly important. The squared norm of a spike train will be written $||\mathbf{S}_i||^2 = (\mathbf{S}_i, \mathbf{S}_i)$. With $K_\Delta(s, s') = \delta(s)\delta(s')$, we observe that $(\mathbf{S}_i, \mathbf{S}_i) = \int_0^T S_i(t)\mathrm{d}t = n_i$ where n_i is the number of spikes in $\mathbf{S}_i$. Therefore the norm of a spike train is related to the total number of spikes it contains. The Victor and Purpura metric is of a different form than the form discussed here, but it has similar properties (see exercises).

The norm readily defines a distance, D_{ij}, between two spike trains

$$D_{ij}^2 = ||\mathbf{S}_i - \mathbf{S}_j||^2 = (\mathbf{S}_i - \mathbf{S}_j, \mathbf{S}_i - \mathbf{S}_j) = ||\mathbf{S}_i||^2 + ||\mathbf{S}_j||^2 - 2(\mathbf{S}_i, \mathbf{S}_j). \qquad (10.47)$$

The right-hand side of Eq. (10.47) shows that that the distance between two spike trains is maximum when $(\mathbf{S}_i, \mathbf{S}_j)$ is zero. On the other hand, D_{ij}^2 becomes zero only when $S_i = S_j$. This implies that $(\mathbf{S}_i, \mathbf{S}_j) = (\mathbf{S}_i, \mathbf{S}_i) = (\mathbf{S}_j, \mathbf{S}_j)$. Again consider $K_\Delta(s, s') = \delta(s)\delta(s')$, then D_{ij} is the total number of spikes in both $\mathbf{S}_i$ and $\mathbf{S}_j$ reduced by 2 for each spike in $\mathbf{S}_i$ that coincided with one in $\mathbf{S}_j$. For the following, it is useful to think of a distance between spike trains as a number of non-coincident spikes.

The cosine of the angle between $\mathbf{S}_i$ and $\mathbf{S}_j$ is

$$\cos \theta_{ij} = \frac{(\mathbf{S}_j, \mathbf{S}_i)}{||\mathbf{S}_i|| \, ||\mathbf{S}_j||}. \qquad (10.48)$$

This angular separation relates to the fraction of coincident spikes. Fig. 10.7 illustrates the concepts of angle and distance for spike trains seen as vectors.

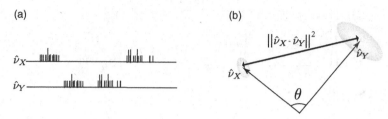

Fig. 10.9 Distance and angular separation between spike densities. (a) Two spike densities corresponding to a sum of spike trains labeled X and Y. (b) Schematic representation of the densities $\hat{v}_X$ and $\hat{v}_Y$ seen as vectors. Both are separated by a distance $||\hat{v}_X - \hat{v}_Y||^2$ and angle θ. The variability is shown as a gray cloud centered on the vectors.

10.3.5 Comparing sets of spike trains

Metrics such as D_{ij} described above can quantify the similarity between two spike trains. In the presence of variability, however, a simple comparison of spike trains is not sufficient. Instead, the spike train similarity measure must be maximally sensitive to differences in the underlying stochastic processes.

We want to know if spike trains generated from a neuron model could well have been generated by a real neuron. We could simply calculate the distance between a spike train from the neuron and a spike train from the model, but neurons are noisy and we will find a different distance each time we repeat the recording. To achieve better statistics, we can compare a set of spike trains from the model with a set of spike trains from the neuron.

Let the two sets of spike trains be denoted by X and Y, containing N_X and N_Y spike trains, respectively. First, it is useful to define some characteristics of such sets of spike trains. A natural quantity to consider is the average of the norms of each spike train within a set, say X,

$$\hat{L}_X = \frac{1}{N_X} \sum_{i=1}^{N_X} ||\mathbf{S}_i^{(x)}||^2, \tag{10.49}$$

where we have used ˆ to denote that the quantity is an experimental estimate. We note that $\hat{L}_X$ is related to the averaged spike count. L_X is exactly the averaged spike count if the inner product satisfies (i) $\int \int K_\Delta(s,s')dsds' = 1$ and (ii) $K_\Delta(s,s') = 0$ whenever $|s - s'|$ is greater than the minimum interspike interval of any of the spike trains considered. The interpretation $L_X \sim$ *spike count* is helpful for the discussion in the remainder of this section. Furthermore, the vector of averaged spike trains,

$$\hat{v}_X = \frac{1}{N_X} \sum_{i=1}^{N_X} \mathbf{s}_i^{(x)}, \tag{10.50}$$

is another occurrence of the spike density seen in Chapter 7. It defines the instantaneous firing rate of the the spiking process, $v(t) = \langle \hat{v} \rangle$. In the vector space, $\hat{v}_X$ can be thought of as lying at the center of the spike trains seen as vectors (Fig. 10.9); note that other "mean spike trains" could be defined (Wu and Srivastava, 2012). The size of the cloud quantifies the variability in the spike timing. The variability is defined as the variance

$$\hat{V}_X = \frac{1}{N_X - 1} \sum_{i=1}^{N_X} ||\mathbf{S}_i^{(x)} - \hat{v}_X||^2. \tag{10.51}$$

A set of spike trains where spikes always occur at the same times has low variability. When the spikes occur with some jitter around a given time, the variability is larger. Variability relates to reliability. While variability is a positive quantity that cannot exceed L_X, reliability is usually defined between zero and 1, where 1 means perfectly reliable spike timing: $\hat{R}_X = 1 - \hat{V}_X / \hat{L}_X$.

Finally, we come to a measure of match between the set of spike trains X and Y. The discussion in Chapter 7 about the neural code would suggest that neuron models should reproduce the detailed time structure of the PSTH. We therefore define

$$\hat{M} = \frac{2(\hat{v}_X, \hat{v}_Y)}{\hat{R}_X \hat{L}_X + \hat{R}_Y \hat{L}_Y}. \tag{10.52}$$

We have M (for match) equal to 1 if X and Y have the same instantaneous firing rate. The smaller M is, the greater the mismatch between the spiking processes. The quantity $R_X L_X$ can be interpreted as a number of reliable spikes. Since $(\hat{v}_X, \hat{v}_Y)$ is interpreted as a number of coincident spikes between X and Y, we can still regard M as a factor counting the fraction of coincident spikes. A similar quantity can be defined for metrics that cannot be cast into an inner product (Naud *et al.*, 2011).

If the kernel $K_\Delta(s, s')$ is chosen to be $k_g(s) k_g(s')$ and k_g is a Gaussian distribution of width Δ, then M relates to a mean square error between PSTHs that were filtered with k_g. Therefore, the kernel used in the definition of the inner product (Eq. (10.46)) can be related to the smoothing filter of the PSTH (see Exercises).

10.4 Closed-loop stimulus design

In the previous sections we have developed robust and tractable approaches to understand neural encoding, based on GLMs, and quantifying the performance of models. The framework we have developed is ultimately data-driven; both our encoding and decoding methods fail if the observed data do not sufficiently constrain our encoding model parameters θ. Therefore we will close by describing how to take advantage of the properties of the GLM to optimize our experiments: the objective is to select, in an online, closed-loop manner, the stimuli that will most efficiently characterize the neuron's response properties.

An important property of GLMs is that not all stimuli will provide the same amount of information about the unknown coefficients k. As a concrete example, we can typically learn much more about a visual neuron's response properties if we place stimulus energy within the receptive field, rather than "wasting" stimulus energy outside the receptive field. To make this idea more rigorous and generally applicable, we need a well-defined objective function that will rank any given stimulus according to its potential informativeness.

Numerous objective functions have been proposed for quantifying the utility of different stimuli (Mackay, 1992; Nelken *et al.*, 1994; Machens, 2002). When the goal is estimating the unknown parameters of a model, it makes sense to choose stimuli x_t which will on average reduce the uncertainty in the parameters θ as quickly as possible (as in the game of 20 questions), given $D = \{x(s), n_s\}_{s<t}$, the observed data up to the current trial. This posterior uncertainty in θ can be quantified using the information-theoretic notion of "entropy"; see Cover and Thomas (1991), Mackay (1992), Paninski (2005) for further details.

In general, information-theoretic quantities such as the entropy can be difficult to compute and optimize in high-dimensional spaces. However, Lewi *et al.* (2009) show that the special structure of the GLM can be exploited (along with a Gaussian approximation to $p(\theta|D)$) to obtain a surprisingly efficient procedure for choosing stimuli optimally in many cases. Indeed, a closed-loop optimization procedure leads to much more efficient experiments than does the standard open-loop approach of stimulating the cell with randomly chosen stimuli that are not optimized adaptively for the neuron under study.

A common argument against online stimulus optimization is that neurons are highly adaptive: a stimulus which might be optimal for a given neuron in a quiescent state may quickly become suboptimal due to adaptation (in the form of short- and long-term synaptic plasticity, slow network dynamics, etc.). Including spike-history terms in the GLM allows us to incorporate some forms of adaptation (particularly those due to intrinsic processes including, for example, sodium channel inactivation and calcium-activated potassium channels), and these spike-history effects may be easily incorporated into the derivation of the optimal stimulus (Lewi *et al.*, 2009). However, extending these results to models with more profound sources of adaptation is an important open research direction; see Lewi *et al.* (2009) and DiMattina and Zhang (2011) for further discussion.

10.5 Summary

With modern statistical methods, we have fast and computationally tractable schemes to fit models of neural encoding and decoding to experimental data. A key insight is that, for a suitable chosen model class, the likelihood of the data being generated by the model is a concave function of the model parameters, i.e., there are no local maxima. Because of this, numerical methods of gradient ascent are bound to lead to the global maximum.

Generalized Linear Models (GLMs) are the representative of this model class. Importantly, a large ensemble of generalized integrate-and-fire models, in particular the SRM with escape noise, belong to the family of GLMs. As we have seen in previous chapters, the SRM can account for a large body of electrophysiological data and firing patterns such as adaptation, burst firing, time-dependent firing threshold, hyperpolarizing spike-afterpotential, etc. The link from SRM to GLM implies that there are systematic and computationally fast methods to fit biologically plausible neuron models to data.

Interestingly, once neuron models are phrased in the language of statistics, the problems of coding and stimulus design can be formulated in a single unified framework. In the following chapter we shall see that the problem of decoding can also be analyzed in the same statistical framework.

Literature

An early application of maximum likelihood approaches to neuronal data can be found in Brillinger (1988). The application of the framework of Generalized Linear Models to the field of neuroscience has been made popular by Truccolo *et al.* (2005) and Pillow *et al.* (2008). A review of Generalized Linear Models can be found in Dobson and Barnett (2008).

The influential book Rieke *et al.* (1997) gives a broad introduction to the field of neural coding. The time-rescaling theorem was exploited by Brown *et al.* (2002) to develop useful goodness-of-fit methods for spike trains. Spike-train metrics were introduced in Victor and Purpura (1996, 1997), but comparisons of spike trains in terms of PSTHs and other features has been commonly used before (Perkel *et al.*, 1967a,b; Gerstein and Perkel, 1972; MacPherson and Aldridge, 1979; Eggermont *et al.*, 1983; Gawne *et al.*, 1991). Many other spike-train distances were also proposed (Kistler *et al.*, 1997; van Rossum, 2001; Quiroga *et al.*, 2002; Hunter and Milton, 2003; Schreiber *et al.*, 2003; Naud *et al.*, 2011) which can be cast in the general framework of a vector space as outlined in Schrauwen and Campenhout (2007), Paiva *et al.* (2009a) and Naud *et al.* (2011); see also Paiva *et al.* (2009b, 2010) and Park *et al.* (2012). Nonlinear functions of the spike trains can also be used to relate to different features of the spiking process such as the interval distribution or the presence of definite firing patterns (Victor and Purpura, 1996; Quiroga *et al.*, 2002; Tiesinga, 2004; Kreuz *et al.*, 2007, 2009; Druckmann *et al.*, 2007).

Exercises

1. **Concave function and non-global optima**
   (a) *Suppose a function $G(x)$ has a global maximum at location x_0. Suppose that $f(y)$ is a strictly increasing function of y (i.e., $df/dy > 0$).*
   Show that $f(G(x))$ has a maximum at x_0. Is it possible that $f(G(x))$ has further maxima as a function of x?
   (b) *A strictly concave function G can be defined as a curve with negative curvature $d^2G/dx^2 < 0$ for all x. Show that a concave function can have at most one maximum.*
   (c) *Give an example of a concave function which does not have a maximum. Give an example of a function G which has a global maximum, but is not concave. Give an example of a function G which is concave and has a global maximum.*
2. **Sum of concave functions.** *Consider a quadratic function $f_k(x) = 1 - (x - \vartheta_k)^2$.*
   (a) *Show that f_k is a concave function of x for any choice of parameter ϑ_k.*
   (b) *Show that $f_1(x) + f_2(x)$ is a concave function.*
   (c) *Show that $\sum_k b_k f_k(x)$ with $b_k > 0$ is a concave function.*
   (d) *Repeat the steps (b) and (c) for a family of functions f_k which are concave, but not necessarily quadratic.*
3. **Comparing PSTHs and spike train similarity measures.** *Experimentally the PSTH is constructed from a set of N_{rep} spike trains, $S_i(t)$, measured from repeated presentations of the same*

stimulus. The ensemble average of the recorded spike trains:

$$\frac{1}{N_{\text{rep}}} \sum_{i=1}^{N_{\text{rep}}} S_i(t) \tag{10.53}$$

is typically convolved with a Gaussian function $h_g(x) = (2\pi\sigma^2)^{-1/2} \exp\left(-x^2/2\sigma^2\right)$ *with* σ *around* $5\,ms$, *such that* $A_1(t) = (h_g * \frac{1}{N_{\text{rep}}} \sum S_i)(t)$ *is a smoothed PSTH. Suppose that two sets of experimental spike trains were recorded in two different conditions, resulting in two smoothed PSTHs* $A_1(t)$ *and* $A_2(t)$.

(a) Show that the sum of the squared error $(A_1(t) - A_2(t))^2$ *can be written as a distance between sets of spike train* D^2 *with the kernel* $K(t,t') = h_g(t)h_g(t')$.

(b) Recall that the correlation coefficient between datasets x *and* y *is*

$$c = \text{cov}(x,y)/\sqrt{\text{cov}(x,x)\text{cov}(y,y)}. \tag{10.54}$$

Show that the correlation coefficient between the two smoothed PSTHs can be written as a angular separation between the sets of spike trains with kernel $K(t,t') = h_g(t)h_g(t')$.

4. **Victor and Purpura metric.** *Consider the minimum cost* C *required to transform a spike train* S_i *into another spike train* S_j *if the only transformations available are:*

- removing a spike has a cost of 1,

- adding a spike has a cost of 1,

- shifting a spike by a distance d has a cost qd *where* q *is a parameter defining temporal precision.*

The C *defines a metric that measures the dissimilarity between spike train* S_i *and spike train* S_j. *The smaller* C *is the more alike the spike trains are in terms of spike timing.*

(a) For $q = 0$ *units of cost per seconds, show that* C *becomes the difference in number of spikes in spike trains* S_i *and* S_j.

(b) For q *greater than four times the maximum firing frequency (i.e., the inverse of the shortest observed interspike interval), show that* C *can be written as a distance* D_{ij}^2 *with kernel* $K(t,t') = h_t(t)\delta(t')$ *and triangular function* $h_t(t) = (1 - |t|q/2)\Theta(1 - |t|q/2)$ *where* $\delta(\cdot)$ *is the Dirac delta function and* $\Theta(\cdot)$ *is the Heaviside function.*

11

Encoding and decoding with stochastic neuron models

In the ten preceding chapters, we have come a long way: starting from the biophysical basis of neuronal dynamics we arrived at a description of neurons that we called generalized integrate-and-fire models. We have seen that neurons contain multiple types of ion channels embedded in a capacitive membrane (Chapter 2). We have seen how basic principles regulate the dynamics of electrical current and membrane potential in synapses, dendrites and axons (Chapter 3). We have seen that sodium and potassium ion channels form an excitable system characterized by a threshold mechanism (Chapter 4) and that other ion channels shape the spike after-effects (Chapter 6). Finally, we have seen in Chapters 4, 5 and 6 how biophysical models can be reduced by successive approximations to other, simpler, models such as the LIF, EIF, AdEx, and SRM. Moreover, we have added noise to our neuron models (Chapters 7 and 9). At this point, it is natural to step back and check whether our assumptions were too stringent, whether the biophysical assumptions were well-founded, and whether the generalized models can explain neuronal data. We laid out the mathematical groundwork in Chapter 10; we can now set out to apply these statistical methods to real data.

We can test the performance of these, and other, models by using them as predictive models of *encoding*. Given a stimulus, will the model be able to predict the neuronal response? Will it be able to predict spike times observed in real neurons when driven by the same stimulus – or only the mean firing rate or PSTH? Will the model be able to account for the variability observed in neuronal data across repetitions?

Testing the performance of models addresses an even bigger question. What information is discarded in the neural code? What features of the stimulus are most important? If we understand the neural code, will we be able to reconstruct the image that the eye is actually seeing at any given moment from spike trains observed in the brain? The problem of *decoding* neuronal activity is central both for our basic understanding of neural information processing (Rieke *et al.*, 1997) and for engineering "neural prosthetic" devices that can interact with the brain directly (Donoghue, 2002). Given a spike train observed in the brain, can we read out intentions, thoughts, or movement plans? Can we use the data to control a prosthetic device?

In Section 11.1 we use the generalized integrate-and-fire models of Chapters 6 and 9 to predict membrane voltage and spike timings of real neurons during stimulation with an arbitrary time-dependent input current in vitro. In Section 11.2, we use the same model class to predict spike timings *in vivo*. Finally, in Section 11.3 we examine the question of decoding: given a measured spike train can we reconstruct the stimulus, or control a prosthetic arm?

11.1 Encoding models for intracellular recordings

We will focus the discussion on generalized integrate-and-fire models with escape noise, also called soft-threshold integrate-and-fire models (Fig. 10.3a). The vast majority of studies achieving good predictions of voltage and spike timing use some variant of this model. The reasons lie in the model's ease of optimization and in its flexibility; see Chapter 6. Also, the possibility of casting them into the GLM formalism allows efficient parameter optimization; see Chapter 10. In Section 11.1.1 we use the SRM as well as soft-threshold integrate-and-fire models to predict the subthreshold voltage of neurons in slices driven by a time-dependent external current. We then use these models to also predict the spike timings of the same neurons (Section 11.1.2).

11.1.1 Predicting membrane potential

The SRM describes somatic membrane potential in the presence of an external current (Section 6.4)

$$u(t) = \sum_f \eta(t - t^f) + \int_0^\infty \kappa(s)\, I^{\text{ext}}(t - s)\, ds + u_{\text{rest}}. \qquad (11.1)$$

The parameters of this model define the functional shape of the functions $\eta(t)$ and $\kappa(t)$. Other parameters such as threshold or, in a stochastic model, the sharpness of threshold β do not contribute to the mean squared error of the membrane potential as defined in Section 10.3.1. Following the methods of Chapter 10, we can estimate the functions $\kappa(t)$ and $\eta(t)$ from recordings of cortical neurons. We note that the spike-afterpotential has units of voltage, whereas the membrane filter κ has units of resistance over time.

Using *in vitro* intracellular recordings of cells in layer 2–3 of the somatosensory cortex, Mensi *et al.* (2012) optimized the functions $\kappa(t)$ and $\eta(t)$ on the recorded potential. For both the main type of excitatory neurons and the main type of inhibitory neurons, the membrane filter $\kappa(t)$ is well described by a single exponential (Fig. 11.1a). Different cell types have different amplitudes and time constants. The inhibitory neurons are typically faster, with a smaller time constant than the excitatory neurons, suggesting we could discriminate between excitatory and inhibitory neurons in terms of the shape of $\kappa(t)$. Discrimination of cell types, however, is much improved when we take into account the spike-afterpotential. The shape of $\eta(t)$ in inhibitory cells is very different than that in excitatory ones (Fig. 11.1b).

While the spike-afterpotential is a monotonically decreasing function in the excitatory cells, in the inhibitory cells the function $\eta(t)$ is better fitted by two exponentials of opposite

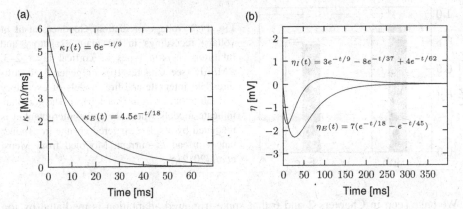

Fig. 11.1 Parameters of voltage recordings in the main excitatory and inhibitory neuron type of cortical layer 2–3. (a) Membrane filter for the main excitatory cell type $\kappa_E(t)$ and the fast-spiking inhibitory cell type $\kappa_I(t)$. (b) Spike-afterpotential for the main excitatory cell type $\eta_E(t)$ and the main inhibitory cell type $\eta_I(t)$. Equations have units of ms for time, mV for η and MΩ/ms for κ. Modified from Mensi *et al.* (2012).

polarity. This illustrates that different cell types differ in the functional shape of the spike-afterpotential $\eta(t)$. This finding is consistent with the predictions of Chapter 6 where we discussed the role of different ion channels in shaping $\eta(t)$. Similar to Fig. 6.14, the spike-afterpotential of inhibitory neurons is depolarizing 30–150 ms after the spike time, another property providing fast-spiking dynamics. Therefore, we conclude that the spike-afterpotential of inhibitory neurons has an *oscillatory* component.

Once the parameters have been extracted from a first set of data, how well does the neuron model predict membrane potential recordings? Qualitatively, we have already seen in Chapter 10 (Fig. 10.5) an example of a typical prediction. Quantitatively, the membrane potential fluctuations of the inhibitory and excitatory neuron have a RMSER (Eq. (10.39)) below one, meaning that the prediction error is smaller than our estimate of the intrinsic error. This indicates that our estimate of the intrinsic error is slightly too large, probably because the actual spike-afterpotential is even longer than a few hundred milliseconds – as we shall see below.

Subthreshold mechanisms that can lead to a resonance (Chapter 6) would cause $\kappa(t)$ to oscillate in time. Mensi *et al.* (2012) have tested for the presence of a resonance in $\kappa(t)$ and found none. Using two exponentials to model $\kappa(t)$ does not improve the prediction of subthreshold membrane potential. Thus, the membrane potential filter is well described by a *single exponential* with time constant $\tau_m = RC$ where R is the passive membrane resistance and C the capacity of the membrane. If we set $\kappa(s) = (1/C)\exp(-s/\tau_m)$, we can take the derivative of Eq. (11.1) and write it in the form of a differential equation

$$C\frac{du(t)}{dt} = -\frac{1}{R}(u - u_{\text{rest}}) + \sum_f \tilde{\eta}(t - t^f) + I^{\text{ext}}(t), \qquad (11.2)$$

where $\tilde{\eta}(s)$ is the time course of the net *current* triggered after a spike.

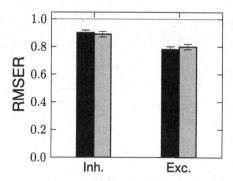

Fig. 11.2 Voltage prediction. Goodness-of-fit of voltage recordings in the main excitatory and inhibitory neuron types of cortical layer 2–3. RMSER (see Chapter 10) for generalized soft-threshold integrate-and-fire models of excitatory and inhibitory neurons (black bars). The gray bars indicate models where the spike-afterpotential is mediated by a spike-triggered change in conductance instead of current. Modified from Mensi *et al.* (2012).

We have seen in Chapters 2 and 6 that spike-triggered adaptation is mediated by ion channels that change the *conductance* of the membrane. Biophysics would therefore suggest a spike-triggered change in conductance, such that after every spike the total current that can charge the membrane capacitance is

$$C\frac{du}{dt} \propto \eta_C(t-\hat{t})(u-E_{\text{rev}}), \tag{11.3}$$

where η_C is the spike-triggered change in conductance and E_{rev} its reversal potential. The reversal potential and the time course η_C can be optimized to yield the best goodness-of-fit. In the excitatory neurons, the resulting conductance change follows qualitatively the current-based $\tilde{\eta}(t)$. The prediction performance, however, is not significantly improved (Fig. 11.2), indicating that describing spike after-effects in terms of current is a good assumption.

11.1.2 Predicting spikes

Using the same intracellular recordings as in Fig. 11.1 (Mensi *et al.*, 2012), we now ask whether spike firing can be predicted from the model. The results of the previous sub-section provide us with the voltage trajectory $u(t)$ of the generalized integrate-and-fire model. Assuming a moving threshold that can undergo a stereotypical change at every spike $\vartheta(t) = \vartheta_0 + \sum_f \theta_1(t-t^f)$ we can model the conditional firing intensity as follows, given the spike train, S (compare Eq. (9.27))

$$\rho(t|S) = \frac{1}{\tau_0} \exp\left[\beta\left(u(t) - \vartheta_0 - \sum_{t^f \in S} \theta_1(t-t^f)\right)\right]. \tag{11.4}$$

Since the parameters regulating $u(t)$ were optimized using the subthreshold membrane potential in Section 11.1.1, the only free parameters left are those of the threshold, i.e., ϑ_0, β, and the function $\theta_1(t)$. Once the function θ_1 is expanded in a linear combination of basis functions, maximizing the likelihood Eq. (10.40), can be done through a convex gradient descent because Eq. (11.4) can be cast into a GLM.

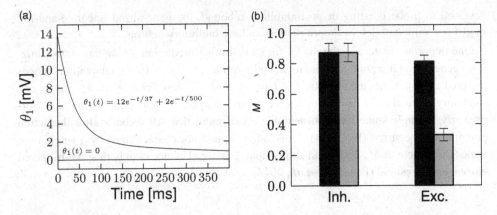

Fig. 11.3 Parameters and spike time prediction in the main excitatory and inhibitory neuron type of cortical layer 2–3. (a) Moving threshold for the main excitatory cell type was found to be an exponentially decaying function (top curve and equation). For the main inhibitory cell type, the fitted moving threshold was not significantly different from zero (bottom curve and equation). Equations have units of ms for time and mV for θ_1. (b) The spike-timing prediction in terms of the similarity measure M (Eq. (10.52)) for models with the moving threshold (black bars) and without the moving threshold (gray bars). Modified from Mensi *et al.* (2012).

Is the dynamic threshold necessary? Optimizing the parameters on a training dataset, we find no need for a moving threshold in the inhibitory neurons (Fig. 11.3a). The threshold in those cells is constant in time. However, the excitatory cells have a strongly moving threshold (Fig. 11.3a) which is characterized by at least two decay time constants. A moving threshold can have several potential biophysical causes. Inactivation of sodium channels is a likely candidate (Fleidervish *et al.*, 1996).

How good is the prediction of spike times in inhibitory and excitatory cortical neurons? Qualitatively, the model spike trains resemble the recorded ones with a similar intrinsic variability (Fig. 10.5). Quantitatively, Mensi *et al.* (2012) used the measure of match M (see Eq. (10.52)) and $K(t,t') = \Theta(t + \Delta)\Theta(\Delta - t)\delta(t')$ with $\Delta = 4$ ms. They found $M = 87\%$ for the inhibitory neurons and $M = 81\%$ for the excitatory neurons (Fig. 11.3b). Intuitively, this result means that these models predict more than 80% of the "predictable" spikes.

These numbers are averaged over a set of cells. Some cells were predicted better than others such that the M reached 95% for inhibitory neurons and 87% for excitatory neurons. Similar results are found in excitatory neurons of layer 5. Spikes from these neurons can be predicted with $M = 81\%$ on average (Pozzorini *et al.*, 2013). Other optimization methods but with similar models could improve the spike-timing prediction of inhibitory neurons, reaching $M = 100\%$ for some cells (Kobayashi *et al.*, 2009). Thus, the case of inhibitory neurons seems well resolved. The almost perfect match between predicted and experimental spike trains leaves little place for model refinement. Unless the stimulus is specifically designed to probe bursting or postinhibitory rebound, the generalized integrate-and-fire model is a sufficient description of the fast-spiking inhibitory neuron.

One important feature of the model for spike-timing prediction is adaptation. Optimizing a generalized integrate-and-fire model with refractory effects but no adaptation reduces the prediction performance by 20–30% (Jolivet *et al.*, 2008b), for both the excitatory and inhibitory cortical cells. How long do the effects of spike-triggered adaptation last? Surprisingly, a single spike has a measurable effect more than 10 seconds after the action potential has occurred (Fig. 11.4). Thus, adaptation is not characterized by a single time scale (Lundstrom *et al.*, 2008) and shows up as a power-law decay in both spike-triggered current and threshold (Pozzorini *et al.*, 2013).

11.1.3 How good are generalized integrate-and-fire models?

For excitatory neurons, a value of $M = 81\%$ implies that there remains nevertheless 19% unexplained PSTH variance. Using state-of-the-art model optimization for a full biophysical model with ion channels and extended dendritic tree does not improve the model performance (Druckmann *et al.*, 2007). Considering a dependence on the voltage derivative in the escape rate (Chapter 9) can slightly improve the performance (Kobayashi and Shinomoto, 2007) but is not sufficient to achieve a flawless prediction. Similarly, taking into account very long spike-history effects (Fig. 11.4) and experimental drifts improves mostly the prediction of time-dependent rate performance on long time scales, and only slightly spike-time prediction at short time scales (Pozzorini *et al.*, 2013). Overall, the situation gives the impression that a mechanism might be missing in the generalized integrate-and-fire model and perhaps in the biophysical description as well.

Nevertheless, more than 80% of PSTH variance *is predicted* by generalized soft-threshold integrate-and-fire models during current injection into the soma. This result holds for a time-dependent current which changes on fast as well as slow time scales – a challenging scenario. The effective current driving single neurons in an awake animal *in vivo* might have comparable characteristics in that it comprises slow fluctuations of the mean as well as fast fluctuations (Crochet *et al.*, 2011; Pozzorini *et al.*, 2013). Similarly, the net driving current in connected model networks (see Part III), typically also shows fluctuations around a mean value that changes on a slower time scale. Taken together, generalized integrate-and-fire models are valid models in the physiological input range observed *in vivo*, and are good candidates for large-scale network simulation and analysis.

Linear dendritic effects show up in the membrane filter and spike-afterpotential; but strongly nonlinear dendrites as observed with multiple recordings from the same neuron (Larkum *et al.*, 2001) cannot be accounted for by a generalized soft-threshold integrate-and-fire model or GLM. If nonlinear interactions between different current injection sites along the dendrite are important, a different class of neuron models needs to be considered (Chapter 3).

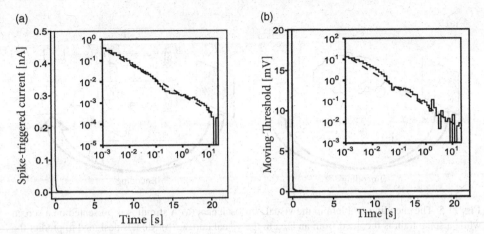

Fig. 11.4 Long spike after-effects in excitatory cortical cells of the layer 5. (a) The spike-triggered current fitted on the membrane potential of layer 5 pyramidal neurons is shown as a function of time since spike emission. Although the effect of a spike appears to be over after a few tens of milliseconds, the log–log scale (inset) reveals that the spike after-current decays with a power law $\tilde{\eta}(t) \propto -t^{-0.8}$ over four orders of magnitude. (b) The moving threshold fitted on the spike timing of layer 5 pyramidal neurons is shown as a function of time since spike emission. As in (a), the log–log scale (inset) reveals a power law $\theta_1(t) \propto t^{-0.8}$ (Pozzorini *et al.*, 2013).

11.2 Encoding models in systems neuroscience

Generalized integrate-and-fire models have been used not only for spike prediction of neurons in brain slices, but also for measurements in systems neuroscience, i.e., in the intact brain driven by sensory stimuli or engaged in a behavioral task. Traditionally, electrophysiological measurements *in vivo* have been performed with extracellular electrodes or multi-electrode probes. With extracellular recording devices, the presence of spikes emitted by one or several neurons can be detected, but the membrane potential of the neuron is unknown. Therefore, in the following we aim at predicting spikes in extracellular recordings from a single neuron, or in groups of connected neurons.

11.2.1 Receptive fields and linear-nonlinear-poisson model

The linear properties of a simple neuron in the primary visual cortex can be identified with its receptive field, i.e., the small region of visual space in which the neuron is responsive to stimuli (see Chapters 1 and 12). Receptive fields as linear filters have been analyzed in a wide variety of experimental preparations.

Experimentally, the receptive field of a simple cell in visual cortex can be determined by presenting a random sequence of spots of lights on a gray screen while the animal is watching the screen (Fig. 11.5a). In a very limited region of the screen, the spot of light leads to an increase in the probability of firing of the cell, in an adjacent small region to a

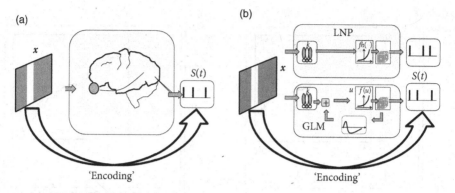

Fig. 11.5 The encoding problem in the visual neuroscience. (a) A stimulus is presented on a screen while a spike train is recorded from an area in the visual cortex. (b) Models designed to predict the spike train first filter the stimulus x with a spatial filter k (linear processing step), pass the result $u = k \cdot x$ through a nonlinearity f and then generate spikes stochastically with Poisson statistics. The main difference between a Linear-Nonlinear-Poisson (LNP, top) and a soft-threshold generalized integrate-and-fire model (GLM, bottom) is the presence of spike-triggered currents $\tilde{\eta}(s)$ in the latter.

decrease. The spatial arrangement of these regions defines the spatial receptive field of the cell and can be visualized as a two-dimensional spatial linear filter (Fig. 11.5b).

Instead of a two-dimensional notation of screen coordinates, we choose in what follows a vector notation where we label all pixels with a single index k. For example, on a screen with 256×256 pixels we have $1 \leq k \leq K$ with $K = 65\,536$. A full image corresponds to a vector $x = (x_1, \ldots, x_K)$ while a single spot of light corresponds to a vector with all components equal to zero except one (Fig. 11.6a).

The spatial receptive field of a neuron is a vector k of the same dimensionality as x. The response of the neuron to an *arbitrary* spatial stimulus x depends on the total drive $k \cdot x_t$, i.e., the similarity between the stimulus and the spatial filter.

More generally, the receptive field filter k can be described not only by a spatial component, but also by a temporal component: an input 100 ms ago has less influence on the spiking probability now than an input 30 ms ago. In other words, the scalar product $k \cdot x_t$ is a short-hand notation for integration over space as well as over time. Such a filter k is called a *spatio-temporal receptive field*.

In the Linear-Nonlinear-Poisson (LNP) model, one assumes that spike trains are produced by an inhomogeneous Poisson process with rate

$$\rho(t) = f(k \cdot x_t), \tag{11.5}$$

given by a cascade of two simple steps (Fig. 11.5b). The linear stage, $k \cdot x_t$, is a linear projection of x_t, the (vector) stimulus at time t, onto the receptive field k; this linear stage is then followed by a simple scalar nonlinearity $f(.)$ which shapes the output (and in particular enforces the non-negativity of the output firing rate $\rho(t)$). A great deal of the systems neuroscience literature concerns the quantification of the receptive field parameters k.

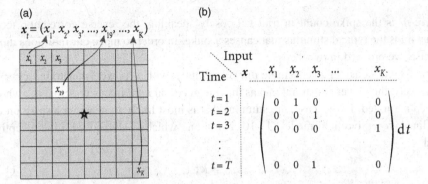

Fig. 11.6 Spatial receptive field measurement. (a) While the animal focuses on the center (star), light dots are presented at random positions on a gray screen; in the present trial, pixel 19 lights up. The input is denoted as a vector x_t. (b) Schematic of input matrix X. Matrix representing a sparse input, such as a single spot of light. Rows of the matrix correspond to different trials, marked by the observation time t.

Note that the LNP model neglects the spike-history effects that are the hallmark of the SRM and the GLM – otherwise the two models are surprisingly similar; see Fig. 11.5b. Therefore, an LNP model cannot account for refractoriness or adaptation, while a GLM in the form of a generalized soft-threshold integrate-and-fire model does. The question arises whether a model with spike-history effects yields a better performance than the standard LNP model.

Both models, LNP and GLM, can be fitted using the methods discussed in Chapter 10. For example, the two models have been compared on a dataset where retinal ganglion cells have been driven by full-field light stimulus, i.e., the stimulus did not have any spatial structure (Pillow *et al.*, 2005). Prediction performance had a similar range of values as for cortical neurons driven by intracellular current injection, with up to 90% of the PSTH variance predicted in some cases. LNP models in this context have significantly worse prediction accuracy; in particular, LNP models greatly overestimate the variance of the predicted spiking responses. See Fig. 11.7 for an example.

Example: Detour on reverse correlation for receptive field estimation

Reverse correlation measurements are an experimental procedure based on spike-triggered averaging (de Boer and Kuyper, 1968; Chichilnisky, 2001). Stimuli x are drawn from some statistical ensemble and presented one after the other. Each time the neuron elicits a spike, the stimulus x presented just before the firing is recorded. The reverse correlation filter is the mean of all inputs that have triggered a spike

$$x_{\text{RevCorr}} = \langle x \rangle_{\text{spike}} = \frac{\sum_t n_t x_t}{\sum_t n_t},$$

(11.6)

where n_t is the spike count in trial t. Loosely speaking, the reverse correlation technique finds the typical stimulus that causes a spike. In order to make our intuitions more precise, we proceed in two steps.

First, let us consider an ensemble $p(x)$ of stimuli x with a "power" constraint $|x|^2 < c$. Intuitively, the power constraint means that the maximal light intensity across the whole screen is limited. In this case, the stimulus that is most likely to generate a spike under the linear receptive field model (11.10) is the one which is aligned with the receptive field

$$x_{\text{opt}} \propto k; \tag{11.7}$$

see Exercises. Thus the receptive field vector k can be interpreted as the optimal stimulus to cause a spike.

Second, let us consider an ensemble of stimuli x with a radially symmetric distribution, where the probability of a possibly multi-dimensional x is equal to the probability of observing its norm $|x| : p(x) = p_c(|x|)$. Examples include the standard Gaussian distribution, or the uniform distribution with power constraint $p(x) = p_0$ for $|x|^2 < c$ and zero otherwise. We assume that spikes are generated with the LNP model of Eq. (11.5). An important result is that the experimental reverse correlation technique yields an unbiased estimator of the filter k, i.e.,

$$\langle x_{\text{RevCorr}} \rangle = k. \tag{11.8}$$

The proof (Bussgang, 1952; Simoncelli *et al.*, 2004) follows from the fact that each arbitrary input vector x_t can be separated into a component parallel to k and one orthogonal to it. Since we are free to choose the scale of the filter k we can impose $|k| = 1$ and write

$$x_t = (k \cdot x_t)k + (e \cdot x_t)e \tag{11.9}$$

where e is a unit vector in the subspace orthogonal to k. For firing, only the component parallel to k matters. The symmetry of the distribution $p(x)$ guarantees that spike-triggered averaging is insensitive to the component orthogonal to k; see Exercises.

In summary, reverse correlations are an experimental technique to determine the receptive field properties of a sensory neuron under an LNP model. The success of the reverse correlation technique as an experimental approach is intimately linked to its interpretability in terms of the LNP model.

Reverse correlations in the LNP model can also be analyzed in a statistical framework. To keep the arguments simple, we focus on the *linear* case and set

$$f(k \cdot x_t) = \rho_0 + k \cdot x_t. \tag{11.10}$$

The parameters minimizing the squared error between the model firing rate $\rho_0 + k \cdot x$ and the observed firing rate n_t are then

$$k_{\text{opt}} = (X^{\mathsf{T}}X)^{-1} \left(\sum_t n_t x_t \right) / dt. \tag{11.11}$$

We note that, for short observation intervals Δ, the spike count n_t is either zero or 1. Therefore the term in parentheses on the right-hand side is proportional to the classical spike-triggered average; see Eq. (11.6). The factor in front of the parentheses, $X^T X$, is a scaled estimate of the covariance of the inputs x. For stimuli consisting of uncorrelated white noise or light dots at random positions, the covariance structure is particularly simple.

See Paninski (2004) for further connections between reverse correlation and likelihood-based estimates of the parameters in the LNP model.

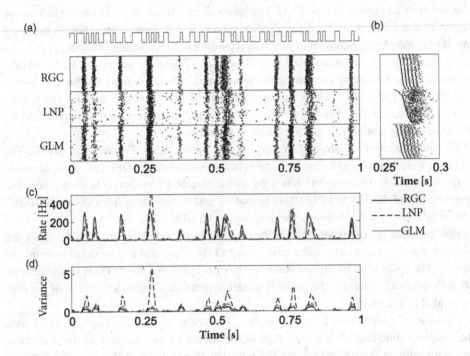

Fig. 11.7 Example predictions of retinal ganglion ON-cell (RGC) activity using the generalized linear encoding model with and without spike-history terms. (a) Recorded responses to repeated full-field light stimulus (top) of true ON cell ("RGC"), simulated LNP model (no spike-history terms; "LNP"), and Generalized Linear Model including spike-history terms ("GLM"). Each row corresponds to the response during a single stimulus presentation. (b) Magnified sections of rasters, with rows sorted in order of first spike time within the window in order to show spike-timing details. Note that the predictions of the model including spike-history terms are in each case more accurate than those of the Poisson (LNP) model. (PSTH variance accounted for: 91%, compared to 39% for the LNP model). (c) Time-dependent firing rate plotted as a PSTH. (d) Variance of the time-dependent firing rate. All data shown here are cross-validated "test" data (i.e., the estimated model parameters were in each case computed based on a non-overlapping "training" dataset not shown here). From Paninski *et al.* (2007) based on data from Uzzell and Chichilnisky (2004).

11.2.2 Multiple neurons

Using multi-electrode arrays, Pillow *et al.* (2008) recorded from multiple ganglion cells in the retina provided with spatio-temporal white noise stimuli. This stimulation reaches the ganglion cells after being transducted by photoreceptors and interneurons of the retina. It is assumed that the effect of light stimulation can be taken into account by a linear filter of the spatio-temporally structured stimulus. An SRM-like model of the membrane potential of a neuron i surrounded by n other neurons is

$$u_i(t) = \sum_f \eta_i(t - t_i^f) + k_i \cdot x(t) + \sum_{j \neq i} \sum_f \varepsilon_{ij}(t - t_j^f) + u_{\text{rest}}. \tag{11.12}$$

The light stimulus $x(t)$ filtered by the receptive field of neuron i, k_i, replaces the artificially injected external current in Eq. (11.1). The spike-afterpotential $\eta_i(t)$ affects the membrane potential as a function of the neuron's own spikes. Spikes from a neighboring neuron j modify the membrane potential of neuron i according to the coupling function $\varepsilon_{ij}(t)$.

The extracellular electrodes used by Pillow *et al.* (2008) did not probe the membrane potential. Nonetheless, by comparing the spike times with the conditional firing intensity $\rho(t|\{S\}) = \frac{1}{\tau_0} \exp(u(t))$ we can maximize the likelihood of observing the set of spike trains $\{S\}$ (Chapter 10). This way we can identify the spatio-temporal receptive field k_i, the spike-afterpotential $\eta(t)$ and the coupling functions $\varepsilon_{ij}(t)$.

The fitted functions k_i showed two types of receptive fields (Pillow *et al.*, 2008). The ON cells were sensitive to recent increase in luminosity while the OFF cells were sensitive to recent decrease. The coupling functions also reflect the two different neuron types. The coupling from ON cells to ON cells is excitatory and the coupling from ON cells to OFF cells is inhibitory, and conversely for couplings from OFF cells.

How accurate are the predictions of the multi-neuron model? Figure 11.8 describes the prediction performance. The spike-trains and PSTHs of the real and modeled neurons are similar. The spike-train likelihood reaches 2 bits per spike and the PSTH is predicted with 80–93% accuracy. Overall, the coupled model appears as a valid description of neurons embedded in a network.

Pillow *et al.* (2008) also asked about the relevance of coupling between neurons. Are the coupling functions an essential part of the model or can the activity be accurately predicted without them? Optimizing the model with and without the coupling function independently, they found that the prediction of PSTH variance was unaffected. The spike prediction performance, however, showed a consistent improvement for the coupled model. (See (Vidne *et al.*, 2012) for further analysis using a model incorporating unobserved common noise effects.) Interneuron coupling played a greater role in decoding, as we shall see in the next section.

11.3 Decoding

"Decoding" refers to the problem of how to "read out" the information contained in a set of neural spike trains (Fig. 11.9) and has both theoretical and practical implications for the

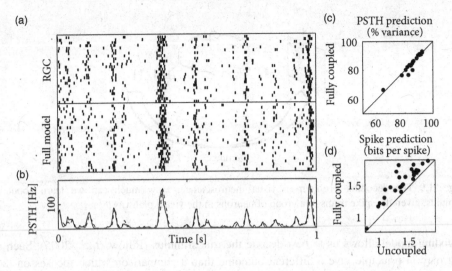

Fig. 11.8 Spike-train prediction of a retinal ganglion cell within its network. (a) Raster of responses of a retinal ganglion cell (RGC; top) to 25 repetitions of 1 s stimulus, and responses of the fully coupled model (Full model; bottom) to the same stimulus. (b) PSTH of the RGC (full black line) and the fully coupled model (dashed black line). (c) PSTH prediction for the fully coupled model of different cells plotted against the the PSTH prediction of a model fitted without interneuron coupling. (d) Log-likelihood (Eq. (10.41)) for the fully coupled model of different cells plotted against the log-likelihood of a model fitted without interneuron coupling. Modified from Pillow *et al.* (2008).

study of neural coding (Rieke *et al.*, 1997; Donoghue, 2002). A variety of statistical techniques have been applied to this problem (Rieke *et al.*, 1997; E. Brown *et al.*, 1998; Pillow *et al.*, 2011; Ahmadian *et al.*, 2011b); in this section, we focus specifically on decoding methods that rely on Bayesian "inversion" of the generalized linear encoding model discussed above and in Chapter 10. That is, we apply Bayes' rule to obtain the posterior probability of the stimulus, conditional on the observed response:

$$p(\boldsymbol{x}|D) \propto p(D|\boldsymbol{x})p(\boldsymbol{x}),$$
(11.13)

where $p(\boldsymbol{x})$ is the prior stimulus probability. As an aside we note that a similar idea was used above when we incorporated prior knowledge to regularize our estimates of the encoding model parameter θ; here we are assuming that θ, or equivalently $p(D|\boldsymbol{x})$, has already been estimated to a reasonable degree of precision, and now we want to incorporate our prior knowledge of the stimulus $\boldsymbol{x}$.

The primary appeal of such Bayesian decoding methods is that they are optimal if we assume that the encoding model $p(D|\boldsymbol{x})$ is correct. Decoding therefore serves as a means for probing which aspects of the stimulus are preserved by the response, and also as a tool for comparing different encoding models. For example, we can decode a spike train using different models (e.g., including vs. ignoring spike-history effects) and examine which

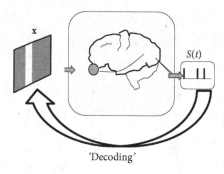

'Decoding'

Fig. 11.9 The decoding problem in visual neuroscience. How much can we learn about a stimulus, given the spike trains of a group of neurons in the visual pathway?

encoding model allows us to best decode the true stimulus (Pillow *et al.*, 2005). Such a test may in principle give a different outcome than a comparison which focuses on the encoding model's ability to predict spike-train statistics. In what follows, we illustrate how to decode using the stimulus which maximizes the posterior distribution $p(x|D)$, and show how a simple approximation to this posterior allows us to estimate how much information the spike-train response carries about the stimulus.

11.3.1 Maximum a posteriori *decoding*

The *maximum a posteriori* (MAP) estimate is the stimulus x that is most probable given the observed spike response D, i.e., the x that maximizes $p(x|D)$. Computing the MAP estimate for x once again requires that we search in a high-dimensional space (the space of all possible stimuli x) to find the maximizer of a nonlinear function, $p(x|D)$. Luckily, in the GLM, the stimulus x interacts linearly with the model parameters θ, implying that concavity of the log-likelihood with respect to x holds under exactly the same conditions as does concavity in θ (Paninski, 2004). Moreover, the sum of two concave functions is concave, so the log-posterior,

$$\log p(x|D) = \log p(D|x) + \log p(x) + c, \qquad (11.14)$$

is concave as long as the stimulus log-prior $\log p(x)$ is itself a concave function of x (e.g., p is Gaussian). In this case, again, we may easily compute $\hat{x}_{MAP}$ by numerically ascending the function $\log p(x|D)$.

We emphasize that the MAP estimate of the stimulus is, in general, a *nonlinear* function of the observed spiking data D. As an empirical test of the MAP estimate, we can compare its performance with that of the optimal *linear* estimate (OLE, see example below), the best linear estimate of the stimulus as a function of the observed spiking data D (Rieke *et al.*, 1997).

Figure 11.10 shows a comparison of the two decoding techniques, given responses D generated by a GLM encoding model with known parameters, as a function of stimulus

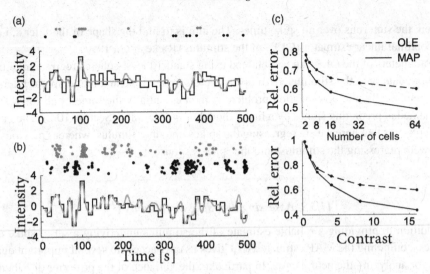

Fig. 11.10 Illustration of MAP (*maximum a posteriori*) decoding. (a) Simulated spike trains from a single pair of simulated ON and OFF retinal ganglion cells (above, gray and block dots) were used to compute the MAP estimate (gray) of a 500 ms Gaussian white noise stimulus (black), sampled at 100 Hz. (b) Spike trains from 10 identical, independent ON and OFF cells in response to the same stimulus, with the associated MAP estimate of the stimulus, illustrating convergence to the true stimulus as the responses of more cells are observed. (c) Comparison of the optimal linear estimate (OLE) and MAP estimate on simulated data, as a function of the number of observed cells (top) and stimulus contrast (variance; bottom). For each data point, the parameters of the OLE were estimated using a long run of simulated data. "Relative error" denotes the average RMS error between the true and estimated stimulus, averaged over 100 trials, divided by the RMS amplitude of the true stimulus.

contrast (variance) and size of the neuronal population. The MAP clearly outperforms the OLE at high contrasts or large population sizes. More importantly, the MAP approach provides us with a great deal of flexibility in considering different encoding models or prior distributions: we can simply substitute in a new $p(D|x)$ or $p(x)$ and recompute the MAP estimator, without having to obtain new estimates of the regression parameters as required by the OLE; see (Ramirez *et al.*, 2011) for an example of this type of analysis. Finally, there are close connections between MAP decoding and the optimal control of neural spiking; see Ahmadian *et al.* (2011a) for further discussion.

Example: Linear stimulus reconstruction

We predict the stimulus x_t by linear filtering of the observed spike times $t^1, t^2, \ldots, t^F < t$,

$$x(t) = x_0 + \sum_f k(t - t^f) \qquad (11.15)$$

where the sum runs over all spike times. The aim is to find the shape of the filter k, i.e., the optimal linear estimator (OLE) of the stimulus (Rieke *et al.*, 1997).

Parameters of the OLE can be obtained using standard least-squares regression of the spiking data onto the stimulus x. To do so, we discretize time and the temporal filter k. Mathematically, the optimization problem is then essentially the same as above where we aimed at predicting spikes by a linear model of the stimulus (Section 10.2). The only difference is that here we are regressing the spikes onto the stimulus, whereas previously we were regressing the stimulus onto the spike response.

11.3.2 Assessing decoding uncertainty (*)

In addition to providing a reliable estimate of the stimulus underlying a set of spike responses, computing the MAP estimate $\hat{x}_{\text{MAP}}$ gives us easy access to several important quantities for analyzing the neural code. In particular, the variance of the posterior distribution around $\hat{x}_{\text{MAP}}$ tells us something about which stimulus features are best encoded by the response D. For example, along stimulus axes where the posterior has small variance (i.e., the posterior declines rapidly as we move away from $\hat{x}_{\text{MAP}}$), we have relatively high certainty that the true x is close to $\hat{x}_{\text{MAP}}$. Conversely, we have relatively low certainty about any feature axis along which the posterior variance is large.

We can measure the scale of the posterior distribution along an arbitrary axis in a fairly simple manner: since we know (by the above concavity arguments) that the posterior is characterized by a single "bump," and the position of the peak of this bump is already characterized by $\hat{x}_{\text{MAP}}$, it is enough to measure the curvature of this bump at the peak $\hat{x}_{\text{MAP}}$. Mathematically, we measure this curvature by computing the "Hessian" matrix A of second derivatives of the log-posterior,

$$A_{ij} = -\frac{\partial^2}{\partial x_i \partial x_j} \log p(x_i | D). \tag{11.16}$$

Moreover, the eigendecomposition of this matrix A tells us exactly which axes of stimulus space correspond to the "best" and "worst" encoded features of the neural response: small eigenvalues of A correspond to directions of small curvature, where the observed data D poorly constrains the posterior distribution $p(x|D)$ (and therefore the posterior variance will be relatively large in this direction), while conversely large eigenvalues in A imply relatively precise knowledge of x, i.e., small posterior variance (Huys *et al.*, 2006) (for this reason the Hessian of the log-likelihood $p(D|x)$ is referred to as the "observed Fisher information matrix" in the statistics literature). In principle, this posterior uncertainty analysis can potentially clarify what features of the stimulus a "downstream" neuron might care most about.

We can furthermore use this Hessian to construct a useful approximation to the posterior $p(x|D)$. The idea is simply to approximate this log-concave bump with a Gaussian function, where the parameters of the Gaussian are chosen to exactly match the peak and curvature of the true posterior. This approximation is quite common in the physics and statistics literature (Kass and Raftery, 1995; E. Brown *et al.*, 1998; Rieke *et al.*, 1997). Specifically,

$$p(x|D) \approx (2\pi)^{-d/2}|A|^{1/2}e^{-(x-\hat{x}_{\text{MAP}})^T A(x-\hat{x}_{\text{MAP}})/2}, \tag{11.17}$$

with $d = \dim(x)$. We can then read off the approximate posterior entropy or variance of x_i: e.g., $\text{var}(x_i|D) \approx [A^{-1}]_{ii}$. As discussed further in Ahmadian *et al.* (2011b) and Pillow *et al.* (2011), the approximation by the Gaussian of Eq. (11.17) is often quite accurate in the context of decoding. See Rieke *et al.* (1997) and Pillow *et al.* (2011) for discussion of a related bound on the posterior entropy, which can be used to bound the mutual information between the stimulus and response.

11.3.3 Decoding in vision and neuroprosthetics

We have established that generalized integrate-and-fire models can predict with good accuracy the activity of real neurons. Is it sensible to assert that we have understood how the neural system translates stimulus into patterns of action potentials? If so we should be able to read the neuronal activity to reconstruct its tangible meaning. As was briefly discussed in the introduction to Section 11.3, reading the neural code has practical applications; a common example of such applications is to help tetraplegic patients to control artificial limbs. In this section, we illustrate decoding in two distinct scenarios. In the first scenario (Fig. 11.11), a monochrome movie is reconstructed from the activity of neurons in the visual pathway. In the second example (Fig. 11.12), it is the time-dependent velocities of hand movements that are decoded from activity in the area MI of the cortex.

Using the methods described in the introduction to Section 11.3, Pillow *et al.* (2008) reconstructed the time-dependent light stimulus from 27 ganglion cells recorded in the retina. First, coupled integrate-and-fire models were optimized on training data (see Section 11.2.2). Once the appropriate set of parameter was determined, spike trains from the data reserved for testing were used to decode the stimulus. Decoding was performed with the methods discussed in the introduction to Section 11.3.

The stimulus was a spatio-temporal binary white noise. The decoding performance can be quantified by evaluating the signal-to-noise ratio for different frequencies (Fig. 11.11). For most of the frequencies, the signal-to-noise ratio of the decoded signal was greater than 1, meaning that the decoded signal was greater than the error. For the fully coupled model discussed in Section 11.2.2, the signal-to-noise ratio can be higher than 3.5 for some frequencies. The decoding performance is expected to grow with the number of recorded neurons, as can be seen in Fig. 11.11c.

We now consider a second example which has applications for neuroprosthetics. The ultimate aim of neuroprosthetics is to help human patients who have lost a limb. Prosthetic limbs are often available for these patients. While prosthesis works from a mechanical point of view, the intuitive control of the prosthetic device poses big challenges. One possible route of research is to read out, directly from the brain, the intentions of the user of the prosthetic device.

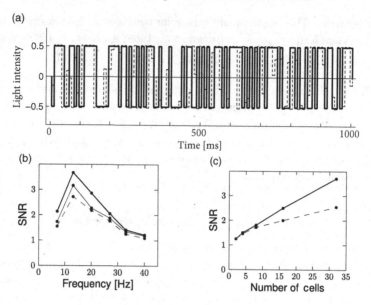

Fig. 11.11 Decoding of light stimulus from recordings of neurons in the retina. (a) Binary light stimulus (thick black) is compared with the decoded stimulus using Bayesian MAP (dashed line, Section 11.3.1). (b) The signal-to-noise ratio (SNR) as function of frequency for decoding using the fully coupled model (thick line), the uncoupled model (thin line) or using an optimal linear decoder (dashed lines). (c) Increasing the number of cells improves the decoding performance of both the coupled model (thick line) and the optimal linear decoder (dashed lines). (a) and (c) are redrawn from Pillow *et al.* (2011), (b) follows a similar figure to one in Pillow *et al.* (2008).

In preliminary experiments, a monkey moves a tracking device with his hand while an electrode records from neurons of its cortex. The electrode is placed in an area associated with planning movements (Donoghue *et al.*, 1998). Truccolo *et al.* (2005) used generalized integrate-and-fire models to decode the hand movements from the recorded activity.

Again here, the first step was to fit the model parameters. The model itself was very similar to the one seen in Section 11.2.2 but without coupling terms and with a different nonlinear relation between model membrane potential and firing intensity. A more noteworthy difference is the input x which consisted of hand velocity such that the receptive field k mapped how the x- and y-components of the velocity influenced the driving potential.

Instead of the method described in Section 11.3.1, Truccolo *et al.* (2005) used a point-process filter (Eden *et al.*, 2004). The decoding algorithm is a recursive algorithm for calculating the Bayesian estimate of the stimulus at time t in term the past activity. This recursive approach is necessary in this real-time application. The decoding performance is illustrated in Fig. 11.12. Signal-to-noise ratio for this decoding was between 1.0 and 2.5, which is rather impressive given the typical variability of cortical neurons and the small number of cells used for decoding (between 5 and 20). This exemplifies that generalized integrate-and-fire models can help in building a brain–machine interface for controlling

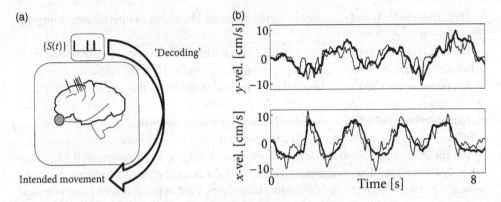

Fig. 11.12 Decoding hand velocity from spiking activity in area MI of cortex. (a) Schematics. (b) The real hand velocity (thin black line) is compared to the decoded velocity (thick black line) for the y- (top) and the x-components (bottom). Modified from Truccolo *et al.* (2005).

prosthetic limbs by "reading" the activity of cortical neurons. A number of groups are now working to further improve these methods for use in prosthetic systems.

11.4 Summary

Generalized integrate-and-fire models can predict the spiking activity of cortical cells such as the main inhibitory and excitatory cell type in layer 2–3 of the cortex. For excitatory neurons, more than 80% of spike timings can be predicted by these models, while for inhibitory neurons the percentage is close to 100%. Similar model performance is seen in the retina, where the activity of up to 250 neurons can be predicted simultaneously (Vidne *et al.*, 2012).

The same models can also be used to decode the activity of neurons. For instance, the spike trains of retinal neurons can be decoded so as to reconstruct a slightly blurred version of the original image movie shown to the retina. Also, the activity of motor cortical neurons can be decoded to reconstruct the intended hand movement in two (or more) dimensions. Thus, the abstract mathematical framework of generalized integrate-and-fire models might ultimately contribute to technical solutions that help human patients.

Literature

The influential book by Rieke *et al.* (1997) gives a broad introduction to the field of neural coding with a special focus on decoding. The LNP model, reverse correlation techniques, and application to receptive field measurements are reviewed in Simoncelli *et al.* (2004).

Predictions of spike timings for a time-dependent input with models including spike-history effects were performed by, for example, Keat *et al.* (2001) and Jolivet *et al.* (2006), and different methods and approaches were compared in a series of international competitions (Jolivet *et al.*, 2008a,b).

The first decoding attempts used time-averaged firing rates to decode information from a diverse population of neurons (Georgopoulos *et al.*, 1986). Then the methods were made more precise in an effort to understand the temporal structure of the neural code (Optican and Richmond, 1987; Bialek *et al.*, 1991). In particular linear stimulus reconstruction from measured spike trains (Rieke *et al.*, 1997) has been widely applied.

Efficient decoding methods are a necessary requirement if a prosthetic arm is controlled by the spikes recorded from cortical neurons. Introducing spike history effects (Truccolo *et al.*, 2005) or interneuron coupling (Pillow *et al.*, 2008) helped to improve decoding accuracy, but the improvement of decoding techniques went in parallel with other technical achievements (Shoham, 2001; Brockwell *et al.*, 2004, 2007; Eden *et al.*, 2004; Truccolo *et al.*, 2005; Srinivasan and Brown, 2007; Kulkarni and Paninski, 2007; Koyama *et al.*, 2010; Paninski *et al.*, 2010).

The discussion of the statistical principles of encoding and decoding in the present and the previous chapter is partly based on the treatment in Paninski *et al.* (2007).

Exercises

1. **Linear filter as optimal stimulus**. *Consider an ensemble of stimuli* x *with a "power" constraint* $|x|^2 < c$.

    (a) Show that, under the linear rate model of Eq.(11.10), the stimulus that maximizes the instantaneous rate is $x = k$.

    Hint: Use Lagrange multipliers to implement the constraint $|x|^2 = c$.

    (b) Assume that the a spatially localized time-dependent stimulus $x(t)$ *is presented in the center of the positive lobe of the neurons receptive field. Describe the neuronal response as*

$$\rho(t) = \rho_0 + \int_0^S \kappa(s) x(t-s) ds, \tag{11.18}$$

    where ρ_0 *is the spontaneous firing rate in the presence of a gray screen and S the temporal extent of the filter* κ. *What stimulus is most likely to cause a spike under the constraint* $\int_0^S [x(t-s)]^2 ds < c$? *Interpret your result.*

2. **LNP model and reverse correlations**. *Show that, if an experimenter uses stimuli* x *with a radially symmetric distribution* $p(x) = q(|x|)$, *then reverse correlation measurements provide an unbiased estimate linear filter* k *under an LNP model*

$$\rho(t) = f(k \cdot x_t); \tag{11.19}$$

    i.e., the expectation of the reverse correlation is parallel to k.

    Hint: Write the stimulus as

$$x = (k \cdot x) k + (e \cdot x) e \tag{11.20}$$

    and determine the reverse correlation measurement by averaging over all stimuli weighted with their probability to cause a spike.

PART THREE

NETWORKS OF NEURONS AND POPULATION ACTIVITY

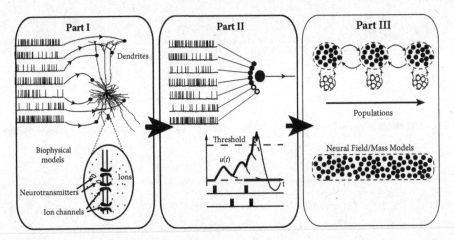

The organization of this book follows a path of successive simplifications so as to ultimately bridge scales from micrometers to centimeters, from single cells to cognition. The first two parts focused on isolated neurons. In Part I, we took as our starting point a rather detailed biophysical description of a neuron, exemplified by the Hodgkin–Huxley model and variants thereof. Working along from Part I to Part II, this description of a neuron was simplified to a point neuron of the integrate-and-fire type.

Part III is the cornerstone for the transition from single neurons to macroscopic phenomena and, ultimately, forms the basis of the cognitive phenomena discussed in Part IV. Chapter 12 starts the transition from single neurons to populations of neurons; the mathematical methods for this transition and the major dynamic phenomena in populations of neurons are explained in Chapters 13 and 14. Because of their complexity, the mathematical equations for the dynamics of populations of neurons are often simplified to so-called rate models. The limitations of the simplification step are highlighted in Chapter 15. The simplified rate equations will then be used for the analysis of a few selected large-scale phenomena in Part IV.

12

Neuronal populations

The brain contains millions of neurons which are organized in different brain areas, within a brain area organized in different subregions, inside each small region into different layers, inside each layer into various cell types. The first two parts of this book focused on the mathematical description of an isolated neuron. Starting with this chapter, we shift our attention to the collective properties of groups of neurons, which we call "neuronal populations." Instead of modeling the spike times of a single neuron which belongs, for example, to the cell class "pyramidal" in layer 5 of subregion C4 in brain region S1 (the numbers here are completely arbitrary), we can ask the question: Suppose a human subject or animal receives a visual, auditory, or somatosensory stimulus – what is the activity of all the cells in this layer of this subregion that are of type "pyramidal" in response to the stimulus? What is the response of this subregion as a whole? What is the response of a brain area? In other words, at any of the scales of spatial resolution (Fig. 12.1), we may be interested in the response of the neuronal population as a whole, rather than in the spikes of individual neurons.

The general idea is presented in Fig. 12.2. A network of 10 000 neurons consisting of $N_E = 8000$ excitatory and $N_I = 2000$ inhibitory neurons, has been simulated while the excitatory neurons received a time-dependent input. Instead of analyzing the spike trains of one or two neurons, we count the number of spikes in a small time step (say $\Delta t = 1$ ms) across all the excitatory neurons in the network. After dividing by Δt and N_E, we arrive at the population activity $A(t)$ of the group of excitatory neurons; see Section 7.2. Analogously, we can determine the population activity of the inhibitory neurons or that of the network as a whole. The central questions of this and the following chapters are: Can we predict the population activity $A(t)$ from the properties of its neurons and the network connectivity? How does the population activity respond to a novel input?

The aim of this chapter is to provide the foundation of the notions of "neuronal population" and "population activity." In the first section we argue that the organization of cortex into columns and layers provides the biological substrate of "neuronal populations." In Section 12.2 we identify the mathematical assumptions and idealizations that will enable us to predict the population activity from single-neuron properties. The basic idea is that, for the definition of a neuronal population, we should group neurons with similar properties together. The aim of Sections 12.2 and 12.3 is to make this intuition more precise.

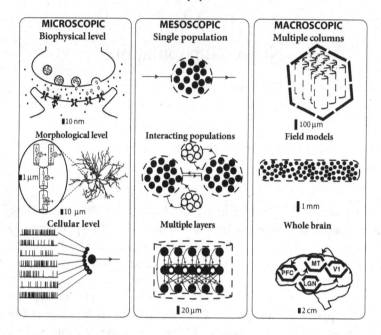

Fig. 12.1 The levels of description in neuroscience models.

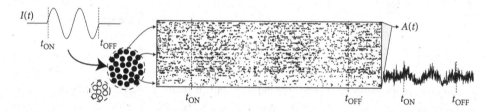

Fig. 12.2 Input and output of a population. A signal $I(t)$, represented by a sinusoidal modulation of the input starting at t_{ON} and ending at t_{OFF}, stimulates the population of 8000 excitatory neurons in a randomly coupled network of 8000 excitatory and 2000 inhibitory neurons (left). Each neuron produces a spike train (middle) illustrated here by lines of dots, each dot corresponding to a spike. Only 1% of the population is shown. The population activity $A(t)$ (right) counts spikes in time bins of 1 ms averaged over the 8000 excitatory neurons.

In Section 12.4 we give a first example of the population activity approach by analyzing stationary activity in a highly connected population. The notions developed in this chapter will be used in the next two chapters in order to analyze the dynamics of one or several connected populations.

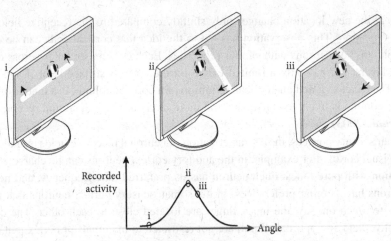

Fig. 12.3 Orientation tuning. The receptive fields of simple cells in the visual cortex have positive and negative subfields. To test orientation tuning, a light bar is slowly moved across the screen (i). The neuron responds maximally if the light bar with an orientation aligned with that of the receptive field moves into the positive subfield (ii) and responds slightly less if the orientation of the bar is not optimal (iii). The response as a function of the orientation of the bar is shown at the bottom (schematic figure).

12.1 Columnar organization

Before we turn, in Section 12.2, to the rather abstract notion of a "neuronal population," we present in this section a short introduction to the structural organization and functional characterization of the cortex. We will argue that a cortical column, or more precisely, a group of cells consisting of neurons of the same type in one layer of a cortical column, can be considered as a plausible biological candidate of a neuronal population.

12.1.1 Receptive fields

Neurons in sensory cortices can be experimentally characterized by the stimuli to which they exhibit a strong response. The receptive field of so-called simple cells in the visual cortex (see Chapter 1) has typically two or three elongated spatial subfields. The neuron responds maximally to a moving light bar with an orientation aligned with the elongation of the positive subfield. If the orientation of the stimulus changes, the activity of the cell decreases (Fig. 12.3). Thus simple cells in the visual cortex are sensitive to the orientation of a light bar (Hubel and Wiesel, 1968).

In this and the following chapters, we exploit the fact that neighboring neurons in the visual cortex have similar receptive fields. If the experimenter moves the electrode vertically down from the cortical surface to deeper layers, the location of the receptive field and its preferred orientation does not change substantially. If the electrode is moved to a neighboring location in the cortex, the location and preferred orientation of the receptive field of neurons at the new location changes only slightly compared to the receptive fields at the previous location. This observation has led to the idea that cortical cells can be grouped into "columns" of neurons with similar properties. Each column stretches across different cortical layers, but has only a limited extent on the cortical surface (Hubel and Wiesel, 1968). The exact size and anatomical definition of a cortical column is a matter of debate, but each column is likely to contain several thousand neurons with similar receptive fields (Lund *et al.*, 2003).

In other sensory cortices, the characterization of neuronal receptive fields is analogous to that in visual cortex. For example, in the auditory cortex, neurons can be characterized by stimulation with pure tones. Each neuron has its preferred tone frequency, and neighboring neurons have similar preferences. In the somatosensory cortex, neurons that respond strongly to touch on, say, the index finger are located close to each other. The concepts of receptive field and optimal stimuli are not restricted to mammals or cortex, but are also routinely used in studies of, for example, retinal ganglion cells, thalamic cells, olfactory bulb, or insect sensory systems.

Example: Cortical maps

Neighboring neurons have similar receptive fields, but the exact characteristics of the receptive fields change slightly as one moves parallel to the cortical surface. This gives rise to cortical maps.

A famous example is the representation of the body surface in the somatosensory area of the human brain. For example, neurons which respond to touch on the thumb are located in the immediate neighborhood of neurons which are activated by touching the index finger, which in turn are positioned next to the subregion of neurons that respond to touching the middle finger. The somatosensory map therefore represents a somewhat stretched and deformed "image" of the surface of the human body projected onto the surface of the cortex. Similarly, the tonotopic map in the auditory cortex refers to the observation that the neurons' preferred pure-tone frequency changes continuously along the cortical surface.

In the visual cortex, the location of the neurons' receptive field changes along the cortical surface giving rise to the retinotopic map. At the same time, the preferred orientation of neurons changes as one moves parallel to the cortical surface giving rise to orientation maps. With modern imaging methods it is possible to visualize the orientation map by monitoring the activity of neuronal populations while the visual cortex is stimulated by the presentation of a slowly moving grating. If the grating is oriented vertically, certain subsets of neurons respond; if the grating is rotated by $60°$, other groups of neurons respond. Thus we can assign to each location on the cortical surface a preferred orientation (see Fig. 12.4), except for a few singular points, called the pinwheels, where regions of different preferred orientations touch each other (Bonhoeffer and Grinvald, 1991; Kaschube *et al.*, 2010).

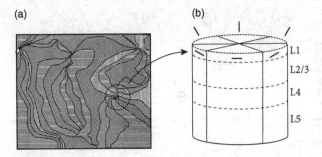

Fig. 12.4 Orientation maps and columns. (a) Top view onto the surface of the visual cortex. Neurons that are optimally activated by a moving grating with an orientation of, say, 60°, form bands. The direction of the hash-line texture in the image indicates the preferred orientation. Iso-orientation contour lines converge to form pinwheels. One of the pinwheels is highlighted by the dashed circle. (b) Side view of a pinwheel (dashed circle in (a)). Orientation selectivity is indicated by thick bars. Neurons with the same orientation form vertical columns. Schematic representation following experimental data shown in Bressloff and Cowan (2002).

12.1.2 How many populations?

The columnar organization of the cortex suggests that all neurons in the same column can be considered as a single population of neurons. Since these neurons share similar receptive fields we should be able to develop mathematical models that describe the net response of the column to a given stimulation. Indeed the development of those abstract models is one of the aims of mathematical neuroscience.

However, the transition from single neurons to a whole column might be too big a challenge to be taken in a single step. Inside a column neurons are organized in different layers. Each layer contains one or several types of neurons. At a first level, we can distinguish excitatory from inhibitory neurons and at an even finer level of detail different types of inhibitory interneurons. As we shall see in the next section, the mathematical transition from single neurons to populations requires that we put only those neurons that have similar intrinsic properties into the same group. In other words, pyramidal neurons in, say, layer 5, of a cortical column are considered as one population whereas pyramidal neurons in layer 2 are a different population; fast-spiking inhibitory neurons in layer 4 form one population while non-fast-spiking interneurons in the same layer form a different group. The number of populations that a theoretician takes into account depends on the level of "coarse-graining" that he is ready to accept, as well as on the amount of information that is available from experiments.

Example: Connectivity in the barrel cortex

The somatosensory cortex of mice contains a region which is sensitive to whisker movement. Each whisker is represented in a different subregion. These subregions are,

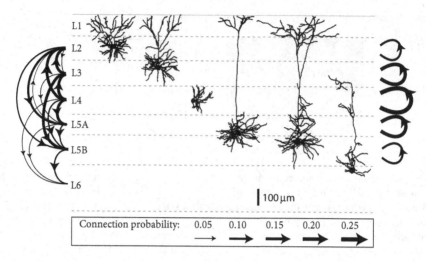

Fig. 12.5 Connectivity patterns inside one column. Examples of shapes of excitatory neurons in different layers. Arrows on the left indicate connection probabilities between excitatory neurons across layers. Arrows on the right show connection probabilities between excitatory neurons within a given layer. Data from a barrel column in the somatosensory cortex of the mouse. After Lefort *et al.* (2009).

at least in layer 4, clearly separated. Neurons are connected vertically across layers so that, in this part of cortex, cortical columns are exceptionally well identifiable. Because of the barrel-shaped subregions in layer 4, this part of the somatosensory cortex is called the barrel cortex (Woosley and Van der Loos, 1970).

Neurons in different layers of a barrel cortex column have various shapes and form connections with each other with different probabilities (Lefort *et al.*, 2009), indicating that excitatory neurons in the column do not form a homogeneous population; see Fig. 12.5. However, if we increase the resolution (i.e., a less "coarse-grained" model) to that of a single layer in one barrel cortex column, then it might be possible to consider all excitatory neurons inside one layer as a rather homogeneous population.

12.1.3 Distributed assemblies

The concept of cortical columns suggests that localized populations of neurons can be grouped together into populations, where each population (e.g., the excitatory neurons in layer 4) can be considered as a homogeneous group of neurons with similar intrinsic properties and similar receptive fields. However, the mathematical notion of a population does not require that neurons need to form local groups to qualify as a homogeneous population.

Donald Hebb (1949) introduced the notion of neuronal assemblies, i.e., groups of cells which get activated together so as to represent a mental concept such as the preparation of a movement of the right arm toward the left. An assembly can be a group of neurons which are distributed across one or several brain areas. Hence, an assembly is not necessarily a local group of neurons. Despite the fact that neurons belonging to one assembly can be widely distributed, we can think of all neurons belonging to the assembly as a homogeneous population of neurons that is activated whenever the corresponding mental concept is evoked. Importantly, such an assignment of a neuron to a population is not fixed, but can depend on the stimulus. We will return to the concept of distributed assemblies in Chapter 17 when we discuss associative memories and the Hopfield model.

12.2 Identical neurons: a mathematical abstraction

As discussed in the previous section, there exist many brain regions where neurons are organized in populations of cells with similar properties. Prominent examples are columns in the somatosensory and visual cortex (Mountcastle, 1957; Hubel and Wiesel, 1962) and pools of motor neurons (Kandel *et al.*, 2000). Given the large number of neurons within such a column or pool it is sensible to describe the mean activity of the neuronal population rather than the spiking of individual neurons.

The definition of population activity has already been introduced earlier, but is repeated here for convenience. In a population of N neurons, we calculate the proportion of active neurons by counting the number of spikes $n_{act}(t; t + \Delta t)$ in a small time interval Δt and dividing by N. Further division by Δt yields the *population activity*

$$A(t) = \lim_{\Delta t \to 0} \frac{1}{\Delta t} \frac{n_{act}(t; t + \Delta t)}{N} = \frac{1}{N} \sum_{j=1}^{N} \sum_{f} \delta(t - t_j^f), \qquad (12.1)$$

where δ denotes the Dirac δ-function. The double sum runs over all firing times t_j^f of all neurons in the population. In other words the activity A is defined by a population average. Even though the activity has units of a rate and indeed is often called the population rate, the population activity is quite different from the concept of a mean firing rate defined by temporal averaging in a single neuron; see Section 7.2.

Theories of population dynamics, sometimes called "neural mass models," have a long tradition (Knight, 1972; Wilson and Cowan, 1972, 1973; Amari, 1974; Abbott and van Vreeswijk, 1993; Gerstner and van Hemmen, 1992; Treves, 1993; Amit and Brunel, 1997b; Brunel and Hakim, 1999; Fusi and Mattia, 1999; Brunel, 2000; Gerstner, 2000; Nykamp and Tranchina, 2000; Omurtag *et al.*, 2000). Their aim is to predict the temporal evolution of the population activity $A(t)$ in large and homogeneous populations of spiking neurons.

Why do we restrict ourselves to large populations? If we repeatedly conduct the same experiment on a population of, say, one hundred potentially noisy neurons, the observed activity $A(t)$ defined in Eq. (12.1) will vary from one trial to the next. Therefore we cannot expect a population theory to predict the activity measurements in a single trial. Rather all population activity equations that we discuss in this chapter predict the *expected* activity. For a large and homogeneous network, the observable activity is very close to the expected activity. For the sake of notational simplicity, we do not distinguish the observed activity from its expectation value and in what follows we denote the expected activity by $A(t)$.

Why do we focus on homogeneous populations? Intuitively, we cannot expect to predict the activity of a population where each neuron receives a different input and has a different, and potentially unknown, set of parameters. However, if all neurons in a population have roughly the same parameters and receive roughly the same input, all neurons are more or less exchangeable and there is a realistic chance that, based on the knowledge of the parameters of a typical neuron in the population, we would be able to predict the activity of the population as a whole. The notion of a homogeneous network will be clarified in the following subsection. In Section 12.2.2 we will ask whether the requirements of homogeneous populations can be relaxed so as to include some degree of heterogeneity within a population.

12.2.1 Homogeneous networks

We study a large and homogeneous population of neurons. By homogeneous we mean that (i) all neurons $1 \leq i \leq N$ are identical; (ii) all neurons receive the same external input $I_i^{\text{ext}}(t) = I^{\text{ext}}(t)$; and (iii) the interaction strength w_{ij} for the connection between any pair j, i of pre- and postsynaptic neurons is "statistically uniform." The notion will be made precise in Section 12.3, but for the moment we can think of connections inside the population as being either absent or "roughly the same," $w_{ij} \approx w_0$, where w_0 is a parameter. For $w_0 = 0$ all neurons are independent; a value $w_0 > 0$ ($w_0 < 0$) implies excitatory (inhibitory) coupling. Not all neurons need to be coupled with each other; connections can, for example, be chosen randomly (see Section 12.3 below).

Example: Homogeneous population of integrate-and-fire neurons

In the case of leaky integrate-and-fire neurons, encountered in Chapters 1 and 5 (Section 5.1), the dynamics are

$$\tau_m \frac{\mathrm{d}}{\mathrm{d}t} u_i = -u_i + R I_i(t) \quad \text{for } u_i < \vartheta \tag{12.2}$$

combined with a reset condition: if $u_i \geq \vartheta$ then integration restarts at u_r. A homogeneous network implies that all neurons have the same input resistance R, the same membrane time constant τ_m, as well as identical thresholds ϑ and reset values u_r. Note that we have shifted the voltage scale such that the resting potential is $u_{\text{rest}} = 0$, which is only possible if all neurons also have the same resting potential.

We assume that a neuron is coupled to all others as well as to itself with coupling strength $w_{ij} = w_0$. The input current I_i in Eq. (12.2) takes care of both the external drive and synaptic coupling

$$I_i = \sum_{j=1}^{N} \sum_f w_{ij} \alpha(t - t_j^f) + I^{\text{ext}}(t). \tag{12.3}$$

Here we have assumed that each input spike generates a postsynaptic current with some generic time course $\alpha(t - t_j^f)$. The sum on the right-hand side of Eq. (12.3) runs over all firing times of all neurons. Because of the homogeneous all-to-all coupling, the total input current is identical for all neurons. To see this, we insert $w_{ij} = w_0$ and use the definition of the population activity, Eq. (12.1). We find a total input current,

$$I(t) = w_0 N \int_0^\infty \alpha(s) A(t-s) \, ds + I^{\text{ext}}(t), \tag{12.4}$$

which is independent of the neuronal index i. Thus, the input current at time t depends on the past population activity and is the same for all neurons.

As an aside we note that for conductance-based synaptic input, the total input current would depend on the neuronal membrane potential which is different from one neuron to the next.

12.2.2 Heterogeneous networks

Our definition of a homogeneous network relied on three conditions: (i) identical parameters for all neurons; (ii) identical external input to all neurons; (iii) statistically homogeneous connectivity within the network. We may wonder whether all three of these are required or whether we can relax our conditions to a certain degree (Tsodyks *et al.*, 1993; Chow, 1998). Potential connectivity schemes will be explored in Section 12.3. Here we focus on the first two conditions.

Let us suppose that all N neurons in the population receive the same input I, considered to be constant for the moment, but parameters vary slightly between one neuron and the next. Because of the difference in parameters, the stationary firing rate $v_i = g_{\theta_i}(I)$ of neuron i is different from that of another neuron j. The index θ_i refers to the set of parameters of neuron i. The mean firing rate averaged across the population is $\langle v \rangle = \sum_i v_i / N$.

Under the condition that, first, the firing rate is a smooth function of the parameters and, second, that the differences between parameters of one neuron and the next are small, we can linearize the function g around the *mean* parameter value $\bar{\theta}$ and find for the mean firing rate averaged across the population

$$\langle v \rangle = g_{\bar{\theta}}(I), \tag{12.5}$$

where we neglected terms $(d^2 g_\theta / d\theta^2)(\theta_i - \bar{\theta})^2$ as well as all higher-order terms. Eq. (12.5) can be phrased as saying that the mean firing rate across a heterogeneous network is equal to the firing rate of the "typical" neuron in the network, i.e., the one with the mean parameters.

However, strong heterogeneity may cause effects that are not well described by the above averaging procedure. For example, suppose that the network contains two subgroups of neurons, each of size $N/2$, one with parameters θ_1 and the other with parameters θ_2. Suppose that the gain function takes a fixed value $v = v_0$ whenever the parameters are smaller than $\hat{\theta}$ and has some arbitrary dependence $v = g_\theta(I) > v_0$ for $\theta > \hat{\theta}$. If $\bar{\theta} = (\theta_1 + \theta_2)/2 < \hat{\theta}$, then Eq. (12.5) would predict a mean firing rate of v_0 averaged across the population, which is not correct. The problem can be solved if we split the population into two populations, one containing all neurons with parameters θ_1 and the other containing all neurons with parameters θ_2. In other words, a strongly heterogeneous population should be split until (nearly) homogeneous groups remain.

The same argument also applies to a population of N neurons with identical parameters, but different inputs I_i. If the differences in the input are small and neuronal output is a continuous function of the input, then we can hope to treat the slight differences in input by a perturbation theory around the homogeneous network, i.e., a generalization of the Taylor expansion used in the previous subsection. If the differences in the input are large, for example, if only a third of the group is strongly stimulated, then the best approach is to split the population into two smaller ones. The first group contains all those that are stimulated, and the second group all the other ones.

12.3 Connectivity schemes

The real connectivity between cortical neurons of different types and different layers, or within groups of neurons of the same type and the same layer, is still partially unknown, because experimental data is limited. At most, some plausible estimates of connection probabilities exist. In some cases the connection probability is considered distance-dependent, in other experimental estimates it is considered uniform in the restricted neighborhood of a cortical column.

In simulations of spiking neurons, there are a few coupling schemes that are frequently adopted (Fig. 12.6). Most of these assume random connectivity within and between populations. In what follows we discuss these schemes with a special focus on the scaling behavior induced by each choice of coupling scheme. Here, scaling behavior refers to a change in the number N of neurons that participate in the population.

An understanding of the scaling behavior is important not only for simulations, but also for the mathematical analysis of the network behavior. However, it should be kept in mind that real populations of neurons have a fixed size because, for example, the number of neurons in a given cortical column is given and, at least in adulthood, does not change dramatically from one day to the next. Typical numbers, counted in one column of mouse somatosensory cortex (barrel cortex, C2), are 5750 excitatory and 750 inhibitory neurons (Lefort *et al.*, 2009). Thus numbers are finite and considerations of the behavior for the number N going to infinity are of little relevance to biology.

We note that numbers are even smaller if we break them down per layer. The estimated mean ($\pm$ standard error of the mean) number of excitatory neurons in each layer (L1 to L6) are as follows: L2, 546 $\pm$ 49; L3, 1145 $\pm$ 132; L4, 1656 $\pm$ 83; L5A, 454 $\pm$ 46; L5B, 641 $\pm$ 50; L6, 1288 $\pm$ 84; and for inhibitory neurons: L1, 26 $\pm$ 8; L2, 107 $\pm$ 7; L3, 123 $\pm$ 19; L4, 140 $\pm$ 9; L5A, 90 $\pm$ 14; L5B, 131 $\pm$ 6; L6, 127 $\pm$ 9 (Lefort *et al.*, 2009).

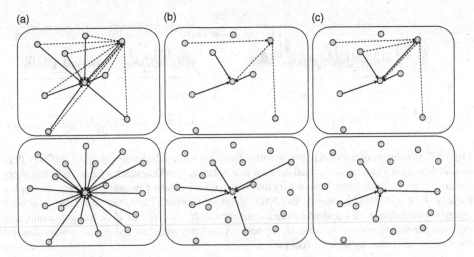

Fig. 12.6 Coupling schemes. (a) Full connectivity: Top: A network of 9 neurons with all-to-all coupling. The input links are shown for two representative neurons. Self-couplings are not indicated. Bottom: The number of input links (indicated for one representative neuron) increases, if the size of the network is doubled. (b) Random coupling with fixed connection probability. In a network of 18 neurons (bottom) the number of input links is larger than in a network of 9 neurons (top). (c) Random coupling with fixed number of inputs. The number of links from presynaptic neurons (top: input links to two representative neurons) does not change when the size of the network is increased (bottom: input links to one representative neuron).

Example: Scaling of interaction strength in networks of different sizes

Suppose we simulate a fully connected network of 1000 noisy spiking neurons. Spikes of each neuron in the population generate in all other neurons an inhibitory input current of strength $w < 0$ which lasts for 20 ms. In addition to the inhibitory inputs, each neuron also receives a fixed constant current I_0^{ext} so that each neuron in the network fires at 5 Hz. Since each neuron receives input from itself and from 999 partner neurons, the total rate of inhibitory input is 5 kHz. Because each input exerts an effect over 20 ms, a neuron is, at each moment in time, under the influence of about 100 inhibitory inputs – generating a total input $I \approx 100w + I_0^{\text{ext}}$.

We now get access to a bigger computer which enables us to simulate a network of 2000 neurons instead of 1000. In the new network each neuron therefore receives inhibitory inputs at a rate of 10 kHz and is, at each moment in time, under the influence of a total input current $I \approx 200w + I_0^{\text{ext}}$. Scaling the synaptic weights w by a factor of $\frac{1}{2}$ leads us back to the same total input as before.

Why should we be interested in changing the size of the network? As mentioned before, in biology the network size is fixed. An experimenter might tell us that the system he studies contains 20 000 neurons, connected with each other with strength $w_{ij} = 1$ (in some arbitrary units) and connection probability of 10%. Running a simulation of the

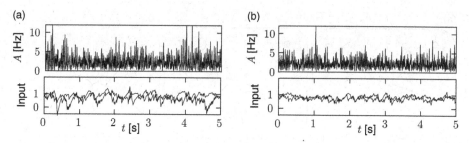

Fig. 12.7 Simulation of a model network with a fixed connection probability $p = 0.1$. (a) Top: Population activity $A(t)$ averaged over all neurons in a network of 4000 excitatory and 1000 inhibitory neurons. Bottom: Total input current $I_i(t)$ into two randomly chosen neurons. (b) Same as (a), but for a network with 8000 excitatory and 2000 inhibitory neurons. The synaptic weights have been rescaled with a factor of $\frac{1}{2}$ and a common input current I^{ext} is given to all neurons to ensure that the same population activity is obtained. All neurons are leaky integrate-and-fire units with identical parameters interacting by short current pulses.

full network of 20 000 neurons is possible, but will take a certain amount of time. We may want to speed up the simulation by simulating a network of 4000 neurons instead. The question arises whether we should increase the interaction strength in the smaller network compared to the value $w_{ij} = 1$ in the big network.

12.3.1 Full connectivity

The simplest coupling scheme is all-to-all connectivity within a population. All connections have the same strength. If we want to change the number N of neurons in the simulation of a population, an appropriate scaling law is

$$w_{ij} = \frac{J_0}{N}. \tag{12.6}$$

This scaling law is a mathematical abstraction that enables us to formally take the limit of $N \to \infty$ while keeping fixed the expected input that a neuron receives from its partners in the population. In the limit of $N \to \infty$, the fluctuations disappear and the expected input can be considered as the actual input to any of the N neurons. Of course, real populations are of finite size, so that some fluctuations always remain. But as N increases the fluctuations decrease.

A slightly more intricate all-to-all coupling scheme is the following: weights w_{ij} are drawn from a Gaussian distribution with mean J_0/N and standard deviation $\sigma_0/\sqrt{N}$. In this case, each neuron in the population sees a somewhat different input, so that fluctuations of the membrane potential are of the order σ_0 even in the limit of large N (Faugeras *et al.*, 2009).

12.3.2 Random coupling: fixed coupling probability

Experimentally the probability p that a neuron inside a cortical column makes a functional connection to another neuron in the same column is in the range of 10%, but varies across layers; see Fig. 12.5.

In simulations, we can fix a connection probability p and choose connections randomly with probability p among all the possible N^2 connections. In this case, the number of presynaptic input links C_j to a postsynaptic neuron j has a mean value of $\langle C_j \rangle = pN$, but fluctuates between one neuron and the next with variance $p(1 - p)N$.

Alternatively, we can take one model neuron $j = 1, 2, 3, \ldots, N$ after the other and choose randomly $C = pN$ presynaptic partners for it (each neuron can be picked only once as a presynaptic partner for a given postsynaptic neuron j). In this case all neurons have, by construction, the same number of input links $C_j = C$. By an analogous selection scheme, we could also fix the number of output links to exactly pN as opposed to simply imposing pN as the average value.

Whatever the exact scheme to construct random connectivity, the number of input connections per neuron increases linearly with the size N of the population; see Fig. 12.6b. It is therefore useful to scale the strength of the connections as

$$w_{ij} = \frac{J_0}{C} = \frac{J_0}{pN},\tag{12.7}$$

so that the mean input to a typical neuron does not change if the number of model neurons in the simulated population is increased. Since in a bigger network individual inputs have smaller effects with the scaling according to Eq. (12.7), the amount of fluctuation in the input decreases with population size; compare Fig. 12.7.

12.3.3 Random coupling: fixed number of presynaptic partners

The number of synapses onto the dendrites of a single pyramidal neuron is estimated to lie in the range of a few thousand (Kandel *et al.*, 2000). Thus, when one simulates networks of a hundred thousand neurons or millions of neurons, a modeling approach based on a fixed connection probability in the range of 10% cannot be correct. Moreover, in an animal participating in an experiment, not all neurons will be active at the same time. Rather only a few subgroups will be active, the composition of which depends on the stimulation conditions and the task. In other words, the number of inputs converging onto a single neuron may be much smaller than a thousand.

We can construct a random network with a fixed number C of inputs by the following procedure. We pick one model neuron $j = 1, 2, 3, \ldots, N$ after the other and choose randomly its C presynaptic partners; see Fig. 12.6c. Whenever the network size N is much bigger than C, the inputs to a given neuron can be thought of as random samples from the current network activity. No scaling of the connections with the population size N is necessary; see Fig. 12.8.

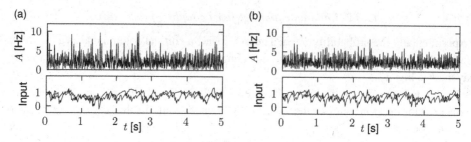

Fig. 12.8 Simulation of a model network with a fixed number of presynaptic partners (400 excitatory and 100 inhibitory cells) for each postsynaptic neuron. (a) Top: Population activity $A(t)$ averaged over all neurons in a network of 4000 excitatory and 1000 inhibitory neurons. Bottom: Total input current $I_i(t)$ into two randomly chosen neurons. (b) Same as (a), but for a network with 8000 excitatory and 2000 inhibitory neurons. The synaptic weights have not been rescaled. While the fluctuations of the population activity $A(t)$ decrease compared to the smaller network (top), the mean and variance of the synaptic input do not change with the size of the network (bottom). All neurons are leaky integrate-and-fire units with identical parameters interacting by current pulses; see Brunel (2000).

12.3.4 Balanced excitation and inhibition

In the simulations of Fig. 12.2, we have assumed a network of excitatory and inhibitory neurons. In other words, our network consists of two interacting populations. The combination of one excitatory and one inhibitory population can be exploited for the scaling of synaptic weights if the effects of excitation and inhibition are "balanced."

In the discussion of scaling in the previous subsections, it was mentioned that a fixed connection probability of p and a scaling of weights $w_{ij} = J_0/(pN)$ leads to a mean neuronal input current that is insensitive to the size of the simulation; however, fluctuations decrease with increasing N. Is there a possibility of working with a fixed connection probability p and yet control the size of the fluctuations while changing N?

In a network of two populations, one excitatory and one inhibitory, it is possible to adjust parameters such that the mean input current into a typical neuron vanishes. The condition is that the total amount of excitation and inhibition cancel each other, so that excitation and inhibition are "balanced." The resulting network is called a balanced network or a population with balanced excitation and inhibition (van Vreeswijk and Sompolinsky, 1996; Vogels *et al.*, 2011).

If the network has balanced excitation and inhibition the mean input current to a typical neuron is automatically zero and we do not have to apply a weight rescaling scheme to control the mean. Instead, we can scale synaptic weights so as to control specifically the amount of fluctuation of the input current around zero. An appropriate choice is

$$w_{ij} = \frac{J_0}{\sqrt{C}} = \frac{J_0}{\sqrt{pN}}. \tag{12.8}$$

With this choice, a change in the size of the network hardly affects the mean and variance of the input current into a typical neuron; see Fig. 12.9. Note that in simulations of

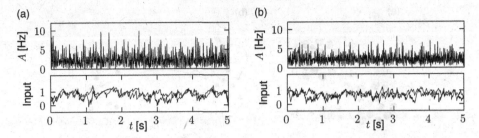

Fig. 12.9 Simulation of a model network with balanced excitation and inhibition and fixed connectivity $p = 0.1$. (a) Top: Population activity $A(t)$ averaged over all neurons in a network of 4000 excitatory and 1000 inhibitory neurons. Bottom: Total input current $I_i(t)$ into two randomly chosen neurons. (b) Same as (a), but for a network with 8000 excitatory and 2000 inhibitory neurons. The synaptic weights have been rescaled by a factor $1/\sqrt{2}$ and the common constant input has been adjusted. All neurons are leaky integrate-and-fire units with identical parameters coupled interacting by short current pulses.

networks of integrate-and-fire neurons, the mean input current to the model neurons is in practice often controlled, and adjusted, through a common constant input to all neurons. In Figs. 12.7–12.9 we simply report the main effects of network size on the population activity and synaptic currents; the analysis of the observed phenomena will be postponed to Section 12.4.

12.3.5 Interacting populations

In the previous subsections we considered two populations, one of them excitatory and the other one inhibitory. Let us generalize the arguments to a network consisting of several populations; see Fig. 12.10. It is convenient to visualize the neurons as being arranged in spatially separate pools, but this is not necessary. All neurons could, for example, be physically localized in the same column of the visual cortex, but of three different types: excitatory, fast-spiking inhibitory, and non-fast-spiking interneurons.

We assume that neurons are homogeneous within each pool. The activity of neurons in pool n is

$$A_n(t) = \frac{1}{N_n} \sum_{j \in \Gamma_n} \sum_f \delta(t - t_j^f), \tag{12.9}$$

where N_n is the number of neurons in pool n and Γ_n denotes the set of neurons that belong to pool n. We assume that each neuron i in pool n receives input from all neurons j in pool m with strength $w_{ij} = J_{nm}/N_m$; see Fig. 12.10. The time course $\alpha_{ij}(s)$ caused by a spike of a presynaptic neuron j may depend on the synapse type, i.e., a connection from a neuron in pool m to a neuron in pool n, but not on the identity of the two neurons. The input current to a neuron i in group Γ_n is generated by the spikes of all neurons in the network,

$$I_{i,n} = \sum_j \sum_f w_{ij} \, \alpha_{ij}(t - t_j^f)$$

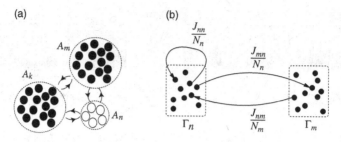

Fig. 12.10 Several interacting populations of neurons. (a) A neuron in population Γ_k is driven by the population activity A_m and A_n of other groups, as well as by the activity A_k of its own population. (b) All neurons in group Γ_n are coupled with synaptic efficacy $w_{ij} = J_{nn}/N_n$. Each pair of neurons i, j with the presynaptic j in groups Γ_m and the postsynaptic neuron i in Γ_n is coupled via $w_{ij} = J_{nm}/N_m$.

$$= \sum_m J_{nm} \int_0^\infty \alpha_{nm}(s) \sum_{j\in\Gamma_m} \sum_f \frac{\delta(t - t_j^f - s)}{N_m} ds,\qquad(12.10)$$

where $\alpha_{nm}(t - t_j^f)$ denotes the time course of a postsynaptic current caused by spike firing at time t_j^f of the presynaptic neuron j which is part of population m. We use Eq. (12.9) to replace the sum on the right-hand side of Eq. (12.10) and obtain

$$I_n = \sum_m J_{nm} \int_0^\infty \alpha(s) A_m(t - s)\, ds.\qquad(12.11)$$

We have dropped the index i since the input current is the same for all neurons in pool n.

Thus, we conclude that the interaction between neurons of different pools can be summarized by the population activity $A(t)$ of the respective pools. Note that Eq. (12.11) is a straightforward generalization of Eq. (12.4) and could have been "guessed" immediately; external input I^{ext} could be added as in Eq. (12.4).

12.3.6 Distance-dependent connectivity

The cortex is a rather thin sheet of cells. Cortical columns extend vertically across the sheet. As we have seen before, the connection probability within a column depends on the layer where pre- and postsynaptic neurons are located. In addition to this vertical connectivity, neurons make many horizontal connections to neurons in other, cortical columns in the same, but also in other, areas of the brain. Within the same brain area the probability of making a connection is often modeled as distance dependent. Note that distance dependence is a rather coarse feature, because the actual connectivity depends also on the function of the pre- and postsynaptic cell. In the primary visual area, for example, it has been found that pyramidal neurons with a preferred orientation for horizontal bars are more likely to make connections to other columns with a similar preferred orientation (Angelucci and Bressloff, 2006).

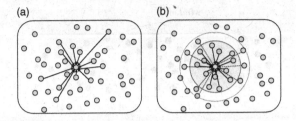

Fig. 12.11 Distance-dependent connectivity. (a) Random coupling where the probability of making a connection falls off with distance. Incoming connections to a single selected neuron are shown. (b) Full connectivity in a local neighborhood, but the connection strength falls off as a function of distance. Incoming connections to a single selected neuron are strong (thick solid arrow among close neighbors), weak (dashed) or non-existent (for distant neurons).

For models of distance-dependent connectivity it is necessary to assign to each model neuron i a location $x(i)$ on the two-dimensional cortical sheet. Two different algorithmic procedures can be used to assign distance-dependent connectivity (Fig. 12.11). The first one assumes full connectivity with a strength w_{ij} which falls off with distance

$$w_{ij} = w(|x(i) - x(j)|),\qquad(12.12)$$

where $x(i)$ and $x(j)$ denote the location of post- and presynaptic neurons, respectively, and w is a function into the real numbers. For convenience, one may assume finite support so that w vanishes for distances $|x(i) - x(j)| > d$.

The second alternative is to give all connections the same weight, but to assume that the probability P of forming a connection depends on the distance

$$\mathrm{Prob}(w_{ij} = 1) = P(|x(i) - x(j)|),\qquad(12.13)$$

where $x(i)$ and $x(j)$ denote the location of post- and presynaptic neurons, respectively and P is a function into the interval $[0,1]$.

Example: Expected number of connections

Let us assume that the density of cortical neurons at location y is $\rho(y)$. The expected number of connections that a single neuron i located at position $x(i)$ receives is then $C_i = \int P(|x(i) - y|)\rho(y)\,dy$. If the density is constant, $\rho(y) = \rho_0$, then the expected number C of input synapses is the same for all neurons and controlled by the integral of the connection probability, i.e., $C_i = \rho_0 \int P(|x(i) - y|)\,dy$.

12.3.7 Spatial continuum limit (*)

The physical location of a neuron in a population often reflects the task of a neuron. In the auditory system, for example, neurons are organized along an axis that reflects the

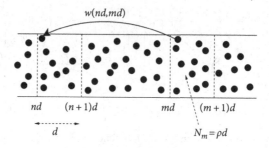

Fig. 12.12 In a spatially continuous ensemble of neurons, the number of neurons in a segment of size d is $N = \rho\, d$. The efficacy w_{ij} between two neurons depends on their location. The coupling strength between a presynaptic neuron j at position $x(j) \approx md$ and a postsynaptic neuron i at location $x(i) \approx nd$ is $w_{ij} \approx w(nd, md)$.

neurons' preferred frequency. A neuron at one end of the axis will respond maximally to low-frequency tones; a neuron at the other end to high frequencies. As we move along the axis the preferred frequency changes gradually. In the visual cortex, the preferred orientation changes gradually as one moves along the cortical sheet. For neurons organized in a spatially extended multi-dimensional network, a description by discrete pools does not seem appropriate. We will indicate in this section that a transition from discrete pools to a continuous population is possible. Here we give a short heuristic motivation of the equations. A thorough derivation along a slightly different line of arguments will be performed in Chapter 18.

To keep the notation simple we consider a population of neurons that extends along a one-dimensional axis; see Fig. 12.12. We assume that the interaction between a pair of neurons i, j depends only on their location x or y on the line. If the location of the presynaptic neuron is y and that of the postsynaptic neuron is x, then $w_{ij} = w(x, y)$. In other words we assume full, but spatially dependent, connectivity and neglect potential random components in the connectivity pattern.

In order to use the notion of population activity as defined in Eq. (12.11), we start by discretizing space in segments of size d. The number of neurons in the interval $[nd, (n+1)d]$ is $N_n = \rho\, d$ where ρ is the spatial density. Neurons in that interval form the group Γ_n. We now change our notation with respect to the discrete population and replace the subscript m in the population activity A_m with the spatial position of the neurons in that group

$$A_m(t) \longrightarrow A(md, t) = A(y, t). \tag{12.14}$$

Since the efficacy of a pair of neurons with $i \in \Gamma_n$ and $j \in \Gamma_m$ is by definition $w_{ij} = J_{nm}/N_m$ with $N_m = \rho\, d$, we have $J_{nm} = \rho\, d\, w(nd, md)$. We use this in Eq. (12.11) and find for the input current

$$I(nd, t) = \rho \sum_m d\, w(nd, md) \int_0^\infty \alpha(s) A(md, t - s)\, ds, \tag{12.15}$$

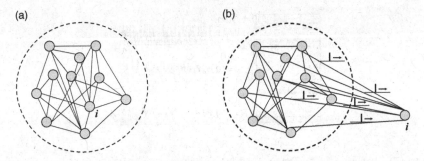

Fig. 12.13 The essence of a mean-field argument. (a) A fully connected population of neurons (not all connections are shown). An arbitrary neuron in the network is marked as i. (b) Neuron i has been pulled out of the network to show that it receives input spikes from the whole population. Hence it is driven by the population activity $A(t)$. The same is true for all other neurons.

where $\alpha(s)$ describes the time course of the postsynaptic current caused by spike firing in one of the presynaptic neurons. For $d \to 0$, the summation on the right-hand side can be replaced by an integral and we arrive at

$$I(x,t) = \rho \int w(x,y) \int_0^\infty \alpha(s) A(y, t-s)\, ds\, dy, \qquad (12.16)$$

which is the final result. To rephrase Eq. (12.16) in words, the input to neurons at location x depends on the spatial distribution of the population activity convolved with the spatial coupling filter $w(x,y)$ and the temporal filter $\alpha(s)$. The population activity $A(y, t-s)\Delta s$ is the number of spikes in a short interval Δs summed across neurons in the neighborhood around y normalized by the number of neurons in that neighborhood.

12.4 From microscopic to macroscopic

In this section we will give a first example of how to make the transition from the properties of single spiking neurons to the population activity in a homogeneous group of neurons. We focus here on stationary activity.

In order to understand the dynamic response of a population of neurons to a changing stimulus, and to analyze the stability of the dynamics with respect to oscillations or perturbations, we will need further mathematical tools to be developed in the next two chapters. As we have see in Chapters 13 and 14, the dynamics depends, apart from the coupling, also on the specific choice of neuron model. However, if we want to predict the level of *stationary activity* in a large network of neurons, i.e., if we do not worry about the temporal aspects of population activity, then knowledge of the single-neuron gain function (f–I curve, or frequency–current relation) is completely sufficient to predict the population activity.

The basic argument is as follows (Fig. 12.13). In a homogeneous population, each

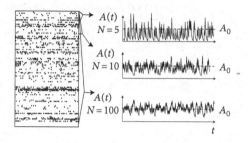

Fig. 12.14 Asynchronous firing. The empirical population activity $A(t)$, defined as an average over the spikes across a group of N neurons, can be plotted after smoothing spikes with a filter $\gamma(s)$ (here the filter is exponential). In the state of stationary asynchronous activity, the filtered population activity converges toward a constant value A_0 if the size N of the group is increased (top: $N = 5$; middle $N = 10$; bottom $N = 100$).

neuron receives input from *many* others, either from the same population, or from other populations, or both. Thus, a single neuron takes as its input a large (and in the case of a fully connected network even a *complete*) sample of the momentary population activity $A(t)$. This has been made explicit in Eq. (12.4) for a single population and in Eq. (12.11) for multiple populations. To keep the arguments simple, in what follows we focus on a single fully connected population. In a homogeneous population, no neuron is different from any other one, so all neurons in the network receive the same input.

Moreover, under the assumption of stationary network activity, the neurons can be characterized by a constant mean firing rate. In this case, the population activity $A(t)$ must be directly related to the constant single-neuron firing rate ν. We show in Section 12.4.2 that, in a homogeneous population, the two are in fact equal: $A(t) = \nu$. We emphasize that the argument sketched here and in the next subsections is completely independent of the choice of neuron model and holds for detailed biophysical models of the Hodgkin–Huxley type just as well as for an adaptive exponential integrate-and-fire model or a spike response model with escape noise. The argument for the stationary activity will now be made more precise.

12.4.1 Stationary activity and asynchronous firing

We define asynchronous firing of a neuronal population as a macroscopic firing state with constant activity $A(t) = A_0$. In this section we show that in a homogeneous population such asynchronous firing states exist and derive the value A_0 from the properties of a single neuron. In fact, we shall see that the only relevant single-neuron property is its gain function, i.e., its mean firing rate as a function of input. More specifically, we will show that the knowledge of the gain function $g(I_0)$ of a *single* neuron and the coupling parameter J_0 is sufficient to determine the activity A_0 during asynchronous firing.

At first glance it might look absurd to search for a constant activity $A(t) = A_0$, because the population activity has been defined in Eq. (12.1) as a sum over δ-functions. Empirically the population activity is determined as the spike count across the population in a finite time interval Δt or, more generally, after smoothing the δ-functions of the spikes with some filter. If the filter is kept fixed, while the population size is increased, the population activity in the stationary state of asynchronous firing approaches the constant value A_0 (Fig. 12.14). This argument will be made more precise below.

12.4.2 Stationary activity as single-neuron firing rate

The population activity A_0 is equal to the mean firing rate ν_i of a single neuron in the population. This result follows from a trivial counting argument and can best be explained by a simple example. Suppose that in a homogeneous population of $N = 1000$ neurons we observe over a time $T = 10$ s a total number of 25 000 spikes. Under the assumption of stationary activity $A(t) = A_0$ the total number of spikes is $A_0 N T$ so that the population firing rate is $A_0 = 2.5$ Hz. Since all 1000 neurons are identical and receive the same input, the total number of 25 000 spikes corresponds to 25 spikes per neuron, so that the firing rate (spike count divided by measurement time) of a single neuron i is $\nu_i = 2.5$ Hz. Thus $A_0 = \nu_i$.

More generally, the assumption of stationarity implies that averaging over time yields, for each single neuron, a good estimate of the firing rate ν_0. The assumption of homogeneity implies that all neurons in the population have the same parameters and are statistically indistinguishable. Therefore a spatial average across the population and the temporal average give the same result:

$$A_0 = \nu_i, \tag{12.17}$$

where the index i refers to the firing rate of a single, but arbitrary neuron.

For an infinitely large population, Eq. (12.17) gives a formula to predict the population activity in the stationary state. However, real populations have a finite size N and each neuron in the population fires at moments determined by its intrinsic dynamics and possibly some intrinsic noise. The population activity $A(t)$ has been defined in Eq. (12.1) as an *empirically observable* quantity. In a finite population, the empirical activity fluctuates and we can, with the above arguments, only predict its expectation value

$$\langle A_0 \rangle = \nu_i. \tag{12.18}$$

The neuron models discussed in Parts I and II enable us to calculate the mean firing rate ν_i for a stationary input, characterized by a mean I_0 and, potentially, fluctuations or noise of amplitude σ. The mean firing rate is given by the gain function

$$\nu_i = g_\sigma(I_0), \tag{12.19}$$

where the subscript σ is intended to remind the reader that the shape of the gain function depends on the level of noise. Thus, considering the pair of equations (12.18) and (12.19), we may conclude that the expected population activity in the stationary state can be predicted from the properties of single neurons.

Example: Theory vs. simulation, expectation vs. observation

How can we compare the population activity $\langle A_0 \rangle$ calculated in Eq. (12.18) with simulation results? How can we check whether a population is in a stationary state of asynchronous firing? In a simulation of a population containing a finite number N of spiking neurons, the observed activity fluctuates. Formally, the (observable) activity $A(t)$ has been defined in Eq. (12.1) as a sum over δ-functions. The activity $\langle A_0 \rangle$ predicted by the theory is the *expectation* value of the observed activity. Mathematically speaking, the observed activity A converges for $N \to \infty$ in the weak topology to its expectation value. More practically this implies that we should convolve the observed activity with a continuous test function $\gamma(s)$ before comparing with A_0. We take a function γ with the normalization $\int_0^{s^{\max}} \gamma(s) \, ds = 1$. For the sake of simplicity we assume furthermore that γ has finite support so that $\gamma(s) = 0$ for $s < 0$ or $s > s^{\max}$. We define

$$\overline{A}(t) = \int_0^{s^{\max}} \gamma(s) A(t - s) \, ds. \tag{12.20}$$

The firing is asynchronous if the averaged fluctuations $\langle |\overline{A}(t) - A_0|^2 \rangle$ decrease with increasing N; see Fig. 12.14.

To keep the notation light, we normally write simply $A(t)$ here, even in places where it would be more precise to write $\langle A(t) \rangle$ (the expected population activity at time t, calculated by theory) or $\overline{A}(t)$ (the filtered population activity, derived from empirical measurement in a simulation or experiment). Only in places where the distinction between $A, \overline{A}$, and $\langle A \rangle$ is crucial do we use the explicit notation with bars or angle brackets.

12.4.3 Activity of a fully connected network

The gain function of a neuron is the firing rate ν as a function of its input current I. In the previous subsection, we have seen that the firing rate is equivalent to the expected value of the population activity A_0 in the state of asynchronous firing. We thus have

$$\langle A_0 \rangle = g_\sigma(I). \tag{12.21}$$

The gain function in the absence of any noise (fluctuation amplitude $\sigma = 0$) will be denoted by g_0.

Recall that the total input I to a neuron of a fully connected population consists of the external input $I^{\text{ext}}(t)$ and a component that is due to the interaction of the neurons within the population. We copy Eq. (12.4) to have the explicit expression of the input current

$$I(t) = w_0 N \int_0^\infty \alpha(s) A(t - s) \, ds + I^{\text{ext}}(t). \tag{12.22}$$

Since the overall strength of the interaction is set by w_0, we can impose a normalization $\int_0^\infty \alpha(s) \, ds = 1$. We now exploit the assumption of stationarity and set $\int_0^\infty \alpha(s) A(t - s) \, ds = A_0$. The left-hand side is the filtered observed quantity which is in reality never exactly

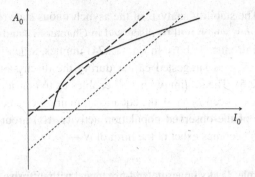

Fig. 12.15 Graphical solution for the fixed point A_0 of the activity in a population of spiking neurons. The intersection of the gain function $A_0 = g_0(I_0)$ (solid line) with the straight line $A_0 = [I_0 - I_0^{\text{ext}}]/J_0$ (dotted) gives the value of the activity A_0. Depending on the parameters, several solutions may coexist (dashed line).

constant, but if the number N of neurons in the network is sufficiently large, we do not have to worry about small fluctuations around A_0. Note that α here plays the role of the test function introduced in the previous example.

Therefore, the assumption of stationary activity A_0 combined with the assumption of constant external input $I^{\text{ext}}(t) = I_0^{\text{ext}}$ yields a constant total driving current

$$I_0 = w_0 N A_0 + I_0^{\text{ext}}. \tag{12.23}$$

Together with Eq. (12.21) we arrive at an *implicit* equation for the population activity A_0,

$$A_0 = g_0 \left(J_0 A_0 + I_0^{\text{ext}} \right), \tag{12.24}$$

where g_0 is the noise-free gain function of single neurons and $J_0 = w_0 N$. In words, the population activity in a homogeneous network of neurons with all-to-all connectivity can be calculated if we know the single-neuron gain function g_0 and the coupling strength J_0. This is the central result of this section, which is independent of any specific assumption about the neuron model.

A graphical solution of Eq. (12.24) is indicated in Fig. 12.15 where two functions are plotted: first, the mean firing rate $\nu = g_0(I_0)$ as a function of the input I_0 (i.e., the gain function); second, the population activity A_0 as a function of the total input I_0 (i.e., $A_0 = [I_0 - I_0^{\text{ext}}]/J_0$; see Eq. (12.23)). The intersections of the two functions yield fixed points of the activity A_0.

As an aside we note that the graphical construction is identical to that of the Curie–Weiss theory of ferromagnetism which can be found in any physics textbook. More generally, the structure of the equations corresponds to the mean-field solution of a system with feedback. As shown in Fig. 12.15, several solutions may coexist. We cannot conclude from the figure whether one or several solutions are stable. In fact, it is possible that *all* solutions are unstable. In the last case, the network leaves the state of asynchronous firing and evolves toward an oscillatory state. The stability analysis of the asynchronous state requires equations for the population *dynamics*, which will be discussed in Chapters 13 and 14.

The parameter J_0 introduced above in Eq. (12.24) implies, at least implicitly, a scaling of weights $w_{ij} = J_0/N$ – as suggested earlier during the discussion of fully connected networks; see Eq. (12.6). The scaling with $1/N$ enables us to consider the limit of a large number of neurons: if we keep J_0 fixed, the equation remains the same, even if N increases. Because fluctuations of the observed population activity $A(t)$ around A_0 decrease as N increases, Eq. (12.24) becomes exact in the limit of $N \to \infty$.

Example: Leaky integrate-and-fire model with diffusive noise

We consider a large and fully connected network of identical leaky integrate-and-fire neurons with homogeneous coupling $w_{ij} = J_0/N$ and normalized postsynaptic currents ($\int_0^\infty \alpha(s)ds = 1$). In the state of asynchronous firing, the total input current driving a typical neuron of the network is then

$$I_0 = I_0^{\text{ext}} + J_0 A_0. \tag{12.25}$$

In addition, each neuron receives individual diffusive noise of variance σ^2 that could represent spike arrival from other populations. The single-neuron gain function (Siegert, 1951) in the presence of diffusive noise has already been stated in Chapter 8; see Eq. (8.54). We use the formula of the gain function to calculate the population activity

$$A_0 = g_\sigma(I_0) = \left\{ \tau_m \sqrt{\pi} \int_{\frac{u_r - RI_0}{\sigma}}^{\frac{\vartheta - RI_0}{\sigma}} du \exp\left(u^2\right) \left[1 + \text{erf}(u)\right] \right\}^{-1}, \tag{12.26}$$

where σ with units of voltage measures the amplitude of the noise. The fixed points for the population activity are once more determined by the intersections of these two functions; see Fig. 12.16.

12.4.4 Activity of a randomly connected network

In the preceding subsections we have studied the stationary state of a large population of neurons for a given noise level. In Fig. 12.16 the noise was modeled explicitly as diffusive noise and can be interpreted as the effect of stochastic spike arrival from other populations or some intrinsic noise source inside each neuron. In other words, noise was added *explicitly* to the model while the input current $I_i(t)$ to neuron i arising from other neurons in the population was constant and the same for all neurons: $I_i = I_0$.

In a randomly connected network (and similarly in a fully connected network of finite size), the summed synaptic input current arising from other neurons in the population is, however, not constant but fluctuates around a mean value I_0, even if the population is in a stationary state of asynchronous activity. In this subsection, we discuss how to mathematically treat the additional noise arising from the network.

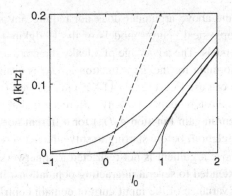

Fig. 12.16 Graphical solution for the fixed point A_0 in the case of a fully connected network of leaky integrate-and-fire neurons. The solid lines show the single-neuron firing rate as a function of the constant input current I_0 for four different noise levels, namely, $\sigma = 1.0, \sigma = 0.5$, $\sigma = 0.1, \sigma = 0.0$ (from top to bottom). The intersection of the gain function with the dashed line with slope $1/J_0$ gives solutions for the stationary activity A_0 in a population with excitatory coupling J_0. Other parameters: $\vartheta = 1, R = 1, \tau = 10$ ms.

We assume that the network is in a stationary state where each neuron fires stochastically, independently, and at a constant rate ν, so that the firing of different neurons exhibits only chance coincidences. Suppose that we have a randomly connected network of N neurons where each neuron receives input from C_{pre} presynaptic partners. All weights are set equal to $w_{ij} = w$.

We are going to determine the firing rate $\nu = A_0$ of a typical neuron in the network self-consistently as follows. If all neurons fire at a rate ν then the mean input current to neuron i generated by its C_{pre} presynaptic partners is

$$\langle I_0 \rangle = C_{\text{pre}} \, q \, w \, \nu + I_0^{\text{ext}}, \tag{12.27}$$

where $q = \int_0^\infty \alpha(s)\,ds$ denotes the integral over the postsynaptic current and can be interpreted as the total electric charge delivered by a single input spike; see Section 8.2.

The input current is not constant but fluctuates with a variance σ_I^2 given by

$$\sigma_I^2 = C_{\text{pre}} \, w^2 \, q_2 \, \nu, \tag{12.28}$$

where $q_2 = \int_0^\infty \alpha^2(s)\,ds$; see Section 8.2.

Thus, if neurons fire at constant rate ν, we know the mean input current and its variance. In order to close the argument we use the single-neuron gain function

$$\nu = g_\sigma(I_0), \tag{12.29}$$

which is supposed to be known for arbitrary noise levels σ_I. If we insert the mean I_0 from Eq. (12.27) and its standard deviation σ_I from Eq. (12.28), we arrive at an implicit equation for the firing rate ν which we need to solve numerically. The mean population activity is then $\langle A_0 \rangle = \nu$.

We emphasize that the above argument does not require any specific neuron model. In fact, it holds for biophysical neuron models of the Hodgkin–Huxley type as well as for integrate-and-fire models. The advantage of a leaky integrate-and-fire model is that an explicit mathematical formula for the gain function $g_\sigma(I_0)$ is available. An example will be given below. But we can use Eqs. (12.27)–(12.29) just as well for a homogeneous population of biophysical neuron models. The only difference is that we have to numerically determine the single-neuron gain function $g_\sigma(I_0)$ for different noise levels (with noise of the appropriate autocorrelation) before starting to solve the network equations.

Note also that the above argument is not restricted to a network consisting of a single population. It can be extended to several interacting populations. In this case, the expressions for the mean and variance of the input current contain contributions from the other populations, as well as from the self-interaction in the network. An example with interacting excitatory and inhibitory populations is given below.

The arguments that have been developed above for networks with a fixed number of presynaptic partners C_{pre} can also be generalized to networks with *asymmetric random connectivity* of fixed connection probability p and synaptic scaling $w_{ij} = J_0/\sqrt{N}$ (Amari, 1972; Sompolinksy *et al.*, 1988; Cessac *et al.*, 1994; van Vreeswijk and Sompolinsky, 1996; Ben Arous and Guionnet, 1995).

Brunel network: excitatory and inhibitory populations

The self-consistency argument will now be applied to the case of two interacting populations, an excitatory population with N_E neurons and an inhibitory population with N_I neurons. The neurons in both populations are modeled by leaky integrate-and-fire neurons. For the sake of convenience, we set the resting potential to zero ($u_{rest} = 0$). We have seen in Chapter 8 that leaky integrate-and-fire neurons with diffusive noise generate spike trains with a broad distribution of interspike intervals when they are driven in the subthreshold regime. We will use this observation to construct a self-consistent solution for the stationary states of asynchronous firing.

We assume that excitatory and inhibitory neurons have the same parameters ϑ, τ_m, R, and u_r. In addition, all neurons are driven by a common external current I^{ext}. Each neuron in the population receives C_E synapses from excitatory neurons with weight $w_E > 0$ and C_I synapses from inhibitory neurons with weight $w_I < 0$. If an input spike arrives at the synapses of neuron i from a presynaptic neuron j, its membrane potential changes by an amount $\Delta u_E = w_E q R/\tau_m$ if j is excitatory and $\Delta u_I = \Delta u_E w_I/w_E$ if j is inhibitory. Here q has units of electric charge. We set

$$\gamma = \frac{C_I}{C_E} \quad \text{and} \quad g = -\frac{w_I}{w_E} = -\frac{\Delta u_I}{\Delta u_E}. \tag{12.30}$$

Since excitatory and inhibitory neurons receive the same number of input connections in our model, we assume that they fire with a common firing rate ν. The total input current generated by the external current and by the lateral couplings is

$$I_0 = I^{\text{ext}} + q \sum_j v_j w_j$$
$$= I_0^{\text{ext}} + q v w_E C_E [1 - \gamma g]. \tag{12.31}$$

Because each input spike causes a jump of the membrane potential, it is convenient to measure the noise strength by the variance σ_u^2 of the membrane potential (as opposed to the variance σ_I^2 of the input). With the definitions of Chapter 8, we set $\sigma_u^2 = 0.5\sigma^2$ where, from Eq. (8.42),

$$\sigma^2 = \sum_j v_j \tau (\Delta u_j^2)$$
$$= v \tau (\Delta u_E)^2 C_E [1 + \gamma g^2]. \tag{12.32}$$

The stationary firing rate A_0 of the population with mean input I_0 and variance σ is copied from Eq. (12.26) and repeated here for convenience

$$A_0 = v = g_\sigma(I_0) = \frac{1}{\tau_m} \left\{ \sqrt{\pi} \int_{\frac{u_r - RI_0}{\sigma}}^{\frac{\vartheta - RI_0}{\sigma}} \exp\left(x^2\right) [1 + \text{erf}(x)] \, dx \right\}^{-1}. \tag{12.33}$$

In a stationary state we must have $A_0 = v$. To get the value of A_0 we must therefore solve Eqs. (12.31)–(12.33) simultaneously for v and σ. Since the gain function, i.e., the firing rate as a function of the input I_0, depends on the noise level σ, a simple graphical solution as in Fig. 12.15 is no longer possible. Numerical solutions of Eqs. (12.31)–(12.33) have been obtained by Amit and Brunel (1997a,b). For a mixed graphical-numerical approach see Mascaro and Amit (1999).

Below we give some examples of how to construct self-consistent solutions. For convenience we always set $\vartheta = 1, q = 1, R = 1$ and $\tau_m = 10$ ms and work with a unit-free current $I \to h$. Our aim is to find connectivity parameters such that the mean input to each neuron is $h = 0.8$ and its variance $\sigma = 0.2$.

Figure 12.17a shows that $h_0 = 0.8$ and $\sigma = 0.2$ correspond to a firing rate of $A_0 = v \approx$ 16 Hz. We set $\Delta u_E = 0.025$, i.e., 40 simultaneous spikes are necessary to make a neuron fire. Inhibition has the same strength $w_I = -w_E$ so that $g = 1$. We constrain our search to solutions with $C_E = C_I$ so that $\gamma = 1$. Thus, on the average, excitation and inhibition balance each other. To get an average input potential of $h_0 = 0.8$ we therefore need a constant driving current $I^{\text{ext}} = 0.8$.

To arrive at $\sigma = 0.2$ we solve Eq. (12.32) for C_E and find $C_E = C_I = 200$. Thus for this choice of the parameters the network generates enough noise to allow a stationary solution of asynchronous firing at 16 Hz.

Note that, for the same parameters, the inactive state where all neurons are silent is also a solution. Using the methods discussed in this section we cannot say anything about the stability of these states. For the stability analysis see Chapter 13.

(a)

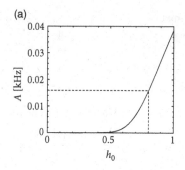

(b)

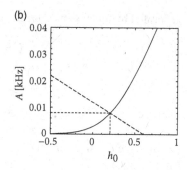

Fig. 12.17 (a) Mean activity of a population of integrate-and-fire neurons with diffusive noise amplitude of $\sigma = 0.2$ as a function of $h_0 = RI_0$. For $h_0 = 0.8$ the population rate is $v \approx 16$ Hz (dotted line). (b) Mean activity of a population of integrate-and-fire neurons with diffusive noise of $\sigma = 0.54$ as a function of $h_0 = RI_0$. For $h_0 = 0.2$ the population rate is $v = 8$ Hz (dotted line). The dashed line shows $A_0 = [h_0 - h_0^{\text{ext}}]/J^{\text{eff}}$ with an effective coupling $J^{\text{eff}} < 0$.

Example: Inhibition dominated network

About 80–90% of the neurons in the cerebral cortex are excitatory and the remaining 10–20% inhibitory. Let us suppose that we have $N_E = 8000$ excitatory and $N_I = 2000$ inhibitory neurons in a cortical column. We assume random connectivity with a connection probability of 10% and take $C_E = 800$, $C_I = 200$ so that $\gamma = 1/4$. As before, spikes arriving at excitatory synapses cause a voltage jump $\Delta u_E = 0.025$, i.e., an action potential can be triggered by the simultaneous arrival of 40 presynaptic spikes at excitatory synapses. If neurons are driven in the regime close to threshold, inhibition is rather strong and we take $\Delta u_I = -0.125$ so that $g = 5$. Even though we have fewer inhibitory than excitatory neurons, the mean feedback is then dominated by inhibition since $\gamma g > 1$. We search for a consistent solution of Eqs. (12.31)–(12.33) with a spontaneous activity of $v = 8$ Hz.

Given the above parameters, the variance is $\sigma \approx 0.54$; see Eq. (12.32). The gain function of integrate-and-fire neurons gives us for $v = 8$ Hz a corresponding total potential of $h_0 \approx 0.2$; see Fig. 12.17b. To attain h_0 we have to apply an external stimulus $h_0^{\text{ext}} = RI^{\text{ext}}$ which is slightly larger than h_0 since the net effect of the lateral coupling is inhibitory. Let us introduce the effective coupling $J^{\text{eff}} = \tau C_E \Delta u_E (1 - \gamma g)$. Using the above parameters we find from Eq. (12.31) that $h_0^{\text{ext}} = h_0 - J^{\text{eff}} A_0 \approx 0.6$.

The external input could, of course, be provided by (stochastic) spike arrival from other columns in the same or other areas of the brain. In this case Eq. (12.31) is to be replaced by

$$h_0 = \tau_m v \Delta u_E C_E [1 - \gamma g] + \tau_m v_{\text{ext}} \Delta u_{\text{ext}} C_{\text{ext}}, \tag{12.34}$$

with C_{ext} the number of connections that a neuron receives from neurons outside the population, Δu_{ext} their typical coupling strength characterized by the amplitude of the voltage jump, and v_{ext} their spike arrival rate (Amit and Brunel, 1997a,b). Owing to the extra stochasticity in the input, the variance σ_u^2 of the membrane voltage is larger

$$\sigma_u^2 = 0.5\sigma^2 = 0.5\tau_m \, v \, (\Delta u_E)^2 C_E \left[1 + \gamma g^2\right] + 0.5\tau_m \, v_{ext}(\Delta u_{ext})^2 C_{ext}. \tag{12.35}$$

The equations (12.33), (12.34) and (12.35) can be solved numerically (Amit and Brunel, 1997a,b). The analysis of the stability of the solution is slightly more involved (Brunel and Hakim, 1999; Brunel, 2000), and will be considered in Chapter 13.

Example: Vogels–Abbott network

The structure of the network studied by Vogels and Abbott (Vogels and Abbott, 2005, 2009; Brette *et al.*, 2007) is the same as that for the Brunel network: excitatory and inhibitory model neurons have the same parameters and are connected with the same probability p within and across the two sub-populations. Therefore inhibitory and excitatory neurons fire with the same mean firing rate (see Section 12.4.4) and with hardly any correlations above chance level (Fig. 12.18). The two main differences to the Brunel network are: (i) the choice of random connectivity in the Vogels–Abbott network does not preserve the number of presynaptic partners per neuron so that some neurons receive more and others less than pN connections; (ii) neurons in the Vogels–Abbott network communicate with each other by conductance-based synapses. A spike fired at time t_j^f causes a change in conductance

$$\tau_g \frac{dg}{dt} = -g + \tau_g \Delta g \sum_f \delta(t - t_j^f). \tag{12.36}$$

Thus, a synaptic input causes for $t > t_j^f$ a contribution to the conductance $g(t) = \Delta g \exp[-(t - t_j^f)/\tau_g]$. The neurons are leaky integrate-and-fire units.

As will be discussed in more detail in Section 13.6.3, the dominant effect of conductance-based input is a decrease of the effective membrane time constant. In other words, if we consider a network of leaky integrate-and-fire neurons (with resting potential $u_{rest} = 0$), we may use again the Siegert formula of Eq. (12.26)

$$A_0 = g_\sigma(I_0) = \left\{ \tau_{eff}(I_0, \sigma)\sqrt{\pi} \int_{\frac{u_r - RI_0}{\sigma}}^{\frac{\vartheta - RI_0}{\sigma}} du \, \exp\left(u^2\right) \left[1 + \mathrm{erf}(u)\right] \right\}^{-1} \tag{12.37}$$

in order to calculate the population activity A_0. The main difference to the current-based model is that the mean input current I_0 and the fluctuations σ of the membrane voltage now also enter into the time constant τ_{eff}. The effective membrane time constant τ_{eff} in simulations of conductance-based integrate-and-fire neurons is sometimes four or five times shorter than the raw membrane time constant τ_m (Destexhe *et al.*, 2003; Vogels and Abbott, 2005, 2009).

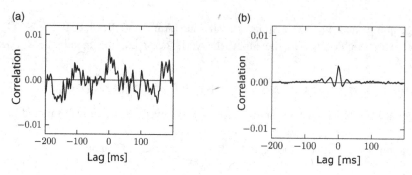

Fig. 12.18 Pairwise correlation of neurons in the Vogels–Abbott network. (a) Excess probability of observing a spike in a neuron i at time t and a spike in neuron j at time t' for various time lags $t - t'$, after subtraction of chance coincidences. Normalization such that two identical spike trains would give a value of 1 at zero time lag. (b) As in (a), but averaged across 171 randomly chosen pairs. The pairwise correlations are extremely small in this randomly connected network of 8000 excitatory and 2000 inhibitory neurons with connection probability $p = 0.02$ and conductance-based synapses; see Vogels *et al.* (2011) for details. The mean firing rate is $A_0 = 5$ Hz.

The Siegert formula holds in the limit of short synaptic time constants ($\tau_E \to 0$ and $\tau_I \to 0$). The assumption of short time constants for the conductances is necessary, because the Siegert formula is valid for white noise, corresponding to short pulses. However, the gain function of integrate-and-fire neurons for colored diffusive noise can also be determined (Fourcaud and Brunel, 2002); see Section 13.6.4.

12.4.5 Apparent stochasticity and chaos in a deterministic network

In this section we discuss how a network of *deterministic* neurons with fixed random connectivity can generate its own noise. In particular, we will focus on spontaneous activity and argue that there exist stationary states of asynchronous firing at low firing rates which have broad distributions of interspike intervals (Fig. 12.19) even though individual neurons are deterministic. The arguments made here have tacitly been used throughout Section 12.4.

Van Vreeswijk and Sompolinsky (1996, 1998) used a network of binary neurons to demonstrate broad interval distribution in deterministic networks. Amit and Brunel (1997a,b) were the first to analyze a network of integrate-and-fire neurons with fixed random connectivity. While they allowed for an additional fluctuating input current, the major part of the fluctuations were in fact generated by the network itself. The theory of randomly connected integrate-and-fire neurons has been further developed by Brunel and Hakim (1999). In a later study, Brunel (2000) confirmed that asynchronous highly irregular firing can be a stable solution of the network dynamics in a completely deterministic network consisting of excitatory and inhibitory integrate-and-fire neurons. Work of Tim Vogels and Larry Abbott has shown that asynchronous activity at low firing rates can indeed be observed reliably

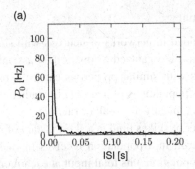
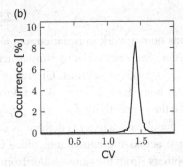

Fig. 12.19 Interspike interval distributions in the Vogels–Abbott network. (a) Interspike interval distribution of a randomly chosen neuron. Note the long tail of the distribution. The width of the distribution can be characterized by a coefficient of variation of $CV = 1.9$. (b) Distribution of the CV index across all 10 000 neurons of the network. Bin width of horizontal axis is 0.01.

in networks of leaky integrate-and-fire neurons with random coupling via conductance-based synapses (Vogels and Abbott, 2005, 2009; Brette *et al.*, 2007). The analysis of randomly connected networks of integrate-and-fire neurons (Brunel, 2000) is closely related to earlier theories for random nets of formal analog or binary neurons (Amari, 1972, 1974, 1977; Kree and Zippelius, 1991; Nützel, 1991; Crisanti and Sompolinsky, 1988; Cessac *et al.*, 1994). However, the reset of neurons after each spike can be the cause of additional instabilities that have been absent in these earlier networks with analog or binary neurons.

   Random connectivity of the network plays a central role in the arguments. We focus on randomness with a fixed number C of presynaptic partners. Sparse connectivity means that the ratio

$$\delta = \frac{C}{N} \ll 1 \qquad (12.38)$$

is a small number. Formally, we may take the limit as $N \to \infty$ while keeping C fixed. As a consequence of the sparse random network connectivity two neurons i and j share only a small number of common inputs. In the limit of $C/N \to 0$ the probability that neurons i and j have a common presynaptic neuron vanishes. Thus, *if* the presynaptic neurons fire stochastically, then the input spike trains that arrive at neuron i and j are independent (Derrida *et al.*, 1987; Kree and Zippelius, 1991). In that case, the input of neurons i and j can be described as an uncorrelated stochastic spike arrival which in turn can be approximated by a diffusive noise model; see Chapter 8. Therefore, in a large and suitably constructed random network, correlations between spiking neurons can be arbitrarily low (Renart *et al.*, 2010); see Fig. 12.18.

   Note that this is in stark contrast to a fully connected network of finite size where neurons receive highly correlated input, but the correlations are completely described by the time course of the population activity.

12.5 Summary

Neurons do not work in isolation, but are embedded in networks of neurons with similar properties. Such networks of similar neurons can be organized as distributed assemblies or as local pools of neurons. Groups of neurons with similar properties can be approximated as homogeneous or weakly heterogeneous populations of neurons. In mathematical models, the connectivity within the population is typically all-to-all or random.

The population activity is defined as the number of spikes fired in a short instant of time, averaged across the population. Since each neuron in a population receives input from many others (from the same and/or from other populations) its total input at each moment in time depends on the activity of the presynaptic population(s). Hence the population activity $A(t)$ controls the mean drive of a postsynaptic neuron.

If the population in a self-connected network is in a state of stationary activity, the expected value $\langle A_0 \rangle$ of the population activity can be determined self-consistently. To do so, we approximate the mean drive of a neuron by $\langle A_0 \rangle$ and exploit that the firing rate of the population must be equal to that of a single neuron. In the stationary state of asynchronous activity the population activity is therefore fully determined by the gain function of a single neuron (i.e., its frequency–current curve) and the strength of feedback connections. This result, which is an example of a (stationary) mean-field theory, is independent of any neuron model. The mean-field solution is exact for a fully connected network in the limit of a large number of neurons ($N \to \infty$), and a good approximation for large randomly connected networks.

The assumption of a stationary state is, of course, a strong limitation. In reality, the activity of populations in the brain responds to external input and may also show non-trivial intrinsic activity changes. In other words, the population activity is in most situations time-dependent. The mathematical description of the dynamics of the population activity is the topic of the next three chapters.

Literature

The development of population equations, also called "neural mass" equations, had a first boom around 1972 with several papers by different researchers (Wilson and Cowan, 1972; Knight, 1972; Amari, 1972). Equations very similar to the population equations have sometimes also been used as effective rate model neurons (Grossberg, 1973). The transition from stationary activity to dynamics of population in the early papers is often ad hoc (Wilson and Cowan, 1972).

The study of randomly connected networks has a long tradition in the mathematical sciences. Random networks of formal neurons have been studied by numerous researchers (e.g., Amari 1972, 1974, 1977; Sompolinksy *et al.* 1988; Cessac *et al.* 1994; van Vreeswijk and Sompolinsky 1996, 1998), and a mathematically precise formulation of mean-field theories for random nets is possible (Faugeras *et al.*, 2009).

The theory for randomly connected integrate-and-fire neurons (Amit and Brunel, 1997a;

Brunel and Hakim, 1999; Brunel, 2000; Renart *et al.*, 2010) builds on earlier studies of formal random networks. The Siegert formula for the gain function of a leaky integrate-and-fire model with diffusive noise appears in several classic papers (Siegert, 1951; Amit and Brunel, 1997a; Brunel and Hakim, 1999; Brunel, 2000). In arbitrarily connected integrate-and-fire networks, the dynamics is highly complex (Cessac, 2008).

Exercises

1. **Fully connected network.** *Assume a fully connected network of N Poisson neurons with firing rate $v_i(t) = g(I_i(t)) > 0$. Each neuron sends its output spikes to all other neurons as well as back to itself. When a spike arrives at the synapse from a presynaptic neuron j to where a postsynaptic neuron i is, it generates a postsynaptic current*

$$I_i^{\text{syn}} = w_{ij} \exp[-(t - t_j^f)/\tau_s] \quad \text{for } t > t_j^f, \tag{12.39}$$

where t_j^f is the moment when the presynaptic neuron j fired a spike and τ_s is the synaptic time constant.

   (a) Assume that each neuron in the network fires at the same rate v. Calculate the mean and the variance of the input current to neuron i.

   Hint: Use the methods of Chapter 8.

   (b) Assume that all weights are of equal weight $w_{ij} = J_0/N$. Show that the mean input to neuron i is independent of N and that the variance decreases with N.

   (c) Evaluate the mean and variance under the assumption that the neuron receives 4000 inputs at a rate of 5 Hz. The synaptic time constant is 5 ms and $J_0 = 1$ μA.

2. **Stochastically connected network.** *Consider a network analogous to that discussed in the previous exercise, but with a synaptic coupling current*

$$I_i^{\text{syn}} = w_{ij} \left\{ \left(\frac{1}{\tau_1}\right) \exp[-(t - t_j^f)/\tau_1] - \left(\frac{1}{\tau_2}\right) \exp[-(t - t_j^f)/\tau_2] \right\} \quad \text{for } t > t_j^f, \tag{12.40}$$

which contains both an excitatory and an inhibitory component.

   (a) Calculate the mean synaptic current and its variance assuming arbitrary coupling weights w_{ij}. How do the mean and variance depend upon the number of neurons N?

   (b) Assume that the weights have a value $J_0/\sqrt{N}$. How do the mean and variance of the synaptic input current scale as a function of N?

3. **Mean-field model.** *Consider a network of N neurons with all-to-all connectivity and scaled synaptic weights $w_{ij} = J_0/N$. The transfer function (rate as a function of input potential) is piecewise linear:*

$$f = g(h) = \frac{h - h_1}{h_2 - h_1} \quad \text{for } h_1 \leq h \leq h_2. \tag{12.41}$$

The rate vanishes for $h < h_1$ and is constant $f = 1$ (in units of the maximal rate) for $h > h_2$.

   The dynamics of the input potential h_i of a neuron i are given by

$$\tau \frac{dh_i}{dt} = -h_i + RI_i(t), \tag{12.42}$$

with

$$I(t) = I^{\text{ext}} + \sum_j w_{ij} \alpha(t - t_j^f). \tag{12.43}$$

   (a) Find graphically the fixed points of the population activity in the network with connections as described above.

   (b) Determine the solutions analytically.

4. **Mean field in a network of two populations.** *We study a network of excitatory and inhibitory neurons. Each excitatory neuron has, in the stationary state, a firing rate*

$$e = f(I) = \gamma I \quad \text{for } I > 0 \quad \text{and } f(I) = 0 \text{ otherwise.} \tag{12.44}$$

Inhibitory neurons have a firing rate

$$s = g(I) = I^2 \quad \text{for } I > 0 \quad \text{and } g(I) = 0 \text{ otherwise.} \tag{12.45}$$

Assume that we have a large network of N excitatory and N inhibitory neurons, where $N \gg 1$. The input to an excitatory neuron i is

$$I_i(t) = I_0 + \sum_{k=1}^{N} \frac{w}{N} e_k - \sum_{n=1}^{N} \frac{1}{N} s_n, \tag{12.46}$$

where e_k is the rate of excitatory neuron k and s_n the rate of inhibitory neuron n. The input to an inhibitory neuron n is

$$I_i(t) = \sum_{k=1}^{N} \frac{w}{N} e_k. \tag{12.47}$$

(a) Give the analytical solution for the steady state of the network. If there are several solutions, indicate the stability of each of these.

Hint: Introduce the parameter $A = \sum_{k=1}^{N} \frac{1}{N} e_k$ for the excitatory population activity; express the activity of the inhibitory population by A and insert the result into the excitatory equation.

(b) Solve graphically for the stationary state of the activity in the network, for two qualitatively different *regimes which you choose. Free parameters are the coupling strength w and the external input I.*

13
Continuity equation and the Fokker–Planck approach

In the previous chapter, the notion of a homogeneous population of neurons was introduced. Neurons within the population can be independent, fully connected, or randomly connected, but they should all have identical, or at least similar, parameters and all neurons should receive similar input. For such a homogeneous population of neurons, it is possible to predict the population activity in the stationary state of asynchronous firing (Section 12.4). While the arguments we made in the previous chapter are general and do not rely on any specific neuron model, they are unfortunately restricted to the stationary state.

In a realistic situation, neurons in the brain receive time-dependent input. Humans change their direction of gaze spontaneously two or three times per second. After each gaze change, a new image impinges on the retina and is transmitted to the visual cortex. Auditory stimuli such as music or traffic noise have a rich intrinsic temporal structure. If humans explore the texture of a surface which by itself is static, they move their fingers so as to actively create temporal structure in the touch perception. If we think back to our last holiday, we recall sequences of events rather than static memory items. When we type a message on a keyboard, we move our fingers in a rapid pattern. In *none* of these situations, is *stationary* brain activity a likely candidate to represent our thoughts and perceptions. Indeed, EEG (electroencephalography) recordings from the surface of the human scalp, as well as multi-unit activity recorded from the cortex of animals, indicate that the activity of the brain exhibits a rich temporal structure.

In this chapter, we present a formulation of population activity equations that can account for the temporal aspects of population dynamics. It is based on the notion of membrane potential densities for which a continuity equation is derived (Section 13.1). In order to illustrate the approach, we consider a population of neurons receiving stochastically arriving spikes (Sections 13.2 and 13.3). For an explicit solution of the equations, we first focus on coupled populations of leaky integrate-and-fire neurons (Sections 13.4), but the mathematical approach can be generalized to arbitrary nonlinear integrate-and-fire neurons (Section 13.5) and generalized integrate-and-fire neurons with adaptation (Section 13.6).

Before we turn to neurons with adaptation, we focus on one-dimensional, but potentially nonlinear integrate-and-fire neurons. Knowledge of the momentary membrane potential and the input is sufficient to predict the future evolution of a single integrate-and-fire neuron. In a large population of neurons, the momentary state of the population as a whole can therefore be characterized by the momentary distribution of membrane potentials. The evolution of this distribution over time is summarized by the continuity equation which is introduced now.

13.1 Continuity equation

In a population of neurons, each neuron may be in a different internal state. In this section we derive partial differential equations that describe how the distribution of internal states evolves as a function of time. We start in Section 13.1.1 with a population of integrate-and-fire neurons. Since the state of an integrate-and-fire neuron is characterized by its membrane potential, we describe the dynamics of the population as the evolution of membrane potential densities.

The population activity, $A(t)$, was introduced in Chapter 7 as the fraction of neurons that fire at time t in a finite population. In this chapter and the next, the population activity is the expected population activity $A(t) \equiv \langle A(t) \rangle$. Since A(t) is self-averaging, it can also be said that we consider the limit of large populations. The finite-size effects will be discussed in Section 14.6.

The formulation of the dynamics of a population of integrate-and-fire neurons on the level of membrane potential densities has been developed by Abbott and van Vreeswijk (1993), Brunel and Hakim (1999), Fusi and Mattia (1999), Nykamp and Tranchina (2000), Brunel (2000), and Omurtag et al. (2000). The closely related formulation in terms of refractory densities has been studied by Wilson and Cowan (1972), Gerstner and van Hemmen (1992), Bauer and Pawelzik (1993), and Gerstner (2000). Generalized density equations have been discussed by Knight (2000) and Fourcaud and Brunel (2002).

13.1.1 Distribution of membrane potentials

We study a homogeneous population of integrate-and-fire neurons. The internal state of a neuron i is determined by its membrane potential which changes according to

$$\tau_m \frac{\mathrm{d}}{\mathrm{d}t} u_i = f(u_i) + R I_i(t) \quad \text{for } u_i < \theta_{\text{reset}}. \tag{13.1}$$

Here R is the input resistance, $\tau_m = RC$ the membrane time constant, and $I_i(t)$ the total input (external driving current and synaptic input). If $u_i \geq \theta_{\text{reset}}$ the membrane potential is reset to $u_i = u_r < \theta_{\text{reset}}$. Here $f(u_i)$ is an arbitrary function of u; see Eq. (5.2). For $f(u_i) = -(u_i - u_{\text{rest}})$ the equation reduces to the standard leaky integrate-and-fire model. For the moment we keep the treatment general and restrict it to the leaky integrate-and-fire model only later.

In a population of N integrate-and-fire neurons, we may ask how many of the neurons have at time t a given membrane potential. As $N \to \infty$ the fraction of neurons i with membrane potential $u_0 < u_i(t) \le u_0 + \Delta u$ is

$$\lim_{N \to \infty} \left\{ \frac{\text{neurons with } u_0 < u_i(t) \le u_0 + \Delta u}{N} \right\} = \int_{u_0}^{u_0 + \Delta u} p(u,t) \, du, \qquad (13.2)$$

where $p(u,t)$ is the *membrane potential density*; see Chapter 8. The integral over this density remains constant over time, i.e.,

$$\int_{-\infty}^{\theta_{\text{reset}}} p(u,t) \, du = 1. \qquad (13.3)$$

The normalization to unity expresses the fact that all neurons have a membrane potential below or equal to the threshold.

The aim of this section is to describe the evolution of the density $p(u,t)$ as a function of time. As we shall see, the equation that describes the dynamics of $p(u,t)$ is nearly identical to that of a single integrate-and-fire neuron with diffusive noise; see Eqs. (8.40) and (8.41).

13.1.2 Flux and continuity equation

Let us consider the portion of neurons with a membrane potential between u_0 and u_1,

$$\frac{n(u_0; u_1)}{N} = \int_{u_0}^{u_1} p(u',t) \, du'. \qquad (13.4)$$

The fraction of neurons with $u_0 < u < u_1$ increases if neurons enter from below through the boundary u_0 or from above through the boundary u_1; see Fig. 13.1. Since there are many neurons in the population, we expect that in each short time interval Δt, many trajectories cross one of the boundaries. The *flux* $J(u,t)$ is the net fraction of trajectories per unit time that crosses the value u. A positive flux $J(u,t) > 0$ is defined as a flux toward increasing values of u. In other words, in a finite population of N neurons, the quantity $N J(u_0,t) \Delta t$ describes the number of trajectories that in the interval Δt cross the boundary u_0 from below, minus the number of trajectories crossing u_0 from above. Note that u_0 here is an arbitrary value that we chose as the lower bound of the integral in Eq. (13.4) and as such has no physical meaning for the neuron model.

Since trajectories cannot simply end, a change in the number $n(u_0; u_1)$ of trajectories in the interval $u_0 < u < u_1$ can be traced back to the flux of trajectories in and out of that interval. We therefore have the conservation law

$$\frac{\partial}{\partial t} \int_{u_0}^{u_1} p(u',t) \, du' = J(u_0,t) - J(u_1,t). \qquad (13.5)$$

Taking the derivative with respect to the upper boundary u_1 and changing the name of the variable from u_1 to u yields the continuity equation,

$$\frac{\partial}{\partial t} p(u,t) = -\frac{\partial}{\partial u} J(u,t) \quad \text{for } u \ne u_r \text{ and } u \ne \theta_{\text{reset}}, \qquad (13.6)$$

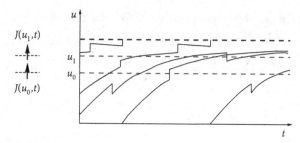

Fig. 13.1 The number of trajectories in the interval $[u_0, u_1]$ changes if one of the trajectories crosses the boundary u_0 or u_1. For a large number of neurons this fact is described by the continuity equation; see Eq. (13.6). Schematic figure where only three trajectories are shown.

which expresses the conservation of the number of trajectories. In integrate-and-fire models, however, there are two special voltage values, u_r and θ_{reset}, where the number of trajectories is *not* conserved, because of the fire-and-reset mechanism.

Since neurons that have fired start a new trajectory at u_r, we have a "source of new trajectories" at $u = u_r$, i.e., new trajectories appear in the interval $[u_r - \varepsilon, u_r + \varepsilon]$ that have not entered the interval through one of the borders. Adding a term $A(t)\,\delta(u - u_r)$ on the right-hand side of (13.6) accounts for this source of trajectories. The trajectories that appear at u_r disappear at θ_{reset}, so that we have

$$\frac{\partial}{\partial t} p(u,t) = -\frac{\partial}{\partial u} J(u,t) + A(t)\,\delta(u - u_r) - A(t)\,\delta(u - \theta_{\text{reset}}). \tag{13.7}$$

The density $p(u,t)$ vanishes for all values $u > \theta_{\text{reset}}$.

The population activity $A(t)$ is, by definition, the fraction of neurons that fire, i.e., those that pass through the threshold. Therefore we find

$$A(t) = J(\theta_{\text{reset}}, t). \tag{13.8}$$

Equations (13.7) and (13.8) describe the evolution of the the membrane potential densities and the resulting population activity as a function of time. We now specify the neuron model so as to have an explicit expression for the flux.

13.2 Stochastic spike arrival

We consider the flux $J(u,t)$ in a homogeneous population of integrate-and-fire neurons with voltage equation (13.1). We assume that all neurons in the population receive the same driving current I^{ext}. In addition each neuron receives independent background input in the form of stochastic spike arrival. We allow for different types of synapses. An input spike at a synapse of type k causes a jump of the membrane potential by an amount w_k. For example, $k = 1$ could refer to weak excitatory synapses with jump size $w_1 > 0$; $k = 2$ to strong excitatory synapses $w_2 > w_1$; and $k = 3$ to inhibitory synapses with $w_3 < 0$. The effective spike arrival rate (summed over all synapses of the same type k) is denoted

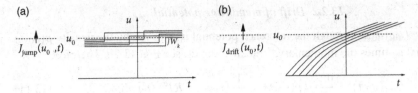

Fig. 13.2 (a) All trajectory that are less than w_k below u_0 cross u_0 upon spike arrival. (b) The drift $J_{\text{drift}}(u_0, t)$ depends on the density of the trajectories and on the slope with which the trajectories cross the boundary u_0.

as v_k. While the mean spike arrival rates $v_k(t)$ are identical for all neurons, we assume that the actual input spike trains at different neurons and different synapses are independent. In a simulation, spike arrival at different neurons is generated by independent Poisson processes with a common spike arrival rate $v_k(t)$ for synapse type k.

Whereas spike arrivals cause a jump of the membrane potential, a finite input current $I^{\text{ext}}(t)$ generates a smooth drift of the membrane potential trajectories. In such a network, the flux $J(u,t)$ across a reference potential u_0 can therefore be generated in two different ways: through a "jump" or a "drift" of trajectories. We separate the two contributions to the flux into J_{jump} and J_{drift}

$$J(u_0, t) = J_{\text{drift}}(u_0, t) + J_{\text{jump}}(u_0, t), \tag{13.9}$$

and treat each of these in turn.

13.2.1 Jumps of membrane potential due to stochastic spike arrival

To evaluate J_{jump}, let us consider an excitatory input $w_k > 0$. All neurons that have a membrane potential u_i with $u_0 - w_k < u_i \leq u_0$ will jump across the reference potential u_0 upon spike arrival at a synapse of type k; see Fig. 13.2a. Since at each neuron spikes arrive stochastically, we cannot predict with certainty whether a single neuron receives a spike around time t or not. But because the Poisson rate v_k of spike arrival at synapses of type k is the same for each neuron, while the actual spike trains are independent for different neurons, the total (expected) flux, or probability current, caused by input spikes at all synapses can be calculated as

$$J_{\text{jump}}(u_0, t) = \sum_k v_k \int_{u_0 - w_k}^{u_0} p(u, t)\, du. \tag{13.10}$$

If the number of neurons is large, the actual flux is very close to the expected flux given in Eq. (13.10).

13.2.2 Drift of membrane potential

The drift flux $J_{\text{drift}}(u_0,t)$ through the reference potential u_0 is given by the density $p(u_0,t)$ at the potential u_0 times the momentary "velocity" du/dt; see Fig. 13.2b. Therefore

$$J_{\text{drift}}(u_0,t) = \left.\frac{du}{dt}\right|_{u_0} p(u_0,t) = \frac{1}{\tau_m}[f(u_0) + RI^{\text{ext}}(t)]\, p(u_0,t), \qquad (13.11)$$

where $f(u_0)$ is the nonlinearity of the the integrate-and-fire model in Eq. (13.1). Note that synaptic δ-current pulses cause a jump of the membrane potential and therefore contribute only to J_{jump} (see Section 13.2.1), but not to the drift flux considered here. Current pulses of finite duration, however, should be included in $I^{\text{ext}}(t)$ in Eq. (13.11).

Example: Leaky integrate-and-fire neurons

With $f(u) = -(u - u_{\text{rest}})$ we have for leaky integrate-and-fire neurons a drift-induced flux

$$J_{\text{drift}}(u_0,t) = \frac{1}{\tau_m}[-u_0 + u_{\text{rest}} + RI^{\text{ext}}(t)]\, p(u_0,t). \qquad (13.12)$$

13.2.3 Population activity

A positive flux through the threshold θ_{reset} yields the population activity $A(t)$. Since the flux has components from the drift and from the jumps, the total flux at the threshold is

$$A(t) = \frac{1}{\tau_m}[f(\theta_{\text{reset}}) + RI^{\text{ext}}(t)]\, p(\theta_{\text{reset}},t) + \sum_k v_k \int_{\theta_{\text{reset}} - w_k}^{\theta_{\text{reset}}} p(u,t)\, du. \qquad (13.13)$$

Since the probability density vanishes for $u > \theta_{\text{reset}}$, the sum over the synapses k can be restricted to all *excitatory* synapses.

If we insert the explicit form of the flux that we derived in Eqs. (13.10) and (13.11) into the continuity equation (13.7), we arrive at the density equation for the membrane potential of integrate-and-fire neurons

$$\begin{aligned}
\frac{\partial}{\partial t}p(u,t) = &-\frac{1}{\tau_m}\frac{\partial}{\partial u}\left\{[f(u) + RI^{\text{ext}}(t)]\, p(u,t)\right\} \\
&+ \sum_k v_k(t)\,[p(u - w_k,t) - p(u,t)] \\
&+ A(t)\,\delta(u - u_r) - A(t)\,\delta(u - \theta_{\text{reset}}).
\end{aligned} \qquad (13.14)$$

The first two terms on the right-hand side describe the continuous drift, the third term the jumps caused by stochastic spike arrival, and the last two terms take care of the reset. Because of the firing condition, we have $p(u,t) = 0$ for $u > \theta_{\text{reset}}$.

Equations (13.13) and (13.14) can be used to predict the population activity $A(t)$ in a population of integrate-and-fire neurons stimulated by an arbitrary common input $I^{\text{ext}}(t)$.

(a)

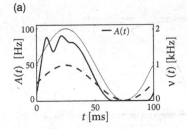

(b)

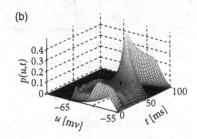

Fig. 13.3 Solution of the membrane potential density equation for time dependent input. The input is sinusoidal with a period of 100 ms. (a) Population activity $A(t)$ (thick solid line; left vertical scale) in response to excitatory and inhibitory spikes arriving with modulated firing rates (thin solid and dashed lines, respectively; right vertical scale). (b) The membrane population density $p(u,t)$ as a function of voltage and time during one period of the periodic stimulation. Adapted from Nykamp and Tranchina (2000) with kind permission from Springer Science and Business Media.

For a numerical implementation of Eq. (13.6) we refer the reader to the literature (Nykamp and Tranchina, 2000; Omurtag *et al.*, 2000).

Example: Transient response of population activity

The population of 10 000 uncoupled leaky integrate-and-fire neurons simulated by Nykamp and Tranchina (2000) receives stochastic spike arrivals at excitatory and inhibitory synapses at rate $v_E(t)$ and $v_I(t)$, respectively. Each input spike causes a voltage jump of amplitude w. The raw jump size is drawn from some distribution and then multiplied with the difference between the synaptic reversal potential and value of the membrane potential just before spike arrival, so as to approximate the effect of conductance based synapses. The average jump size in the simulation was about 0.5 mV at excitatory synapses and -0.33 mV at inhibitory synapses (Nykamp and Tranchina, 2000).

The input rates are periodically modulated with frequency $f = 10$ Hz

$$v_{E/I}(t) = \bar{v}_{E/I}[1 + \sin(2\pi f t)], \qquad (13.15)$$

with $\bar{v}_E = 2$ kHz and $\bar{v}_I = 1$ kHz. Integration of the population equations (13.13) and (13.14) yields a population activity $A(t)$ that responds strongly during the rising phase of the input, well before the excitatory input reaches its maximum; see Fig. 13.3a.

We compare the solution of the population activity equations with the explicit simulation of 10 000 uncoupled neurons. The simulated population activity of the finite network (Fig. 13.4a) is well approximated by the predicted activity $A(t)$ which becomes correct if the number of neurons goes to infinity. The density equations also predict the voltage distribution at each moment in time (Fig. 13.3b). The empirical histogram of voltages in a finite population of 10 000 neurons (Fig. 13.4b) is close to the smooth voltage distribution predicted by the theory.

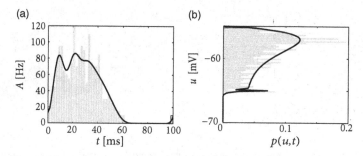

Fig. 13.4 Comparison of theory and simulation. (a) Population firing rate $A(t)$ as a function of time in a simulation of 100 neurons (gray histogram bars) compared to the prediction by the theory (solid line) while the population receives periodically modulated excitatory and inhibitory conductance input with period $T = 100$ ms. (b) Histogram of voltage distribution (gray horizontal bars) at $t_0 = 20$ ms in a population of 1000 neurons compared to the solution $p(u, t_0)$ of the density equation during the periodic stimulation. Adapted from Nykamp and Tranchina (2000) with kind permission from Springer Science and Business Media.

13.2.4 Single neuron versus population of neurons

Equation (13.14), which describes the dynamics of $p(u,t)$ in a population of integrate-and-fire neurons, is nearly identical to that of a single integrate-and-fire neuron with stochastic spike arrival; see Eq. (8.40). Apart from the fact that we have formulated the problem here for arbitrary nonlinear integrate-and-fire models, there are three subtle differences.

First, while $p(u,t)$ was introduced in Chapter 8 as *probability* density for the membrane potential of a *single* neuron, it is now interpreted as the density of membrane potentials in a large population of uncoupled neurons.

Second, the normalization is different. In Chapter 8, we considered a single neuron which was initialized at time $\hat{t}$ at a voltage u_r. For $t > \hat{t}$, the integrated density $\int_{-\infty}^{\theta_{\text{reset}}} p(u,t)\, du \leq 1$ was interpreted as the probability that the neuron under consideration has not yet fired since its last spike at $\hat{t}$. The value of the integral therefore decreases over time. In the present treatment of a population of neurons, a neuron remains part of the population even if it fires. Thus the integral over the density remains constant over time; see Eq. (13.3).

Third, the fraction of neurons that "flow" across threshold per unit of time is the (expected value of) the population activity $A(t)$. Thus, the population activity has a natural interpretation in terms of the flux $J(\theta_{\text{reset}}, t)$.

13.3 Fokker–Planck equation

The equation for the membrane potential density in a population of integrate-and-fire neurons (see Eq. (13.14) in the previous section) can, in the limit of small jump amplitudes w_k, be approximated by a diffusion equation. To show this, we expand the right-hand side of Eq. (13.14) into a Taylor series up to second order in w_k. The result is the Fokker–Planck equation,

$$
\tau_m \frac{\partial}{\partial t} p(u,t) = -\frac{\partial}{\partial u} \left\{ \left[f(u) + R I^{\text{ext}}(t) + \tau_m \sum_k v_k(t) w_k \right] p(u,t) \right\}
$$

$$
+ \frac{1}{2} \left[\tau_m \sum_k v_k(t) w_k^2 \right] \frac{\partial^2}{\partial u^2} p(u,t) \tag{13.16}
$$

$$
+ \tau_m A(t) \, \delta(u - u_r) - \tau_m A(t) \, \delta(u - \theta_{\text{reset}}) + \mathcal{O}(w_k^3).
$$

The term with the second derivative describes a "diffusion" in terms of the membrane potential.

It is convenient to define the total "drive" in voltage units as

$$
\mu(t) = R I^{\text{ext}}(t) + \tau_m \sum_k v_k(t) w_k \tag{13.17}
$$

and the amount of diffusive noise (again in voltage units) as

$$
\sigma^2(t) = \tau_m \sum_k v_k(t) w_k^2. \tag{13.18}
$$

The firing threshold acts as an absorbing boundary so that the density at threshold vanishes:

$$
p(\theta_{\text{reset}}, t) = 0. \tag{13.19}
$$

The boundary condition $p(\theta_{\text{reset}}, t) = 0$ arises from the mathematical limiting process: We consider that all weights go to zero, $w_k \to 0$, while the total drive μ and the amount of diffusive noise remains constant. This is only possible if we have at least two different types of synapse (excitatory and inhibitory) and we increase the rate of both while decreasing the weights of synapses. In other words, the spike arrival rates at the synapses go to infinity so that the "shot noise" generated by spike arrivals turns into a white Gaussian distributed noise. Any neuron with a membrane potential just below the threshold would then immediately fire because of the noise. Therefore the density at the threshold has to be zero. This argument is no longer valid if spike arrival rates are finite, or if synapses react slowly so that the noise is colored (see Section 13.6.4 below).

In order to calculate the flux through the reset threshold we expand Eq. (13.13) in w_k about $u = \theta_{\text{reset}}$ and obtain

$$
A(t) = -\frac{\sigma^2(t)}{2\tau_m} \frac{\partial p(u,t)}{\partial u} \bigg|_{u=\theta_{\text{reset}}}, \tag{13.20}
$$

Eqs. (13.16)–(13.20), together with the normalization (13.3), define the dynamics of a homogeneous population of integrate-and-fire neurons with "diffusive" noise. For a more detailed discussion of the diffusion limit see Chapter 8, in particular Eqs. (8.41) and (8.43).

Example: Flux in the diffusion limit

If we compare the continuity equation (13.7) with the explicit form of the Fokker–Planck equation (13.16), we can identify the flux caused by stochastic spike arrival and external current in the diffusion limit

$$J^{\text{diff}}(u,t) = \frac{f(u) + \mu(t)}{\tau_m} p(u,t) - \frac{1}{2} \frac{\sigma^2(t)}{\tau_m} \frac{\partial}{\partial u} p(u,t). \tag{13.21}$$

We emphasize that stochastic spike arrival contributes to the mean drive $\mu(t) = RI^{\text{ext}}(t) + \tau_m \sum_k v_k(t) w_k$ as well as to the diffusive noise $\sigma^2(t) = \tau_m \sum_k v_k(t) w_k^2$.

13.3.1 Stationary solution for leaky integrate-and-fire neurons (*)

The stationary distribution $p(u)$ of the membrane potential is of particular interest, since it is experimentally accessible (Calvin and Stevens, 1968; Destexhe *et al.*, 2003; Crochet and Petersen, 2006). We now derive the stationary solution $p(u,t) \equiv p(u)$ of the Fokker–Planck equation (13.16) for a population of leaky integrate-and-fire neurons. Neurons are described by Eq. (13.1) with $f(u) = -u$, i.e., the voltage scale is shifted so that the equilibrium potential is at zero. For leaky integrate-and-fire neurons, the reset threshold is the same as the rheobase firing threshold and will be denoted by $\vartheta = \theta_{\text{reset}} = \vartheta_{\text{rh}}$.

We assume that the total input $h_0 = RI^{\text{ext}} + \tau_m \sum_k v_k w_k$ is constant. In the stationary state, the temporal derivative on the left-hand side of Eq. (13.16) vanishes. The terms on the right-hand side can be transformed so that the stationary Fokker–Planck equation reads (for $u < \vartheta$)

$$0 = -\frac{\partial}{\partial u} J(u) + A_0 \delta(u - u_r), \tag{13.22}$$

where A_0 is the population activity (or mean firing rate) in the stationary state and

$$J(u) = \frac{-u + h_0}{\tau_m} p(u) - \frac{1}{2} \frac{\sigma^2}{\tau_m} \frac{\partial}{\partial u} p(u) \tag{13.23}$$

is the total flux; see Eqs. (13.6) and (13.21). The meaning of Eq. (13.22) is that the flux is constant except at $u = u_r$ where it jumps by an amount A_0. Similarly, the boundary condition $p(\vartheta,t) = 0$ implies a second discontinuity of the flux at $u = \vartheta$.

With the results from Chapter 8 in mind, we expect that the stationary solution approaches a Gaussian distribution for $u \to -\infty$. In fact, we can check easily that for any constant c_1

$$p(u) = \frac{c_1}{\sigma} \exp\left[-\frac{(u - h_0)^2}{\sigma^2}\right] \quad \text{for } u \leq u_r \tag{13.24}$$

is a solution of Eq. (13.22) with flux $J(u) = 0$. However, for $u > u_r$ a simple Gaussian distribution cannot be a solution since it does not respect the boundary condition $p(\vartheta) = 0$.

Nevertheless, we can make an educated guess and try a modified Gaussian (Giorno *et al.*, 1992; Brunel and Hakim, 1999)

$$p(u) = \frac{c_2}{\sigma^2} \exp\left[-\frac{(u-h_0)^2}{\sigma^2}\right] \cdot \int_u^\vartheta \exp\left[\frac{(x-h_0)^2}{\sigma^2}\right] dx \quad \text{for } u_r < u \le \vartheta, \quad (13.25)$$

with some constant c_2. We have written the above expression as a product of two terms. The first factor on the right-hand side is a standard Gaussian while the second factor guarantees that $p(u) \to 0$ for $u \to \vartheta$. If we insert Eq. (13.25) in (13.22) we can check that it is indeed a solution. The constant c_2 is proportional to the flux,

$$c_2 = 2\tau_m J(u) \quad \text{for } u_r < u \le \vartheta. \quad (13.26)$$

The solution defined by Eqs. (13.24) and (13.25) must be continuous at $u = u_r$. Hence

$$c_1 = \frac{c_2}{\sigma} \int_{u_r}^\vartheta \exp\left[\frac{(x-h_0)^2}{\sigma^2}\right] dx. \quad (13.27)$$

Finally, the constant c_2 is determined by the normalization condition (13.3). We use Eqs. (13.24), (13.25), and (13.27) in (13.3) and find

$$\frac{1}{c_2} = \int_{-\infty}^{u_r} \int_{u_r}^\vartheta f(x,u) \, dx \, du + \int_{u_r}^\vartheta \int_u^\vartheta f(x,u) \, dx \, du = \int_{u_r}^\vartheta \int_{-\infty}^x f(x,u) \, du \, dx, \quad (13.28)$$

with

$$f(x,u) = \frac{1}{\sigma^2} \exp\left[-\frac{(u-h_0)^2}{\sigma^2}\right] \exp\left[\frac{(x-h_0)^2}{\sigma^2}\right]. \quad (13.29)$$

Figure 13.5b shows the resulting stationary density $p(u)$ for different noise amplitudes.

The activity A_0 is identical to the flux $J(u)$ between u_r and ϑ and therefore proportional to the constant c_2; see Eq. (13.26). If we express the integral over u in Eq. (13.28) in terms of the error function, $\text{erf}(x) = \frac{2}{\sqrt{\pi}} \int_0^x \exp(-u^2) \, du$, we obtain

$$A_0^{-1} = \tau_m \sqrt{\pi} \int_{\frac{u_r-h_0}{\sigma}}^{\frac{\vartheta-h_0}{\sigma}} \exp(x^2) \left[1 + \text{erf}(x)\right] dx, \quad (13.30)$$

which is identical to the Siegert formula (Siegert, 1951) of the single-neuron firing rate [see Eq. (8.54) or (12.26)] that we used previously in Chapters 8 and 12. An alternative formulation (see Exercises) of the remaining integral in Eq. (13.30) is also possible (Brunel and Hakim, 1999).

13.4 Networks of leaky integrate-and-fire neurons

In the previous section, the formalism of membrane potential densities was applied to a single population driven by spikes arriving at some rate v_k at the synapse of type k, where $k = 1, \ldots, K$. In a population that is coupled to itself, the spikes that drive a given neuron

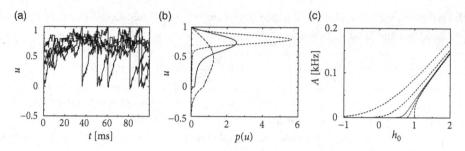

Fig. 13.5 (a) Membrane potential trajectories of five neurons ($R = 1$ and $\tau_m = 10\,\text{ms}$) driven by a constant background current $I_0 = 0.8$ and stochastic background input with $\nu_+ = \nu_- = 0.8\,\text{kHz}$ and $w_\pm = \pm 0.05$. These parameters correspond to $h_0 = 0.8$ and $\sigma = 0.2$ in the diffusive noise model. (b) Stationary membrane potential distribution in the diffusion limit for $\sigma = 0.2$ (solid line), $\sigma = 0.1$ (short-dashed line), and $\sigma = 0.5$ (long-dashed line). (Threshold $\vartheta = 1$.) (c) Mean activity of a population of integrate-and-fire neurons with diffusive noise as a function of h_0 for four different noise levels: (from top to bottom) $\sigma = 1.0, \sigma = 0.5, \sigma = 0.2$ (solid line), $\sigma = 0.1, \sigma = 0.0$.

are, at least partially, generated within the same population. For a homogeneous population with self-coupling the feedback is then proportional to the population activity $A(t)$; see Chapter 12.

We now formulate the interaction between several coupled populations using the Fokker–Planck equation for the membrane potential density (Section 13.4.1) and apply it subsequently to the special cases of a population of excitatory integrate-and-fire neurons interacting with a population of inhibitory ones (Section 13.4.2).

13.4.1 Multiple populations

We consider multiple populations $k = 1, \ldots, K$. The population with index k contains N_k neurons and its activity is denoted by A_k. We recall that $N_k A_k(t) \Delta t$ is the total number of spikes emitted by population k in a short interval Δt.

Let us suppose that population k sends its spikes to another population n. If each neuron in population n receives input from *all* neurons in k the total spike arrival rate from population k is therefore $\nu_k(t) = N_k A_k(t)$ ("full connectivity"). If each neuron in population n receives connections only from a subset of C_{nk} randomly chosen neurons of population k, then the total spike arrival rate is $\nu_k(t) = C_{nk} A_k(t)$ ("random connectivity" with a connection probability $p_{nk} = C_{nk}/N_k$ from population k to population n). We assume that all connections from k to n have the same weight w_{nk} and that spike arrival from population k can be approximated by a Poisson process with rate $\nu_k(t)$.

For each population $n = 1, \ldots, K$ we write down a Fokker–Planck equation analogous to Eq. (13.16). Neurons are leaky integrate-and-fire neurons. Within a population n, all neurons have the same parameters τ_n, R_n, u_r^n, and in particular the same firing threshold ϑ_n. For population n the Fokker–Planck equation for the evolution of membrane potential

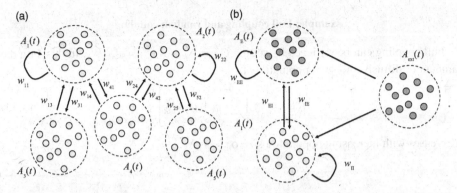

Fig. 13.6 Interacting populations. (a) Five populations interact via their population activities A_k. The parameter w_{nk} gives the synaptic weight of a connection from a presynaptic neuron in population k to a postsynaptic neuron in population n. Not all populations are coupled with each other. (b) Brunel network: an excitatory population of leaky integrate-and-fire neurons is coupled to itself and to an inhibitory population. Neurons in both populations receive also external input from a third population with population activity $A_{\text{ext}} = v^{\text{ext}}$ described as a homogeneous Poisson process.

densities is then

$$\tau_n \frac{\partial}{\partial t} p_n(u,t) = -\frac{\partial}{\partial u} \left\{ \left[-u + R_n I_n^{\text{ext}}(t) + \tau_n \sum_k C_{nk} A_k(t) w_{nk} \right] p_n(u,t) \right\}$$

$$+ \frac{1}{2} \left[\tau_n \sum_k C_{nk} A_k(t) w_{nk}^2 \right] \frac{\partial^2}{\partial u^2} p_n(u,t) \qquad (13.31)$$

$$+ \tau_n A_n(t) \, \delta(u - u_r^n) - \tau_n A_n(t) \, \delta(u - \vartheta_n) .$$

The population activity A_n is the flux through the threshold (see Eq. (13.20)), which gives in our case

$$A_n(t) = -\frac{1}{2} \left[\sum_k C_{nk} A_k(t) w_{nk}^2 \right] \left(\frac{\partial p_n(u,t)}{\partial u} \right)_{u=\vartheta_n} . \qquad (13.32)$$

Thus populations interact with each other via the variable $A_k(t)$; see Fig. 13.6.

Example: Background input

Sometimes it is useful to focus on a single population, coupled to itself, and replace the input arising from other populations by background input. For example, we may focus on population $n = 1$, which is modeled by Eq. (13.31), but use as the inputs A_k spikes generated by a homogeneous or inhomogeneous Poisson process with rate $A_k = v_k$.

Example: Full coupling and random coupling

Full coupling can be retrieved by setting $C_{nk} = N_k$ and $w_{nk} = J_{nk}/N_k$. In this case the amount of diffusive noise in population n,

$$\sigma_n^2(t) = \tau_n \left[\sum_k C_{nk} A_k(t) w_{nk}^2 \right], \tag{13.33}$$

decreases with increasing population size $\sigma_n^2 \propto 1/N_k$.

13.4.2 *Synchrony, oscillations, and irregularity*

In Chapter 12 we have already discussed the stationary state of the population activity in a population coupled to itself. With the methods discussed in Chapter 12 we were, however, unable to study the stability of the stationary state; nor were we able to make any prediction about potential time-dependent solutions.

We now give a more complete characterization of a network of leaky integrate-and-fire neurons consisting of two populations: a population of N_E excitatory neurons coupled to a population with $N_I = N_E/4$ inhibitory neurons (Brunel, 2000). The structure of the network is shown in Fig. 13.6b. Each neuron (be it excitatory or inhibitory) receives C_E connections from the excitatory population, each with weight $w_{EE} = w_{IE} = w_0$; it also receives $C_I = C_E/4$ connections from the inhibitory population ($w_{EI} = w_{II} = -g w_0$) and furthermore C_E connections from an external population (weight w_{EE}) with neurons that fire at a fixed rate v^{ext}. Each spike causes, after a delay of $\Delta = 1.5 \, \text{ms}$ a voltage jump of $w_0 = 0.1 \, \text{mV}$ and the threshold is $20 \, \text{mV}$ above resting potential. Note that each neuron receives four times as many excitatory than inhibitory inputs so that the total amount of inhibition balances excitation if inhibition is four times stronger ($g = 4$), but the relative strength g is kept as a free parameter. Also note that, in contrast to Chapter 12, the weight here has units of voltage and directly gives the amplitude of the voltage jump: $w_0 = \Delta u_E$.

The population can be in a state of asynchronous irregular activity (AI), where neurons in the population fire at different times ("asynchronous" firing) and the distribution of interspike intervals is fairly broad ("irregular" firing of individual neurons); see Fig. 13.7b. This is the state that corresponds to the considerations of stationary activity in Chapter 12. However, with a slight change of parameters, the same network can also be in a state of fast synchronous regular (SR) oscillations. It is characterized by periodic oscillations of the population activity *and* a sharply peaked interval distribution of individual neurons. The network can also be in the state of synchronous irregular firing (SI) either with fast (SI fast) or with slow (SI slow) oscillations of the population activity. The oscillatory temporal structure emerges despite the fact that the input has a constant spike arrival rate. It can be traced back to an instability of the asynchronous firing regime toward oscillatory activity.

With the mathematical approach of the Fokker–Planck equations, it is possible to determine the instabilities analytically. The mathematical approach will be presented in

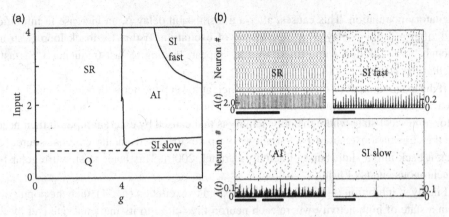

Fig. 13.7 Population of pulse-coupled leaky integrate-and-fire neurons (Brunel network). (a) Phase diagram of the Brunel network. The population activity can be in a state of asynchronous irregular (AI), synchronous regular (SR) or synchronous irregular (SI) activity. The horizontal axis indicates the relative importance of inhibition ($g = 4$ corresponds to balance between excitation and inhibition). The vertical axis is the amount of external input each neuron receives. Input $I = 1$ corresponds to a mean input just sufficient to reach the neuronal firing threshold (in the absence of recurrent input from the network). Stability of the asynchronous irregular firing state (AI) breaks down at the dashed or solid lines and can lead to synchronous regular (SR), or synchronous irregular (SI, either fast or slow) activity, or to a near-quiescent state (Q); redrawn after Brunel (2000). (b) Typical time course of the population activity $A(t)$ (bottom part of each subgraph, units in kHz) and associated spike patterns (50 randomly chosen neurons are plotted along the vertical axis in the top part of each subgraph; each dot indicates a spike) in different firing regimes. "SI fast" refers to fast and regular oscillations, but individual neurons fire irregularly with intervals at random multiples of the oscillation period. Horizontal black bar: 50 ms. Simulation of 10 000 excitatory and 2500 inhibitory neurons with connection probability $p = 0.1$. Each spike causes, after a delay of $\Delta = 1.5$ ms a voltage jump of 0.1 mV; distance from equilibrium potential to the threshold is 20 mV; absolute refractory period 2 ms; membrane time constant 20 ms. Parameters are top left: $g = 3$, input = 2 (SR); top right: $g = 6$, input = 4 (SI fast); bottom left: $g = 5$, input = 2 (AI) bottom right $g = 4.5$, input = 0.9 (SI slow). Adapted from Brunel (2000) with kind permission from Springer Science and Business Media.

Section 13.5.2, but Fig. 13.7a already shows the result. Stability of a stationary state of asynchronous firing is most easily achieved in the regime where inhibition dominates excitation. Since each neuron receives four times as many excitatory as inhibitory inputs, inhibition must be at least four times as strong ($g > 4$) as excitation. In order to get nonzero activity despite the strong inhibition, the external input alone must be sufficient to make the neurons fire. "Input = 1" corresponds to an average external input just sufficient to reach the firing threshold, without additional input from the network.

Consider now the regime of strong inhibition ($g > 4$) and strong input, say spikes from the external source arrive at a rate leading to a mean input of amplitude 4. To understand how the network can run into an instability, let us consider the following intuitive argument. Suppose a momentary fluctuation leads to an increase in the total amount of activity in the excitatory population. This causes, after a transmission delay Δ, an increase in inhibition and, after a further delay Δ, a suppression of excitation. If this feedback loop is strong enough, an oscillation with period 4Δ may appear, leading to fast-frequency ("SI fast") oscillations (Brunel, 2000).

If the external input is, on its own, not sufficient to keep the network going ("input < 1"), then a similar small fluctuation may eventually turn the network from a self-activated state into a quiescent state where the only activity is that caused by external input. It then needs another fluctuation (caused by variations of spike arrivals from the external source) to kick it back into a short burst of activity (Brunel, 2000). This leads to slow irregular but synchronous bursts of firing ("SI slow").

Finally, if inhibition is globally weak compared to excitation ($g < 4$), then the population is in a state of high activity where each neuron fires close to its maximal rate (set by the inverse of an absolute refractory period). This high-activity state is unstable compared to fast but regular oscillations ("SR"). Typically, the population can split up into two or more subgroups, the number of which depends on the transmission delay (Brunel, 2000; Gerstner and van Hemmen, 1993).

Example: Analysis of the Brunel network

All neurons have the same parameters, so that we can assume that they all fire at the same time-dependent firing rate $v(t) = A(t)$. We assume that the network is large $N \gg C_E$, so that it is unlikely that neurons share a large fraction of presynaptic neurons; therefore inputs can be considered as uncorrelated, except for the trivial correlations induced by their common modulation of the firing rate $A(t)$.

The mean input at time t to a neuron in either the excitatory or the inhibitory population is (in voltage units)

$$\mu(t) = \tau_m w_0 C_E [1 - g/4] A(t - \Delta) + \tau_m w_0 C_E v^{\text{ext}}, \qquad (13.34)$$

and the input also generates diffusive noise (in voltage units) of strength

$$\sigma^2(t) = \tau_m w_0^2 C_E [(1 + g^2/4) A(t - \Delta) + v_{\text{ext}}]. \qquad (13.35)$$

The mean and σ^2 are inserted in the Fokker–Planck equation (see Eq. 13.31)

$$\tau_m \frac{\partial}{\partial t} p(u,t) = -\frac{\partial}{\partial u} \{[-u + \mu(t)]\, p(u,t)\}$$

$$+ \frac{1}{2} \sigma^2(t) \frac{\partial^2}{\partial u^2} p(u,t) \qquad (13.36)$$

$$+ \tau_m A(t)\, \delta(u - u_r) - \tau_m A(t)\, \delta(u - \vartheta) + \mathcal{O}(w_k^3).$$

The main difference to the stationary solution considered in Section 13.3.1 and Chapter 12 is that mean input and noise amplitude are kept time-dependent.

We first solve to find the stationary solution of the Fokker–Planck equation, denoted as $p_0(u)$ and activity A_0. This step is completely analogous to the calculation in Section 13.3.1.

In order to analyze the stability of the stationary solution, we search for solutions of the form $A(t) = A_0 + A_1 e^{\lambda t} \cos(\omega t)$ (for details, see Section 13.5.2). Parameter combinations that lead to a value $\lambda > 0$ indicate an instability of the stationary state of asynchronous firing for a network with this set of parameters.

Figure 13.7a indicates that there is a broad regime of *stability* of the asynchronous irregular firing state (AI). This holds even if the network is completely deterministic (Brunel, 2000) and driven by a constant input I_0 (i.e., we set $v^{\text{ext}} = 0$ in the noise term, Eq. (13.35), and replace spike arrivals by a constant current $RI_0^{\text{ext}} = w_0 C_E v^{\text{ext}}$ in Eq. (13.34).

Stability of the stationary state of asynchronous irregular activity is most easily achieved if the network is in the regime where inhibition slightly dominates excitation and external input is sufficient to drive neurons to the threshold. This is called the "inhibition dominating" regime. The range of parameters where asynchronous firing is stable can, however, be increased into the range of dominant excitation, if delays are not fixed at $D = 1.5$ ms, but drawn from the range $0 < D < 3$ ms. Finite size effects can also be taken into account (Brunel, 2000).

13.5 Networks of nonlinear integrate-and-fire neurons

In Chapter 5 it was shown that nonlinear integrate-and-fire neurons such as the exponential integrate-and-fire model provide an excellent approximation to the dynamics of single neurons, much better than the standard leaky integrate-and-fire model. This section indicates how the Fokker–Planck approach can be used to analyze networks of such nonlinear integrate-and-fire models.

We determine, for arbitrary nonlinear integrate-and-fire models driven by a diffusive input with constant mean $\mu = RI_0$ and noise σ^2, the distribution of membrane potentials $p_0(u)$ as well as the linear response of the population activity

$$A(t) = A_0 + A_1(t) = A_0 + \int_0^\infty G(s) I_1(t - s) \, ds \qquad (13.37)$$

to a drive $\mu(t) = R[I_0 + I_1(t)]$ (Richardson, 2007). As explained in Section 13.4, knowledge of p_0 is sufficient to predict, for coupled populations of integrate-and-fire neurons, the activity A_0 in the stationary state of asynchronous firing. Moreover, we shall see that the filter $G(s)$ contains all the information needed to analyze the stability of the stationary state of asynchronous firing. In this section we focus on one-dimensional nonlinear integrate-and-fire models, and add adaptation later on, in Section 13.6.

13.5.1 Steady-state population activity

We consider a population of nonlinear integrate-and-fire models in the diffusion limit. We start with the continuity equation (13.7)

$$\frac{\partial}{\partial t} p(u,t) = -\frac{\partial}{\partial u} J(u,t) + A(t)\,\delta(u-u_r) - A(t)\,\delta(u-\theta_{\text{reset}}). \tag{13.38}$$

In the stationary state, the membrane potential density does not depend on time, $p(u,t) = p_0(u)$, so that the left-hand side of (13.38) vanishes. Eq. (13.38) therefore simplifies to

$$\frac{\partial}{\partial u} J(u,t) = A(t)\,\delta(u-u_r) - A(t)\,\delta(u-\theta_{\text{reset}}). \tag{13.39}$$

Therefore the flux takes a constant value, except at two values: at the numerical threshold θ_{reset}, at which the membrane potential is reset; and at the potential u_r, to which the reset occurs. The flux vanishes for $u > \theta_{\text{reset}}$ and for $u < u_r$. For $u_r < u < \theta_{\text{reset}}$ the constant value $J(u,t) = c > 0$ still needs to be determined.

A neuron in the population under consideration is driven by the action potentials emitted by presynaptic neurons from the same or other populations. For stochastic spike arrivals at rate v_k, where each spike causes a jump of the voltage by an amount w_k, the contributions to the flux have been determined in Eqs. (13.10) and (13.11). In the diffusion limit the flux according to Eq. (13.21) is

$$J(u,t) = \frac{1}{\tau_m}\left[f(u) + \mu(t) - \frac{1}{2}\sigma^2(t)\frac{\partial}{\partial u} \right] p(u,t). \tag{13.40}$$

In the stationary state, we have $p(u,t) = p_0(u)$ and $J(u,t) = c$ for $u_r < u < \theta_{\text{reset}}$. (For $u < u_r$ we have $J(u,t) = 0$.) Hence Eq. (13.40) simplifies to a first-order differential equation

$$\frac{dp_0(u)}{du} = \frac{2\tau_m}{\sigma^2}\left[\frac{f(u)+\mu}{\tau_m} p_0(u) - c \right]. \tag{13.41}$$

The differential equation (13.41) can be integrated numerically starting at the upper bound $u = \theta_{\text{reset}}$ with initial condition $p_0(\theta_{\text{reset}}) = 0$ and $dp_0/du|_{\theta_{\text{reset}}} = -1 = -2c\tau_m/\sigma^2$. When the integration passes $u = u_r$ the constant switches from c to zero. The integration is stopped at a lower bound u_{low} when p_0 has approached zero. The exact value of the lower bound is of little importance.

At the end of the integration, the surface under the voltage distribution $\int_{u_{\text{low}}}^{\theta_{\text{reset}}} p_0(u)\,du = 1$, which determines the constant c and therefore the firing rate A_0 in the stationary state.

Example: Exponential integrate-and-fire model

The exponential integrate-and-fire model (Fourcaud-Trocme *et al.*, 2003) as defined in Eq. (5.6) is characterized by the differential equation

$$\tau\frac{d}{dt}u = -(u-u_{\text{rest}}) + \Delta_T \exp\left(\frac{u-\vartheta_{\text{rh}}}{\Delta_T}\right) + \mu, \tag{13.42}$$

where μ is the total drive in units of the membrane potential. The result of the numerical integration of Eqs. (13.39) and (13.41) depends critically on the relative value of the reset potential, the driving potential μ with respect to the reset u_r, and the rheobase firing

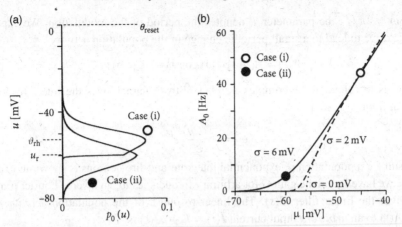

Fig. 13.8 Exponential integrate-and-fire neurons. (a) The stationary membrane potential density $p_0(u)$ in the regime of low noise and superthreshold drive (case (i): $\sigma = 2$ mV, $\mu = -45$ mV $>$ $\vartheta_{rh} = -53$ mV $> u_r = -60$ mV) and in the regime of high noise and subthreshold drive (case (ii): $\sigma = 6$ mV, $\mu = u_r = -60$ mV $< \vartheta_{rh} = -53$ mV). Note that the exact value of the numerical firing threshold ($\theta_{reset} = 0$ mV) is irrelevant because the membrane $p_0(u)$ is, for all potentials above -30 mV, very small. (b) The stationary population firing rate $A_0 = g_\sigma(I_0)$ as a function of the total drive $\mu = RI_0$ of the population, in the regimes of high noise (solid line, $\sigma = 6$ mV), low noise (dashed line, $\sigma = 2$ mV), and in the absence of noise (dotted, $\sigma = 0$). The two cases depicted in (a) are marked by open and solid symbols. Adapted from Richardson (2007).

threshold ϑ_{rh}, as well as on the level σ of diffusive noise. Two representative scenarios are shown in Fig. 13.8a. Case (i) has very little noise ($\sigma = 2$ mV) and the total drive ($\mu = -45$ mV) is above the rheobase firing threshold ($\vartheta_{rh} = -53$ mV). In this case, the membrane potential density a few millivolts below the reset potential ($u_r = -60$ mV) is negligible. Because of the strong drive, the model neuron model is in the superthreshold regime (see Section 8.3) and fires regularly with a rate of about 44 Hz.

Case (ii) is different, because it has a larger amount of noise ($\sigma = 6$ mV) and a negligible drive of $\mu = u_r = -60$ mV. Therefore, the distribution of membrane potentials is broad, with a maximum at u_r, and firing is noise driven and occurs at a low rate of 5.6 Hz.

For both noise levels, the frequency–current curve $A_0 = \nu = g_\sigma(I_0)$ is shown in Fig. 13.8b, as a function of the total drive $\mu = RI$. We emphasize that for very strong superthreshold drive, the population firing rate A_0 of noisy neurons is lower than that of noise-free neurons.

13.5.2 Response to modulated input (*)

So far we have restricted the discussion to a constant input I_0. We now add a small periodic perturbation

$$I(t) = I_0 + \varepsilon \cos(\omega t), \tag{13.43}$$

where $\omega = 2\pi/T$; the parameter T denotes the period of the modulation. We expect the periodic drive to lead to a small periodic change in the population activity

$$A(t) = A_0 + A_1(\omega)\cos(\omega t + \phi_A(\omega)). \tag{13.44}$$

Our aim is to calculate the complex number $\hat{G}$ that characterizes the linear response or "gain" at frequency ω

$$\hat{G}(\omega) = \frac{A_1(\omega)}{\varepsilon}\, e^{i\phi_A(\omega)}. \tag{13.45}$$

The result for a population of exponential integrate-and-fire neurons is shown in Fig. 13.9.

Once we have found the gain $\hat{G}$ for arbitrary frequencies ω, an inverse Fourier transform of $\hat{G}$ gives the linear filter $G(s)$. The linear response of the population activity $A(t) = A_0 + \Delta A(t)$ to an *arbitrary* input current $I(t) = I_0 + \Delta I(t)$ is

$$\Delta A(t) = \int_0^\infty G(s)\,\Delta I(t-s)\,ds. \tag{13.46}$$

A linear response is a valid description if the change is small:

$$\Delta A(t) \ll A(t). \tag{13.47}$$

In our case of periodic stimulation, the amplitude of the input current is scaled by ε. We are free to choose ε small enough to fulfill condition (13.47).

The small periodic drive at frequency ω leads to a small periodic change in the density of membrane potentials

$$p(u,t) = p_0(u) + p_1(u)\cos(\omega t + \phi_p(u)), \tag{13.48}$$

which has a phase lead ($\phi_p > 0$) or lag ($\phi_p < 0$) with respect to the periodic drive. We assume that the modulation amplitude in the input current ε is small so that $p_1(u) \ll p_0(u)$ for most values of u. We say that the change is at most of "order ε."

Similarly to the membrane potential density, the flux $J(u,t)$ will also exhibit a small perturbation of order ε. For the exponential integrate-and-fire model of Eq. (13.42) with $u_{\text{rest}} = 0$ the flux is (see Eq. (13.40))

$$J(u,t) = \left[\frac{-u + RI(t)}{\tau_m} + \frac{\Delta_T}{\tau_m}\exp\left(\frac{u - \vartheta_{\text{rh}}}{\Delta_T}\right) - \frac{\sigma^2(t)}{2\tau_m}\frac{\partial}{\partial u}\right]p(u,t) = Q(u,t)\,p(u,t),$$

$$\tag{13.49}$$

where we have introduced on the right-hand side a linear operator Q that comprises all the terms inside the square brackets. The stationary state that we analyzed in the previous subsection under the assumption of constant input $I(t) = I_0$ has a flux $J_0(u) = Q_0(u)\,p_0(u)$. In the presence of the periodic perturbation, the flux is

$$J(u,t) = J_0(u) + J_1(u)\cos(\omega t + \phi_J(u)) \tag{13.50}$$

with

$$J_1(u)\cos(\omega t + \phi_J(u)) = Q_0(u)\,p_1(u)\cos(\omega t + \phi_p(u)) + Q_1(u,t)\,p_0(u) + 0_{\text{order}}(\varepsilon^2),$$

$$\tag{13.51}$$

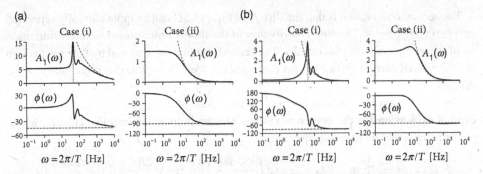

Fig. 13.9 Frequency response of a population of exponential integrate-and-fire neurons, with parameter settings as in Fig. 13.8. Solid line: theoretical Dashed line: analytical prediction for high frequencies. (a) Case (i): The population response $A_1(\omega)$ (top) to a periodic stimulation of frequency $\omega = 2\pi/T$ in the situation of low noise ($\sigma = 2$ mV) shows a resonance at the population firing rate $A_0 = 44$ Hz. The phase shift $\phi(\omega)$ for low noise (bottom) approaches $-45°$ for high frequencies. Case (ii): The population response $A_1(\omega)$ for high noise ($\sigma = 6$ mV, population firing rate $A_0 = 5.6$ Hz) has no resonance (top) and the phase shift $\phi(\omega)$ approaches $-90°$ (bottom). The combination of amplitude and phase $A_1(\omega)\exp(i\phi(\omega))$ defines the complex frequency-dependent gain factor $\hat{G}(\omega)$ in response to modulation of the input current. (b) Gain factor G_σ for a modulation of the noise strength $\sigma^2(t)$ while the input current is constant. Case (i): low noise. Case (ii): high noise. (a) and (b) adapted from Richardson (2007). © 2007 The American Physical Society.

where $Q_1(u,t) = \varepsilon R \cos(\omega t)/\tau_m$ is the change of the operator Q to order ε. Note that the flux through the threshold θ_{reset} gives the periodic modulation of the population activity.

We insert our variables A, p, J into the differential equation (13.38) and find that the stationary terms with subscript zero cancel each other, as should be the case, and only the terms with subscript "1" survive. To simplify the notation, it is convenient to switch from real to complex numbers and include the phase in the definition of $A_1, p_1(u), J_1(u)$, for example, $\hat{A}_1 = A_1 \exp(i\phi_A)$; the hat indicates the complex number. If we take the Fourier transform over time, Eq. (13.38) becomes

$$-\frac{\partial}{\partial u}\hat{J}_1(u) = i\omega \hat{p}_1(u) + \hat{A}_1\left[\delta(u - \theta_{\text{reset}}) - \delta(u - u_r)\right]. \qquad (13.52)$$

Before we proceed further, let us have a closer look at Eqs. (13.51) and (13.52). We highlight three aspects (Richardson, 2007). The first observation is that we have, quite arbitrarily, normalized the membrane potential density to an integral of unity. We could have chosen, with equal rights, a normalization to the total number N of neurons in the population. Then the flux on the left-hand side of Eq. (13.52) would be enlarged by a factor of N, but so would the membrane potential density and the population activity, which appear on the right-hand side. We could also multiply both sides of the equation by any other (complex) number. As a consequence, we can, for example, try to solve Eq. (13.52) for a population activity modulation $\hat{A}_1 = 1$ and take care of the correct normalization only later.

The second observation is that the flux J_1 in Eq. (13.51) can be quite naturally separated into two components. The first contribution to the flux is proportional to the perturbation p_1 of the membrane potential density. The second component is caused by the direct action of the external current $Q_1(u,t) = \varepsilon R \cos(\omega t)/\tau_m$. We will exploit this separability of the flux later.

The third observation is that, for the case of exponential integrate-and-fire neurons, the explicit expression for the operators Q_0 and Q_1 can be inserted into Eq. (13.51), which yields a first-order differential equation

$$\frac{\partial}{\partial u}\hat{p}_1(u) = \frac{2}{\sigma^2}\left[-u + RI_0 + \Delta_T \exp\left(\frac{u - \vartheta_{\text{rh}}}{\Delta_T}\right)\right]\hat{p}_1(u) + \frac{2R\varepsilon}{\sigma^2}p_0(u) - \frac{2\tau_m}{\sigma^2}\hat{f}_1(u).$$

(13.53)

We therefore have two first-order differential equations (13.52) and (13.53) which are coupled to each other. In order to solve the two equations, we now exploit our second observation and split the flux into two components. We drop the hats on J_1, p_1, A_1 to lighten the notation.

(i) A "free" component $J_1^{\text{free}}(u)$ describes the flux that would occur in the absence of external drive ($\varepsilon = 0$), but in the presence of a periodically modulated population activity A_1. Intuitively, the distribution of the membrane potential density $p_1^{\text{free}}(u)$ and the flux J_1^{free} must exhibit some periodic "breathing pattern" to enable the periodic modulation of the flux through the threshold of strength $\hat{A}_1$. We find the "free" component by integrating Eq. (13.53) with $\varepsilon = 0$ in parallel with Eq. (13.52) with parameter $A_1 = 1$ (i.e., the periodic flow through threshold is of unit strength). The integration starts at the initial condition $p_1(\theta_{\text{reset}}) = 0$ and $J_1^{\text{free}}(\theta_{\text{reset}}) = A_1 = 1$ and continues toward decreasing voltage values. Integration stops at a lower bound u_{low} which we place at an arbitrarily large negative value.

(ii) A "driven" component J_1^ε accounts for the fact that the periodic modulation is in fact caused by the input. We impose for the "driven" component that the modulation of the flux through threshold vanishes: $A_1 = 0$. We can therefore find the "driven" component by integrating Eq. (13.53) with a finite $\varepsilon > 0$ in parallel with Eq. (13.52) with parameter $A_1 = 0$ starting at the initial condition $p_1(\theta_{\text{reset}}) = 0$ and $J_1^\varepsilon(\theta_{\text{reset}}) = A_1 = 0$ and integrating toward decreasing voltage values. As before, integration stops at a lower bound u_{low} which we can shift to arbitrarily large negative values.

Finally we add the two solutions together: any combination of parameters a_1, a_2 for the total flux $a_1 J_1^{\text{free}}(u) + a_2 J_1^\varepsilon(u)$ and the total density $a_1 p_1^{\text{free}}(u) + a_2 p_1^\varepsilon(u)$ will solve the pair of differential equations (13.53) and (13.52). Which one is the right combination?

The total flux must vanish at large negative values. Therefore we require a boundary condition

$$0 = J(u_{\text{low}}) = a_1 J_1^{\text{free}}(u_{\text{low}}) + a_2 J_1^\varepsilon(u_{\text{low}}).$$

(13.54)

We recall that $J_1^\varepsilon(u)$ is proportional to the drive ε. Furthermore, the initial condition was chosen such that $J_1^{\text{free}}(\theta_{\text{reset}})$ yields a population response $A_1 = 1$ so that, in the combined solution, the factor a_1 is the population response!

We are interested in the "gain factor" at stimulation frequency ω. We started this section by applying a periodic stimulus of strength ε and observing, at the same periodic frequency, a modulation of strength A_1. The gain factor is defined as $\hat{G}(\omega) = A_1/\varepsilon$. With the above arguments the gain factor is (Richardson, 2007)

$$\hat{G}(\omega) = \frac{a_1}{\varepsilon} = -\frac{a_2}{\varepsilon} \frac{J_1^{\varepsilon}(u_{\text{low}})}{J_1^{\text{free}}(u_{\text{low}})}. \tag{13.55}$$

The gain factor $\hat{G}(\omega)$ has an amplitude $|\hat{G}(\omega)|$ and a phase ϕ_G. Amplitude and phase of the gain factor of a population of exponential integrate-and-fire neurons are plotted in Fig. 13.9a.

The same numerical integration scheme that starts at the numerical threshold θ_{reset} and integrates downward with appropriate initial conditions can also be applied to other, linear as well as nonlinear, neuron models. Furthermore, with the same scheme it is also possible to calculate the gain factor G_σ in response to a modulation of the variance $\sigma^2(t)$ (Fig. 13.9b), or the response G_ϑ to periodic modulation of model parameters such as the rheobase threshold ϑ_{rh} (Richardson, 2007). For earlier results on G_σ see also Brunel and Hakim (1999), Lindner and Schimansky-Geier (2001) and Silberberg et al. (2004).

13.6 Neuronal adaptation and synaptic conductance

In the previous section we analyzed a population of exponential integrate-and-fire neurons driven by diffusive noise with mean $\mu(t)$ and strength $\sigma(t)$. At first glance, the results might seem of limited relevance and several concerns may be raised.

(i) What happens if we replace the one-dimensional exponential integrate-and-fire model by a neuron model with adaptation?

(ii) What happens if neurons are embedded into a network with coupling within and between several populations?

(iii) What happens if neurons don't receive synaptic current pulses that lead to a jump of the membrane potential but rather, more realistically, conductance-based input?

(iv) What happens if the input noise is not "white" but colored?

All of these questions can be answered and will be answered in this section. In fact, all questions relate to the same, bigger picture: suppose we would like to simulate a large network consisting of K populations. In each population, neurons are described by a multi-dimensional integrate-and-fire model, similar to the adaptive integrate-and-fire models of Chapter 6.

The set of equations (6.1) and (6.2) that controls the dynamics of a single neuron i is repeated here for convenience

$$\tau_m \frac{du_i}{dt} = f(u_i) - R \sum_k w_{k,i} + RI_i(t), \tag{13.56}$$

$$\tau_k \frac{dw_{k,i}}{dt} = a_k(u - u_{\text{rest}}) - w_{k,i} + b_k \tau_k \sum_{t^f} \delta(t - t_i^f), \tag{13.57}$$

where $f(u) = -(u - u_{\text{rest}}) + \Delta_T \exp[(u - \vartheta_{\text{rh}})/\Delta_T]$ is the nonlinear spike generation mechanism of the exponential integrate-and-fire model. The voltage equation (13.56) is complemented by a set of adaptation variables $w_{k,i}$ which are coupled to the voltage and the spike firing via Eq. (13.57). The first of the above questions concerns the treatment of these slow adaptation variables in the Fokker–Planck framework.

In a network with a more realistic synapse model, the input current I_i of neuron i is generated as a conductance change, caused by the spike firings of other neurons j

$$I_i(t) = \sum_j \sum_f g_{ij}(t - t_j^f)(u_i - E_{ij}^{\text{syn}}), \tag{13.58}$$

where $g_{ij}(s)$ for $s > 0$ describes the time course of the conductance change and E_{ij}^{syn} is the reversal potential of the synapse from j to i. Question (ii) concerns the fact that the spike firings are generated by the network dynamics, rather than by a Poisson process. Questions (iii) and (iv) focus on the aspects of conductance (rather than current) input and temporal extension of the conductance pulses.

Let us now discuss each of the four points in turn.

13.6.1 Adaptation currents

To keep the treatment simple, we consider the adaptive exponential integrate-and-fire model (AdEx) with a single adaptation current (see Eq. (6.3)). We drop the neuron index i, and consider, just as in the previous sections, that the stochastic spike arrival can be modeled by a mean $\mu(t) = R\langle I(t)\rangle$ plus a white-noise term ξ

$$\tau_m \frac{du}{dt} = -(u - u_{\text{rest}}) + \Delta_T \exp\left(\frac{u - \vartheta_{\text{rh}}}{\Delta_T}\right) - Rw + \mu(t) + \xi(t), \tag{13.59}$$

$$\tau_w \frac{dw}{dt} = a(u - u_{\text{rest}}) - w + b\tau_w \sum_{t^f} \delta(t - t^f). \tag{13.60}$$

The stochastic input drives the neuron into a regime where the voltage fluctuates and the neuron occasionally emits a spike. Let us now assume that the input is stationary, i.e., the mean and variance of the input are constant. Suppose furthermore that the time constant τ_w of the adaptation variable w is larger than the membrane time constant and that the increase of w during spike firing is small: $b \ll 1$. In this case, the fluctuations of the adaptation variable w around its mean value $\langle w \rangle$ are small. Therefore, for the solution of the membrane potential density equations $p_0(u)$ the adaptation variable can be approximated by a constant $w_0 = \langle w \rangle$ (Richardson *et al.*, 2003; Gigante *et al.*, 2007). This separation-of-time-scales approach can also be extended to calculate the steady-state rate and time-dependent response for neurons with biophysically detailed voltage-gated currents (Richardson, 2009).

13.6.2 Embedding in a network

Embedding the model neurons into a network consisting of several populations proceeds along the same line of argument as in Section 13.4 or Chapter 12.

The mean input $\mu(t)$ to neuron i arriving at time t from population k is proportional to its activity $A_k(t)$. Similarly, the contribution of population k to the variance σ^2 of the input to neuron i is also proportional to $A_k(t)$; see Eq. (13.31). The stationary states and their stability in a network of adaptive model neurons can therefore be analyzed as follows.

(i) Determine the stationary state A_0 self-consistently. To do so, we use the gain function $g_\sigma(I_0)$ for our neuron model of choice, where the mean current $I_0 = \mu/R$ and the noise level σ depend on the activity A_0. The gain function $g_\sigma(I_0)$ of adaptive nonlinear integrate-and-fire neurons can be found using the methods discussed above.

(ii) Determine the response to periodic modulation of input current and input variance, $\hat{G}_\mu(\omega)$ and $\hat{G}_\sigma(\omega)$, respectively, using the methods discussed above.

(iii) Use the inverse Fourier transform to find the linear response filters $G_\mu(s)$ and $G_\sigma(s)$ that describes the population activity with respect to small perturbations of the input current $\Delta I(t)$ and to small perturbations in the noise amplitude $\sigma(t)$

$$A(t) = A_0 + \int_0^\infty G_\mu(s)\,\Delta I(t-s)\,ds + \int_0^\infty G_\sigma(s)\,\Delta\sigma(t-s)\,ds. \qquad (13.61)$$

(iv) Exploit the fact that the current $I(t)$ and its fluctuations $\sigma(t)$ in a network with self-coupling, Eq. (13.31), are proportional to the current activity $A(t)$. If we set $\Delta A(t) = A(t) - A_0(t)$ we therefore have for the case of a single population feeding its activity back to itself

$$\Delta A(t) = \int_0^\infty [J_\mu\,G_\mu(s) + J_\sigma\,G_\sigma(s)]\,\Delta A(t-s)\,ds, \qquad (13.62)$$

where the constants J_μ and J_σ depend on the coupling parameters.

(v) Search for solutions $\Delta A(t) = \varepsilon\exp[\lambda(\omega)t]\cos(\omega t)$. The stationary state of asynchronous firing with activity A_0 is unstable if there exists a frequency for which $\lambda(\omega) > 0$.

The arguments in steps (i) to (v) do not rely on the assumption of current-based synapses. In fact, as we shall see now, conductance-based synapses can be, in the stationary state, well approximated by an equivalent current-based scheme.

13.6.3 Conductance input vs. current input

Throughout this chapter we assumed that spike firing by a presynaptic neuron j at time t_j^f generates in the postsynaptic neuron i an excitatory or inhibitory postsynaptic *current* pulse $w_{ij}\,\delta(t - t_j^f)$. However, synaptic input is more accurately described as a change in conductance $g(t - t_j^f)$, rather than as current injection (Destexhe *et al.*, 2003). As mentioned in Eq. (13.58), a time-dependent synaptic conductance leads to a total synaptic current into neuron i

$$I_i(t) = \sum_j \sum_f w_{ij} g_{ij}(t - t_j^f)\,(u_i(t) - E_{\text{syn}}), \qquad (13.63)$$

which depends on the momentary difference between the reversal potential E_{syn} and the membrane potential $u_i(t)$ of the postsynaptic neuron. A spike fired by a presynaptic neuron

j at time t_j^f can therefore have a bigger or smaller effect, depending on the state of the postsynaptic neuron; see Chapter 3.

Nevertheless we will now show that, in the state of stationary asynchronous activity, conductance-based input can be approximated by an effective current input (Lansky and Lanska, 1987; Richardson, 2004; Richardson and Gerstner, 2005; Wolff and Lindner, 2011). The main effect of conductance-based input is that the membrane time constant of the stochastically driven neuron is shorter than the "raw" passive membrane time constant (Bernander *et al.*, 1991; Destexhe *et al.*, 2003).

To keep the arguments transparent, we consider N_E excitatory and N_I inhibitory leaky integrate-and-fire neurons in the subthreshold regime

$$C\frac{du}{dt} = -g_L(u - E_L) - g_E(t)(u - E_E) - g_I(t)(u - E_I), \tag{13.64}$$

where C is the membrane capacity, g_L the leak conductance and E_L, E_E, E_I are the reversal potentials for leak, excitation, and inhibition, respectively. We assume that input spikes at excitatory synapses lead to an increased conductance

$$g_E(t) = \Delta g_E \sum_j \sum_f \exp[-(t - t_j^f)/\tau_E]\Theta(t - t_j^f) \tag{13.65}$$

with amplitude Δg_E and decay time constant τ_E. The Heaviside step function Θ assures causality in time. The sum over j runs over all excitatory synapses. Input spikes at inhibitory synapses have a similar effect, but with jump amplitude Δg_I and decay time constant τ_I. We assume that excitatory and inhibitory input spikes arrive with a total rate ν_E and ν_I, respectively. For example, in a population of excitatory and inhibitory neurons the total excitatory rate to neuron i would be the number of excitatory presynaptic partners C_E of neuron i times the typical firing rate of a single excitatory neuron.

Using the methods from Chapter 8 we can calculate the mean excitatory conductance

$$g_{E,0} = \Delta g_E \, \nu_E \, \tau_E, \tag{13.66}$$

where ν_E is the total spike arrival rate at excitatory synapses, and analogously for the mean inhibitory conductance. The variance of the conductance is

$$\sigma_E^2 = 0.5(\Delta g_E)^2 \, \nu_E \, \tau_E. \tag{13.67}$$

The mathematical analysis of conductance input proceeds in two steps. First, we write the conductance as the mean $g_{E,0}$ plus a fluctuating component $g_{E,f}(t) = g_E(t) - g_{E,0}$. This turns Eq. (13.64) into a new equation

$$C\frac{du}{dt} = -g_0(u - \mu) - g_{E,f}(t)(u - E_E) - g_{I,f}(t), (u - E_I), \tag{13.68}$$

with a total conductance $g_0 = g_L + g_{E,0} + g_{I,0}$ and an input-dependent equilibrium potential

$$\mu = \frac{g_L E_L + g_{E,0} E_E + g_{I,0} E_I}{g_0}. \tag{13.69}$$

We emphasize that Eq. (13.68) looks just like the original equation (13.64). The major differences are, however, that the dynamics in Eq. (13.64) is characterized by a raw membrane time constant C/g_L whereas Eq. (13.68) is controlled by an *effective* membrane time constant

$$\tau_{\text{eff}} = \frac{C}{g_0} = \frac{C}{g_L + g_{E,0} + g_{I,0}}, \tag{13.70}$$

and a mean depolarization μ which acts as an effective equilibrium potential (Johannesma, 1968).

In the second step we compare the momentary voltage $u(t)$ with the effective equilibrium potential μ. The fluctuating part of the conductance in Eq. (13.68) can therefore be written as

$$g_{E,f}(t)(u - E_E) = g_{E,f}(t)(\mu - E_E) + g_{E,f}(t)(u - \mu), \tag{13.71}$$

and similarly for the inhibitory conductance. The second term on the right-hand side of Eq. (13.71) is small compared to the first term and needs to be dropped to arrive at a consistent diffusion approximation (Richardson and Gerstner, 2005). The first term on the right-hand side of Eq. (13.71) does not depend on the membrane potential and can therefore be interpreted as the summed effects of postsynaptic *current* pulses. Thus, in the stationary state, a conductance-based synapse model is well approximated by a current-based model of synaptic input. However, we need to use the *effective* membrane time constant τ_{eff} introduced above in Eq. (13.70) in the voltage equation.

Example: Response to conductance-modulating input

Suppose we have a population of uncoupled exponential integrate-and-fire neurons. Using the methods discussed above in Section 13.5, we can calculate the linear response $G(s)$ of the population to a short conductance pulse $g_E(t)$ at an excitatory synapse (Fig. 13.10). The response to some arbitrary time-dependent conductance input can then be predicted by convolving the conductance change with the filter response. The Fourier transform of the filter predicts the response to sinusoidal conductance modulation with period T (Fig. 13.10).

13.6.4 Colored noise (*)

In the previous subsection, we replaced synaptic conductance pulses by current input. If the time constants τ_E and τ_I of excitatory and inhibitory synapses are sufficiently short, we may approximate stochastic spike arrivals by white noise. Some synapse types, such as the NMDA component of excitatory synapses, are, however, rather slow (see Chapter 3). As a result of this, a spike that has arrived at an NMDA synapse at time t_0 generates a fluctuation of the input current that persists for tens of milliseconds. Thus the fluctuations in the input exhibit temporal correlations, a situation that is termed colored noise, as opposed to white noise; see Chapter 8. Colored noise represents the temporal smoothing caused by slow synapses in a compact form.

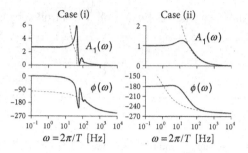

Fig. 13.10 Conductance input. Frequency response of the population of exponential integrate-and-fire neurons as in Fig. 13.9, but to conductance modulation. For high frequencies, the phase slowly approaches a lag of 270° which can be interpreted as a phase advance of 90°. Solid line: numerical solution. Dashed line: analytical high-frequency response; cases (i) and (ii) correspond to low noise and high noise, respectively. Adapted from Richardson (2007). © (2007) The American Physical Society.

There are two different approaches to colored noise in the membrane potential density equations.

The first approach is to approximate colored noise by white noise and replace the temporal smoothing by a broad distribution of delays. To keep the treatment transparent, let us assume a current-based description of synaptic input. The mean input to a neuron i in population n arising from other populations k is

$$I_i(t) = \sum_k C_{nk} w_{nk} \int_0^\infty \alpha_{nk}(s) A_k(t-s)\, ds, \tag{13.72}$$

where C_{nk} is the number of presynaptic partner neurons in population k, w_{nk} is the typical weight of a connection from k to a neuron in population n and $\alpha_{nk}(s)$ is the time course of a synaptic current pulse caused by a spike fired in population k at $s = 0$. Suppose C_{nk} is a large number, say $C_{nk} = 1000$, but the population k itself is at least 10 times larger (e.g., $N_k = 10\,000$) so that the connectivity $C_{nk}/N_k \ll 1$. We now replace the broad current pulses $\alpha(s)$ by short pulses $q\,\delta(s - \Delta)$ where δ denotes the Dirac δ-function and $q = \int_0^\infty \alpha(s)\, ds$ and $\Delta > 0$ is a transmission delay. For each of the C_{nk} connections we randomly draw the delay Δ from a distribution $p(\Delta) = \alpha(\Delta)/q$. Because of the low connectivity, we may assume that the firing of different neurons is uncorrelated. The mean input current $I_i(t)$ to neuron i is then given again by Eq. (13.72), with fluctuations around the mean that are approximately white, because each spike arrival causes only a momentary current pulse. The broad distribution of delays stabilizes the stationary state of asynchronous firing (Brunel, 2000).

The second approach consists in an explicit model of the synaptic current variables. To keep the treatment transparent and minimize the number of indices, we focus on a single population coupled to itself and suppose that the synaptic current pulses are exponential $\alpha(s) = (q/\tau_q)\exp(-s/\tau_q)$. The driving current of a neuron i in a population n arising from spikes of the same population is then described by the differential equation

$$\frac{\mathrm{d}I_i}{\mathrm{d}t} = -\frac{I_i}{\tau_q} + C_{nn}w_{nn}\frac{q}{\tau_q}A_n(t), \tag{13.73}$$

which we can verify by taking the temporal derivative of Eq. (13.72). As before the population activity $A_n(t)$ can be decomposed into a mean $\mu(t)$ (which is the same for all neurons) and a fluctuating part $\xi_i(t)$ with white-noise characteristics:

$$\frac{\mathrm{d}I_i}{\mathrm{d}t} = -\frac{I_i}{\tau_q} + \mu(t) + \xi_i(t). \tag{13.74}$$

However, Eq. (13.74) does not lead directly to spike firing but needs to be combined with the differential equation for the voltage

$$\tau_m \frac{\mathrm{d}u_i}{\mathrm{d}t} = f(u_i) + RI_i(t), \tag{13.75}$$

and the reset condition: if $u = \theta_{\text{reset}}$ then $u = u_r$. Since we now have two coupled differential equations, the momentary state of a population of N neurons is described by a two-dimensional density $p(u,I)$.

We recall that, in the case of white noise, the membrane potential density at threshold vanishes. The main insight for the mathematical treatment of the membrane potential density equations in two dimensions is that the density at threshold $p(\theta_{\text{reset}}, I(t))$ is finite, whenever the momentary slope of the voltage $\mathrm{d}u/\mathrm{d}t \propto RI(t) + f(\theta_{\text{reset}})$ is positive (Fourcaud and Brunel, 2002).

13.7 Summary

The momentary state of a population of one-dimensional integrate-and-and fire neurons can be characterized by the membrane potential density $p(u,t)$. The continuity equation describes the evolution of $p(u,t)$ over time. In the special case that neurons in the population receive many inputs that each cause a small change of the membrane potential, the continuity equation has the form of a Fokker–Planck equation. Several populations of integrate-and-fire neurons interact via the population activity $A(t)$, which is identified with the flux across the threshold.

The stationary state of the Fokker–Planck equation and the stability of the stationary solution can be calculated by a mix of analytical and numerical methods, be it for a population of independent or interconnected neurons. The mathematical and numerical methods developed for membrane potential density equations apply to leaky as well as to arbitrary nonlinear one-dimensional integrate-and-fire models. A slow adaptation variable such as in the adaptive exponential integrate-and-fire model can be treated as quasi-stationary in the proximity of the stationary solution. Conductance input can be approximated by an equivalent current-based model.

Literature

The formulation of the dynamics of a population of integrate-and-fire neurons on the level of membrane potential densities has been developed by Abbott and van Vreeswijk (1993), Brunel and Hakim (1999), Fusi and Mattia (1999), Nykamp and Tranchina (2000), Omurtag *et al.* (2000), and Knight (2000), but the Fokker–Planck equation has been used much earlier for the probabilistic description of a single neuron driven by stochastic spike arrivals (Johannesma, 1968; Capocelli and Ricciardi, 1971; Ricciardi, 1976). The classic application of the Fokker–Planck approach to a network of excitatory and inhibitory leaky integrate-and-fire neurons is Brunel (2000). For the general theory of Fokker–Planck equations see Risken (1984).

Efficient numerical solutions of the Fokker–Planck equation, for both stationary input and periodic input, have been developed by M. J. E. Richardson (2007, 2009). These methods can be used to find activity in networks of nonlinear integrate-and-fire models, and also of generalized neuron models with slow spike-triggered currents or conductances (Richardson, 2009). For the treatment of colored noise, see Fourcaud and Brunel (2002).

Exercises

1. **Diffusion limit in the quadratic integrate-and-fire model**. *Consider a population of quadratic integrate-and-fire models. Assume that spikes from external sources arrive at excitatory and inhibitory synapses stochastically, and independently for different neurons, at a rate $v_E(t)$ and $v_I(t)$, respectively.*
   (a) Write down the membrane potential density equations assuming that each spike causes a voltage jump by an amount $\pm\Delta u$.
   (b) Take the diffusion limit so as to arrive at a Fokker–Planck equation.
2. **Voltage distribution of the quadratic integrate-and-fire model**. *Find the stationary solution of the membrane potential distribution for the quadratic integrate-and-fire model with white diffusive noise.*
3. **Non-leaky integrate-and-fire model**. *Consider a non-leaky integrate-and-fire model subject to stochastic spike arrival*

$$\frac{du}{dt} = \frac{1}{C}I(t) = \frac{q}{C}\sum_f \delta(t - t^f),\tag{13.76}$$

   where q is the charge that each spike puts on the membrane and the spike arrival rate is constant and equal to v. At $u = \vartheta = 1$ the membrane potential is reset to $u = u_r = 0$.
   (a) Formulate the continuity equation for the membrane potential density equation.
   (b) Make the diffusion approximation.
   (c) Solve for the stationary membrane potential density distribution under the assumption that the flux through u_r vanishes.
4. **Linear response**. *A population is driven by a current $I_0 + I_1(t)$. The response of the population is described by*

$$A(t) = A_0 + A_1(t) = A_0 + \int_0^\infty G(s)I_1(t - s)\, ds,\tag{13.77}$$

   where G is called the linear response filter.

(a) *Take the Fourier transformation and show that the convolution with the filter G turns into a simple multiplication:*

$$\hat{A}_1(\omega) = \hat{G}(\omega)\,\hat{I}_1(\omega),\tag{13.78}$$

where the hats denote the Fourier transformed variable.

Hint: *Replace $G(s)$ in Eq. (13.77) by a causal filter $G_c(s) = 0$ for $s \le 0$ and $G_c(s) = G(s)$ for $s > 0$, extend the lower integral bound to $-\infty$, and apply standard rules for Fourier transforms.*

(b) *The squared quantity $|\hat{I}_1(\omega)|^2$ is the power of the input at frequency ω. What is the power $|\hat{A}_1(\omega)|^2$ of the population activity at frequency ω?*

(c) *Assume that the filter is given by $G(s) = \exp[-(s-\Delta)/\tau_g]$ for $s > \Delta$ and zero otherwise. Calculate $\hat{G}(\omega)$.*

(d) *Assume that the input current has a power spectrum $|\hat{I}_1(\omega)|^2 = (c/\omega)$ with $c > 0$ for $\omega > \omega_0$ and zero otherwise.*

What is the power spectrum of the population activity with a linear filter as in (iii)?

5. **Stability of stationary state**. *The response of the population is described by*

$$A(t) = A_0 + A_1(t) = A_0 + \int_0^\infty G(s)\,I_1(t-s)\,ds,\tag{13.79}$$

where G is the linear response filter. Set $G(s) = \exp[-(s-\Delta_g)/\tau_g]$ for $s > \Delta_g$ and zero otherwise. Assume that the input arises due to self-coupling with the population:

$$I_1(t) = \int_0^\infty \alpha(s)\,A_1(t-s)\,ds.\tag{13.80}$$

Set $\alpha(s) = (\alpha_0/\tau_\alpha)\exp[-(s-\Delta_\alpha)/\tau_\alpha]$ for $s > \Delta_\alpha$ and zero otherwise.

(a) *Search for solutions $A_1(t) \propto \exp[\lambda(\omega)t]\cos(\omega t)$. The stationary state A_0 is stable if $\lambda < 0$ for all frequencies ω.*

(b) *Analyze the critical solutions $\lambda = 0$ as a function of the delays Δ_G and Δ_α and the feedback strength α_0.*

6. **Conductance input**. *Consider N_E excitatory and N_I inhibitory leaky integrate-and-fire neurons in the subthreshold regime*

$$C\frac{du}{dt} = -g_L(u-E_L) - g_E(t)(u-E_E) - g_I(t)(u-E_I),\tag{13.81}$$

where C is the membrane capacity, g_L the leak conductance and E_L, E_E, E_I are the reversal potentials for leak, excitation, and inhibition, respectively. Assume that input spikes at excitatory arrive at a rate ν_E and lead to a conductance change

$$g_E(t) = \Delta g_E \sum_j \sum_f \exp[-(t-t_j^f)/\tau_E] \quad \text{for } t > t_j^f\tag{13.82}$$

(and zero otherwise) with amplitude Δg_E and decay time constant τ_E. A similar expression holds for inhibition with $\Delta g_I = 2\Delta g_E$ and $\tau_I = \tau_E/2$. Spike arrival rates are identical $\nu_I = \nu_E$.

(a) *Determine the mean potential μ.*

(b) *Introduce*

$$\alpha_E(t-t_j^f) = a_E \exp[-(t-t_j^f)/\tau_E]\Theta(t-t_j^f)(\mu - E_E)\tag{13.83}$$

and an analogous expression for inhibitory input currents α_I.

Show that the membrane with conductance-based synapses Eq. (13.81) can be approximated by a model with current-based *synapses*

$$\tau_{\text{eff}}\frac{du}{dt} = -(u-E_L) + \sum_{j\in N_E}\sum_f \alpha_E(t-t_j^f) + \sum_{j\in N_I}\sum_f \alpha_I(t-t_j^f),\tag{13.84}$$

where E_L is the leak potential defined earlier in Eq. (13.81). Determine a_E, a_I and τ_{eff}. What are the terms that are neglected in this approximation? Why are they small?

(c) Assume that the reversal potential for inhibition and leak are the same $E_I = E_L$. What is the mean potential μ in this case? How does inhibitory input manifest itself? What would change if you replaced inhibition by a constant current that sets the mean membrane potential (in the presence of the same amount of excitation as before) to μ?

7. **Firing rate of leaky integrate-and-fire neurons in the Brunel–Hakim formulation.**

Show that the Siegert formula of Eq. (13.30) can be also written in the form (Brunel and Hakim, 1999)

$$\frac{1}{A_0\,\tau_m} = 2\int_0^\infty du\, e^{-u^2}\left[\frac{e^{2y_2 u} - e^{2y_1 u}}{u}\right] \tag{13.85}$$

with $y_2 = (\vartheta - h_0)/\sigma$ and $y_1 = (u_r - h_0)/\sigma$.

Hint: Use the definition of the error function erf given above Eq. (13.30).

14

Quasi-renewal theory and the integral-equation approach

In the previous chapter it was shown that an approach based on membrane potential densities can be used to analyze the dynamics of networks of integrate-and-fire neurons. For neuron models that include biophysical phenomena such as refractoriness and adaptation on multiple time scales, however, the resulting system of partial differential equations is situated in more than two dimensions and therefore difficult to solve analytically; even the numerical integration of partial differential equations in high dimensions is slow. To cope with these difficulties, we now indicate an alternative approach to describing the population activity in networks of model neurons. The central concept is expressed as an integral equation of the population activity.

The advantage of the integral equation approach is four-fold. First, the approach works for a broad spectrum of neuron models, such as the Spike Response Model with escape noise and other Generalized Linear Models (see Chapter 9) for which parameters can be directly extracted from experiments (see Chapter 11). Second, it is easy to assign an intuitive interpretation to the quantities that show up in the integral equation. For example, the interspike interval distribution plays a central role. Third, an approximative mathematical treatment of adaptation is possible not only for the stationary population activity, but also for the case of arbitrary time-dependent solutions. Fourth, the integral equations provide a natural basis for the transition to classical "rate equations," which will be discussed in Chapter 15.

In Section 14.1, we derive, starting from a small set of assumptions, an integral equation for the population activity. The essential idea of the mathematical formulation is to remain at the macroscopic level as much as possible, without reference to a specific model of neuronal dynamics. Knowledge of the interval distribution $P_I(t|\hat{t})$ for arbitrary input $I(t)$ is enough to formulate the population equations.

For didactic purposes, we begin by treating neurons without adaptation. In this case, the internal state of the neurons depends solely on the input and on the time since the last spike. The formulation of the macroscopic integral equation exploits the concepts of a time-dependent version of renewal theory that we have already encountered in Chapter 7. In the presence of adaptation, however, the state of the neuron depends not only on the last spike, but also on all the previous spike times. But since the refractoriness caused by the last spike dominates over the effects of earlier spikes we can approximate the interval distribution for adaptive neurons by a "quasi-renewal" theory.

A theory for networks consisting of several interacting populations of spiking neurons is formulated in Section 14.2. To analyze the stability of stationary solutions of asynchronous firing with population activity A_0 in connected networks of integrate-and-fire neurons, we need to know the linear response filter. The linearization of the integral equations under the assumption of a small perturbation is presented in Section 14.3.

The integral equation of Section 14.1 is exact in the limit of a large number of neurons and can be interpreted as a solution to partial differential equations analogous to those of the previous chapter. Section 14.4, which is slightly more technical, presents the relation of the integral equation to an approach by membrane potential density equations.

Section 14.5 describes in detail how we can formulate integral equations for adaptive neurons. Finally, Section 14.6 contains variants of the theory that are applicable to populations of a finite number of neurons.

14.1 Population activity equations

The interval distribution $P_I(t|\hat{t})$, which has already been introduced in Chapter 7, plays a central role in the formulation of the population equation. Before we formulate the evolution of the population activity $A(t)$ in terms of this interval distribution $P_I(t|\hat{t})$, we specify some necessary assumptions. Two key assumptions are that the population is homogeneous and contains non-adaptive neurons so that we can work in the framework of a time-dependent renewal theory. These assumptions will eventually be relaxed in Section 14.1.4 where we extend the theory to the case of a population of adaptive neurons and in Section 14.6 where we treat populations of finite size.

14.1.1 Assumptions of time-dependent renewal theory

To formulate a first version of an integral equation for a population of neurons, we start in the framework of time-dependent renewal theory (Chapter 7). To do so, we have to assume the state of a neuron i at time t to be completely described by (i) its last firing time $\hat{t}_i$; (ii) the input $I(t')$ it received for times $t' < t$; (iii) the characteristics of potential noise sources, be it noise in the input, noise in the neuronal parameters, or noise in the output.

Are these assumptions overly restrictive or can we still place an interesting and rich set of neuron models in the class of models consistent with assumptions (i)–(iii) of time-dependent renewal theory?

The state of a single-variable integrate-and-fire neuron i, for example one of the nonlinear integrate-and-fire models of Chapter 5, is completely characterized by its momentary membrane potential $u_i(t)$. After firing at a time $\hat{t}_i$, the membrane potential is reset, so that all information that arrived before the firing is "forgotten." Integration continues with $u = u_r$. Therefore knowledge of the last firing time $\hat{t}_i$ and the input current $I(t')$ for $\hat{t}_i < t' \leq t$ is sufficient to predict the momentary state of neuron i at time t and therefore (for a deterministic model) its next firing time. If the integrate-and-fire model is furthermore subject to noise in the form of stochastic spike arrivals of known rate (but unknown spike arrival times), we will not be able to predict the neuron's exact firing time. Instead we are interested in the probability density

$$P_I(t|\hat{t}_i) \tag{14.1}$$

that the next spike occurs around time t given that the last spike was at time $\hat{t}_i$ and the neuron was subject to an input $I(t')$ for $t' \leq t$. In practice, it might be difficult to write down an exact analytical formula for $P_I(t|\hat{t}_i)$ for noise models corresponding to stochastic spike arrival or diffusive noise (see Chapter 8), but the quantity $P_I(t|\hat{t}_i)$ is still well defined. We call $P_I(t|\hat{t}_i)$ the generalized interval distribution (see Chapter 9).

For several other noise models, there exist explicit mathematical expressions for $P_I(t|\hat{t}_i)$. Consider, for example, integrate-and-fire models with slow noise in the parameters, defined as follows. After each firing time, the value u_r for the reset or the value τ_m of the membrane time constant is drawn from a predefined distribution. Between two resets, the membrane potential evolves deterministically. As a consequence, the distribution $P_I(t|\hat{t}_i)$ of the next firing time can be predicted from the distribution of parameters and the deterministic solution of the threshold crossing equations (Gerstner, 2000). Such a model of slow noise in the parameters can also be considered as an approximation to a heterogeneous population of neurons where different neurons in the population have slightly different, but fixed, parameters.

Another tractable noise model is the "escape noise" model, which is also the basis for the Generalized Linear Models of spiking neurons already discussed in Chapter 9. The short-term memory approximation SRM_0 of the Spike Response Model with escape noise (see Eq. (9.19)) is a prime example of a model that fits into the framework of renewal theory specified by assumptions (i)–(iii).

The escape noise model can be used in combination with any linear or nonlinear integrate-and-fire model. For a suitable choice of the escape function f it provides also an excellent approximation to diffusive noise in the input; see Section 9.4. An example of how to formulate a nonlinear integrate-and-fire model with escape noise is given below.

The major limitation of time-dependent renewal theory is that, for the moment, we need to exclude adaptation effects, because the momentary state of adaptive neurons depends not only on the last firing time (and the input in the past) but also on the firing times of earlier spikes. Section 14.1.4 shows that adaptation can be included by extending the renewal theory to a quasi-renewal theory. The treatment of adaptive neurons is important because most cortical neurons exhibit adaptation (Chapter 6).

Example: Escape noise in integrate-and-fire models

Consider an arbitrary (linear or nonlinear) integrate-and-fire model with refractoriness. The neuron has fired its last spike at $\hat{t}$ and enters thereafter an absolute refractory period of time Δ^{abs}. Integration of the differential equation of the membrane potential u,

$$\tau \frac{d}{dt}u = f(u) + R(u)I(t),$$ (14.2)

restarts at time $\hat{t} + \Delta^{abs}$ with initial condition u_r. The input current $I(t)$ can have an arbitrary temporal structure.

In the absence of noise, the neuron would emit its next spike at the moment when the membrane potential reaches the numerical threshold θ^{reset}. In the presence of escape noise, the neuron fires in each short time interval $\Delta t \to 0$, a spike with probability $P_F(t; t + \Delta t) = \rho(t)\Delta t$ where

$$\rho(t) = f(u(t) - \theta^{reset}, \dot{u}(t))$$ (14.3)

is the escape rate which typically depends on the distance between the membrane potential and the threshold, and potentially also on the derivative $\dot{u} = (du/dt)$ of the membrane potential; see Section 9.4.

Knowledge of the input $I(t')$ for $t' > \hat{t} + \Delta^{abs}$ is sufficient to calculate the membrane potential $u(t)$ by integration of Eq. (14.2). The time course of $u(t)$ is inserted into Eq. (14.3) to get the instantaneous rate or firing "hazard" $\rho(t)$ for all $t > \hat{t} + \Delta^{abs}$. By definition, the instantaneous rate vanishes during the absolute refractory time: $\rho(t) = 0$ for $\hat{t} < t < \hat{t} + \Delta^{abs}$. With this notation, we can use the results of Chapter 7 to arrive at the generalized interval distribution

$$P_I(t|\hat{t}) = \rho(t) \exp\left[-\int_{\hat{t}}^{t} \rho(t')dt'\right].$$ (14.4)

Note that, in order to keep notation light, we simply write $\rho(t)$ instead of the more explicit $\rho(t|\hat{t}, I(t'))$ which would emphasize that the hazard depends on the last firing time $\hat{t}$ and the input $I(t')$ for $\hat{t} < t' \leq t$; for the derivation of Eq. 14.4, see also Eq. (7.28).

14.1.2 Integral equations for non-adaptive neurons

The integral equation (Gerstner, 1995, 2000; Wilson and Cowan, 1972) for activity dynamics with time-dependent renewal theory states that the activity at time t depends on the fraction of active neurons at earlier times $\hat{t}$ multiplied by the probability of observing a spike at t given a spike at $\hat{t}$:

$$A(t) = \int_{-\infty}^{t} P_I(t|\hat{t})A(\hat{t})d\hat{t}.$$ (14.5)

Equation (14.5) is easy to understand. The kernel $P_I(t|\hat{t})$ is the probability density that the next spike of a neuron, which is under the influence of an input I, occurs at time t given that its last spike was at $\hat{t}$. The number of neurons which have fired at $\hat{t}$ is proportional to $A(\hat{t})$ and the integral runs over all times in the past. The interval distribution $P_I(t|\hat{t})$ depends on the total input (both the external input and the synaptic input from other neurons in the population). For an unconnected population, $I(t)$ corresponds to the external drive.

For connected neurons, $I(t)$ is the sum of the external input and the recurrent input from other neurons in the population; the case of connected neurons will be further analyzed in Section 14.2.

We emphasize that $A(t)$ on the left-hand side of Eq. (14.5) is the *expected* activity at time t, while $A(\hat{t})$ on the right-hand side is the *observed* activity in the past. In the limit of the number N of neurons in the population going to infinity, the fraction of neurons that actually fire in a short time Δt is the same as its expected value $A(t)\Delta t$. Therefore, Eq. (14.5) becomes exact in the limit of $N \to \infty$, so that we can use the same symbol for $A(t)$ on both sides of the equation. Finite-size effects are discussed in Section 14.6.

We conclude this section with some final remarks on the form of Eq. (14.5). First, we observe that we can multiply the activity value A on both sides of the equation with a constant c and introduce a new variable $A' = cA$. If $A(t)$ solves the equation, then $A'(t)$ will solve it as well. Thus, Eq. (14.5) cannot predict the correct normalization of the activity A. This reflects the fact that, instead of defining the activity by a spike count divided by the number N of neurons, we could have chosen to work directly with the spike count per unit of time or any other normalization. The proper normalization consistent with our definition of the population activity $A(t)$ is derived below in Section 14.1.3.

Second, even though Eq. (14.5) is linear in the variable A, it is in fact a highly nonlinear equation in the drive, because the kernel $P_I(t|\hat{t})$ depends nonlinearly on the input $I(t)$. However, numerical implementations of the integral equations lead to rapid schemes that predict the population activity in response to changing input, even in the highly nonlinear regime when strong input transiently synchronizes neurons in the population (Fig. 14.1).

Example: Leaky integrate-and-fire neurons with escape noise

Using appropriate numerical schemes, the integral equation can be used to predict the activity in a homogeneous population of integrate-and-fire neurons subject to a time-dependent input. In each time step, the fraction of neurons that fire is calculated as $A(t)\Delta t$ using (14.5). The value of $A(t)$ then becomes part of the observed history and we can evaluate the fraction of neurons in the next time step $t + \Delta t$. For the sake of the implementation, the integral over the past can be truncated at some suitable lower bound (see Section 14.1.5). The numerical integration of Eq. (14.5) predicts well the activity pattern observed in a simulation of 4000 independent leaky integrate-and-fire neurons with exponential escape noise (Fig. 14.1).

14.1.3 Normalization and derivation of the integral equation

To derive Eq. (14.5), we recall that $P_I(t|\hat{t})$ is the probability density that a neuron fires at time t given its last spike at $\hat{t}$ and an input $I(t')$ for $t' \leq t$. Integration of the probability density over time $\int_{\hat{t}}^{t} P_I(s|\hat{t})ds$ gives the probability that a neuron which has fired at $\hat{t}$ fires its next spike at some arbitrary time between $\hat{t}$ and t. Just as in Chapter 7, we can define a

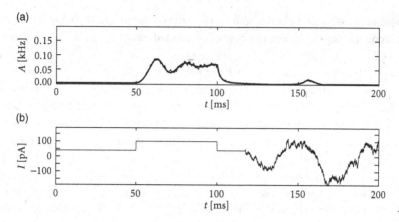

Fig. 14.1 Population activity $A(t)$ (top) in a population of leaky integrate-and-fire neurons with escape noise in response to a time-dependent input (bottom). After a strong step, neurons in the population synchronize, which leads to a transient oscillation. The numerical solution of the integral equation is compared with a simulation of 4000 neurons.

survival probability,

$$S_I(t|\hat{t}) = 1 - \int_{\hat{t}}^{t} P_I(s|\hat{t})\mathrm{d}s, \tag{14.6}$$

i.e., the probability that a neuron which has fired its last spike at $\hat{t}$ "survives" without firing up to time t.

We now return to the homogeneous population of neurons in the limit of $N \to \infty$ and assume that the firing of different neurons at time t is independent, given that we know the history (the input and last spike) of each neuron. The technical term for such a situation is "conditional independence." We consider the network state at time t and label all neurons by their last firing time $\hat{t}$. The proportion of neurons at time t which have fired their last spike between t_0 and $t_1 < t$ (and have not fired since) is expected to be

$$\left\langle \frac{\text{number of neurons at } t \text{ with last spike in } [t_0, t_1]}{\text{total number of neurons}} \right\rangle = \int_{t_0}^{t_1} S_I(t|\hat{t})A(\hat{t})\mathrm{d}\hat{t}. \tag{14.7}$$

For an interpretation of the integral on the right-hand side of Eq. (14.7), we recall that $A(\hat{t})\mathrm{d}\hat{t}$ is the fraction of neurons that have fired in the interval $[\hat{t}, \hat{t}+\Delta\hat{t}]$. Of these a fraction $S_I(t|\hat{t})$ are expected to survive from $\hat{t}$ to t without firing. Thus among the neurons that we observe at time t the proportion of neurons that have fired their last spike between t_0 and t_1 is expected to be $\int_{t_0}^{t_1} S_I(t|\hat{t})A(\hat{t})\mathrm{d}\hat{t}$; see Fig. 14.2.

Finally, we use the fact that the total number of neurons remains constant. All neurons have fired at *some* point in the past.[1] Thus, if we extend the lower bound t_0 of the integral on the right-hand side of Eq. 14.7 to $-\infty$ and the upper bound to t, the left-hand side becomes

---

[1] Neurons which have never fired before are assigned a formal firing time $\hat{t} = -\infty$.

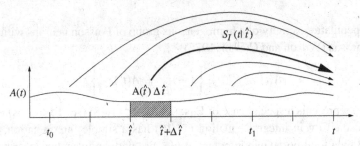

Fig. 14.2 Derivation of the population equation in discretized time. Of the $NA(\hat{t})\Delta\hat{t}$ neurons that have fired between $\hat{t}$ and $\hat{t}+\Delta\hat{t}$, a fraction $S_I(t|\hat{t})$ is expected to "survive" up to time t without firing another spike. Thus (with $t_1 = \hat{t}_0 + k^{\max}\Delta\hat{t}$) the Riemann sum $\sum_{k=0}^{k^{\max}} S(t|t_0 + k\Delta\hat{t})A(t_0 + k\Delta\hat{t})\Delta\hat{t} \approx \int_{t_0}^{t_1} S_I(t|\hat{t})A(\hat{t})\,d\hat{t}$ gives the expected fraction of neurons at time t that have fired their last spike between t_0 and t_1.

equal to one,

$$1 = \int_{-\infty}^{t} S_I(t|\hat{t})A(\hat{t})\,d\hat{t}, \tag{14.8}$$

because all N neurons have fired their last spike in the interval $[-\infty, t]$. Since the number of neurons remains constant, the normalization of Eq. 14.8 must hold at arbitrary times t. Eq. (14.8) is an implicit equation for the population activity A and the starting point for the discussions in this and the following chapters.

Since Eq. (14.8) is rather abstract, we will put it into a form that is easier to grasp intuitively. To do so, we take the derivative of Eq. (14.8) with respect to t. We find

$$0 = S_I(t|t)A(t) + \int_{-\infty}^{t} \frac{\partial S_I(t|\hat{t})}{\partial t}A(\hat{t})\,d\hat{t}. \tag{14.9}$$

We now use $P_I(t|\hat{t}) = -\frac{\partial}{\partial t}S_I(t|\hat{t})$ and $S_I(t|t) = 1$, which is a direct consequence of Eq. (14.6). This yields the activity dynamics of Eq. (14.5).

We repeat an important remark concerning the normalization of the activity. Since Eq. (14.5) is defined as the *derivative* of Eq. (14.8), the integration constant on the left-hand side of Eq. (14.8) is lost. This is most easily seen for constant activity $A(t) = A_0$. In this case the variable A_0 can be eliminated on both sides of Eq. (14.5) so that it yields the trivial statement that the interval distribution is normalized to unity. Equation (14.5) is therefore invariant under a rescaling of the activity $A_0 \to cA_0$ with any constant c, as mentioned earlier. To get the correct normalization of the activity we have to return to Eq. (14.8).

Example: Absolute refractoriness and the Wilson–Cowan integral equation

Let us consider a population of Poisson neurons with an absolute refractory period Δ^{abs}. A neuron that is not refractory fires stochastically with a rate $f[h(t)]$ where $h(t) = \int_0^{\infty} \kappa(s)I(t-s)\,ds$ is the total input potential caused by an external driving current or synaptic input from other neurons. After firing, a neuron is inactive during a time

Δ^{abs}. The population activity of a homogeneous group of Poisson neurons with absolute refractoriness is (Wilson and Cowan, 1972)

$$A(t) = f[h(t)] \left\{ 1 - \int_{t-\Delta^{\text{abs}}}^{t} A(t')dt' \right\}. \tag{14.10}$$

Eq. (14.10) represents a special case of Eqs. (14.5) and (14.8) (see Exercises).

The Wilson–Cowan integral equation (14.10) has a simple interpretation. Neurons stimulated by a total postsynaptic potential $h(t)$ fire with an instantaneous rate $f[h(t)]$. If there were no refractoriness, we would expect a population activity $A(t) = f[h(t)]$. However, not all neurons may fire, since some of the neurons are in the absolute refractory period. The fraction of neurons that participate in firing is $1 - \int_{t-\Delta^{\text{abs}}}^{t} A(t')dt'$, which explains the factor in curly brackets.

The function f in Eq. (14.10) was introduced here as the stochastic intensity of an inhomogeneous Poisson process describing neurons in a *homogeneous* population. In this interpretation, Eq. (14.10) is the exact equation for the population activity of neurons with absolute refractoriness in the limit of $N \to \infty$. In their original paper, Wilson and Cowan motivated the function f by a distribution of threshold values in an *inhomogeneous* population. In this case, the population equation (14.10) is only an approximation since correlations are neglected (Wilson and Cowan, 1972).

For constant input potential, $h(t) = h_0 = I_0 \int_0^{\infty} \kappa(s)I(t-s)ds$, the population activity has a stationary solution (see Fig. 14.3)

$$A_0 = \frac{f(h_0)}{1 + \Delta^{\text{abs}} f(h_0)} = g(h_0). \tag{14.11}$$

For the last equality sign we have used the definition of the gain function of Poisson neurons with absolute refractoriness in Eq. (7.50). Equation (14.11) tells us that in a homogeneous population of neurons the population activity in a stationary state is equal to the firing rate of individual neurons, as expected from the discussion in Chapter 12.

Sometimes the stationary solution from Eq. (14.11) is also used in the case of time-dependent input. However, the expression $A_0(t) = g(h(t))$ [with g from Eq. (14.11)] does not correctly reflect the transients that are seen in the solution of the integral equation (14.10); see Fig. 14.3b and Chapter 15.

14.1.4 Integral equation for adaptive neurons

The integral equations presented so far are restricted to non-adapting neurons, because we assumed that the knowledge of the input and of the last firing time was sufficient to characterize the state of a neuron. For adapting neurons, however, the whole spiking history can shape the interspike interval distribution. In this section we extend the integral equation (14.5) to the case of adapting neurons.

For an *isolated* adaptive neuron in the presence of noise, the probability density of firing around time t will, in general, depend on its past firing times $\hat{t}_n < \hat{t}_{n-1} \cdots < \hat{t}_2 < \hat{t}_1 = \hat{t} < t$

(a)
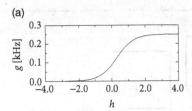

(b)
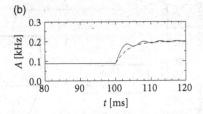

Fig. 14.3 Wilson–Cowan model. (a) Stationary activity calculated from the gain function $A_0 = g(h)$ of Poisson neurons with absolute refractoriness of $\Delta^{abs} = 4$ ms; see Eq. (14.11). (b) The response of the population activity to an abrupt change of the input current shows an oscillatory behavior (solid line) in the approach to the new stationary state. The oscillations are absent in a quasi-stationary approximation $A_0(t) = g(h(t))$ where the stationary solution from Eq. (14.11) is applied to explain time-dependent behavior (dashed line). The input potential vanishes for $t_0 < 100$ ms and is $h(t) = 1 - \exp[-(t-t_0)/\tau_m]$ for $t > t_0$ with $\tau_m = 4$ ms. The exponential escape rate $f(h) = \tau_0^{-1} \exp[\beta(h - \vartheta)]$ with $\vartheta = 1$, $\tau_0 = 1$ ms, and $\beta = 2$. No lateral coupling ($w_0 = 0$).

where $\hat{t} = \hat{t}_1$ denotes the *most recent* spike time. The central insight is that, in a *population* of neurons, we can approximate the past firing times by the population activity $A(\hat{t})$ in the past. Indeed, the probability of one of the neurons having a past spike time $\hat{t}_k = t'$ in the interval $\hat{t} < t' < \hat{t} + \Delta t$ is $A(\hat{t})\Delta t$.

Just as in the time-dependent renewal theory, we will treat the most recent spike $\hat{t}_1 = \hat{t}$ of each neuron explicitly. For all spikes $\hat{t}_k$ with $k \geq 2$ we approximate the actual spike-train history of an individual by the *average* history as summarized in the population activity $A(t)$. Let $P_{I,A}(t|\hat{t})$ be the probability of observing a spike at time t given the last spike at time $\hat{t}$, the input current *and* the activity history $A(t)$ until time t; then we can rewrite Eq. (14.5) in a form suitable for adaptive neurons

$$A(t) = \int_{-\infty}^{t} P_{I,A}(t|\hat{t})A(\hat{t})d\hat{t}. \tag{14.12}$$

In Section 14.5 we explain the methods to describe populations of adaptive neurons in more detail. Appropriate numerical schemes (Section 14.1.5) make it possible to describe the response of a population of adaptive neurons to arbitrary time-dependent input; see Fig. 14.4.

14.1.5 Numerical methods for integral equations (*)

Integral equations can be solved numerically. However, the type of equation we face in Eq. (14.5) or Eq. (14.12) cannot be cast in the typical Volterra or Fredholm forms for which efficient numerical methods have been extensively studied (Linz, 1985; Atkinson, 1997). In what follows, we describe a method that can be used to solve Eq. (14.5), Eq. (14.12) or

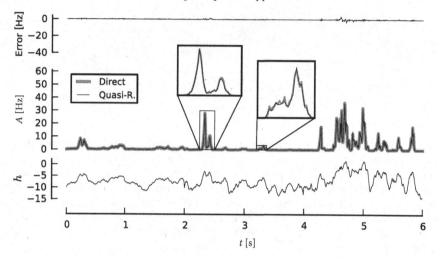

Fig. 14.4 Population of adaptive neurons. Middle: The solution (black solid line) of the integral equation for adaptive neurons (14.12) is compared with the population activity during a simulation of 25 000 model neurons (thick gray line). Model neurons are Generalized Linear Models of spiking neurons with parameters from cortical cells; see Chapter 11. Top: Error (theory minus simulations) in the prediction of the population activity. Bottom: Driving stimulus $h(t) = \int_0^\infty \exp(-s/\tau_m)I(t-s)\,\mathrm{d}s$ in arbitrary units. Threshold in the limit of deterministic neurons located at $h = 0$ so that $h < 0$ indicates the subthreshold regime. Modified from Naud and Gerstner (2012a).

Eq. (14.8), but we take as an example the quasi-renewal equivalent of Eq. (14.8)

$$1 = \int_{-\infty}^{t} S_{I,A}(t|\hat{t})A(\hat{t})\mathrm{d}\hat{t}. \tag{14.13}$$

To derive a numerical algorithm, we proceed in three steps: first, truncation of the integral in Eq. (14.13) at some lower bound; second, the discretization of this integral; and, third, the discretization of the integral defining the survivor function. Here we will use the rectangle rule for the discretization of every integral. Note that adaptive quadratures or Monte-Carlo methods could present more efficient alternatives.

The first step is the truncation. The probability of surviving a very long time is essentially zero. Let τ_c be a period of time such that the survivor $S_{I,A}(t|t - \tau_c)$ is very small. Then, we can truncate the infinite integral in (14.13)

$$1 = \int_{t-\tau_c}^{t} S_{I,A}(t|\hat{t})A(\hat{t})\mathrm{d}\hat{t}. \tag{14.14}$$

Next, we proceed to discretize the integral on small bins of size Δt. Let $\mathbf{m}^{(t)}$ be the vector made up of the fraction of neurons at t with last spike within $\hat{t}$ and $\hat{t} + \Delta t$. This definition means that the kth element is $m_k^{(t)} = S(t|t - k\Delta t)A(t - k\Delta t)\Delta t$. The element with $k = 0$ is then the momentary population activity in the time step starting at time t, $m_0^{(t)} = A_t\Delta t$, since

$S(t|t) = 1$. Therefore we arrive at

$$A_t \Delta t = 1 - \sum_{k=1}^{K} m_k^{(t)}. \tag{14.15}$$

Finally, we discretize the integral defining the survival function to obtain $m_k^{(t)}$ as a function $m_k^{(t-\Delta t)}$. Because of $S(t|\hat{t}) = \exp[-\int_{\hat{t}}^{t} \rho(t'|\hat{t}) dt'] = \exp[-\int_{t-\Delta t}^{t} \rho(t'|\hat{t}) dt'] S(t - \Delta t|\hat{t})$, we find for sufficiently small time steps

$$m_k^{(t)} = m_{k-1}^{(t-\Delta t)} \exp[-\rho(t|t - k\Delta t) \Delta t] \quad \text{for} \quad k \geq 1. \tag{14.16}$$

Note that we work in a moving coordinate because the index k always counts time steps backward starting from the present time t. Therefore $m_k^{(t)}$ and $m_{k-1}^{(t-\Delta t)}$ refer to the same group of neurons, i.e., those that have fired their last spike around time $\hat{t} = t - k\Delta t = (t - \Delta t) - (k-1)(\Delta t)$. Equation (14.16) indicates that the number of neurons that survive from $\hat{t}$ up to t decreases in each time step by an exponential factor. In Eq. (14.16), $\rho(t|t')$ can be either the renewal conditional intensity of a non-adaptive neuron model (e.g., Eq. (14.3)) or the effective "quasi-renewal" intensity of adaptive neurons (see Section 14.5). Together, Eqs. (14.15) and (14.16) can be used to solve A_t iteratively.

14.2 Recurrent networks and interacting populations

The integral equation (14.5) derived in the previous section can be applied to interacting populations of connected neurons. In Section 14.2.1 we present the mathematical framework of the integral equations so as to describe several populations that interact with each other.

Using the methods discussed in Chapter 12, we can find the activity A_0 of a recurrent network in the regime of stationary asynchronous firing (Section 14.2.2). Using the linear response filter, which will be derived in Section 14.3, the stability of the solutions can further be analyzed for different levels of noise and arbitrary delays (Section 14.2.3).

14.2.1 Several populations and networks with self-interaction

In Section 14.1 we discussed a single homogeneous population of N neurons. The formalism of integral equations introduced there can readily be adapted to several populations with recurrent interactions within and across populations.

We consider a coupled network of spiking neurons of the renewal type, such as nonlinear (or leaky) integrate-and-fire neurons with escape noise or a Spike Response Model SRM$_0$. Neurons within a population have the same set of parameters whereas neurons of different populations can have different parameters. The activity of population k is described by Eq. (14.5)

$$A_k(t) = \int_{-\infty}^{t} P_{I_k}(t|\hat{t}) A_k(\hat{t}) d\hat{t}, \tag{14.17}$$

(a)

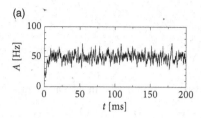

(b)

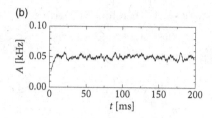

Fig. 14.5 Asynchronous firing. For a sufficient amount of noise, the population activity in a network of coupled spiking neurons with constant external input approaches a stationary value A_0. (a) The population activity of 1000 neurons has been filtered with a time window of 1 ms duration. (b) Same parameters as before, but the size of the population has been increased to $N = 4000$. Fluctuations decrease with N and approach the value of $A_0 = 50$ Hz predicted by theory.

where $P_{I_k}(t|\hat{t})$ is the input-dependent interval distribution of population k. The input to population k is

$$I_k(t) = \sum_n N_n w_{kn} \int_0^\infty \alpha_{kn}(s) A_n(t-s)\, ds + I_k^{ext}. \tag{14.18}$$

Here N_n is the number of neurons in the presynaptic population n, w_{kn} is the strength of a synaptic connection of a neuron in population n to a neuron in population k, and α_{kn} the time course of the postsynaptic current into a neuron in population k, caused by spike firing of a neuron in population n. Conductance-based synapses are treated in the current-based approximation (see Section 13.6.3). Connections can be excitatory or inhibitory, depending on the choice of w_{kn}. Because the overall strength of the connection is incorporated in w_{kn}, we can, without loss of generality, assume a normalization $\int_0^\infty \alpha_{kn}(s) ds = 1$.

The noise level of each neuron in population k is fixed to a value of σ_k. The choice of noise is arbitrary. If our aim is to mimic stochastic spike arrivals in randomly connected networks by an escape rate, a suitable choice of escape function has been given in Chapter 9. In practice this implies that noise in the *input* to a neuron is effectively described and replaced by escape noise in its *output*.

In the following we assume a fully connected network with interaction strength $w_{kn} = J_{kn}/N_n$; see Chapter 12. If the theory is applied to a random network where each neuron in population k has a fixed number of presynaptic partners C_{kn} in population n, we can use the same theory, except that (i) we use $w_{kn} = J_{kn}/C_{kn}$; and (ii) we increase the noise level σ in the escape rate function so as to mimic the additional noise caused by stochastic spike arrival; see Section 9.4.

14.2.2 Stationary states and fixed points of activity

We are interested in the value $A_k(t) \doteq A_{k,0}$ of the population activity in the stationary state of asynchronous firing. We recall from Chapter 12 that stationary activity means that the *expected* value of the population activity is constant whereas in a simulation the actual value $A(t)$ always fluctuates (Fig. 14.5). To lighten the notation, we consider a single population k with self-interaction $w_{kk} = J_0/N_k$ and drop the index k subsequently. The input from other populations is summarized as a constant external input I^{ext}. According to our assumptions, all neurons in the population have the same parameters and can be described by time-dependent renewal theory. The level of noise is indicated by an index σ.

A stationary state of asynchronous firing requires that the total input I_0 is constant (or at least stationary). In Chapter 12, we have seen that the population activity A_0 in the state of asynchronous firing is given by the single-neuron firing rate $v = g_\sigma(I_0)$. We thus have

$$A_0 = v = g_\sigma(I_0). \tag{14.19}$$

Given constant activity A_0 of the population and constant external input I_0^{ext}, the total input I_0 to each neuron is constant. From Eq. (14.18) we find the total input to a neuron in population k

$$I_0 = I_0^{\text{ext}} + J_0 \int_0^\infty \alpha(s) A_0(t-s) \, ds = I_0^{\text{ext}} + J_0 A_0. \tag{14.20}$$

Equations (14.19) and (14.20) together yield the following equation for the population activity A_0

$$A_0 = g_\sigma(J_0 A_0 + I_0^{\text{ext}}). \tag{14.21}$$

This result agrees with the general result found in Chapter 12 for the stationary state in a network with self-coupling. Solutions can be found graphically (Fig. 14.6) using the same method as in Chapter 12.

The advantage of the integral equation approach is two-fold. First, for the integral equations we have transparent mathematical tools to analyze the stability of the stationary solution, as shown in Section 14.2.3.

Second, we can write down the gain function $g_\sigma(I)$ and an expression for A_0 in a compact form, as will be shown now. Because the input is constant, the state of each neuron depends only on the time since the last spike $t - \hat{t}$. We are thus in the situation of stationary renewal theory. Therefore, the survivor function and the interval distribution cannot depend explicitly upon the absolute time, but only on the time difference $s = t - \hat{t}$. Hence we set

$$S_I(\hat{t} + s | \hat{t}) \rightarrow S_0(s), \tag{14.22}$$

$$P_I(\hat{t} + s | \hat{t}) \rightarrow P_0(s). \tag{14.23}$$

The value of the stationary activity A_0 now follows directly from the normalization Equation (14.8),

$$1 = A_0 \int_0^\infty S_0(s) \, ds. \tag{14.24}$$

We use $\frac{d}{ds} S_0(s) = -P_0(s)$ and integrate by parts

$$1 = A_0 \int_0^\infty s P_0(s) \, ds = A_0 \langle T \rangle, \tag{14.25}$$

where the last equality follows from the definition of the mean interspike interval

(a)

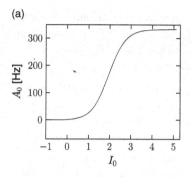

(b)

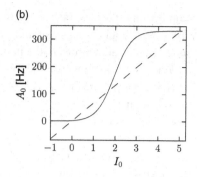

Fig. 14.6 Gain function and stationary activity in a population of SRM neurons with exponential escape noise. (a) Gain function (single neuron firing frequency ν as a function of constant current I_0) for neurons with refractoriness given by Eq. (14.29). (b) Self-consistent solution for the population activity $A(t) = A_0$ in a recurrent network of SRM neurons coupled to itself with strength J_0. Neurons are characterized by the same gain function as in part (a) of the figure.

(see Chapter 9). Hence

$$A_0 = \frac{1}{\int_0^\infty S_0(s)\,\mathrm{d}s} = \frac{1}{\langle T \rangle} = \nu. \tag{14.26}$$

The result has an intuitively appealing interpretation: if everything is constant, then averaging over time (for a single neuron) is the same as averaging over a population of identical neurons; see the discussion in Chapter 12.

Example: Population of SRM neurons with escape noise

Consider a population of SRM_0 neurons with exponential escape noise and membrane potential

$$u(t) = \eta(t - \hat{t}) + \int_0^\infty \kappa(s)\, I(t - s)\,\mathrm{d}s = \eta(t - \hat{t}) + h(t). \tag{14.27}$$

We assume that the input current is constant so that $h(t) = h_0 = R I_0$ with $R = \int_0^\infty \kappa(s)\,\mathrm{d}s$. With exponential escape noise, the hazard function (Chapter 9) is $\rho(t - \hat{t}) = \rho_0 \exp[\beta(h_0 + \eta(t - \hat{t}))]$ and the gain function is given by Eq. (14.26)

$$A_0 = \left[\int_0^\infty \mathrm{d}x \exp\left(-\int_0^x \rho_0 e^{\beta[h_0 + \eta(s)]}\mathrm{d}s \right) \right]^{-1} = g_\sigma(I_0) \tag{14.28}$$

where $\sigma = 1/\beta$ indicates the level of noise.

We now set $\beta = 1$ and consider a specific choice of η that includes absolute and relative refractoriness

$$\eta(t) = \begin{cases} -\infty & \text{if } t < \Delta^{\mathrm{abs}} \\ \ln\left[1 - e^{-(t - \Delta^{\mathrm{abs}})/\tau}\right] & \text{otherwise.} \end{cases} \tag{14.29}$$

With this choice of η it is possible to calculate the gain function in terms of the incomplete gamma function $\gamma(a,x) = \int_0^x t^{a-1} e^{-t} dt$.

$$A_0 = g_\sigma(I_0) = \left(\Delta^{\text{abs}} + \frac{\tau \gamma(r,r)}{r^r e^{-r}} \right)^{-1}, \tag{14.30}$$

where $r = \tau \rho_0 e^{h_0}$ (see Exercises). The result is shown in Fig. 14.6a.

If the population of neurons is coupled to itself with synapses $w_0 = J_0/N$, the stationary value of asynchronous activity can be found graphically by plotting on the same graph $A_0 = g_\sigma(I_0)$ and

$$A_0 = [I_0 - I_0^{\text{ext}}]/J_0, \tag{14.31}$$

which follows from Eq. (14.20); see Fig. 14.6b.

14.2.3 Oscillations and stability of the stationary state (*)

In the previous subsection we assumed that the network is in a state of asynchronous firing. In this section, we study whether asynchronous firing can indeed be a stable state of a fully connected population of spiking neurons – or whether the connectivity drives the network toward oscillations. For the sake of simplicity, we restrict the analysis to SRM$_0$ neurons; the same methods can, however, be applied to integrate-and-fire neurons or spiking neurons formulated in the framework of Generalized Linear Models.

For SRM$_0$ neurons (see Chapter 9), the membrane potential is given by

$$u_i(t) = \eta(t - \hat{t}_i) + h(t), \tag{14.32}$$

where $\eta(t - \hat{t}_i)$ is the effect of the last firing of neuron i (i.e., the spike-afterpotential) and $h(t)$ is the total postsynaptic potential caused by presynaptic firing. If all presynaptic spikes are generated within the homogeneous population under consideration, we have

$$h(t) = \sum_j w_{ij} \sum_f \varepsilon_0(t - t_j^f) = J_0 \int_0^\infty \varepsilon_0(s) A(t-s) \, ds. \tag{14.33}$$

Here $\varepsilon_0(t - t_j^f)$ is the time course of the postsynaptic potential generated by a spike of neuron j at time t_j^f and $w_{ij} = J_0/N$ is the strength of lateral coupling within the population. The second equality sign follows from the definition of the population activity, i.e., $A(t) = N^{-1} \sum_j \sum_f \delta(t - t_j^f)$; see Chapter 12. For the sake of simplicity, we have assumed in Eq. (14.33) that there is no external input.

The state of asynchronous firing corresponds to a fixed point $A(t) = A_0$ of the population activity. We have already seen in the previous subsection as well as in Chapter 12 how the fixed point A_0 can be determined either numerically or graphically. To analyze its stability we assume that for $t > 0$ the activity is subject to a small perturbation,

$$A(t) = A_0 + A_1 e^{i\omega t + \lambda t} \tag{14.34}$$

with $A_1 \ll A_0$. This perturbation in the activity induces a perturbation in the input potential,

$$h(t) = h_0 + h_1\, e^{i\omega t + \lambda t}. \tag{14.35}$$

The perturbation of the potential causes some neurons to fire earlier (when the change in h is positive) and others to fire later (whenever the change is negative). The perturbation may therefore build up ($\lambda > 0$, the asynchronous state is unstable) or decay back to zero ($\lambda < 0$, the asynchronous state is stable). At the transition between the region of stability and instability the amplitude of the perturbation remains constant ($\lambda = 0$, marginal stability of the asynchronous state). These transition points, defined by $\lambda = 0$, are determined now.

We start from the population integral equation $A(t) = \int_{-\infty}^{t} P_I(t|\hat{t})A(\hat{t})\,d\hat{t}$ that was introduced in Section 14.1. Here $P_I(t|\hat{t})$ is the input-dependent interval distribution, i.e., the probability density of emitting a spike at time t given that the last spike occurred at time $\hat{t}$. The linearized response of the population activity to a small change ΔI in the input can, under general smoothness assumptions, always be written in the form

$$A(t) = A_0 + \int_0^{\infty} G(s)\,\Delta I(t - s)\,ds, \tag{14.36}$$

where $G(s)$ is the linear response filter in the time domain. The Fourier transform $\hat{G}(\omega)$ is the frequency-dependent gain function. The explicit form of the filter will be derived in the framework of the integral equations in Section 14.3.

Instead of thinking of a stimulation by an input current $\Delta I(t)$, it is more convenient to work with the input potential $h(t) = \int_0^{\infty} \kappa(s)I(t - s)\,ds$, because the neuron model equations have been defined on the level of the potential; see Eq. (14.32). We use $\Delta A(t) = A_1\, e^{i\omega t + \lambda t}$ and $\Delta h(t) = h_1\, e^{i\omega t + \lambda t}$ in Eq. (14.36) and search for the critical value $\lambda = 0$ where the stable solution turns into an unstable one. After cancellation of a common factor $A_1 \exp(i\omega t)$ the result can be written in the form

$$1 = J_0\, \frac{\hat{G}(\omega)\,\hat{\varepsilon}(\omega)}{\hat{\kappa}(\omega)} = S_f(\omega)\, \exp[i\Phi(\omega)]. \tag{14.37}$$

Here, $\hat{\kappa}(\omega)$ and $\hat{\varepsilon}(\omega)$ are the Fourier transform of the membrane kernel $\kappa(s)$ and the time course of the postsynaptic potential $\varepsilon_0(s)$ caused by an input spike, respectively. Typically, $\kappa(s) = (R/\tau_m)\exp(-s/\tau_m)$ where τ_m is the membrane time constant. If the synaptic input is a short current pulse of unit charge, ε_0 and κ are identical, but we would also like to include the case of synaptic input currents with arbitrary time dependence and therefore keep separate symbols for ε_0 and κ. The second equality sign defines the real-valued functions $S_f(\omega)$ and $\Phi(\omega)$.

Equation (14.37) is thus equivalent to

$$S_f(\omega) = 1 \quad \text{and} \quad \Phi(\omega)\, \mathrm{mod}\, 2\pi = 0. \tag{14.38}$$

Solutions of Eq. (14.38) yield bifurcation points where the asynchronous firing state loses its stability toward an oscillation with frequency ω.

We have written Eq. (14.38) as a combination of two requirements, i.e., an *amplitude* condition $S_f(\omega) = 1$ and a *phase* condition $\Phi(\omega) \bmod 2\pi = 0$. Let us discuss the general structure of the two conditions. First, if $S_f(\omega) \leq 1$ for all frequencies ω, an oscillatory perturbation cannot build up. All oscillations decay and the state of asynchronous firing is stable. We conclude from Eq. (14.37) that by increasing the absolute value $|J_0|$ of the coupling constant, it is always possible to increase $S_f(\omega)$. The amplitude condition can thus be met if the excitatory or inhibitory feedback from other neurons in the population is sufficiently strong. Second, for a bifurcation to occur we need in addition that the phase condition is met. Loosely speaking, the phase condition implies that the feedback from other neurons in the network must arrive just in time to keep the oscillation going. Thus the axonal signal transmission time and the rise time of the postsynaptic potential play a critical role during oscillatory activity (Abbott and van Vreeswijk, 1993; Gerstner and van Hemmen, 1993; Treves, 1993; Tsodyks *et al.*, 1993; Gerstner, 1995; Brunel and Hakim, 1999; Brunel, 2000; Gerstner, 2000).

Example: Slow noise and phase diagram of instabilities

Let us apply the above results to leaky integrate-and-fire neurons with slow noise in the parameters. After each spike the neuron is reset to a value u_r which is drawn from a Gaussian distribution with mean $\bar{u}_r$ and width $\sigma_r \ll [\vartheta - \bar{u}_r]$. After the reset, the membrane potential evolves deterministically according to

$$\tau_m \frac{du}{dt} = -u + RI(t). \qquad (14.39)$$

The next firing occurs if the membrane potential hits the threshold ϑ.

We assume that neurons are part of a large population $N \to \infty$ which is in a state of asynchronous firing with activity A_0. In this case, each neuron receives a constant input I_0. For constant input, a neuron which was reset to a value $\bar{u}_r$ will fire again after a period T_0. Because of the noisy reset with $\sigma_r \ll [\vartheta - \bar{u}_r]$, the interval distribution is approximately a Gaussian centered at T_0. We denote the standard deviation of the interval distribution by σ. The stationary population activity is simply $A_0 = 1/T_0$. The width of the Gaussian interval distribution σ is linearly related to σ_r with a proportionality factor that represents the (inverse of the) slope of the membrane potential at the firing threshold (Gerstner, 2000).

In order to analyze the stability of the stationary state, we have to specify the time course of the excitatory or inhibitory postsynaptic potential ε_0. For the sake of simplicity we choose a delayed alpha function,

$$\varepsilon_0(s) = \frac{s - \Delta^{\mathrm{ax}}}{\tau^2} \exp\left(-\frac{s - \Delta^{\mathrm{ax}}}{\tau}\right) \Theta(s - \Delta^{\mathrm{ax}}). \qquad (14.40)$$

The Fourier transform of ε has an amplitude $|\hat{\varepsilon}(\omega)| = (1 + \omega^2 \tau^2)^{-1}$ and a phase $|\psi(\omega)| = \omega \Delta^{\mathrm{ax}} + 2\arctan(\omega \tau)$. Note that a change in the delay Δ^{ax} affects only the phase of the Fourier transform and not the amplitude.

Figure 14.7 shows S_f defined in the second equality sign of Eq. (14.37) as a function of ωT_0. Since $S_f = 1$ is a necessary condition for a bifurcation, it is apparent that bifurcations can occur only for frequencies $\omega \approx \omega_n = n 2\pi/T_0$ with integer n where $T_0 = 1/A_0$ is the typical interspike interval. We also see that higher harmonics are only relevant for low levels of noise. At a high noise level, however, the asynchronous state is stable even with respect to perturbations at $\omega \approx \omega_1$.

A bifurcation at $\omega \approx \omega_1$ implies that the period of the perturbation is identical to the firing period of individual neurons. Higher harmonics correspond to instabilities of the asynchronous state toward cluster states (Golomb et al., 1992; Gerstner and van Hemmen, 1993; Ernst et al., 1995; Golomb and Rinzel, 1994; Brunel, 2000): each neuron fires with a mean period of T_0, but the population of neurons splits up in several groups that fire alternately so that the overall activity oscillates several times faster. In terms of the terminology introduced in Chapter 13, the network is in the synchronous regular (SR) state of fast oscillations.

Figure 14.7 illustrates the amplitude condition for the solution of Eq. (14.38). The numerical solutions of the full equation (14.38) for different values of the delay Δ^{ax} and different levels of the noise σ are shown in the bifurcation diagram of Fig. 14.8. The insets show simulations that illustrate the behavior of the network at certain combinations of transmission delay and noise level.

Let us consider, for example, a network with transmission delay $\Delta^{ax} = 2$ ms, corresponding to an x-value of $\Delta^{ax}/T_0 = 0.25$ in Fig. 14.8. The phase diagram predicts that, at a noise level of $\sigma = 0.5$ ms, the network is in a state of asynchronous firing. The simulation shown in the inset in the upper right-hand corner confirms that the activity fluctuates around a constant value of $A_0 = 1/T_0 = 0.125$ kHz.

If the noise level of the network is significantly reduced, the system crosses the short-dashed line. This line is the boundary at which the constant activity state becomes unstable with respect to an oscillation with $\omega \approx 3 (2\pi/T_0)$. Accordingly, a network simulation with a noise level of $\sigma = 0.1$ exhibits an oscillation of the population activity with period $T^{osc} \approx T_0/3 \approx 2.6$ ms.

Keeping the noise level constant but reducing the transmission delay corresponds to a horizontal move across the phase diagram in Fig. 14.8. At some point, the system crosses the solid line that marks the transition to an instability with frequency $\omega_1 = 2\pi/T_0$. Again, this is confirmed by a simulation shown in the inset in the upper left corner. If we now decrease the noise level, the oscillation becomes even more pronounced (bottom left).

In the limit of low noise, the asynchronous network state is unstable for virtually all values of the delay. The region of the phase diagram in Fig. 14.8 around $\Delta^{ax}/T_0 \approx 0.1$, which looks stable, hides instabilities with respect to the higher harmonics ω_6 and ω_5, which are not shown. We emphasize that the specific location of the stability borders depends on the form of the postsynaptic response function ε. The qualitative features of the phase diagram in Fig. 14.8 are generic and hold for all kinds of response kernels.

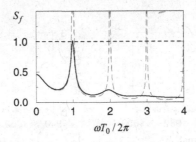

Fig. 14.7 Amplitude condition for instabilities in the asynchronous state. The amplitude S_f is plotted as a function of the normalized frequency ωT_0 for two different values of the noise: $\sigma = 1$ ms (solid line) and $\sigma = 0.1$ ms (dashed line). Instabilities of the asynchronous firing state are possible at frequencies where $S_f > 1$. For low noise S_f crosses unity (broken horizontal line) at frequencies $\omega \approx \omega_n = n2\pi/T_0$. For $\sigma = 1$ ms there is a single instability region for $\omega T_0 \approx 1$. For the plot we have set $T_0 = 2\tau$.

What happens if the excitatory interaction is replaced by inhibitory coupling? A change in the sign of the interaction corresponds to a phase shift of π. For each harmonic, the region along the delay axis where the asynchronous state is *unstable* for excitatory coupling (see Fig. 14.8) becomes *stable* for inhibition and vice versa. In other words, we simply have to shift the instability tongues for each harmonic frequency $\omega_n = 2n\pi/T_0$ horizontally by half the period of the harmonic, i.e., $\Delta/T_0 = 1/(2n)$. Apart from that the pattern remains the same.

14.3 Linear response to time-dependent input

We consider a homogeneous population of independent neurons. All neurons receive the same time-dependent input current $I(t)$ which varies about the mean I_0. For constant input I_0 the population would fire at an activity A_0 which we can derive from the neuronal gain function. We require that the variations of the input

$$I(t) = I_0 + \Delta I(t) \tag{14.41}$$

are small enough for the population activity to stay close to the value A_0

$$A(t) = A_0 + \Delta A(t), \tag{14.42}$$

with $|\Delta A| \ll A_0$.

In that case, we may expand the right-hand side of the population equation $A(t) = \int_{-\infty}^{t} P_I(t|\hat{t}) A(\hat{t}) \, d\hat{t}$ into a Taylor series about A_0 to linear order in ΔA. In this section, we want to show that for spiking neuron models (either integrate-and-fire or SRM$_0$ neurons) the linearized population equation can be written in the form

$$\Delta A(t) = \int_{-\infty}^{t} P_0(t - \hat{t}) \Delta A(\hat{t}) \, d\hat{t} + A_0 \frac{d}{dt} \int_{0}^{\infty} \mathscr{L}(x) \Delta h(t - x) \, dx, \tag{14.43}$$

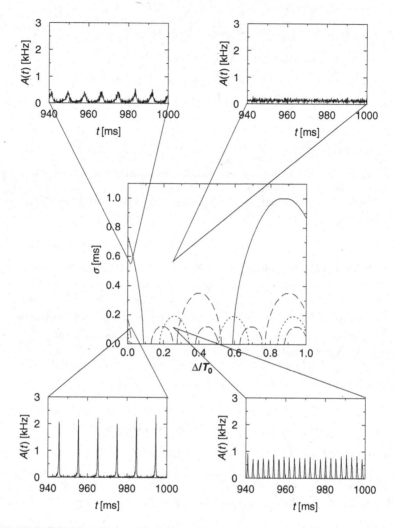

Fig. 14.8 Stability diagram (center) for the state of asynchronous firing in a network of SRM_0 neurons with reset noise as a function of the noise level (y-axis) and the delay Δ^{ax} (x-axis). The noise level is characterized by the standard deviation σ_{ISI} of the interspike-interval distribution divided by the mean interval T_0. The diagram shows the borders of the stability region with respect to $\omega_1, \ldots, \omega_4$. For high values of noise, the asynchronous firing state is always stable. If the noise is reduced, the asynchronous state becomes unstable with respect to an oscillation either with frequency ω_1 (solid border lines), or ω_2 (long-dashed border lines), ω_3 (short-dashed border lines), or ω_4 (long-short-dashed border lines). Four insets show typical patterns of the activity as a function of time taken from a simulation with $N = 1000$ neurons. Parameters are $\sigma_{ISI} = 0.5$ ms and $\Delta^{ax} = 0.2$ ms (top left); $\sigma_{ISI} = 0.5$ ms and $\Delta^{ax} = 2.0$ ms (top right); $\sigma_{ISI} = 0.1$ ms and $\Delta^{ax} = 0.2$ ms (bottom left); $\sigma_{ISI} = 0.1$ ms and $\Delta^{ax} = 2.0$ ms (bottom right). Neuronal parameters are $J_0 = 1$ and $\tau = 4$ ms. The threshold ϑ was adjusted so that the mean interspike interval is $T_0 = 2\tau = 8$ ms. Adapted from Gerstner (2000).

where $P_0(t - \hat{t})$ is the interval distribution for constant input I_0, $\mathcal{L}(x)$ is a real-valued function that plays the role of an integral kernel, and

$$\Delta h(t) = \int_0^\infty \kappa(s)\,\Delta I(t-s)\,\mathrm{d}s \qquad (14.44)$$

is the input potential generated by the time-dependent part of the input current. The first term of the right-hand side of Eq. (14.43) takes into account that previous perturbations $\Delta A(\hat{t})$ with $\hat{t} < t$ have an after-effect one interspike interval later. The second term describes the immediate response to a change in the input potential. If we want to understand the response of the population to an input current $\Delta I(t)$, we need to know the characteristics of the kernel $\mathcal{L}(x)$. The main task of this section is therefore the calculation of $\mathcal{L}(x)$ to be performed in Section 14.3.1.

The linearization of the integral equation (Gerstner, 2000) is analogous to the linearization of the membrane potential density equations (Brunel and Hakim, 1999) that was presented in Chapter 13. In order to arrive at the standard formula for the linear response,

$$A(t) = A_0 + \int_0^\infty G(s)\,\Delta I(t-s)\,\mathrm{d}s, \qquad (14.45)$$

we insert Eq. (14.44) into Eq. (14.43) and take the Fourier transform. For $\omega \neq 0$ we find

$$\hat{A}(\omega) = i\omega \frac{A_0 \hat{\mathcal{L}}(\omega)\,\hat{\kappa}(\omega)}{1 - \hat{P}(\omega)}\,\hat{I}(\omega) = \hat{G}(\omega)\,\hat{I}(\omega). \qquad (14.46)$$

Hats denote transformed quantities, i.e., $\hat{\kappa}(\omega) = \int \kappa_0(s)\exp(-i\omega s)\,\mathrm{d}s$ is the Fourier transform of the response kernel; $\hat{P}(\omega)$ is the Fourier transform of the interval distribution $P_0(t - \hat{t})$; and $\hat{\mathcal{L}}(\omega)$ is the transform of the kernel $\mathcal{L}$. Note that for $\omega \neq 0$ we have $\hat{A}(\omega) = (\hat{\Delta A})(\omega)$ and $I(\omega) = (\hat{\Delta I})(\omega)$ since A_0 and I_0 are constant.

The frequency-dependent gain $\hat{G}(\omega)$ describes the linear response of the population activity to a periodic input current $\hat{I}(\omega)$. The linear response filter $G(s)$ in the time domain is found by inverse Fourier transform

$$G(s) = \frac{1}{2\pi}\int_{-\infty}^\infty \hat{G}(\omega)\,\mathrm{e}^{+i\omega s}\mathrm{d}\omega. \qquad (14.47)$$

A_0 is the mean rate for constant drive I_0. The filter G plays an important role for the analysis of the stability of the stationary state in recurrent networks (Section 14.2).

Example: Leaky integrate-and-fire with escape noise

The frequency-dependent gain $\hat{G}$ depends on the filter $\mathcal{L}(s)$, which in turns depends on the width of the interval distribution $P_0(s)$ (Fig. 14.9b and a, respectively). In Fig. 14.9c we have plotted the signal gain $\hat{G}(\omega)$ for integrate-and-fire neurons with escape noise at different noise levels. At low noise, the signal gain exhibits resonances at the frequency that corresponds to the inverse of the mean interval and multiples thereof. Increasing the noise level, however, lowers the signal gain of the system. For high noise

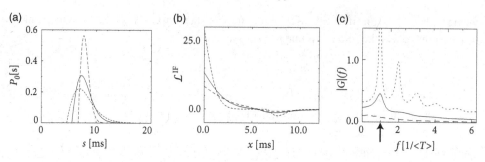

Fig. 14.9 Response properties of a population of leaky integrate-and-fire neurons with escape noise. (a) Interval distribution for three different noise levels. The escape rate has been taken as piecewise linear $\rho = \rho_0 [u - \vartheta] \Theta(u - \vartheta)$. The value of the bias current I_0 has been adjusted so that the mean interval is always $\langle T \rangle = 8$ ms. (b) The corresponding kernel $\mathscr{L}^{\mathrm{IF}}(x)$. The dip in the kernel around $x = \langle T \rangle$ is typical for integrate-and-fire neurons. (c) Frequency-dependent gain $|G(f)| = |\hat{G}(\omega = 2\pi f)|$. Low noise (short-dashed line): the sharply peaked interval distribution (standard deviation 0.75 ms) and rapid fall-off of kernel $\mathscr{L}$ lead to a linear response gain $\hat{G}$ with strong resonances at multiples of the intrinsic firing frequency $1/\langle T \rangle$. High noise (long-dashed line): the broad interval distribution (standard deviation 4 ms) and broad kernel $\mathscr{L}$ suppress resonances in the frequency dependent gain. Medium noise (solid line): a single resonance for an interval distribution with standard deviation 2 ms. Adapted from Gerstner (2000).

(long-dashed line in Fig. 14.9c) the signal gain at 1000 Hz is ten times lower than the gain at zero frequency. The cut-off frequency depends on the noise level. The gain at zero frequency corresponds to the slope of the gain function $g_\sigma(I_0)$ and changes with the level of noise.

14.3.1 Derivation of the linear response filter (*)

In order to derive the linearized response ΔA of the population activity to a change in the input we start from the conservation law,

$$1 = \int_{-\infty}^{t} S_I(t \,|\, \hat{t}) A(\hat{t}) \, d\hat{t};   \tag{14.48}$$

compare Eq. (14.8). As we have seen in Section 14.1 the population equation (14.5) can be obtained by taking the derivative of Eq. (14.8) with respect to t, i.e.,

$$0 = \frac{d}{dt} \int_{-\infty}^{t} S_I(t \,|\, \hat{t}) A(\hat{t}) \, d\hat{t}.   \tag{14.49}$$

For constant input I_0, the population activity has a constant value A_0. We consider a small perturbation of the stationary state, $A(t) = A_0 + \Delta A(t)$, that is caused by a small change in the input current, $\Delta I(t)$. The time-dependent input generates a total postsynaptic potential, $h(t) = h_0 + \Delta h(t, \hat{t})$ where h_0 is the postsynaptic potential for constant input I_0 and

$$\Delta h(t, \hat{t}) = \int_{0}^{b(\hat{t})} \kappa(s) \Delta I(t - s) \, ds   \tag{14.50}$$

is the change of the postsynaptic potential generated by ΔI. Note that we keep the notation general and include a dependence upon the last firing time $\hat{t}$. For leaky integrate-and-fire neurons, we set $b(\hat{t}) = t - \hat{t}$ whereas for SRM$_0$ neurons we set $b(\hat{t}) = \infty$. We expand Eq. (14.49) to linear order in ΔA and Δh and find

$$0 = \frac{d}{dt} \int_{-\infty}^{t} S_0(t-\hat{t}) \Delta A(\hat{t}) \, d\hat{t}$$

$$+ A_0 \frac{d}{dt} \left\{ \int_{-\infty}^{t} ds \int_{-\infty}^{t} d\hat{t} \, \Delta h(s,\hat{t}) \left. \frac{\partial S_I(t \mid \hat{t})}{\partial \Delta h(s,\hat{t})} \right|_{\Delta h=0} \right\}. \quad (14.51)$$

We have used the notation $S_0(t-\hat{t}) = S_{I_0}(t \mid \hat{t})$ for the survivor function of the asynchronous firing state. To take the derivative of the first term in Eq. (14.51) we use $dS_0(s)/ds = -P_0(s)$ and $S_0(0) = 1$. This yields

$$\Delta A(t) = \int_{-\infty}^{t} P_0(t-\hat{t}) \Delta A(\hat{t}) \, d\hat{t}$$

$$- A_0 \frac{d}{dt} \left\{ \int_{-\infty}^{t} ds \int_{-\infty}^{t} d\hat{t} \, \Delta h(s,\hat{t}) \left. \frac{\partial S_I(t \mid \hat{t})}{\partial \Delta h(s,\hat{t})} \right|_{\Delta h=0} \right\}. \quad (14.52)$$

We note that the first term on the right-hand side of Eq. (14.52) has the same form as the population integral equation (14.5), except that P_0 is the interval distribution in the stationary state of asynchronous firing.

To make some progress in the treatment of the second term on the right-hand side of Eq. (14.52), we now restrict the choice of neuron model and focus on either SRM$_0$ or integrate-and-fire neurons.

(i) For SRM$_0$ neurons, we may drop the $\hat{t}$ dependence of the potential and set $\Delta h(t,\hat{t}) = \Delta h(t)$ where Δh is the input potential caused by the time-dependent current ΔI; compare Eqs. (14.44) and (14.50). This allows us to pull the variable $\Delta h(s)$ in front of the integral over $\hat{t}$ and write Eq. (14.52) in the form

$$\Delta A(t) = \int_{-\infty}^{t} P_0(t-\hat{t}) \Delta A(\hat{t}) \, d\hat{t} + A_0 \frac{d}{dt} \int_{0}^{\infty} \mathcal{L}(x) \Delta h(t-x) \, dx, \quad (14.53)$$

with a kernel

$$\mathcal{L}(x) = - \int_{x}^{\infty} d\xi \, \frac{\partial S(\xi \mid 0)}{\partial \Delta h(\xi - x)} \equiv \mathcal{L}^{\text{SRM}}(x). \quad (14.54)$$

(ii) For leaky integrate-and-fire neurons we set $\Delta h(t,\hat{t}) = \Delta h(t) - \Delta h(\hat{t}) \exp[-(t-\hat{t})/\tau]$, because of the reinitialization of the membrane potential after the reset (Gerstner, 2000). After some rearrangements of the terms, Eq. (14.52) becomes identical to Eq. (14.53) with a kernel

$$\mathcal{L}(x) = - \int_{x}^{\infty} d\xi \, \frac{\partial S(\xi \mid 0)}{\partial \Delta h(\xi - x)} + \int_{0}^{x} d\xi \, e^{-\xi/\tau} \frac{\partial S(x \mid 0)}{\partial \Delta h(\xi)} \equiv \mathcal{L}^{\text{IF}}(x). \quad (14.55)$$

Let us discuss Eq. (14.53). The first term on the right-hand side of Eq. (14.53) is of the same form as the dynamic equation (14.5) and describes how perturbations $\Delta A(\hat{t})$ in the

(a)

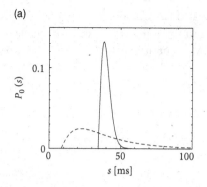

(b)

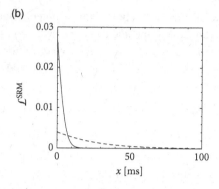

Fig. 14.10 Interval distribution (a) and the kernel $\mathscr{L}^{SRM}(x)$ (b) for SRM_0 neurons with escape noise. The escape rate has been taken as piecewise linear $\rho = \rho_0 [u - \vartheta] \Theta(u - \vartheta)$. For low noise (solid lines in (a) and (b)) the interval distribution is sharply peaked and the kernel $\mathscr{L}^{SRM}$ has a small width. For high noise (dashed line) both the interval distribution and the kernel $\mathscr{L}^{SRM}$ are broad. The value of the bias current I_0 has been adjusted so that the mean interval is always 40 ms. The kernel has been normalized to $\int_0^\infty \mathscr{L}(x)\,dx = 1$.

past influence the present activity $\Delta A(t)$. The second term gives an additional contribution which is proportional to the derivative of a *filtered* version of the potential Δh.

We see from Fig. 14.10 that the width of the kernel $\mathscr{L}$ depends on the noise level. For low noise, it is significantly sharper than for high noise.

Example: The kernel $\mathscr{L}(x)$ for escape noise (*)

In the escape noise model, the survivor function is given by

$$S_I(t|\hat{t}) = \exp\left\{ -\int_{\hat{t}}^{t} f[\eta(t' - \hat{t}) + h(t', \hat{t})]\,dt' \right\}, \tag{14.56}$$

where $f[u]$ is the instantaneous escape rate across the noisy threshold; see Chapter 7. We write $h(t, \hat{t}) = h_0(t - \hat{t}) + \Delta h(t, \hat{t})$. Taking the derivative with respect to Δh yields

$$\left. \frac{\partial S_I(t|\hat{t})}{\partial \Delta h(s, \hat{t})} \right|_{\Delta h=0} = -\Theta(s - \hat{t})\Theta(t - s) f'[\eta(s - \hat{t}) + h_0(s - \hat{t})] S_0(t - \hat{t}), \tag{14.57}$$

where $S_0(t - \hat{t}) = S_{h_0}(t|\hat{t})$ and $f' = df(u)/du$. For SRM_0 neurons, we have $h_0(t - \hat{t}) \equiv h_0$ and $\Delta h(t, \hat{t}) = \Delta h(t)$, independent of $\hat{t}$. The kernel $\mathscr{L}$ is therefore

$$\mathscr{L}^{SRM}(t - s) = \Theta(t - s) \int_{-\infty}^{s} d\hat{t}\, f'[\eta(s - \hat{t}) + h_0] S_0(t - \hat{t}). \tag{14.58}$$

Example: Absolute refractoriness (*)

Absolute refractoriness is defined by a refractory kernel $\eta(s) = -\infty$ for $0 < s < \delta^{abs}$ and zero otherwise. We take an arbitrary escape rate $f(u) \geq 0$. The only condition on f is that the escape rate goes rapidly to zero for voltages far below threshold: $\lim_{u \to -\infty} f(u) = 0 = \lim_{u \to -\infty} f'(u)$.

This yields $f[\eta(t - \hat{t}) + h_0] = f(h_0)\Theta(t - \hat{t} - \delta^{\mathrm{abs}})$ and hence

$$f'[\eta(t - \hat{t}) + h_0] = f'(h_0)\Theta(t - \hat{t} - \delta^{\mathrm{abs}}). \tag{14.59}$$

The survivor function $S_0(s)$ is unity for $s < \delta^{\mathrm{abs}}$ and decays as $\exp[-f(h_0)(s - \delta^{\mathrm{abs}})]$ for $s > \delta^{\mathrm{abs}}$. Integration of Eq. (14.58) yields

$$\mathscr{L}(t - t_1) = \Theta(t - t_1)\frac{f'(h_0)}{f(h_0)}\exp[-f(h_0)(t - t_1)]. \tag{14.60}$$

As we have seen in Section 14.1, absolute refractoriness leads to the Wilson–Cowan integral equation (14.10). Thus $\mathscr{L}$ defined in (14.60) is the kernel relating to Eq. (14.10). It could have been derived directly from the linearization of the Wilson–Cowan integral equation (see Exercises). We note that it is a low-pass filter with cut-off frequency $f(h_0)$, which depends on the input potential h_0.

14.4 Density equations vs. integral equations

In this section we relate the integral equation (14.5) to the membrane potential density approach for integrate-and-fire neurons that we discussed in Chapter 13. The two approaches are closely related. For noise-free neurons driven by a constant suprathreshold stimulus, the two mathematical formulations are, in fact, equivalent and related by a simple change of variables. Even for noisy neurons with subthreshold stimulation, the two approaches are comparable. Both methods are linear in the densities and amenable to efficient numerical implementations. The formal mathematical relation between the two approaches is shown in Section 14.4.3.

We use Section 14.4.1 to introduce a "refractory density" which is analogous to the membrane potential density that we saw in Chapter 13. In particular, the dynamics of refractory density variables follow a continuity equation. The solution of the continuity equation (14.4.2) transforms the partial differential equation into the integral equations that we saw in Section 14.1.

14.4.1 Refractory densities

In this section we develop a density formalism for spike response neurons, similar to the membrane potential density approach for integrate-and-fire neurons that we discussed in Chapter 13. The main difference is that we replace the membrane potential density $p(u,t)$ by a refractory density $q(r,t)$, to be introduced below.

We study a homogeneous population of neurons with escape noise. The neuron model should be consistent with time-dependent renewal theory. In this case, we can write the membrane potential of a neuron i in general form as

$$u_i(t, \hat{t}) = \eta(t - \hat{t}_i) + h(t, \hat{t}_i). \tag{14.61}$$

For example, a nonlinear integrate-and-fire model which has fired the last time at $\hat{t}_i$ and follows a differential equation $\dot{u}(t) = [f(u) + RI(t)]$ has for $t > \hat{t}_i$ a potential $u_i(t, \hat{t}_i) = h(t, \hat{t}_i) = u_r + \int_{\hat{t}_i}^{t} \dot{u}(t')dt'$ and $\eta = 0$. An SRM$_0$ neuron has a potential $u_i(t, \hat{t}) = \eta(t - \hat{t}_i) + h(t)$ with an arbitrary spike-afterpotential $\eta(t - \hat{t}_i)$ and an input potential h.

The notation in Eq. (14.61) emphasizes the importance of the last firing time $\hat{t}$. We denote the refractory state of a neuron by the variable

$$r = t - \hat{t} \geq 0, \tag{14.62}$$

i.e., by the time that has passed since the last spike. If we know r and the total input current in the past, we can calculate the membrane potential, $u(t) = \eta(r) + h(t, t - r)$. Given the importance of the refractory variable r, we may wonder how many neurons in the population have a refractory state between r_0 and $r_0 + \Delta r$. For a large population ($N \to \infty$) the fraction of neurons with a momentary value of r in the interval $[r_0, r_0 + \Delta r]$ is given by

$$\lim_{N \to \infty} \left\{ \frac{\text{neurons with } r_0 < r(t) \leq r_0 + \Delta r}{N} \right\} = \int_{r_0}^{r_0 + \Delta r} q(r, t)\, dr, \tag{14.63}$$

where $q(r, t)$ is the *refractory density*. The aim of this section is to describe the dynamics of a population of SRM neurons by the evolution of $q(r, t)$.

We start from the continuity equation (see Chapter 13),

$$\frac{\partial}{\partial t} q(r, t) = -\frac{\partial}{\partial r} J_{\text{refr}}(r, t), \tag{14.64}$$

where we have introduced the flux J_{refr} along the axis of the refractory variable r. As long as the neuron does not fire, the variable $r = t - \hat{t}$ increases at a speed of $dr/dt = 1$. The flux is the density q times the velocity, hence

$$J_{\text{refr}}(r, t) = q(r, t) \frac{dr}{dt} = q(r, t). \tag{14.65}$$

The continuity equation (14.64) expresses the fact that, as long as a neuron does not fire, its trajectories $r(t)$ can neither start nor end. On the other hand, if a neuron fires, the trajectory stops at the current value of r and "reappears" at $r = 0$. In the escape rate formalism, the instantaneous firing rate of a neuron with refractory variable r is given by the hazard

$$\rho(t|t - r) = f[\eta(r) + h(t|t - r)]. \tag{14.66}$$

If we multiply the hazard (14.66) with the density $q(r, t)$, we get the loss per unit of time,

$$J_{\text{loss}} = -\rho(t|t - r)\, q(r, t). \tag{14.67}$$

The total number of trajectories that disappear at time t due to firing is equal to the population activity, i.e.,

$$A(t) = \int_0^{\infty} \rho(t|t - r)\, q(r, t)dr. \tag{14.68}$$

The loss (14.67) has to be added as a "sink" term on the right-hand side of the continuity equation, while the activity $A(t)$ acts as a source at $r = 0$. The full dynamics is

$$\frac{\partial}{\partial t}q(r,t) = -\left[\frac{\partial}{\partial r}q(r,t)\right] - \rho(t|t-r)\,q(r,t) + \delta(r)A(t)\,. \qquad (14.69)$$

This partial differential equation is the analog of the Fokker–Planck equation (13.16) for the membrane potential density of integrate-and-fire neurons. The relation between the two equations will be discussed in Section 14.4.3.

Equation (14.69) can be integrated analytically and rewritten in the form of an integral equation for the population activity. The mathematical details of the integration will be presented below. The final result is

$$A(t) = \int_{-\infty}^{t} P_I(t|\hat{t})A(\hat{t})\,d\hat{t}\,, \qquad (14.70)$$

where

$$P_I(t|\hat{t}) = \rho(t|\hat{t})\exp\left[-\int_{\hat{t}}^{t} \rho(t'|\hat{t})\,dt'\right] \qquad (14.71)$$

is the interval distribution of neurons with escape noise; see Eq. (7.28). Thus, neurons that have fired their last spike at time $\hat{t}$ contribute with weight $P_I(t|\hat{t})$ to the activity at time T. Integral equations of the form (14.70) are the starting point for the formal theory of population activity presented in Section 14.1.

14.4.2 From refractory densities to the integral equation (*)

All neurons that have fired together at time $\hat{t}$ form a group that moves along the r-axis at constant speed. To solve Eq. (14.69) we turn to a frame of reference that moves along with the group. We replace the variable r by $t - r \equiv \hat{t}$ and define a new density

$$Q(\hat{t},t) = q(t-\hat{t},t)\,, \qquad (14.72)$$

with $\hat{t} \leq t$. The total derivative of Q with respect to t is

$$\frac{d}{dt}Q(\hat{t},t) = \frac{\partial}{\partial r}\,q(r,t)|_{r=t-\hat{t}}\,\frac{dr}{dt} + \frac{\partial}{\partial t}\,q(r,t)|_{r=t-\hat{t}} \qquad (14.73)$$

with $dr/dt = 1$. We insert Eq. (14.69) on the right-hand side of (14.73) and obtain for $t > \hat{t}$

$$\frac{d}{dt}Q(\hat{t},t) = -\rho(t|\hat{t})Q(\hat{t},t)\,. \qquad (14.74)$$

The partial differential equation (14.69) has thus been transformed into an ordinary differential equation that is solved by

$$Q(\hat{t},t) = Q(\hat{t},t_0)\exp\left[-\int_{t_0}^{t} \rho(t'|\hat{t})\,dt'\right]\,, \qquad (14.75)$$

where $Q(\hat{t},t_0)$ is the initial condition, which is still to be fixed.

From the definition of the refractory density $q(r,t)$ we conclude that $q(0,t)$ is the proportion of neurons at time t that have just fired, i.e., $q(0,t) = A(t)$ or, in terms of the new refractory density, $Q(t,t) = A(t)$. We can thus fix the initial condition in Eq. (14.75) at $t_0 = \hat{t}$ and find

$$Q(\hat{t},t) = A(\hat{t})\exp\left[-\int_{\hat{t}}^{t} \rho(t'|\hat{t})\,dt'\right]\,. \qquad (14.76)$$

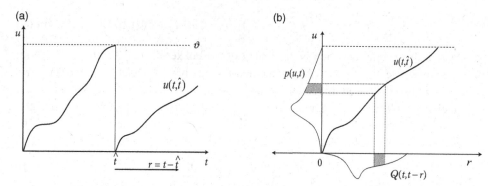

Fig. 14.11 (a) In a noise-free (nonlinear) integrate-and-fire neuron we define a refractory variable $r = t - \hat{t}$ and write the trajectory as $u(t, \hat{t})$. (b) The membrane potential density $p(u, t)$ at time t is plotted to the left as a function of the membrane potential u (vertical axis). The fraction of neurons $p(u, t) \Delta u$ with membrane potentials around u (gray shaded area) is proportional to the refractory density $Q(t, \hat{t}) \Delta \hat{t}$ (shaded area at the bottom).

On the other hand, from (14.68) we have

$$A(t) = \int_{-\infty}^{t} \rho(t|\hat{t}) \, Q(\hat{t}, t) \, d\hat{t} . \tag{14.77}$$

If we insert (14.76) into (14.77), we find

$$A(t) = \int_{-\infty}^{t} \rho(t|\hat{t}) \exp\left[-\int_{\hat{t}}^{t} \rho(t'|\hat{t}) \, dt' \right] A(\hat{t}) \, d\hat{t}, \tag{14.78}$$

which is the population equation (14.70) mentioned above. It has been derived from refractory densities in Gerstner and van Hemmen (1992) and similarly in the appendix of the papers by Wilson and Cowan (1972). If we insert Eq. (14.76) into the normalization condition $1 = \int_{-\infty}^{t} Q(\hat{t}, t) \, d\hat{t}$ we arrive at

$$1 = \int_{-\infty}^{t} \exp\left[-\int_{\hat{t}}^{t} \rho(t'|\hat{t}) \, dt' \right] A(\hat{t}) \, d\hat{t} . \tag{14.79}$$

Both the population equation (14.78) and the normalization condition (14.79) play an important role in the general theory outlined in Section 14.1.

For a numerical implementation of population dynamics, it is more convenient to take a step back from the integral equations to the iterative updates that describe the survival $Q(\hat{t}, t)$ of the group of neurons that has fired the last time at time $\hat{t}$. In other words, efficient numerical implementation schemes work directly on the level of the density equations (14.74). A simple discretization scheme for numerical implementations has been discussed above in Section 14.1.5.

14.4.3 From refractory densities to membrane potential densities (*)

In this section we want to show the formal relation between the dynamics of $p(u,t)$ and the evolution of the refractory densities $q(r,t)$. We focus on a population of nonlinear or leaky integrate-and-fire neurons with escape noise. For a known time-dependent input we can calculate the membrane potential $u(t,\hat{t})$ where the notation with $\hat{t}$ highlights that, in addition to external input, we also need to know the last firing time (and the reset value u_r) in order to predict the voltage at time t. We require that the input is constant or only weakly modulated so that the trajectory is increasing monotonously ($\partial u/\partial t > 0$).

To stay concrete, we focus on leaky integrate-and-fire neuron for which the membrane potential is

$$u(t,\hat{t}) = u_r \exp\left(-\frac{t-\hat{t}}{\tau_m}\right) + \frac{R}{\tau_m}\int_{\hat{t}}^{t}\exp\left(-\frac{t-t'}{\tau_m}\right)I(t')\,dt'. \qquad (14.80)$$

Knowledge of $u(t,\hat{t})$ can be used to define a transformation from voltage to refractory variables: $u \longleftrightarrow r = t - \hat{t}$; see Fig. 14.11a. It turns out that the final equations are even simpler if we take $\hat{t}$ instead of r as our new variable. We therefore consider the transformation $u \longrightarrow \hat{t}$.

Before we start, we calculate the derivatives of Eq. (14.80). The derivative with respect to t yields $\partial u/\partial t = [-u+RI(t)]/\tau_m$ as expected for integrate-and-fire neurons. According to our assumption, $\partial u/\partial t > 0$ or $RI(t) > u$ (for all neurons in the population). The derivative with respect to $\hat{t}$ is

$$-\frac{\partial u}{\partial \hat{t}} = \frac{RI(t)-u_r}{\tau_m}\exp\left(-\frac{t-\hat{t}}{\tau_m}\right) = F(t,\hat{t}) > 0, \qquad (14.81)$$

where the function F is defined by Eq. (14.81).

The densities in the variable $\hat{t}$ are denoted as $Q(\hat{t},t)$. From $Q(\hat{t},t)\,|d\hat{t}| = p(u,t)\,|du|$ we have

$$Q(\hat{t},t) = p[u(t,\hat{t}),t]\,F(t,\hat{t}). \qquad (14.82)$$

We now want to show that the differential equation for the density $Q(\hat{t},t)$ that we derived in (14.74),

$$\frac{\partial}{\partial t}Q(\hat{t},t) = -\rho(t|\hat{t})\,Q(\hat{t},t), \quad \text{for } \hat{t} < t, \qquad (14.83)$$

is equivalent to the partial differential equation for the membrane potential densities. If we insert Eq. (14.82) into Eq. (14.83) we find

$$\frac{\partial p}{\partial u}\frac{\partial u}{\partial t}F + \frac{\partial p}{\partial t}F + p\frac{\partial F}{\partial t} = -\rho\,pF. \qquad (14.84)$$

For the linear integrate-and-fire neuron and $I(t) = \text{const.}$ we have $\partial F/\partial t = -F/\tau_m$. Furthermore, according to our assumption of monotonously increasing trajectories, we have $F \neq 0$. Thus we can divide (14.84) by F and rewrite Eq. (14.84) in the form

$$\frac{\partial p(u,t)}{\partial t} = -\frac{\partial}{\partial u}\left[\frac{-u+RI(t)}{\tau_m}p(u,t)\right] - f(u-\vartheta)\,p(u,t), \quad \text{for } u_r < u < \vartheta, \qquad (14.85)$$

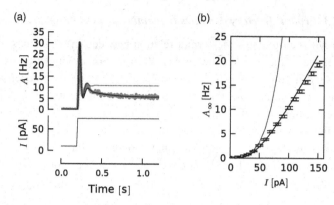

Fig. 14.12 Population of adaptive neurons in response to a step stimulus. The results from quasi-renewal theory are compared to a direct simulation of 25 000 neurons with parameters optimized for cortical cells. (a) The solution of the integral equation Eqs. (14.86) and (14.96) for the population activity (thin black line) is overlaid on the population activity calculated by simulating 25 000 SRM neurons with parameters capturing properties of cortical cells (see Chapter 11). The dotted line, which gives the solution of the integral equation of non-adapting neurons (time-dependent renewal theory, Eq. (14.5)), indicates that adaptation makes a major contribution to the observed population activity. (b) Comparing adapted activity A_∞ from simulations (squares, error bars correspond to one standard deviation) to predictions from renewal (dotted line) and quasi-renewal (black line) theory. Modified from Naud and Gerstner (2012a).

where we have used the definition of the hazard via the escape function $\rho(t|\hat{t}) = f[u(t,\hat{t}) - \vartheta]$ and the definition of the reset potential $u_r = \eta_0$. If we compare Eq. (14.85) with the Fokker–Planck equation (13.16), we see that the main difference is the treatment of the noise. For noise-free integrate-and-fire neurons (i.e., $\rho(t|\hat{t}) = 0$ for $u \neq \vartheta$) the equation (13.16) for the membrane potential densities is therefore equivalent to the density equation $\partial Q(\hat{t},t)/\partial t = 0$; see Eq. (14.83).

14.5 Adaptation in population equations

The integral equations presented so far apply only to neurons whose state does not depend on the spiking history, except on the most recent spike. Cortical neurons, however, show pronounced adaptation, as discussed in Chapter 11. Since time-dependent renewal theory cannot account for adaptation, the predicted population activity does not match the one observed in simulations; see Fig. 14.12.

As indicated in Eq. (14.12), the intuitions that have led to the integral equation (14.5) of time-dependent renewal theory, are still applicable, but the interval distribution must take into account the past history.

Let $P_{I,A}(t|\hat{t})$ be, again, the probability of observing a spike at time t given the last spike at time $\hat{t}$, the input current *and* the activity history $A(t)$ until time t; then the integral equation for adapting neurons is Eq. (14.12), which we recall here for convenience

$$A(t) = \int_{-\infty}^{t} P_{I,A}(t|\hat{t}) A(\hat{t}) d\hat{t}.$$ (14.86)

In this section, we develop the methods necessary to describe adapting neuron populations. First we present the systematic derivation of the integral equation Eq. (14.86). Then, in Section 14.5.2 we describe the event-based moment expansion which provides a framework for approximating $P_{I,A}(t|\hat{t})$.

14.5.1 Quasi-renewal theory (*)

Chapter 12 discussed the concept of a homogeneous population. We have seen that the activity of a homogeneous population of uncorrelated neurons can be seen as an average of the spike trains across the population, $A(t) = \langle S(t) \rangle_N$ where the subscript N denotes an average across the N neurons. Because neurons are stochastic, all neurons have different spiking histories. Accordingly, an average over a population is equivalent to an average over all possible past spike trains,

$$A(t) = \langle \rho(t|S) \rangle_S,$$ (14.87)

where $\rho(t|S)$ is the hazard (or instantaneous firing rate) at time t given the previous spikes in the spike-train $S(t)$ and the average $\langle \cdot \rangle_S$ is over all spike-train histories. In other words, $A(t)$ can be calculated as the expected activity averaged over *all* possible spike train histories, whereas $\rho(t|S)$ gives the stochastic intensity of generating a spike around time t given the *specific* history summarized by the past spike train S (Naud and Gerstner, 2012a).

The spike train S consists of a series of spikes $\hat{t}_1, \hat{t}_2, \dots, \hat{t}_n$. To average over all possible spike trains requires that we consider spike trains made of $n = 0$ to ∞ spikes. Moreover, for a given number n of spikes, all possible time sequences of the n spikes must be considered. This average takes the form of a path integral (Feynman et al., 2010) where the *path* here is the spike trains. Therefore, the average in Eq. (14.87) is

$$A(t) = \sum_{n=0}^{\infty} \int_{-\infty}^{t} \int_{-\infty}^{\hat{t}_1} \dots \int_{-\infty}^{\hat{t}_{n-1}} \rho(t|\hat{t}_1, \hat{t}_2, \dots, \hat{t}_n) P(\hat{t}_1, \hat{t}_2, \dots) d\hat{t}_n \dots d\hat{t}_1.$$ (14.88)

We emphasize that in Eq. (14.88) the spikes are ordered counting backward in time; therefore $\hat{t}_1$ is the most recent spike so that $t > \hat{t}_1 > \hat{t}_2 > \dots > \hat{t}_n$.

Each spike train can occur with a probability entirely defined by the hazard function

$$P(\hat{t}_1, \hat{t}_2, \dots, \hat{t}_n) = \left[\prod_{[\hat{t}_i \in S_n]} \rho(\hat{t}_i|S_n) \right] e^{-\int_{-\infty}^{t} \rho(x|S_n) dx}.$$ (14.89)

The equality follows from the product of two probabilities: the probabilities of observing the spikes at the times $\hat{t}$ given the rest of the history (the hazard function) and the probability of not spiking between each of the spikes (the survivor function). Again, it is a generalization of the quantities seen in Chapters 7 and 9. Writing the complete path integral, we have

$$A(t) = \rho(t)e^{-\int_{-\infty}^{t} \rho(x)dx} + \sum_{n=1}^{\infty} \int_{-\infty}^{t} \int_{-\infty}^{\hat{t}_1} \cdots \int_{-\infty}^{\hat{t}_{n-1}} \left[e^{-\int_{\hat{t}_1}^{t} \rho(x|\hat{t}_1,\ldots,\hat{t}_n)dx} \rho(t|\hat{t}_1,\ldots,\hat{t}_n) \right]$$

$$\times \rho(\hat{t}_1|\hat{t}_2,\ldots,\hat{t}_n)\rho(\hat{t}_2|\hat{t}_3,\ldots,\hat{t}_n)\ldots\rho(\hat{t}_n)e^{-\int_{\hat{t}_2}^{\hat{t}_1} \rho(x|\hat{t}_2,\ldots,\hat{t}_n)dx-\ldots-\int_{-\infty}^{\hat{t}_n} \rho(x)dx} d\hat{t}_n\ldots d\hat{t}_2 d\hat{t}_1.$$

$$(14.90)$$

The case with zero spikes in the past (the first term on the right-hand-side of Eq. (14.90)) can be neglected, because we can always formally assign a firing time at $\hat{t} = -\infty$ to neurons that have not fired in the recent past. We now focus on the factor enclosed in square brackets on the right-hand side of Eq. (14.90). This factor resembles $P_I(t|\hat{t})$. In fact, if, for a moment, we made a renewal assumption, the most recent spike were the only one that mattered. This would imply that we could set $\rho(t|\hat{t}_1,\ldots,\hat{t}_n) = \rho(t|\hat{t})$ inside the square brackets (where $\hat{t} = \hat{t}_1$ is the most recent spike) and shift the factor enclosed by square brackets in front of the $n-1$ integral over $\hat{t}_2,\hat{t}_3,\ldots,\hat{t}_n$. In this case, the factor in square brackets would become exactly $P_I(t|\hat{t})$. The remaining integrals over the $n-1$ variables can be recognized as the average of $\rho(\hat{t}_1|S)$ over the possible histories, i.e., $A(\hat{t}_1)$. Therefore the renewal assumption leads back to Eq. (14.5), as it should.

In quasi-renewal theory, instead of assuming $\rho(t|S) = \rho(t|\hat{t}_1)$ we assume that

$$\langle\rho(t|S)\rangle \approx \langle\rho(t|\hat{t}_1,S')\rangle_{S'}, \qquad (14.91)$$

where S' is made of all the spikes in S but $\hat{t}_1$. This assumption is reasonable given the following two observations in real neurons. First, the strong effect of the most recent spike needs to be considered explicitly. Second, the rest of the spiking history only introduces a self-inhibition that is similar for all neurons in the population and that depends only on the expected distribution of spikes in the past (Naud and Gerstner, 2012a). The approximation (14.91) is not appropriate for intrinsically bursting neurons, but should apply well to other cell types (fast-spiking, non-fast-spiking, adapting, delayed, ...). If we insert Eq. (14.91) into the terms inside the square brackets of Eq. (14.90), we can define the interspike interval distribution

$$P_{I,A}(t|\hat{t}) = \langle\rho(t|\hat{t},S')\rangle_{S'} \exp\left(-\int_{\hat{t}}^{t} \langle\rho(x|\hat{t},S')\rangle_{S'}dx\right), \qquad (14.92)$$

such that Eq. (14.90) becomes Eq. (14.86).

14.5.2 Event-based moment expansion (*)

The development in the previous subsection is general and does not rely on a specific neuron model nor on a specific noise model. In this section, we now introduce approximation methods that are valid for the broad class of Generalized Linear Models of spiking neurons with exponential escape noise, for example the Spike Response Model (see Chapter 9). The aim is to find theoretical expressions for $P_{I,A}(t|\hat{t})$ according to quasi-renewal theory

(Eq. (14.92)). In particular we need to evaluate the average of the likelihood over the past history $\langle \rho(t|\hat{t}_1, S') \rangle_{S'}$.

We recall the SRM model with exponential escape noise (Chapter 9). The instantaneous stochastic intensity at time t, given the spike history, is

$$\rho(t|S) = \overline{\rho} \exp \left(h(t) + \sum_{\hat{t}_k \in S} \eta(t - \hat{t}_k) \right) = \overline{\rho} e^{h(t) + [\eta * S](t)}. \tag{14.93}$$

Here, $h(t) = \int_0^\infty \kappa(s) I(t - s)\, ds$ is the input potential, $\eta(s)$ describes the spike-afterpotential introduced by each spike and $u(t) = h(t) + \sum_{\hat{t}_k \in S} \eta(t - \hat{t}_k)$ is the total membrane potential. The standard formulation of exponential escape noise, $\rho(t) = f(u(t) - \vartheta) = \rho_0 \exp[\beta\,(u(t) - \vartheta)]$, contains two extra parameters (ϑ for the threshold and $1/\beta$ for the noise level), but we can rescale the voltage and rate units so as to include the parameters β and ϑ in the definition of u and $\overline{\rho}$, respectively. The time course of η and κ and the parameter $\overline{\rho}$ can be optimized so as to describe the firing behavior of cortical neurons; see Chapter 11.

In the model defined by Eq. (14.93), all the history dependence is contained in a factor, $e^{\eta * S}$, which can be factorized into the contribution from the last spike and that of all previous spikes,

$$\langle \rho(t|I, \hat{t}, S') \rangle_{S'} = \overline{\rho} e^{h(t) + \eta(t - \hat{t})} \langle e^{[\eta * S'](t)} \rangle_{S'}. \tag{14.94}$$

In order to evaluate the expected values on the right-hand side of Eq. (14.92), we need to calculate the quantity $M_S[\eta] = \langle e^{\eta * S} \rangle_S$.

M_S is called a moment-generating functional because the functional derivative with respect to $\eta(t)$ and evaluated at $\eta(t) = 0$ yields the moments of S: $\frac{\delta M_S}{\delta \eta}[\eta = 0] = \langle S(t) \rangle$, $\frac{\delta^2 M_S}{\delta \eta^2}[\eta = 0] = \langle S(t) S(t') \rangle, \dots$. Explicit formulas for the moment-generating functional are known (van Kampen, 1992). One of the expansion schemes unfolds in terms of the correlation functions $g_k(t_1, t_2, \dots, t_k)$ and provides a useful framework for the approximation of our functional at hand.

We have already seen two examples of such correlation functions in various chapters of the book. The first term is simply the population activity $g_1(t_1) = \langle S(t_1) \rangle = A(t_1)$, i.e., the expectation value or "mean" of the spike count in a short interval $\Delta t \to 0$. The second term in the expansion scheme is the second-order correlation function which we encountered in Chapter 7 in the context of autocorrelation and the noise spectrum. There, the quantity $C_{ii}^0(s)$ is the stationary version of the slightly more general time-dependent correlation term $g_2(t_1, t_2) = \langle S(t_1) S(t_2) \rangle - \langle S(t_1) \rangle \langle S(t_2) \rangle$. Higher orders would follow the same pattern (van Kampen, 1992), but they will play no role in what follows.

Using the moment expansion, the expected value in Eq. (14.94) becomes

$$\langle e^{[\eta * S'](t)} \rangle_{S'} = \exp \left(\sum_{m=1}^\infty \frac{1}{m!} \int_{-\infty}^{\hat{t}} \left(e^{\eta(t - s_1)} - 1 \right) \cdots \left(e^{\eta(t - s_m)} - 1 \right) g_m(s_1, \dots, s_m)\, ds_1 \dots ds_m \right). \tag{14.95}$$

We call the expansion the event-based moment expansion. As a physical rule of thumb, the contribution of terms $m \geq 2$ in Eq. (14.95) decreases rapidly with increasing m, whenever the events (i.e., spike times at times t and t') are weakly coupled. For the purpose of Eq. (14.92), we can effectively ignore all second- and higher-order correlations and keep only the term with $m = 1$. This gives

$$\langle \rho(t|\hat{t}, S') \rangle_{S'} = \bar{\rho} e^{h(t) + \eta(t-\hat{t}) + \int_{-\infty}^{\hat{t}} (e^{\eta(t-z)} - 1) A(z) dz}. \tag{14.96}$$

Eq. (14.96) can be used as an excellent approximation in the survivor function as well as in the formula for the interval distribution $P_{I,A}(t|\hat{t})$ in Eq. (14.92). Used within the integral equation (14.12) it gives an implicit description of the population activity for infinite an population of adapting neurons.

14.6 Heterogeneity and finite size

Neuronal populations in biology are neither completely homogeneous nor infinitely large. In order to treat heterogeneity in local neuronal parameters, the variability of a parameter between one neuron and the next is often replaced by slow noise in the parameters. For example, a population of integrate-and-fire neurons where the reset value u_r is different for each neuron is replaced by a population where the reset values are randomly chosen after each firing (and not only once at the beginning). Such a model of slow noise in the parameters has been discussed in the example of Section 14.3. The replacement of heterogeneity by slow noise neglects, however, correlations that would be present in a truly heterogeneous model. To replace a heterogeneous model by a noisy version of a homogeneous model is somewhat ad hoc, but common practice in the literature.

The second question is whether we relax the condition of a *large network*. For $N \to \infty$ the population activity shows no fluctuations and this fact has been used for the derivation of the population equation. For systems of finite size fluctuations are important since they limit the amount of information that can be transmitted by the population activity. For a population without internal coupling ($J_0 = 0$), fluctuations can be calculated directly from the interval distribution $P_I(t|\hat{t})$ if the population consists of neurons that can be described by renewal theory; see Chapter 9. For networks with recurrent connections, several attempts toward a description of the fluctuations have been made (Spiridon *et al.*, 1998; Meyer and van Vreeswijk, 2002; Lindner *et al.*, 2005). Here we present a different approach.

If we consider a network with a finite number N of neurons, the integral equation (14.5), which describes the evolution of the population activity $A(t)$ in terms of the input-dependent interval distribution $P_I(t|\hat{t})$, should be written more carefully with expectation signs,

$$\langle A(t) \rangle = \int_{-\infty}^{t} P_I(t|\hat{t}) A(\hat{t}) d\hat{t} \tag{14.97}$$

so as to emphasize that the left-hand side is the *expected* population activity at time t, given the observed population activity at earlier times $\hat{t}$. In other words $N \langle A(t) \rangle \Delta t = N \langle m_0(t) \rangle$ is the expected number of spikes to occur in a short interval Δt. Here we have defined $m_0(t)$ as the fraction of neurons that fire in a time step Δt, just as in Section 14.1.5. Given the past input for $t' < t$ (which is the same for all the N neurons in the group), the firing of the neurons is independent in the next time step ("conditional independence"). Therefore in the limit of $N \to \infty$ the observed variable $m_0(t)$ approaches $\langle m_0(t) \rangle$ and we can drop the expectation signs.

For finite N, the variable $m_0(t)$ fluctuates around $\langle m_0(t) \rangle$. To determine these fluctuations, we assume that N is large, but finite. For finite N the population activity $A(t)$ can be written in the form of a "noisy" integral equation

$$A(t) = \langle A(t) \rangle + \sigma(t)\xi(t) = \int_{-\infty}^{t} \rho^{\text{noise}}(t|\hat{t}) S_I^{\text{noise}}(t|\hat{t}) A(\hat{t}) d\hat{t}, \qquad (14.98)$$

where $\xi(t)$ is a Gaussian colored noise, $A(\hat{t})$ is the observed activity in the past, $S_I^{\text{noise}}(t|\hat{t})$ is the fraction of neurons that have survived up to time t after a last spike at time $\hat{t}$, and $\rho(t|\hat{t})^{\text{noise}}$ is the stochastic intensity of that group of neurons. Starting from discrete time steps, and then taking the continuum limit, it is possible to determine the amplitude of the fluctuations as $\sigma(t) = \sqrt{\langle A(t) \rangle / N}$. Equation (14.98) can be used to evaluate the correlations $\langle A(t) A(t') \rangle$, in coupled networks of finite size (Deger *et al.*, 2013).

14.6.1 Finite number of neurons (*)

For the development of the arguments, it is convenient to work in discrete time. We use the formalism developed in Section 14.1.5. We introduce the variable $m_k^N(t) = N m_k^{(t)}$ to denote the number of neurons that have fired in the interval $[t - k\Delta t, t - (k-1)\Delta t]$ and have "survived" up to time t without firing again. With this definition, $m_0^N(t) = N A(t) \Delta t$ denotes the number of neurons that fire in the time step from t to $t + \Delta t$.

We start with the normalization condition in the quasi-renewal equivalent of Eq. (14.8) and multiply both sides by the number of neurons

$$N = \int_{-\infty}^{t} S_{I,A}(t|\hat{t}) N A(\hat{t}) d\hat{t}. \qquad (14.99)$$

This normalization must hold at any moment in time, therefore

$$m_0^N(t) = N - \sum_{k=1}^{K} m_k^N(t), \qquad (14.100)$$

where K is chosen big enough so that all neurons have fired at least once in the last K time bins.

In order to determine the value of $m_k^N(t)$ for $k \geq 2$, we focus on the group of neurons that has fired at time $\hat{t} \approx t - (k-1)\Delta t$. The number of neurons that have "survived" up to time $t - \Delta t$ without emitting a further spike is $m_{k-1}^N(t - \Delta t)$. In the time step starting at time t, all of these neurons have the same stochastic intensity $\rho(t|\hat{t})$ and fire independently with probability $p_F(t|\hat{t}) = 1 - \exp[-\rho(t|\hat{t})\Delta t]$. In a finite-$N$ discrete-time update scheme, the actual number of neurons $n_k(t)$ of neurons that fire in time step t is therefore drawn from the binomial distribution

$$P(n_k) = \left(\frac{[m_{k-1}^N(t - \Delta t)]!}{[n_k]! \, [m_{k-1}^N(t - \Delta t) - n_k]!} \right) [p_F(t|\hat{t})]^{n_k} \, [1 - p_F(t|\hat{t})]^{m_{k-1}^N(t - \Delta t) - n_k}. \quad (14.101)$$

In the time step starting at time t, the number of neurons that have last fired at $\hat{t}$ is therefore (for $k \geq 2$)

$$m_k^N(t) = m_{k-1}^N(t - \Delta t) - n_k(t). \quad (14.102)$$

Because of the shifting time frame used for the index k, neurons that are at time $t - \Delta t$ in group $(k-1)$ will be at time t in group k, except those that fired in the previous time step – and this is expressed in Eq. (14.102). Note that $m_k^N(t)$ is the *actual* number of neurons remaining in the group of neurons that fired the last spike at $\hat{t}$. Its *expected* value is

$$\langle m_k^N(t) \rangle = m_{k-1}^N(t - \Delta t) \exp \left[-\rho(t|t - k\Delta t) \, \Delta t \right] \qquad \text{for } k > 1 \quad (14.103)$$

as already discussed in Eq. (14.16). In the limit $N \to \infty$, the actual value will approach the expectation value, but for finite N the actual value fluctuates. The finite-N update scheme in discrete time is given by the iteration of Eqs. (14.102) and (14.100).

To arrive at an equation in continuous time, two further steps are needed. First, the binomial distribution in Eq. (14.101) is approximated by a Gaussian distribution with the same mean and variance. Second, we take the limit of Δt to zero and keep track of terms to order $1/N$ but not $1/N^2, 1/N^3, \ldots$. The result is Eq. (14.98). Note that for an uncoupled network of N neurons in the stationary case, fluctuations can also be directly calculated from the interval distribution as discussed in Chapter 7. The advantage of the approach presented here is that it works also for coupled networks.

14.7 Summary

Relating the microscopic level of single neurons to the macroscopic level of neuronal populations, the integral equation approach offers an interpretation of neuronal activity in terms of the interspike interval distribution. The integral approach can be related to partial differential equations. The formulation of partial differential equations with refractory densities exhibits a close formal relation with the membrane potential density equations of Chapter 13. In a direct comparison of the two theories, the first one developed in Chapter 13, the second here, it turns out that the integral equation approach is particularly useful in modeling populations of neurons that have multiple intrinsic time scales in refractoriness, synapses, or adaptation and escape noise as the model of stochasticity.

Population equations can be formulated for several coupled populations. At the steady state, the population can be in a state of asynchronous and irregular firing, but the stability of these solutions against emergence of oscillations needs to be checked. Stability can be analyzed using the linearization of the integral equations around a stationary state.

Heterogeneity in the population can be treated as slow noise in the parameters and finite size effects can be analyzed and included in the numerical integration scheme.

Literature

The original paper of Wilson and Cowan (1972) can be recommended as the classical reference for population equations. The paper contains the integral equation for neurons with absolute refractoriness as well as, in the appendix, the case of relative refractoriness. Note, however, that the paper is most often cited for a differential equation for an "ad hoc" rate model that does not correctly reflect the dynamics of neurons with absolute refractoriness. It is worth while also consulting the papers of Knight (1972) and Amari (1972) that each take a somewhat different approach toward a derivation of population activity equations.

The presentation of the integral equations for time-dependent renewal theory (Eqs. (14.5) and (14.8)) in this chapter follows the general arguments developed in Gerstner (1995, 2000) emphasizing that the equations do not rely on any specific noise model. The same integral equations can also be found in the appendix of Wilson and Cowan (1972) as an approximation to a model with heterogeneity in the firing thresholds and have been derived by integration of the partial differential equations for refractory densities with escape noise in Gerstner and van Hemmen (1992). The integral approach for adaptive neurons and the approximation scheme based on the moment-generating function were introduced in Naud and Gerstner (2012a).

The linearization of the integral equation can be found in Gerstner (2000) and Gerstner and van Hemmen (1993). The model of slow noise in the parameters is taken from Gerstner (2000). The escape noise model – which turns out to be particularly convenient for the integral equation approach – is intimately linked to the noise model of Generalized Linear Models, as discussed in Chapter 9, where references to the literature are given.

Exercises

1. **Integral equation of neurons with absolute refractory period**
   (a) Apply the population equation (14.5) to SRM neurons with escape noise which have an absolute refractory period

$$\eta(t) = \begin{cases} -\infty & \text{if } t < \Delta^{\text{abs}} \\ 0 & \text{otherwise.} \end{cases} \qquad (14.104)$$

   (b) Introduce the normalization condition Eq. (14.8) so as to arrive at the Wilson–Cowan integral equation (14.10).
   (c) Use Eq. (14.8) to show that the mean interspike interval of neurons firing stochastically with a rate $f(h_0)$ is

$$A_0^{-1} = \Delta^{\text{abs}} + f(h_0)^{-1}, \qquad (14.105)$$

   where h_0 is a constant input potential.

2. **Gain function of SRM neurons.** *Consider SRM neurons with escape noise such that the hazard function is given by* $\rho(s) = \overline{\rho}e^{h+\eta(s)}$ *with* $\eta(s) = \ln\left[1 - e^{-s/\tau}\right]$.
   (a) *Show that the survivor function in the asynchronous state is*

$$. S_0(t) = \exp\left(-\frac{rt}{\tau} + r(1 - e^{-t/\tau})\right),\tag{14.106}$$

   where $r = \tau\overline{\rho}e^h$.
   (b) *Using your results in (a), find the gain function* $A_0 = g(h_0)$ *for neurons.*
   Hint: Remember that the mean firing rate for fixed h_0 *is the inverse of the mean interval. You will have to use the lower incomplete gamma function* $\gamma(a,x) = \int_0^x t^{a-1}e^{-t}dt$.
   (c) *Suppose that you have SRM$_0$ neurons with an absolute and a relative refractory period as in Eq. (14.29). Calculate* A_0 *using your result from (b) and compare with Eq. (14.30).*

3. **Linearization of the Wilson–Cowan integral equation.** *The aim is to find the frequency-dependent gain* $\hat{G}(\omega)$ *for a population of neurons with absolute refractoriness.*
   (a) *Start from the Wilson–Cowan integral equation and linearize around a stationary state* A_0.
   (b) *Start with the filter in Eq. (14.60) and derive directly the filter* $\hat{G}$.

4. **Slow noise in the parameters.** *Consider a population of leaky integrate-and-fire neurons with time constant* τ_m *and resistance R, driven by a constant superthreshold input* I_0. *After each firing, the membrane potential is reset to* u_r, *which is chosen randomly from a distribution* $P(u_r)$ *with mean* $\langle u_r\rangle$.
   (a) *Calculate the interspike interval* T_0 *for a neuron i which was reset at time* t_0 *to a value* $u_i(t_0) = \langle u_r\rangle$ *and that of another neuron j which was reset at* t_0 *to* $u_j(t_0) = \langle u_r\rangle + \Delta u$.
   (b) *Suppose a Gaussian distribution of reset values with standard deviation* σ_r. *Show that the standard deviation* σ_{ISI} *of the interval distribution is* $\sigma_{ISI} = \sigma_r/\dot{u}(T_0)$ *where* $\dot{u}(T_0)$ *is the derivative of the membrane potential at the moment of threshold crossing.*

5. **Linear response filter with step-function escape rate.** *Consider* $f(u) = \rho\,\Theta(u - \vartheta)$, *i.e., a step-function escape rate. For* $\rho \to \infty$ *neurons fire immediately as soon as* $u(t) > \vartheta$ *and we are back to a noise-free sharp threshold. For finite* ρ, *neurons respond stochastically with time constant* ρ^{-1}. *The neuron mode is an SRM$_0$ with arbitrary refractoriness* $\eta(t - \hat{t})$ *driven by a constant input* h_0 *and a time-dependent component* $h_1(t)$. *The total membrane potential at time t is* $u(t) = \eta(t - \hat{t}) + h_0 + h_1(t)$ *where* $h_1(t) = \int_0^\infty \exp(-s/\tau_m) I_1(t - s)\,ds$.
   (i) *Show that the kernel* $\mathcal{L}(x)$ *for neurons with step-function escape rate is an exponential function.*
   Hint: Denote by T_0 *the time between the last firing time* $\hat{t}$ *and the formal threshold crossing,* $T_0 = \min\{s\,|\,\eta(s) + h_0 = \vartheta\}$. *The derivative of f is a* δ-*function in time. Use a short-hand notation* $\eta' = \frac{d\eta(s)}{ds}\big|_{s=T_0}$ *and exploit Eq. (14.58).*
   (ii) *Calculate the linear filter* $G(s)$ *and the response to an input current* $I_1(t)$.

15

Fast transients and rate models

The mathematical formalism necessary for a correct description of the population activity $A(t)$ in homogeneous networks of neurons is relatively involved – as we have seen in Chapters 13 and 14. However, the population activity A_0 in a *stationary* state of asynchronous firing can simply be predicted by the neuronal gain function $g_\sigma(I)$ of isolated neurons; see Chapter 12. It is therefore tempting to extend the results that are valid in the stationary state to the case of time-dependent input. Let us write

$$A(t) = F(h(t)),\tag{15.1}$$

where F is the gain function expressed with the input *potential* $h(t)$ as an argument, as opposed to input *current*. We choose a different symbol, because the units of the argument are different, but the relation of $F(h)$ to the normal frequency–current curve is simply $F(h) = g_\sigma(h/R)$ where $g_\sigma(I_0)$ is the single-neuron gain function for constant input I_0 at some noise level σ and R the membrane resistance.

The input potential h in the argument on the right-hand side of Eq. (15.1) is the contribution to the membrane potential that is caused by the input

$$h(t) = \frac{R}{\tau_m} \int_0^\infty e^{-\frac{s}{\tau_m}} I(t - s)\,\mathrm{d}s,\tag{15.2}$$

where τ_m is the membrane time constant. Eq. (15.2) can also be written in the form of a differential equation

$$\tau_m \frac{\mathrm{d}h(t)}{\mathrm{d}t} = -h + RI(t).\tag{15.3}$$

Integration of Eq. (15.3) with initial conditions $h(-\infty) = 0$ in the far past leads back to Eq. (15.2) so that the two formulations are equivalent.

By construction, Eqs. (15.1) and (15.2) predict the correct population activity for a *constant* mean input I_0. From Eq. (15.2) we have $h_0 = RI_0$ so that Eq. (15.1) yields the stationary activity $A_0 = F(h_0) = g_\sigma(I_0)$, as it should.

The question arises whether the rate model defined by Eqs. (15.1) and (15.2) (or, equivalently, by Eqs. (15.1) and (15.3)) is also a valid description for *time-dependent* stimuli. In other words, we ask whether the stationary solution of the population activity can be

(a)

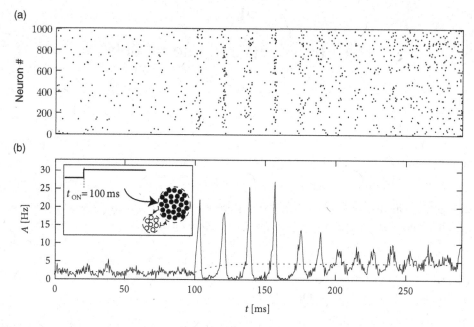

(b)

Fig. 15.1 Transients and rate models. All neurons receive the same step current stimulus at time $t_{ON} = 100$ ms. A randomly connected network of 8000 excitatory and 2000 inhibitory neurons exhibits an abrupt response to the change in the input. (a) The spike trains of 1000 excitatory neurons are shown. Vertical bands of greater spike density are short periods of high activity as shown in the population activity A to the right. Scale bars are 200 ms and 10 Hz. (b) The population activity $A(t)$ exhibits fast transients (full line). In a Standard Rate Model with population activity $A(t) = F(h(t))$, the new stationary state is approached on the time scale defined by the membrane time constant τ_m (here $\tau_m = 4$ ms, dotted line). The response to the input switch at $t_0 = 200$ ms is therefore comparatively slow.

extended to a "quasi-stationary" rate model of the population activity. To answer this question we focus in this chapter on the special case of step stimuli. Strong step stimuli cause a transient response, which can be abrupt in networks of spiking neurons (Fig. 15.1a), but is systematically smooth and slow in the rate model defined above (Fig. 15.1b).

Therefore the question arises whether the "normal" case for neurons *in vivo* is that of an abrupt and *fast* response (which would be absent in the rate model), or that of a smooth and *slow* response as predicted by the rate model. To answer this question, we start in Section 15.1 by taking a closer look at experimental data.

In Section 15.2 we use modeling approaches to give an answer to the question of whether the response to a step stimulus is fast or slow. As we shall see, the response of generalized integrate-and-fire models to a step input can be rapid, if the step is either strong and the noise level is low or if the noise is slow, i.e., not white. However, if the noise is white and the noise level is high, the response to the step input is slow. In this case the rate model defined above in Eqs. (15.1) and (15.2) provides an excellent approximation to the population dynamics.

(a)   (b)

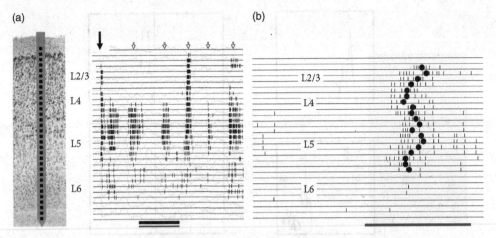

Fig. 15.2 Response of auditory neurons across different layers to short stimuli. (a) Left: Schematic drawing of an electrode with 32 sites overlayed on top of stained cortical tissue in order to show that the electrode crosses all cortical layers. Right: Spike responses of multiple neurons to a short click stimulus (solid arrows) and during spontaneous activity (open arrows). Horizontal scale bar: 500 ms. (b) Responses to a tone sustained during the shaded period. Solid circles indicate estimated peak of response. Scale bar: 50 ms. Neuron recordings in (a) and (b) are from primary auditory cortex. Figures adapted from Sakata and Harris (2009) with permission from Elsevier.

Finally, in Section 15.3, we discuss several variants of rate models. We emphasize that all of the rate models discussed in this section are intended to describe the response of a *population* of neurons to a changing input – as opposed to rate models for single neurons. However, it is also possible to reinterpret a population model as a rate model of a single stochastically firing neuron. Indeed, the single-neuron PSTH accumulated over 200 repetitions of the same time-dependent stimulus is identical to the population activity of 200 neurons in a single trial.

15.1 How fast are population responses?

Simultaneous measurements from many neurons *in vivo* with spike-time resolution are difficult. Fig. 15.2 shows two examples of simultaneous recordings across different layers in the primary auditory cortex. Each of the 32 recording sites is able to pick up activity of several neurons (Fig. 15.2a). The group of recorded neurons in layer 4 responds to a short tone stimulus with a delay of about 15 ms (Fig. 15.2b); the neurons in other layers follow shortly thereafter. Based on several such experiments, we may conclude that population activity in layer 4 exhibits an initial sharp peak less than 20 ms after stimulus onset (Sakata and Harris, 2009). Unfortunately, the number of neurons that are recorded simultaneously in one layer is limited so that an interpretation in terms of population activity is difficult; nevertheless, the data suggests that transients can be fast and reliable on the time scale of 10 ms.

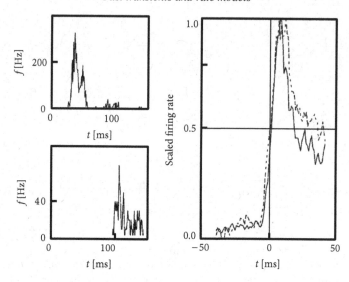

Fig. 15.3 Transient response of neurons in the visual cortex. At $t = 0$ a high-contrast grating is flashed on a gray screen. Top left: A neuron in visual cortex V1 of a behaving monkey responds with a sharp onset after a latency of 27 ms, as shown by the PSTH. Bottom left: Another neuron in V1 responds after a latency of 99 ms. Right: PSTHs of 73 neurons in V1 (solid line) and of 183 neurons in V4 (dashed line) were normalized to an amplitude of 1.0 and onsets were aligned at half the peak value (horizontal and vertical solid lines) and finally averaged. The rise time of the averaged PSTH is less than 10 ms. After the first peak, the firing rate drops off rapidly; adapted from Marsalek *et al.* (1997).

Alternatively, one can attempt to study population activity across many experiments with single-neuron recordings. Neurons in visual cortex V1 and V4 respond reliably to the onset of spatial gratings (Fig. 15.3), as seen in the PSTH accumulated over several repetitions of the stimulus presentation (Marsalek *et al.*, 1997). However, different neurons have different delays. If the PSTHs from many neurons are aligned onto the moment of the sharp rise of the PSTH response, then the resulting population activity exhibits an extremely sharp and abrupt onset peak, followed by a rapid decrease (Marsalek *et al.*, 1997). However, if the responses of different cells were aligned on the moment of stimulus onset, then the population response would look slower, which is not surprising given that the recordings do not come from a single homogeneous population.

In an *in vitro* preparation, the same step current input can be repeatedly given to the same neuron. In order to mimic additional stochastic spike arrivals that would be present *in vivo*, during each repetition a different realization of a noisy current can be added to the step current. Fig. 15.4 shows the response of pyramidal neurons in cortical layer 2/3 to such noisy step inputs, averaged over 12 different cells. The population activity in Fig. 15.4a exhibits a rapid transient, followed by a strongly damped oscillation (Tchumatchenko *et al.*, 2011). As we shall see in the following sections, the oscillatory component indicates

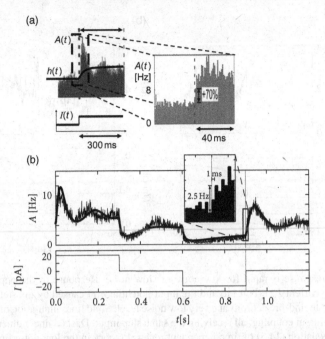

Fig. 15.4 Response of pyramidal cells *in vitro* to step input. (a) The PSTH response of pyramidal cells in cortical layers 2 and 3 averaged across 12 cells gives an estimate of the population activity $A(t)$. The step current ($I(t)$, bottom) generates an input potential $h(t)$ which responds much slower than the population activity $A(t)$. Right: Zoom into $A(t)$. Vertical dashed line indicates stimulus onset. Adapted from Tchumatchenko *et al.* (2011). (b) Experimental data from Tchumatchenko *et al.* (2011) are compared with the numerical integration of the integral equations for adaptive neurons (see Section 14.5). The input current is shown below.

that the noise level of the stochastic input component was chosen fairly low. For low noise, those neurons that fire together at stimulus onset enter together into a state of refractoriness and fire again after a time corresponding to the mean interspike interval. We can therefore conclude that populations of neurons *in vitro* exhibit, in the regime of low noise, a sharp transient, indicating a very fast response to step current input.

The theory of population activity (Fig. 15.4b) enables us to understand the responses found in the experiments, as we shall see in the next section.

15.2 Fast transients vs. slow transients in models

Populations of model neurons can exhibit fast abrupt responses or slow responses to a step current input. To predict whether the response is fast or slow, knowledge of the type and magnitude of noise turns out to be more critical than the details of the neuron model.

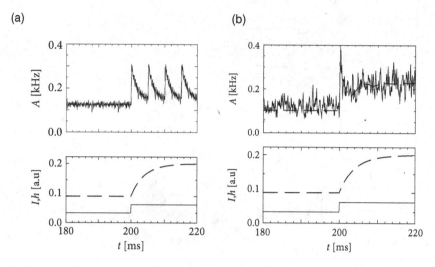

Fig. 15.5 The response is rapid for low noise or slow noise. Response of the population activity (top) to the step current $I(t)$ (bottom) and the input potential $h(t)$ caused by the step at $t = 100$ ms. (a) Leaky integrate-and-fire neurons at a very low noise level. Solid line: simulation of a population of 1000 neurons without coupling, all receiving the same step input. Dashed line: numerical integration of the integral equation (14.5) of time-dependent renewal theory in the low-noise limit; see Chapter 14. (b) Slow noise. Transients for SRM_0 neurons with noisy reset in response to the same step current. The results of a simulation of 1000 SRM_0-neurons (solid line) are compared with a numerical integration (dashed line) of the integral equation; see Eq. (14.5). The instantaneous response is typical for "slow" noise models. Bottom: Step current input I (solid line) and input potential $h(t)$ (dashed line). Note that the population responds instantaneously to the input switch at $t_0 = 100$ ms even though the membrane potential responds only slowly; taken from Gerstner (2000).

15.2.1 Fast transients for low noise or "slow" noise

A homogeneous population of independent leaky integrate-and-fire neurons with a low level of noise exhibits a sharp transient after the onset of a step current as shown in Fig. 15.5a. The onset transiently synchronizes a subgroup of neurons. Since all the neurons are of the same type and have the same parameters, the synchronized subgroup fires again some time later, such that the population activity oscillates with a period corresponding to the interspike interval of single neurons.

The oscillation is suppressed, and neurons desynchronize, if the population is heterogeneous or, for a homogeneous population, if neurons have slow noise in the parameters (Fig. 15.5b). The abrupt onset, however, remains, so that the transient after a switch in the input is extremely fast.

We can conclude that *fast transients* occur in a population of leaky integrate-and-fire neurons:

(i) at a low noise level and strong step current stimulation;

(ii) at a high level of "slow" noise, for example, slow variations in the parameters of the neurons or heterogeneity across the group of neurons.

In the first case, the onset triggers oscillations, while in the second case the oscillations are suppressed. The rapid transients in spiking models without noise or with slow noise have been reported by several researchers (Knight, 1972; Gerstner, 2000; Brunel *et al.*, 2001; Moreno-Bote and Parga, 2004).

Note that the time course of the response in the simulations with slow noise in Fig. 15.5b is reminiscent of the neuronal responses measured in the visual cortex; see Fig. 15.3. In particular, we find in the simulations that the rapid onset is followed by a decay of the activity immediately thereafter. This indicates that the decay of the activity is due to the reset or, more generally, to refractoriness after firing, and not due to adaptation or input from inhibitory neurons.

Whereas the low-noise result is independent of the specific noise model, the results for high noise depend on the characteristics of the noise. We analyze in Sections 15.2.2 and 15.2.3 the response to step currents for two different noise models. We start with escape noise and turn thereafter to diffusive noise. Before we do so, let us discuss a concrete example of slow noise.

Example: Fast transients with noise in parameters

We consider a population of SRM_0 neurons with noise in the duration of the absolute refractoriness. The membrane potential is $u(t) = \eta_r(t - \hat{t}) + h(t)$ where $h(t)$ is the input potential and

$$\eta_r(s) = \begin{cases} -c & \text{for} \quad 0 < s \leq \Delta^{\text{abs}} + r \\ \eta_0(s - \Delta^{\text{abs}} - r) & \text{for} \quad s > \Delta^{\text{abs}} + r. \end{cases}$$

The constant c is large enough to prevent firing during absolute refractoriness. After each spike the reset variable r is chosen independently from a Gaussian distribution $\mathscr{G}_\sigma(r)$ with variance $\sigma_r \ll \Delta^{\text{abs}}$. This is an example of a "slow" noise model, because a new value of the stochastic variable r is chosen only once per interspike interval. The approach of the neuron to the threshold is noise-free.

A neuron which was reset at time $\hat{t}$ with a value r fires again after an interval $T(\hat{t}, r)$ which is defined by the next threshold crossing $u(t) = \vartheta$. The interval distribution of the noisy reset model is

$$P_I(t|\hat{t}) = \int_{-\infty}^{\infty} dr \, \delta[t - \hat{t} - T(\hat{t}, r)] \mathscr{G}_\sigma(r). \tag{15.4}$$

The population equation (14.5) from Chapter 14 is thus

$$A(t) = \int_{-\infty}^{t} d\hat{t} \int_{-\infty}^{\infty} dr \, \delta[t - \hat{t} - T(\hat{t}, r)] \mathscr{G}_\sigma(r) A(\hat{t}). \tag{15.5}$$

A neuron that has been reset at time $\hat{t}$ with value r behaves identically to a noise-free neuron that has fired its last spike at $\hat{t} + r$. In particular we have the relation $T(\hat{t}, r) = r + T_0(\hat{t} + r)$ where $T_0(t')$ is the next interspike interval of a noiseless neuron ($r = 0$) that has fired its last spike at t'. The integration over $\hat{t}$ in Eq. (15.5) can therefore be done and yields

$$A(t) = \left[1 + \frac{h'}{\eta'}\right] \int_{-\infty}^{\infty} dr \, \mathscr{G}_\sigma(r) A[t - T_b(t) - r], \tag{15.6}$$

where $T_b(t)$ is the backward interval, i.e., the distance to the previous spike for a noise-less neuron ($r = 0$) that fires at time t. The factor $[1 + (h'/\eta')]$ arises due to the integration over the δ-function. We use the short-hand h' for the derivative $dh(t)/dt$ and η' for $d\eta_0(T(\hat{t}, 0))/dt$. We remind the reader that the interval $T(\hat{t}, r)$ is defined by the threshold condition $u(t) = \vartheta$ which gives, more explicitly, $\eta_r(T(\hat{t}, r)) + h(\hat{t} + T(\hat{t}, r)) = \vartheta$ (see Exercises).

We can interpret Eq. (15.6) as follows.

(i) The activity at time t is proportional to the activity $A(t - T_b(t))$ one interspike interval earlier.

(ii) Compared to $A(t - T_b(t))$, the activity is smoother, because interspike intervals vary across different neurons in the population, which gives rise to an integration over the Gaussian $\mathscr{G}_\sigma$.

(iii) Most importantly, compared to the activity $A(t - T_b(t))$ one interspike interval earlier, the activity at time t is increased by a factor $[1 + \frac{h'}{\eta'}]$. This factor is proportional to the *derivative* of the input potential as opposed to the potential itself. As we can see from Eq. (15.3), the derivative of h is discontinuous at the moment when the step current switches. Therefore, the response of the population activity $A(t)$ to a step current is instantaneous and exhibits an abrupt change, as confirmed by the simulation of Fig. 15.5b. We emphasize that the mathematical arguments that lead to Eq. (15.6) require neither an assumption of small input steps nor a linearization of the population dynamics, but are applicable to arbitrary time-dependent and strong inputs.

15.2.2 Populations of neurons with escape noise

For neurons with escape noise, the level of noise determines whether transients are sharp and fast or smooth and slow. For low noise the response to a step current is fast (Fig. 15.6a) whereas for a high noise level the response is slow and follows the time course of the input potential $h(t)$ (Fig. 15.6b). Analogous results hold for a large class of generalized integrate-and-fire models with escape noise, including SRMs and leaky integrate-and-fire models (Gerstner, 2000).

To analyze the response to step current inputs, we assume that the step amplitude ΔI of the input is small so that the population activity $A(t)$ after the step can be considered as a small perturbation of the asynchronous firing state with activity A_0 before the step. With these assumptions, we can use the linearized population activity equations (14.43) that were derived in Section 14.3. For the sake of convenience we copy the equation here

$$\Delta A(t) = \int_{-\infty}^{t} P_0(t - \hat{t}) \Delta A(\hat{t}) \, d\hat{t} + A_0 \frac{d}{dt} \int_0^{\infty} \mathscr{L}(x) \Delta h(t - x) \, dx. \tag{15.7}$$

(a)

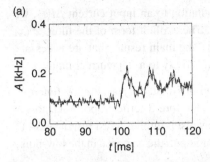

(b)

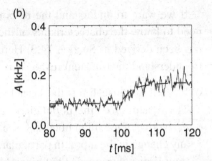

Fig. 15.6 Escape noise. Response of a network of 1000 SRM_0 neurons with exponential escape noise to step current input. The input is switched at $t = 100$ ms. Simulations (fluctuating solid line) are compared to the numerical integration of the integral equation (14.5) (thick dashed line). (a) For low noise the transition is comparatively sharp. (b) For high noise the response to the change in the input is smooth and slow.

We recall that $P_0(t - \hat{t})$ is the interval distribution for constant input I_0 before the step; $\mathscr{L}(x)$ is a real-valued function that plays the role of an integral kernel; and

$$\Delta h(t) = \int_0^{t-t_0} \frac{R}{\tau_m} e^{-\frac{s}{\tau_m}} \Delta I \, ds = R \Delta I \left[1 - \exp\left(-\frac{t-t_0}{\tau_m} \right) \right] \quad \text{for } t > t_0 \qquad (15.8)$$

is the input potential generated by step input of amplitude ΔI, switched on at time t_0.

The first term on the right-hand side of Eq. (15.7) describes that perturbations $\Delta A(\hat{t})$ in the past ($\hat{t} < t$) have an after-effect about one interspike interval later. Thus, if the switch in the input at time t_0 has caused a momentary increase of the population activity $A(t)$, then the first peak in A around t_0 can generate a second, slightly broader, peak one interspike interval later – exactly as seen in the experimental data of Fig. 15.4a. If the second peak is again prominent, it can cause a further peak one period later, so that the population activity passes through a phase of transient oscillations; see Fig. 15.6a. The oscillation decays rapidly, however, if the noise level is high, because a high noise level corresponds to a broad interspike interval distribution $P_0(t - \hat{t})$ so that successive peaks are "smeared out." Thus, the first term on the right-hand side of Eq. (15.7) explains the potential "ringing" of the population activity after a momentary synchronization of neurons around time t_0; it does not, however, predict whether the transient at time t_0 is sharp or not.

It is the second term on the right-hand side of Eq. (15.7) which predicts the immediate response to a change in the input potential Δh. In what follows, we are mainly interested in the *initial* phase of the transient, i.e., $0 < t - t_0 \ll T$ where $T = 1/A_0$ is the mean interspike interval. During the initial phase of the transient, the first term on the right-hand side of Eq. (15.7) does not contribute, since $\Delta A(\hat{t}) = 0$ for $\hat{t} < t_0$. Therefore, Eq. (15.7) reduces to

$$\Delta A(t) = A_0 \frac{\mathrm{d}}{\mathrm{d}t} \int_0^{t-t_0} \mathscr{L}(s) \Delta h(t-s) \, ds, \quad \text{for } t - t_0 \ll T. \qquad (15.9)$$

In the upper bound of the integral we have exploited that $\Delta h = 0$ for $t < t_0$.

If we want to understand the response of the population to an input current $\Delta I(t)$, we need to know the characteristics of the kernel $\mathscr{L}(x)$. The explicit form of the filter $\mathscr{L}(x)$ has been derived in Section 14.3. Here we summarize the main results that are necessary to understand the transient response of the population activity to a step current input.

(i) In the low-noise limit, the kernel $\mathscr{L}(x)$ can be approximated by a Dirac δ-function. The dynamics of the population activity ΔA has therefore a term proportional to the *derivative* of the input potential; see Eq. (15.9). This result implies a fast response ΔA to any change in the input. In particular, for step current input, the response in the low-noise limit is discontinuous at the moment of the step.

(ii) For a large amount of escape noise, the kernel $\mathscr{L}(x)$ is broad. This implies that the dynamics of the population activity is proportional to the *input potential h* rather than to its derivative. Therefore the response to a step input is slow and consistent with that of a rate model, $A(t) = F(h(t))$.

A summary of the mathematical results for the filter $\mathscr{L}(x)$ is given in Table 15.1. The formulas for leaky integrate-and-fire models differ slightly from those for SRM$_0$, because of the different treatment of the reset.

Example: Slow response for large escape noise

To understand how the slow response to a step at time t_0 arises, we focus on the right-hand side of Eq. (15.9) and approximate the kernel $\mathscr{L}(x)$ by a small constant c over the interval $0 < x < 1/c$. For $t - t_0 < 1/c$ (and as before $t - t_0 \ll T$), the integral then simplifies to $\int_0^\infty \mathscr{L}(s) \Delta h(t - s) \, ds \approx c \int_{t_0}^t \Delta h(t') \, dt'$; i.e., a simple integral over the input potential.

In front of the integral on the right-hand side of Eq. (15.9) we see the temporal derivate. The derivate undoes the integration so that

$$\Delta A(t) \propto \Delta h(t). \qquad (15.10)$$

This implies that the response to a change in the input is as slow as the input potential and controlled by the membrane time constant.

15.2.3 *Populations of neurons with diffusive noise*

Simulation results for a population of integrate-and-fire neurons with diffusive noise are similar to those reported for escape noise. For a small to medium amount of diffusive noise, the transient is fairly sharp and followed by a damped oscillation (Fig. 15.7a). For a large amount of noise, the oscillation is suppressed and the response of the population activity $A(t)$ is slower (Fig. 15.7b).

In the discussion of escape noise in the preceding section, we saw that the response to a

Definition	$\mathscr{L}^{\mathrm{SRM}}(x) =$	$-\int_x^\infty \mathrm{d}\xi\, \frac{\partial S(\xi\mid 0)}{\partial \Delta h(\xi - x)}$
	$\mathscr{L}^{\mathrm{IF}}(x) =$	$\mathscr{L}^{\mathrm{SRM}}(x) + \int_0^x \mathrm{d}\xi\, e^{-\xi/\tau}\, \frac{\partial S(x\mid 0)}{\partial \Delta h(\xi)}$
No noise	$\mathscr{L}_0^{\mathrm{SRM}}(x) =$	$\delta(x)/\eta'$
	$\mathscr{L}_0^{\mathrm{IF}}(x) =$	$\left[\delta(x) - \delta(x - T_0)\, e^{-T_0/\tau}\right]/u'$
Escape noise	$\mathscr{L}^{\mathrm{SRM}}(x) =$	$\int_x^\infty \mathrm{d}\xi\, f'[u(\xi - x)]\, S_0(\xi)$
	$\mathscr{L}^{\mathrm{IF}}(x) =$	$\mathscr{L}^{\mathrm{SRM}}(x) - S_0(x) \int_0^x \mathrm{d}\xi\, e^{-\xi/\tau}\, f'[u(\xi)]$
Reset noise	$\mathscr{L}^{\mathrm{SRM}}(x) =$	$\delta(x)/\eta'$
	$\mathscr{L}^{\mathrm{IF}}(x) =$	$\left[\delta(x) - \mathscr{G}_\sigma(x - T_0)\, e^{-T_0/\tau}\right]/u'$

Table 15.1 *The kernel $\mathscr{L}(x)$ that appears in Eq. (15.7) is given each time for integrate-and-fire neurons and SRM$_0$ neurons (upper index IF and SRM, respectively). Top row: The general case ("Definition"). Second row: Deterministic neuron model without noise. Third row: Neuron model with escape noise. Bottom: Neuron model with slow noise in the form of "reset noise," where the value of the reset has a small jitter. $S_0(s)$ is the survivor function in the asynchronous state and $\mathscr{G}_\sigma$ a normalized Gaussian with width σ. Primes denote derivatives with respect to the argument.*

step input is fast if the population activity reflects the *derivative h'* of the input potential. To understand when and how the derivative h' can play a role with diffusive noise, it is convenient to consider for a moment not a step current input but a current *pulse*. According to Eq. (15.3), a current pulse $I(t) = q\,\delta(t - t_0)$ which deposits at time t_0 a charge q causes a discontinuous jump of the input potential

$$\Delta h(t) = \begin{cases} 0 & \text{for } t \le t_0, \\ Rq/\tau_m & \text{for } t > t_0. \end{cases} \tag{15.11}$$

The central idea of the following arguments is shown schematically in Fig. 15.8. According to Eq. (15.11), all membrane potential trajectories jump at time t_0 by the amount $\Delta u = Rq/\tau_m$. The distribution of membrane potentials across the different neurons in the population, just before t_0, is described by $p(u)$. The step increase in the membrane potential kicks all neurons i with membrane potential u_i in the range $\vartheta - \Delta u < u_i < \vartheta$ instantaneously across the threshold which generates an activity pulse

$$\Delta A(t_0) \propto \frac{N_F(t_0)}{N}\, \delta(t - t_0), \tag{15.12}$$

where $N_F(t_0)/N = \int_{\vartheta - \Delta u}^{\vartheta} p(u)\,\mathrm{d}u$ is the fraction of neurons that fire because of the input

(a)

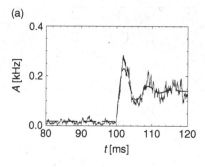

(b)

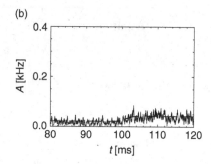

Fig. 15.7 Diffusive noise. Response of a network of 1000 integrate-and-fire neurons with diffusive noise to step current input. Simulations (fluctuating solid line) are compared to a numerical integration of the density equations (thick dashed line). (a) For low noise and a big (superthreshold) current step the response is rapid. (b) For high noise and a small current step the response is slower and does not exhibit oscillations.

current pulse. The Dirac δ-pulse in the activity indicates that $\Delta A(t)$ is proportional to the *derivative* h' of the input potential of Eq. (15.11). A population response proportional to h' is the signature of an immediate response to step currents.

The above argument assumes that the jump size is finite. The linearization of the membrane potential density equations (see Chapter 13) corresponds to the limit where the jump size goes to zero. Two different situations may occur, which are visualized in Figs. 15.8a and b. Let us start with the situation depicted in Fig. 15.8b. As the jump size Δu goes to zero, the fraction of neurons that fire (i.e., the shaded area under the curve of $p(u)$) remains proportional to Δu. Therefore, even in the limit of Δu to zero the linearized population equations predict a rapid response component. The fast response component is proportional to $p(\vartheta)$, i.e., to the density of the membrane potential at the threshold. For colored noise, the density at threshold is finite. Therefore, for colored noise, the response is fast (Fig. 15.9), even after linearization of the equations of the population dynamics (Brunel *et al.*, 2001; Fourcaud and Brunel, 2002).

For diffusive noise with white-noise characteristics, however, the membrane potential density vanishes at the threshold. The area under the curve therefore has the shape of a triangle (Fig. 15.8a) and is proportional to $(\Delta u)^2$. In the limit as Δu tends to zero, a linearization of the equation thus predicts that the response loses its instantaneous component (Brunel and Hakim, 1999; Lindner and Schimansky-Geier, 2001; Richardson, 2007).

The linearization of the membrane potential density equations leads to the linear response filter $G(s)$. The Fourier transform of G is the frequency-dependent gain $\hat{G}(\omega)$; see Chapter 13. After linearization of the population activity equations, the question of fast or slow response to a step input is equivalent to the question of the high-frequency behavior of $\hat{G}(\omega)$. Table 15.2 summarizes the main results from the literature. A cut-off frequency proportional to $1/\tau_m$ implies that the dynamics of the population activity is "slow" and roughly follows the input potential. Exponential integrate-and-fire neurons, which we identified in

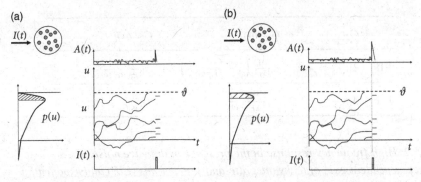

Fig. 15.8 Transients in a population of neurons with diffusive noise. (a) Rapid response to strong stimuli. A population of neurons (top left) is characterized by its distribution of membrane potentials (below left). Four representative trajectories are shown (right). In the stationary state of asynchronous firing, the population activity $A(t)$ fluctuates about a constant value A_0. Bottom right: If all neurons receive a common current pulse at time t_0, the membrane potential jumps by a small amount Δu. Therefore, all neurons with a membrane potential just below threshold (shaded area below $p(u)$) fire synchronously at time t_0, which gives rise to an instantaneous peak in $A(t)$. With white diffusive noise, the density $p(u)$ vanishes at the threshold ϑ. Therefore, the amplitude of the peak vanishes quadratically as the charge deposited by the current pulse decreases. (b) Rapid response to strong and weak stimuli. Same as in (a), except that the noise is slow, either slow noise in the parameters or colored diffusive noise. In this case, the area under the curve and therefore the amplitude of the peak in $A(t)$ vanishes linearly with the charge delivered by the current pulse. This gives rise to a rapid linear response. Schematic figure.

Chapter 5 as a good model of cortical neurons, are always slow in this sense. If there is no cut-off, the population activity can respond rapidly. With this definition, leaky integrate-and-fire neurons respond rapidly to a change in the input variance σ^2 of the diffusive noise (Lindner and Schimansky-Geier, 2001; Silberberg *et al.*, 2004; Richardson, 2007). A cut-off proportional to $1/\sqrt{\tau_m}$ means that the response of a population of leaky integrate-and-fire neurons to a step is slightly faster than that of the membrane potential but must still be considered as "fairly slow" (Brunel and Hakim, 1999).

We close with a conundrum: Why is the linear response of the leaky integrate-and-fire model fairly slow for all noise levels, yet the noise-free response that we have seen in Fig. 15.5a is fast? We emphasize that the linearization of the noise-free population equations does indeed predict a fast response, because, if there is no noise, the membrane potential density at the threshold is finite. However, already for a very small amount of white diffusive noise, the formal membrane potential density at the threshold vanishes, so that the linearized population equations predict a slow response. This is, however, to a certain degree an artifact of the diffusion approximation. For a small amount of diffusive noise, the layer below ϑ over which the membrane potential density drops from its maximum to zero becomes very thin. For any finite spike arrival rate and finite EPSP size in the background input or finite signal amplitude ΔI, the immediate response is strong and fast – as seen from the general arguments in Fig. 15.8.

	$G_I(\omega)$	$G_\sigma(\omega)$	$G_g(\omega)$
LIF	$A_0 \frac{R}{\sigma} \frac{1}{\sqrt{\omega\tau_m}}$	$A_0 \frac{1}{\sigma^2}\left(1 + \frac{\vartheta - h_0}{\sigma\sqrt{\omega\tau_m}}\right)$	$A_0 \frac{1}{g_0} \frac{\vartheta - h_0}{\sigma\sqrt{\omega\tau_m}}$
EIF	$A_0 \frac{R}{\Delta_T} \frac{1}{\omega\tau_m}$	$A_0 \frac{1}{(\Delta_T)^2} \frac{1}{\omega\tau_m}$	$A_0 \frac{1}{g_0} \frac{1}{\omega\tau_m} \log(\omega\tau_m)$

Table 15.2 *High-frequency response in the presence of diffusive noise. The frequency-dependent gain of leaky integrate-and-fire neurons (LIF) and exponential integrate-and-fire neurons (EIF) in response to a periodic modulation of the input current G_I, of the noise variance G_σ, or of the input conductance G_g. The neurons are subject to diffusive noise and described by the Fokker–Planck equation; see Chapter 13. The response G_σ of the LIF to modulations in the noise level is rapid, since it approaches a finite value for $\omega \to \infty$. The response G_I or G_g of the LIF to changes in input current or input conductance is fairly slow, since it decays at high frequencies with $1/\sqrt{\omega\tau_m}$. The response of the EIF is always slow (decay with $1/\omega\tau_m$) whatever the type of input. Parameters denote the input resistance R, membrane time constant τ_m, noise level σ_0, population activity in the stationary state A_0, and slope factor Δ_T of the exponential integrate-and-fire model (see Chapter 5). The table (adapted from Richardson (2007)) summarizes mathematical results of various sources (Brunel and Hakim, 1999; Lindner and Schimansky-Geier, 2001; Fourcaud and Brunel, 2005; Richardson, 2007).*

15.3 Rate models

The gain function $F(h)$ of rate models can always be chosen such that, for constant input $h_0 = RI_0$, the population activity $A_0 = F(h_0)$ in the stationary state of asynchronous firing is correctly described. The dynamic equations that describe the approach to the stationary state in a rate model are, however, to a certain degree ad hoc. This means that the analysis of transients as well as the stability analysis in recurrent networks will, in general, give different results in rate models than in spiking neuron models.

15.3.1 Rate models have slow transients

In Section 15.2 we saw that spiking neuron models with a large amount of escape noise exhibit a population activity $A(t)$ that follows the input potential $h(t)$. In this case, it is therefore reasonable to define a rate model $A(t) = F(h(t))$ in which the momentary activity $A(t)$ reflects the momentary input potential $h(t)$. An example is Eq. (15.1), which corresponds to a "quasi-stationary" treatment of the population activity, because the transform F is identical to the stationary gain function, except for a change in the units of the argument, as discussed in the text after Eq. (15.1). A similar argument can also be made for

(a)

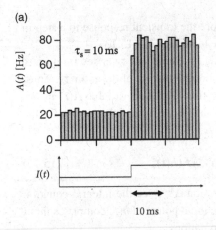

(b)

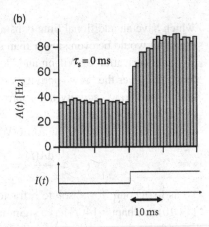

Fig. 15.9 Slow (colored) diffusive noise versus white diffusive noise. A population of integrate-and- fire models with a time constant of $\tau_m = 20$ ms was simulated and responses to a step stimulus reported in time bins of 1 ms. (a) Colored noise with a filtering time constant $\tau_s = 10$ ms leads to an abrupt, instantaneous response. (b) White noise leads to a smoothly increasing, fairly slow response. Figures adapted from Brunel *et al.* (2001). Copyright (2001) The American Physical Society.

exponential integrate-and-fire neurons with diffusive noise, as we shall see later in this section.

If we insert Eq. (15.2) into Eq. (15.1) we obtain

$$A(t) = F[h(t)] = F\left[\frac{R}{\tau_m}\int_0^\infty \exp\left(-\frac{s}{\tau_m}\right)I(t-s)\mathrm{d}s\right].\qquad(15.13)$$

Eq. (15.13) makes explicit that the population activity in the rate model reflects a *low-pass filtered* version of the input current. The transient response to a step in the input current is therefore slow.

Since differential equations are more convenient than integrals, we rewrite the input potential in the form of Eq. (15.3), which we repeat here for convenience

$$\tau_m\frac{\mathrm{d}h(t)}{\mathrm{d}t} = -h + RI(t).\qquad(15.14)$$

The input potential $h(t)$ resulting from the integration of Eq. (15.14) is to be inserted into the function F to arrive at the population activity $A(t) = F[h(t)]$. Note that the input current $I(t)$ in Eq. (15.14) can arise from external sources, from other populations or from recurrent activity in the network itself.

Example: Wilson–Cowan differential equation

Sometimes one finds in the literature rate models of the form

$$\tau_A\frac{\mathrm{d}\bar{A}(t)}{\mathrm{d}t} = -\bar{A}(t) + F(h(t)),\qquad(15.15)$$

which have an additional time constant τ_A. Therefore the transient response to a step in the input would be even slower than that of the rate model in Eq. (15.13).

In the derivation of Wilson and Cowan (1973) the time constant τ_A arises from time-averaging over the "raw" activity variable with a sliding window of duration τ_A. Thus, even if the "raw" activity has sharp transients, the time-averaged variable $\bar{A}(t)$ in Eq. (15.15) is smooth. In the theory of Wilson and Cowan, the differential equation for the population activity takes the form (Wilson and Cowan, 1972, 1973)

$$\tau_A \frac{d\bar{A}(t)}{dt} = -\bar{A}(t) + (1 - \Delta^{abs}) F(h(t))$$

(15.16)

so as to account for absolute refractoriness of duration Δ^{abs}; see the integral equation (14.10) in Chapter 14. F has a sigmoidal shape. The input potential $h(t)$ comprises input from the same population as well as from other populations.

Since there is no reason to introduce the additional low-pass filter with time constant τ_A, we advise against the use of the model defined in Eqs. (15.15) or (15.16). However, we may set

$$\tau_m \frac{dA(t)}{dt} = -A(t) + g_\sigma(I(t)),$$

(15.17)

where $I(t)$ is the input *current* (as opposed to the input potential). The current can be attributed to input from other populations or from recurrent coupling within the population. The low-pass filter in Eq. (15.17) replaces the low-pass filter in Eq. (15.14) so that the two rate models are equivalent after an appropriate rescaling of the input, even for complex networks (Miller and Fumarola, 2012); see also Exercises.

15.3.2 Networks of rate models

Let us consider a network consisting of K populations. Each population contains a homogeneous population of neurons. The input into population k arising from other populations n and from recurrent coupling within the population is described as

$$I_k(t) = \sum_n C_{kn} w_{kn} \int_0^\infty \alpha(s) A_n(t - s) \, ds.$$

(15.18)

Here $A_n(t)$ is the activity of population n and C_{kn} is the number of presynaptic neurons in population n that are connected to a typical neuron in population k; the time course and strength of synaptic connections are described by α and w_{kn}, respectively; see Chapter 12.

We describe the dynamics of the input potential h_k of population k with the differential equation (15.14) and use for each population the quasi-stationary rate model $A_n(t) = F_n(h_n)$ where F_n is the gain function of the neurons in population n. The final result is

$$\tau_m \frac{dh_k(t)}{dt} = -h_k + R \sum_n C_{kn} w_{kn} \int_0^\infty \alpha(s) F_n(h_n(t - s)) \, ds.$$

(15.19)

Eq. (15.19) is the starting point for some of the models in Part IV of this book.

Example: Population with self-coupling

If we have a single population, we can drop the indices in Eq. (15.19) so as to arrive at

$$\tau_m \frac{dh(t)}{dt} = -h + J_0 \int_0^\infty \alpha(s) F(h(t-s)) \, ds, \tag{15.20}$$

where J is the strength of the feedback. Thus, a single population with self-coupling is described by a single differential equation for the input potential h. The population activity is simply $A(t) = F(h(t))$.

Stationary states are found as discussed in Chapter 12. If there are three fixed points, the middle one is unstable while the other two (at low and high activity) are stable under the dynamics (15.20). The fixed points calculated from Eq. (15.20) are correct. However, stability under the dynamics (15.20) does *not* guarantee stability of the original network of spiking neurons. Indeed, as we have seen in Chapters 13 and 14, the fixed points of high and low activity may lose stability with respect to oscillations, even in a single homogeneous population. The rate dynamics of Eq. (15.20) cannot correctly account for these oscillations. In fact, for instantaneous synaptic current pulses $\alpha(s) = q\delta(s)$, where δ denotes the Dirac δ-function, Eq. (15.20) reduces to a one-dimensional differential equation which can never give rise to oscillatory solutions.

15.3.3 Linear-Nonlinear-Poisson and improved transients

To improve the description of transients, we start from Eq. (15.13), but insert an arbitrary filter κ,

$$A(t) = F(h(t)) = F\left[\int_0^\infty \kappa(s) I(t-s) ds\right]. \tag{15.21}$$

Equation (15.21) is called the Linear-Nonlinear-Poisson (LNP) model (Chichilnisky 2001; Simoncelli *et al.* 2004). It is also called a cascade model because it can be interpreted as a sequence of three processing steps. First, input is filtered with an arbitrary linear filter κ, which yields the input potential h. Second, the result is passed through a nonlinearity F. Third, in case of a single neuron, spikes are generated by an inhomogeneous Poisson process with rate $F(h(t))$. Since, in our model of a homogeneous population, we have many similar neurons, we drop the third step and interpret the rate $F(h(t))$ directly as the population activity.

For $\kappa(s) = (R/\tau_m) \exp(-s/\tau_m)$ we are back at Eq. (15.13). The question arises whether we can make a better choice of the filter κ than a simple low-pass with the membrane time constant τ_m. In Chapter 11 it was shown how an optimal filter κ can be determined experimentally by reverse correlation techniques.

Here we are interested in deriving the optimal filter from the complete population dynamics. The LNP model in Eq. (15.21) is an approximation of the population dynamics that is more correctly described by the Fokker–Planck equations in Chapter 13 or by the integral equation of time-dependent renewal theory in Chapter 14. Let us recall that, in both approaches, we can linearize the population equations around a stationary state of asynchronous firing A_0 which is obtained with a mean input I_0 at some noise level σ. The linearization of the population dynamics about A_0 yields a filter $G_I(s)$. We use this filter, and arrive at a variant of Eq. (15.21)

$$A(t) = \tilde{F}\left(\int_0^\infty G_I(s)I(t-s)\mathrm{d}s\right),\tag{15.22}$$

where $\tilde{F}(x) = g_\sigma(x/c)$ is a scaled version of the frequency–current curve $g_\sigma(I)$ and $c = \int_0^\infty G_I(s)\mathrm{d}s$ a constant which matches the slope of the gain function at the reference point for the linearization (Ostojic and Brunel, 2011). Models with this, or similar, choices of $\tilde{F}$ describe transient peaks in the population activity surprisingly well (see, e.g., Herrmann and Gerstner, 2001; Aviel and Gerstner, 2006; Ostojic and Brunel, 2011). Rate models based on Eq. (15.22) can also be used to describe coupled populations. Stability of a stationary state A_0 is correctly described by Eq. (15.22), if the filter $G_I(s)$ in the argument on the right-hand-side reflects the linearization of the full population dynamics around A_0, but not if the filter is derived by linearization around some other value of the activity.

Example: Effective rate model for exponential integrate-and-fire neurons

We denote the stationary gain function of exponential integrate-and-fire neurons by $g_\sigma(I)$ and the linear filter arising from linearization around a stationary activity A_0 by $G_I(s)$. For exponential integrate-and-fire neurons $G_I(s)$ has the high-frequency behavior of a low-pass filter that varies as $A_0 \frac{R}{\Delta_T \tau_m} \frac{1}{\omega}$; see Table 15.2.

We recall that the Fourier transform of an exponential filter also yields a high-frequency behavior that varies as $1/\omega$ with the inverse filter time constant as cut-off frequency. This suggests that, for the exponential integrate-and-fire model, we can approximate the time course of $G_I(s)$ as an exponential filter with an effective time constant $\tau_{\mathrm{eff}} \propto \tau_m/A_0$. This leads back to Eq. (15.22), but with an *exponential* filter $G(s)$. Hence, we are now nearly back to Eq. (15.13), except that the time constant of the exponential is different.

We now switch from the frequency current curve $g_\sigma(I)$ to the equivalent description of the gain function $F(h) = g_\sigma(h/R)$ where the argument of F has units of a potential. It is convenient to implement the exponential filter in the form of a differential equation for the effective input potential (Ostojic and Brunel, 2011)

$$\tau_{\mathrm{eff}}(t)\frac{\mathrm{d}h}{\mathrm{d}t} = -h + RI(t),\tag{15.23}$$

with an effective time constant

$$\tau_{\mathrm{eff}}(t) = \tau_m \frac{\Delta_T F'}{A_0(t)},\tag{15.24}$$

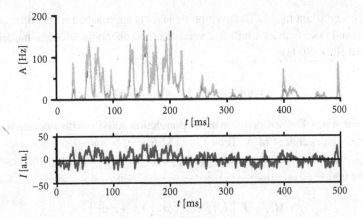

Fig. 15.10 Population of exponential integrate-and-fire neurons. The population activity $A(t)$ arising from a explicit simulation of N model neurons (black solid line) can be approximated by a rate model with effective time constant $\tau_{\text{eff}}(t)$ (gray overlaid). The stimulation is shown in the bottom panel. Figure adapted from (Ostojic and Brunel, 2011).

where $A_0(t)$ is the activity averaged over one or a few previous time steps and $F' = dF/dh$ is the derivative of the gain function at an appropriately chosen reference point h_0, so that $F(h_0) \approx \langle A_0(t) \rangle$ is the long-term average of the activity.

In each time step, we update the input using Eq. (15.23) and calculate the activity as $A(t) = F(h(t))$ with $F(h) = g_\sigma(h/R)$. Such a rate model gives an excellent approximation of the activity in a population of exponential integrate-and-fire neurons (Fig. 15.10). Note that fast transients are well described, because the effective time constant is shortened as soon as the population activity increases.

15.3.4 Adaptation

So far we have focused on the initial transient after a step in the input current. After the initial transient, however, follows a second, much slower phase of adaptation during which the population response decreases, even if the stimulation is kept constant. For single neurons, adaptation has been discussed in Chapter 6.

In a population of neurons, adaptation can be described as an effective decrease in the input potential. If a population of non-adaptive neurons has an activity described by the gain function $A(t) = F(h(t))$, then the population rate model for adaptive neurons is

$$A(t) = F(h(t) - a(t)), \tag{15.25}$$

where $a(t)$ describes the amount of adaptation that neurons have accumulated, and

$$\tau_a(A)\frac{da}{dt} = a_\infty(A) - a, \tag{15.26}$$

where $a_\infty(A)$ is the asymptotic level of adaptation that is attained if the population continuously fires at a constant rate A. The asymptotic level is approached with a time constant τ_a. Eqs. (15.25) and (15.26) are a simplified version of the phenomenological model proposed in Benda and Herz (2003).

Example: Effective adaptation filter

Suppose that $a_\infty(A) = cA$ is linear in the population activity with a constant $c > 0$ and $\tau_a(A) = \tau_a$ is independent of A. Then Eq. (15.26) can be integrated and yields $a(t) = \int_0^\infty \gamma(s) A(t-s) ds$ with a filter $\gamma(s) = (c/\tau_a) \exp(-s/\tau_a)$. We insert the result in Eq. (15.25) and find

$$A(t) = F\left(h(t) - \int_0^\infty \gamma(s) A(t-s) ds \right). \tag{15.27}$$

Equation (15.27) nicely describes the adaptation process but it misses, like other rate models, the sharp initial transient, and potential transient oscillation, caused by the synchronization of the population at the moment of the step (Naud and Gerstner, 2012a).

15.4 Summary

The population activity of spiking neuron models responds to a big and rapid change in the input current much faster than the input potential. The response of the input potential is characterized by the membrane time constant τ_m and therefore exhibits the properties of a low-pass filter. In an asynchronously firing population of neurons, however, there are always a few neurons with membrane potential just below the threshold. These neurons respond quasi-instantaneously to a step in the input current, despite the fact that the input potential, i.e., the contribution to the membrane potential that is caused by the input, responds slowly.

The details of the response depend on the neuron model as well as on the amplitude of the signal and the type of noise. With slow noise as the dominant noise source, model neurons respond quickly and reliably to a step input. For white noise, the picture is more complicated.

For Spike Response Model neurons with escape noise, the speed of the response depends on the noise level. While the response is fast for low noise, it is as slow as the membrane potential in the limit of high noise.

For a large amount of diffusive white noise and a small amplitude of the input signal, the choice of neuron model plays an important role. Leaky integrate-and-fire models respond fairly slowly, but faster than the input potential. The response of exponential integrate-and-fire models follows that of the effective membrane potential, but the effective membrane time constant depends on the population activity.

The fact that spiking neuron models in the high-noise limit respond slowly can be used to derive rate models for the population activity. Such rate models are the basis for the analysis of cognitive dynamics in Part IV of the book. Nevertheless, it should be kept in mind that standard rate models miss the rapid transients that a population of spiking models exhibits in response to signals that are strong compared to the level of noise.

Literature

The rapid transients in spiking models without noise or with slow noise have been reported by several researchers, probably first by Knight (1972) and have later been rediscovered several times (Gerstner, 2000; Brunel et al., 2001; Moreno-Bote and Parga, 2004).

The analysis of transients in the escape rate has been performed in Gerstner (2000), where the limits of high noise and low noise are also discussed. For the linearization of the membrane potential density equations and analysis of transient behavior in neuron models with diffusive noise see Brunel and Hakim (1999); Lindner and Schimansky-Geier (2001); Fourcaud and Brunel (2005); and Richardson (2007). Experimental data on transients in the linearized regime can be found in Silberberg et al. (2004) and Tchumatchenko et al. (2011).

Simoncelli et al. (2004) give an authoritative summary of LNP models. How generalized integrate-and-fire models can be mapped to LNP models has been discussed in Aviel and Gerstner (2006) and Ostojic and Brunel (2011). An excellent overview of the central concepts of rate models with adaptation can be found in Benda and Herz (2003).

Exercises

1. **Population of noise-free neurons**
   (a) *Show that for noise-free neurons the population activity equation yields*

   $$A(t) = \frac{1}{1 + T'(\hat{t})} A(\hat{t}), \tag{15.28}$$

   where $T(\hat{t})$ is the interspike interval of a neuron that has fired its last spike at time $\hat{t}$, and the prime denotes the derivative.
   Hints: In the limit of no noise, the input-dependent interval distribution $P_I(t|\hat{t})$ reduces to a Dirac δ-function, i.e.,

   $$P_I(t|\hat{t}) = \delta[t - \hat{t} - T(\hat{t})], \tag{15.29}$$

   where $T(\hat{t})$ is given implicitly by the threshold condition

   $$T(\hat{t}) = \min\{(t - \hat{t})\,|\,u(t) = \vartheta; \dot{u} > 0, t > \hat{t}\}. \tag{15.30}$$

   Recall from the rules for δ-functions that

   $$\int_a^b \delta[f(x)]\,g(x)\,dx = \frac{g(x_0)}{|f'(x_0)|}, \tag{15.31}$$

   if f has a single zero-crossing $f(x_0) = 0$ in the interval $a < x_0 < b$ with $f'(x_0) \neq 0$.
   (b) *Assume SRM_0 neurons with $u(t) = \eta(t - \hat{t}) + h(t)$. Show that*

   $$A(t) = \frac{h'(t)}{\eta'T} A(\hat{t}). \tag{15.32}$$

Hint: Use the results from (a).

(c) *An input current of amplitue I_1 is switched on at time $t = 0$. Assume an input potential $h(t) = h_0$ for $t < 0$ and $h(t) = (R/\tau) \int_0^t \exp(-s/\tau) I_1$ for $t > 0$. Show that the transient of the population activity after the step at $t = 0$ is instantaneous, despite the fact that the input potential responds slowly.*

2. **LNP and frequency–current curve.** *Around Eq. (15.22), it was argued that a model*

$$A(t) = \hat{F} \left(\int_0^\infty G_I(s) I(t - s) \mathrm{d}s \right) \tag{15.33}$$

with a choice $\hat{F}(x) = g_\sigma(x/[\int_0^\infty G_I(s) \mathrm{d}s])$ is optimal. The aim is to make the notion of optimality more precise.

(a) *Show that for constant, but arbitrary, input I_0, Eq. (15.33) leads to $A_0 = g_\sigma(I_0)$, consistent with the general results of Chapter 12.*

(b) *Suppose that $G_I(s)$ is the linearization of the population activity equations around A_0 which is achieved for a constant input I_0. Show that linearization of Eq. (15.33) leads to $\Delta A(t) = \int_0^\infty G(s) \Delta I(t - s) \mathrm{d}s$.*

Hint: Recall that the response at zero frequency, $\hat{G}(0) = \int_0^\infty G(s) \mathrm{d}s$, is related to the slope of the gain function.

(c) *Interpret the results from (a) and (b) and explain the range of validity of the model defined in Eq. (15.33). What can happen if the input varies about a mean $I_1 \neq I_0$? What happens if the variations around I_0 are big?*

3. **Leaky integrate-and-fire with white diffusive noise.** *According to the results given in Table 15.2, the linear filter $G_I(s)$ of leaky integrate-and-fire neurons has a high-frequency behavior $\tilde{G}_I(\omega) = A_0 \frac{R}{\sigma} \frac{1}{\sqrt{\omega \tau_m}}$.*

(a) *Calculate the response to a step current input.*

Hint: Use $\Delta A(t) = \int_0^\infty G(s) \Delta I(t - s) \mathrm{d}s$. Insert the step current, take the Fourier transform, perform the multiplication in frequency space, and finish with the inverse Fourier transform.

(b) *Compare with the simulation results in Fig. 15.9b.*

4. **Rate model for a population of exponential integrate-and-fire with white diffusive noise.** *The aim is to derive the effective time constant given in Eq. (15.24) which characterizes a population of exponential integrate-and-fire neurons.*

(a) *Write $A(t) = F[h(t)]$. Linearize about a reference value $A_0 = F(h_0)$ and prove that $\mathrm{d}A/\mathrm{d}t = F' \, \mathrm{d}h/\mathrm{d}t$.*

(b) *Assume that Eq. (15.23) holds with the unknown time constant τ_{eff}. Assume periodic stimulation $I(t) = I_0 + \Delta I \exp(i\omega t)$ with a high frequency ω. This will lead to a periodic perturbation $\Delta A \exp[i(\omega t + \phi)]$. Find the ratio $c(\omega) = \Delta A / \Delta I$.*

(c) *Match the high-frequency behavior of $c(\omega)$ to $\tilde{G}_I(\omega)$ so as to find the time constant τ_{eff}.*

Hint: Recall from Table 15.2 that the linear filter $G_I(s)$ of the exponential integrate-and-fire neurons has a high-frequency behavior $\tilde{G}_I(\omega) = A_0 \frac{R}{\Delta_T} \frac{1}{\omega \tau_m}$.

5. **Equivalence of rate models.** *We use the rate model defined in Eqs. (15.1) and (15.3) with $R = 1$ in order to describe coupled populations*

$$\tau_m \frac{\mathrm{d}h_i}{\mathrm{d}t} = -h_i + I_i + \sum_k w_{ik} F(h_k). \tag{15.34}$$

Compare this model to another rate model

$$\tau_m \frac{\mathrm{d}A_i}{\mathrm{d}t} = -A_i + F \left(\sum_k w_{ik} A_k + \hat{I}_i \right). \tag{15.35}$$

Show that Eq. (15.35) implies Eq. (15.34) under the assumption that $I = \hat{I} + \tau_m \mathrm{d}\hat{I}/\mathrm{d}t$.
Hint: Set $h_i = \sum_k w_{ik} A_k + I$ and take the derivative (Miller and Fumarola, 2012).

PART FOUR
DYNAMICS OF COGNITION

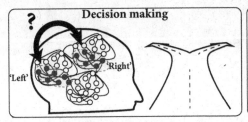
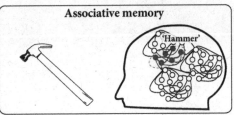

Cognitive science is an academic field of research with its own questions, paradigms, and models. The aim of Part IV is not to review the field of cognitive science, but rather to show by way of four examples how models of neuronal activity can be linked to fundamental questions of cognition. To do so, we use the population rate equations resulting from the mathematical developments of Part III and apply them to questions of cognition.

In Chapter 16 we describe the process of decision making using a network of interacting neurons. Different neuronal populations, each one representing a different option, compete with each other. The population with the highest activity eventually wins the competition, suppresses the others, and determines the choice. The dynamics of decision making can be visualized as a ball rolling down on one side rather than the other side of a hill.

Humans keep memories of important events of their life and can recall these events if they receive appropriate cues or questions. Similarly, humans remember objects and tools, such as a hammer, and can recognize these from noisy images. In Chapter 17, we describe the recall of previously stored items using a model of associative memory. In this model, neuronal assemblies of strongly connected neurons play an important role.

Human visual perception does not give rise to a precise photographic image of the environment, but interprets and reconstructs the outside world based on the raw retinal image. Many models of the visual cortex are formulated as field models, which are reviewed in Chapter 18 and discussed in relation to common visual illusions.

Finally, strong brain oscillations are related to many severe brain diseases. Understanding the mechanisms that would allow suppression of brain oscillations could eventually help patients, as discussed in Chapter 20.

16
Competing populations and decision making

We make multiple decisions in daily life. Should I cut across a busy street or take the safer pedestrian underground path which causes a 2-minute detour? Should I say "Hello" to the person I see on the other side of the street or move on? Should I spend money on a simple and cheap bicycle which is less likely to be stolen, or on a faster, shiny, expensive one? Which college should I choose after high school? Should I continue after college for graduate studies and get a PhD? Some of these are small decisions of minor relevance, but there are also important decisions that can influence the course of life for several years.

Decisions are most easily analyzed in the context of games. Small children already learn in board games that they need to decide between several possibilities. A typical example is shown in Fig. 16.1a. Would you advise a child to take the safe long path to the left, or the shorter one with the risk of being reset to "Start"? What would you decide?

The situation depicted in the board game presents a choice between a safe and a risky option. It is typical for decision problems that are empirically studied in the field of neuroeconomics (Platt and Huettel, 2008; Rangel *et al.*, 2008; Glimcher *et al.*, 2008). Suppose that you have a choice between winning 100 dollars with 100% probability or 200

(a)   (b)

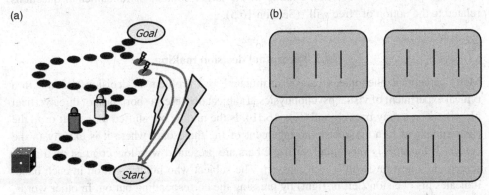

Fig. 16.1 Decision processes. (a) In a board game, your die shows the digit 4, and you have to move the white token. The right path is shorter, but more risky, because the token has to restart if it ends on one of the flashed fields. How would you decide? (b) Perceptual decision making. Three vertical bars are presented on a gray screen (four examples are shown): Is the central bar shifted left or right compared to a perfectly symmetrical arrangement?

dollars with 50% probability, which option would you choose? Suppose you just received 200 dollars, but you now have the unfortunate choice between losing half of it (100 dollars) with 100% probability or even all of it (200 dollars) with 50% probability, which option would you choose? If the brain activity of a human subject is imaged, while he answers these or similar monetary questions, the areas of highest activity associated with value, risk, and loss can be identified, at the coarse resolution of brain regions (Platt and Huettel, 2008; Rangel *et al.*, 2008).

In this chapter we work on a more microscopic level, i.e., that of neuronal activity during decision making (Gold and Shadlen, 2007). Decision making requires (i) a suitable representation of inputs and potential outcomes as well as of the values attached to the options; (ii) a selection process that picks one of the options; and (iii) potentially also some feedback that enables learning so as to achieve improved performance over several trials (Rangel *et al.*, 2008). Decision making involves different brain systems and has conscious as well as unconscious aspects (Sanfey and Chang, 2008). Here, we focus on the dynamic *selection* between different options in the context of perceptual decision making. There are three reasons for this focus. First, measurements of neuronal activity of single neurons or groups of neurons are available that indicate a correlation of neural activity with the choice made during a decision. Second, these experimental measurements can be linked to neuronal models of decision making. And, finally, the moment of the final selection between different choices lies at the heart of decision making.

In Section 16.1, we review some of the classic recordings of neural activity during decision making in monkeys (Gold and Shadlen, 2007). In Section 16.2, a model is presented that describes the process of decision making as a competition between neuronal populations that share the same pool of inhibitory neurons (Wang, 2002). The mathematical analysis of the dynamics in such a model of competition is outlined in Section 16.3. Alternative descriptions of decision making are presented in Section 16.4. We close the chapter by situating models of decision making in the larger context of fundamental questions related to the notion of "free will" (Section 16.5).

16.1 Perceptual decision making

Many perceptual phenomena can be formulated as a problem of decision making. In a typical experiment of visual psychophysics, a subject observes a short flash of three vertical black bars on a gray background (Fig. 16.1b). Is the middle bar shifted to the left or to the right compared to a symmetric arrangement of the three bars where it is exactly in the center? If the shift is very small, or if the bars are presented with low contrast on a noisy screen, the question is difficult to answer. The subject who holds a button in each hand, indicates his decision (left or right) by pressing the corresponding button. In other words, he reports his perception as a decision.

In what follows, we focus on an experimental paradigm with visual random dot motion stimuli used for the study of perceptual decision making in monkeys (Salzman *et al.*, 1990; Roitman and Shadlen, 2002; Gold and Shadlen, 2007). The stimulus consists of a random pattern of moving dots, where most, but not necessarily all, of the dots move coherently in the same direction; see Fig. 16.2. Typically, two different directions of motion are used, for example upward or downward. The monkey has been trained to indicate the perceived motion direction by saccadic eye movements to one of two targets see Fig. 16.2b.

Note that, in contrast to the examples given at the beginning of this chapter, problems of perceptual decision making typically have no direct monetary value or risk associated with them. Normally we do not care whether a bar is shifted to the left or to the right, or whether dots move upward or downward. Nevertheless, a correct perceptual decision might be life-saving if a moving stripe pattern in the bush is correctly recognized as an approaching tiger as opposed to a movement of the leaves in the wind.

16.1.1 Perception of motion

Neurons in the middle temporal visual area (MT, also called V5) are activated by large-scale motion stimuli. The receptive field of an MT neuron, i.e., the region of visual space that is sensitive to motion stimuli, is considerably larger than that of a neuron in the primary visual cortex; see Chapter 12. Different neurons in MT respond to different directions of motion, but just as in other parts of the visual cortex, area MT has a columnar structure so that clusters of neighboring neurons share receptive fields with a similar preferred direction of motion (Albright *et al.*, 1984).

At the beginning of a typical recording session with an extracellular electrode in MT (Salzman *et al.*, 1990), the location of the receptive field and the preferred direction of motion of a single neuron or cluster of neighboring neurons is determined by varying the movement angle and the location of the random dot stimulus. Once the receptive properties of the local MT neurons have been determined, only two different classes of stimuli are used, i.e., dots moving coherently in the preferred direction of the recorded neuron, and dots moving coherently in the opposite direction.

After each presentation of a random dot motion pattern, two targets are switched on, one at a location in the direction of stimulus motion, the other one on the opposite side. The monkey is trained to indicate the movement direction of the stimulus by a saccadic eye movement to the corresponding target. After training, the perceptual decision between a dot movement in the cell's preferred direction (P) or the null direction (N) is reliably performed by the monkey if a noise-free stimulus is used where all dots move in the same direction. However, the task becomes more difficult if only a small fraction of dots move coherently in one of the two directions while the rest of the dots move in a random direction. The behavioral performance can be assessed with the psychometric function which represents the percentage of saccades to the target P as a function of coherence, where coherence indicates the fraction of coherently moving dots (Fig. 16.2b).

An electrode in MT can be used not only to record neural activity, but also to stimulate a cluster of neurons in the neighborhood of the electrode. Since neighboring neurons have similar preferred directions of motion, current injection into the electrode can bias the perception of the monkey in favor of the neurons' preferred direction, even if the random

(a)

(b)

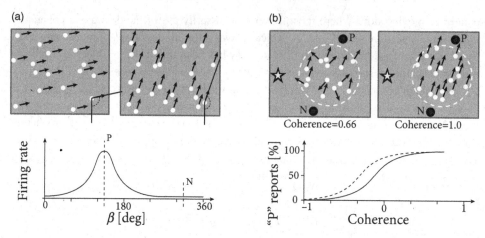

Fig. 16.2 Random dot stimuli and perception of motion. (a) Top: A pattern of random dots moving in direction β is presented on the screen. Different motion directions are tested. Bottom: The firing rate response of a neuron in area MT depends on the direction of motion β of the random dot stimulus. The preferred direction is marked "P," the null direction "N" (schematic figure). (b) Top: In the first phase of each trial, the monkey fixates on the star while a moving random dot stimulus is presented inside the receptive field (dashed circle) of a neuron. After visual stimulation is switched off, the monkey indicates by eye movements to one of the two targets (solid black circles, marked P and N) whether the perceived motion is in the direction "P" or "N." Bottom: The percentage of "P" reports (vertical axis) is plotted as a function of the coherence (horizontal axis) of the stimulus (solid line). If, during presentation of a random dot motion pattern, the MT column of neurons with preferred direction "P" is electrically stimulated, the percentage of times the monkey reports a perception of "P" is increased (dashed line). Coherence of 1 indicates that all points move in the P direction, while coherence of 0.66 indicates that one third of the points move in a random direction. Coherence of -1 indicates coherent motion in the "N" direction; schematically redrawn after Salzman *et al.* (1990).

dot pattern has no or only a small amount of coherence (Fig. 16.2b). This indicates that the perceptual decision of the monkey relies on the motion information represented in the activity of MT neurons (Salzman *et al.*, 1990).

While the monkey's perceptual decision is influenced by the manipulation of MT neurons, this result does not imply that the decision itself is made in MT. It is likely to be made at a later stage, in an area that uses the information of MT neurons.

16.1.2 Where is the decision taken?

The short answer is: we do not know. However, an interesting observation has been made in the lateral intra-parietal (LIP) area during experiments of perceptual decision making with moving random dot stimuli (Roitman and Shadlen, 2002).

Before discussing the experiment, we need to present a few facts about the properties of LIP neurons. Area LIP is located in the visual processing stream between the primary visual cortex and the frontal eye field region involved in control of saccadic eye movements. Neurons in area LIP respond during the *preparation* of saccadic eye movements. Different neurons in LIP have different receptive fields. The location of the receptive field corresponds to a potential target region of eye movements. In other words, a LIP neuron responds just *before* a saccadic eye movement into its receptive field occurs.

As in the previous subsection, monkeys in the experiment of Roitman and Shadlen are trained to indicate the direction of a moving dot pattern by saccadic eye movements to one of two visual targets. The first target is located in the receptive field of a LIP neuron. Therefore, the recorded neuron is expected to respond whenever the monkey prepares a movement to the first target. The second target is located in the opposite direction. The task is designed such that a random dot stimulus moving in the direction of the first target indicates that the monkey should make an eye movement toward it; the correct response to a stimulus moving in the opposite direction is a saccade to the second target (Fig. 16.3a). The difficulty of the task can be varied by changing the fraction of coherently moving

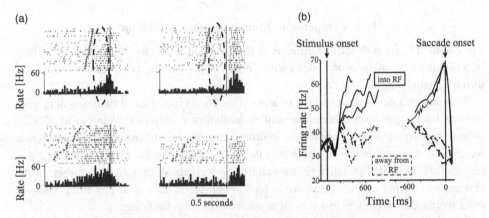

Fig. 16.3 (a) Neurons in the lateral intra-parietal (LIP) area have receptive fields (RF) that represent potential targets of a saccade. A LIP neuron responds strongly just before the saccade, if the saccadic movement is *into* its RF (left, dashed line surrounds region of interest), and is suppressed if the movement is in the opposite direction, away from its RF (right). Monkeys observed random dot motion stimuli and had been trained to report the direction of the stimulus by saccadic eye movements either "into" or "away from" the RF of the recorded neuron. For histograms and spike raster, trials were aligned to saccade onset (sac, vertical line). Filled triangles indicate onset of motion stimulus. Responses were faster for stimuli with larger coherence (top row, coherence = 51.2%) than small coherence (bottom row, coherence = 6.4%), and stronger for movements into the RF (left column) than away from the RF (right column). (b) Firing rate response of LIP neurons (averaged over 54 neurons) aligned to stimulus onset (left part of graph) or saccade onset (right part of graph). The stronger the coherence (thick solid line: coherence = 51.2%, other solid lines: 12.8% and 3.2%) of a random dot motion stimulus initiating a saccade "into" the RF, the faster the rise of the initial response of LIP neurons (left). However, whatever the coherence, the LIP neurons always reach the same firing rate, at the moment when a saccade into the RF starts (right). The neurons are suppressed, if the monkey chooses the opposite saccadic target ("away from the RF," dashed lines, left and right). Adapted from Roitman and Shadlen (2002).

dots. The behavioral reaction time of the monkey was measured as a function of stimulus coherence. At the same time, the activity of neurons in LIP was recorded.

Roitman and Shadlen found that, during the presentation of the moving dot stimulus, the activity of LIP neurons increased. The rate of increase after stimulus onset was higher for stimuli with a large fraction of coherent points than for stimuli with little or no coherence. Importantly, when the responses were averaged and aligned to the onset of the *saccade*, LIP neurons always reached the same level of activity just before a saccade *into* their receptive field (Fig. 16.3b).

These findings are consistent with the idea that the decision to perform a saccade occurs at the moment when LIP neurons reach a threshold value. For stimuli with a high degree of coherence, the activity increases more rapidly, the threshold is reached earlier, and reaction times are shorter than for stimuli with a low degree of coherence. Therefore, Roitman and Shadlen suggest that "a threshold level of LIP activity appears to mark the completion of the decision process" (Roitman and Shadlen, 2002).

16.2 Competition through common inhibition

The essential features of the experiments of Roitman and Shadlen (2002) can be described by a simple model of decision making where neuronal populations compete with each other through shared inhibition.

We consider a network of spiking neurons (Fig. 16.4) consisting of two excitatory populations interacting with a common pool in inhibitory neurons (Y. Wang *et al.*, 2002). Within the two excitatory populations neurons are randomly connected with connection weight w_{EE}. Connections to and from the inhibitory populations have weights w_{IE} and w_{EI}, respectively. Neuronal parameters and connection weights are adjusted such that, in the absence of external input, all neurons exhibit spontaneous activity at low firing rates. In other words, the network is in a state of asynchronous irregular firing.

Stimulation corresponds to a positive mean input into one or both groups of excitatory neurons. For example, for a description of the experiments of Roitman and Shadlen discussed in the previous section, we can identify input into population 1 as indicating

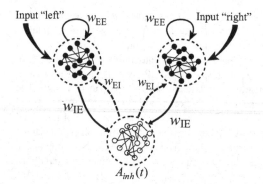

Fig. 16.4 Competition between neuronal pools. Two populations of excitatory neurons interact with a common pool of inhibitory neurons. Input signals indicating movement to the left are fed into population 1 with activity $A_{E,1}(t)$. Each population of excitatory neurons makes excitatory connections of strength w_{EE} onto itself. The inhibitory population receives input of strength w_{IE} from the two excitatory populations and sends back inhibition of strength w_{EI}.

coherent motion of the random dot pattern to the left whereas input into population 2 indicates motion to the right (Fig. 16.4). Since the stimulus in the experiments has a random component (e.g., the fraction of coherent dots is less than 100%), the input into each population is described as a mean plus some noise.

If the pattern has a high degree of coherence and moves to the left, the mean input to population 1 is high. This induces a high activity $A_{E,1}$ which in turn excites the inhibitory population which transmits inhibition to both excitatory pools. However, only the stimulated pool can overcome the inhibition so that the activity of the other excitatory population is suppressed. Since, at most one of the two populations can be active at the same time, the two populations are said to "compete" with each other. The competition is induced by the shared inhibition. If the external stimulus favors one of the two populations, the population receiving the stronger stimulus "wins" the competition. In the absence of external stimulation, or for a weak unbiased stimulus, both populations exhibit low activity.

To highlight the dynamics of competition, let us now focus on a strong, but unbiased stimulus. Here, unbiased means that, after stimulus onset, both excitatory populations receive an input of the same mean, but with a different realization of the noise (Fig. 16.5a). Immediately after the onset of stimulation, both excitatory populations increase their firing rates. Soon afterward, however, one of the activities grows further at the expense of the other one, which is suppressed. The population which develops a high activity is called the "winner" of the competition. In the next section, we will show mathematically how the shared inhibition induces a competition between the two excitatory populations.

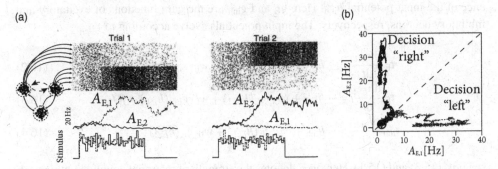

Fig. 16.5 Competition between neuronal pools. (a) Top: Spiking activity of two populations in trial 1 (left) and trial 2 (right). Dots denote spikes. Average across the population gives the population activities $A_{E,1}(t)$ and $A_{E,2}(t)$. During presentation of an unbiased stimulus (e.g., equal number of points moving to the left and to the right), one of the excitatory population develops a high population activity, while the other one is suppressed, indicating a spontaneous decision to the left (trial 1) or to the right (trial 2). Bottom: An unbiased stimulus corresponds to an input to the left and right populations of equal mean, but different realizations of noise. (b) The dynamics of population activities $A_{E,1}(t), A_{E,2}(t)$ can be visualized in the phase plane. In the absence of stimulation, the activity of both excitatory populations exhibits a low firing rate of less than 5 Hz (circle). Upon stimulation, the dynamics converge either to the region corresponding to "decision left" (characterized by high values of $A_{E,1}$) or to "decision right" (characterized by high values of $A_{E,2}$). Adapted from Wang *et al.* (2002).

16.3 Dynamics of decision making

In this section, we present a mathematical analysis of decision making in models of interacting populations. We start in Section 16.3.1 with the rate equations for a model with three populations, two excitatory ones which interact with a common inhibitory population. In Section 16.3.2, the rate model with three populations is reduced to a simplified system described by two differential equations. The fixed points of the two-dimensional dynamical system are analyzed in the phase plane (Section 16.3.3) for several situations relevant to experiments on decision making. Finally, in Section 16.3.4 the formalism of competition through shared inhibition is generalized to the case of K competing populations.

16.3.1 Model with three populations

In order to analyze the model of Fig. 16.4, we use the rate equations of Chapter 15 and formulate for each of the three interacting populations a differential equation for the input potential. Let

$$A_{E,k} = g_E(h_{E,k}) \tag{16.1}$$

denote the population activity of an excitatory population k driven by an input potential $h_{E,k}$. Similarly, $A_{inh} = g_{inh}(h_{inh})$ is the activity of the inhibitory population under the influence of the input potential h_{inh}. Here g_E and g_{inh} are the gain functions of excitatory and inhibitory neurons, respectively. The input potentials evolve according to

$$\tau_E \frac{dh_{E,1}}{dt} = -h_{E,1} + w_{EE} g_E(h_{E,1}) + w_{EI} g_{inh}(h_{inh}) + R I_1, \tag{16.2}$$

$$\tau_E \frac{dh_{E,2}}{dt} = -h_{E,2} + w_{EE} g_E(h_{E,2}) + w_{EI} g_{inh}(h_{inh}) + R I_2, \tag{16.3}$$

$$\tau_{inh} \frac{dh_{inh}}{dt} = -h_{inh} + w_{IE} g_E(h_{E,1}) + w_{IE} g_E(h_{E,2}); \tag{16.4}$$

see Eqs. (15.3) and (15.1). Here w_{EE} denotes the strength of recurrent coupling within each of the excitatory populations and w_{EI} the coupling from the inhibitory to the excitatory population of neurons. Inhibitory neurons are driven by the input from excitatory populations via connections of strength w_{IE}. We assume that inhibitory neurons have no self-coupling, but feed their activity A_{inh} back to both excitatory populations with a negative coupling coefficient, $w_{EI} < 0$. Note that the two excitatory populations are completely equivalent, i.e., they contain neurons of the same type and the same coupling strength. However, the two populations receive separate inputs, I_1 and I_2, respectively. We call an input "biased" (i.e., favoring one of the two options represented by the excitatory populations) if $I_1 \neq I_2$. We emphasize that the only interaction between the two excitatory populations is indirect via the shared inhibitory population.

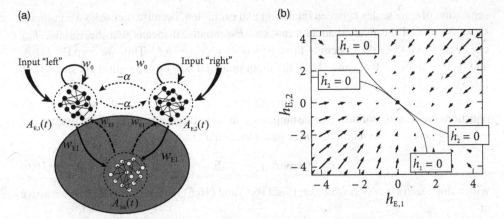

Fig. 16.6 Effective inhibition. (a) Two populations of excitatory neurons interact with a common pool of inhibitory neurons. The inhibitory population is replaced by an effective inhibitory coupling of strength α between the two excitatory populations. In addition, both populations of excitatory neurons make excitatory connections of strength $w_0 = w_{EE} - \alpha$ onto itself. (b) Phase plane analysis in the absence of stimulation. The nullclines $dh_{E,1}/dt = 0$ and $dh_{E,2}/dt = 0$ are shown as a function of $h_{E,1}$ (horizontal axis) and $h_{E,2}$ (vertical axis). There is a single crossing point corresponding to a stable fixed point close to $h_{E,1} = h_{E,2} = 0$. Arrows indicate the flow toward the fixed point.

16.3.2 *Effective inhibition*

The system of three differential equations (16.2)–(16.4) is still relatively complicated. However, from Chapter 4 we know that for a two-dimensional system of equations we can use the powerful mathematical tools of phase plane analysis. This is the main reason why we now reduce the three equations to two.

To do so, we make two assumptions. First, we assume that the membrane time constant of inhibition is shorter than that of excitation, $\tau_{inh} \ll \tau_E$. Formally, we consider the limit of a separation of time scales $\tau_{inh}/\tau_E \to 0$. Therefore we can treat the dynamics of h_{inh} in Eq. (16.4) as instantaneous, so that the inhibitory potential is always at its fixed point

$$h_{inh} = w_{IE} \left[g_E(h_{E,1}) + g_E(h_{E,2}) \right]. \tag{16.5}$$

Is this assumption justified? Inhibitory neurons do indeed fire at higher firing rates than excitatory ones and are in this sense "faster." However, this observation on its own does not imply that the membrane time constants of excitatory and inhibitory neurons, respectively, would differ by a factor of 10 or more; in fact, they don't. Nevertheless, a focus on the raw membrane time constant is also too limited in scope, since we should also take into account synaptic processes. Excitatory synapses typically have an NMDA component with time constants in the range of a hundred milliseconds or more, whereas inhibitory synapses are fast. We recall from Chapter 15 that the rate equations that we use here are in any case highly simplified and do not fully reflect the potentially much richer dynamics of neuronal populations.

Intuitively, the assumption of a separation of time scales implies that inhibition reacts faster to a change in the input than excitation. In the following we simply assume the separation of time scales between inhibition and excitation, because it enables a significant simplification of the mathematical treatment. Essentially, it means that the variable h_{inh} can be removed from the system of three equations (16.2)–(16.4). Thus we drop Eq. (16.4) and replace in Eqs. (16.2) and (16.3) the input potential h_{inh} by the right-hand side of Eq. (16.5).

The second assumption is not absolutely necessary, but it makes the remaining two equations more transparent. The assumption concerns the shape of the gain function of inhibitory neurons. We require a linear gain function and set

$$g_{\text{inh}}(h_{\text{inh}}) = \gamma h_{\text{inh}},\tag{16.6}$$

with a slope factor $\gamma > 0$. If we insert Eqs. (16.5) and (16.6) into (16.2) and (16.3) we arrive at

$$\tau_{\text{E}}\frac{dh_{E,1}}{dt} = -h_{E,1} + (w_{\text{EE}} - \alpha)\,g_{\text{E}}(h_{E,1}) - \alpha\,g_{\text{E}}(h_{E,2}) + RI_1,\tag{16.7}$$

$$\tau_{\text{E}}\frac{dh_{E,2}}{dt} = -h_{E,2} + (w_{\text{EE}} - \alpha)\,g_{\text{E}}(h_{E,2}) - \alpha\,g_{\text{E}}(h_{E,1}) + RI_2,\tag{16.8}$$

where we have introduced a parameter $\alpha = -\gamma w_{\text{EI}} w_{\text{IE}} > 0$. Thus, the model of three populations has been replaced by a model with two excitatory populations that interact with an *effective inhibitory* coupling of strength α; see Fig. 16.6a. Even though neurons make either excitatory or inhibitory synapses, never both ("Dale's law"), the above derivation shows that, under appropriate assumptions, there is a mathematically *equivalent* description where explicit inhibition by inhibitory neurons is replaced by *effective inhibition* between excitatory neurons. The effective inhibitory coupling allows us to discuss competition between neuronal groups in a transparent manner.

16.3.3 Phase plane analysis

The advantage of the reduced system with two differential equations (16.7) and (16.8) and effective inhibition is that it can be studied using phase plane analysis; see Figs. 16.6b and 16.7.

In the absence of stimulation, there exists only a single fixed point $h_{E,1} = h_{E,2} \approx 0$, corresponding to a small level of spontaneous activity (Fig. 16.6b).

If a stimulus $I_1 > 0$ favors the first population, the fixed point moves to an asymmetric position where population 1 exhibits much stronger activity $A_{E,1} = g(h_{E,1})$ than population 2 (Fig. 16.7a). Note that, at the fixed point, $h_{E,2} \ll 0$. In other words, the effective interaction between the two populations causes a strong inhibitory input potential to population 2. This is a characteristic feature of a competitive network. If one of the populations exhibits a strong activity, it inhibits activity of the others so that only the activity of a single winning population "survives." This principle can also be applied to more than two interacting populations, as we shall see in Section 16.3.4.

A particularly interesting situation arises with a strong but unbiased stimulus, as we have

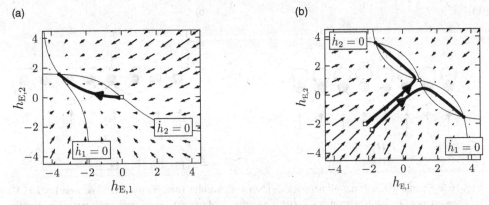

Fig. 16.7 Phase plane analysis of the competition model during stimulation. (a) A strong stimulus $I_1 > 0 = I_2$ gives rise to a single stable fixed point, corresponding to high firing rates $A_{E,1}$ of the first population. This indicates a choice "left." The nullclines $dh_{E,1}/dt = 0$ (solid line) and $dh_{E,2}/dt = 0$ (solid line) are shown as a function of $h_{E,1}$ (horizontal axis) and $h_{E,2}$ (vertical axis). Arrows indicate the flow toward the fixed point. A sample trajectory is indicated (thick line). (b) Phase plane analysis with strong, but ambiguous stimulation $I_1 = I_2 > 0$. The symmetric fixed point is unstable, and the flow converges to one of the two stable fixed points. Two sample trajectories are shown.

already seen in the simulations of Fig. 16.5. The phase plane analysis of Fig. 16.7b shows that, with a strong unbiased stimulus $I_1 = I_2 \gg 0$, three fixed points exist. The symmetric fixed point $h_{E,1} = h_{E,2}$ is a saddle point and therefore unstable. The two other fixed points occur at equivalent positions symmetrically to the left and right of the diagonal. These are the fixed points that enforce a decision "left" or "right."

It depends on the initial conditions, or on tiny fluctuations in the noise of the input, whether the system ends up in the left or right fixed point. If, before the onset of the unbiased strong stimulation, the system was at the stable resting point close to $h_{E,1} = h_{E,2} \approx 0$, then the dynamics is first attracted toward the saddle point, before it bends over to either the left or right stable fixed point (Fig. 16.7b). Thus, the phase plane analysis of the two-dimensional system correctly reflects the dynamics observed in the simulations of the model with populations of hundreds of spiking neurons (Fig. 16.5b).

16.3.4 *Formal winner-take-all networks*

The arguments that were developed above for the case of a binary choice between two options can be generalized to a situation with K possible outcomes. Each outcome is represented by one population of excitatory neurons. Analogous to the arguments in Fig. 16.6a, we work with an effective inhibition of strength $\alpha > 0$ between the K pools of neurons and with a self-interaction of strength w_0 within each pool of neurons.

The activity of population k is then

$$A_k(t) = g(h_k(t)) \tag{16.9}$$

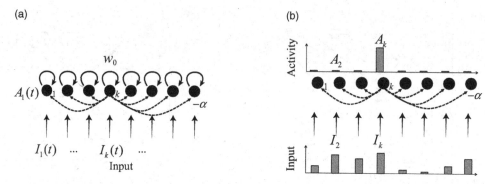

Fig. 16.8 Formal winner-take-all network. (a) Network architecture: each artificial neuron $1 \leq k \leq K$ receives an input I_k. Each neuron has a positive feedback of magnitude w_0 onto itself but inhibits with strength α all other neurons. (b) In a pattern of fixed inputs $I_k > 0$, $1 \leq k \leq K$ switched on at time t_0, the network converges to a state where only a single "winner" neuron is active, i.e., the one which receives the strongest input.

with input potential

$$\tau \frac{dh_k}{dt} = -h_k + w_0 \, g(h_k) - \alpha \sum_{j \neq k} g_{\mathrm{E}}(h_j) + R I_k, \qquad (16.10)$$

where the sum runs over all neurons $1 \leq j \leq K$, except neuron k. Note that we assume here a network of interacting *populations*, but it is common to draw the network as an interaction between formal units. Despite the fact that, in our interpretation, each unit represents a whole population, the units are often called "artificial neurons;" see Fig. 16.8a. Winner-take-all networks are a standard topic of artificial neural networks (Hertz *et al.*, 1991; Kohonen, 1984; Haykin, 1994).

For a suitable choice of coupling parameters w_0 and α the network implements a competition between artificial neurons, as highlighted in the following example.

Example: Competition

Consider a network of formal neurons described by activities $A_k = [1 + \tanh(h - \theta)] \, A_{\max}/2$. We work in unit-free variables and set $A_{\max} = 1$ and $\theta = 5$. Thus, for an input potential $h = 0$ the activity is nearly zero while for $h = 10$ it is close to 1. The input potential, given by Eq. (16.10), contains contributions from external input as well as contributions from recurrent interactions within the network.

Suppose that for all times $t < t_0$ the external input vanishes, $I_k = 0$ for all k. Thus, at time t_0 the input potential h_k and the activity A_k are negligible for all units k. Therefore the interactions within the network are negligible as well.

At time t_0 the input is switched on to a new fixed value I_k which is different for each neuron; see Fig. 16.8b. The activity of the neuron k which receives the strongest input grows more rapidly than that of the others so that its activity also increases more rapidly.

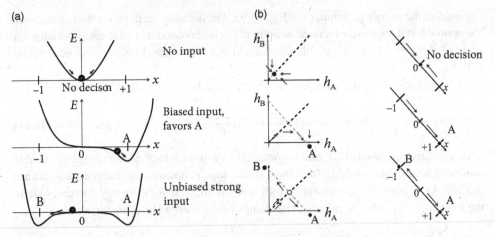

Fig. 16.9 Energy picture of decision making. (a) Decisions correspond to a ball rolling down an energy landscape, plotted as a function of a formal decision variable x. A value of $x = 0$ indicates that no decision is taken (top, no input), whereas a value of $x = \pm 1$ reflects a decision for options A or B, respectively. An input favoring option A deforms and tilts the energy landscape so that the minimum of the energy is in the neighborhood of $x = 1$ (middle). A strong but unbiased input creates two energy minima corresponding to options A and B. Only one of the two options can be taken by the rolling ball (bottom). (b) The corresponding phase plane diagram of the input potentials h_A (horizontal axis) and h_B (vertical axis). Fixed points are indicated as solid (stable) or empty (saddle) circles. The decision variable x moves along the axis (dashed gray line) perpendicular to the diagonal (dashed black line) and is replotted again as a one-dimensional flow on the right-hand side of the figure.

The strong activity of neuron k inhibits the development of activity in the other neurons so that, in the end, the neuron with the strongest input wins the competition and its activity is the only one to survive.

16.4 Alternative decision models

In the previous two sections, we discussed decision models as the competitive interaction between two or more populations of excitatory neurons. In this section we present two different models of decision making, i.e., the energy picture in Section 16.4.1 and the drift-diffusion model in Section 16.4.2. Both models are phenomenological concepts to describe decision making. However, both models are also related to the phase diagram of the model of two neuronal populations, encountered in Section 16.3.

16.4.1 The energy picture

Binary decisions can be visualized as a ball in a hilly energy landscape. Once the ball rolls in a certain direction, a decision starts to form. The decision is finalized when the ball approaches the energy minimum; see Fig. 16.9a. The decision variable x reflects a decision for option A if it approaches a fixed point in the neighborhood of $x \approx 1$, and a decision for option B for $x \approx -1$. If the variable x is trapped in a minimum close to $x = 0$, no decision is taken.

The dynamics of the decision process can be formulated as gradient descent

$$\frac{dx}{dt} = -\eta \frac{dE}{dx} \tag{16.11}$$

with a positive constant η. In other words, in a short time step Δt, the decision variable moves by an amount $-\eta \Delta t \, dE/dx$. Thus, if the slope is positive, the movement is toward the left. As a result, the movement is always downhill, so that the energy decreases along the trajectory $x(t)$. We can calculate the change of the energy along the trajectory:

$$\frac{dE(x(t))}{dt} = \frac{dE}{dx} \frac{dx}{dt} = -\eta \left(\frac{dE}{dx} \right)^2 \leq 0. \tag{16.12}$$

Therefore the energy plays the role of a Liapunov function of the system, i.e., a quantity that cannot increase along the trajectory of a dynamical system .

Interestingly, the energy picture can be related to the phase plane analysis of the two-dimensional model that we encountered earlier in Figs. 16.6b and 16.7. The diagonal of the phase plane plays the role of the boundary between the options A and B while the variable x indicates the projection onto an axis orthogonal to the diagonal. Position $x = 0$ is the unbiased, undecided position on the diagonal; see Fig. 16.9. In the case of strong unbiased input, the one-dimensional flow diagram of the variable x presents a reasonable summary of the flow pattern in the two-dimensional system, because the saddle point in the phase plane is attractive along the diagonal and is reached rapidly while the flow in the perpendicular direction is much slower (Wang *et al.*, 2002; Bogacz *et al.*, 2006; Wong and Wang, 2006).

The above arguments regarding the Liapunov function of the network can be made more precise and formulated as a general theorem (Cohen and Grossberg, 1983; Hopfield, 1984). We consider an arbitrary network of K neuronal populations $1 \leq j \leq K$ with population rate $A_j = g(h_j) \geq 0$ where g is a gain function with derivative $g' > 0$ and h follows the dynamics

$$\tau \frac{dh_j}{dt} = -h_j + RI_j + \sum_k w_{jk} g(h_k) \tag{16.13}$$

with fixed inputs I_j. If the coupling is *symmetric*, i.e., $w_{ij} = w_{ji}$, then the energy

$$E = -\sum_i \sum_j w_{ij} A_i A_j - \sum_i A_i RI_i + \sum_i \int_0^{A_i} g^{-1}(a) \, da \tag{16.14}$$

is a Liapunov function of the dynamics.

The proof follows by taking the derivative. We exploit the fact that $w_{ij} = w_{ji}$ and apply

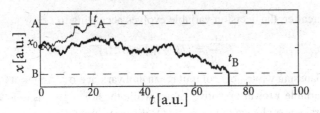

Fig. 16.10 Drift-diffusion model. The decision variable $x(t)$ starts from x_0 and undergoes a biased random walk toward one of the two thresholds, marked by horizontal dashed lines. In the first trial (thin solid line), the choice is option A and the reaction time indicated as t_A. In another trial (thick solid line) the trajectory hits, after a time t_B the threshold for option B.

the chain rule $dA_i/dt = g'(h_i)dh_i/dt$ so as to find

$$\frac{dE}{dt} = -\sum_i \left[\sum_j w_{ij}A_j\right] g'(h_i)\frac{dh_i}{dt} - \sum_i RI_i g'(h_i)\frac{dh_i}{dt} + \sum_i g^{-1}(A_i) g'(h_i)\frac{dh_i}{dt}$$

$$= -\tau \sum_i g'(h_i)\left[\frac{dh_i}{dt}\right]^2 \leq 0. \tag{16.15}$$

In the second line we have used Eq. (16.13). Furthermore, since the neuronal gain function stays below a biologically sustainable firing rate $g(x) \leq A^{max}$, the energy is bounded from below. Therefore the flow of a symmetric network of interacting populations will always converge to one of the stable fixed points corresponding to an energy minimum, unless the initial condition is chosen to lie on an unstable fixed point, in which case the dynamics stays there until it is perturbed by some input.

Example: Binary decision network revisited

The binary decision network of Eqs. (16.7) and (16.8) with effective inhibition α and recurrent interactions w_0 consists of two populations. Interactions are symmetric since $w_{12} = w_{21} = -\alpha$. Therefore the energy function

$$E = -w_0[A_1^2 + A_2^2] + 2\alpha A_1 A_2 - R[I_1 A_1 + I_2 A_2] + \int_0^{A_1} g^{-1}(x)dx + \int_0^{A_2} g^{-1}(y)dy \tag{16.16}$$

is a Liapunov function of the dynamics defined in Eqs. (16.7) and (16.8). Since the dynamics is bounded, there must be stable fixed points.

16.4.2 Drift-diffusion model

The drift-diffusion model is a phenomenological model to describe choice preferences and distributions of reaction times in binary decision making tasks (Ratcliff and Rouder, 1998). At each trial of a decision experiment, a decision variable x is initialized at time t_0 at a value

$x(t_0) = x_0$. Thereafter, the decision variable evolves according to

$$\frac{dx}{dt} = (I_A - I_B) + \sigma \xi(t) \tag{16.17}$$

where $\xi(t)$ is Gaussian white noise of unit mean and variance σ^2. An input $I_A > I_B$ causes a "drift" of the variable x toward positive values while the noise ξ leads to a "diffusion"-like motion of the trajectory; hence the name "drift-diffusion model."

The reaction time is the time at which the variable x reaches one of two thresholds, Θ_A or Θ_B, respectively (Fig. 16.10). For example t_B, defined by $t_B = \min\{t | x(t) = \Theta_B\}$, is the reaction time in a trial where the choice falls on option B.

Parameters of the phenomenological drift-diffusion model are the values of thresholds Θ_A and Θ_B, and the strength of the input $I_A - I_B$ compared to that of the noise. The initial condition x_0 can be identical in all trials or chosen in each trial independently from a small interval that reflects uncontrolled variations in the bias of the subject. The time t_0 is typically the moment when the subject receives the choice stimulus, but it is also possible to start the drift-diffusion process a few milliseconds later so as to account for the propagation delay from the sensors to the brain (Ratcliff and Rouder, 1998; Ratcliff and McKoon, 2008).

Example: Drift-diffusion model versus neuronal models

In the original formulation, the drift-diffusion model was used as a "black box," i.e., a phenomenological model with parameters that can be fitted to match the distribution of reaction times and choice preferences to behavioral experiments. Interestingly, however, variants of one-dimensional drift-diffusion models can be derived from the models of neural populations with competitive interaction that we have discussed in earlier sections of this chapter (Bogacz *et al.*, 2006; Wong and Wang, 2006; Roxin and Ledberg, 2008). The essential idea can be best explained in the energy picture; see Fig. 16.9. We assume a small amount of noise. In the absence of input, the decision variable jitters around the stable fixed point $x = 0$. Its momentary value $x \approx 0$ serves as an initial condition, once the input is switched on. Suppose the input is strong but unbiased. Two new valleys form around $x \approx \pm 1$. However, in the neighborhood of $x = 0$ the landscape is flat, so that noise leads to a diffusive motion of the trajectory. A biased input $I_A > I_B$ tilts the energy landscape to the right which causes a corresponding drift term in the diffusion process. The location where the slope of the valley becomes steep can be associated with the threshold Θ_A in the diffusion model.

16.5 Human decisions, determinism, and free will

In the previous section, we compared the process of decision making to a ball in an energy landscape. However, as outlined in the introduction to this chapter, decision

(a)   (b)

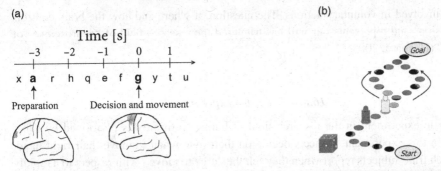

Fig. 16.11 Decision processes and the notion of free will. (a) In a modern variant of the Libet experiment (Libet, 1985), a subject lies in the fMRI-scanner while watching a rapid sequence of letters
(Soon *et al.*, 2008) that appear at a rate of 2 Hz (top; horizontal axis shows time in seconds). The
subject spontaneously decides to move his left or right index finger and reports the letter he saw at
the moment when he felt the "urge to move" interpreted as the moment when he took a decision
(right; letter "g" defines time zero). However, already a few seconds earlier (e.g., when the letter "a"
was shown, left) the brain activity in frontal areas of the subject has a high correlation with his final
decision; schematic figure, adapted from Soon *et al.* (2008) and Haggard (2008). (b) The decision
to move the left or right index finger is completely irrelevant, similar to a game where a decision
between two equivalent choices has to be made.

making incorporates a broad set of phenomena and processes (Rangel *et al.*, 2008; Sanfey
and Chang, 2008). Here we sketch a link from the simplified model from decision making
to the bigger picture.

Adult humans in a state of normal health feel that they are in control of their actions:
"The street is too busy, therefore I decide to take the safer underground pathway"; "Because
there have been many accidents at this crossing, I decide to break early and be particularly
careful"; "I would rather prepare for the exams than go to the movies." We all know examples of consciously controlling our decisions and actions.

Voluntary control of actions can be understood in opposition to pure reflexes (Haggard,
2008). If the doctor hits the right spot on your knee, your foot moves without you intend-
ing it. If an object approaches your eyes from the front, you automatically move your head.
There are also cases where reflexes have been learned from experience. For example, during your first driving lessons you had to consciously control your foot in order to step on
the brakes when a red traffic light appeared in front of your car. After years of experience,
you start to break even before you become aware of a conscious decision. Similarly, if you
are a good tennis player you will respond to a serve with an arm movement that was trained
so often that it has become as fast as a reflex. Nevertheless, you could decide to take back
control and try to inhibit your automatic response, if for some reason you want to disturb
your opponent. The feeling of voluntary control is what makes you feel responsible for the
things you do.

The movement of our arms and legs is controlled by muscles which in turn receive action
potentials from the brain via the spinal cord. The human cortex contains several areas

that are involved in voluntary actions. The question of where and how the brain controls our decisions and represents our will has triggered the research field of "neuroscience of volition" (Haggard, 2008).

16.5.1 *The Libet experiment*

The classic experiment in the research field of human volition was performed by Libet (1985). In this experiment, subjects decide on their own when to move their right hand. After each trial, subjects report when they felt the "urge to move," with respect to a rapidly rotating hand of a clock. The reported "urge to move" is in fact about 200 ms earlier than the actual movement. Most interestingly, however, electrical brain activity measured by EEG recordings indicates that the brain exhibits signals of preparatory activity several hundred milliseconds *before* the reported "urge to move." Thus, if we agree to interpret the felt "urge to move" as the conscious decision to move the hand, then we must also accept the fact that the brain has unconsciously prepared our decision.

A modern and debated variant of the Libet experiment is shown in Fig. 16.11a. The main difference to the original Libet experiment (where the decision was limited to "move" or "not move") is that subjects now hold two buttons, one in the left and the other in the right hand (Soon *et al.*, 2008). Subjects are free to decide when to move and press either of the two buttons. While subjects perform the experiment, they watch a stream of letters at a rate of two letters per second. At the end of each trial, they indicate at which letter they had felt the "urge to move." The reported letter serves as a timing reference for the subsequent analysis.

During the experiment, brain activity was recorded through functional magnetic resonance imaging (fMRI). Using statistical pattern classification techniques, the authors aimed at predicting the final response outcome (left or right) based on the activity patterns in localized brain areas. If brain activity contained no cue about the final decision, the prediction would always be 50%. However, the authors found that activity patterns in fronto-polar cortex 5 seconds before the reported "urge to move" allowed them to predict the final choice (left or right) with a precision of 55–60% (Soon *et al.*, 2008) which is above chance but far from a reliable prediction.

16.5.2 *Relevant and irrelevant decisions – a critique*

What, if anything, can we learn about decision making and volition from these and similar experiments? In a naive interpretation, the results seem to suggest that the brain has taken its own decision a long time before the subject becomes aware of it. As Wolfgang Prinz puts it: "We don't do what we want, but we want what we do" (Prinz, 2004).

There is little doubt that our actions, plans, and wishes are represented in the brain. Our childhood memories are stored in our brain; our knowledge of the world is memorized in the brain; our values and priorities acquired through education, reading, understanding, trial and error, or simply through being embedded in our culture, must also be stored in the brain. Thus, a large fraction, if not all, of what we consider our conscious personality is located in the brain.

Most actions where we care about our decision are relevant choices. The decision of whether to take the risky shortcut across a busy street or the safer underground pathway depends on what we have experienced in the past. Similarly, the decision in the board game of Fig. 16.1a depends on the player's attitude toward risk, which has been formed by previous experiences in similar situations. However, the decision task in the scientific experiment of Libet (1985) or Soon *et al.* (2008) is a completely irrelevant one. Subjects don't really care whether they move the left or right finger. The decision has nothing to do with life-long experience or attitude toward risk. In cases like this one, any decision is arbitrary and therefore easily influenced by noise. Think of the board game of Fig. 16.1a and compare it with the situation in Fig. 16.11b. While the first one asks for a decision between a risky and a safe path, the second one poses an irrelevant choice. In the latter case, we might, just for the sake of advancing the game, decide to go left, based on the whim of the moment, but we know that right would do just as well.

Interestingly, even in the irrelevant situation of the experiment of Soon *et al.* (2008), the predictive power of the brain activity five seconds before the conscious "urge to move" is only in the range of 60%. Moreover, in a different experimental design, the subject could "veto" at the last moment a previously prepared movement suggesting the possibility of voluntary inhibition of actions that are only weakly predicted (Brass and Haggard, 2007). Finally, there is also the problem of whether we can really identify a reported "urge to move" with a precise moment of decision. If we take the picture of the ball in the energy landscape, the ball starts to roll in a certain direction while still remaining in the flat region. But this does not yet imply a final decision, because novel input could tilt the energy landscape in the opposite direction.

16.6 Summary

Decisions are prepared and made in the brain so that numerous physiological correlates of decision making can be found in the human and monkey cortex. The fields of cognitive neuroscience associated with these questions are called "neuroeconomics" and "neuroscience of volition."

An influential computational model describes decision making as the competition of several populations of excitatory neurons which share a common pool of inhibitory neurons. Under suitable conditions, the explicit model of inhibitory neurons can be replaced by an effective inhibitory coupling between excitatory populations. In a rate model, the competitive interactions between two excitatory populations can be understood using phase plane analysis. Equivalently, the decision process can be described as downward motion in an energy landscape which plays the role of a Liapunov function. The energy picture is valid for any rate model where all units of the network are coupled by symmetric interactions.

The drift-diffusion model, which has been used in the past as a black-box model for reaction time distributions and choice preferences, can, under appropriate assumptions, be related to a rate model of competitively interacting populations of neurons.

Literature

There are several accessible introductions to the problem of decision making in neuro-economics (Platt and Huettel, 2008; Rangel *et al.*, 2008; Glimcher *et al.*, 2008). The neurophysiological correlates of decision making are reviewed in Gold and Shadlen (2007), Romo and Salinas (2003) and Deco *et al.* (2009, 2010).

The competitive model of decision making that we presented in this chapter is discussed in Y. Wang *et al.* (2002) and Wong and Wang (2006), but competitive interaction through inhibition is a much older topic in the field of computational neuroscience and artificial neural networks (Grossberg, 1969; Kohonen, 1984; Hertz *et al.*, 1991; Haykin, 1994). Competitive models of spiking neurons with shared inhibition have also been applied to other tasks of perceptual decision making, (see e.g., Machens *et al.*, 2005).

Energy as a Liapunov function for rate models of neurons has been introduced by Cohen and Grossberg (1983). In the context of associative memories (to be discussed in the next chapter) energy functions have been used for binary neuron models by Hopfield (1982) and for rate models by Hopfield (1984).

Drift-diffusion models have been reviewed by Ratcliff and Rouder (1998) and Ratcliff and McKoon (2008). The relation of drift-diffusion models to neuronal decision models has been discussed by Bogacz *et al.* (2006) and Wong and Wang (2006) and has been worked out in the general case by Roxin and Ledberg (2008).

A highly recommended overview of neuroscience around the questions of volition is given by Haggard (2008), who reviews both the original Libet experiment (Libet, 1985) and its modern variants. The fMRI study of Soon *et al.* (2008) is also accessible to the non-specialized reader.

Exercises

1. **Phase plane analysis of a binary decision process.** *Consider the following system (in unit-free variables)*

$$\frac{dh_{E,1}}{dt} = -h_{E,1} + (w_{EE} - \alpha) g_E(h_{E,1}) - \alpha g_E(h_{E,2}) + h_1^{ext}, \qquad (16.18)$$

$$\frac{dh_{E,2}}{dt} = -h_{E,2} + (w_{EE} - \alpha) g_E(h_{E,2}) - \alpha g_E(h_{E,1}) + h_2^{ext}, \qquad (16.19)$$

where $\alpha = 1$ and $w_{EE} = 1.5$. The function $g(h)$ is piecewise linear: $g(h) = 0$ for $h < -0.2$; $g(h) = 0.1 + 0.5h$ for $-0.2 \leq h \leq 0.2$; $g(h) = h$ for $0.2 < h < 0.8$ $g(h) = 0.4 + 0.5h$ for $0.8 \leq h \leq 1.2$; and $g(h) = 1$ for $h > 1.2$.
(a) Draw the two nullclines ($dh_1/dt = 0$ and $dh_2/dt = 0$) in the phase plane with horizontal axis h_1 and vertical axis h_2 for the case $h_1^{ext} = h_2^{ext} = 0.8$.
(b) Add flow arrows on the nullclines.
(c) Set $h_1^{ext} = h_2^{ext} = b$ and study the fixed point on the diagonal $h_1 = h_2 = h^*$. Find an expression

for $h^*(b)$ under the assumption that the fixed point is in the region where $g(h) = h$. Analyze the stability of this fixed point.

(d) We now drop the assumption that the fixed point is in the region where $g(h) = h$. Consider an arbitrary sufficiently smooth function $g(h)$ as well as arbitrary couplings α and w_{EE}, and give a formula for the fixed point on the diagonal.

(e) Assume now that $\alpha = 0.75$ and $w_{EE} = 1.5$. Linearize about the fixed point in (d) and calculate the two eigenvalues.
Hint: Introduce a parameter $\beta = 0.75 g'(h^*)$.

(f) Show that the fixed point is stable for $g'(h^*) = 0$ and unstable for $g'(h^*) = 1$. At which value of β does it change stability?

(g) Describe in words your findings. What happens with a weak or a strong unbiased input to the decision model?

2. **Winner-take-all in artificial neural networks.** *Consider a network of formal neurons described by activities $A_k = (h_k - 1)$ for $1 \le h_k \le 2$, $A_k = 0$ for $h_k < 1$, and $A_k = 1$ for $h_k > 2$. We write $A_k = g_E(h_k)$.*
The update happens in discrete time according to

$$h_k(t + \Delta t) = w_0 g(h_k(t)) - \alpha \sum_{j \ne k} g_E(h_j(t)) + h_k^{ext}(t). \qquad (16.20)$$

The external input vanishes for $t \le 0$. For $t > 0$ the input to unit k is $h_k^{ext} = (0.5)^k + 1.0$.
(a) Set $w_0 = 2$ and $\alpha = 1$. Follow the evolution of the activities for three time steps.
(b) What happens if you change α? What happens if you keep $\alpha = 1$ but decrease w_0?
(c) Derive sufficient conditions so that the only fixed point is $A_k = \delta_{k,1}$, i.e., only the unit with the strongest input is active. Assume that the maximal external input to the maximally excited neuron is $h_k^{ext} \le 2$.

3. **Energy picture.** *Consider the energy function*

$$E(x) = [1 - (I_A + I_B)]x^2 + \frac{1}{4}x^4 + (I_A - I_B)x \qquad (16.21)$$

where I_A and I_B are inputs in support of options A and B, respectively.
(a) Draw qualitatively the energy landscape in the absence of input, $I_A = I_B = 0$.
(b) Draw qualitatively the energy landscape for $I_B = 0$ when I_A takes one of the three values $\{0.5, 1.0, 1.5\}$.
(c) Draw the energy landscape for $I_A = I_B = c$ when c varies in the range $[0.5, 1.5]$.
(d) Determine the flow $\Delta x = -\Delta t \, \eta \, dE/dx$ for a small positive parameter η for all the relevant cases from (a)–(c).
(e) Compare your results with Fig. 16.9.

17

Memory and attractor dynamics

Humans remember important events in their lives. You might be able to recall every detail of your first exam at college, or of your first public speech, or of your first day in kindergarten, or of the first time you went to a new school after your family moved to a new city. Human memory works with associations. If you hear the voice of an old friend on the phone, you may spontaneously recall stories that you had not thought of for years. If you are hungry and see a picture of a banana, you might vividly recall the taste and smell of a banana ... and thereby realize that you are indeed hungry.

In this chapter, we present models of neural networks that describe the recall of previously stored items from memory. In Section 17.1 we start with a few examples of associative recall to prepare the stage for the modeling work later on. In Section 17.2 we introduce an abstract network model of memory recall, known as the Hopfield model. We take this network as a starting point and add, in subsequent sections, some biological realism to the model.

17.1 Associations and memory

A well-known demonstration of the strong associations which are deeply embedded in the human brain is given by the following task. The aim is to respond as quickly as possible to three questions. Think of the first answer that comes to mind! Are you ready? Here are the questions: (i) Can you give me an example of a color? (ii) Can you give me an example of a tool? (iii) Can you give me an example of a fruit? For each of these, what was the very first example that came to your mind? Chances are high that your examples are "red" for color and "hammer" for tool. In fact, most humans have particularly strong associations from tool to hammer and from color to red. Regarding fruit, the cultural background plays a more important role (apple, orange, banana), but since the text at the beginning of this chapter mentioned bananas, you probably had a slightly stronger bias toward banana at the moment when you answered the above questions than what you would have had under normal circumstances. This bias through an earlier word or context is a highly significant effect, called "priming" in psychophysics.

Not surprisingly, the word "red" is associated with seeing the color red and vice versa. If you read a list of words that contains names of colors, you are normally fast in doing

(a)

I find it rea*l* amazin* t*at y*u ar*
abl* to re*d t*is tex* despit* th*
fac* *hat more t*an t* ent* perc*n*
of t** char* cte*s a*e mis*ing.
his mean t*at you* brai* i* abl*
** fill in missin* info* matio*.

(b)

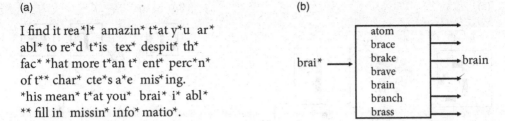

Fig. 17.1 Memory recall cued by partial information. (a) Read it! (b) Schematic view of the recall process. Your brain has memorized a list of words. Based on partial information and the context, your brain is able to complete the missing characters.

so and do not experience any particular difficulty. Similarly, you can easily name the color of objects. However, people find it difficult to name the ink color in lists of words that contain entries such as *red, green, blue*, but are written in colors that are inconsistent with the word (e.g., the word *red* is written in green, whereas the word *green* is written in blue). In this case responses in the color-naming task are slower compared to naming the color of geometric objects. The measurable difference in reaction time in naming the color of (inconsistent) words compared to the color of objects is called the Stroop effect (Stroop, 1935; MacLeod, 1991). The association of the color "red" with the word *red* makes it difficult to name the ink color (e.g., green) in which the word *red* is written.

In this chapter we mainly focus on association in the sense of completing partial information. Take a look at Fig. 17.1a. Nearly all words are incomplete, but your brain is able to cope with this situation, just as you are able to follow a phone conversation over a noisy line, recognize a noisy image of a handwritten character or associate the picture of an orange with its taste to retrieve your concept of an orange as a tasty fruit.

17.1.1 Recall, recognition, and partial information

If half of an orange is hidden behind a coffee mug, you can still recognize it as an orange based on the partial information you have. Recognition works because you have seen oranges before and have memorized the concept "orange," including a prototypical image of this fruit. More generally, when you see a noisy image of a known object (e.g., the letter "T") your brain is able to retrieve from memory the prototype version of the object (e.g., an idealized "T"). Thus recognizing an object in a noisy environment involves the process of "memory recall."

A highly simplified schematic view of memory recall based on partial information is shown in Fig. 17.1b. The input (e.g., an incomplete word) is compared to a list of all possible words. The most likely entry (i.e., the one which is most similar to the input) in the list is given as the output of memory recall.

Similarly, noisy images of objects are recognized if the brain finds, among the memorized items, one which is highly similar (Fig. 17.2). Let us call the "pure" noise-free memory item a prototype p^μ, where the index $1 \leq \mu \leq M$ labels all different memory

(a)

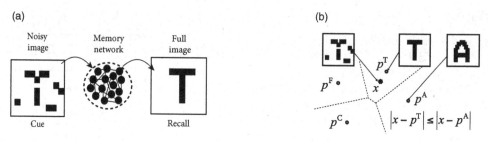

Fig. 17.2 Recall and recognition as search for nearest prototype. (a) A letter "T" in a noisy image (left) serves as a cue in order to recall a noise-free prototype letter "T" from the memory embedded in a neural network. (b) Recognition of the input x (black star, representing a noisy "T") can be interpreted as an algorithm that searches for the nearest prototype p^α such that $|x - p^\alpha| \leq |x - p^\mu|$ for all μ, and p^μ denotes all possible prototypes (gray circles). The dashed lines are the sets of points with equal distance to two different prototypes.

items. The prototype can be visualized as a point in some high-dimensional space. A noisy input cue x corresponds to another point in the same space. Suppose that we have a similarity measure which enables us to calculate the distance $|x - p^\mu|$ between the input cue and each of the prototypes. A simple method of memory recall is a search algorithm that goes through the list of all available prototypes to find the nearest one. More formally, the output of the recall process is the prototype p^α with

$$|x - p^\alpha| \leq |x - p^\mu| \quad \text{for all } \mu, \tag{17.1}$$

which gives rise to a simple geometric picture (Fig. 17.2b).

The aim of this chapter is to replace the explicit algorithmic search for the nearest prototype by the dynamics of interacting neurons. Instead of an *explicit* algorithm working through a list of stored prototypes, the mere cross-talk of neurons embedded in a large network will find the prototype that corresponds best to the noisy cue – in a highly distributed and automatic fashion, reminiscent of what we believe is happening in the brain (Fig. 17.2a). Brain-style computation implements an *implicit* algorithm, as we shall see in Sections 17.2 and 17.3.

17.1.2 Neuronal assemblies

Neural assemblies play a central role in the implicit algorithm for memory retrieval that we will discuss in Section 17.2. Neuronal assemblies (Hebb, 1949) are subnetworks of strongly connected neurons that, together, represent an abstract concept. For example, your mental concept of a "banana" containing the mental image of its form, color, taste, and texture could be represented by one assembly of strongly connected neurons, while another

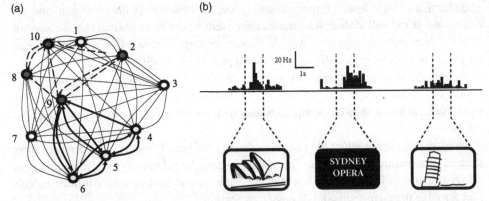

Fig. 17.3 Assemblies and responses to abstract concepts. (a) Schematic diagram of a network of 10 neurons containing two assemblies, defined as strongly connected subgroups (thick solid and dashed lines, respectively). Note that neuron 9 participates in both assemblies. Assemblies could represent abstract mental concepts. (b) Response of a single unit in the human hippocampus (Quiroga *et al.*, 2005). The same neuron responds strongly to an image of the Sydney opera house and the words "Sydney opera," but much more weakly to images of other landmarks such as the Pisa tower. Vertical lines indicate the one-second period of stimulation with images of Sydney opera house, words, or Pisa tower, respectively. The photographic images used in the real experiment are replaced here by sketches. Adapted from Quiroga *et al.* (2005).

might represent your concept of Paris with mental pictures of the Eiffel Tower and the Louvre, and yet another your concept of Sydney with its famous opera house.

The assembly as a subgroup of strongly connected neurons has been an influential theoretical notion, introduced by Hebb (1949). Do such assemblies exist? The short answer is: We don't know. Neurons belonging to an assembly do not have to be neighbors but can be widely distributed across one, or even several, brain areas. Experimentally, it is therefore difficult to check for the presence of an assembly as a *group* of neurons. However, Quiroga *et al.* (2005) found individual neurons in human patients that code for abstract mental concepts such as the Sydney opera house. These patients suffer from severe treatment-resistant epilepsy which makes a surgical intervention necessary. In order to precisely locate the focus of the epilepsy in relation to important brain areas (such as those for speech or motor control), electrophysiological recordings are made while the patient performs various tasks. In contrast to neurons in the visual cortex which respond in the presence of an appropriate visual stimulus, single neurons in the medial temporal lobe of the human cortex (in particular, in the hippocampus) do not respond to a specific stimulus, but to a much broader set of stimuli that are linked to the same mental concept. For example, the written word "Sydney" and a picture of the opera house in Sydney both cause a response in the same neuron (Fig. 17.3), which we can therefore interpret as one of the neurons belonging to the assembly of neurons encoding the mental concept "Sydney."

Three aspects are worth emphasizing. First, it is unlikely that the neuron responding to the Sydney opera house is the only one to do so. Therefore, we should not think of a *single* neuron as representing a concept or memory item, but rather a group of neurons.

The idea that a single neuron represents one concept is sometimes called the "grandmother cell" code: if the cell coding for grandmother were to die in our brain, our memory of grandmother would disappear as well. At the current stage of research, neural codes based on groups of cells are a more likely code than a grandmother cell code.

Second, the same neuron participates in several assemblies. In the recording sessions of Quiroga *et al.* where a large collection of pictures of famous individuals and landmarks were used, each unit showed strong responses to about 3% of the stimuli (Quiroga *et al.*, 2005).

Third, some, but not all, of the neurons showed prolonged responses that persisted after the end of stimulus presentation. This could potentially indicate that a memory item is retrieved and kept in the brain even after the stimulus has disappeared. All three aspects play a role in the memory model discussed in Section 17.2.

17.1.3 *Working memory and delayed matching-to-sample tasks*

In contrast to long-term memory, items in working memory do not have to be kept for a lifetime. For example, humans use their working memory when they write down a phone number that they just received or search in the supermarket for items on their shopping list. Neural activity during working memory tasks has been recorded in monkeys, in the particular in the prefrontal and inferotemporal cortex (Miyashita, 1988a; Fuster and Jervey, 1982; Miller and Cohen, 2001). In a delayed matching-to-sample task, a monkey has to indicate whether a second stimulus is, or is not, identical to a first stimulus received one or several seconds earlier.

To correctly perform the task, the monkey has to remember the sample stimulus during the delay period where no stimulation is given. Some neurons in the prefrontal cortex show sustained activity during the delay period (Fig. 17.4a). This has been interpreted as a neural signature of working memory. During the delay period, the time course of neural activity varies widely between different objects for one neuron (Fig. 17.4b). and across a population of neurons (Rainer and Miller, 2002), which indicates that simple models such as the ones discussed in this chapter do not explain all aspects of working memory.

17.2 Hopfield model

The Hopfield model (Hopfield, 1982), consists of a network of N neurons, labeled by a lower index i, with $1 \le i \le N$. Similar to some earlier models (McCulloch and Pitts, 1943; Little, 1974; Willshaw *et al.*, 1969), neurons in the Hopfield model have only two states. A neuron i is "ON" if its state variable takes the value $S_i = +1$ and "OFF" (silent) if $S_i = -1$. The dynamics evolve in discrete time with time steps Δt. There is no refractoriness and the duration of a time step is typically not specified. If we take $\Delta t = 1$ ms, we can interpret $S_i(t) = +1$ as an action potential of neuron i at time t. If we take $\Delta t = 500$ ms, $S_i(t) = +1$ should rather be interpreted as an episode of high firing rate.

(a)   (b)

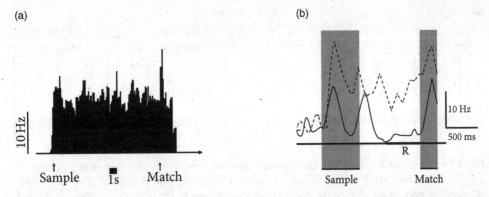

Fig. 17.4 Delayed matching-to-sample task. (a) PSTH of a neuron in the anterior ventral temporal cortex in a visual working memory task. The monkey has to indicate whether a first stimulus (sample, presented for 0.2 s at time marked by arrow) is identical to a second one which can be either a matching (arrow) or an unfamiliar stimulus; adapted from Miyashita (1988a). (b) PSTH of a single neuron in the prefrontal cortex in response to two different images, one object (dashed line) and one different noise pattern (solid line). Sample stimuli were presented for 650 ms. After a delay period of 1 s, a matching stimulus was presented. "R" marks a period when responses tend to recover after a transient dip. Vertical axis: firing rate measured with respect to baseline activity. Adapted from Rainer and Miller (2002).

Neurons interact with each other with weights w_{ij}. The input potential of neuron i, influenced by the activity of other neurons is

$$h_i(t) = \sum_j w_{ij} S_j(t).$$ (17.2)

The input potential at time t influences the probabilistic update of the state variable S_i in the next time step:

$$\text{Prob}\{S_i(t + \Delta t) = +1 | h_i(t)\} = g(h_i(t)) = g\left(\sum_j w_{ij} S_j(t)\right),$$ (17.3)

where g is a monotonically increasing gain function with values between zero and 1. A common choice is $g(h) = 0.5[1 + \tanh(\beta h)]$ with a parameter β. For $\beta \to \infty$, we have $g(h) = 1$ for $h > 0$ and zero otherwise. The dynamics are therefore deterministic and summarized by the update rule

$$S_i(t + \Delta t) = \text{sgn}[h(t)].$$ (17.4)

For finite β the dynamics are stochastic. In the following we assume that in each time step all neurons are updated synchronously (parallel dynamics), but an update scheme where only one neuron is updated per time step is also possible.

The aim of this section is to show that, with a suitable choice of the coupling matrix w_{ij}, memory items can be retrieved by the collective dynamics defined in Eq. (17.3), applied to all N neurons of the network. In order to illustrate how collective dynamics can lead

(a)   (b)

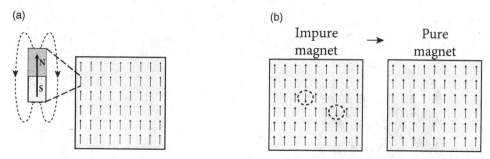

Fig. 17.5 Physics of ferromagnets. (a) Magnetic materials consist of atoms, each with a small magnetic moment, here visualized as an arrow, a symbol for a magnetic needle. At low temperature,
all magnetic needles are aligned. Inset: Field lines around one of the magnetic needles. (b) At high
temperature, some of the needles are misaligned (dashed circles). Cooling the magnet leads to a
spontaneous alignment and reforms a pure magnet. Schematic figure.

to meaningful results, we start, in Section 17.2.1, with a detour through the physics of
magnetic systems. In Section 17.2.2, the insights from magnetic systems are applied to the
case at hand, i.e., memory recall.

17.2.1 Detour: magnetic analogy

Magnetic material contains atoms which carry a so-called spin. The spin generates a magnetic moment at the microscopic level visualized graphically as an arrow (Fig. 17.5a). At
high temperature, the magnetic moments of individual atoms point in all possible directions. Below a critical temperature, however, the magnetic moment of all atoms spontaneously align with each other. As a result, the microscopic effects of all atomic magnetic
moments add up and the material exhibits the macroscopic properties of a ferromagnet.

In order to understand how a spontaneous alignment can arise, let us study Eqs. (17.2)
and (17.3) in the analogy of magnetic materials. We assume that $w_{ij} = w_0 > 0$ between all
pairs of neurons $i \neq j$, and that self-interaction vanishes, $w_{ii} = 0$.

Each atom is characterized by a spin variable $S_i = \pm 1$ where $S_i = +1$ indicates that the
magnetic moment of atom i points "upward." Suppose that, at time $t = 0$, all spins take a
positive value ($S_I = +1$), except that of atom i which has a value $S_i(0) = -1$ (Fig. 17.5a).
We calculate the probability that, at time step $t = \Delta t$, the spin of neuron i will switch to
$S_i = +1$. This probability is according to Eq. (17.3)

$$\text{Prob}\{S_i(t + \Delta t) = +1 | h_i(t)\} = g(h_i(t)) = g\left(\sum_{j=1}^{N} w_{ij} S_j(t)\right) = g(w_0 (N - 1)), \quad (17.5)$$

where we have used our assumptions. With $g(h) = 0.5[1 + \tanh(\beta h)]$ and $w_0 = \beta = 1$,
we find that, for any network of more than three atoms, the probability that the magnetic
moments of all atoms would align is extremely high. In physical systems, β plays the role

of an inverse temperature. If β becomes small (high temperature), the magnetic moments no longer align and the material loses its spontaneous magnetization.

According to Eq. (17.5) the probability of alignment increases with the network size. This is an artifact of our model with all-to-all interaction between all atoms. Physical interactions, however, rapidly decrease with distance, so that the sum over j in Eq. (17.5) should be restricted to the nearest neighbors of neuron i, e.g., about 4 to 20 atoms depending on the configuration of the atomic arrangement and the range of the interaction. Interestingly, neurons, in contrast to atoms, are capable of making long-range interactions because of their far-reaching axonal cables and dendritic trees. Therefore, the number of topological neighbors of a given neuron is in the range of thousands.

An arrangement of perfectly aligned magnetic elements looks rather boring, but physics offers more interesting examples as well. In some materials, typically consisting of two different types of atoms, say A and B, an anti-ferromagnetic ordering is possible (Fig. 17.6). While one layer of magnetic moments points upward, the next one points downward, so that the macroscopic magnetization is zero. Nevertheless, a highly ordered structure is present. Examples of anti-ferromagnets are some metallic oxides and alloys.

To model an anti-ferromagnet, we choose interactions $w_{ij} = +1$ if i and j belong to the same class (e.g., both are in a layer of type A or both in a layer of type B), and $w_{ij} = -1$ if one of the two atoms belongs to type A and the other to type B. A simple repetition of the calculation in Eq. (17.5) shows that an anti-ferromagnetic organization of the spins emerges spontaneously at low temperature.

The same idea of positive and negative interactions w_{ij} can be used to embed an arbitrary pattern into a network of neurons. Let us draw a pattern of black and white pixels corresponding to active ($p_i = +1$) and inactive ($p_i = -1$) neurons, respectively. The rule extracted from the anti-ferromagnet implies that pixels of opposite color are connected by negative weights, while pixels of the same color have connections with positive weight. This rule can be formalized as

$$w_{ij} = p_i p_j . \tag{17.6}$$

This rule forms the basis of the Hopfield model.

17.2.2 Patterns in the Hopfield model

The Hopfield model consists of a network of N binary neurons. A neuron i is characterized by its state $S_i = \pm 1$. The state variable is updated according to the dynamics defined in Eq. (17.3).

The task of the network is to store and recall M different patterns. Patterns are labeled by the index μ with $1 \leq \mu \leq M$. Each pattern μ is defined as a desired configuration $\{p_i^\mu = \pm 1; 1 \leq i \leq N\}$. The network of N neurons is said to correctly represent pattern μ, if the state of all neurons $1 \leq i \leq N$ is $S_i(t) = S_i(t + \Delta t) = p_i^\mu$. In other words, patterns must be fixed points of the dynamics (17.3).

For us as human observers, a meaningful pattern could, for example, be a configuration

(a)   (b)

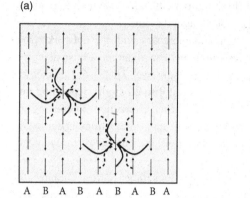

A B A B   A B   A B

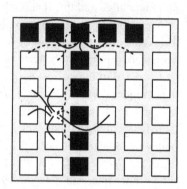

Fig. 17.6 Storing patterns. (a) Physical anti-ferromagnets consist of layers of atoms A and B. All magnetic moments are aligned within a layer of identical neurons, but exhibit different orientations between layers. A model where interactions within atoms of the same type are positive (solid lines) and interactions between atoms of different type are negative (dashed lines) can explain the spontaneous order in the arrangement of magnetic moments. The interaction scheme for two atoms with their ten nearest neighbors is indicated. (b) If we replace magnetic moments by black and white pixels (squares), represented by active and inactive neurons, respectively, the neuronal network can store a pattern, such as T. Interactions are positive (solid lines) between pixels of the same color (black-to-black or white-to-white) and negative otherwise. Only a few representative interactions are shown. Schematic figure.

in form of a "T," such as depicted in Fig. 17.6b. However, visually attractive patterns have large correlations between each other. Moreover, areas in the brain related to memory recall are situated far from the retinal input stage. Since the configuration of neurons in memory-related brain areas is probably very different from those at the retina, patterns in the Hopfield model are chosen as fixed random patterns; see Fig. 17.7.

During the set-up phase of the Hopfield network, a random number generator generates, for each pattern μ, a string of N independent binary numbers $\{p_i^{\mu} = \pm 1; 1 \leq i \leq N\}$ with expectation value $\langle p_i^{\mu} \rangle = 0$. Strings of different patterns are independent. The weights are chosen as

$$w_{ij} = c \sum_{\mu=1}^{M} p_i^{\mu} p_j^{\mu}, \tag{17.7}$$

with a positive constant $c > 0$. The network has full connectivity. Note that for a single pattern and $c = 1$, Eq. (17.7) is identical to the connections of the anti-ferromagnet, Eq. (17.6). For reasons that become clear later on, the standard choice of the constant c is $c = 1/N$.

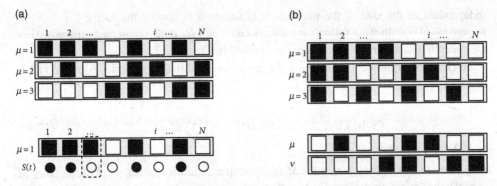

Fig. 17.7 Hopfield model. (a) Top: Three random patterns $\mu = 1, 2, 3$ in a network of $N = 8$ neurons. Black squares ($p_i^\mu = +1$) and white squares ($p_i^\mu = -1$) are arranged in random order. Bottom: The overlap $m^1 = (1/N) \sum_i p_i^1 S_i(t)$ measures the similarity between the current state $S(t) = \{S_i(t); 1 \leq i \leq N\}$ and the first pattern. Here only a single neuron exhibits a mismatch (dotted line). The desired value in the pattern is shown as black and white squares, while the current state is indicated as black and white circles. Schematic figure. (b) Orthogonal patterns have a mutual overlap of zero so that correlations are $C^{\mu\nu} = (1/N) \sum_i p_i^\mu p_i^\nu = \delta^{\mu\nu}$ (top) whereas random patterns exhibit a small residual overlap for $\mu \neq \nu$ (bottom).

17.2.3 Pattern retrieval

In many memory retrieval experiments, a cue with partial information is given at the beginning of a recall trial. The retrieval of a memory item is verified by the completion of the missing information.

To mimic memory retrieval in the Hopfield model, an input is given by initializing the network in a state $S(t_0) = \{S_i(t_0); 1 \leq i \leq N\}$. After initialization, the network evolves freely under the dynamics (17.3). Ideally the dynamics should converge to a fixed point corresponding to the pattern μ which is most similar to the initial state.

To measure the similarity between the current state $S(t) = \{S_i(t); 1 \leq i \leq N\}$ and a pattern μ, we introduce the overlap (Fig. 17.7a)

$$m^\mu(t) = \frac{1}{N} \sum_i p_i^\mu S_i(t). \tag{17.8}$$

The overlap takes a maximum value of 1 if $S_i(t) = p_i^\mu$, i.e., if the pattern is retrieved. It is close to zero if the current state has no correlation with pattern μ. The minimum value $m^\mu(t) = -1$ is achieved if each neuron takes the opposite value to that desired in pattern μ.

The overlap plays an important role in the analysis of the network dynamics. In fact, using Eq. (17.2) the input potential h_i of a neuron i is

$$h_i(t) = \sum_j w_{ij} S_j(t) = c \sum_{j=1}^{N} \sum_{\mu=1}^{M} p_i^\mu p_j^\mu S_j(t) = cN \sum_{\mu=1}^{M} p_i^\mu m^\mu(t), \tag{17.9}$$

where we have used Eqs. (17.7) and (17.8). To make the results of the calculation independent of the size of the network, it is standard to choose the factor $c = 1/N$, as mentioned above. In what follows we always take $c = 1/N$ unless indicated otherwise. For an in-depth discussion, see the scaling arguments in Chapter 12.

To close the argument, we now use the input potential in the dynamics equation (17.3) and find

$$\text{Prob}\{S_i(t + \Delta t) = +1 | h_i(t)\} = g \left[\sum_{\mu=1}^{M} p_i^{\mu} m^{\mu}(t) \right]. \tag{17.10}$$

Equation (17.10) highlights that the M macroscopic similarity values m^{μ} with $1 \leq \mu \leq M$ completely determine the dynamics of the network.

Example: Memory retrieval

Let us suppose that the initial state has a significant similarity with pattern $\mu = 3$, for example an overlap of $m^{\mu}(t_0) = 0.4$ and no overlap with the other patterns $m^{\nu} = 0$ for $\nu \neq 3$.

In the noiseless case Eq. (17.10) simplifies to

$$S_i(t_0 + \Delta t) = \text{sgn} \left[\sum_{\mu=1}^{M} p_i^{\mu} m^{\mu} \right] = \text{sgn} \left[p_i^3 m^3(t_0) \right] = p_i^3 \quad \text{for all } i. \tag{17.11}$$

Hence, each neuron takes, after a single time step, the desired state corresponding to the pattern. In other words, the pattern with the strongest similarity to the input is retrieved, as it should be.

For stochastic neurons we find

$$\text{Prob}\{S_i(t_0 + \Delta t) = +1 | h_i(t)\} = g[p_i^3 m^3(t_0)]. \tag{17.12}$$

We note that, given the overlap $m^3(t_0)$, the right-hand side of Eq. (17.12) can take only two different values, corresponding to $p_i^3 = +1$ and $p_i^3 = -1$. Thus, all neurons that *should* be active in pattern 3 share the same probabilistic update rule:

$$\text{Prob}\{S_i(t_0 + \Delta t) = +1 | h_i(t)\} = g[m^3(t_0)] \quad \text{for all } i \text{ with } p_i^3 = +1. \tag{17.13}$$

Similarly all those that *should* be inactive share another rule:

$$\text{Prob}\{S_i(t_0 + \Delta t) = +1 | h_i(t)\} = g[-m^3(t_0)] \quad \text{for all } i \text{ with } p_i^3 = -1. \tag{17.14}$$

Thus, despite the fact that there are N neurons and M different patterns, during recall the network breaks up into two macroscopic populations: those that should be active and those that should be inactive. This is the reason why we can expect to arrive at macroscopic population equations, similar to those encountered in Part III of the book.

Let us use this insight for the calculation of the overlap at time $t_0 + \Delta t$. We denote the size of the two populations (active, inactive) by N_+^3 and N_-^3, respectively, and find

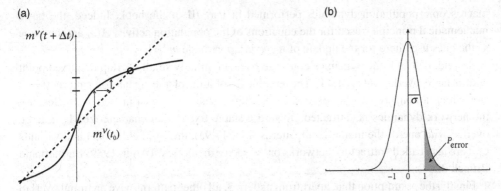

Fig. 17.8 Memory retrieval in the Hopfield model. (a) The overlap $m^v(t+\Delta t)$ with a specific pattern v is given as a function of the overlap with the same pattern $m^v(t)$ in the previous time step (solid line); see Eq. (17.16). The overlap with the $M-1$ other patterns is supposed to vanish. The iterative update can be visualized as a path (arrow) between the overlap curve and the diagonal (dashed line). The dynamics approach a fixed point (circle) with high overlap corresponding to the retrieval of the pattern. (b) The probability P_{error} that during retrieval an erroneous state flip occurs corresponds to the shaded area under the curve; see Eq. (17.20). The width σ of the curve is proportional to the pattern load M/N. Schematic figure.

$$m^3(t_0+\Delta t) = \frac{1}{N}\sum_i p_i^3 S_i(t_0+\Delta t) \qquad (17.15)$$

$$= \frac{N_+^3}{N}\left[\frac{1}{N_+^3}\sum_{i \text{ with } p_i^3=+1} S_i(t_0+\Delta t)\right] - \frac{N_-^3}{N}\left[\frac{1}{N_-^3}\sum_{i \text{ with } p_i^3=+1} S_i(t_0+\Delta t)\right].$$

We can interpret the two terms enclosed by the square brackets as the average activity of those neurons that should, or should not, be active, respectively. In the limit of a large network ($N\to\infty$) both groups are very large and of equal size $N_+^3 = N_-^3 = N/2$. Therefore, the averages inside the square brackets approach their expectation values. The technical term, used in the physics literature, is that the network dynamics are "self-averaging." Hence, we can evaluate the square brackets with probabilities introduced in Eqs. (17.13) and (17.14). With $\text{Prob}\{S_i(t_0+\Delta t) = -1|h_i(t)\} = 1 - \text{Prob}\{S_i(t_0+\Delta t) = +1|h_i(t)\}$, we find

$$m^3(t_0+\Delta t) = \frac{1}{2}\{2g[m^3(t_0)]-1\} - \frac{1}{2}\{2g[-m^3(t_0)]-1\}. \qquad (17.16)$$

In the special case that $g(h) = 0.5[1+\tanh(\beta h)]$ Eq. (17.16) simplifies to an update law

$$m^3(t+\Delta t) = \tanh[\beta\, m^3(t)], \qquad (17.17)$$

where we have replaced t_0 by t, in order to highlight that updates should be iterated over several time steps.

We close with three remarks. First, the dynamics of N neurons has been replaced, in a mathematically precise limit, by the iterative update of one single macroscopic variable, i.e., the overlap with one of the patterns. The result is reminiscent of the analysis of the macroscopic population dynamics performed in Part III of the book. Indeed, the basic mathematical principles used for the equations of the population activity $A(t)$ are the same as the ones used here for the update of the overlap variable $m^\mu(t)$.

Second, if $\beta > 1$, the dynamics converge from an initially small overlap to a fixed point with a large overlap, close to 1. The graphical solution of the update of pattern $v = 3$ (for which a nonzero overlap existed in the initial state) is shown in Fig. 17.8. Because the network dynamics is "attracted" toward a stable fixed point characterized by a large overlap with one of the memorized patterns (Fig. 17.9a), the Hopfield model and variants of it are also called "attractor" networks or "attractor memories" (Amit, 1989; Barbieri and Brunel, 2008).

Finally, the assumption that, apart from pattern 3, all other patterns have an initial overlap exactly equal to zero is artificial. For random patterns, we expect a small overlap between arbitrary pairs of patterns. Thus, if the network is exactly in pattern 3 so that $m^3 = 1$, the other patterns have a small but finite overlap $|m^\mu| \neq 0$, because of spurious correlations $C^{\mu v} = (1/N) \sum_i p_i^\mu p_i^v$ between any two random patterns μ and v; Fig. 17.7b. If the number of patterns is large, the spurious correlations between the patterns can generate problems during memory retrieval, as we shall see now.

17.2.4 Memory capacity

How many random patterns can be stored in a network of N neurons? Memory retrieval implies pattern completion, starting from a partial cue. An absolutely minimal condition for pattern completion is that at least the dynamics should not move *away* from the pattern, if the initial cue is *identical* to the complete pattern (Hertz *et al.*, 1991). In other words, we require that a network with initial state $S_i(t_0) = p_i^v$ for $1 \leq i \leq N$ stays in pattern v. Therefore pattern v must be a fixed point under the dynamics.

We study a Hopfield network at zero temperature ($\beta = \infty$). We start the calculation as in Eq. (17.9) and insert $S_j(t_0) = p_j^v$. This yields

$$S_i(t_0 + \Delta t) = \text{sgn} \left[\frac{1}{N} \sum_{j=1}^{N} \sum_{\mu=1}^{M} p_i^\mu p_j^\mu p_j^v \right]$$

$$= \text{sgn} \left[p_i^v \left(\frac{1}{N} \sum_{j=1}^{N} p_j^v p_j^v \right) + \frac{1}{N} \sum_{\mu \neq v} \sum_j p_i^\mu p_j^\mu p_j^v \right], \qquad (17.18)$$

where we have separated the pattern v from the other patterns. The factor in parentheses on the right-hand side adds up to 1 and can therefore be dropped. We now multiply the second term on the right-hand side by a factor $1 = p_i^v p_i^v$. Finally, because $p_i^v = \pm 1$, a factor p_i^v can be pulled out of the argument of the sign-function:

$$S_i(t_0 + \Delta t) = p_i^v \, \text{sgn} \left[1 + \frac{1}{N} \sum_j \sum_{\mu \neq v} p_i^\mu p_i^v p_j^\mu p_j^v \right] = p_i^v \, \text{sgn}[1 - a_{iv}]. \qquad (17.19)$$

The desired fixed point exists only if $1 > a_{iv} = \frac{1}{N}\sum_j \sum_{\mu \neq v} p_i^\mu p_i^v p_j^\mu p_j^v$ for all neurons i. In other words, even if the network is initialized in perfect agreement with one of the patterns, it can happen that one or a few neurons flip their sign. The probability of moving away from the pattern is equal to the probability of finding a value $a_{iv} > 1$ for one of the neurons i.

Because patterns are generated from independent random numbers $p_i^\mu = \pm 1$ with zero mean, the product $p_i^\mu p_i^v p_j^\mu p_j^v = \pm 1$ is also a binary random number with zero mean. Since the values p_i^μ are chosen independently for each neuron i and each pattern μ, the term a_{iv} can be visualized as a random walk of $N(M-1)$ steps and step size $1/N$. For a large number of steps, the positive or negative walking distance can be approximated by a Gaussian distribution with zero mean and standard deviation $\sigma = \sqrt{(M-1)/N} \approx \sqrt{M/N}$ for $M \gg 1$. The probability that the activity state of neuron i erroneously flips is therefore proportional to (Fig. 17.86)

$$P_{\text{error}} = \frac{1}{\sqrt{2\pi}\sigma} \int_1^\infty e^{\frac{-x^2}{2\sigma^2}} \, dx \approx \frac{1}{2}\left[1 - \text{erf}\left(\sqrt{\frac{N}{2M}}\right)\right], \qquad (17.20)$$

where we have introduced the error function

$$\text{erf}(x) = \frac{1}{\sqrt{\pi}} \int_0^x e^{-y^2} \, dy. \qquad (17.21)$$

The most important insight is that the probability of an erroneous state flip increases with the ratio M/N. Formally, we can define the storage capacity C_{store} of a network as the maximal number M^{max} of patterns that a network of N neurons can retrieve

$$C_{\text{store}} = \frac{M^{\text{max}}}{N} = \frac{M^{\text{max}} N}{N^2}. \qquad (17.22)$$

For the second equality sign we have multiplied both numerator and denominator by a common factor N which gives rise to the following interpretation. Since each pattern consists of N neurons (i.e., N binary numbers), the total number of bits that need to be stored at maximum capacity is $M^{\text{max}} N$. In the Hopfield model, patterns are stored by an appropriate choice of the synaptic connections. The number of available synapses in a fully connected network is N^2. Therefore, the storage capacity measures the number of bits stored per synapse.

Example: Erroneous bits

We can evaluate Eq. (17.20) for various choices of P_{error}. For example, if we accept an error probability of $P_{\text{error}} = 0.001$, we find a storage capacity of $C_{\text{store}} = 0.105$.

Hence, a network of 10 000 neurons is capable of storing about 1000 patterns with $P_{\text{error}} = 0.001$. Thus in each of the patterns, we expect that about 10 neurons exhibit erroneous activity. We emphasize that the above calculation focuses on the *first* iteration step only. If we start in the pattern, then about 10 neurons will flip their state in the first iteration. But these flips could in principle cause further neurons to flip in the second iteration and eventually initiate an avalanche of many other changes.

(a)   (b)

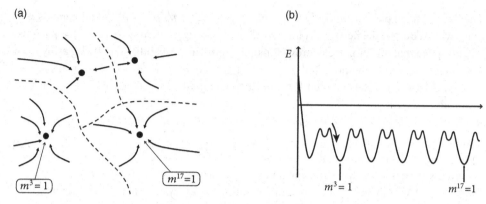

Fig. 17.9 Attractor picture and energy landscape. (a) The dynamics are attracted toward fixed points corresponding to memory states (overlap $m^\nu = 1$). Four attractor states are indicated. The dashed lines show the boundaries of the basin of attraction of each memory. (b) The Hopfield model has multiple equivalent energy minima, each one corresponding to the retrieval (overlap $m^\nu = 1$) of one pattern. Between the main minima, additional local minima (corresponding to mixtures of several patterns) may also exist.

A more precise calculation shows that such an avalanche does not occur if the number of stored patterns stays below a limit such that $C_{\text{store}} = 0.138$ (Amit *et al.*, 1985, 1987b).

17.2.5 The energy picture

The Hopfield model has symmetric interactions $w_{ij} = w_{ji} = c \sum_{\mu=1}^{M} p_i^\mu p_j^\mu$. We now show that, in any network with symmetric interactions and asynchronous deterministic dynamics

$$S_i(t + \Delta t) = \text{sgn}[h(t)] = \text{sgn}\left[\sum_j w_{ij} S_j(t)\right], \tag{17.23}$$

the energy

$$E = -\sum_i \sum_j w_{ij} S_i S_j \tag{17.24}$$

decreases with each state flip of a single neuron (Hopfield, 1982).

In each time step only one neuron is updated (asynchronous dynamics). Let us assume that after application of Eq. (17.23) neuron k has changed its value from S_k at time t to $S_k' = -S_k$ while all other neurons keep their value $S_j' = S_j$ for $j \neq k$. The prime indicates values evaluated at time $t + \Delta t$. The change in energy caused by the state flip of neuron k is

$$E' - E = -\sum_i w_{ik} S_i (S_k' - S_k) - \sum_j w_{kj} S_j (S_k' - S_k). \tag{17.25}$$

First, because of the update of neuron k, we have $S_k' - S_k = 2S_k'$. Second, because of the symmetry $w_{ij} = w_{ji}$, the two terms on the right-hand side are identical, and $\sum_i w_{ik} S_i = \sum_i w_{ki} S_i = h_k$. Third, because of Eq. (17.23), the sign of h_k determines the new value S_k' of neuron k. Therefore the change in energy is $E' - E = -4h_k \operatorname{sgn} h_k < 0$. In other words, the energy E is a Liapunov function of the deterministic Hopfield network.

Since the dynamics leads to a decrease of the energy, we may wonder whether we can say something about the global or local minimum of the energy. If we insert the definition of the connection weights into the energy function (17.24), we find

$$E = -\sum_i \sum_j \left(c \sum_\mu p_i^\mu p_j^\mu \right) S_i S_j = -cN^2 \sum_\mu (m^\mu)^2, \qquad (17.26)$$

where we have used the definition of the overlap; see Eq. (17.8).

The maximum value of the overlap with a fixed pattern v is $m^v = 1$. Moreover, for random patterns, the correlations between patterns are small. Therefore, if $m^v = 1$ (i.e., recall of pattern v) the overlap with other patterns $\mu \neq v$ is $m^\mu \approx 0$. Therefore, the energy landscape can be visualized with multiple minima of the same depth, each minimum corresponding to retrieval of one of the patterns (Fig. 17.9b).

17.2.6 Retrieval of low-activity patterns

There are numerous aspects in which the Hopfield model is rather far from biology. One of these is that, in each memory pattern, 50% of the neurons are active.

To characterize patterns with a lower level of activity, let us introduce random variables $\xi_i^\mu \in \{0,1\}$ for $1 \leq i \leq N$ and $1 \leq \mu \leq M$ with mean $\langle \xi_i^\mu \rangle = a$. For $a = 0.5$ and $p_i^\mu = 2\xi_i^\mu - 1$ we are back to the patterns in the Hopfield model. In the following we are, however, interested in patterns with an activity $a < 0.5$. To simplify some of the arguments below, we suppose that patterns are generated under the constraint $\sum_i \xi_i^\mu = N a$ for each μ, so that all patterns have *exactly* the same target activity a.

The weights in the Hopfield model of Eq. (17.7) are replaced by

$$w_{ij} = c' \sum_{\mu=1}^{M} (\xi_i^\mu - b)(\xi_j^\mu - a), \qquad (17.27)$$

where a is the mean activity of the stored patterns, $0 \leq b \leq 1$ a constant, and $c' = [2a(1-a)N]^{-1}$. Note that Eq. (17.7) is a special case of Eq. (17.27) with $a = b = 0.5$ and $c' = 2c$.

As before, we work with binary neurons $S_i = \pm 1$ defined by the stochastic update rule in Eqs. (17.2) and (17.3). To analyze pattern retrieval we proceed analogously to Eq. (17.10). Introducing the overlap of low-activity patterns

$$m^\mu = \frac{1}{2a(1-a)N} \sum_j (\xi_j^\mu - a) S_j, \qquad (17.28)$$

we find

$$\operatorname{Prob}\{S_i(t+\Delta t) = +1 | h_i(t)\} = g \left[\sum_{\mu=1}^{M} (\xi_i^\mu - b) m^\mu(t) \right]. \qquad (17.29)$$

Example: Memory retrieval and attractor dynamics

Suppose that at time t the overlap with one of the patterns, say pattern 3, is significantly above zero while the overlap with all other patterns vanishes $m^\mu \approx m\,\delta^{\mu 3}$, where δ^{nm} denotes the Kronecker-δ. The initial overlap is $0.1 < m \le 1$. Then the dynamics of the low-activity networks split up into two groups of neurons, i.e., those that should be "ON" in pattern 3 ($\xi_i^3 = 1$) and those that should be "OFF" ($\xi_i^3 = 0$).

The size of both groups scales with N: there are $a \cdot N$ "ON" neurons and $(1-a) \cdot N$ "OFF" neurons. For $N \to \infty$, the population activity A^{ON} of the "ON" group (i.e., the fraction of neurons with state $S_i = +1$ in the "ON" group) is therefore well described by its expectation value

$$A^{\text{ON}}(t + \Delta t) = g[(1-b)\,m^3(t)]. \qquad (17.30)$$

Similarly, the "OFF" group has activity

$$A^{\text{OFF}}(t + \Delta t) = g[(-b)\,m^3(t)]. \qquad (17.31)$$

To close the argument we determine the overlap at time $t + \Delta t$. Exploiting the split into two groups of size $a \cdot N$ and $(1-a) \cdot N$, respectively, we have

$$m^3(t + \Delta t) = \frac{1}{2a(1-a)N} \left[\sum_{j \text{ with } \xi_j^3 = 1} (1-a)\,S_j(t+\Delta t) + \sum_{j \text{ with } \xi_j^3 = 0} (-a)\,S_j(t+\Delta t) \right]$$

$$= \frac{1}{2}\left[A^{\text{ON}}(t+\Delta t) - A^{\text{OFF}}(t+\Delta t) \right]. \qquad (17.32)$$

Thus, the overlap with pattern 3 has changed from the initial value $m^3(t) = m$ to a new value $m^3(t+\Delta t)$. Retrieval of memories works if iteration of Eqs. (17.30)–(17.32) makes m^3 converge to a value close to unity while, at the same time, the other overlaps m^ν (for $\nu \ne 3$) stay close to zero.

We emphasize that the analysis of the network dynamics presented here does not require symmetric weights but is possible for arbitrary values of the parameter b. However, a standard choice is $b = a$, which leads to symmetric weights and to a high memory capacity (Tsodyks and Feigelman, 1986).

17.3 Memory networks with spiking neurons

The Hopfield model is an abstract conceptual model and rather far from biological reality. In this section we aim at pushing the abstract model in the direction of increased biological plausibility. We focus on two aspects. In Section 17.3.1 we replace the binary neurons of the Hopfield model with spiking neuron models of the class of Generalized Linear Models or Spike Response Models; see Chapter 9. Then, in Section 17.3.2 we ask whether it is possible to store multiple patterns in a network where excitatory and inhibitory neurons are functionally separated from each other.

17.3.1 Activity of spiking networks

Neuron models such as the Spike Response Model with escape noise, formulated in the framework of Generalized Linear Models, can predict spike times of real neurons to a high degree of accuracy; see Chapters 9 and 11. We therefore choose the Spike Response Model (SRM) as our candidate for a biologically plausible neuron model. Here we use these neuron models to analyze the macroscopic dynamics in attractor memory networks of spiking neurons.

As discussed in Chapter 9, the membrane potential u_i of a neuron i embedded in a large network can be described as

$$u_i(t) = \sum_f \eta(t - t_i^f) + h_i(t) + u_{\text{rest}}, \tag{17.33}$$

where $\eta(t - t_i^f)$ summarizes the refractoriness caused by the spike-afterpotential and $h_i(t)$ is the (deterministic part of the) input potential

$$h_i(t) = \sum_j w_{ij}\varepsilon(t - t_j^f) = \sum_j w_{ij} \int_0^\infty \varepsilon(s) S_j(t - s)\mathrm{d}s. \tag{17.34}$$

Here i denotes the postsynaptic neuron, w_{ij} is the coupling strength from a presynaptic neuron j to i, and $S_j(t) = \sum_f \delta(t - t_j^f)$ is the spike train of neuron j.

Statistical fluctuations in the input as well as intrinsic noise sources are both incorporated into an escape rate (or stochastic intensity) $\rho_i(t)$ of neuron i,

$$\rho_i(t) = f(u_i(t) - \vartheta), \tag{17.35}$$

which depends on the momentary distance between the (noiseless) membrane potential and the threshold ϑ.

In order to embed memories in the network of SRM neurons we use Eq. (17.27) and proceed as in Section 17.2.6. There are three differences compared to the previous section: First, while previously S_j denoted a binary variable ± 1 in *discrete* time, we now work with spikes $\delta(t - t_j^f)$ in *continuous* time. Second, in the Hopfield model a neuron can be active in every time step while here spikes must have a minimal distance because of refractoriness. Third, the input potential h is only one of the contributions to the total membrane potential.

Despite these differences the formalism of Section 17.2.6 can be directly applied to the case at hand. Let us define the *instantaneous* overlap of the spike pattern in the network with pattern μ as

$$m^\mu(t) = \frac{1}{2a(1 - a)N} \sum_j (\xi_j^\mu - a) S_j(t), \tag{17.36}$$

where $S_j(t) = \sum_f \delta(t - t_j^f)$ is the spike train of neuron j. Note that, because of the Dirac δ-function, we need to integrate over m^μ in order to arrive at an observable quantity. Such

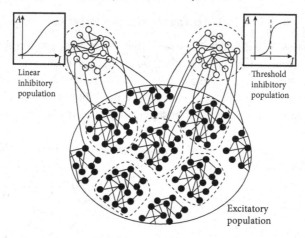

Fig. 17.10 A population of excitatory neurons interacts with two populations of inhibitory neurons. Memory patterns are embedded as Hebbian assemblies in the excitatory population. All neurons are integrate-and-fire neurons. Theory predicts that the first inhibitory population should be activated to levels where the gain function (left inset) is approximately linear. The second inhibitory population is activated if the total input is above some threshold value (right inset).

an integration is automatically performed by each neuron. Indeed, the input potential Eq. (17.34) can be written as

$$h_i(t) = \sum_j \left(\frac{1}{2a(1-a)N} \sum_{\mu=1}^{M} (\xi_i^\mu - b)(\xi_j^\mu - a) \right) \int_0^\infty \varepsilon(s) S_j(t-s)\,ds$$

$$= \sum_{\mu=1}^{M} (\xi_i^\mu - b) \int_0^\infty \varepsilon(s) m^\mu (t-s)\,ds, \tag{17.37}$$

where we have used Eqs. (17.27) and (17.36).

Thus, in a network of N neurons (e.g., $N = 100\,000$) which has stored M patterns (e.g., $M = 2000$) the input potential is completely characterized by the M overlap variables, which reflects an enormous reduction in the complexity of the mathematical problem. Nevertheless, each neuron keeps its identity for two reasons:

(i) Each neuron i is characterized by its "private" set of past firing times t_i^f. Therefore each neuron is in a different state of refractoriness and adaptation which manifests itself by the term $\sum_f \eta(t - t_i^f)$ in the total membrane potential.

(ii) Each neuron has a different functional role during memory retrieval. This role is defined by the sequence $\xi_i^1, \xi_i^2, \ldots, \xi_i^M$. For example, if neuron i is part of the active assembly in patterns $\mu = 3, \mu = 17, \mu = 222, \mu = 1999$ and should be inactive in the other 1996 patterns, then its functional role is defined by the set of numbers $\xi_i^3 = \xi_i^{17} = \xi_i^{222} = \xi^{1999} = 1$ and $\xi_i^\mu = 0$ otherwise. In a network that stores M different patterns there are 2^M different functional roles so it is extremely unlikely that two neurons play the same role. Therefore each of the N neurons in the network is different!

However, during retrieval we can reduce the complexity of the dynamics drastically. Suppose that during the interval $t_0 < t < t_0 + T$ all overlaps are negligible, except the overlap with one of the patterns, say pattern v. Then the input potential in Eq. (17.37) reduces for $t > t_0 + T$

$$h_i(t) = (\xi_i^v - b) \int_0^\infty \varepsilon(s) m^v(t-s) \, ds, \qquad (17.38)$$

where we have assumed that $\varepsilon(s) = 0$ for $s > T$. Therefore, the network with its N different neurons splits up into two homogeneous populations: the first one comprises all neurons with $\xi_i^v = +1$, i.e., those that should be "ON" during retrieval of pattern v; and the second comprises all neurons with $\xi_i^v = 0$, i.e., those that should be "OFF" during retrieval of pattern v.

In other words, we can apply the mathematical tools of population dynamics that were presented in Part III of this book to analyze memory retrieval in a network of N different neurons.

Example: Spiking neurons without adaptation

In the absence of adaptation, the membrane potential depends only on the input potential and the time since the last spike. Thus, Eq. (17.33) reduces to

$$u_i(t) = \eta(t - \hat{t}_i) + h_i(t) + u_{\text{rest}}, \qquad (17.39)$$

where $\hat{t}_i$ denotes the last firing time of neuron i and $\eta(t - \hat{t}_i)$ summarizes the effect of refractoriness. Under the assumption of an initial overlap with pattern v and no overlap with other patterns, the input potential is given by Eq. (17.38). Thus, the network of N splits into an "ON" population with input potential

$$h^{\text{ON}}(t) = (1 - b) \int_0^\infty \varepsilon(s) m^v(t-s) \, ds \qquad (17.40)$$

and an "OFF" population with input potential

$$h^{\text{OFF}}(t) = (-b) \int_0^\infty \varepsilon(s) m^v(t-s) \, ds. \qquad (17.41)$$

For each of the populations, we can write down the integral equation of the population dynamics that we saw in Chapter 14. For example, the "ON"-population evolves according to

$$A^{\text{ON}}(t) = \int_{-\infty}^t P_I(t|\hat{t}) A(\hat{t}) d\hat{t} \qquad (17.42)$$

with

$$P_I(t|\hat{t}) = \rho(t) \exp\left[-\int_{\hat{t}}^t \rho(t') dt'\right], \qquad (17.43)$$

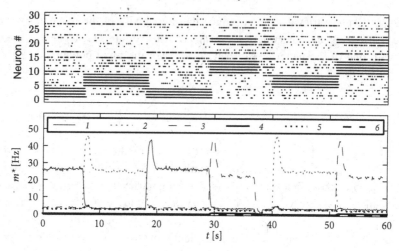

Fig. 17.11 Attractor network with spiking neurons. Memory retrieval in a network of 8000 excitatory neurons which stores 90 different patterns. Top: The spike raster shows 30 neurons selected and relabeled so that the first five neurons respond to pattern 1, the second group of five neurons to pattern 2, etc. Bottom: Overlap defined here as $m^{\mu*} = A^{ON}(t)$ with the first six patterns $1 \leq \mu \leq 6$. After a partial cue ($t = 8, 18.5, 19.5, 40, 51$ s), one of the patterns is retrieved and remains stable without further input during a delay period of 10 seconds. Occasionally a global input to the inhibitory neurons is given leading to a reset of the network ($t = 38$ s). After the reset, the network remains in the spontaneously activity state.

where $\rho(t) = f(\eta(t - \hat{t}) + h^{ON}(t) + u_{rest} - \vartheta)$. An analogous equation holds for the "OFF"-population.

Finally, we use Eq. (17.36) to close the system of equations. The sum over all neurons can be split into one sum over the "ON"-population and another over the "OFF"-population, of size $a \cdot N$ and $(1 - a) \cdot N$, respectively. If the number N of neurons is large, the overlap is therefore

$$m^{\nu}(t) = \frac{1}{2}[A^{ON}(t) - A^{OFF}(t)]. \qquad (17.44)$$

Thus, the retrieval of pattern ν is controlled by a small number of macroscopic equations.

In an analogous sequence of calculations one needs to check that the overlap with the other patterns μ (with $\mu \neq \nu$) does not increase during retrieval of pattern ν.

17.3.2 *Excitatory and inhibitory neurons*

Synaptic weights in the Hopfield model can take both positive and negative values. However, in the cortex, all connections originating from the same presynaptic neuron have the same sign, either excitatory or inhibitory. This experimental observation, called Dale's law, gives rise to a primary classification of neurons as excitatory or inhibitory.

In Chapter 16 we started with models containing separate populations of excitatory and inhibitory neurons, but could show that the model dynamics are, under certain conditions, equivalent to an effective network where the excitatory populations excite themselves but inhibit each other. Thus explicit inhibition was replaced by an effective inhibition. Here we take the inverse approach and transform the effective mutual inhibition of neurons in the Hopfield network into an *explicit* inhibition via populations of inhibitory neurons.

To keep the arguments transparent, let us stick to discrete time and work with random patterns $\xi_i^\mu \in \{0,1\}$ with mean activity $(\sum_i \xi_i^\mu)/N = a$. We take weights $w_{ij} = c' \sum_\mu (\xi_i^\mu - b)(\xi_j^\mu - a)$ and introduce a discrete-time spike variable $\sigma_i = 0.5(S_i + 1)$ so that $\sigma_i = 1$ can be interpreted as a spike and $\sigma_i = 0$ as the quiescent state. Under the assumption that each pattern μ has exactly $a \cdot N$ entries with $\xi_i^\mu = 1$, we find that the input potential $h_i = \sum_j w_{ij} S_j$ can be rewritten with the spike variable σ

$$h_i(t) = 2c' \sum_j \sum_\mu (\xi_i^\mu - b) \xi_j^\mu \sigma_j - 2c' \sum_j \sum_\mu (\xi_i^\mu - b) a \sigma_j. \tag{17.45}$$

In what follows we choose $b = 0$ and $c' = 1/4N$. Then the first sum on the right-hand side of Eq. (17.45) describes excitatory and the second one inhibitory interactions.

To interpret the second term as arising from inhibitory neurons, we make the following assumptions. First, inhibitory neurons have a linear gain function and fire stochastically with probability

$$\text{Prob}\{\sigma_k = +1 | h_k^{\text{inh}}\} = g(h_k^{\text{inh}}(t))\Delta t = \gamma h_k^{\text{inh}}(t), \tag{17.46}$$

where the constant γ takes care of the units and k is the index of the inhibitory neuron with $1 \leq k \leq N^{\text{inh}}$. Second, each inhibitory neuron k receives input from C excitatory neurons. Connections are random and of equal weight $w^{E \to I} = 1/C$. Thus, the input potential of neuron k is $h_k^{\text{inh}} = (1/C)\sum_{j \in \Gamma_k} \sigma_j$ where Γ_k is the set of presynaptic neurons. Third, the connection from an inhibitory neuron k back to an excitatory neuron i has weight

$$w_{ik}^{I \to E} = \frac{a}{\gamma N^{\text{inh}}} \sum_\mu \xi_i^\mu. \tag{17.47}$$

Thus, inhibitory weights onto a neuron i which participates in many patterns are stronger than onto one which participates in only a few patterns. Fourth, the number N^{inh} of inhibitory neurons is large. Taken together, the four assumptions give rise to an average inhibitory feedback to each excitatory neuron proportional to $\sum_j \sum_\mu \xi_i^\mu a \sigma_j$. In other words, the inhibition caused by the inhibitory population is equivalent to the second term in Eq. (17.45).

Because of our choice $b = 0$, patterns are only in weak competition with each other and several patterns can become active at the same time. In order to also limit the total activity of the network, it is useful to add a second pool of inhibitory neurons which turn on whenever the total number of spikes in the network exceeds $a \cdot N$. Note that biological cortical tissue contains many different types of inhibitory interneurons, which are thought to play different functional roles; Fig. 17.10.

Figure 17.11 shows that the above argument carries over to the case of integrate-and-fire neurons in continuous time. We emphasize that the network of 8000 excitatory and two groups of inhibitory neurons (2000 neurons each) has stored 90 patterns of activity $a \approx 0.1$. Therefore each neuron participates in many patterns (Curti *et al.*, 2004).

In practice, working memory models with spiking neurons require some parameter tuning. Adding to working models a mechanism of synaptic short-term facilitation (see Chapter 3) improves stability of memory retrieval during the delay period (Mongillo *et al.*, 2008).

17.4 Summary

The Hopfield model is an abstract model of memory retrieval. After a cue with a partial overlap with one of the stored memory patterns is presented, the memory item is retrieved. Because the Hopfield model has symmetric synaptic connections, memory retrieval can be visualized as downhill movement in an energy landscape. An alternative view is that of memories forming attractors of the collective network dynamics. While the energy picture does not carry over to networks with asymmetric interactions, the attractor picture remains applicable even for biologically more plausible network models with spiking neurons.

Attractor networks where each neuron participates in several memory patterns can be seen as a realization of Hebb's idea of neuronal assemblies. At the current state of research, it remains unclear whether increased spiking activity observed in the cortex during delayed matching-to-sample tasks has a relation to attractor dynamics. However, the ideas of Hebb and Hopfield have definitely influenced the thinking of many researchers.

Literature

Precursors of the Hopfield model are the networks models of Willshaw *et al.* (1969), Kohonen (1972), Anderson (1972), and Little (1974). The model of associative memory of Willshaw *et al.* (1969) was designed for associations between a binary input pattern $\xi^{\mu,A}$ and a binary output vector $\xi^{\mu,B}$, where $\xi_i^{\mu,A/B} \in \{0,1\}$ and interactions weights w_{ij} are taken to vary as $\xi_i^{\mu,B} \xi_j^{\mu,A}$ where j is a component of the input and i a component of the desired output pattern. A recurrent network can be constructed if the dimensionality of inputs and outputs match and the output from step n is used as input to step $n+1$.

Intrinsically recurrent models of memory were studied with linear neurons by Kohonen (1972) and Anderson (1972) and with stochastic binary units by Little (1974). The latter showed that, under some assumptions, persistent states that can be identified with potential memory states can exist in such a network.

Hopfield's (1982) paper has influenced a whole generation of physicists and is probably the most widely cited paper in computational neuroscience. It initiated a wave of studies of storage capacity and retrieval properties in variants of the Hopfield model using the tools of statistical physics (Amit *et al.*, 1985, 1987b) including extensions to low-activity patterns (Amit *et al.*, 1987a; Tsodyks and Feigelman, 1986), sparsely connected networks (Derrida *et al.*, 1987) and temporal sequences (Sompolinsky and Kanter, 1986; Herz *et al.*, 1989). The energy function in Hopfield (1982) requires symmetric interactions, but the dynamics can also be analyzed directly on the level of overlaps. The book by Hertz *et al.* (1991) presents an authoritative overview of these and related topics in the field of associative memory networks.

The transition from abstract memory networks to spiking network models began after 1990 (Amit and Tsodyks, 1991; Gerstner, 1991; Gerstner and van Hemmen, 1992; Treves, 1993; Amit and Brunel, 1997a,b) and continued after 2000 (Curti *et al.*, 2004; Mongillo *et al.*, 2008), but a convincing memory model of spiking excitatory and inhibitory neurons where each neuron participates in several memory patterns is still missing. The relation of attractor network models to persistent activity in electrophysiological recordings in monkey prefrontal cortex during memory tasks is discussed in the accessible papers of Barbieri and Brunel (2008) and Balaguer-Ballester *et al.* (2011).

Exercises

1. **Storing one or several patterns.**

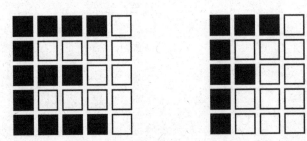

Fig. 17.12 Patterns for "E" and "F" in a Hopfield network of 25 neurons.

(a) *In a Hopfield network of 25 binary neurons (Fig. 17.12), how would you encode the letter E? Write down couplings w_{ij} from arbitrary neurons onto neuron i if i is either the black pixel in the lower left corner of the image or the white pixel in the lower right corner.*

(b) *Suppose the initial state is close to the stored image, except for m pixels which are flipped. How many time steps does the Hopfield dynamics take to correct the wrong pixels? What is the maximum number of pixels that can be corrected? What happens if 20 pixels are flipped?*

(c) *Store as a second pattern the character F using the Hopfield weights $w_{ij} = \sum_\mu p_i^\mu p_j^\mu$. Write down the dynamics in terms of overlaps. Suppose that the initial state is exactly F. What is the overlap with the first pattern?*

2. **Mixture states.** *Use the rule of the Hopfield network to store the six orthogonal patterns such as those shown in Fig. 17.7b but of size 8×8.*

(a) *Suppose the initial state is identical to pattern $v = 4$. What is the overlap with the other patterns $\mu \neq v$?*
Hint: Why are these patterns orthogonal?

(b) *How many pixels can be wrong in the initial state, so that pattern $v = 4$ is retrieved with deterministic dynamics?*

(c) *Start with an initial state which has overlap with two patterns: $m^1 = (1 - \alpha)m$ and $m^2 = \alpha m$ and $m^\mu = 0$ for $\mu \geq 3$. Analyze the evolution of the overlap over several time steps, using deterministic dynamics.*

(d) *Repeat the calculation in (c) but for a mixed cue $m^1(t) = m^2(t) = m^3(t) = m < 1$ and $m^v(t) = 0$ for $v > 3$. Is the mixture of three patterns a stable attractor of the dynamics?*

(e) Repeat the calculation in (d), for stochastic dynamics.

3. **Binary codes and spikes.** *In the Hopfield model, neurons are characterized by a binary variable $S_i = \pm 1$. For an interpretation in terms of spikes it is, however, more appealing to work with a binary variable $\sigma_i \in \{0, 1\}$.*

(a) Write $S_i = 2\sigma_i - 1$ and rewrite the Hopfield model in terms of the variable σ_i. What are the conditions so that the the input potential in the rewritten model is simply $h_i = \sum_j w_{ij}\sigma_j$?

(b) Repeat the same calculation for low-activity patterns and weights $w_{ij} = c' \sum_\mu (\xi_i^\mu - b)(\xi_j^\mu - a)$ with some constants a, b, c' and $\xi_i^\mu \in \{0, 1\}$. What are conditions such that $h_i = \sum_j w_{ij}\sigma_j$?

18

Cortical field models for perception

The world is continuous. Humans walk along corridors and streets, move their arms, turn their head, and orient the direction of gaze. All of these movements and gestures can be described by continuous variables such as position, head direction, gaze orientation, etc. These continuous variables need to be represented in the brain. Field models are designed to encode such continuous variables.

Objects such as houses, trees, cars, pencils have a finite extension in three-dimensional space. Visual input arising from these and other objects is projected onto the retinal photo-receptors and gives rise to a two-dimensional image in the retina. This image is already preprocessed by nerve cells in the retina and undergoes some further processing stages before it arrives in the cortex. A large fraction of the primary visual cortex is devoted to processing of information from the retinal area around the fovea. As a consequence, the activation pattern on the cortical surface resembles a coarse, deformed and distorted image of the object (Fig. 18.1). Topology is largely preserved so that neighboring neurons in the cortex process neighboring points of retinal space. In other words, neighboring neurons have similar receptive fields, which give rise to cortical maps; see Chapter 12.

In this chapter we describe the activity of local groups of cortical neurons. We exploit the fact that neighboring neurons have similar receptive fields so as to arrive at a continuum model of cortical activity. Neural continuum models are often called field models. Neurons in a field model typically receive input on a forward path, from sensory modalities such as vision, audition, or touch, but they also interact with each other. Field models of sensory areas in the cortex are suitable to explain some, but not all, aspects of perception. For example, the lateral interaction of neurons in the visual cortex (and also in the retina!) gives rise to visual phenomena such as Mach bands or grid illusions (Fig. 18.2).

Field models are also used for some forms of working memory. As an example, let us focus on the sense of orientation. Normally, when reading this book for example, you are able to point spontaneously in the direction of the door of your room. Let us imagine that you spin around with closed eyes until you get dizzy and lose your sense of orientation. When you open your eyes your sense of orientation will re-establish itself based on the visual cues in your surroundings. Thus, visual input strongly influences self-orientation. Nevertheless, the sense of orientation also works in complete darkness. If somebody turns the lights off, you still remember where the door is. Thus, humans (and animals) have a

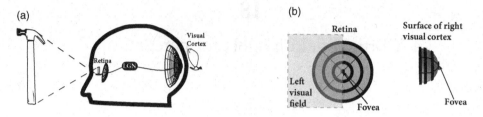

Fig. 18.1 Transformation from visual space to the cortex. (a) The image of an object is projected onto the retina and from there transmitted, via the optic tract and lateral geniculate nucleus (LGN), to the visual cortex. The pattern of activation on the medial surface of visual cortex represents a "distorted" image. (b) Concentric rings on the retina give rise to vertical stripes of activation along the surface of the cortical tissue. A large fraction of neurons in V1 process information from a small region around the fovea in the retina. From Kandel *et al.* (2000).

rather stable "internal compass" which can be used, even in complete darkness, to walk a few steps in the right direction.

While the memory effect of the "internal compass" can be related to the regime of bump attractors in a continuum model, perceptual phenomena can be described by the same class of continuum models, but in the input-driven regime. Both regimes will be discussed in this chapter. We start with a general introduction to continuum models in Section 18.1. We then turn to the input-driven regime in Section 18.2 in order to account for some perceptual and cortical phenomena. Finally we discuss the regime of bump attractors in the context of the sense of orientation (Section 18.3).

18.1 Spatial continuum model

We focus on networks that have a spatial structure. In doing so we emphasize two characteristic features of the cerebral cortex, namely the high density of neurons and its virtually two-dimensional architecture.

Each cubic millimeter of cortical tissue contains more than 10^4 neurons. This impressive number suggests that a description of neuronal dynamics in terms of an averaged *population activity* is more appropriate than a description on the single-neuron level. Furthermore, the cerebral cortex is huge. More precisely, the unfolded cerebral cortex of humans covers a surface of 2200–2400 cm², but its thickness amounts on average to only 2.5–3.0 mm. If we do not look too closely, the cerebral cortex can hence be treated as a continuous two-dimensional sheet of neurons. Neurons will no longer be labeled by discrete indices but by continuous variables that give their spatial position on the sheet. The coupling of two neurons i and j is replaced by the *average* coupling strength between neurons at position x and those at position y, or, even more radically simplified, by the average coupling strength of two neurons being separated by the distance $|x - y|$. Similarly to the notion of an average coupling strength we will also introduce the *average activity* of neurons located at position x and describe the dynamics of the network in terms of these averaged quantities only. The details of how these average quantities are defined have been discussed in Chapter 12.

(a)

(b)

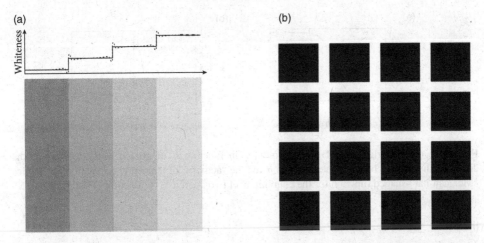

Fig. 18.2 Visual illusions. (a) Mach bands. Gray stripes touching each other are perceived as non-uniform, despite the fact that inside each stripe the gray value is constant. Top: Actual (solid line) and perceived (dashed line) whiteness (vertical axis) as a function of position along the horizontal axis of the image. (b) Helmholtz grid illusion. A grid of black squares on a white background gives rise to scintillating bright or gray dots at the intersections of the white bands.

We now introduce – without a formal justification – field equations for the spatial activity $A(x,t)$ in a spatially extended, but otherwise homogeneous, population of neurons.

We work with the population rate equations that we introduced in Chapter 15. As we have seen, these equations neglect rapid transients and oscillations that can show up in simulations of spiking neurons. On the other hand, in the limit of high noise and short refractoriness, the approximation of population dynamics by differential equations is good; see Chapter 15.

Consider a single sheet of densely packed neurons. We assume that all neurons have similar properties and that the connectivity is homogeneous and isotropic, i.e., that the coupling strength of two neurons is a function of their distance only. We loosely define a quantity $h(x,t)$ as the average input potential at time t of the group of neurons located at position x. We have seen in Chapter 12 that in the stationary state the "activity" of a population of neurons is strictly given by the single-neuron gain function $A_0(x) = F[h(x)]$; see Fig. 18.3. If we *assume* that changes of the input potential are slow enough so that the population always remains in a state of incoherent firing, then we can set

$$A(x,t) = F[h(x,t)], \qquad (18.1)$$

even for time-dependent situations. According to Eq. (18.1), the activity $A(x,t)$ of the population around location x is a function of the input potential at that location.

The synaptic input current to a given neuron depends on the level of activity of its presynaptic neurons and on the strength of the synaptic couplings. We assume that the amplitude of the input current is simply the presynaptic activity scaled by the average coupling strength of these neurons. The total input current $I^{\text{syn}}(x,t)$ to a neuron at position x is (a)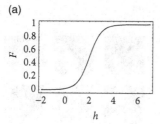

(b)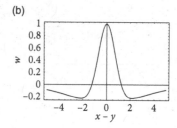

Fig. 18.3 (a) Generic form of the sigmoidal gain function F of graded response neurons that describes the relation between the potential h and the "activity" of the neural population. (b) Typical "Mexican-hat"-shaped function for the coupling w of two neurons as a function of their distance x.

therefore

$$I^{\text{syn}}(x,t) = \int \mathrm{d}y\, w\,(|x-y|)\,A(y,t).\qquad(18.2)$$

Here, w is the average coupling strength of two neurons as a function of their distance.

To complete the definition of the model, we need to specify a relation between the input current and the resulting membrane potential. To keep things simple we treat each neuron as a leaky integrator. The input potential is thus given by a differential equation of the form

$$\tau\frac{\partial h}{\partial t} = -h + RI^{\text{syn}} + RI^{\text{ext}},\qquad(18.3)$$

with τ being the time constant of the integrator and I^{ext} an additional external input. In what follows we work with unit-free variables and set $R = 1$. If we put things together we obtain the field equation

$$\tau\frac{\partial h(x,t)}{\partial t} = -h(x,t) + \int \mathrm{d}y\, w\,(|x-y|)\,F[h(y,t)] + I^{\text{ext}}(x,t);\qquad(18.4)$$

see Wilson and Cowan (1973); Feldman and Cowan (1975); Amari (1977). This is a nonlinear integro-differential equation for the average membrane potential $h(x,t)$.

18.1.1 Mexican-hat coupling

In order to be more specific, we now specify the connection strength w as a function of interneuron distance. In what follows we consider a connectivity pattern that is excitatory for proximal neurons and predominantly inhibitory for distal neurons. Figure 18.3b shows the typical "Mexican-hat" shape of the corresponding coupling function.

There are a few simplifying assumptions in the choice of the Mexican-hat function which are worth mentioning. First, Eq. (18.2) assumes that synaptic interaction is instantaneous. In a more detailed model we could include the axonal transmission delay and synaptic time constants. In that case, $A(y,t)$ on the right-hand side of Eq. (18.2) should be replaced by $\int \alpha(s)A(y,t-s)\,\mathrm{d}s$ where $\alpha(s)$ is the temporal interaction kernel.

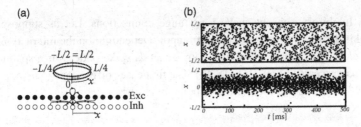

Fig. 18.4 Ring model with spiking neurons. (a) Neurons are organized on a ring, i.e., neurons at position $x = L/2$ are neighbors of neurons at position $x = -L/2$ (top). The dashed vertical line indicates the position where the ring was cut for the unfolded figure at the bottom. At each position x excitatory and inhibitory neurons interact with each other. Inhibitory interactions have a longer range than the excitatory ones. Both neuron types are integrate-and-fire models with identical model parameters and interaction patterns. (b) Spike patterns of sample neurons. In the input-driven regime, activity is spatially homogeneous (top) while for stronger lateral interactions an activation bump forms spontaneously (bump attractor, bottom). Vertical axis shows different neurons, plotted according to their position on the ring. In both cases input is spatially uniform. From Shriki *et al.* (2003) by permission of MIT Press Journals.

Second, in Eq. (18.2) presynaptic neurons at location x can give rise to both excitatory and inhibitory input whereas cortical neurons are either excitatory or inhibitory. The reason is that our population model is meant to be an effective model. There are two alternative ways to arrive at such an effective model. Either we work out the effective coupling model using the mathematical steps of Chapter 16 starting from a common pool of inhibitory neurons shared by all excitatory cells. Or we assume that excitatory and inhibitory neurons at each location receive the same mean input and have roughly the same neuronal parameters (Shriki *et al.*, 2003), but have slightly different output pathways (Fig. 18.4a). In both cases, inhibition needs to be of longer range than excitation to arrive at the effective Mexican-hat coupling. A third, and biologically more plausible alternative is discussed in Section 18.2.4.

With Mexican-hat coupling, two different regimes emerge (Fig. 18.4):

(i) In the *input-driven regime* the activity pattern is, in the absence of input, spatially uniform. In other words, any spatial structure in the neuronal activity pattern is causally linked to the input.

(ii) In the *regime of bump attractors*, spatially localized activity patterns develop even in the absence of input (or with spatially uniform input).

The two regimes are discussed in Sections 18.2 and 18.3, respectively.

Example: Ring model with spiking neurons

Excitatory and inhibitory integrate-and-fire models are coupled with a ring-like topology (Fig. 18.4a). Excitatory neurons make connections to their excitatory and inhibitory neighbors. Inhibitory neurons make long-range connections. Let us suppose that the ring model is driven by a spatially uniform input. Depending on the interaction strength (Shriki *et al.*, 2003), either a spatially homogeneous spike pattern or a spatially localized spike pattern can emerge (Fig. 18.4b). The first case corresponds to the input-driven regime, the second case to the regime of bump attractors.

18.2 Input-driven regime and sensory cortex models

In this section we study the field equation (18.4) in the input-driven regime. Thus, if the input is spatially uniform, the activity pattern is also spatially uniform. From a mathematical perspective, the spatially uniform activity pattern is the homogeneous solution of the field equation (Section 18.2.1). The stability of the homogeneous solution is discussed in Section 18.2.2.

A non-trivial spatial structure in the input gives rise to deviations from the homogeneous solution. Thus the input drives the formation of spatial activity patterns. This regime can account for perceptual phenomena such as contrast enhancement as shown in Section 18.2.3. Finally, we discuss how the effective Mexican-hat interaction, necessary for contrast enhancement, could be implemented in the cortex with *local* inhibition (Section 18.2.4).

18.2.1 Homogeneous solutions

Although we have kept the above model as simple as possible, the field equation (18.4) is complicated enough to prevent comprehensive analytical treatment. We therefore start our investigation by looking for a special type of solution, i.e., a solution that is uniform over space, but not necessarily constant over time. We call this the homogeneous solution and write $h(x,t) \equiv h(t)$. We expect that a homogeneous solution exists if the external input is homogeneous as well, i.e., if $I^{\text{ext}}(x,t) \equiv I^{\text{ext}}(t)$.

Substitution of the ansatz $h(x,t) \equiv h(t)$ in Eq. (18.4) yields

$$\tau \frac{dh(t)}{dt} = -h(t) + \bar{w} F[h(t)] + I^{\text{ext}}(t), \qquad (18.5)$$

with $\bar{w} = \int dy \, w(|y|)$. This is a nonlinear ordinary differential equation for the average input potential $h(t)$. We note that the equation for the homogeneous solution is identical to that of a single population without spatial structure; see Chapter 15.

The fixed points of the above equation with $I^{\text{ext}} = 0$ are of particular interest because they correspond to a resting state of the network. More generally, we search for stationary solutions for a given constant external input $I^{\text{ext}}(x,t) \equiv I^{\text{ext}}$. The fixed points of Eq. (18.5) are solutions of

$$F(h) = \frac{h - I^{\text{ext}}}{\bar{w}}, \qquad (18.6)$$

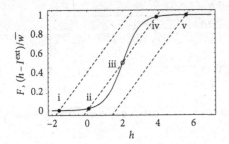

Fig. 18.5 Graphical representation of the fixed-point equation (18.6). The solid line corresponds to the neuronal gain function $F(h)$ and the dashed lines to $(h - I^{\text{ext}})/\bar{w}$ for different amounts of external stimulation I^{ext}. Depending on the amount of I^{ext} there is either a stable fixed point at low activity (i), a stable fixed point at high activity (v), or a bistable situation with stable fixed points (ii–iv) separated by an unstable fixed point at intermediate level of activity (iii).

which is represented graphically in Fig. 18.5.

Depending on the strength of the external input three qualitatively different situations can be observed. For low external stimulation there is a single fixed point at a very low level of neuronal activity. This corresponds to a quiescent state where the activity of the whole network has ceased. Large stimulation results in a fixed point at an almost saturated level of activity which corresponds to a state where all neurons are firing at their maximum rate. Intermediate values of external stimulation, however, may result in a situation with more than one fixed point. Depending on the shape of the output function and the mean synaptic coupling strength $\bar{w}$, three fixed points may appear. Two of them correspond to the quiescent and the highly activated state, which are separated by the third fixed point at an intermediate level of activity.

Any potential physical relevance of fixed points clearly depends on their stability. Stability under the dynamics defined by the ordinary differential equation (18.5) is readily checked using standard analysis. Stability requires that at the intersection

$$F'(h) < \bar{w}^{-1}. \tag{18.7}$$

Thus all fixed points corresponding to quiescent or highly activated states are stable whereas the middle fixed point in the case of multiple solutions is unstable; see Fig. 18.5. This, however, is only half the truth because Eq. (18.5) describes only homogeneous solutions. Therefore, it may well be that the solutions are stable with respect to Eq. (18.5), but unstable with respect to *inhomogeneous* perturbations, i.e., to perturbations that do not have the same amplitude everywhere in the net.

18.2.2 Stability of homogeneous states (*)

In what follows we will perform a linear stability analysis of the homogeneous solutions found in the previous section. Readers not interested in the mathematical details can jump directly to Section 18.2.3.

We study the field equation (18.4) and consider small perturbations about the homogeneous solution. A linearization of the field equation will lead to a linear differential equa-

(a)

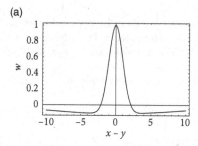

(b)

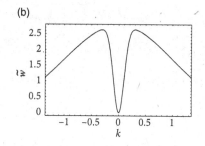

Fig. 18.6 (a) Synaptic coupling function with zero mean as in Eq. (18.14) with $\sigma_1 = 1$ and $\sigma_2 = 10$. (b) Fourier transform of the coupling function shown in (a); see Eq. (18.16).

tion for the amplitude of the perturbation. The homogeneous solution is said to be stable if the amplitude of every small perturbation is *decreasing* whatever its shape.

Suppose $h(x,t) \equiv h_0$ is a homogeneous solution of Eq. (18.4), i.e.,

$$0 = -h_0 + \int dy\, w(|x-y|)\, F[h_0] + I^{\text{ext}}. \tag{18.8}$$

Consider a small perturbation $\delta h(x,t)$ with initial amplitude $|\delta h(x,0)| \ll 1$. We substitute $h(x,t) = h_0 + \delta h(x,t)$ in Eq. (18.4) and linearize with respect to δh,

$$\tau \frac{\partial}{\partial t} \delta h(x,t) = -h_0 - \delta h(x,t)$$
$$+ \int dy\, w(|x-y|)\,[F(h_0) + F'(h_0)\,\delta h(y,t)] + I^{\text{ext}}(x,t) + \mathcal{O}(\delta h^2). \tag{18.9}$$

Here, a prime denotes the derivative with respect to the argument. Zero-order terms cancel each other because of Eq. (18.8). If we collect all terms linear in δh we obtain

$$\tau \frac{\partial}{\partial t} \delta h(x,t) = -\delta h(x,t) + F'(h_0) \int dy\, w(|x-y|)\,\delta h(y,t). \tag{18.10}$$

We make two important observations. First, Eq. (18.10) is *linear* in the perturbations δh – simply because we have neglected terms of order $(\delta h)^n$ with $n \geq 2$. Second, the coupling between neurons at locations x and y is mediated by the coupling kernel $w(|x-y|)$ that depends only on the distance $|x-y|$. If we apply a Fourier transform over the spatial coordinates, the convolution integral turns into a simple multiplication. It suffices therefore to discuss a single (spatial) Fourier component of $\delta h(x,t)$. Any specific initial form of $\delta h(x,0)$ can be created from its Fourier components by virtue of the superposition principle. We can therefore proceed without loss of generality by considering a single Fourier compo-

(a)

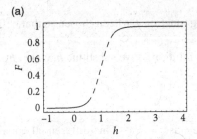

(b)

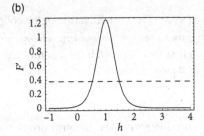

Fig. 18.7 (a) Gain function $F(h) = \{1 + \exp[\beta(x - \theta)]\}^{-1}$ with $\beta = 5$ and $\theta = 1$. The dashed line indicates that part of the graph where the slope exceeds the critical slope s^*. (b) Derivative of the gain function shown in (a) (solid line) and critical slope s^* (dashed line).

nent, namely, $\delta h(x,t) = c(t)\,e^{ikx}$. If we substitute this ansatz in Eq. (18.10) we obtain

$$\tau c'(t) = -c(t)\left[1 - F'(h_0)\int dy\, w(|x - y|)\,e^{ik(y-x)}\right]$$

$$= -c(t)\left[1 - F'(h_0)\int dz\, w(|z|)\,e^{ikz}\right], \tag{18.11}$$

which is a *linear* differential equation for the amplitude c of a perturbation with wave number k. This equation is solved by

$$c(t) = c(0)\,e^{-\kappa(k)t}, \tag{18.12}$$

with

$$\kappa(k) = 1 - F'(h_0)\int dz\, w(|z|)\,e^{ikz}. \tag{18.13}$$

Stability of the solution h_0 with respect to a perturbation with wave number k depends on the sign of the real part of $\kappa(k)$. Note that – quite intuitively – only two quantities enter this expression, namely the slope of the activation function evaluated at h_0 and the Fourier transform of the coupling function w evaluated at k. If the real part of the Fourier transform of w stays below $1/F'(h_0)$, then h_0 is stable. Note that Eqs. (18.12) and (18.13) are valid for an arbitrary coupling function $w(|x - y|)$. In the following, we illustrate the typical behavior for a specific choice of the lateral coupling.

Example: "Mexican-hat" coupling with zero mean

We describe Mexican-hat coupling by a combination of two bell-shaped functions with different width. For the sake of simplicity we will again consider a one-dimensional sheet of neurons. For the lateral coupling we take

$$w(x) = \frac{\sigma_2\,e^{-x^2/(2\sigma_1^2)} - \sigma_1\,e^{-x^2/(2\sigma_2^2)}}{\sigma_2 - \sigma_1}, \tag{18.14}$$

with $\sigma_1 < \sigma_2$. The normalization of the coupling function has been chosen so that $w(0) = 1$ and $\int \mathrm{d}x\, w(x) = \bar{w} = 0$; cf Fig. 18.6a.

As a first step we search for a homogeneous solution. If we substitute $h(x,t) = h(t)$ in Eq. (18.4) we obtain

$$\tau \frac{\mathrm{d}h(t)}{\mathrm{d}t} = -h(t) + I^{\mathrm{ext}}.\tag{18.15}$$

The term containing the integral drops out because $\bar{w} = 0$. This differential equation has a single stable fixed point at $h_0 = I^{\mathrm{ext}}$. This situation corresponds to the graphical solution of Fig. 18.5 with the dashed lines replaced by vertical lines ("infinite slope").

We still have to check the stability of the homogeneous solution $h(x,t) = h_0$ with respect to inhomogeneous perturbations. In the present case, the Fourier transform of w,

$$\int \mathrm{d}x\, w(x)\, \mathrm{e}^{ikx} = \frac{\sqrt{2\pi}\,\sigma_1\,\sigma_2}{\sigma_2 - \sigma_1}\left(\mathrm{e}^{-k^2\sigma_1^2/2} - \mathrm{e}^{-k^2\sigma_2^2/2}\right),\tag{18.16}$$

vanishes at $k = 0$ and has its maximum at

$$k_m = \pm\left[\frac{2\ln(\sigma_2^2/\sigma_1^2)}{\sigma_2^2 - \sigma_1^2}\right]^{1/2}.\tag{18.17}$$

At the maximum, the amplitude of the Fourier transform has a value of

$$\hat{w}_m = \max_k \int \mathrm{d}x\, w(x)\, \mathrm{e}^{ikx} = \frac{\sqrt{2\pi}\,\sigma_1\,\sigma_2}{\sigma_2 - \sigma_1}\left[\left(\frac{\sigma_1^2}{\sigma_2^2}\right)^{\frac{\sigma_1^2}{\sigma_2^2 - \sigma_1^2}} - \left(\frac{\sigma_1^2}{\sigma_2^2}\right)^{\frac{\sigma_2^2}{\sigma_2^2 - \sigma_1^2}}\right],\tag{18.18}$$

see Fig. 18.6b. We use this result in Eqs. (18.12) and (18.13) and conclude that stable homogeneous solutions can only be found for those parts of the graph of the output function $F(h)$ where the slope $s = F'(h)$ does not exceed the critical value $s^* = 1/\hat{w}_m$,

$$s^* = \frac{\sigma_2 - \sigma_1}{\sqrt{2\pi}\,\sigma_1\,\sigma_2}\left[\left(\frac{\sigma_1^2}{\sigma_2^2}\right)^{\frac{\sigma_1^2}{\sigma_2^2 - \sigma_1^2}} - \left(\frac{\sigma_1^2}{\sigma_2^2}\right)^{\frac{\sigma_2^2}{\sigma_2^2 - \sigma_1^2}}\right]^{-1}.\tag{18.19}$$

Figures 18.6 and 18.7 show that, depending on the choice of coupling w and gain functions F, a certain interval for the external input exists without a corresponding stable homogeneous solution. In this parameter domain a phenomenon called *pattern formation* can be observed: small fluctuations around the homogeneous state grow exponentially until a characteristic pattern of regions with low and high activity has developed; see Fig. 18.8.

18.2.3 Contrast enhancement

More than a hundred years ago Mach described the psychophysical phenomenon of edge enhancement or contrast enhancement (Mach, 1906): the sharp transition between two

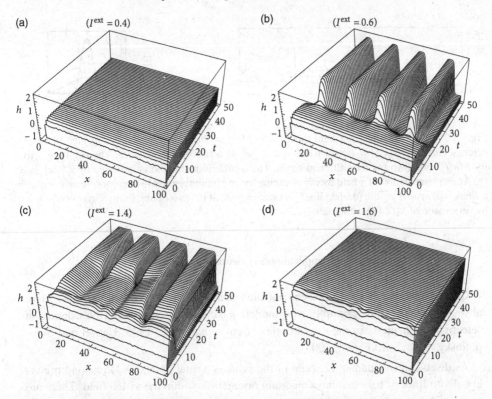

Fig. 18.8 Spontaneous pattern formation in a one-dimensional sheet of neurons with "Mexican-hat" type of interaction and homogeneous external stimulation. The parameters for the coupling function and the output function are the same as in Figs. 18.6–18.7. The graphs show the evolution in time of the spatial distribution of the average membrane potential $h(x,t)$. (a) For $I^{\text{ext}} = 0.4$ the homogeneous low-activity state is stable, but it loses stability at $I^{\text{ext}} = 0.6$. (b) Here, small initial fluctuations in the membrane potential grow exponentially and result in a global pattern of regions with high and low activity. (c) Similar situation to that in (b), but with $I^{\text{ext}} = 1.4$. (d) Finally, at $I^{\text{ext}} = 1.6$ the homogeneous high-activity mode is stable.

regions of different intensities generates perceptual bands along the borders that enhance the perceived intensity difference (Fig. 18.2a). Edge enhancement is already initiated in the retina (Mach, 1865), but likely to have cortical components as well.

Field models with a Mexican-hat interaction kernel generically generate contrast enhancement in the input-driven regime (Fig. 18.9a). Because of the nonlinear lateral interactions, an incoming spatial input pattern is transformed (Wilson and Cowan, 1973; Grossberg, 1973). For example, a spatial input with rectangular profile boosts activity at the borders, while a smooth input with sinusoidal modulation across space boosts activity at the maximum (Fig. 18.9b). A spatial input with a staircase intensity profile generates activity patterns that resemble the perceptual phenomenon of Mach bands.

(a)

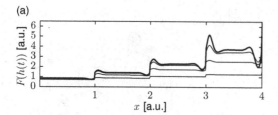

(b)

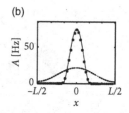

Fig. 18.9 (a) Mach bands in a field model with Mexican-hat coupling. Reflecting Fig. 18.2a, the external current $I^{\text{ext}}(x,t) = I^{\text{ext}}(x)$ forms a staircase as a function of distance. The resulting activity $F(h(t))$ is shown for four different times. The equilibrium solution is indicated by a thick line. (b) An implementation of a field model of excitatory and inhibitory spiking neurons, stimulated with a sinusoidal spatial profile (dashed line) generates a peak at the maximum. From Shriki *et al.* (2003) by permission of MIT Press Journals.

Example: An application to orientation selectivity in V1

Continuum models can represent not only spatial position profiles, but also more abstract variables. For example, ring models have been used to describe orientation selectivity of neurons in the visual cortex (Ben-Yishai *et al.*, 1995; Hansel and Sompolinsky, 1998; Shriki *et al.*, 2003).

As discussed in Chapter 12, cells in the primary visual cortex (V1) respond preferentially to lines or bars that have a certain orientation within the visual field. There are neurons that "prefer" vertical bars; others respond maximally to bars with a different orientation (Hubel, 1988). Up to now it is still a matter of debate where this orientation selectivity comes from. It may be the result of the wiring of the input to the visual cortex, i.e., the wiring of the projections from the LGN to V1, or it may result from intra-cortical connections, i.e., from the wiring of the neurons within V1, or both. Here we will investigate the extent to which intracortical projections can contribute to orientation selectivity.

We consider a network of neurons forming a so-called hyper column. These are neurons with receptive fields which correspond to roughly the same zone in the visual field but with different preferred orientations. The orientation of a bar at a given position within the visual field can thus be coded faithfully by the population activity of the neurons from the corresponding hyper column.

Instead of using spatial coordinates to identify a neuron in the cortex, we label the neurons in this section by their preferred orientation θ which may vary from $-\pi/2$ to $+\pi/2$. In doing so we assume that the preferred orientation is indeed a good "name tag" for each neuron so that the synaptic coupling strength can be given in terms of the preferred orientations of presynaptic and postsynaptic neuron. Following the formalism developed in the previous sections, we assume that the synaptic coupling strength w of neurons with preferred orientation θ and θ' is a symmetric function of the difference

$\theta - \theta'$, i.e., $w = w(|\theta - \theta'|)$. Since we are dealing with angles from $[-\pi/2, +\pi/2]$ it is natural to assume that all functions are π-periodic so that we can use Fourier series to characterize them. Non-trivial results are obtained even if we retain only the first two Fourier components of the coupling function,

$$w(\theta - \theta') = w_0 + w_2 \cos[2(\theta - \theta')]. \tag{18.20}$$

Similarly to the intracortical projections we take the (stationary) external input from the LGN as a function of the difference of the preferred orientation θ and the orientation of the stimulus θ_0,

$$I^{\text{ext}}(\theta) = c_0 + c_2 \cos[2(\theta - \theta_0)]. \tag{18.21}$$

Here, c_0 is the mean of the input and c_2 describes the modulation of the input that arises from anisotropies in the projections from the LGN to V1.

Analogously to Eq. (18.4) the field equation for the present setup thus has the form

$$\tau \frac{\partial h(\theta, t)}{\partial t} = -h(\theta, t) + \int_{-\pi/2}^{+\pi/2} \frac{d\theta'}{\pi} \, w(|\theta - \theta'|) \, F[h(\theta', t)] + I^{\text{ext}}(\theta). \tag{18.22}$$

We are interested in the distribution of the neuronal activity within the hyper column as it arises from a stationary external stimulus with orientation θ_0. This will allow us to study the role of intracortical projections in sharpening orientation selectivity.

In order to obtain conclusive results we have to specify the form of the gain function F. A particularly simple case is the piecewise linear function,

$$F(h) = [h]_+ \equiv \begin{cases} h, & h \geq 0, \\ 0, & h < 0, \end{cases} \tag{18.23}$$

so that neuronal firing increases linearly monotonously once the input potential exceeds a certain threshold.

If we assume that the average input potential $h(\theta, t)$ is always above threshold, then we can replace the gain function F in Eq. (18.22) by the identity function. We are thus left with the following *linear* equation for the stationary distribution of the average membrane potential,

$$h(\theta) = \int_{-\pi/2}^{+\pi/2} \frac{d\theta'}{\pi} \, w(|\theta - \theta'|) \, h(\theta') + I^{\text{ext}}(\theta). \tag{18.24}$$

This equation is solved by

$$h(\theta) = h_0 + h_2 \cos[2(\theta - \theta_0)], \tag{18.25}$$

with

$$h_0 = \frac{c_0}{1 - w_0} \quad \text{and} \quad h_2 = \frac{2 c_2}{2 - w_2}. \tag{18.26}$$

As a result of the intracortical projections, the modulation h_2 of the response of the (a)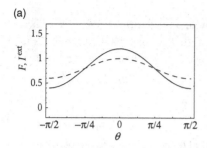

(b)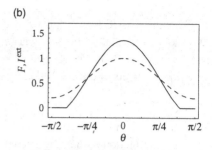

Fig. 18.10 Activity profiles (solid line) that result from stationary external stimulation (dashed line) in a model of orientation selectivity. (a) Weak modulation ($c_0 = 0.8$, $c_2 = 0.2$) of the external input results in a broad activity profile; see Eq (18.24). (b) Strong modulation ($c_0 = 0.6$, $c_2 = 0.4$) produces a narrow profile; see Eq. (18.27). Other parameters are $\omega_0 = 0$, $\omega_2 = 1$, $\theta_0 = 0$.

neurons from the hyper column is thus amplified by a factor $2/(2-w_2)$ compared to the modulation of the input c_2.

In deriving Eq. (18.24) we have assumed that h always stays above threshold so that we have an additional condition, namely, $h_0 - |h_2| > 0$, in order to obtain a self-consistent solution. This condition may be violated depending on the stimulus. In that case the above solution is no longer valid and we have to take the nonlinearity of the gain function into account (Ben-Yishai *et al.*, 1995), i.e., we have to replace Eq. (18.24) by

$$h(\theta) = \int_{\theta_0 - \theta_c}^{\theta_0 + \theta_c} \frac{d\theta'}{\pi} \, w(|\theta - \theta'|) \, h(\theta') + I^{\text{ext}}(\theta). \tag{18.27}$$

Here, $\theta_0 \pm \theta_c$ are the cut-off angles that define the interval where $h(\theta)$ is positive. If we use (18.25) in the above equation, we obtain together with $h(\theta_0 \pm \theta_c) = 0$ a set of equations that can be solved for h_0, h_2, and θ_c. Figure 18.10 shows two examples of the resulting activity profiles $F[h(\theta)]$ for different modulation depths of the input.

Throughout this example we have described neuronal populations in terms of an averaged input potential and the corresponding firing rate. At least for stationary input and a high level of noise this is indeed a good approximation of the dynamics of spiking neurons. Figure 18.11 shows two examples of a simulation based on SRM_0 neurons with escape noise and a network architecture that is equivalent to what we have used above. The stationary activity profiles shown in Fig. 18.11 for a network of spiking neurons are qualitatively similar to those of Fig. 18.10 derived for a rate-based model. For low levels of noise, however, the description of spiking networks in terms of a firing rate is no longer valid, because the state of asynchronous firing becomes unstable (see Section 14.2.3) and neurons tend to synchronize (Laing and Chow, 2001).

18.2.4 Inhibition, surround suppression, and cortex models

There are several concerns when writing down a standard field model such as Eq. (18.4) with Mexican-hat interaction. In this section, we aim to move field models closer to biology and consider three of these concerns.

(a)

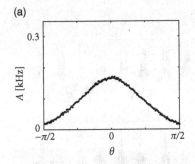

(b)

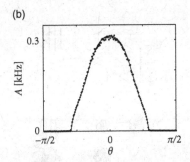

Fig. 18.11 Activity profiles in a model of orientation selectivity obtained by simulations based on SRM_0 neurons (dots) compared to the theoretical prediction (solid line) during stimulation with a low-contrast orientation input at $\theta = 0$. (a) If lateral coupling is not distance-dependent $[\omega_2 = 0;$ see Eq. (18.20)] the activity profile reflects the weak modulation of the input pattern. (b) Excitatory coupling between cells of the same orientation and long-range inhibition ($\omega_2 = 10$) generates a sharp activity profile centered at $\theta = 0$. From Spiridon and Gerstner (2001) with permission of Informa Healthcare.

A. Does Mexican-hat connectivity exist in the cortex? The Mexican-hat interaction pattern has a long tradition in theoretical neuroscience (Wilson and Cowan, 1973; Grossberg, 1973; Kohonen, 1984), but, from a biological perspective, it has two major shortcomings. First, in field models with Mexican-hat interaction, the same presynaptic population gives rise to both excitation and inhibition whereas in the cortex excitation and inhibition require separate groups of neurons (Dale's law). Second, inhibition in Mexican-hat connectivity is of longer range than excitation whereas biological data suggests the opposite. In fact, inhibitory neurons are sometimes called local interneurons because they make only local interactions. Pyramidal cells, however, make long-range connections within and beyond cortical areas.

B. Are there electrophysiological correlates of contrast enhancement? Simple and complex cells in the visual cortex respond best if they are stimulated by a slowly moving grating with optimal orientation and of a size that is matched to the cells' receptive field; see Chapter 12. If the grating is optimally oriented but larger than the receptive field, the response is reduced compared to that of a smaller grating (Fig. 18.12). At first sight, this finding is consistent with contrast enhancement through Mexican-hat interaction: a uniform large stimulus evokes a smaller response because it generates inhibition from neurons which are further apart. Paradoxically, however, neurons receive *less* inhibition (Fig. 18.13) with the larger stimulus than with the smaller one (Ozeki *et al.*, 2009).

C. How can we interpret the "position" variable in field models? In the previous sections we varied the interpretation of the "space" variable from physical position in the cortex to an abstract variable representing the preferred orientation of cells in the primary visual cortex. Indeed, in the visual cortex several variables need to be encoded in parallel: the location of a neuron's receptive field *and* its preferred orientation *and* potentially its preferred color *and* potentially the relative importance of input from left and right eye – while

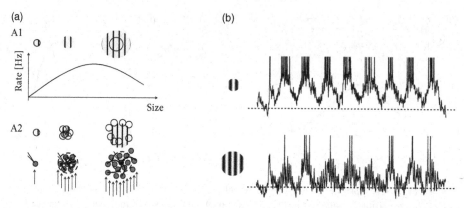

Fig. 18.12 Surrounding suppression. (a) Schematic. A1. Firing rate of a V1 cell as a function of the size of a moving grid stimulus. The grid has optimal orientation and optimal line spacing. Larger grids cause weaker responses than smaller ones. A2. Heuristic interpretation of surrounding suppression. The feedforward pathway from LGN to a cell (arrow, bottom row) gives rise to a small receptive field (RF size and location indicated above cell). Neighboring neurons with overlapping receptive fields excite each other and can be grouped into a local population (dashed circle). If the size of the stimulus is slightly larger, the response of the recorded neuron (middle) is enhanced because of excitatory input from neighboring cells. Right: Distal neurons inhibit the central neuron. Therefore an even larger stimulus suppresses the firing rate of the recorded neuron. (b) Experimental data. A moving grating causes a modulation of the membrane potential and spike firing. The number of spikes and the membrane potential are larger for a small grating than for a bigger one. Dashed horizontal line: mean membrane potential in the absence of stimulation. From Ozeki *et al.* (2009) with permission from Elsevier.

each neuron also has a physical location in the cortex. Therefore a distance-dependent connectivity pattern needs to be distance dependent for several dimensions in parallel while respecting the physical properties of a nearly two-dimensional cortical sheet.

In what follows, we present a model by Ozeki *et al.* (2009) that addresses concerns A and B and enables us to comment on point C.

We group neurons with overlapping receptive fields of similar orientation preference (Fig. 18.12a) into a single population. Inside the population neurons excite each other. We imagine that we record from a neuron in the center of the population. Neurons with receptive fields far away from the recorded neuron inhibit its activity.

Inhibition is implemented indirectly as indicated in Fig. 18.13c. The excitatory neurons in the central population project onto a group of local inhibitory interneurons, but also onto populations of other inhibitory neurons further apart. Each population of inhibitory neurons makes only *local* connections to the excitatory population in their neighborhood. Input to the central group of excitatory neurons therefore induces indirect inhibition of excitatory neurons further apart. Such a network architecture therefore addresses concern A.

To address concern B, the network parameters are set such that the network is in the inhibition-stabilized regime. A network is said to be inhibition-stabilized if the positive feedback through recurrent connections within an excitatory population is strong enough

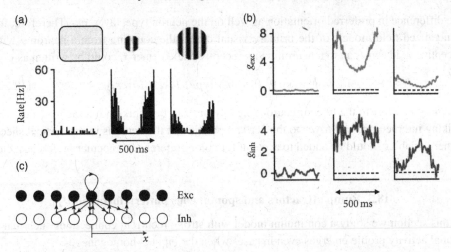

Fig. 18.13 Network stabilized by local inhibition. The schematic model could potentially explain why larger gratings lead not only to less excitatory input g_{exc}, but also to less inhibitory input g_{inh}. (a) The firing rate as a function of the phase of the moving grating for the three stimulus conditions (blank screen, small grating, and large grating). (b) Top: Excitatory input into the cell. Bottom: Inhibitory input into the same cell. As in (a), left, middle, and right correspond to a blank screen, a small grating, and a large grating. Note that the larger grating leads to a reduction of both excitation and inhibition. Adapted from Ozeki *et al.* (2009). (c) Network model with long-range excitation and local inhibition. Excitatory neurons within a local population excite themselves (feedback arrow), and also send excitatory input to inhibitory cells (downward arrows). Inhibitory neurons project to local excitatory neurons.

to cause run-away activity in the absence of inhibition. To counterbalance the positive excitatory feedback, inhibition needs to be even stronger (Tsodyks *et al.*, 1997). As a result, an inhibition-stabilized network responds to a positive external stimulation of inhibitory neurons with a decrease of both excitatory and inhibitory activity (see Exercises).

If the coupling from excitatory populations to neighboring inhibitory populations is stronger than that to neighboring excitatory populations, an inhibition-stabilized network can explain the phenomenon of surrounding suppression *and* at the same time account for the fact that during surrounding suppression both inhibitory and excitatory drive are reduced (Fig. 18.13b). Such a network architecture therefore addresses concern B (Ozeki *et al.*, 2009).

In the above simplified model we focused on populations of neurons with the same preferred orientation, say vertical. However, in the same region of the cortex, there are also neurons with other preferred orientations, such as diagonal or horizontal. The surrounding suppression effect is much weaker if the stimulus in the surroundings has a different orientation than in the central region. We therefore conclude that the cortical connectivity pattern does not simply depend on the physical distance between two neurons, but also on the difference in preferred orientation as well on the neuron type, layer, etc. Therefore, for generalized field models of the primary visual cortex the coupling from a neuron j with receptive field center x_j to a neuron i with receptive field center x_i could be written as

$$w_{ij} = w(x_i, x_j, \theta_i, \theta_j, type_i, type_j, layer_i, layer_j), \tag{18.28}$$

where *type* refers to the type of neuron (e.g., pyramidal, fast-spiking interneuron, non-fast spiking interneuron) and *layer* to the vertical position of the neurons in the cortical sheet. Other variables should be added to account for color preference, binocular preference, etc.

18.3 Bump attractors and spontaneous pattern formation

In this section we study a continuum model with strong recurrent connections such that a spatial activity profile emerges even in cases when the input is homogeneous.

18.3.1 "Blobs" of activity: inhomogeneous states

From a computational point of view bistable systems are of particular interest because they can be used as "memory units." For example, a homogeneous population of neurons with all-to-all connections can exhibit a bistable behavior where either all neurons are quiescent or all neurons are firing at their maximum rate. By switching between the inactive and the active state, the neuronal population is able to represent, store, or retrieve one bit of information. The exciting question that arises now is whether a neuronal net with distance-dependent coupling $w(|x - y|)$ can store more than just a single bit of information, but *spatial patterns* of activity. Sensory input, such as visual stimulation, could switch part of the network to its excited state whereas the unstimulated part would remain in its resting state. Owing to bistability this pattern of activity could be preserved even if the stimulation is turned off again and thus provide a neuronal correlate of working memory.

Let us suppose we prepare the network in a state where neurons in one spatial domain are active and all remaining neurons are quiescent. Will the network stay in that configuration? In other words, we are looking for an "interesting" stationary solution $h(x)$ of the field equation (18.4). The borderline where quiescent and active domains of the network meet is obviously most critical to the function of the network as a memory device. To start with the simplest case with a single borderline, we consider a one-dimensional spatial pattern where the activity changes at $x = 0$ from the low-activity to the high-activity state. This pattern could be the result of inhomogeneous stimulation in the past, but since we are interested in a memory state we now assume that the external input is simply constant, i.e., $I^{ext}(x,t) = I^{ext}$. Substitution of $h(x)$ for $h(x,t)$ in the field equation yields

$$h(x) - I^{ext} = \int dy\, w(|x - y|)\, F[h(y)]. \tag{18.29}$$

This is a nonlinear integral equation for the unknown function $h(x)$.

We can find a particular solution of Eq. (18.29) if we replace the output function by a simple step function, for example

$$F(h) = \begin{cases} 0, & h < \vartheta, \\ 1, & h \geq \vartheta. \end{cases} \tag{18.30}$$

In this case $F[h(x)]$ is either zero or 1 and we can exploit translation invariance to define $F[h(x)] = 1$ for $x > 0$ and $F[h(x)] = 0$ for $x < 0$ without loss of generality. The right-hand side of Eq. (18.29) now no longer depends on h and we find

$$h(x) = I^{\text{ext}} + \int_{-\infty}^{x} dz\, w(|z|), \tag{18.31}$$

and in particular

$$h(0) = I^{\text{ext}} + \frac{1}{2}\bar{w}, \tag{18.32}$$

with $\bar{w} = \int dy\, w(|y|)$. We have calculated this solution under the assumption that $F[h(x)] = 1$ for $x > 0$ and $F[h(x)] = 0$ for $x < 0$. This assumption imposes a self-consistency condition on the solution, namely that the membrane potential reaches the threshold ϑ at $x = 0$. A solution in the form of a stationary border between quiescent and active neurons can therefore only be found if

$$I^{\text{ext}} = \vartheta - \frac{1}{2}\bar{w}. \tag{18.33}$$

If the external stimulation is either smaller or greater than this critical value, then the border will propagate to the right or to the left.

Following the same line of reasoning, we can also look for a localized "blob" of activity. Assuming that $F[h(x)] = 1$ for $x \in [x_1, x_2]$ and $F[h(x)] = 0$ outside this interval leads to a self-consistency condition of the form

$$I^{\text{ext}} = \vartheta - \int_{0}^{\Delta} dx\, w(x), \tag{18.34}$$

with $\Delta = x_2 - x_1$. The mathematical arguments are qualitatively the same if we replace the step function by a more realistic smooth gain function.

Figure 18.14 shows that solutions in the form of sharply localized excitations exist for a broad range of external stimulations. A simple argument also shows that the width Δ of the blob is stable if $w(\Delta) < 0$ (Amari, 1977). In this case blobs of activity can be induced without the need for fine tuning the parameters in order to fulfill the self-consistency condition, because the width of the blob will adjust itself until stationarity is reached and Eq. (18.34) holds; see Fig. 18.14a.

18.3.2 Sense of orientation and head direction cells

Head direction cells in the rodent entorhinal cortex are thought to be a neural correlate of the internal compass of rodents. A head direction cell responds maximally if the head of

(a)   (b)

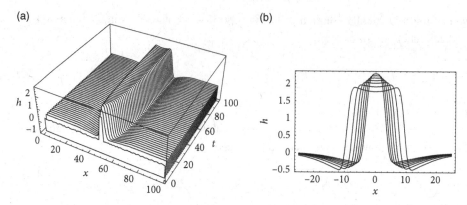

Fig. 18.14 Localized "blobs" of activity. (a) A small initial perturbation develops into a stable blob of activity. (b) Stationary profile of a localized excitation for various amounts of external stimulation ($I^{\text{ext}} = 0, 0.5, \ldots, 0.3$ in order of increasing width). Note that, for strong stimuli, neurons in the center of the activity blob are less active than those close to the edge of the blob.

the animal points in the direction preferred by this cell (Taube and Muller, 1998). Different head direction cells have different receptive fields. The preferred direction of head direction cells depends not on absolute north and south, but rather on visual cues. In a laboratory setting, one specific head direction cell will, for example, always fire when a salient cue card is 60° to the left of the body axis, another one when it is 40° to the right (Fig. 18.15a).

In an experiment during recordings from the entorhinal cortex (Zugaro *et al.*, 2003), a rat was trained to sit still while eating food with its head pointing in the preferred direction of one of the cells in the entorhinal cortex. Recordings from this cell show high activity (Fig. 18.15b). The cell remains active after the light has been switched off, indicating that the rat has memorized its momentary orientation. We emphasize that the orientation of the head can be described by a continuous variable. It is therefore this continuous value which needs to be kept in memory!

During the second phase of the experiment, while lights are switched off, the cues are rotated. Finally, in the last phase of the experiment, lights are switched on again. After a few milliseconds, the internal compass aligns with the new position of the cues. The activity of the recorded cell drops (Fig. 18.15b), because, in the new frame of reference, the head direction is now outside its receptive field (Zugaro *et al.*, 2003). Two aspects are important from a modeling perspective. First, memory content depends on the external input. Second, the memory must be capable of storing a continuous variable – in contrast to the memory models of Chapter 17 where discrete memory items are stored.

In order to represent the continuous head direction variable, ring models have been used (Redish *et al.*, 1996; Zhang, 1996). The location of a neuron on the ring represents its preferred head direction (Fig. 18.16). Cells with similar preferred head direction excite each other whereas cells with opposite preferred head direction inhibit each other. Thus,

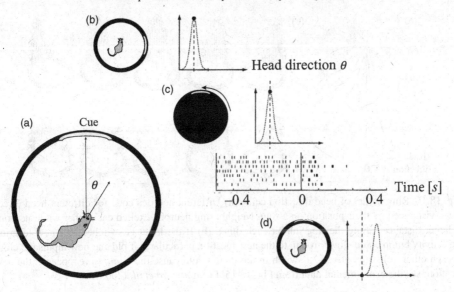

Fig. 18.15 Head direction cells. (a) The head direction θ is defined with respect to salient cues in the environment. (b) Firing rate as a function of θ. The cell responds maximally when the head points in the cell's preferred direction. (c) The cell remains active, even if the lights are switched off. Spike raster shows action potentials of a single head direction cell. For $t < 0$ the room is dark. During the lights-off phase, the cue is manually rotated. At $t = 0$ the light is switched on again, with the cue in the new position. (d) Compared to the new cue position, the head of the rat no longer points in the cell's preferred direction and, after a few milliseconds, the cell becomes silent. Adapted from Zugaro et al. (2003).

the ring model has a Mexican-hat connectivity. Parameters are chosen such that the model is in the regime of bump attractors, so that the present value of presumed head direction is kept in memory, even if stimulation stops.

Example: Activation of head direction cells

Head direction cells rely on visual cues, but also on information arising from the acceleration sensors in the inner ears. One of the intriguing open questions is how the sensory information from the inner ear is transformed into updates of the head direction system (Redish et al., 1996; Zhang, 1996). A second question is how head direction information can be maintained in the absence of further visual or acceleration input. Here we focus on this second question.

Since the activity of head direction cells does not stop when the light is turned off, interactions in a ring model of head direction must be chosen such that activity bumps are stable in the absence of input. Initially, a strong visual cue fixates the bump of activity at one specific location on the ring. If the visual input is switched off, the bump remains at

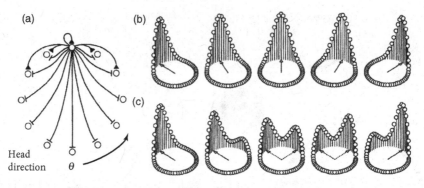

Fig. 18.16 Ring model of head direction cells. (a) Different neurons code for different head directions, visualized by their position on a ring. Neighboring neurons excited each other while neurons at larger distances along the ring inhibit each other. (b) If the input is switched to a new location the activity bump could slowly rotate to the new location particularly if old and new inputs are close to each other. (c) Alternatively, a switch in the input could cause the bump to reappear at the new location; see the experimental data from Fig. 18.15. From Zugaro *et al.* (2003).

its location so that the past head direction is memorized. When a new input with rotated cues is switched on, the activity bump could either rotate towards the new location or disappear at the old and reappear at the new location (Fig. 18.16). For large jumps in the input, the latter seems to be more likely in view of the existing experimental data (Zugaro *et al.*, 2003).

18.4 Summary

The cortex is a large, but thin sheet of neurons. Field models, in their spatial interpretation, describe the population activity of neurons as a function of the location on the cortical sheet.

Field models are, however, also used in a more general setting. In sensory cortices, neuronal activity encodes continuous variables, such as position of an object, orientation of edges, direction of movement etc. Field models, in their more abstract interpretation, represent the distribution of activity along the axes representing one or several of these variables.

In field models, interactions between populations of neurons depend on the distance of neurons in the physical, or abstract, space. Classical field models assume a Mexican-hat interaction pattern where local excitation is combined with long-range inhibition. Field models with Mexican-hat interaction have two important regimes of parameter settings. In the input-driven regime, spatial activity patterns can only arise if the input has a non-trivial spatial structure. In the bump-attractor regime, however, localized blobs of activity emerge even in the absence of input.

Mexican-hat interaction combines excitation and inhibition from the same presynaptic population and must therefore be considered as an *effective, mathematical* coupling scheme between neurons. It is, however, possible to construct similar field models with separate populations of excitatory neurons with long-range interactions, and inhibitory neurons with short-range interactions. These models bring the main results of field models a step closer to biological reality.

Exercises

1. **Bump formation.** *Consider a one-dimensional discrete recurrent network with population units $1 \leq i \leq N$ and update rule*

$$A_i(t+1) = F\left(\sum_k w_{ik} x_k(t) + \sum_j B_{ij} A_j(t) \right), \qquad (18.35)$$

where w_{ik} is the coupling strength to the input x_k and B_{ij} are the recurrent weights. Each neuron receives local excitation from its d neighbors on both sides, $B_{ij} = 1$ for $|i - j| \leq d$, and inhibition from all others, $B_{ij} = -\beta \leq -1$ for $|i - j| > d$. The gain function $F(h)$ is the Heaviside step function, i.e., $F(h) = 1$ for $h > 0$ and $F(h) = 0$ for $h \leq 0$.
(a) Imagine that one single unit is stimulated and therefore becomes active. This neuron will excite its neighbors. Show that in the steady state of the network the number N of active neurons is larger than 2d.
Hint: Consider the balance of excitation and inhibition at the border of the blob.
(b) How does the value of β influence the number of active neurons? What happens in the limit of $\beta \to 1$?
(c) Assume that $d = 5$, $N = 1000$ and the input to neuron $i = 17$ is 1. Compute the first three time steps of the network dynamics.

2. **Stability of homogeneous solution with excitatory coupling.**
(a) Consider the purely excitatory coupling

$$w(x) = \frac{\bar{w}}{\sqrt{2\pi\sigma^2}} e^{-x^2/(2\sigma^2)}, \qquad (18.36)$$

with the mean strength $\int dx \, w(x) = \bar{w}$ and Fourier transform

$$\int dx w(x) e^{ikx} = \bar{w} e^{-k^2 \sigma^2/2}. \qquad (18.37)$$

Under what conditions is the homogeneous solution stable (assume $F'(h_0) > 0$)?
(b) Consider a general coupling function $w(x)$ such that this function can be written as an auto-correlation

$$w(x) = \bar{w} \int_{-\infty}^{\infty} f(x' - x) f(x') dx', \qquad (18.38)$$

for some real function $f(x)$. Under what conditions is the homogeneous solution stable? Hint: The convolution theorem.

3. **Phase plane analysis of inhibition-stabilized network.** *An excitatory population is coupled to an inhibitory population, controlled by the activity equations*

$$\tau_E \frac{dA_E}{dt} = -A_E + F(w_{EE} A_E - w_{EI} A_I + I_E),$$

$$\tau_I \frac{dA_I}{dt} = -A_I + F(w_{IE} A_E - w_{II} A_I + I_I - \vartheta). \qquad (18.39)$$

Assume that $F(h) = 0$ for $h < 0$; $F(h) = h$ for $0 \leq h \leq 1$ and $F(h) = 1$ for $h > 1$.

(a) *Draw the nullclines in the phase plane spanned by the variables A_E (x-axis) and A_I (y-axis) in the absence of input $I_E = I_I = 0$ and $\vartheta = 0.5$. Assume that $w_{EE} = w_{EI} = 2$, $w_{IE} = 1$ and $w_{II} = 0$.*
(b) *Assume that the inhibitory population receives positive input $I_I = 0.2$. Redraw the nullclines. Does the population activity of excitatory or inhibitory populations increase or decrease? Does this correspond to your intuition? Can you interpret the result?*

4. **Surrounding inhibition.** *We study the model of the previous exercise in the linear region ($F(h) = h$). Two instantiations $i = 1, 2$ of the model are coupled via an additional connection from $A_{E,1}$ to $A_{i,2}$ and from $A_{E,2}$ to $A_{i,1}$ with lateral connections $w_{\text{lat}} > 0$.*
(a) *Assume that the first excitatory population receives an input $I_{E,1} = 0.3$. Calculate the stationary population activity of all four populations.*
(b) *Assume that both excitatory populations receive an input $I_{E,1} = 0.3 = I_{E,2}$. Calculate the stationary population activity of $A_{E,1}$ and $A_{I,1}$. Do the population activities increase or decrease compared to the case considered in (a)?*
(c) *Can you interpret your result in the context of the surrounding suppression?*

19

Synaptic plasticity and learning

In the network models discussed in Parts III and IV, each synapse has so far been characterized by a single *constant* parameter w_{ij}, called the synaptic weight, synaptic strength, or synaptic efficacy. If w_{ij} is constant, the amplitude of the response of a postsynaptic neuron i to the arrival of action potentials from a presynaptic neuron j should always be the same. Electrophysiological experiments, however, show that the response amplitude is not fixed but can change over time. In experimental neuroscience, changes of the synaptic strength are called synaptic plasticity.

Appropriate stimulation paradigms can induce changes of the postsynaptic response that last for hours or days. If the stimulation paradigm leads to a persistent *increase* of the synaptic efficacy, the effect is called long-term potentiation of synapses, or LTP for short. If the result is a *decrease* of the synaptic efficacy, it is called long-term depression (LTD). These persistent changes are thought to be the neuronal correlate of learning and memory. LTP and LTD are different from short-term synaptic plasticity such as synaptic facilitation or depression that we have encountered in Section 3.1. Facilitated or depressed synapses decay back to their normal strength within less than a few seconds, whereas, after an LTP or LTD protocol, synapses keep their new values for hours. The long-term storage of the new values is thought to be the basis of long-lasting memories.

In the formal theory of neural networks, the weight w_{ij} of a connection from neuron j to i is considered a parameter that can be adjusted so as to optimize the performance of a network for a given task. The process of parameter adaptation is called *learning* and the procedure for adjusting the weights is referred to as a *learning rule*. Here learning is meant in its widest sense. It may refer to synaptic changes during development just as much as to the specific changes necessary to memorize a visual pattern or to learn a motor task. There are many different learning rules, all of which we cannot cover in this chapter. In particular, we leave aside the large class of "supervised" learning rules which are an important topic in the fields of artificial neural networks and machine learning. Here we focus on two other classes of learning rules that are of biological relevance.

In Section 19.1 we introduce the Hebb rule and discuss its relation to experimental protocols for long-term potentiation (LTP) and spike-timing-dependent plasticity (STDP). In Section 19.2 we formulate mathematical models of Hebbian plasticity. We shall see in Section 19.3 that Hebbian plasticity causes synaptic connections to tune to the statistics of the

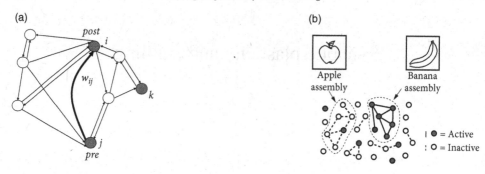

Fig. 19.1 Hebbian learning. (a) The change of a synaptic weight w_{ij} depends on the state of the presynaptic neuron j and the postsynaptic neuron i and the present efficacy w_{ij}, but not on the state of other neurons k. (b) Hebbian learning strengthens the connectivity within assemblies of neurons that fire together, for example during the perception of a banana. Schematic figure.

input. Such a self-tuning of network properties is an example of unsupervised learning. While unsupervised learning is thought to be a major drive for developmental plasticity in the brain, it is not sufficient to learn specific behaviors such as pressing a button in order to receive a reward. In Section 19.4 we discuss reward-based learning rules in the form of STDP modulated by reward. Reward-modulated synaptic plasticity is thought to be the basis of behavioral learning observed in animal conditioning experiments.

19.1 Hebb rule and experiments

Since the 1970s, a large body of experimental results on synaptic plasticity has been accumulated. Many of these experiments are inspired by Hebb's postulate (Hebb, 1949), which describes how the connection from a presynaptic neuron A to a postsynaptic neuron B should be modified:

> When an axon of cell A is near enough to excite cell B and repeatedly or persistently takes part in firing it, some growth process or metabolic change takes place in one or both cells such that A's efficiency, as one of the cells firing B, is increased.

Today this famous postulate is often rephrased in the sense that modifications of the synaptic transmission efficacy are driven by correlations in the firing activity of pre- and postsynaptic neurons; see Fig. 19.1a. The shortest summary is: neurons that "fire together, wire together" (Shatz, 1992). Note that the term "fire together" is less precise than Hebb's original formulation which contains an asymmetry since a neuron that "contributes to firing" another one has to be active slightly *before* the latter. Even though the idea of learning through correlations dates further back in the past (James, 1890), correlation-based learning is now generally called *Hebbian learning*.

Hebb formulated his principle on purely theoretical grounds. He realized that such a mechanism would help to stabilize specific neuronal activity patterns in the brain; see

Fig. 19.1b. If neuronal activity patterns correspond to behavior, then stabilization of specific patterns implies learning of specific types of behaviors (Hebb, 1949). We emphasize that Hebbian learning is unsupervised, because there is no notion of "good" or "bad" changes of a synapse. Synaptic changes happen whenever there is joint activity of pre- and postsynaptic neurons, i.e., they are driven by the neuronal firing patterns. These patterns may reflect sensory stimulation as well as ongoing brain activity, but there is no feedback signal from a "supervisor" or from the environment.

In this section we review experimental protocols that induce lasting synaptic changes and discuss their relation to Hebbian learning.

19.1.1 Long-term potentiation

The classic paradigm of LTP induction is, very schematically, the following (Brown *et al.*, 1989; Bliss and Collingridge, 1993). Neuronal activity is monitored by an extracellular or intracellular electrode, while presynaptic fibers are stimulated by means of a second (extracellular) electrode. Small pulses are applied to the presynaptic fibers in order to measure the strength of the postsynaptic response (Fig. 19.2a). The amplitude of the test pulse is chosen such that the stimulation evokes a postsynaptic potential, but no action potentials.

In a second step, the input fibers are strongly stimulated by a sequence of high-frequency pulses so as to evoke postsynaptic firing (Fig. 19.2b). After that, the strength of the postsynaptic response to small pulses is tested again and a significantly increased amplitude of postsynaptic potentials is found (Fig. 19.2c). This change in the synaptic strength persists over many hours and is thus called *long-term potentiation* or LTP (Fig. 19.2d).

The increase of the synaptic weights can be interpreted as "Hebbian," because it occurred after an episode of joint activity of pre- and postsynaptic neurons. Early LTP experiments were done with two extracellular electrodes (one for the stimulation of presynaptic fibers, the other for the measurement of the neuronal response), but in later experiments LTP was also studied with intracellular recordings.

Example: Voltage dependence of LTP

With an intracellular electrode, an experimenter can not only record the response to an incoming spike, but also manipulate the membrane potential of the postsynaptic neuron; see Fig. 19.3. If presynaptic spikes arrive during a period where the neuron is strongly depolarized, LTP is induced at the activated synapses. On the other hand, spike arrival combined with weak depolarization causes LTD (Artola *et al.*, 1990; Artola and Singer, 1993; Ngezahayo *et al.*, 2000). These and similar experiments reveal the importance of the postsynaptic voltage during the induction of synaptic plasticity. If we interpret strong depolarization of the postsynaptic neuron as a substitute of neuronal activity, the above protocol for LTP induction can be called "Hebbian."

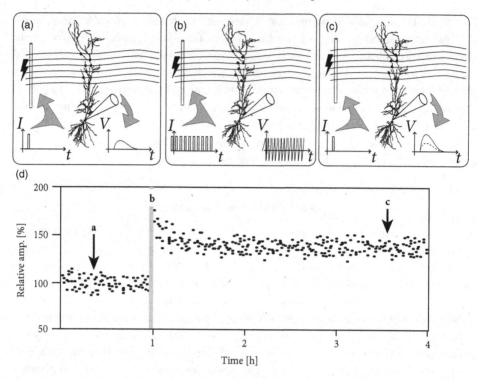

Fig. 19.2 Schematic drawing of a paradigm of LTP induction. (a) A weak test pulse (left) evokes the postsynaptic response sketched on the right-hand side of the figure. (b) A strong stimulation sequence (left) triggers postsynaptic firing (right, the peak of the action potential is out of bounds). (c) A test pulse applied some time later evokes a larger postsynaptic response (right; solid line) than the initial response. The dashed line is a copy of the initial response in (a). (d) The relative amplitude as measured with the test pulses illustrated in (a) and (c) is increased after the strong stimulation at $t = 1$ h. Schematic figure.

19.1.2 Spike-timing-dependent plasticity

Pairing experiments with multiple intracellular electrodes in synaptically coupled neurons have opened the possibility of studying synaptic plasticity at an excellent spatial and temporal resolution (Markram *et al.*, 1997; Zhang *et al.*, 1998; Debanne *et al.*, 1998; Bi and Poo, 1998, 1999; Sjöström *et al.*, 2001); see Bi and Poo (2001) and Sjöström and Gerstner (2010) for reviews.

Figure 19.4 illustrates a pairing experiment with cultured hippocampal neurons where the presynaptic neuron (j) and the postsynaptic neuron (i) are forced to fire spikes at time t_j^f and t_i^f, respectively (Bi and Poo, 1998). The resulting change in the synaptic efficacy Δw_{ij} after several repetitions of the experiment turns out to be a function of the difference $t_j^f - t_i^f$ between the firing times of the pre- and postsynaptic neuron. This observation

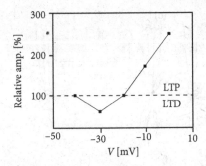

Fig. 19.3 Voltage dependence of LTP. Repeating the experiment shown in Fig. 19.2 while holding the membrane potential of the postsynaptic neuron shows a decrease in EPSP amplitude when holding at -30 mV and an increase when holding a higher voltage. Vertical axis: Ratio of EPSP amplitude $w_{ij}(T)/w_{ij}(0)$ before ($t = 0$) and after ($t = T$) the plasticity inducing protocol. Adapted from Ngezahayo et al. (2000).

has given rise to the term "spike-timing-dependent plasticity" (STDP). Most notably, the direction of the change depends critically on the relative timing of pre- and postsynaptic spikes on a millisecond time scale (Markram *et al.*, 1997). The synapse is strengthened if the presynaptic spike occurs shortly before the postsynaptic neuron fires, but the synapse is weakened if the sequence of spikes is reversed; see Fig. 19.4b. This observation is indeed in agreement with Hebb's postulate because presynaptic neurons that are active slightly *before* the postsynaptic neuron are those which "take part in firing it" whereas those that fire later obviously did not contribute to the postsynaptic action potential. An asymmetric learning window such as the one in Fig. 19.4f is thus an implementation of the causality requirement that is implicit in Hebb's principle.

Similar results on spike-time-dependent synaptic plasticity have been found in various neuronal systems (Abbott and Nelson, 2000; Bi, 2002; Caporale and Dan, 2008), but there are also characteristic differences. Synapses between parallel fibers and "Purkinje-cells" in the cerebellar-like structure of electric fish, for example, show the opposite dependence on the relative timing of presynaptic input and the (so-called "broad") postsynaptic spike (Bell *et al.*, 1997). In this case the synapse is weakened if the presynaptic input arrives shortly before the postsynaptic spike (anti-Hebbian plasticity).

19.2 Models of Hebbian learning

Before we turn to spike-based learning rules, we first review the basic concepts of correlation-based learning in a firing rate formalism. Firing rate models (see Chapter 15) have been used extensively in the field of artificial neural networks; see Hertz *et al.* (1991); Haykin (1994) for reviews.

19.2.1 A mathematical formulation of Hebb's rule

In order to find a mathematically formulated learning rule based on Hebb's postulate we focus on a single synapse with efficacy w_{ij} that transmits signals from a presynaptic neuron j to a postsynaptic neuron i. For the time being we content ourselves with a description in

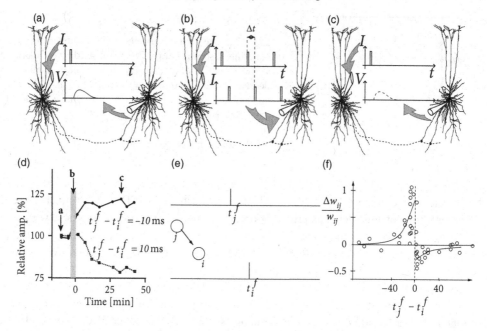

Fig. 19.4 Spike-Timing Dependent Plasticity. (a) Intracellular electrodes are used to manipulate two synaptically coupled neurons (axons are shown as dashed lines). A test pulse (I) injected into the presynaptic neuron causes an EPSP in the postsynaptic neuron (V). (b) During the plasticity induction protocol of a few seconds ("pairing"), both neurons are stimulated with current pulses forcing spikes at precise moments in time. (c) After the pairing protocol, the presynaptic neuron is stimulated by another current pulse, testing the level of potentiation of the synapse (before pairing protocol, dashed line; after, full line). (d) Amplitude of EPSP relative to initial amplitude as a function of time after the pairing protocol. If the presynaptic spike is 10 ms before the postsynaptic one, potentiation occurs (full line). If the order of the spikes is inverted, depression occurs (data points redrawn after Markram *et al.* (1997)). (e) Synaptic changes Δw_{ij} occur only if presynaptic firing at t_j^f and postsynaptic activity at t_i^f occur sufficiently close to each other. (f) The STDP window summarizes the timing requirements between pre- and postsynaptic spikes. Experimentally measured weight changes (circles) as a function of $t_j^f - t_i^f$ in milliseconds overlaid on a schematic two-phase learning window (solid line). A positive change (LTP) occurs if the presynaptic spike *precedes* the postsynaptic one; for a reversed timing, synaptic weights are decreased (data points redrawn after the experiments of Bi and Poo (1998)).

terms of mean firing rates. In what follows, the activity of the presynaptic neuron is denoted by v_j and that of the postsynaptic neuron by v_i.

There are two aspects of Hebb's postulate that are particularly important: *locality* and *joint activity*. Locality means that the change of the synaptic efficacy can depend only on local variables, i.e., on information that is available at the site of the synapse, such as pre- and postsynaptic firing rate, and the actual value of the synaptic efficacy, but not on the activity of other neurons. Based on the locality of Hebbian plasticity we can write down a rather general formula for the change of the synaptic efficacy,

$$\frac{\mathrm{d}}{\mathrm{d}t} w_{ij} = F(w_{ij}; v_i, v_j).$$ (19.1)

Here, $\mathrm{d}w_{ij}/\mathrm{d}t$ is the rate of change of the synaptic coupling strength and F is a so-far-undetermined function (Sejnowski and Tesauro, 1989). We may wonder whether there are other local variables (e.g., the input potential h_i; see Chapter 15) that should be included as additional arguments of the function F. It turns out that in standard rate models this is not necessary, since the input potential h_i is uniquely determined by the postsynaptic firing rate, $v_i = g(h_i)$, with a monotone gain function g.

The second important aspect of Hebb's postulate is the notion of "joint activity" which implies that pre- and postsynaptic neurons have to be active *simultaneously* for a synaptic weight change to occur. We can use this property to learn something about the function F. If F is sufficiently well behaved, we can expand F in a Taylor series about $v_i = v_j = 0$,

$$\frac{\mathrm{d}}{\mathrm{d}t} w_{ij} = c_0(w_{ij}) + c_1^{\mathrm{pre}}(w_{ij}) v_j + c_1^{\mathrm{post}}(w_{ij}) v_i + c_2^{\mathrm{pre}}(w_{ij}) v_j^2$$
$$+ c_2^{\mathrm{post}}(w_{ij}) v_i^2 + c_{11}^{\mathrm{corr}}(w_{ij}) v_i v_j + \mathcal{O}(v^3).$$ (19.2)

The term containing c_{11}^{corr} on the right-hand side of (19.2) is bilinear in pre- and postsynaptic activity. This term implements the AND condition for joint activity. If the Taylor expansion had been stopped before the bilinear term, the learning rule would be called "non-Hebbian," because pre- or postsynaptic activity alone induces a change of the synaptic efficacy, and joint activity is irrelevant. Thus a Hebbian learning rule needs either the bilinear term $c_{11}^{\mathrm{corr}}(w_{ij}) v_i v_j$ with $c_{11}^{\mathrm{corr}} > 0$ or a higher-order term (such as $c_{21}(w_{ij}) v_i^2 v_j$) that involves the activity of both pre- and postsynaptic neurons.

Example: Hebb rules, saturation, and LTD

The simplest choice for a Hebbian learning rule within the Taylor expansion of Eq. (19.2) is to fix c_{11}^{corr} at a positive constant and to set all other terms in the Taylor expansion to zero. The result is the prototype of Hebbian learning,

$$\frac{\mathrm{d}}{\mathrm{d}t} w_{ij} = c_{11}^{\mathrm{corr}} v_i v_j.$$ (19.3)

We note in passing that a learning rule with $c_{11}^{\mathrm{corr}} < 0$ is usually called anti-Hebbian because it weakens the synapse if pre- and postsynaptic neuron are active simultaneously, a behavior that is just contrary to that postulated by Hebb.

Note that, in general, the coefficient c_{11}^{corr} may depend on the current value of the weight w_{ij}. This dependence can be used to limit the growth of weights at a maximum value w^{max}. The two standard choices of weight-dependence are called "hard bound" and "soft bound," respectively. Hard bound means that $c_{11}^{\mathrm{corr}} = \gamma_2$ is constant in the range $0 < w_{ij} < w^{\mathrm{max}}$ and zero otherwise. Thus, weight growth stops abruptly if w_{ij} reaches the upper bound w^{max}.

Post v_i	Pre v_j	$dw_{ij}/dt \propto$ $v_i v_j$	$dw_{ij}/dt \propto$ $v_i v_j - c_0$	$dw_{ij}/dt \propto$ $(v_i - v_\theta) v_j$	$dw_{ij}/dt \propto$ $v_i (v_j - v_\theta)$	$dw_{ij}/dt \propto$ $(v_i - \langle v_i \rangle)(v_j - \langle v_j \rangle)$
ON	ON	+	+	+	+	+
ON	OFF	0	−	0	−	−
OFF	ON	0	−	−	0	−
OFF	OFF	0	−	0	0	+

Table 19.1 *The change $\frac{d}{dt} w_{ij}$ of a synapse from j to i for various Hebb rules as a function of pre- and postsynaptic activity. "ON" indicates a neuron firing at high rate ($v > 0$), whereas "OFF" means an inactive neuron ($v = 0$). From left to right: Standard Hebb rule, Hebb with decay, Hebb with postsynaptic or presynaptic LTP/LTD threshold, covariance rule. The parameters are $0 < v_\theta < v^{\max}$ and $0 < c_0 < (v^{\max})^2$.*

A soft bound for the growth of synaptic weights can be achieved if the parameter c_{11}^{corr} in Eq. (19.3) tends to zero as w_{ij} approaches its maximum value $w^{\max}$,

$$c_{11}^{\text{corr}}(w_{ij}) = \gamma_2 (w^{\max} - w_{ij})^\beta, \tag{19.4}$$

with positive constants γ_2 and β. The typical value of the exponent is $\beta = 1$, but other choices are equally possible (Gütig *et al.*, 2003). For $\beta \to 0$, the soft-bound rule (19.4) converges to the hard-bound one.

Note that neither Hebb's original proposal nor the simple rule (19.3) contains a possibility for a decrease of synaptic weights. However, in a system where synapses can only be strengthened, all efficacies will eventually saturate at their upper maximum value. Our formulation (19.2) is sufficiently general to allow for a combination of synaptic potentiation and depression. For example, if we set $w^{\max} = \beta = 1$ in (19.4) and combine it with a choice $c_0(w_{ij}) = -\gamma_0 w_{ij}$, we obtain a learning rule

$$\frac{d}{dt} w_{ij} = \gamma_2 (1 - w_{ij}) v_i v_j - \gamma_0 w_{ij}, \tag{19.5}$$

where, in the absence of stimulation, synapses spontaneously decay back to zero. Many other combinations of the parameters $c_0, \ldots, c_{11}^{\text{corr}}$ in Eq. (19.2) exist. They all give rise to valid Hebbian learning rules that exhibit both potentiation and depression; see Table 19.1.

Example: Covariance rule

Sejnowski (1977) has suggested a learning rule of the form

$$\frac{d}{dt} w_{ij} = \gamma (v_i - \langle v_i \rangle) (v_j - \langle v_j \rangle), \tag{19.6}$$

called the covariance rule. This rule is based on the idea that the rates $v_i(t)$ and $v_j(t)$ fluctuate around mean values $\langle v_i \rangle, \langle v_j \rangle$ that are taken as running averages over the recent firing history. To allow a mapping of the covariance rule to the general framework of Eq. (19.2), the mean firing rates $\langle v_i \rangle$ and $\langle v_j \rangle$ have to be constant in time.

Example: Oja's rule

All of the above learning rules had $c_2^{\text{pre}} = c_2^{\text{post}} = 0$. Let us now consider a nonzero quadratic term $c_2^{\text{post}} = -\gamma w_{ij}$. We take $c_{11}^{\text{corr}} = \gamma > 0$ and set all other parameters to zero. The learning rule

$$\frac{\mathrm{d}}{\mathrm{d}t} w_{ij} = \gamma [v_i v_j - w_{ij} v_i^2] \tag{19.7}$$

is called Oja's rule (Oja, 1982). Under some general conditions Oja's rule converges asymptotically to synaptic weights that are normalized to $\sum_j w_{ij}^2 = 1$ while keeping the essential Hebbian properties of the standard rule of Eq. (19.3); see Exercises. We note that normalization of $\sum_j w_{ij}^2$ implies competition between the synapses that make connections to the same postsynaptic neuron, i.e., if some weights grow, others must decrease.

Example: Bienenstock–Cooper–Munro rule

Higher-order terms in the expansion on the right-hand side of Eq. (19.2) lead to more intricate plasticity schemes. Let us consider

$$\frac{\mathrm{d}}{\mathrm{d}t} w_{ij} = \phi (v_i - v_\theta) v_j \tag{19.8}$$

with a nonlinear function ϕ and a reference rate v_θ. If we take v_θ to be a function $f(\langle v_i \rangle)$ of the average output rate $\langle v_i \rangle$, then we obtain the so-called Bienenstock–Cooper–Munro (BCM) rule (Bienenstock *et al.*, 1982).

The basic structure of the function ϕ is sketched in Fig. 19.5. If presynaptic activity is combined with moderate levels of postsynaptic excitation, the efficacy of synapses activated by presynaptic input is *decreased*. Weights are *increased* only if the level of postsynaptic activity exceeds a threshold, v_θ. The change of weights is restricted to those synapses which are activated by presynaptic input. A common choice for the function ϕ is

$$\frac{\mathrm{d}}{\mathrm{d}t} w_{ij} = \eta \, v_i (v_i - v_\theta) v_j = c_{21} v_i^2 v_j - c_{11}^{\text{corr}} v_i v_j, \tag{19.9}$$

which can be mapped to the Taylor expansion of Eq. (19.2) with $c_{21} = \eta$ and $c_{11}^{\text{corr}} = -\eta v_\theta$.

For stationary input, it can be shown that the postsynaptic rate v_i under the BCM-rule (19.9) has a fixed point at v_θ which is unstable (see Exercises). To avoid the postsynaptic firing rate blowing up or decaying to zero, it is therefore necessary to turn v_θ into an adaptive variable which depends on the average rate $\langle v_i \rangle$. The BCM rule leads to input

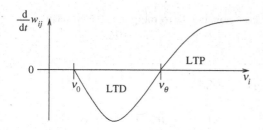

Fig. 19.5 BCM rule. Synaptic plasticity is characterized by two thresholds for the post-synaptic activity (Bienenstock *et al.*, 1982). Below v_0 no synaptic modification occurs, between v_0 and v_θ synapses are depressed, and for postsynaptic firing rates beyond v_θ synaptic potentiation can be observed. Often v_0 is set to zero.

selectivity (see Exercises) and has been successfully used to describe the development of receptive fields (Bienenstock *et al.*, 1982).

19.2.2 Pair-based models of STDP

We now switch from rate-based models of synaptic plasticity to a description with spikes. Suppose a presynaptic spike occurs at time t_{pre} and a postsynaptic one at time t_{post}. Most models of STDP interpret the biological evidence in terms of a pair-based update rule, i.e., the change in weight of a synapse depends on the temporal difference $|\Delta t| = |t_{\mathrm{post}} - t_{\mathrm{pre}}|$; see Fig. 19.4f. In the simplest model, the updates are

$$\Delta w_+ = A_+(w) \cdot \exp(-|\Delta t|/\tau_+) \text{ at } t_{\mathrm{post}} \quad \text{for } t_{\mathrm{pre}} < t_{\mathrm{post}},$$
$$\Delta w_- = A_-(w) \cdot \exp(-|\Delta t|/\tau_-) \text{ at } t_{\mathrm{pre}} \quad \text{for } t_{\mathrm{pre}} < t_{\mathrm{post}}, \quad (19.10)$$

where $A_\pm(w)$ describes the dependence of the update on the current weight of the synapse. The update of synaptic weights happens immediately after each presynaptic spike (at time t_{pre}) and each postsynaptic spike (at time t_{post}). A pair-based model is fully specified by defining: (i) the weight-dependence of the amplitude parameter $A_\pm(w)$; (ii) which pairs are taken into consideration to perform an update. A simple choice is to take all pairs into account. An alternative is to consider for each postsynaptic spike only the nearest presynaptic spike or vice versa. Note that spikes that are far apart hardly contribute because of the exponentially fast decay of the update amplitude with the interval $|\Delta t|$. Instead of an exponential decay (Song *et al.*, 2000), some other arbitrary time dependence, described by a learning window $W_+(s)$ for LTP and $W_-(s)$ for LTD is also possible (Gerstner *et al.*, 1996a; Kempter *et al.*, 1999a).

If we introduce $S_j = \sum_f \delta(t - t_j^f)$ and $S_i = \sum_f \delta(t - t_i^f)$ for the spike trains of pre- and postsynaptic neurons, respectively, then we can write the update rule in the form (Kistler and van Hemmen, 2000)

$$\frac{d}{dt}w_{ij}(t) = S_j(t) \left[a_1^{\mathrm{pre}} + \int_0^\infty A_-(w_{ij})W_-(s)S_i(t-s)\,ds \right]$$
$$+ S_i(t) \left[a_1^{\mathrm{post}} + \int_0^\infty A_+(w_{ij})W_+(s)S_j(t-s)\,ds \right], \quad (19.11)$$

where $W_\pm$ denotes the time course of the learning window while a_1^{pre} and a_1^{post} are non-Hebbian contributions, analogous to the parameters c_1^{pre} and c_1^{post} in the rate-based model of Eq. (19.2). In the standard pair-based STDP rule, we have $W_\pm(s) = \exp(-s/\tau_\pm)$ and $a_1^{\text{pre}} = a_1^{\text{post}} = 0$; see 19.10.

Example: Implementation by local variables

The pair-based STDP rule of 19.10 can be implemented with two local variables, i.e., one for a low-pass filtered version of the presynaptic spike train and one for the postsynaptic spikes. Suppose that each presynaptic spike at synapse j leaves a trace x_j, i.e., its update rule is

$$\frac{dx_j}{dt} = -\frac{x_j}{\tau_+} + \sum_f \delta(t - t_j^f),\qquad(19.12)$$

where t_j^f is the firing time of the presynaptic neuron. In other words, the variable is increased by an amount of one at the moment of a presynaptic spike and decreases exponentially with time constant τ_+ afterward. Similarly, each postsynaptic spike leaves a trace y_i

$$\frac{dy_i}{dt} = -\frac{y_i}{\tau_-} + \sum_f \delta(t - t_i^f).\qquad(19.13)$$

The traces x_j and y_i play an important role during the weight update. At the moment of a presynaptic spike, a decrease of the weight is induced proportional to the value of the postsynaptic trace y_i. Analogously, potentiation of the weight occurs at the moment of a postsynaptic spike proportional to the trace x_j left by a previous presynaptic spike,

$$dw_{ij}/dt = -A_-(w_{ij})y_i(t)\sum_f \delta(t - t_j^f) + A_+(w_{ij})x_j(t)\sum_f \delta(t - t_i^f).\qquad(19.14)$$

The traces x_j and y_i correspond here to the factors $\exp(-|\Delta t|/\tau_\pm)$ in 19.10. For the weight dependence of the factors A_- and A_+, one can use either hard bounds or soft bounds; see Eq. (19.4).

19.2.3 *Generalized STDP models*

There is considerable evidence that the pair-based STDP rule discussed above cannot give a full account of experimental results with STDP protocols. Specifically, they reproduce neither the dependence of plasticity on the repetition frequency of pairs of spikes in an experimental protocol, nor the results of triplet and quadruplet experiments.

STDP experiments are usually carried out with about 50−60 pairs of spikes. The temporal distance of the spikes in the pair is of the order of a few to tens of milliseconds, whereas

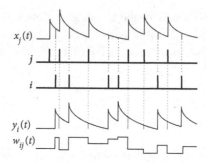

Fig. 19.6 Implementation of pair-based plasticity by local variables: The presynaptic spikes leave a trace $x_j(t)$, postsynaptic spikes a trace $y_i(t)$. The weight increases at the moment of a postsynaptic spike proportional to the momentary value of the trace $x_j(t)$ left by previous presynaptic spike arrivals. Analogously we get depression for post-before-pre pairings at the moment of a presynaptic spike (vertical dashed lines highlight moments of spike firing). From Morrison *et al.* (2008).

the temporal distance between the pairs is of the order of hundreds of milliseconds to seconds. In the case of a potentiation protocol (i.e., pre-before-post), standard pair-based STDP models predict that if the repetition frequency ρ is increased, the strength of the depressing interaction (i.e., post-before-pre) becomes greater, leading to less net potentiation. However, experiments show that increasing the repetition frequency leads to an increase in potentiation (Sjöström *et al.*, 2001; Senn *et al.*, 2001). Other experimenters have employed multiple-spike protocols, such as repeated presentations of symmetric triplets of the form pre-post-pre and post-pre-post (Bi, 2002; Froemke and Dan, 2002; Wang *et al.*, 2005; Froemke *et al.*, 2006). Standard pair-based models predict that the two sequences should give the same results, as they each contain one pre-post pair and one post-pre pair. Experimentally, this is not the case.

Here we review two examples of simple models which account for these experimental findings (Pfister and Gerstner, 2006; Clopath *et al.*, 2010), but there are other models which also reproduce frequency dependence, (e.g., Senn, 2002).

Triplet model

One simple approach to modeling STDP which addresses the issues of frequency dependence is the triplet rule developed by Pfister and Gerstner (2006). In this model, LTP is based on sets of three spikes (one presynaptic and two postsynaptic). The triplet rule can be implemented with local variables as follows. Similarly to pair-based rules, each spike from the presynaptic neuron j contributes to a trace x_j at the synapse:

$$\frac{\mathrm{d}x_j}{\mathrm{d}t} = -\frac{x_j}{\tau_+} + \sum_{t_j^f} \delta\left(t - t_j^f\right),$$

where t_j^f denotes the firing times of the presynaptic neuron. Unlike pair-based rules, each spike from postsynaptic neuron i contributes to a fast trace $y_{i,1}$ and a slow trace $y_{i,2}$ at the

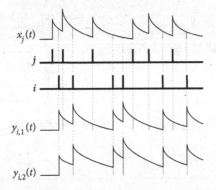

Fig. 19.7 Implementation of the triplet rule by local variables. The spikes of a presynaptic neuron j contribute to a trace $x_j(t)$, the spikes of postsynaptic neuron i contribute to a fast trace $y_{i,1}(t)$ and a slow trace $y_{i,2}(t)$. The update of the weight w_{ij} at the moment of a presynaptic spike is proportional to the momentary value of the fast trace $y_{i,1}(t)$, as in the pair-based model of Fig. 19.6. The update of the weight w_{ij} at the moment of a postsynaptic spike is proportional to the momentary value of the trace $x_j(t)$ and the value of the slow trace $y_{i,2}(t)$ just before the spike. Moments of weight update are indicated by vertical dashed lines. From Morrison et al. (2008).

synapse:

$$\frac{dy_{i,1}}{dt} = -\frac{y_{i,1}}{\tau_1} + \sum_f \delta(t - t_i^f),$$

$$\frac{dy_{i,2}}{dt} = -\frac{y_{i,2}}{\tau_2} + \sum_f \delta(t - t_i^f),$$

where $\tau_1 < \tau_2$; see Fig. 19.7. The new feature of the rule is that LTP is induced by a triplet effect: the weight change is proportional to the value of the presynaptic trace x_j evaluated at the moment of a postsynaptic spike and also to the slow postsynaptic trace $y_{i,2}$ remaining from previous postsynaptic spikes:

$$\Delta w_{ij}^+ \left(t_i^f\right) = A_+ (w_{ij}) \, x_j \left(t_i^f\right) y_{i,2} \left(t_i^{f-}\right) \tag{19.15}$$

where t_i^{f-} indicates that the function $y_{i,2}$ is to be evaluated before it is incremented due to the postsynaptic spike at t_i^f. LTD is analogous to the pair-based rule, given in (19.14), i.e., the weight change is proportional to the value of the fast postsynaptic trace $y_{i,1}$ evaluated at the moment of a presynaptic spike.

The triplet rule reproduces experimental data from visual cortical slices (Sjöström et al., 2001) that increasing the repetition frequency in the STDP pairing protocol increases net potentiation (19.8). It also gives a good fit to experiments based on triplet protocols in hippocampal culture (H.-X.Wang et al., 2005).

The main functional advantage of such a triplet learning rule is that it can be mapped to the BCM rule of Eqs. (19.8) and (19.9): if we assume that the pre- and postsynaptic spike trains are governed by Poisson statistics, the triplet rule exhibits depression for low

(a)

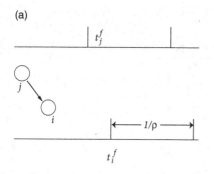

(b)

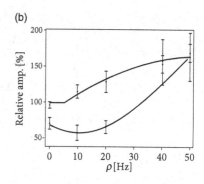

Fig. 19.8 Frequency dependence of STDP. (a) The experimental protocol depicted in Fig. 19.4 was repeated for different frequency, ρ, of pre-post pairs. (b) The triplet rule reproduces the finding that increased frequency of pair repetition leads to increased potentiation in visual cortex pyramidal neurons. Top curve $t_j^f - t_i^f = 10$ ms, bottom curve -10 ms. Data from Sjöström *et al.* (2001), figure adapted from Pfister *et al.* (2006).

postsynaptic firing rates and potentiation for high postsynaptic firing rates (Pfister and Gerstner, 2006); see Exercises. If we further assume that the triplet term in the learning rule depends on the mean postsynaptic frequency, a sliding threshold between potentiation and depression can be defined. In this way, the learning rule matches the requirements of the BCM theory and inherits the properties of the BCM learning rule such as the input selectivity (see Exercises). From the BCM properties, we can immediately conclude that the triplet model should be useful for receptive field development (Bienenstock *et al.*, 1982).

Example: Plasticity model with voltage dependence

Spike timing dependence is only one of several manifestations of synaptic plasticity. Apart from spike timing, synaptic plasticity also depends on several other variables, in particular on postsynaptic voltage (Fig. 19.3). In this example, we present the voltage-dependent model of Clopath *et al.* (2010).

The Clopath model exhibits separate additive contributions to the plasticity rule, one LTD and another for LTP. For the LTD part, presynaptic spike arrival at a synapse from a presynaptic neuron j to a postsynaptic neuron i induces depression of the synaptic weight w_{ij} by an amount $-A_{\mathrm{LTD}}\left[\bar{u}_{i,-}(t) - \theta_-\right]_+$ that is proportional to the average postsynaptic depolarization $\bar{u}_{i,-}$. The brackets $[]_+$ indicate rectification, i.e., any value $\bar{u}_{i,-} < \theta_-$ does not lead to a change; see Artola *et al.* (1990) and Fig. 19.3. The quantity $\bar{u}_{i,-}(t)$ is an low-pass filtered version of the postsynaptic membrane potential $u(t)$ with a time constant τ_-:

$$\tau_- \frac{\mathrm{d}}{\mathrm{d}t}\bar{u}_{i,-}(t) = -\bar{u}_{i,-}(t) + u_i(t).$$

Introducing the presynaptic spike train $S_j(t) = \sum_f \delta(t - t_j^f)$, the update rule for depression is (Fig. 19.9)

$$\frac{\mathrm{d}}{\mathrm{d}t} w_{ij}^{\mathrm{LTD}} = -A_{\mathrm{LTD}}(\bar{u}_i) \, S_j(t) \, [\bar{u}_{i,-}(t) - \theta_-]_+ \qquad \text{if } w_{ij} > w_{\min}, \qquad (19.16)$$

where $A_{\mathrm{LTD}}(\bar{u}_i)$ is an amplitude parameter that depends on the mean depolarization $\bar{u}$ of the postsynaptic neuron, averaged over a time scale of 1 second. A choice $A_{\mathrm{LTD}}(\bar{u}_i) = \alpha \frac{\bar{u}_i^2}{u_{\mathrm{ref}}^2}$ where u_{ref}^2 is a reference value, is a simple method to avoid a run-away of the rate of the postsynaptic neuron, analogous to the sliding threshold in the BCM rule of Eq. (19.9). A comparison with the triplet rule above shows that the role of the trace y_i (which represents a low-pass filter of the postsynaptic spike train, see Eq. (19.13)) is taken over by the low-pass filter $\bar{u}_{i,-}$ of the postsynaptic voltage.

For the LTP part, we assume that each presynaptic spike at the synapse w_{ij} increases the trace $\bar{x}_j(t)$ of some biophysical quantity, which decays exponentially with a time constant τ_+ in the absence of presynaptic spikes; see Eq. (19.12). The potentiation of w_{ij} depends on the trace $\bar{x}_j(t)$ and the postsynaptic voltage via (see also Fig. 19.9)

$$\frac{\mathrm{d}}{\mathrm{d}t} w_i^{\mathrm{LTP}} = +A_{\mathrm{LTP}} \, \bar{x}_j(t) \, [u_i(t) - \theta_+]_+ \, [\bar{u}_{i,+}(t) - \theta_-]_+ \quad \text{if } w_{ij} < w_{\max}. \quad (19.17)$$

Here, $A_{\mathrm{LTP}} > 0$ is a constant parameter and $\bar{u}_{i,+}(t)$ is another low-pass filtered version of $u_i(t)$ similar to $\bar{u}_-(t)$ but with a shorter time constant τ_+ around 10 ms. Thus positive weight changes can occur if the momentary voltage $u_i(t)$ surpasses a threshold θ_+ and, at the same time the average value $\bar{u}_{i,+}(t)$, is above θ_-. Note again the similarity to the triplet STDP rule. If the postsynaptic voltage is dominated by spikes, so that $u_i(t) = \sum_f \delta(t - t_i^f)$, the Clopath model and the triple STDP rule are in fact equivalent.

The Clopath rule is summarized by the equation

$$\frac{\mathrm{d}}{\mathrm{d}t} w_{ij} = -A_{\mathrm{LTD}}(\bar{u}) \, S_j(t) \, [\bar{u}_{i,-}(t) - \theta_-]_+ + A_{\mathrm{LTP}} \, \bar{x}_i(t) \, [u_i(t) - \theta_+]_+ \, [\bar{u}_{i,+}(t) - \theta_-]_+ (19.18)$$

combined with hard bounds $0 \leq w_{ij} \leq w_{\max}$.

The plasticity rule can be fitted to experimental data and can reproduce several experimental paradigms (Sjöström *et al.*, 2001) that cannot be explained by pair-based STDP or other phenomenological STDP rules without voltage dependence.

19.3 Unsupervised learning

In artificial neural networks some, or even all, neurons receive input from external sources as well as from other neurons in the network. Inputs from external sources are typically described as a statistical ensemble of potential stimuli. Unsupervised learning in the field of artificial neural networks refers to changes of synaptic connections which are driven by the statistics of the input stimuli – in contrast to supervised learning or reward-based learning where the network parameters are optimized to achieve, for each stimulus, an optimal behavior. Hebbian learning rules, as introduced in the previous section, are the prime example of unsupervised learning in artificial neural networks.

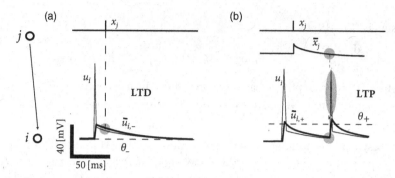

Fig. 19.9 Clopath model of voltage-dependent plasticity. Synaptic weights react to presynaptic events (top) and postsynaptic membrane potential (bottom) (a) The synaptic weight is decreased if a presynaptic spike x_j (dashed vertical line) arrives when the low-pass filtered value $\bar{u}_{i,-}$ (thick black line) of the membrane potential is above θ_- (dashed horizontal line). (b) The synaptic weight is increased if three criteria are met (shaded ellipses): (i) the membrane potential u_i (thin black line) is above a threshold θ^+ (horizontal dashed line); (ii) the low-pass filtered value of the membrane potential $\bar{u}_{i,+}$ (thick black line) is higher than a threshold θ^-; and (iii) the presynaptic low-pass filter $\bar{x}$ is above zero; adapted from Clopath *et al.* (2010).

In the following we always assume that there are N input neurons $1 \leq j \leq N$. Their firing rates v_j are chosen from a set of P firing rate patterns with index $1 \leq \mu \leq P$. While one of the patterns, say pattern μ with $\xi^\mu = (\xi^\mu_1, \ldots, \xi^\mu_N)$, is presented to the network, the firing rates of the input neurons are $v_j = \xi^\mu_j$. In other words, the input rates form a vector $v = \xi^\mu$ where $v = (v_1, \ldots, v_N)$. After a time Δt a new input pattern is randomly chosen from the set of available patterns. We call this the static pattern scenario.

19.3.1 *Competitive learning*

In the framework of Eq. (19.2), we can define a Hebbian learning rule of the form

$$\frac{d}{dt} w_{ij} = \gamma v_i \left[v_j - v_\theta(w_{ij}) \right], \tag{19.19}$$

where γ is a positive constant and v_θ is some reference value that may depend on the current value of w_{ij}. A weight change occurs only if the postsynaptic neuron is active, $v_i > 0$. The direction of the weight change depends on the sign of the expression in the rectangular brackets.

Let us suppose that the postsynaptic neuron i is driven by a subgroup of highly active presynaptic neurons ($v_i > 0$ and $v_j > v_\theta$). Synapses from one of the highly active presynaptic neurons onto neuron i are strengthened while the efficacy of other synapses that have not been activated is decreased. Firing of the postsynaptic neuron thus leads to LTP at the active pathway ("homosynaptic LTP") and at the same time to LTD at the inactive synapses ("heterosynaptic LTD"); for reviews see Brown *et al.* (1991) and Bi and Poo (2001).

A particularly interesting case from a theoretical point of view is the choice $v_\theta(w_{ij}) = w_{ij}$, i.e.,

$$\frac{\mathrm{d}}{\mathrm{d}t} w_{ij} = v_i [v_j - w_{ij}].$$ (19.20)

The synaptic weights thus move toward the fixed point $w_{ij} = v_j$ whenever the postsynaptic neuron is active. In the stationary state, the set of weight values w_{ij} reflects the presynaptic firing pattern $v_j, 1 \le j \le N$. In other words, the presynaptic firing pattern is *stored* in the weights.

The above learning rule is an important ingredient of competitive unsupervised learning (Kohonen, 1984; Grossberg, 1976). To implement competitive learning, an array of K (postsynaptic) neurons receive input from the same set of N presynaptic neurons which serve as the input layer. The postsynaptic neurons inhibit each other via strong lateral connections, so that, whenever a stimulus is applied at the input layer, the K postsynaptic neurons compete with each other and only a single postsynaptic neuron responds. The dynamics in such competitive networks where only a single neuron "wins" the competition have already been discussed in Chapter 16.

In a learning paradigm with the static pattern scenario, all postsynaptic neurons use the same learning rule (19.20), but only the active neuron i' (i.e., the one which "wins" the competition) will effectively update its weights (all others have zero update because $v_i = 0$ for $i \ne i'$). The net result is that the weight vector $w_{i'} = (w_{i'1} \ldots w_{i'N})$ of the winning neuron i' moves closer to the current vector of inputs $v = \xi^\mu$. For a different input pattern μ' the same or another postsynaptic neuron may win the competition. Therefore, different neurons specialize for different subgroups ("clusters") of patterns and each neuron develops a weight vector which represents the center of mass of "its" cluster.

Example: Developmental learning with STDP

The results of simulations of the Clopath model shown in Fig. 19.10 can be interpreted as a realization of a soft form of competitive learning. Neurons form subnetworks that specialize on the same features of the input. Because of inhibition, different subnetworks specialize on different segments of the input space.

Ten excitatory neurons (with all-to-all connectivity) are linked to three inhibitory neurons. Each inhibitory neuron receives input from eight randomly selected excitatory neurons and randomly projects back to six excitatory neurons (Clopath *et al.*, 2010). In addition to the recurrent input, each excitatory and inhibitory neuron receives feedforward spike input from 500 presynaptic neurons j that generate stochastic Poisson input at a rate v_j. The input neurons can be interpreted as a sensory array. The rates of neighboring input neurons are correlated, mimicking the presence of a spatially extended object stimulating the sensory layer. Spiking rates at the sensory layer change every 100 ms.

Feedforward connections and lateral connections between model pyramidal neurons are plastic whereas connections to and from inhibitory neurons are fixed. In a simulation

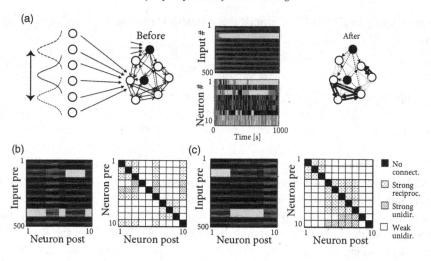

Fig. 19.10 Receptive field development and lateral connectivity. (a) A network of ten excitatory neurons (empty circles, not all neurons are shown) is connected to three inhibitory neurons (solid circles) and receives feedforward inputs from 500 Poisson spike trains with a Gaussian profile of firing rates. The center of the Gaussian is shifted randomly every 100 ms. Between the two schematic figures representing the network before (left) and after the plasticity experiment (right), we depict the evolution of input weights and recurrent excitatory weights onto one selected excitatory neuron. (b) Mean feedforward weights (left) and recurrent excitatory weights (right) averaged over 100 s. The gray level graph for the feedforward weights (left) indicates that neurons develop receptive fields that are localized in the input space. The diagonal in the matrix of recurrent connectivity is black, since self-connections do not exist in the model. (c) Same as (b) but for the sake of visual clarity the index of neurons is reordered so that neurons with similar receptive fields have adjacent numbers, highlighting that neurons with similar receptive fields (e.g., neurons 1 to 3) have strong bilateral connections. Adapted from Clopath *et al.* (2010).

of the model network, the excitatory neurons developed localized receptive fields, i.e., weights from *neighboring* inputs to the same postsynaptic neuron become either strong or weak *together* (Fig. 19.10a). Similarly, lateral connections onto the same postsynaptic neuron develop strong or weak synapses, that remain, apart from fluctuations, stable thereafter (Fig. 19.10a) leading to a structured pattern of synaptic connections (Fig. 19.10b). While the labeling of the excitatory neurons at the beginning of the experiment was randomly assigned, we can relabel the neurons after the formation of lateral connectivity patterns so that neurons with similar receptive fields have similar indices. After reordering we can clearly distinguish that two groups of neurons have been formed, characterized by similar receptive fields and strong bidirectional connectivity within the group, and different receptive fields and no lateral connectivity between groups (Fig. 19.10c).

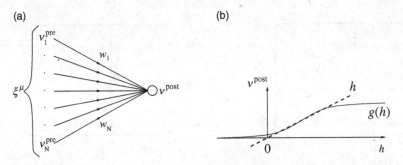

Fig. 19.11 Elementary model. (a) Patterns ξ^μ are applied as a set of presynaptic firing rates v_j, i.e., $\xi_j^\mu = v_j^{\text{pre}}$ for $1 \le j \le N$. (b) The gain function of the postsynaptic neuron is taken as linear, i.e., $v^{\text{post}} = h$. It can be seen as a linearization of the sigmoidal gain function $g(h)$.

19.3.2 Learning equations for rate models

We focus on a *single* analog neuron that receives input from N presynaptic neurons with firing rates v_j^{pre} via synapses with weights w_j; see Fig. 19.11a. Note that we have dropped the index i of the postsynaptic neuron since we focus in this section on a single output neuron. We think of the presynaptic neurons as "input neurons," which, do not, however, have to be sensory neurons. The input layer could, for example, consist of neurons in the lateral geniculate nucleus (LGN) that project to neurons in the visual cortex. As before, the firing rate of the input neurons is modeled by the static pattern scenario. We will show that the statistical properties of the input control the evolution of synaptic weights. In particular, we identify the conditions under which unsupervised Hebbian learning is related to principal component analysis (PCA).

In the following we analyze the evolution of synaptic weights using the simple Hebbian learning rule of Eq. (19.3). The presynaptic activity drives the postsynaptic neuron and the joint activity of pre- and postsynaptic neurons triggers changes of the synaptic weights:

$$\Delta w_i = \gamma v^{\text{post}} v_i^{\text{pre}} . \tag{19.21}$$

Here, $0 < \gamma \ll 1$ is a small constant called the "learning rate." The learning rate in the static pattern scenario is closely linked to the correlation coefficient c_{11}^{corr} in the continuous-time Hebb rule introduced in Eq. (19.3). In order to highlight the relation, let us assume that each pattern ξ^μ is applied during an interval Δt. For Δt sufficiently small, we have $\gamma = c_{11}^{\text{corr}} \Delta t$.

In a general rate model, the firing rate v^{post} of the postsynaptic neuron is given by a nonlinear function of the total input

$$v^{\text{post}} = g \left(\sum_j w_j v_j^{\text{pre}} \right) ; \tag{19.22}$$

see Fig. 19.11b and Chapter 15. For the sake of simplicity, we restrict our discussion in the

(a)

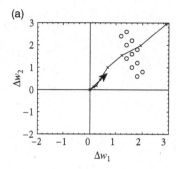

(b)

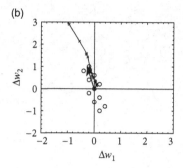

Fig. 19.12   Weight changes induced by the standard Hebb rule. Input patterns $\xi^\mu \in \mathbb{R}^2$ are marked as circles. The sequence of weight vectors $w(1)$, $w(2)$, ... is indicated by crosses connected by a solid line. (a) The weight vector evolves in the direction of the center of mass of the cloud of data points, because this is the dominant eigenvector of the (non-normalized) correlation matrix of the data. (b) If the input patterns are normalized so that their center of mass is at the origin, then the weight vector becomes parallel to the first principal component e_1 of the dataset.

following to a *linear* rate model with

$$v^{\mathrm{post}} = \sum_j w_j v_j^{\mathrm{pre}} = w \cdot v^{\mathrm{pre}}, \tag{19.23}$$

where we have introduced vector notation for the weights $w = (w_1, \dots, w_N)$, the presynaptic rates $v^{\mathrm{pre}} = (v_1, \dots, v_N)$ and the dot denotes a scalar product. Hence we can interpret the output rate v^{post} as a projection of the input vector onto the weight vector.

If we combine the learning rule (19.21) with the linear rate model of Eq. (19.23) we find after the presentation of pattern ξ^μ

$$\Delta w_i = \gamma \sum_j w_j v_j^{\mathrm{pre}} v_i^{\mathrm{pre}} = \gamma \sum_j w_j \xi_j^\mu \xi_i^\mu. \tag{19.24}$$

The evolution of the weight vector $w = (w_1, \dots, w_N)$ is thus determined by the iteration

$$w_i(n+1) = w_i(n) + \gamma \sum_j w_j \xi_j^{\mu_n} \xi_i^{\mu_n}, \tag{19.25}$$

where μ_n denotes the pattern that is presented during the nth time step. Eq. (19.25) is called an "online" rule, because the weight update happens immediately after the presentation of each pattern. The evolution of the weight vector $w = (w_1, \dots, w_N)$ during the presentation of several patterns is shown in Fig. 19.12.

If the learning rate γ is small, a large number of patterns has to be presented in order to induce a substantial weight change. In this case, there are two equivalent routes to proceed with the analysis. The first one is to study a version of learning where all P patterns are presented before an update occurs. Thus, Eq. (19.25) is replaced by

$$w_i(n+1) = w_i(n) + \tilde{\gamma} \sum_j w_j \sum_{\mu=1}^{P} \xi_j^\mu \xi_i^\mu \tag{19.26}$$

with a new learning rate $\tilde{\gamma} = \gamma/P$. This is called a "batch update." With the batch update rule, the right-hand side can be rewritten as

$$w_i(n+1) = w_i(n) + \gamma \sum_j C_{ij} w_j(n), \tag{19.27}$$

where we have introduced the correlation matrix

$$C_{ij} = \frac{1}{P} \sum_{\mu=1}^{P} \xi_i^\mu \xi_j^\mu = \langle \xi_i^\mu \xi_j^\mu \rangle_\mu. \tag{19.28}$$

Thus, the evolution of the weights is driven by the correlations in the input.

The second, alternative, route is to stick to the online update rule, but study the *expectation* value of the weight vector, i.e., the weight vector $\langle w(n) \rangle$ averaged over the sequence $(\xi^{\mu_1}, \xi^{\mu_2}, \ldots, \xi^{\mu_n})$ of all patterns that so far have been presented to the network. From Eq. (19.25) we find

$$\langle w_i(n+1) \rangle = \langle w_i(n) \rangle + \gamma \sum_j \left\langle w_j(n) \, \xi_j^{\mu_{n+1}} \xi_i^{\mu_{n+1}} \right\rangle$$

$$= \langle w_i(n) \rangle + \gamma \sum_j \langle w_j(n) \rangle \left\langle \xi_j^{\mu_{n+1}} \xi_i^{\mu_{n+1}} \right\rangle$$

$$= \langle w_i(n) \rangle + \gamma \sum_j C_{ij} \langle w_j(n) \rangle. \tag{19.29}$$

The angle brackets denote an ensemble average over the whole sequence of input patterns $(\xi^{\mu_1}, \xi^{\mu_2}, \ldots)$. The second equality is due to the fact that input patterns are chosen *independently* in each time step, so that the average over $w_j(n)$ and $(\xi_j^{\mu_{n+1}} \xi_i^{\mu_{n+1}})$ can be factorized. Note that Eq. (19.29) for the *expected* weights in the online rule is equivalent to Eq. (19.27) for the weights in the *batch* rule.

Expression (19.29), or equivalently (19.27), can be written in a more compact form using matrix notation (we drop the angle brackets in the following)

$$w(n+1) = (\mathbf{1} + \gamma C) w(n) = (\mathbf{1} + \gamma C)^{n+1} w(0), \tag{19.30}$$

where $w(n) = (w_1(n), \ldots, w_N(n))$ is the weight vector and $\mathbf{1}$ is the identity matrix.

If we express the weight vector in terms of the eigenvectors e_k of C,

$$w(n) = \sum_k a_k(n) e_k, \tag{19.31}$$

we obtain an explicit expression for $w(n)$ for any given initial condition $a_k(0)$, namely,

$$w(n) = \sum_k (1 + \lambda_k)^n a_k(0) e_k. \tag{19.32}$$

Since the correlation matrix is positive semi-definite, all eigenvalues λ_k are real and positive. Therefore, the weight vector is growing exponentially, but the growth will soon be dominated by the eigenvector with the largest eigenvalue, i.e., the *first principal component*,

$$w(n) \xrightarrow{n \to \infty} (1 + \lambda_1)^n a_1(0) e_1 . \tag{19.33}$$

Recall that the output of the linear neuron model (19.23) is proportional to the projection of the current input pattern ξ^μ on the direction w. For $w \propto e_1$, the output is therefore proportional to the projection on the first principal component of the input distribution. A Hebbian learning rule such as (19.21) is thus able to extract the first principal component of the input data.

From a data-processing point of view, the extraction of the first principal component of the input dataset by a biologically inspired learning rule seems to be very compelling. There are, however, a few drawbacks and pitfalls when using the above simple Hebbian learning scheme. Interestingly, all three can be overcome by slight modifications in the Hebb rule.

First, the above statement about the Hebbian learning rule is limited to the *expectation value* of the weight vector. However, it can be shown that if the learning rate is sufficiently low, then the actual weight vector is very close to the expected one so that this is not a major limitation.

Second, while the direction of the weight vector moves in the direction of the principal component, the *norm* of the weight vector grows without bounds. However, variants of Hebbian learning such as the Oja learning rule (19.7) allow us to normalize the length of the weight vector without changing its direction; see Exercises.

Third, principal components are only meaningful if the input data is normalized, i.e., distributed around the origin. This requirement is not consistent with a rate interpretation because rates are usually positive. This problem can, however, be overcome by learning rules such as the covariance rule of Eq. (19.6) that are based on the deviation of the rates from a certain mean firing rate. Similarly, STDP rules can be designed in such a way that the output rate remains normalized so that learning is sensitive only to deviations from the mean firing rate and can thus find the first principal component even if the input is not properly normalized (Kempter *et al.*, 1999a; Song *et al.*, 2000; Kempter *et al.*, 2001).

Example: Correlation matrix and principal component analysis

For readers not familiar with principal component analysis (PCA) we review here the basic ideas and main results. PCA is a standard technique to describe statistical properties of a set of high-dimensional data points and is performed to find the direction in which the data shows the largest variance. If we think of the input dataset as a cloud of points in a high-dimensional vector space centered around the origin, then the first principal component is the direction of the longest axis of the ellipsoid that encompasses the cloud; see Fig. 19.13a. In what follows, we will explain the basic idea and show that the first principal component gives the direction where the variance of the data is maximal.

Let us consider an ensemble of data points $\{\xi^1, \ldots, \xi^P\}$ drawn from a (high-dimensional) vector space, for example $\xi^\mu \in \mathbb{R}^N$. For this set of data points we define the *correlation matrix C_{ij}* as

$$C_{ij} = \frac{1}{P} \sum_{\mu=1}^{P} \xi_i^\mu \xi_j^\mu = \left\langle \xi_i^\mu \xi_j^\mu \right\rangle_\mu. \tag{19.34}$$

Angle brackets $\langle \cdot \rangle_\mu$ denote an average over the whole set of data points. In a similar way to the variance of a single random variable we can also define the *covariance matrix V_{ij}* of our dataset,

$$V_{ij} = \left\langle (\xi_i^\mu - \langle \xi_i^\mu \rangle_\mu)(\xi_j^\mu - \langle \xi_j^\mu \rangle_\mu) \right\rangle_\mu. \tag{19.35}$$

Here we will assume that the coordinate system is chosen so that the center of mass of the set of data points is located at the origin, i.e., $\langle \xi_i \rangle_\mu = \langle \xi_j \rangle_\mu = 0$. In this case, correlation matrix and covariance matrix are identical.

The *principal components* of the set $\{\xi^1, \ldots, \xi^P\}$ are defined as the eigenvectors of the covariance matrix V. Note that V is symmetric, i.e., $V_{ij} = V_{ji}$. The eigenvalues of V are thus real-valued and different eigenvectors are orthogonal (Horn and Johnson, 1985). Furthermore, V is positive semi-definite since

$$y^\mathsf{T} V y = \sum_{ij} y_i \left\langle \xi_i^\mu \xi_j^\mu \right\rangle_\mu y_j = \left\langle \left[\sum_i y_i \xi_i^\mu \right]^2 \right\rangle_\mu \geq 0 \tag{19.36}$$

for any vector $y \in \mathbb{R}^N$. Therefore, all eigenvalues of V are non-negative.

We can sort the eigenvectors e_i according to the size of the corresponding eigenvalues $\lambda_1 \geq \lambda_2 \geq \cdots \geq 0$. The eigenvector with the largest eigenvalue is called the first principal component.

The first principal component points in the direction where the variance of the data is maximal. To see this we calculate the variance of the projection of ξ^μ onto an arbitrary direction y (Fig. 19.13b) that we write as $y = \sum_i a_i e_i$ with $\sum_i a_i^2 = 1$ so that $\|y\| = 1$. The variance σ_y^2 along y is

$$\sigma_y^2 = \left\langle \left[\xi^\mu \cdot y \right]^2 \right\rangle_\mu = y^\mathsf{T} V y = \sum_i \lambda_i a_i^2. \tag{19.37}$$

The right-hand side is maximal under the constraint $\sum_i a_i^2 = 1$ if $a_1 = 1$ and $a_i = 0$ for $i = 2, 3, \ldots, N$, i.e., if $y = e_1$.

19.3.3 Learning equations for STDP models (*)

The evolution of synaptic weights in the pair-based STDP model of 19.10 can be assessed by assuming that pre- and postsynaptic spike trains can be described by Poisson processes.

(a)   (b)

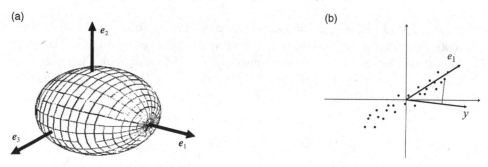

Fig. 19.13 Principal component analysis. (a) Ellipsoid approximating the shape of a cloud of data points. The first principal component e_1 corresponds to the principal axis of the ellipsoid. (b) Sample distribution of data points in two dimensions. The first principal component e_1 points in the direction where the variance of the data is maximal. Projection (dashed line) of data points onto an arbitrary other axis y gives a distribution of smaller variance.

For the postsynaptic neuron, we take the linear Poisson model in which the output spike train is generated by an inhomogeneous Poisson process with rate

$$v_i(u_i) = [\alpha u_i - v_0]_+ \tag{19.38}$$

with scaling factor α, threshold v_0 and membrane potential $u_i(t) = \sum_j w_{ij}\varepsilon\left(t - t_j^f\right)$, where $\varepsilon(t)$ denotes the time course of an excitatory postsynaptic potential generated by a presynaptic spike arrival. The notation $[x]_+$ denotes a piecewise linear function: $[x]_+ = x$ for $x > 0$ and zero otherwise. In the following we assume that the argument of our piecewise linear function is positive so that we can suppress the square brackets.

For the sake of simplicity, we assume that all input spike trains are Poisson processes with a *constant* firing rate v_j. In this case the *expected* firing rate of the postsynaptic neuron is simply:

$$\langle v_i \rangle = -v_0 + \alpha \bar{\varepsilon} \sum_j w_{ij} v_j, \tag{19.39}$$

where $\bar{\varepsilon} = \int \varepsilon(s)\mathrm{d}s$ is the total area under an excitatory postsynaptic potential. The *conditional* rate of firing of the postsynaptic neuron, given an input spike at time t_j^f, is given by

$$v_i(t) = -v_0 + \alpha \bar{\varepsilon} \sum_j w_{ij} v_j + \alpha w_{ij} \varepsilon\left(t - t_j^f\right). \tag{19.40}$$

Since the conditional rate is different from the expected rate, the postsynaptic spike train $S_i(t)$ is correlated with the presynaptic spike trains $S_j(t')$. The correlations can be calculated to be

$$\Gamma_{ji}(s) = \langle S_i(t+s)S_j(t)\rangle = \langle v_i \rangle v_j + \alpha w_{ij} v_j \varepsilon(s). \tag{19.41}$$

In a similar way to the expected weight evolution for rate models in Section 19.3.2, we now study the expected weight evolution in the spiking model with the pair-based plasticity rule of Eq. (19.10). The result is (Kempter *et al.*, 1999a)

$$\langle \dot{w}_{ij} \rangle = \nu_j \langle \nu_i \rangle \left[-A_-(w_{ij})\tau_- + A_+(w_{ij})\tau_+ \right] + \alpha w_{ij}\nu_j A_+(w_{ij}) \int W_+(s)\varepsilon(s)\mathrm{d}s. \quad (19.42)$$

The first term is reminiscent of rate-based Hebbian learning, Eq. (19.3), with a coefficient c_{11}^{corr} proportional to the integral under the learning window. The last term is due to pre-before-post spike timings that are absent in a pure rate model. Hence, despite the fact that we started off with a pair-based STDP rule, the synaptic dynamics contains a term of the form $\alpha \nu_j w A_+(w) \int W_+(s)\varepsilon(s)\mathrm{d}s$ that is *linear* in the presynaptic firing rate (Kempter *et al.*, 1999a, 2001).

Example: Stabilization of postsynaptic firing rate

If spike arrival rates $\nu_j = \nu$ at all synapses are identical, we expect a solution of the learning equation to exist where all weights are identical, $w_{ij} = w$. For simplicity we drop the averaging signs. Eq. (19.42) then becomes

$$\frac{\dot{w}}{\nu} = \nu_i \left[-A_-(w)\tau_- + A_+(w)\tau_+ \right] + \alpha w A_+(w) \int W_+(s)\varepsilon(s)\mathrm{d}s. \quad (19.43)$$

Moreover, we can use Eq. (19.39) to express the postsynaptic firing rate in terms of the input rate ν:

$$\nu_i = -\nu_0 + \alpha \nu \bar{\varepsilon} N w. \quad (19.44)$$

If the weight w increases, the postsynaptic firing rate also increases. We now ask whether the postsynaptic firing has a fixed point ν_{FP}.

The fixed point analysis can be performed for a broad class of STDP models. However, for the sake of simplicity we focus on the model with hard bounds in the range where $0 < w < w^{\mathrm{max}}$. We introduce a constant $C = A_-(w)\tau_- - A_+(w)\tau_+$. If the integral of the learning window is negative, then $C > 0$ and LTD dominates over LTP. In this case, a fixed point exists at

$$\nu_{\mathrm{FP}} = \frac{C_{\mathrm{ss}}\nu_0}{NC\nu\bar{\varepsilon} - C_{\mathrm{ss}}} \quad (19.45)$$

where $C_{\mathrm{ss}} = A_+(w) \int W_+(s)\varepsilon(s)\mathrm{d}s$ denotes the contribution of the spike–spike correlations. The mean firing rate of the neuron is, under rather general conditions, stabilized at the fixed point (Kempter *et al.*, 2001). Hence STDP can lead to a control of the postsynaptic firing rate (Kempter *et al.*, 1999a; Song *et al.*, 2000; Kempter *et al.*, 2001). We emphasize that the existence of a fixed point and its stability does not crucially depend on the presence of soft or hard bounds on the weights. Since, for constant input rates ν, we have $\nu_i = \nu_0 + \alpha \nu \bar{\varepsilon} \sum_j w_{ij}$, stabilization of the output rate automatically implies normalization of the summed weights.

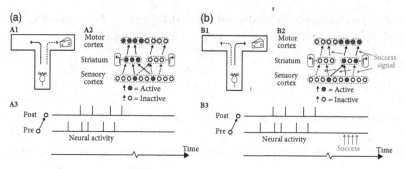

Fig. 19.14 Hebbian learning versus reward-modulated Hebbian learning in a T-maze decision task (schematic). The momentary sensory state of the animal is encoded by the layer of sensory cortex neurons, the action plan by a set of striatal neurons, and the motor output by neurons in motor cortex. (a) Hebbian learning. Joint activity of neurons in sensory, striatal, and motor areas strengthens the links between the active neurons, despite the fact that turning left does not lead to success. (b) Reward-modulated Hebbian learning. Joint activity of pre- and postsynaptic neurons strengthens connections only if, within a delay of a few seconds, a success signal is broadcast in the brain.

19.4 Reward-based learning

In conditioning experiments, animals learn complex action sequences if the desired behavior is rewarded. For example, in a simple T-maze an animal has to decide at the bifurcation point whether to turn left or right (Fig. 19.14a). In each of several trials, the same arm of the maze is baited with a piece of cheese that is hidden in a hole in the floor and therefore neither visible nor smellable. After a few trials the animal has learned to reliably turn into the baited arm of the maze.

Unsupervised Hebbian learning is of limited use for behavioral learning, because it makes no distinction between actions that do and those that do not lead to a successful outcome. The momentary sensory state at the bifurcation point is represented by activity in the sensory cortices and, possibly, in hippocampal place cells. The action plan "turn left" is represented by groups of cells in several brain areas likely to include the striatum, whereas the final control of muscle activity involves areas in the motor cortex. Therefore, during the realization of the action plan "turn left," several groups of neurons are jointly active (Fig. 19.14a). Unsupervised Hebbian learning strengthens the connections between the jointly active cells so that, at the next trial, it becomes more likely that the animal takes the same decision again. However, turning left does not lead to success if the cheese is hidden in the other branch of the maze.

In order to solve the above task, two important aspects have to be taken into account that are neglected in unsupervised Hebbian learning rules. First, rules of synaptic plasticity have to take into account the success of an action. Neuromodulators such a dopamine are ideal candidates to broadcast a success signal in the brain (Fig. 19.15), where success can loosely be defined as "reward minus expected reward" (Schultz *et al.*, 1997; Schultz, 2007,

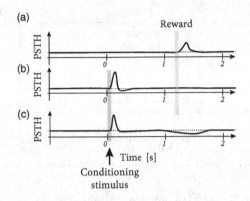

(a)

Reward

(b)

(c)

↑ Time [s]

Conditioning
stimulus

Fig. 19.15 Dopamine encodes reward minus expected reward. (a) The activity of dopaminergic neurons (PSTH) increases at the moment when a reward R occurs. (b) If a conditioning stimulus (CS) such as a tone beep or a light reliably occurs one second before the reward, the same neurons no longer respond to the reward but instead respond after the CS that predicts the reward. (c) If the reward is predicted by the CS but not given, the PSTH exhibits a dip below the baseline (dashed lines) at the moment when the reward is expected. Schematic figure summarizing data from Schultz *et al.* (1997).

2010). Second, the success often comes with a delay of a few seconds after an action has been taken; see Fig. 19.14b. Thus, the brain needs somehow to store a short-term memory of past actions. A suitable location for such a memory is the synapses themselves.

The above two points can be used to formulate a first qualitative model of reward-modulated Hebbian learning. In Hebbian learning, weight changes Δw_{ij} depend on the spikes *pre$_j$* of the presynaptic neuron j and the state *post$_i$* of the postsynaptic neuron i. Correlations between the pre- and postsynaptic activity are picked up by the Hebbian function $H(pre_j, post_i)$. We assume that synapses keep track of correlations by updating a synaptic eligibility trace

$$\tau_e \frac{d}{dt} e_{ij} = -e_{ij} + H(pre_j, post_i). \tag{19.46}$$

If the joint activity of pre- and postsynaptic neurons stops, the Hebbian term H vanishes and the eligibility trace decays back to zero with a time constant τ_e. The Hebbian term H could be modeled by one of the rate models in the framework of Eq. (19.2) or an STDP model such as the one defined in 19.10.

The update of synaptic weights requires a nonzero-eligibility trace as well as the presence of a neuromodulatory success signal M

$$\frac{d}{dt} w_{ij} = M \cdot e_{ij}. \tag{19.47}$$

While in standard Hebbian learning synaptic plasticity depends on two factors (i.e., pre- and postsynaptic activity), weight changes in Eq. (19.47) now depend on three factors, i.e., the two Hebbian factors and the neuromodulator M. The class of plasticity rules encompassed by Eq. (19.47) is therefore called three-factor learning rules. In models of reward-based learning, the modulator signal M is most often taken as "reward minus expected reward,"

$$M(t) = R(t) - \langle R \rangle, \tag{19.48}$$

where R denotes the reward and the expectation $\langle R \rangle$ is empirically estimated as a running

(a)

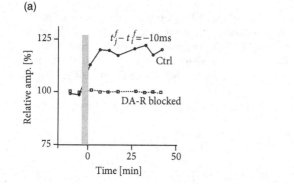

(b)

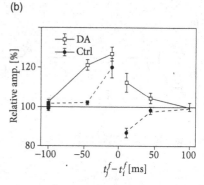

Fig. 19.16 Dopamine-modulated Hebbian learning. (a) An STDP protocol normally gives rise to long-term potentiation (pre-before-post, solid black line as in Fig. 19.4d). However, if dopamine receptors are blocked, no change occurs (schematic representation of experiments in Pawlak and Kerr (2008)). (b) The STDP window in a control situation (dashed line and solid data points) changes if additional extracellular dopamine is present (solid lines, open squares). Adapted from Zhang *et al.* (2009).

average. The time constant τ_e is typically chosen in the range of one second, so as to bridge the delay between action choice and final reward signal.

Three-factor rules have been suggested for rate-based (Reynolds and Wickens, 2002; Loewenstein, 2008) as well as spike-based Hebbian models. In spike-based Hebbian models, the Hebbian term is often taken as a standard pair-based STDP function (Izhikevich, 2007a; Legenstein *et al.*, 2008; Florian, 2007) or an STDP model that also depends on postsynaptic voltage (Pfister *et al.*, 2006; Florian, 2007; Baras and Meir, 2007). Experiments have shown that the shape of the STDP window is indeed modulated by dopamine as well as other neuromodulators (Fig. 19.16); for a review see Pawlak *et al.* (2010).

Example: R-STDP and learning of spike sequences

Suppose a table tennis player plays a serve or a piano player a rapid scale. In both cases the executed movements are extremely rapid, have been practiced many times, and are often performed in "open loop" mode, for example, without visual feedback during the movement. There is, however, feedback after some delay which signals the success (or failure) of the performed action, for example the ball went off the table or the scale contained a wrong note.

A rapid scale on a piano means touching about 10 different keys per second. Similarly, the complex gliding movement to give the ball its spin takes less than a second. It is likely that for such fast movements spike timing plays an important role. The motor cortex is involved in the control of limb movements. Experimental data from the arm area of the primary motor cortex indicates that populations of neurons encode the direction of hand motion during reaching movements in three-dimensional space (Georgopoulos *et al.*, 1988). Each neuron *i* has a preferred direction of motion represented as a vector d_i. The vectors of different neurons are added up with a weighting function proportional to the cell's firing rate (Georgopoulos *et al.*, 1988). For the rapid movements of less than one second that we consider here, a single neuron is expected to emit at most a few spikes. Therefore a desired trajectory can be represented as a target spatio-temporal spike pattern; see Fig. 19.17.

Model neurons in the motor cortex receive spike input from neurons in sensory areas that represent, for example, the vertical movement of the ball that is launched at the beginning of the serve, as well as the intention of the player. During practice sessions, the aim is to associate the spatio-temporal spike pattern in the input layer with the target spike pattern in the layer of motor cortex neurons while the only feedback is the success signal available at the *end* of the movement.

Figure 19.17 shows that a two-layer network of spiking neurons can learn this task if synaptic connections use a reward-modulated STDP rule (R-STDP) where the Hebbian term *H* in Eq. (19.47) is the pair-based STDP rule defined in (19.10). It is important that the global neuromodulatory signal provided at the end of each trial is *not* the raw reward, but success defined as "reward – expected reward" as in Eq. (19.48). If a single task has to be learned, the expected reward can be estimated from the running average over past trials. However, if several trajectories (e.g., two different serves or two different scales) have to be learned in parallel, then the expected reward needs to be estimated separately for each trajectory (Fremaux *et al.*, 2010).

R-STDP rules have also been used for several other tasks, see, (e.g., Izhikevich, 2007a; Florian, 2007).

19.5 Summary

The Hebb rule (19.2) is an example of a *local* unsupervised learning rule. It is a local rule, because it depends only on pre- and postsynaptic firing rates and the present state w_{ij} of the synapse, i.e., information that is easily "available" at the location of the synapse. Experiments have shown that not only the firing rates, but also the membrane voltage of the postsynaptic neuron, as well as the relative timing of pre- and postsynaptic spikes, determine the amplitude and direction of change of the synaptic efficacy. To account for spike timing effects, classical pair-based models of STDP are formulated with a learning window that consists of two parts: If the presynaptic spike arrives before a postsynaptic output spike, the synaptic change is positive. If the timing is reversed, the synaptic change is negative. However, classical pair-based STDP models neglect the frequency and voltage dependence of synaptic plasticity, which are included in modern variants of STDP models.

The synaptic weight dynamics of Hebbian learning can be studied analytically if weights are changing slowly compared to the time scale of the neuronal activity. Weight changes are driven by correlations between pre- and postsynaptic activity. More specifically, simple

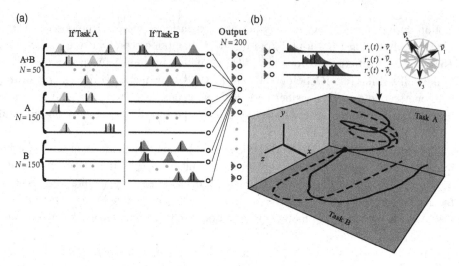

Fig. 19.17 Learning with R-STDP. (a) The input consists of 350 spike trains with a temporal precision of 20 ms. Fifty unspecific neurons fired for both tasks, whereas half of the other neurons fired only for task A or task B. The output consists of 200 spiking model neurons. (b) Output spike trains were convolved with a filter (top). The resulting continuous signal for neuron i is interpreted as the speed of movement in direction d_i, where different neurons code for different directions. The two target trajectories (bottom, dashed lines) correspond to two different target spatio-temporal spike-train patterns. After a learning period of 10 000 trials, the network output generates a trajectory (full black lines) close to the target trajectories.

Hebbian learning rules in combination with a linear neuron model find the first principal component of a normalized input dataset. Generalized Hebb rules, such as Oja's rule, keep the norm of the weight vector approximately constant during plasticity.

The interesting aspect of STDP is that it naturally accounts for *temporal* correlations by means of a learning window. Explicit expressions for temporal spike–spike correlations can be obtained for certain simple types of neuron model such as the linear Poisson model. Spike-based and rate-based rules of plasticity are equivalent as long as *temporal* spike–spike correlations are disregarded. If firing rates vary slowly, then the integral over the learning window plays the role of the Hebbian correlation term.

Hebbian learning and STDP are examples of unsupervised learning rules. Hebbian learning is considered to be a major principle of neuronal organization during development and a driving force for receptive field formation. However, Hebbian synaptic plasticity is not useful for behavioral learning, since it does not take into account the success (or failure) of an action. Three-factor learning rules combine the two Hebbian factors (i.e., pre- and postsynaptic activity) with a third factor (i.e., a neuromodulator such as dopamine) which conveys information about an action's success. Three-factor rules with an eligibility trace can be used to describe behavioral learning, in particular during conditioning experiments.

Literature

Correlation-based learning can be traced back to Aristoteles[1] and has been discussed extensively by James (1890), who formulated a learning principle on the level of "brain processes" rather than neurons:

> When two elementary brain-processes have been active together or in immediate succession, one of them, on re-occurring, tends to propagate its excitement into the other.

A chapter of James' book is reprinted in volume 1 of Anderson and Rosenfeld's collection on neurocomputing (Anderson and Rosenfeld, 1988). The formulation of synaptic plasticity in Hebb's book (Hebb, 1949), of which two interesting sections are reprinted in the collection of Anderson and Rosenfeld (1988), has had a long-lasting impact on the neuroscience community. The historical context of Hebb's postulate is discussed in the reviews of Sejnowski (1999) and Makram *et al.* (2011).

There are several classical experimental studies on STDP (Markram *et al.*, 1997; Zhang *et al.*, 1998; Debanne *et al.*, 1998; Bi and Poo, 1998, 1999; Sjöström *et al.*, 2001), but precursors of timing-dependent plasticity can be found even earlier (Levy and Stewart, 1983). Note that for some synapses, the learning window is reversed (Bell *et al.*, 1997). For reviews on STDP, see Abbott and Nelson (2000), Bi and Poo (2001), Caporale and Dan (2008), and Sjöström and Gerstner (2010).

The theory of unsupervised learning and principal component analysis is reviewed in the textbook by Hertz *et al.* (1991). Models of the development of receptive fields and cortical maps have a long tradition in the field of computational neuroscience (see, e.g., von der Malsburg, 1973; Willshaw and von der Malsburg, 1976; Sejnowski, 1977; Bienenstock *et al.*, 1982; Kohonen, 1984; Linsker, 1986; Miller *et al.*, 1989; MacKay and Miller, 1990; Miller, 1994; for reviews see, e.g., Erwin *et al.*, 1995; Wiskott and Sejnowski, 1998). The essential aspects of the weight dynamics in linear networks are discussed in Oja (1982) and Miller and MacKay (1994). Articles by Grossberg (1976) and Bienenstock *et al.* (1982) or the book by Kohonen (1984) illustrate the early use of the rate-based learning rules in computational neuroscience.

The early theory of STDP was developed by Gerstner *et al.* (1993, 1996a); Kempter *et al.* (1999a); Roberts and Bell (2000); van Rossum *et al.* (2000); Song *et al.* (2000); Rubin *et al.* (2001) but precursors of timing-dependent plasticity can be found in earlier rate-based formulations (Herz *et al.*, 1988; Sompolinsky and Kanter, 1986). Modern theories of STDP go beyond the pair-based rules (Senn *et al.*, 2001; Pfister and Gerstner, 2006), consider voltage effects (Clopath *et al.*, 2010), variations of boundary conditions (Gütig *et al.*, 2003) or calcium-based models (Lisman *et al.*, 2002; Lisman, 2003) and for reviews see Morrison *et al.* (2008) and Sjöström and Gerstner (2010).

Experimental support for three-factor learning rules is reviewed in Reynolds and Wickens (2002) and Pawlak *et al.* (2010). Model studies to reward modulated STDP are

---

[1] Aristoteles, "De memoria et reminiscentia": There is no need to consider how we remember what is distant, but only what is neighboring, for clearly the method is the same. For the changes follow each other by habit, one after another. And thus, whenever someone wishes to recollect he will do the following: He will seek to get a starting point for a change after which will be the change in question.

Izhikevich (2007a); Legenstein *et al.* (2008); Florian (2007); Fremaux *et al.* (2010). The consequences for behavior are discussed in Loewenstein and Seung (2006) and Loewenstein (2008). The classic reference for dopamine in relation to reward-based learning is Schultz *et al.* (1997). Modern reviews on the topic are Schultz (2007, 2010).

Exercises

1. **Normalization of firing rate.** *Consider a learning rule* $\frac{d}{dt}w_{ij} = \gamma(v_i - v_\theta)v_j$, *i.e., a change of synaptic weights can only occur if the presynaptic neuron is active* $(v_j > 0)$*. The direction of the change is determined by the activity of the postsynaptic neuron. The postsynaptic firing rate is given by* $v_i = g(\sum_{j=1}^N w_{ij}v_j)$*. We assume that presynaptic firing rates* v_j *are constant.*
   (a) Show that v_i *has a fixed point at* $v_i = v_\theta$*.*
   (b) Discuss the stability of the fixed point. Consider the cases $\gamma > 0$ *and* $\gamma < 0$*.*
   (c) Discuss whether the learning rule is Hebbian, anti-Hebbian, or non-Hebbian.
2. **Fixed point of BCM rule.** *Assume a single postsynaptic neuron* v_i *which receives constant input* $v_j > 0$ *at all synapses* $1 \le j \le N$*.*
   (a) Show that the weights w_{ij} *have a fixed point under the BCM rule (19.9).*
   (b) Show that this fixed point is unstable.
3. **Receptive field development with BCM rule.** *Twenty presynaptic neurons with firing rates* v_j *connect onto the same postsynaptic neuron which fires at a rate* $v_i^{post} = \sum_{j=1}^{20} w_{ij}v_j$*. Synaptic weights change according to the BCM rule (19.9) with a hard lower bound* $0 \le w_{ij}$ *and* $v_\theta = 10\,Hz$*.*
   The 20 inputs are organized in two groups of 10 inputs each. There are two possible input patterns ξ^μ*, with* $\mu = 1, 2$*.*
   (a) The two possible input patterns are: $\mu = 1$*, a group 1 fires at 3 Hz and group 2 is quiescent; and* $\mu = 2$*, group 2 fires at 1 Hz and group 1 is quiescent. Inputs alternate between both patterns several times back and forth. Each pattern presentation lasts for* Δt*. How do weights* w_{ij} *evolve? Show that the postsynaptic neuron becomes specialized to one group of inputs.*
   (b) Similar to (a), except that that the second pattern is now $\mu = 2$*: group 2 fires at 2.5 Hz and group 1 is quiescent. How do weights* w_{ij} *evolve?*
   (c) As in (b), but you are allowed to make v_θ *a function of the time-averaged firing rate* $\bar{v}_i^{post}$ *of the postsynaptic neuron. Is* $v_\theta = \bar{v}_i^{post}$ *a good choice? Why is* $v_\theta = (\bar{v}_i^{post})^2/10\,Hz$ *a better choice?*
   Hint: Consider the time it takes to update your time-averaged firing rate in comparison to the presentation time Δt *of the patterns.*
4. **Weight matrix of Hopfield model.** *Consider synaptic weights that change according to the following Hebbian learning rule:* $\frac{d}{dt}w_{ij} = c(v_i - v_0)(v_j - v_0)$*.*
   (a) Identify the parameters c and v_0 *with the parameters of Eq. (19.2).*
   (b) Assume a fully connected network of N neurons. Suppose that the initial weights w_{ij} *vanish. During presentation of a pattern* μ*, activities of all neurons* $1 \le k \le N$ *are fixed to values* $v_k = p_k^\mu$*, where* $p_k^\mu \in \{0, 1\}$ *and synapses change according to the Hebbian learning rule. Patterns are applied one after the other, each for a time* Δt*. Choose an appropriate value for* v_0 *so that, after application of P patterns, the final weights are* $w_{ij} = \gamma\sum_{j=1}^P p_i^\mu p_j^\mu$*. Express the parameter* γ *by* $c, v_0, \Delta t$*.*
   (c) Compare your results with the weight matrix of the Hopfield model in Chapter 17. Is the above learning procedure realistic? Can it be classified as unsupervised learning?
   Hint: Consider not only the learning phase, but also the recall phase. Consider the situation where input patterns are chosen stochastically.
5. **PCA with Oja's learning rule.** *In order to show that Oja's learning rule (19.7) selects the first principal component proceed in three steps.*
   (a) Show that the eigenvectors $\{e_1, \dots, e_N\}$ *of C are fixed points of the dynamics.*

Hint: Apply the methods of Section 19.3 to the batch version of Oja's rule and show that

$$\Delta w = \gamma C w - \gamma w [w \cdot C w].\qquad(19.49)$$

The claim then follows.

(b) Show that only the eigenvector e_1 with the largest eigenvalue is stable.

Hint: Assume that the weight vector $w = e_1 + \varepsilon e_k$ has a small perturbation $\varepsilon \ll 1$ in one of the principal direction. Derive an equation for $d\varepsilon / dt$ and show that the perturbation grows if $k \neq 1$.

(c) Show that the output rate represents the projection of the input onto the first principal component.

6. **Triplet STDP rule and BCM**. *Show that for Poisson spike arrival and output spike generated by an independent Poisson process of rate v_i, the triplet STDP model gives rise to a rate-based plasticity model identical to BCM. Identify the function ϕ in Eqs. (19.8) and (19.9) with the parameters of the triplet model in (19.15).*

Hint: Use the methods of Section 19.3.3. Independent Poisson output means that you can neglect the pre-before-post spike correlations.

20

Outlook: dynamics in plastic networks

In this final chapter, we combine the dynamics of single neurons (Parts I and II) and networks (Part III) with synaptic plasticity (Chapter 19) and illustrate their interaction in a few applications.

In Section 20.1 on "reservoir computing" we show that the network dynamics in random networks of excitatory and inhibitory neurons is sufficiently rich to serve as a computing device that buffers past inputs and computes on present ones. In Section 20.2 we study oscillations that arise in networks of spiking neurons and outline how synaptic plasticity interacts with oscillations. Finally, in Section 20.3, we illustrate why the study of neuronal dynamics is not just an intellectual exercise, but might, one day, become useful for applications or, eventually, benefit human patients.

20.1 Reservoir computing

One of the reasons the dynamics of neuronal networks are rich is that networks have a nontrivial connectivity structure linking different neuron types in an intricate interaction pattern. Moreover, network dynamics are rich because they span many time scales. The fastest time scale is set by the duration of an action potential, i.e., a few milliseconds. Synaptic facilitation and depression (Chapter 3) or adaptation (Chapter 6) occur on time scales from a few hundred milliseconds to seconds. Finally, long-lasting changes of synapses can be induced in a few seconds, but last from hours to days (Chapter 19).

These rich dynamics of neuronal networks can be used as a "reservoir" for intermediate storage and representation of incoming input signals. Desired outputs can then be constructed by reading out appropriate combinations of neuronal spike trains from the network. This kind of "reservoir computing" encompasses the notions of "liquid computing" (Maass *et al.*, 2002) and "echo state networks" (Jaeger and Haas, 2004). Before we discuss some mathematical aspects of randomly connected networks, we illustrate rich dynamics by a simulated model network.

20.1.1 Rich dynamics

A nice example of rich network dynamics is the work by Maass *et al.* (2007). Six hundred leaky integrate-and-fire neurons (80 % excitatory and 20 % inhibitory) were placed on a three-dimensional grid with distance-dependent random connectivity of small probability so that the total number of synapses is about 10 000. Synaptic dynamics included short-term plasticity (Chapter 3) with time constants ranging from a few tens of milliseconds to a few seconds. Neuronal parameters varied from one neuron to the next and each neuron received independent noise.

To check the computational capabilities of such a network, Maass *et al.* stimulated it with four input streams targeting different subgroups of the network (Fig. 20.1). Each input stream consisted of Poisson spike trains with time-dependent firing rate $v(t)$.

Streams 1 and 2 fired at a low background rate but switched occasionally to a short period of high firing rate ("burst"). In order to build a memory of past bursts, synaptic weights from the network onto a group of eight integrate-and-fire neurons ("memory" in Fig. 20.1) were adjusted by an optimization algorithm, so that the spiking activity of these eight neurons reflects whether the last firing rate burst happened in stream 1 (memory neurons are active = memory "on") or 2 (the same neurons are inactive = memory "off"). Thus, these neurons provided a 1-bit memory ("on"/"off") of past events.

Streams 3 and 4 were used to perform a non-trivial online computation. A network output with value v_{online} was optimized to calculate the sum of activity in streams 3 and 4, but only if the memory neurons were active (memory "on"). Optimization of weight parameters was achieved in a series of preliminary training trials by minimizing the squared error (Chapter 10) between the target and the actual output.

Figure 20.1 shows that, after optimization of the weights, the network could store a memory and, at the same time, perform the desired online computation. Therefore, the dynamics in a randomly connected network with feedback from the output are rich enough to generate an output stream which is a non-trivial nonlinear transformation of the input streams (Maass *et al.*, 2007; Jaeger and Haas, 2004; Sussillo and Abbott, 2009).

In the above simulation, the tunable connections (Fig. 20.1a) have been adjusted "by hand" (or rather by a suitable algorithm), in a biologically non-plausible fashion, so as to yield the desired output. However, it is possible to learn the desired output with the three-factor learning rules discussed in Section 19.4. This has been demonstrated on a task and set-up very similar to Fig. 20.1, except that the neurons in the network were modeled by rate units (Hoerzer *et al.*, 2012). The neuromodulatory signal M (see Section 19.4) took a value of 1 if the momentary performance was better than the average performance in the recent past, and zero otherwise.

20.1.2 Network analysis (*)

Networks of randomly connected excitatory and inhibitory neurons can be analyzed for the case of rate units (Rajan and Abbott, 2006). Let x_i denote the deviation from a spontaneous

(a)   (b)

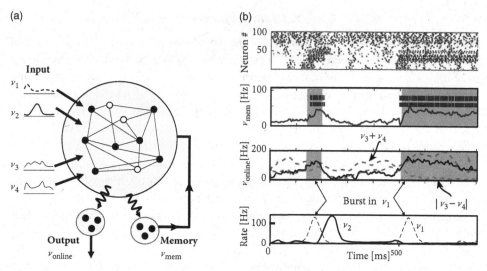

Fig. 20.1 Reservoir computing. (a) A randomly connected network of integrate-and-fire neurons receives four input streams, each characterized by spike trains with a time-dependent Poisson firing rate v_k. The main network is connected to two further pools of neurons, called "memory" and "output." Memory neurons are trained to fire at high rates if the last burst in v_1 is more recent than the last burst in v_2. Spike trains of the memory neurons are fed back into the network. The output v_{online} is trained to calculate either the sum $v_3 + v_4$ or the difference $|v_3 - v_4|$ of the two other input streams, depending on the current setting of the memory unit. The tunable connections onto the memory and output neurons are indicated by curly arrows. (b) Spiking activity of the main network (top) and of two memory neurons (second from top) as well as mean firing rate of memory neurons (second from top), and online output (third, thick solid line; the dashed lines give the momentary targets). The two input streams v_1, v_2 are shown at the bottom. The periods when the memory unit should be active are shaded. Adapted from Maass *et al.* (2007).

background rate v_0, i.e., the rate of neuron i is $v_i = v_0 + x_i$. Let us consider the update dynamics

$$x_i(t+1) = g\left(\sum_j w_{ij} x_j\right) \tag{20.1}$$

for a monotone transfer function g with $g(0) = 0$ and derivative $g'(0) = 1$.

The background state ($x_i = 0$ for all neurons i) is stable if the weight matrix has no eigenvalues with real part larger than 1. If there are eigenvalues with real part larger than 1, spontaneous chaotic network activity may occur (Sompolinksy *et al.*, 1988).

For weight matrices of random networks, a surprising number of mathematical results exist. We focus on mixed networks of excitatory and inhibitory neurons. In a network of N neurons, there are fN excitatory and $(1-f)N$ inhibitory neurons where f is the fraction of excitatory neurons. Outgoing weights from an excitatory neuron j take values $w_{ij} \geq 0$ for all i (and $w_{ij} \leq 0$ for weights from inhibitory neurons), so that all columns

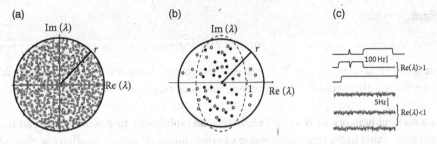

Fig. 20.2 Random networks. (a) Distribution of eigenvalues in the complex plane for a network of excitatory and inhibitory neurons with detailed balance. The distribution is circular and stays within a spectral radius r. Adapted from Rajan and Abbott (2006). (b) Inhibitory plasticity quenches the real part of eigenvalues into a smaller band (dashed ellipse). Thus an unstable random network (where some eigenvalues have $\text{Re}(\lambda) > 1$, open circles) can be turned into stable one ($\text{Re}(\lambda) < 1$, solid circles); schematic figure. (c) Time course of the activity of three sample neurons while the network is driven with a small amount of noise. Neuronal activity in unstable random networks exhibits chaotic switching between maximally low and high rates (top three traces) whereas the same neurons show only a small amount of fluctuations after stabilization through inhibitory plasticity (bottom three traces). Adapted from Hennequin (2014).

of the weight matrix have the same sign. We assume non-plastic random weights with the following three constraints: (i) Input to each neuron is balanced so that $\sum_j w_{ij} = 0$ for all i ("detailed balance"). In other words, if all neurons are equally active, excitation and inhibition cancel each other on a neuron-by-neuron level. (ii) Excitatory weights are drawn from a distribution with mean $\mu_E/\sqrt{N} > 0$ and variance r/N. (iii) Inhibitory weights are drawn from a distribution with mean $\mu_I/\sqrt{N} < 0$ and variance r/N. Under the conditions (i)–(iii), the eigenvalues of the weight matrix all lie within a circle (Fig. 20.2a) of radius r, called the spectral radius (Rajan and Abbott, 2006).

The condition of detailed balance stated above as item (i) may look artificial at first sight. However, experimental data supports the idea of detailed balance (Froemke *et al.*, 2007; Okun and Lampl, 2008). Moreover, plasticity of inhibitory synapses can be used to achieve such a balance of excitation and inhibition on a neuron-by-neuron basis (Vogels *et al.*, 2011).

To understand how inhibitory plasticity comes into play, consider a rate model in continuous time

$$\tau \frac{dx_i}{dt} = -x_i + g\left(\sum_j w_{ij} x_j\right) + \xi(t), \qquad (20.2)$$

where τ is a time constant and x_i is, as before, the deviation of the firing rate from a background level v_0. The gain function $g(h)$ with $g(0)$ and $g'(0) = 1$ is bounded between $x^{\min} = -v_0$ and $x^{\max}$. Gaussian white noise $\xi(t)$ of small amplitude is added on the right-hand side of Eq. (20.2) to kick network activity out of the fixed point at $x = 0$.

We subject inhibitory weights $w_{ij} < 0$ (where j is one of the inhibitory neurons) to

Hebbian plasticity

$$\frac{d}{dt}w_{ij} = -\gamma x_i(t)\bar{x}_j(t),\tag{20.3}$$

where $\bar{x}_j(t) = \int_0^\infty \exp(-s/\tau)x_j(t-s)ds$ is the synaptic trace left by earlier presynaptic activity. For $\gamma > 0$, this is a Hebbian learning rule because the absolute size of the *inhibitory* weight increases if postsynaptic and presynaptic activity are correlated (Chapter 19).

In a random network of $N = 200$ excitatory and inhibitory rate neurons with an initial weight matrix that had a large distribution of eigenvalues, inhibitory plasticity according to Eq. (20.3) led to a compression of the real parts of the eigenvalues (Hennequin, 2013). Hebbian inhibitory plasticity can therefore push a network from the regime of unstable dynamics into a stable regime (Fig. 20.2b,c) while keeping the excitatory weights strong. Such networks, which have strong excitatory connections, counterbalanced by equally strong precisely tuned inhibition, can potentially explain patterns of neural activity in the motor cortex during arm movements (Churchland *et al.*, 2012). In-depth understanding of patterns in the motor cortex could eventually contribute to the development of neural prosthesis (Shenoy *et al.*, 2011) that detect and decode neural activity in motor-related brain areas and translate it into intended movements of a prosthetic limb; see Chapter 11.

Example: Generating movement trajectories with inhibition stabilized networks

During the preparation and performance of arm movements (Fig. 20.3a) neurons in the motor cortex exhibit collective dynamics (Churchland *et al.*, 2012). In particular, during the preparation phase just before the start of the movement, the network activity approaches a stable pattern of firing rates, which is similar across different trials. This stable pattern can be interpreted as an initial condition for the subsequent evolution of the network dynamics during arm movement, which is rather stereotypical across trials (Shenoy *et al.*, 2011).

Because of its sensitivity to small perturbations, a random network with chaotic network dynamics may not be a plausible candidate for stereotypical dynamics, necessary for reliable arm movements. On the other hand, in a stable random network with a circular distribution of eigenvalues with spectral radius $r < 1$, transient dynamics after release from an initial condition are short and dominated by the time constant τ of the single-neuron dynamics (unless one of the eigenvalues is hand-tuned to lie very close to unity). Moreover, as discussed in Chapter 18, the cortex is likely to work in the regime of an inhibition-stabilized network (Tsodyks *et al.*, 1997; Ozeki *et al.*, 2009) where excitatory connections are strong, but counterbalanced by even stronger inhibition.

Inhibitory plasticity is helpful to generate inhibition-stabilized random networks. Because excitatory connections are strong but random, transient activity after release from an appropriate initial condition is several times longer than the single-neuron time constant τ. Different initial conditions put the network onto different, but reliable trajectories. These trajectories of the collective network dynamics can be used as a reservoir to generate simulated muscle output for different arm trajectories (Fig. 20.3).

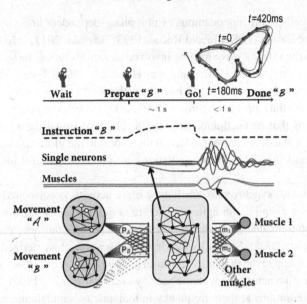

Fig. 20.3 Movement preparation and execution. Top: A typical delayed movement generation task in behavioral neuroscience starts with the instruction of what movement must be prepared. The arm must be held still until the go cue is given. Middle: During the preparatory period, model neurons receive a ramp input (dashed) which is withdrawn when the go cue is given. Thereafter the network dynamics move freely from the initial condition set during the preparatory period. Model neurons (four sample black lines) then exhibit transient oscillations which drive muscle activation (gray lines). Bottom: To prepare the movement $\mathcal{B}$ (e.g., butterfly movement), the network (gray box, middle) is initialized in the desired state by the slow activation of the corresponding pool of neurons (gray circle). Muscles (right) in the model are activated by a suitable combination of neuronal activity read out from the main network. Note that no feedback is given during the drawing movement. Adapted from Hennequin *et al.* (2014).

20.2 Oscillations: good or bad?

Oscillations are a prevalent phenomenon in biological neural systems and manifest themselves experimentally in electroencephalograms (EEG), recordings of local field potentials (LFP), and multi-unit recordings. Oscillations are thought to stem from synchronous network activity and are often characterized by the associated frequency peak in the Fourier spectrum. For example, oscillations in the range 30–70 Hz are called gamma oscillations and those above 100 Hz "ultrafast" or "ripples" (Traub, 2006; Buzsaki, 2011). Among the slower oscillations, prominent examples are delta oscillations (1–4 Hz) and spindle oscillations in the EEG during sleep (7–15 Hz) (Bazhenov and Timofeev, 2006) or theta oscillations (4–10 Hz) in the hippocampus and other areas (Buzsaki, 2011).

Oscillations are thought to play an important role in the coding of sensory information. In the olfactory system an ongoing oscillation of the population activity provides a temporal frame of reference for neurons coding information about the odorant (Laurent, 1996).

Similarly, place cells in the hippocampus exhibit phase-dependent firing activity relative to a background oscillation (O'Keefe and Recce, 1993; Buzsaki, 2011). Moreover, rhythmic spike patterns in the inferior olive may be involved in various timing tasks and motor coordination (Welsh *et al.*, 1995; Kistler and van Hemmen, 2000). Finally, synchronization of firing across groups of neurons has been hypothesized to provide a potential solution to the so-called binding problem (Singer, 1993, 2007). The common idea across all the above examples is that an oscillation provides a reference signal for a "phase code": the significance of a spike depends on its phase with respect to the global oscillatory reference; see Section 7.6 and Fig. 7.17. Thus, oscillations are potentially useful for intricate neural coding schemes.

On the other hand, synchronous oscillatory brain activity is correlated with numerous brain diseases. For example, an epileptic seizure is defined as "a transient occurrence of signs and/or symptoms due to abnormal excessive or synchronous neuronal activity in the brain" (Fisher *et al.*, 2005). Similarly, Parkinson's disease is characterized by a high level of neuronal synchrony in the thalamus and basal ganglia (Pare *et al.*, 1990) while neurons in the same areas fire asynchronously in the healthy brain (Nini *et al.*, 1995). Moreover, local field potential oscillations at theta frequency in thalamic or subthalamic nuclei are linked to tremor in human Parkinsonian patients, i.e., rhythmic finger, hand or arm movement at 3–6 Hz (Pare *et al.*, 1990; Tass *et al.*, 2010). Therefore, in these and in similar situations, it seems to be desirable to suppress abnormal, highly synchronous oscillations so as to shift the brain back into its healthy state.

Simulations of the population activity in homogeneous networks typically exhibit oscillations when driven by a constant external input. For example, oscillations in networks of purely excitatory neurons arise because, as soon as some neurons in the network fire, they contribute to exciting others. Once the avalanche of firing has run across the network, all neurons pass through a period of refractoriness, until they are ready to fire again. In this case the time scale of the oscillation is set by neuronal refractoriness (Fig. 20.4a). A similar argument can be made for a homogeneous network of inhibitory neurons driven by a constant external stimulus. After a first burst by a few neurons, mutual inhibition will silence the population until inhibition wears off. Thereafter, the whole network fires again.

Oscillations also arise in networks of coupled excitatory and inhibitory neurons. The excitatory connections cause a synchronous bursts of the network activity leading to a build-up of inhibition which, in turn, suppresses the activity of excitatory neurons. The oscillation period in the two latter cases is therefore set by the build-up and decay time of inhibitory feedback (Fig. 20.4b).

Even slower oscillations can be generated in "winner-take-all" networks (see Chapter 16) with dynamic synapses (see Chapter 3) or adaptation (see Chapter 6). Suppose the networks consists of K populations of excitatory neurons which share a common pool of inhibitory neurons. Parameters can be set such that excitatory neurons within the momentarily "winning" population stimulate each other so as to overcome inhibition. In the presence of synaptic depression, however, the mutual excitation fades away after a short time, so that now a different excitatory population becomes the new "winner" and switches on.

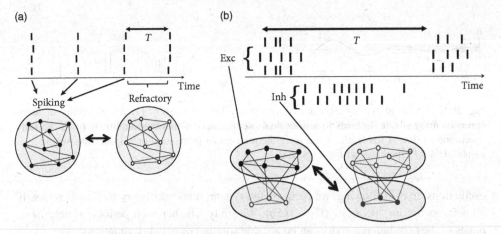

Fig. 20.4 Types of network oscillation. (a) In a homogeneous network of excitatory neurons, near-synchronous firing of all neurons is followed by a period of refractoriness, leading to fast oscillations with period T. Active neurons: vertical dash in spike raster and solid circle in network schema. Silent neurons: open circle in schema. (b) In a network of excitatory and inhibitory neurons, activity of the excitatory population alternates with activity of the inhibitory one. The period T is longer than in (a).

As a result, inhibition arising from inhibitory neurons turns the activity of the previously winning group off, until inhibition has decayed and excitatory synapses have recovered from depression. The time scale is then set by a combination of the time scales of inhibition and synaptic depression. Networks of this type have been used to explain the shift of attention from one point in a visual scene to the next (Itti *et al.*, 1998).

In this section, we briefly review mathematical theories of oscillatory activity (Sections 20.2.1–20.2.3) before we study the interaction of oscillations with STDP (Section 20.2.4) The results of this section will form the basis for the discussion of Section 20.3.

20.2.1 Synchronous oscillations and locking

Homogeneous networks of spiking neurons show a natural tendency toward oscillatory activity. In Sections 13.4.2 and 14.2.3, we analyzed the stability of asynchronous firing. In the stationary state the population activity is characterized by a constant value A_0 of the population activity. An instability of the dynamics with respect to oscillations at period T, appears as a sinusoidal perturbation of increasing amplitude; see Fig. 20.5a as well as Fig. 14.8. The analysis of the stationary state shows that a high level of noise, network heterogeneity, or a sufficient amount of inhibitory plasticity, all contribute to stabilizing the stationary state. The linear stability analysis, however, is only valid in the vicinity of the stationary state. As soon as the amplitude ΔA of the oscillations is of the same order of magnitude as A_0, the solution found by linear analysis is no longer valid since the population activity cannot become negative.

Oscillations can, however, also be analyzed from a completely different perspective. In a homogeneous network with fixed connectivity in the limit of low noise we expect strong

(a)

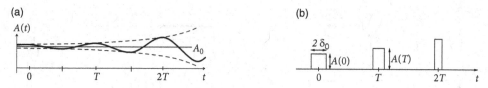

(b)

Fig. 20.5 Population activity $A(t)$ during oscillations and synchrony. (a) An instability of asynchronous firing at rate A_0 leads to a sinusoidal oscillation of increasing amplitude. (b) If the fully synchronized state is stable, the width δ_0 of the rectangular population pulses decreases while their amplitude $A(kT)$ increases with each period.

oscillations. In the following, we focus on the synchronous oscillatory mode where nearly all neurons fire in "lockstep" (Fig. 20.5b). We study whether such periodic synchronous bursts of the population activity can be a stable solution of network equations.

To keep the arguments simple, we consider a homogeneous population of identical SRM$_0$ neurons (Chapter 6 and Section 9.3) which is nearly perfectly synchronized and fires almost regularly with period T. To analyze the existence and stability of a fully locked synchronous oscillation we approximate the population activity by a sequence of square pulses k, $k \in \{0, \pm 1, \pm 2, \ldots\}$, centered around $t = kT$. Each pulse k has a certain half-width δ_k and amplitude $(2\delta_k)^{-1}$ – since all neurons are supposed to fire once in each pulse; see Fig. 20.5b. If we find that the amplitude of subsequent pulses increases while their width decreases (i.e., $\lim_{k \to \infty} \delta_k = 0$), we conclude that the fully locked state in which all neurons fire simultaneously is stable.

In the examples below, we will prove that the condition for stable locking of all neurons in the population can be stated as a condition on the *slope* h' of the input potential h at the moment of firing. More precisely, if the last population pulse occurred at about $t = 0$ with amplitude $A(0)$ the amplitude of the population pulse at $t = T$ increases if $h'(T) > 0$:

$$h'(T) > 0 \quad \Longleftrightarrow \quad A(T) > A(0). \tag{20.4}$$

If the amplitude of subsequent pulses increases, their width must decrease accordingly. In other words, we have the following *locking theorem*. In a homogeneous network of SRM$_0$ neurons, a necessary and, in the limit of a large number of presynaptic neurons ($N \to \infty$), also sufficient condition for a coherent oscillation to be asymptotically stable is that firing occurs when the postsynaptic potential arising from all previous spikes in the population is increasing in time (Gerstner *et al.*, 1996b).

Example: Perfect synchrony in network of inhibitory neurons

Locking in a population of spiking neurons can be understood by simple geometrical arguments. To illustrate this argument, we study a homogeneous network of N identical SRM$_0$ neurons which are mutually coupled with strength $w_{ij} = J_0/N$. In other words, the interaction is scaled with $1/N$ so that the total input to a neuron i is of order 1 even if the number of neurons is large ($N \to \infty$). Since we are interested in synchrony we suppose that all neurons have fired simultaneously at $\hat{t} = 0$. When will the neurons fire again?

Since all neurons are identical we expect that the next firing time will also be synchronous. Let us calculate the period T between one synchronous pulse and the next. We start from the firing condition of SRM$_0$ neurons

$$\vartheta = u_i(t) = \eta(t - \hat{t}_i) + \sum_j w_{ij} \sum_f \varepsilon \left(t - t_j^f\right) + h_0, \tag{20.5}$$

where $\varepsilon(t)$ is the postsynaptic potential. The axonal transmission delay Δ^{ax} is included in the definition of ε, i.e., $\varepsilon(t) = 0$ for $t < \Delta^{ax}$. Since all neurons have fired synchronously at $t = 0$, we set $\hat{t}_i = t_j^f = 0$. The result is a condition of the form

$$\vartheta - \eta(t) = J_0 \varepsilon(t) + h_0, \tag{20.6}$$

since $w_{ij} = J_0/N$ for $j = 1, \ldots, N$. Note that we have neglected the postsynaptic potentials that may have been caused by earlier spikes $t_j^f < 0$ back in the past.

The graphical solution of Eq. (20.6) for the case of inhibitory neurons (i.e., $J_0 < 0$) is presented in Fig. 20.6. The first crossing point of the effective dynamic threshold $\vartheta - \eta(t)$ and $J_0 \varepsilon(t) + h_0$ defines the time T of the next synchronous pulse.

What happens if synchrony at $t = 0$ was not perfect? Let us assume that one of the neurons is slightly late compared to the others (Fig. 20.6b). It will receive the input $J_0 \varepsilon(t)$ from the others, thus the right-hand side of Eq. (20.6) remains the same. The left-hand side, however, is different since the last firing was at δ_0 instead of zero. The next firing time is at $t = T + \delta_1$ where δ_1 is found from

$$\vartheta - \eta(T + \delta_1 - \delta_0) = h_0 + J_0 \varepsilon(T + \delta_1). \tag{20.7}$$

Linearization with respect to δ_0 and δ_1 then yields:

$$\delta_1 < \delta_0 \quad \Longleftrightarrow \quad J_0 \varepsilon'(T) > 0, \tag{20.8}$$

where we have exploited that neurons with "normal" refractoriness and adaptation properties have $\eta' > 0$. From Eq. (20.8) we conclude that the neuron which has been late is "pulled back" into the synchronized pulse of the others if the postsynaptic potential $J_0 \varepsilon$ is rising at the moment of firing at T. Equation (20.8) is a special case of the locking theorem.

Example: Proof of the locking theorem (*)

To check whether the fully synchronized state is a stable solution of the network dynamics, we exploit the population integral equation (14.5) and assume that the population has already fired a couple of narrow pulses for $t < 0$ with widths $\delta_k \ll T, k \leq 0$, and calculate the amplitude and width of subsequent pulses.

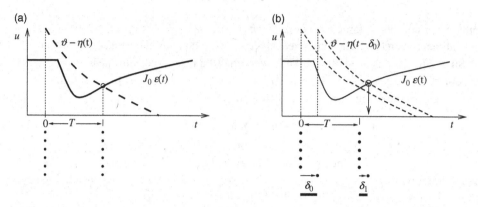

Fig. 20.6 Synchronous firing in a network with inhibitory coupling. (a) Bottom: Spike raster – all neurons have fired synchronously at $\hat{t} = 0$. Top: The next spike occurs when the total input potential $h_0 + J_0\varepsilon(t)$ (solid line; the offset corresponds to a constant background input $h_0 > 0$) has increased sufficiently to cross the dynamic threshold $\vartheta - \eta(t)$. (b) Stability of perfect synchrony. The last neuron is out of tune. The firing time difference at $t = 0$ is δ_0. One period later the firing time difference is reduced ($\delta_1 < \delta_0$), since the threshold is reached at a point where $J_0\varepsilon(t)$ is rising. Therefore this neuron is eventually pulled back into the synchronous group.

To translate the above idea into a step-by-step demonstration, we use

$$A(t) = \sum_{k=-\infty}^{\infty} \frac{1}{2\delta_k}\Theta[t - (kT - \delta_k)]\,\Theta[(kT + \delta_k) - t] \qquad (20.9)$$

as a parameterization of the population activity; see Fig. 20.5b. Here, $\Theta(.)$ denotes the Heaviside step function with $\Theta(s) = 1$ for $s > 0$ and $\Theta(s) = 0$ for $s \leq 0$. For stability, we need to show that the amplitude $A(0), A(T), A(2T), \ldots$ of the rectangular pulses increases while the width δ_k of subsequent pulses decreases.

To prove the theorem, we assume that (i) all neurons in the network have identical refractoriness $\eta(s)$ with $d\eta/ds > 0$ for all $s > 0$; (ii) all neurons have identical shape $\varepsilon(s)$ of the postsynaptic potential; (iii) all couplings are identical, $w_{ij} = w_0 = J_0/N$; and (iv) all neurons receive the same constant external drive h_0. The sequence of rectangular activity pulses in the past therefore gives rise to an input potential

$$h(t) = h_0 + J_0 \int_0^{\infty} \varepsilon(s)A(t - s)\mathrm{d}s = h_0 + \sum_{k=0}^{\infty} J_0\varepsilon(t + kT) + \mathcal{O}\left[(\delta_k)^2\right], \qquad (20.10)$$

which is identical for all neurons.

To determine the period T, we consider a neuron in the *center* of the square pulse which has fired its last spike at $\hat{t} = 0$. The next spike of this neuron must occur at $t = T$, i.e., in the center of the next square pulse. We use $\hat{t} = 0$ in the threshold condition for spike firing, which yields

$$T = \min \left\{ t \mid \eta(t) + h_0 + J_0 \sum_{k=0}^{\infty} \varepsilon(t + kT) = \vartheta \right\}. \tag{20.11}$$

If a synchronized solution exists, (20.11) defines its period.

We now use the population equation of renewal theory, Eq. (14.5). In the limit of low noise, the interval distribution $P_I(t|\hat{t})$ becomes a δ-function: neurons that have fired at time $\hat{t}$ fire again at time $t = \hat{t} + T(\hat{t})$. Using the rules for calculation with δ-functions and the threshold condition (Eq. (20.11)) for firing, we find

$$A(t) = \left[1 + \frac{h'}{\eta'} \right] A(t - T_b), \tag{20.12}$$

where the prime denotes the temporal derivative. T_b is the "backward interval:" neurons that fire at time t have fired their previous spike at time $t - T_b$. According to our assumption $\eta' > 0$. A necessary condition for an increase of the activity from one cycle to the next is therefore that the derivative h' is positive – which is the essence of the locking theorem.

The locking theorem is applicable in a large population of SRM neurons (Gerstner *et al.*, 1996b). As discussed in Chapter 6, the framework of SRM encompasses many neuron models, in particular the leaky integrate-and-fire model. Note that the above locking argument is a "local" stability argument and requires that network firing is already close to the fully synchronized state. A related but *global* locking argument has been presented by Mirollo and Strogatz (1990).

20.2.2 Oscillations with irregular firing

In the previous subsection, we have studied fully connected homogeneous network models which exhibit oscillations of the neuronal activity. In the locked state, all neurons fire regularly and in near-perfect synchrony. However, experiments show that, though oscillations are a common phenomenon, spike trains of individual neurons are often highly irregular.

Periodic large-amplitude oscillations of the population activity are compatible with irregular spike trains if individual neurons fire at an average frequency that is significantly lower than the frequency of the population activity (Fig. 20.7). If the subgroup of neurons that is active during each activity burst changes from cycle to cycle, then the distribution of interspike intervals can be broad, despite a prominent oscillation. For example, in the inferior olivary nucleus, individual neurons have a low firing rate of one spike per second while the population activity oscillates at about 10 Hz. Strong oscillations with irregular spike trains have interesting implications for short-term memory and timing tasks (Kistler and De Zeeuw, 2002).

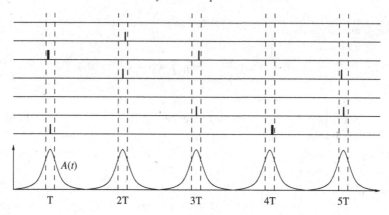

Fig. 20.7 Synchronous oscillation with irregular spike trains. Neurons tend to fire synchronously but with an average rate that is significantly lower than the oscillation frequency of the population activity (bottom). Each neuron is thus firing only in one out of approximately four cycles, giving rise to highly irregular spike trains. Short vertical lines indicate the spikes of a set of six neurons (schematic figure).

20.2.3 Phase models

For weak coupling, synchronization and locking of periodically firing neurons can be systematically analyzed in the framework of phase models (Kuramoto, 1984; Ermentrout and Kopell, 1984; Kopell, 1986; Pikovsky and Rosenblum, 2007).

Suppose a neuron driven by a constant input fires regularly with period T, i.e., it evolves on a periodic limit cycle. We have already seen in Chapter 4 that the position on the limit cycle can be represented by a phase ϕ. In contrast to Chapter 4, we adopt here the conventions that (i) spikes occur at phase $\phi = 0$ (Fig. 20.8) and (ii) between spikes the phase increases from zero to 1 at a constant speed $f_0 = 1$, where $f_0 = 1/T$ is the frequency of the periodic firing. In more formal terms, the phase of an uncoupled neural "oscillator" evolves according to the differential equation

$$\frac{d}{dt}\phi = f_0 \tag{20.13}$$

and we identify the value 1 with zero. Integration yields $\phi(t) = (t/T)_{\text{mod1}}$ where "mod1" means "modulo 1." The phase ϕ represents the position on the limit cycle (Fig. 20.8a).

Phase models for networks of N interacting neurons are characterized by the intrinsic frequencies f_j of the neurons ($1 \leq j \leq N$) as well as the mutual coupling. For weak coupling, the interaction can be directly formulated for the phase variables ϕ_j,

$$\frac{d}{dt}\phi_i = f_i + \varepsilon \sum_j w_{ij} P(\phi_i, \phi_j), \tag{20.14}$$

where $\varepsilon \ll 1$ is the overall coupling strength, w_{ij} are the relative pairwise coupling, and P the phase coupling function. For pulse-coupled oscillators, an interaction from neuron j to

(a)

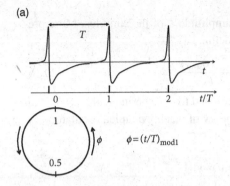

(b)

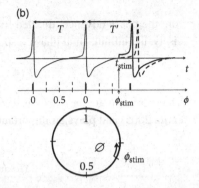

Fig. 20.8 Phase models. (a) For a neuron firing with period T (top), we can introduce a phase variable $\phi = (t/T)_{\mathrm{mod}1}$ (bottom). (b) If a weak input pulse of amplitude ε is given at a phase ϕ_{stim}, the interspike interval T' is shorter. The phase response curve $\tilde{F}(\phi_{\mathrm{stim}})$ measures the phase advance $\Delta\phi = (T - T')/T$ as a function of the stimulation phase ϕ_{stim}.

neuron i happens only at the moment when the presynaptic neuron j emits a spike. Hence the phase coupling function $P(\phi_i, \phi_j)$ is replaced by

$$P(\phi_i, \phi_j) \longrightarrow F(\phi_i) \sum_f \delta(t - t_j^f), \qquad (20.15)$$

where $\{t_j^1, t_j^2, t_j^3, \ldots\}$ are the spike times of the presynaptic neuron, defined by the zero-crossings of ϕ_j, i.e., $\{t \,|\, \phi_j(t) = 0\}$. The function F is the "phase response curve": the effect of an input pulse depends on the momentary state (i.e., the phase ϕ_i) of the receiving neuron (see the below example below).

For neurons with synaptic currents of finite duration, phase coupling is not restricted to the moment of spike firing ($\phi_j = 0$) of the presynaptic neuron, but extends also to phase values $\phi_j > 0$. The phase coupling can be positive or negative. Positive values of P lead to a phase advance of the postsynaptic neuron. Phase models are widely used to study synchronization phenomena (Pikovsky and Rosenblum, 2007).

Example: Phase response curve

The idea of a phase response curve is illustrated in Fig. 20.8b. A short positive stimulating input pulse of amplitude ε perturbs the period of an oscillator from its reference value T to a new value T', which might be shorter or longer than T (Canavier, 2006; Winfree, 1980). The phase response curve $\tilde{F}(\phi_{\mathrm{stim}})$ measures the phase advance $\Delta\phi = (T - T')/T$ as a function of the phase ϕ_{stim} at which the stimulus was given.

Knowledge of the stimulation phase is, however, not sufficient to characterize the effect on the period, because a stimulus of amplitude 2ε is expected to cause a larger phase shift than a stimulus of amplitude 1ε. The mathematically relevant notion is therefore the phase advance, divided by the (small) amplitude ε of the stimulus. More precisely, the infinitesimal phase response curve is defined as

$$F(\phi_{\text{stim}}) = \lim_{\varepsilon \to 0} \frac{T - T'(\phi_{\text{stim}})}{\varepsilon T}. \tag{20.16}$$

The infinitesimal phase response curve can be extracted from experimental data (Gutkin *et al.*, 2005) and plays an important role in the theory of weakly coupled oscillators.

Example: Kuramoto model

The Kuramoto model (Kuramoto, 1984; Acebron *et al.*, 2005) describes a network of N phase oscillators with homogeneous all-to-all connections $w_{ij} = J_0/N$ and a sinusoidal phase coupling function

$$\frac{\mathrm{d}}{\mathrm{d}t}\phi_i = f_i + \frac{J_0}{N}\sum_{j=1}^{N}\sin(2\pi(\phi_j - \phi_i)), \tag{20.17}$$

where f_i is the intrinsic frequency of oscillator i. For the analysis of the system, it is usually assumed that both the coupling strength J_0 and the frequency spread $(f_i - \overline{f})/\overline{f}$ are small. Here $\overline{f}$ denotes the mean frequency.

If the spread of intrinsic frequencies is zero, then an arbitrary small coupling $J_0 > 0$ synchronizes all units at the same phase $\phi_i(t) = \phi(t) = \overline{f}t$. This is easy to see. First, synchronous dynamics $\phi_i(t) = \phi_j(t) = \phi(t)$ for all i, j are a solution of Eq. (20.17). Second, if one of the oscillators is late by a small amount, say oscillator n has a phase $\phi_n(t) < \phi(t)$, then the interaction with the others makes it speed up (if the phase difference is smaller than 0.5) or slow down (if the phase difference is larger than 0.5), until it is synchronized with the group of other neurons. More generally, for a fixed (small) spread of intrinsic frequencies, there is a minimal coupling strength J_c above which global synchronization sets in.

We note that, in contrast to pulse-coupled models, units in the Kuramoto model can interact at arbitrary phases.

20.2.4 Synaptic plasticity and oscillations

During an oscillation a large fraction of excitatory neurons fires near-synchronously (Fig. 20.4). What happens to the oscillation if the synaptic efficacies between excitatory neurons are not fixed but subject to spike-timing dependent plasticity (STDP)? In this subsection we sketch some of the theoretical arguments (Lubenov and Siapas, 2008; Pfister and Tass, 2010)

In Fig. 20.9 near synchronous spikes in a pair of pre- and postsynaptic neurons are shown together with a schematic STDP window; see Section 19.1.2. Note that the horizontal axis of the STDP window is the difference between the spike *arrival* time t^{pre} at the

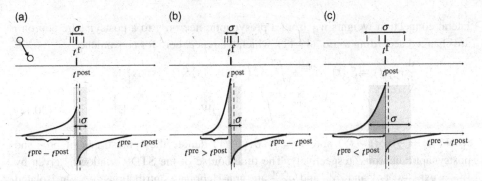

Fig. 20.9 Network oscillations and STDP. (a) Top: During a near-synchronous oscillation presynaptic spike timings t^f have a jitter σ with respect to the spike of a given postsynaptic neuron. Bottom: Because of axonal transmission delay, the spike *arrival* time $t^{pre} = t^f + \Delta^{ax}$ of presynaptic spikes at the synapse, is slightly shifted (light shaded area) to the regime "post-before-pre." Therefore, for an antisymmetric STDP window, synaptic depression dominates; compare the dark shaded areas for potentiation and depression. (b) Same as in (a), except that the amplitude of potentiation for near-synchronous firing is larger. As before, the total area under the STDP curve is balanced between potentiation and depression (the integral over the STDP curve vanishes). (c) Same as in (b), except that the integral over the STDP curve is now positive, as is likely to be the case at high firing rates. For large jitter σ potentiation dominates over depression (compare the dark-shaded areas).

presynaptic terminal and the spike firing time $t_i^f = t^{post}$ of the postsynaptic neuron. This choice (where the presynaptic spike arrival time is identified with the onset of the EPSP) corresponds to one option, but other choices (Markram *et al.*, 1997; Sjöström *et al.*, 2001) are equally common. With our convention, the jump from potentiation to depression occurs if postsynaptic firing coincides with presynaptic spike arrival. However, because of axonal transmission delays, synchronous firing leads to spike arrival that is *delayed* with respect to the postsynaptic spike. Therefore, consistent with experiments (Sjöström *et al.*, 2001), synchronous spike firing with small jitter leads, at low repetition frequency, to a depression of synapses (Fig. 20.9a). Lateral connections within the population of excitatory neurons are therefore weakened (Lubenov and Siapas, 2008).

However, the shape of the STDP window is frequency dependent with a marked dominance of potentiation at high repetition frequencies (Sjöström *et al.*, 2001). Therefore, near-synchronous firing with a large jitter σ leads to a strengthening of excitatory connections (Fig. 20.9c) in the synchronously firing group (Pfister and Tass, 2010). In summary, synchronous firing and STDP tightly interact.

Example: Bistability of plastic networks

Since we are interested in the interaction of STDP with oscillations, we focus on a recurrent network driven by periodically modulated spike input (Fig. 20.10a). The lateral connection weights w_{ij} from a presynaptic neuron j to a postsynaptic neuron i are changed according to Eq. (19.11), which we repeat here for convenience

$$\frac{\mathrm{d}}{\mathrm{d}t}w_{ij}(t) = S_j(t)\left[a_1^{\text{pre}} + \int_0^\infty A_-(w_{ij})W_-(s)S_i(t-s)\,\mathrm{d}s\right]$$
$$+ S_i(t)\left[a_1^{\text{post}} + \int_0^\infty A_+(w_{ij})W_+(s)S_j(t-s)\,\mathrm{d}s\right], \qquad (20.18)$$

where $S_j = \sum_f \delta(t - t_j^f)$ and $S_i = \sum_f \delta(t - t_i^f)$ denote the spike trains of pre- and postsynaptic neurons, respectively. The time course of the STDP window is given by $W_\pm = \exp(-s/\tau_\pm)$ and a_1^{pre} and a_1^{post} are non-Hebbian contributions, i.e., an isolated presynaptic or postsynaptic spike causes a small weight change, even if it is not paired with activity of the partner neuron. Non-Hebbian terms $a_1^{\text{pre}} + a_1^{\text{post}} < 0$ are linked to "homeostatic" or "heterosynaptic" plasticity and are useful to balance weight growth caused by Hebbian terms (Chapter 19). The amplitude factors $A_\pm$ are given by soft-bounds analogous to Eq. 19.4:

$$A_+(w_{ij}) = A_+^0 (w^{\text{max}} - w_{ij})^\beta \quad \text{for } 0 < w < w^{\text{max}}, \qquad (20.19)$$
$$A_-(w_{ij}) = A_-^0 (w_{ij})^\beta \qquad \quad \text{for } 0 < w < w^{\text{max}}, \qquad (20.20)$$

with $\beta = 0.05$. An exponent β close to zero implies that there is hardly any weight dependence except close to the bounds at zero and w^{max}.

The analysis of the network dynamics in the presence of STDP (Pfister and Tass, 2010; Gilson *et al.*, 2009; Kempter *et al.*, 1999a) shows that the most relevant quantities are (i) the integral over the STDP window $A_+(w)\tau_+ + A_-(w)\tau_-$ evaluated at a value w far away from the bounds; (ii) the Fourier transform of the STDP window at the frequency $1/T$, where T is the period of the oscillatory drive; (iii) the sum of the non-Hebbian terms $a_1^{\text{pre}} + a_1^{\text{post}}$.

Oscillations of brain activity in the δ or θ frequency band are relatively slow compared to the time scale of STDP. If we restrict the analysis to oscillations with a period T that is long compared to the time scale $\tau_{+/-}$ of the learning window, the Fourier transform of the STDP window mentioned in (ii) can be approximated by the integral mentioned in (i). Note that slow sinusoidal oscillations correspond to a large jitter σ of spike times (Fig. 20.9c).

Pfister and Tass (2010) found that the network dynamics are bistable if the integral over the learning window is positive (which causes an increase of weights for uncorrelated Poisson firing), but weight increase is counterbalanced by weight decrease caused by homeostatic terms in the range $C < a_1^{\text{pre}} + a_1^{\text{post}} < c < 0$ with suitable negative constants C and c. Therefore, for the same periodic stimulation paradigm, the network can be in either a stable state where the average weight is close to zero, or a different stable state where the average weight is significantly positive (Fig. 20.10b). In the latter case, the oscillation amplitude in the network is enhanced (Fig. 20.10c).

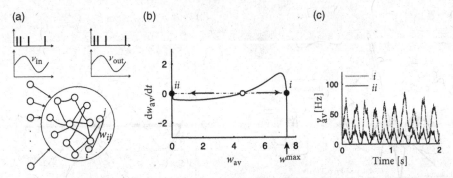

Fig. 20.10 Bistability of plastic networks. (a) A model network of spiking neurons receives spike input at a periodically modulated rate v^{in}, causing a modulation of the firing rate v_i^{out} of network neurons $1 \leq i \leq N$. Lateral weights w_{ij} are subject to STDP. (b) Change dw_{av}/dt of the average weight as a function of w_{av}. For an STDP window with positive integral the average network weight w_{av} exhibits bistability (arrows indicate direction of change) in the presence of the periodic input drive. The maximum weight is w^{max}. (c) Bistability of the average network output rate $v_{av} = (1/N)\sum_{i=1}^{N} v_i^{out}$ in the presence of a periodic drive. The weights w_{ij} in the two simulations have an average value w_{av} given by the two fixed points in (b). Adapted from Pfister and Tass (2010).

20.3 Helping patients

We would like to close this chapter – and indeed the whole book – with an inspiring application of insights derived from the theory of neuronal dynamics to animals and, potentially, humans. Initial results at the current state of research are encouraging, so that mathematical considerations could ultimately increase the quality of life of, among others, Parkinsonian patients.

Parkinson's is a severe brain disease. A prominent symptom in human patients suffering from Parkinson's disease is involuntary shaking of arms and fingers in a periodic movement of about 3–6 Hz, called resting tremor. Some patients also exhibit muscle rigidity or akinesia where they are unable to move. Tremor as well as rigidity are correlated with overly strong oscillatory synchronization in brain areas such as thalamus and basal ganglia, whose activity in the healthy state is asynchronous (Pare *et al.*, 1990; Nini *et al.*, 1995; Tass *et al.*, 2010). Moreover, the oscillation frequency of neural activity is related to the tremor frequency.

One of the presently available treatments of Parkinsonian symptoms is "deep brain stimulation" (DBS) (Benabid *et al.*, 1991, 2009). DBS reduces both tremor and rigidity of Parkinsonian patients. To perform DBS, a high-frequency stimulus is applied to an electrode implanted in the subthalamic nucleus or globus pallidus (which project indirectly or directly onto the thalamus) of the patient (Fig. 20.11a). The treatment is reversible so that, when stimulation is stopped, patients rapidly fall back into tremor or rigidity.

If we view the brain as a dynamical system, we can say that classical DBS shifts the state of the brain so as to reduce the symptoms of Parkinson's during stimulation, but does not return the brain's autonomous dynamics back to a healthy state. In other words, the

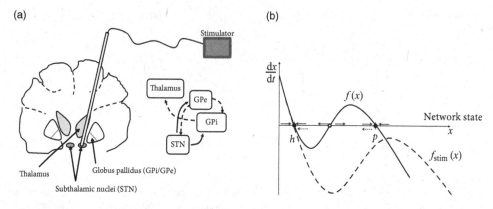

Fig. 20.11 Deep brain stimulation. (a) Schema showing a vertical cut through the brain with implanted electrode. The tip of the electrode reaches one of the subthalamic nuclei. The electrode is connected with a wire to the stimulator. The box diagram shows some of the major excitatory (solid arrows) and inhibitory (dashed arrows) connections from the subthalamic nucleus (STN) to thalamus. (b) Bistability of a healthy (h) and pathological network state (p, circle), described by the flow (solid arrows) of an abstract differential equation $dx/dt = f(x)$ (solid line). To kick the network out of the pathological state, an appropriate stimulus has to be applied that destabilizes p and drives the network state toward h by changing the right-hand side of the differential equation to $f_{stim}(x)$ (dashed line and arrows); adapted from Pfister and Tass (2010).

patient relies on continuous treatment through DBS. We may visualize the pathological and healthy conditions as two different configuration in some abstract space of network states. It is reasonable to assume that brain dynamics in the healthy state is at a stable equilibrium point – despite ongoing spike firing and plasticity on different time scales; otherwise our brains would rapidly stop functioning. The fact that, after the end of DBS, the brain returns to the pathological state indicates that this state is also stable (Fig. 20.11b).

The question arises whether, by suitable stimulation protocols, it would be possible to shift the pathological brain back into its healthy state. Work of the group of Peter Tass (Tass, 2003; Tass *et al.*, 2012b), but also other groups (Rubin and Terman, 2004; Rosin *et al.*, 2011; Wilson *et al.*, 2011) suggests that this may be possible. The treatment relies on the idea that the pathological state of strong oscillations is probably linked to pathologically strong intranetwork connections (Fig. 20.10c). An ideal stimulation protocol should thus not only interfere with the oscillations but also lead to a rewiring of the network with weaker connections so that, even when the stimulus is removed, the network does not immediately fall back into the strong oscillatory mode.

How can we interfere with an ongoing synchronized oscillation? As discussed in Section 20.2, neurons in an oscillatory state can be described by a phase ϕ. An electric pulse delivered by an electrode tends to synchronize neurons in the neighborhood of the electrode by shifting their phases by an amount that depends on the current phase of the neuron. If several electrode fibers are used in the same network, local groups surrounding the tips of the fibers can be stimulated at different moments in time. Therefore, the phase within each

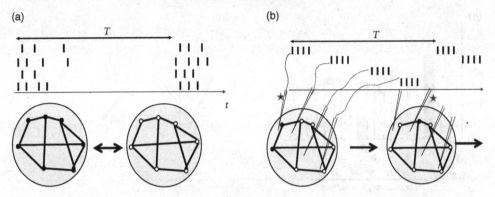

Fig. 20.12 Coordinated reset stimulation. (a) A population of neurons exhibits synchronous firing activity with period T (schematic). (b) If subgroups of neurons are stimulated at intervals $T/4$, the synchronous oscillation is interrupted ("coordinated reset" of oscillators). The stimulation can be delivered directly in the population or in one of the nuclei projecting onto it. Schematic, after Tass (2003).

group is reset by roughly the same amount, but the phase shift varies between groups. Consider a stimulation of four fibers given at a relative interval of $T/4$ (Fig. 20.12). With such a stimulation paradigm, the global network synchronization is perturbed by the "coordinated reset" of the four subpopulations (Tass, 2003). With eight or twenty independent electrode fibers one could spread out the stimulation (and therefore the phases of neuronal oscillators) even more equally over one period. However, the number four is a reasonable compromise and bundles of four fibers attached together so as to form one single electrode device are readily available.

If a single sequence of four "coordinated reset" pulses is given to four electrode fibers, the network returns, after some transients, to the synchronized oscillation. In order to make the asynchronous state stable, the network wiring needs to be changed. Hebbian synaptic plasticity requires neurons to be active. It is therefore important to choose a stimulation protocol which suppresses synchronous oscillations, but not neuronal activity *per se*. The "coordinated reset" fulfills this condition since it does not silence the neural oscillators but just shifts their phases. Therefore, if the "coordinated reset" stimulation is repeated again and again, so as to keep network activity in a state of asynchronous firing for a sufficiently long time, we may expect that synaptic plasticity causes a rewiring of the network connectivity. Once the network is rewired, the stimulus can be removed.

Indeed, when monkeys suffering from Parkinsonian symptoms have received a few hours of DBS with the "coordinated reset" protocol, symptoms are reduced and remain at a reduced level for more than 24 hours (Fig. 20.13b), before they slowly drift back into the oscillatory state (Tass *et al.*, 2012b). The beneficial effects of "coordinated reset" stimulation therefore last at least 10 times longer than those of traditional DBS where tremor reappears rapidly.

From the perspective of dynamical systems, these results suggest that the healthy state of Parkinsonian patients is not globally stable. However, since the "ruins" (see Chapter 4)

(a)

(b)

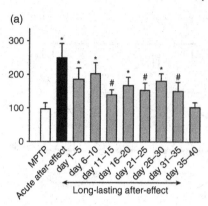
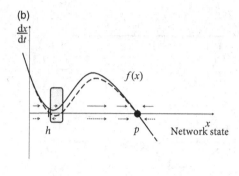

Fig. 20.13 Long-lasting plasticity effects. (a) Behavioral performance (vertical) of monkeys suffering from Parkinsonian symptoms before ("MPTP") and after treatment with coordinated reset stimulation. Stimulation led to an improvement of behavior that persisted for many days after the end of stimulation. From Tass *et al.* (2012b) with permission from IOS Press. (b) Dynamical systems interpretation: In contrast to Fig. 20.11b, the healthy state *h* of MPTP monkeys is either not a fixed point at all (solid line) or a marginally stable one (dashed line), but in both cases the flow in the vicinity of the healthy state (gray area) is slowed down, so that the return to the pathological state takes some time.

of the fixed point corresponding to healthy asynchronous activity persist, a shift of the network into the neighborhood of the healthy state leads to a slow down of the dynamics so that the network remains for a long time in the neighborhood of the healthy condition (Fig. 20.13c).

Traditional protocols of DBS have been found by trial and error. The standard protocol consists of continuous high-frequency stimulation (>100 Hz) at rather large amplitude (Benabid *et al.*, 1991). Remarkably, the mathematical perspective provided by the theory of dynamical systems together with intensive computational modeling (Tass, 2003; Rubin and Terman, 2004; Wilson *et al.*, 2011; Pfister and Tass, 2010) has now led to protocols that work with reduced amplitude and do not require continuous stimulation. Instead, only a few hours of stimulation per day promise to suffice (Tass *et al.*, 2012b). Eventually, we may hope that these or related (Rosin *et al.*, 2011) protocols will be translated from monkeys to humans and increase the quality of life of patients suffering from severe forms of Parkinson's disease. Interestingly, the "coordinated reset" protocol has already found a first successful application in humans suffering from tinnitus (Tass *et al.*, 2012a).

20.4 Summary

Reservoir computing uses the rich dynamics of randomly connected networks as a representation on which online computation can be performed. Inhibitory synaptic plasticity may tune networks into a state of detailed balance where strong excitation is counterbalanced by strong inhibition. The resulting network patterns exhibit similarities with cortical data.

Oscillations are present in multiple brain areas, and at various frequencies. Oscillations in networks of coupled model neurons can be mathematically characterized as an instability of the stationary state of irregular firing (see Chapters 13 and 14) or as a stable limit cycle where all neurons fire in synchrony. The stability of perfectly synchronized oscillation is clarified by the locking theorem: a synchronous oscillation is stable if the spikes are triggered during the rising phase of the input potential, which is the summed contribution of all presynaptic neurons. Stable synchronous oscillations can occur for a wide range of parameters and for both excitatory and inhibitory couplings.

Phase models describe neurons in the oscillatory state. If a stimulus is given while the neuron is at a certain phase, its phase shifts by an amount predicted by the phase response curves and the size of the stimulus.

Oscillatory activity has been linked to numerous brain diseases, in particular Parkinson's. Modern protocols of DBS aim at exploiting the interaction between phase response curves, oscillations, and synaptic plasticity so as to reduce the motor symptoms of Parkinson's disease.

Literature

The potential computational use of the rich network dynamics of randomly connected networks has been emphasized in the framework of "liquid computing" (Maass et al., 2002) and "echo state networks" (Jaeger and Haas, 2004). The network dynamics can be influenced by a variety of optimization algorithms (Jaeger and Haas, 2004; Maass et al., 2007; Sussillo and Abbott, 2009; Hoerzer et al., 2012) and the resulting networks can be analyzed with principles from dynamical systems (Ganguli et al., 2008; Sussillo and Barak, 2013). The theory of random neural networks has been developed around the eigenvalue spectrum of connectivity matrices (Rajan and Abbott, 2006) and the notion of chaos (Sompolinksy et al., 1988).

Synchronization is a traditional topic of applied mathematics (Winfree, 1980; Kuramoto, 1984). For pulse-coupled units, synchronization phenomena in pulse-coupled units have been widely studied in a non-neuronal context, such as the synchronous flashing of tropical fireflies (Buck and Buck, 1976), which triggered a whole series of theoretical papers on synchronization of pulse-coupled oscillators (see, e.g., Mirollo and Strogatz, 1990). The locking theorem (Gerstner et al., 1996b) is formulated for SRM neurons which cover a large class of neuronal firing patterns and includes the leaky integrate-and-fire model as a special case (see Chapter 6). The more traditional mathematical theories are typically formulated in the phase picture (Winfree, 1980; Kuramoto, 1984; Pikovsky and Rosenblum, 2007) and have found ample applications in the mathematical neurosciences (Gutkin et al., 2005; Canavier, 2006).

Oscillations in the visual system and the role of synchrony for feature binding have been reviewed by Singer (1993, 2007). Oscillations in sensory systems have been reviewed by Ritz and Sejnowski (1997) and, specifically in the context of the olfactory system, by Laurent (1996), and the hippocampus by O'Keefe and Recce (1993) and Buzsaki (2011). For oscillations in EEG, see Bazhenov and Timofeev (2006).

The classic work on DBS is Benabid *et al.* (1991). The interplay between mathematical theories of neuronal dynamics and DBS is highlighted in the papers of Rubin and Terman (2004), Wilson *et al.* (2011), Pfister and Tass (2010), and Tass (2003).

References

Abbott, L. (1994) Decoding neuronal firing and modeling neural networks. *Quart. Rev. Biophys.*, **27**:291–331.

Abbott, L. F. (1991) Realistic synaptic inputs for model neural networks. *Network*, **2**: 245–258.

Abbott, L. F. and Kepler, T. B. (1990) Model neurons: from Hodgkin–Huxley to Hopfield. In Garrido, L., ed., *Statistical Mechanics of Neural Networks*, pp. 5–18. Springer, Berlin.

Abbott, L. F. and Nelson, S. B. (2000) Synaptic plastictiy – taming the beast. *Nature Neurosci.*, **3**:1178–1183.

Abbott, L. F. and van Vreeswijk, C. (1993) Asynchronous states in a network of pulse-coupled oscillators. *Phys. Rev. E*, **48**:1483–1490.

Abbott, L. F., Fahri, E., and Gutmann, S. (1991) The path integral for dendritic trees. *Biol. Cybern.*, **66**:49–60.

Abeles, M. (1991) *Corticonics*. Cambridge University Press, Cambridge.

Acebron, J., Bonilla, L., Perez Vicente, C., Ritort, F., and Spigler, R. (2005) The Kuramoto model: A simple paradigm for synchronization phenomena. *Rev. Mod. Phys.*, **77**: 137–185.

Adrian, E. D. (1926) The impulses produced by sensory nerve endings. *J. Physiol. (Lond.)*, **61**:49–72.

Ahmadian, Y., Packer, A. M., Yuste, R., and Paninski, L. (2011a) Designing optimal stimuli to control neuronal spike timing. *J. Neurophys.*, **106**(2):1038–1053.

Ahmadian, Y., Pillow, J., and Paninski, L. (2011b) Efficient Markov Chain Monte Carlo methods for decoding population spike trains. *Neural Comput.*, **1**(23):46–96.

Ahrens, M., Paninski, L., and Sahani, M. (2008) Inferring input nonlinearities in neural encoding models. *Network*, **19**:35–67.

Aizenman, C. and Linden, D. (1999) Regulation of the rebound depolarization and spontaneous firing patterns of deep nuclear neurons in slices of rat cerebellum. *J. Neurophysiol.*, **82**:1697–1709.

Albright, T., Desimone, R., and Gross, C. (1984) Columnar organization of directionally selective cells in visual area MT of the macaque. *J. Neurophysiol.*, **51**:16–31.

Amari, S. (1972) Characteristics of random nets of analog neuron-like elements. *IEEE Trans. Syst. Man. Cyber.*, **2**:643–657.

Amari, S. (1974) A method of statistical neurodynamics. *Kybernetik*, **14**:201–215.

Amari, S. (1977) A mathematical foundation of statistical neurodynamics. *SIAM J. Appl. Math.*, **33**:95–126.

Amit, D. J. (1989) *Modeling Brain Function: The World of Attractor Neural Networks*. Cambridge University Press, Cambridge.

Amit, D. J. and Brunel, N. (1997a) Dynamics of a recurrent network of spiking neurons before and following learning. *Network*, **8**:373–404.

Amit, D. J. and Brunel, N. (1997b) A model of spontaneous activity and local delay activity during delay periods in the cerebral cortex. *Cerebral Cortex*, **7**:237–252.

Amit, D. J., Gutfreund, H., and Sompolinsky, H. (1985) Storing infinite numbers of patterns in a spin-glass model of neural networks. *Phys. Rev. Lett.*, **55**:1530–1533.

Amit, D. J., Gutfreund, H., and Sompolinsky, H. (1987a) Information storage in neural networks with low levels of activity. *Phys. Rev. A*, **35**:2293–2303.

Amit, D. J., Gutfreund, H., and Sompolinsky, H. (1987b) Statistical mechanics of neural networks near saturation. *Ann. Phys. (NY)*, **173**:30–67.

Amit, D. J. and Tsodyks, M. V. (1991) Quantitative study of attractor neural networks retrieving at low spike rates. 1: Substrate — spikes, rates, and neuronal gain. *Network*, **2**:259–273.

Anderson, J. A. (1972) A simple neural network generating an interactive memory. *Math. Biosci.*, **14**:197–220.

Anderson, J. A. and Rosenfeld, E., eds (1988) *Neurocomputing: Foundations of Research*. MIT Press, Cambridge, MA.

Angelucci, A. and Bressloff, P. (2006) Contribution of feedforward, lateral and feedback connections to the classical receptive field center and extra-classical receptive field surround of primate v1 neurons. *Prog. Brain Res.*, **154**:93–120.

Aracri, P., Colombo, E., Mantegazza, M., *et al.* (2006) Layer-specific properties of the persistent sodium current in sensorimotor cortex. *J. Neurophysiol.*, **95**(6):3460–3468.

Artola, A. and Singer, W. (1993) Long-term depression of excitatory synaptic transmission and its relationship to long-term potentiation. *Trends Neurosci.*, **16**(11):480–487.

Artola, A., Bröcher, S., and Singer, W. (1990) Different voltage dependent thresholds for inducing long-term depression and long-term potentiation in slices of rat visual cortex. *Nature*, **347**:69–72.

Atkinson, K. (1997) *The Numerical Solution of Integral Equations of the Second Kind*, Vol. 4. Cambridge University Press, Cambridge.

Avery, R. B. and Johnston, D. (1996) Multiple channel types contribute to the low-voltage-activated calcium current in hippocampal CA3 pyramidal neurons. *J. Neurosci*, **16**(18):5567–82.

Aviel, Y. and Gerstner, W. (2006) From spiking neurons to rate models: a cascade model as an approximation to spiking neuron models with refractoriness. *Phys. Rev. E*, **73**:51908.

Badel, L., Lefort, S., Berger, T., Petersen, C., Gerstner, W., and Richardson, M. (2008a) Extracting non-linear integrate-and-fire models from experimental data using dynamic I-V curves. *Biol. Cybernetics*, **99**(4–5):361–370.

Badel, L., Lefort, S., Brette, R., Petersen, C., Gerstner, W., and Richardson, M. (2008b) Dynamic I-V curves are reliable predictors of naturalistic pyramidal-neuron voltage traces. *J. Neurophysiol*, **99**:656–666.

Bair, W. and Koch, C. (1996) Temporal precision of spike trains in extrastriate cortex of the behaving macaque monekey. *Neural Comput.*, **8**:1185–1202.

Bair, W., Koch, C., Newsome, W., and Britten, K. (1994) Power spectrum analysis of MT neurons in the behaving monkey. *J. Neurosci.*, **14**:2870–2892.

Balaguer-Ballester, E., Lapish, C., Seamans, J., and Durstewitz, D. (2011) Dynamics of frontal cortex ensembles during memory-guided decision-making. *PLOS Comput. Biol.*, **7**:e1002057.

Baras, D. and Meir, R. (2007) Reinforcement learning, spike-time-dependent plasticity, and the BCM rule. *Neural Comput.*, **19**(8):2245–2279.

Barbieri, F. and Brunel, N. (2008) Can attractor network models account for the statistics of firing during persistent activity in prefrontal cortex? *Front. Neurosci.*, **2**:114–122.

Bauer, H. U. and Pawelzik, K. (1993) Alternating oscillatory and stochastic dynamics in a model for a neuronal assembly. *Physica D*, **69**:380–393.

Bazhenov, M. and Timofeev, I. (2006) Thalamocortical oscillations. *Scholarpedia*, **1**:1319.

Bell, C., Han, V., Sugawara, Y., and Grant, K. (1997) Synaptic plasticity in a cerebellum-like structure depends on temporal order. *Nature*, **387**:278–281.

Ben Arous, G. and Guionnet, A. (1995) Large deviations for Langevin spin glass dynamics. *Prob. Theory Rel. Fields*, **102**:455–509.

Ben-Yishai, R., Bar-Or, R., and Sompolinsky, H. (1995) Theory of orientation tuning in visual cortex. *Proc. Natl. Acad. Sci. USA*, **92**:3844–3848.

Benabid, A., Chabardes, S., Mitrofanis, J., and Pollak, P. (2009) Deep brain stimulation of the subthalamic nucleus for the treatment of Parkinson's disease. *Lancet Neurol.*, **8**:67–81.

Benabid, A., Pollak, P., *et al.* (1991) Long-term suppression of tremor by chronic stimulation of the ventral intermediate thalamic nucleus. *Lancet*, **337**:403–406.

Benda, J. and Herz, A. V. M. (2003) A universal model for spike-frequency adaptation. *Neural Comput.*, **15**(11):2523–2564.

Berger, T. K., Perin, R., Silberberg, G., and Markram, H. (2009) Frequency-dependent disynaptic inhibition in the pyramidal network: a ubiquitous pathway in the developing rat neocortex. *J. Physiol.*, **587**(22):5411–5425.

Bernander, Ö., Douglas, R. J., Martin, K. A. C., and Koch, C. (1991) Synaptic background activity influences spatiotemporal integration in single pyramidal cells. *Proc. Natl. Acad. Sci. USA*, **88**:11569–11573.

Berry, M. and Meister, M. (1998) Refractoriness and neural precision. *J. Neurosci.*, **18**:2200–2211.

Berry, M. J., Warland, D. K., and Meister, M. (1997) The structure and precision of retinal spike trains. *Proc. Natl. Acad. Sci. USA*, **94**:5411–5416.

Bi, G. and Poo, M. (1998) Synaptic modifications in cultured hippocampal neurons: dependence on spike timing, synaptic strength, and postsynaptic cell type. *J. Neurosci.*, **18**:10464–10472.

Bi, G. and Poo, M. (1999) Distributed synaptic modification in neural networks induced by patterned stimulation. *Nature*, **401**:792–796.

Bi, G. and Poo, M. (2001) Synaptic modification of correlated activity: Hebb's postulate revisited. *Ann. Rev. Neurosci.*, **24**:139–166.

Bi, G.-Q. (2002) Spatiotemporal specificity of synaptic plasticity: cellular rules and mechanisms. *Biol. Cybernetics*, **87**(5–6):319–332.

Bialek, W., Rieke, F., de Ruyter van Stevenick, R. R., and Warland, D. (1991) Reading a neural code. *Science*, **252**:1854–1857.

Bienenstock, E., Cooper, L., and Munroe, P. (1982) Theory of the development of neuron selectivity: orientation specificity and binocular interaction in visual cortex. *J. Neurosci.*, **2**:32–48.

Binczak, S., Eilbeck, J., and Scott, A. C. (2001) Ephaptic coupling of myelinated nerve fibers. *Physica D*, **148**(1):159–174.

Bliss, T. V. P. and Collingridge, G. L. (1993) A synaptic model of memory: long-term potentiation in the hippocampus. *Nature*, **361**:31–39.

Bogacz, R., Brown, E., Moehlis, J., Holmes, P., and Cohen, J. (2006) The physics of optimal decision making: a formal analysis of models of performance in two-alternative forced-choice tasks. *Psychol. Rev.*, **113**:700–765.

Bonhoeffer, T. and Grinvald, A. (1991) Iso-orientation domains in cat visual cortex are arranged in pinwheel-like patterns. *Nature*, **353**:429–431.

Bower, J. M. and Beeman, D. (1995) *The Book of Genesis*. Springer, New York.

Brass, M. and Haggard, P. (2007) To do or not to do: the neural signature of self-control. *J. Neurosci.*, **27**:9141–9145.

Bressloff, P. C. and Cowan, J. D. (2002) The visual cortex as a crystal. *Physica D: Nonlinear Phenomena*, **173**(3-4):226–258.

Bressloff, P. C. and Taylor, J. G. (1994) Dynamics of compartmental model neurons. *Neural Networks*, **7**:1153–1165.

Brette, R. and Gerstner, W. (2005) Adaptive exponential integrate-and-fire model as an effective description of neuronal activity. *J. Neurophysiol.*, **94**:3637–3642.

Brette, R., Rudolph, M., *et al.* (2007) Simulation of networks of spiking neurons: a review of tools and strategies. *J. Comput. Neurosci.*, **23**(3):349–398.

Brillinger, D. R. (1988) Maximum likelihood analysis of spike trains of interacting nerve cells. *Biol. Cybern.*, **59**:189–200.

Brillinger, D. R. (1992) Nerve cell spike train data analysis: a progression of techniques. *J. Am. Stat. Assoc.*, **87**:260–271.

Brockwell, A., Rojas, A., and Kass, R. (2004) Recursive Bayesian decoding of motor cortical signals by particle filtering. *J. Neurophysiol.*, **91**(4):1899–1907.

Brockwell, A., Kass, R. E., and Schwartz, A. (2007) Statistical signal processing and the motor cortex. *Proc. IEEE*, **95**(5):881–898.

Brown, E., Barbieri, R., Ventura, V., Kass, R., and Frank, L. (2002) The time-rescaling theorem and its application to neural spike train data analysis. *Neural Comput.*, **14**: 325–346.

Brown, E., Frank, L., Tang, D., Quirk, M., and Wilson, M. (1998) A statistical paradigm for neural spike train decoding applied to position prediction from ensemble firing patterns of rat hippocampal place cells. *J. Neurosci.*, **18**:7411–7425.

Brown, T. H., Ganong, A. H., Kairiss, E. W., Keenan, C. L., and Kelso, S. R. (1989) Long-term potentiation in two synaptic systems of the hippocampal brain slice. In Byrne, J. and Berry, W., eds, *Neural Models of Plasticity*, pp. 266–306. Academic Press, San Diego, CA.

Brown, T. H., Zador, A. M., Mainen, Z. F., and Claiborne, B. J. (1991) Hebbian modifications in hippocampal neurons. In Baudry, M. and Davis, J., eds, *Long–term Potentiation*, pp. 357–389. MIT Press, Cambridge, MA.

Brunel, N. (2000) Dynamics of sparsely connected networks of excitatory and inhibitory neurons. *Comput. Neurosci.*, **8**:183–208.

Brunel, N., Chance, F., Fourcaud, N., and Abbott, L. (2001) Effects of synaptic noise and filtering on the frequency response of spiking neurons. *Phys. Rev. Lett.*, **86**: 2186–2189.

Brunel, N. and Hakim, V. (1999) Fast global oscillations in networks of integrate-and-fire neurons with low firing rates. *Neural Comput.*, **11**:1621–1671.

Bryant, H. L. and Segundo, J. P. (1976) Spike initiation by transmembrane current: a white noise analysis. *J. Physiol.*, **260**:279–314.

Buck, J. and Buck, E. (1976) Synchronous fireflies. *Scientific American*, **234**:74–85.

Bugmann, G., Christodoulou, C., and Taylor, J. G. (1997) Role of temporal integration and fluctuation detection in the highly irregular firing of a leaky integrator neuron model with partial reset. *Neural Comput.*, **9**:985–1000.

Burkitt, A. N. and Clark, G. M. (1999) Analysis of integrate-and-fire neurons: synchronization of synaptic input and spike output. *Neural Comput.*, **11**:871–901.

Bussgang, J. J. (1952) Cross-correlation function of amplitude-distorted Gaussian signals. In *Tech. Rep. 216, Research Lab. Electronics*, Institute of Technology, Cambridge, MA.

Buzsaki, G. (2011) Hippocampus. *Scholarpedia*, **6**:1468.

Calvin, W. and Stevens, C. (1968) Synaptic noise and other sources of randomness in motoneuron interspike intervals. *J. Neurophysiol.*, **31**:574–587.

Canavier, C. (2006) Phase response curve. *Scholarpedia*, **1**:1332.

Capocelli, R. M. and Ricciardi, L. M. (1971) Diffusion approximation and first passage time problem for a neuron model. *Kybernetik*, **8**:214–223.

Caporale, N. and Dan, Y. (2008) Spike timing-dependent plasticity: a Hebbian learning rule. *Ann. Rev. Neurosci.*, **31**:25–46.

Carnevale, N. and Hines, M. (2006) *The Neuron Book*. Cambridge University Press, Cambridge.

Cessac, B. (2008) A discrete time neural network model with spiking neurons: rigorous results on the spontaneous dynamics. *J. Math. Biol.*, **56**:311–345.

Cessac, B., Doyon, B., Quoy, M., and Samuleides, M. (1994) Mean-field equations, bifurcation map and route to chaos in discrete time neural networks. *Physica D*, **74**:24–44.

Chacron, M., Longtin, A., St-Hilaire, M., and Maler, L. (2000) Suprathreshold stochastic firing dynamics with memory in *P*-type electroreceptors. *Phys. Rev. Lett.*, **85**: 1576–1579.

Chichilnisky, E. J. (2001) A simple white noise analysis of neuronal light responses. *Network*, **12**:199-213.

Chornoboy, E., Schramm, L., and Karr, A. (1988) Maximum likelihood identification of neural point process systems. *Biol. Cybernetics*, **59**:265–275.

Chow, C. C. (1998) Phase-locking in weakly heterogeneous neuronal networks. *Physica D*, **118**:343–370.

Chow, C. C. and White, J. (1996) Spontaneous action potential fluctuations due to channel fluctuations. *Biophys. J.*, **71**:3013–3021.

Churchland, M., Cunningham, J., Kaufman, *et al.* (2012) Neural population dynamics during reaching. *Nature*, **487**:51–56.

Clopath, C., Busing, L., Vasilaki, E., and Gerstner, W. (2010) Connectivity reflects coding: A model of voltage-based spike-timing-dependent-plasticity with homeostasis. *Nature Neurosci.*, **13**:344–352.

Cohen, M. A. and Grossberg, S. (1983) Absolute stability of global pattern formation and parallel memory storage by competitive neural networks. *IEEE Trans. Sys. Man Cybernetics*, **13**:815–823.

Collins, J., Chow, C., Capela, A., and Imhoff, T. (1996) Aperiodic stochastic resonance. *Phy. Rev. E*, **54**:5575–5584.

Connors, B. W. and Gutnick, M. J. (1990) Intrinsic firing patterns of diverse cortical neurons. *Trends Neurosci.*, **13**:99–104.

Contreras, D., Destexhe, A., and Steriade, M. (1997) Intracellular and computational characterization of the intracortical inhibitory control of synchronized thalamic inputs in vivo. *J. Neurophysiol.*, **78**(1):335–350.

Cover, T. and Thomas, J. (1991) *Elements of Information Theory*. Wiley, New York.

Cox, D. R. (1962) *Renewal Theory*. Methuen, London.

Cox, D. R. and Lewis, P. A. W. (1966) *The Statistical Analysis of Series of Events*. Methuen, London.

Crisanti, A. and Sompolinsky, H. (1988) Dynamics of spin systems with randomly asymmetric bonds – Ising spins and Glauber dynamics. *Phys. Rev. A*, **37**:4865–4874.

Crochet, S. and Petersen, C. (2006) Correlating whisker behavior with membrane potential in barrel cortex of awake mice. *Nature Neurosci.*, **9**:608–610.

Crochet, S., Poulet, J. F. A., Kremer, Y., and Petersen, C. C. H. (2011) Synaptic mechanisms underlying sparse coding of active touch. *Neuron*, **69**(6):1160–75.

Cullheim, S., Fleshman, J. W., Glenn, L. L., and Burke, R. E. (1987) Membrane area and dendritic structure in type-identified triceps surae alpha motoneurons. *J. Comp. Neurol.*, **255**(1):68–81.

Curti, E., Mongillo, G., La Camera, G., and Amit, D. (2004) Mean field and capacity in realistic networks of spiking neurons storing sparsely coded random memories. *Neural Comput.*, **16**:2597–2637.

Dayán, P. and Abbott, L. F. (2001) *Theoretical Neuroscience*. MIT Press, Cambridge, MA.

de Boer, E. and Kuyper, P. (1968) Triggered correlation. *IEEE Trans. Biomed. Enging*, **15**:169–179.

de Ruyter van Steveninck, R. R. and Bialek, W. (1988) Real-time performance of a movement-sensitive neuron in the blowfly visual system: coding and information transfer in short spike sequences. *Proc. R. Soc. Lond. B*, **234**:379–414.

de Ruyter van Steveninck, R. R., Lowen, G. D., Strong, S. P., Koberle, R., and Bialek, W. (1997) Reproducibility and variability in neural spike trains. *Science*, **275**:1805.

Debanne, D., Gähwiler, B., and Thompson, S. (1998) Long-term synaptic plasticity between pairs of individual CA3 pyramidal cells in rat hippocampal slice cultures. *J. Physiol.*, **507**:237–247.

Debanne, D., Campanac, E., Bialowas, A., Carlier, E., and Alcaraz, G. (2011) Axon physiology. *Phys. Rev.*, **91**(2):555–602.

deCharms, R. and Merzenich, M. (1996) Primary cortical representation of sounds by the coordination of action-potential timing. *Nature*, **381**:610–613.

Deco, G., Rolls, E., and Romo, R. (2009) Stochastic dynamics as a principle of brain function. *Progr. Neurobiol.*, **88**:1–16.

Deco, G., Rolls, E., and Romo, R. (2010) Synaptic dynamics and decision-making. *Proc. Natl. Acad. Sci. USA*, **107**:7545–7549.

Deger, M., Schwalger, T., Naud, R., and Gerstner, W. (2013) Dynamics of interacting finite-sized networks of spiking neurons with adaptation. *arXiv*: 1311.4206.

DeAngelis, G. C., Ohzwaw, I., and Freeman, R. D. (1995) Receptive-field dynamics in the central visual pathways. *Trends Neurosci.*, **18**:451–458.

Derrida, B., Gardner, E., and Zippelius, A. (1987) An exactly solvable asymmetric neural network model. *Europhys. Lett.*, **4**:167–173.

Destexhe, A., Contreras, D., Sejnowski, T. J., and Steriade, M. (1994a) A model of spindle rhythmicity in the isolated thalamic reticular nucleus. *J. Neurophysiol.*, **72**(2): 803–818.

Destexhe, A., Mainen, Z., and Sejnowski, T. (1994b) Synthesis of models for excitable membranes, synaptic transmission and neuromodulation using a common kinetic formalism. *J. Comput. Neurosci.*, **1**:195–230.

Destexhe, A. and Pare, D. (1999) Impact of network activity on the integrative properties of neocortical pyramidal neurons in vivo. *J. Neurophysiol.*, **81**:1531–1547.

Destexhe, A., Rudolph, M., and Pare, D. (2003) The high-conductance state of neocortical neurons in vivo. *Nature Rev. Neurosci.*, **4**:739–751.

DiMattina, C. and Zhang, K. (2011) Active data collection for efficient estimation and comparison of nonlinear neural models. *Neural Comput.*, **23**(9):2242–88.

Dobson, A. and Barnett, A. (2008) *Introduction to Generalized Linear Models*, 3rd edn. Chapman and Hall, London.

Donoghue, J. (2002) Connecting cortex to machines: recent advances in brain interfaces. *Nature Neurosci.*, **5**:1085–1088.

Donoghue, J. P., Sanes, J. N., Hatsopoulos, N. G., and Gaál, G. (1998) Neural discharge and local field potential oscillations in primate motor cortex during voluntary movements. *J. Neurophys.*, **79**(1):159–173.

Douglass, J., Wilkens, L., Pantazelou, E., and Moss, F. (1993) Noise enhancement of information transfer in crayfish mechanoreceptors by stochastic resonance. *Nature*, **365**:337–340.

Druckmann, S., Bannitt, Y., Gidon, A. A., Schuermann, F., and Segev, I. (2007) A novel multiple objective optimization framework for constraining conductance-based neuron models by experimental data. *Front Neurosci*, **1**:1.

Eckhorn, R., Bauer, R., Jordan, W., Brosch, M., Kruse, W., Munk, M., and Reitboeck, H. J. (1988) Coherent oscillations: a mechanism of feature linking in the visual cortex? *Biol. Cybern.*, **60**:121–130.

Eckhorn, R., Krause, F., and Nelson, J. L. (1993) The RF-cinematogram: a cross-correlation technique for mapping several visual fields at once. *Biol. Cybern.*, **69**:37–55.

Eden, U., Truccolo, W., Fellows, M., Donoghue, J., and Brown, E. (2004) Reconstruction of hand movement trajectories from a dynamic ensemble of spiking motor cortical neurons. In *Engineering in Medicine and Biology Society, 2004. IEMBS '04. 26th Annual International Conference of the IEEE*, Vol. 2, pp. 4017–4020. IEEE.

Edwards, B. and Wakefield, G. H. (1993) The spectral shaping of neural discharges by refractory effects. *J. Acoust. Soc. Am.*, **93**:3553–3564.

Eggermont, J. J., Aertsen, A. M., and Johannesma, P. I. (1983) Quantitative characterisation procedure for auditory neurons based on the spectro-temporal receptive field. *Hearing Res.*, **10**(2):167–90.

Ermentrout, G. B. (1996) Type I membranes, phase resetting curves, and synchrony. *Neural Comput.*, **8**(5):979–1001.

Ermentrout, G. B. and Kopell, N. (1984) Frequency plateaus in a chain of weakly coupled oscillators. *SIAM J. Math. Anal.*, **15**:215–237.

Ermentrout, G. B. and Kopell, N. (1986) Parabolic bursting in an excitable system coupled with a slow oscillation. *SIAM J. Appl. Math.*, **46**:233–253.

Erneux, T. and Nicolis, G. (1993) Propagating waves in discrete bistable reaction-diffusion systems. *Physica D*, **67**(1):237–244.

Ernst, U., Pawelzik, K., and Geisel, T. (1995) Synchronization induced by temporal delays in pulse-coupled oscillators. *Phys. Rev. Lett.*, **74**:1570–1573.

Erwin, E., Obermayer, K., and Schulten, K. (1995) Models of orientation and ocular dominance columns in the visual cortex: a critcal comparison. *Neural Comput.*, **7**:425–468.

Faisal, A., Selen, L., and Wolpert, D. (2008) Noise in the nervous system. *Nat. Rev. Neurosci.*, **9**:202.

Faugeras, O., Touboul, J., and Cessac, B. (2009) A constructive mean-field analysis of multi-population neural networks with random synaptic weights and stochastic inputs. *Front. Comput. Neurosci.*, **3**:1.

Feldman, J. L. and Cowan, J. D. (1975) Large-scale activity in neural nets I: Theory with application to motoneuron pool responses. *Biol. Cybern.*, **17**:29–38.

Feng, J. (2001) Is the integrate-and-fire model good enough? – a review. *Neural Networks*, **14**:955–975.

Feynman, R. P., Hibbs, A. R., and Styer, D. F. (2010) *Quantum Mechanics and Path Integrals*, 2nd edn. Dover, New York.

Fisher, R., van Emde Boas, W., Blume, W., *et al.* (2005) Epileptic seizures and epilepsy: definitions proposed by the International League Against Epilepsy (ILAE) and the International Bureau for Epilepsy (IBE). *Epilepsia*, **46**:470–472.

Fishman, H. M., Poussart, D. J. M., Moore, L. E., and Siebenga, E. (1977) Conduction description from the low frequency impedance and admittance of squid axon. *J. Membrane Biol.*, **32**:255–290.

FitzHugh, R. (1961) Impulses and physiological states in models of nerve membrane. *Biophys. J.*, **1**:445–466.

Fleidervish, I. A., Friedman, A. and Gutnick, M. J. (1996) Slow inactivation of Na^+ current and slow cumulative spike adaptation in mouse and guinea-pig neocortical neurones in slices. *J. Physiol.*, **493**:83–97.

Florian, R. V. (2007) Reinforcement learning through modulation of spike-timing-dependent synaptic plasticity. *Neural Comput.*, **19**:1468–1502.

Fourcaud, N. and Brunel, N. (2002) Dynamics of the firing probability of noisy integrate-and-fire neurons. *Neural Comput.*, **14**:2057–2110.

Fourcaud, N. and Brunel, N. (2005) Dynamics of the instantaneous firing rate in response to changes in input statistics. *J. Comput. Neurosci.*, **18**:311–321.

Fourcaud-Trocme, N., Hansel, D., van Vreeswijk, C., and Brunel, N. (2003) How spike generation mechanisms determine the neuronal response to fluctuating input. *J. Neurosci.*, **23**:11628–11640.

Fremaux, N., Sprekeler, H., and Gerstner, W. (2010) Functional requirements for reward-modulated spike-timing-dependent plasticity. *J. Neurosci.*, **40**:13326–13337.

French, A. and Stein, R. (1970) A flexible neural analog using integrated circuits. *IEEE Trans. Bio-med. Enging.*, **17**(3):248–253.

Froemke, R. and Dan, Y. (2002) Spike-timing dependent plasticity induced by natural spike trains. *Nature*, **416**:433–438.

Froemke, R. C., Merzenich, M. M., and Schreiner, C. E. (2007) A synaptic memory trace for cortical receptive field plasticity. *Nature*, **450**:425–429.

Froemke, R. C., Tsay, I., Raad, M., Long, J., and Dan, Y. (2006) Contribution of individual spikes in burst-induced long-term synaptic modification. *J. Neurophysiol.*, **95**:1620–1629.

Fuortes, M. and Mantegazzini, F. (1962) Interpretation of the repetitive firing of nerve cells. *J. Gen. Physiol.*, **45**:1163–1179.

Fusi, S. and Mattia, M. (1999) Collective behavior of networks with linear (VLSI) integrate and fire neurons. *Neural Comput.*, **11**:633–652.

Fuster, J. and Jervey, J. (1982) Neuronal firing in the inferotemporal cortex of the monkey in a visual memory task. *J. Neurosci.*, **2**:361–375.

Gabbiani, F. and Koch, C. (1998) Principles of spike train analysis. In Koch, C. and Segev, I., eds, *Methods in Neuronal Modeling*, 2nd edn, pp. 312–360. MIT Press, Cambridge, MA.

Gabbiani, F., Midtgaard, J., and Knopfel, T. (1994) Synaptic integration in a model of cerebellar granule cells. *J. Neurophys.*, **72**(2):999–1009.

Gammaitoni, L., Hänggi, P., Jung, P., and Marchesoni, F. (1998) Stochastic resonance. *Rev. Mod. Phys.*, **70**:223–287.

Ganguli, S., Huch, D., and Sompolinsky, H. (2008) Memory traces in dynamics systems. *Proc. Natl. Acad. Sci. USA*, **105**:18970–18975.

Gawne, T. J., Richmond, B. J., and Optican, L. M. (1991) Interactive effects among several stimulus parameters on the response of striate cortical complex cells. *J. Neurophys.*, **66**(2):379–389.

Geisler, C. and Goldberg, J. (1966) A stochastic model of repetitive activity of neurons. *Biophys. J.*, **6**:53–69.

Georgopoulos, A. P., Schwartz, A., and Kettner, R. E. (1986) Neuronal population coding of movement direction. *Science*, **233**:1416–1419.

Georgopoulos, A., Kettner, R., and Schwartz, A. (1988) Primate motor cortex and free arm movements to visual targets in three-dimensional space. II. Coding of the direction of movement by a neuronal population. *J. Neurosci.*, **8**:2928–2937.

Gerhard, F., Haslinger, R., and Pipa, G. (2011) Applying the multivariate time-rescaling theorem to neural population models. *Neural Comput.*, **23**:1452–1483.

Gerstein, G. L. and Perkel, D. H. (1972) Mutual temporal relations among neuronal spike trains. *Biophys. J.*, **12**:453–473.

Gerstner, W. (1991) Associative memory in a network of 'biological' neurons. In Lippmann, R. P., Moody, J. E., and Touretzky, D. S., eds, *Advances in Neural Information Processing Systems 3*, pp. 84–90. Morgan Kaufmann, San Mates, CA. Conference in Denver 1990.

Gerstner, W. (1995) Time structure of the activity in neural network models. *Phys. Rev. E*, **51**(1):738–758.

Gerstner, W. (2000) Population dynamics of spiking neurons: fast transients, asynchronous states and locking. *Neural Comput.*, **12**:43–89.

Gerstner, W. (2008) Spike-response model. *Scholarpedia*, **3**(12):1343.

Gerstner, W. and Brette, R. (2009) Adaptive exponential integrate-and-fire model. *Scholarpedia*, **4**:8427.

Gerstner, W. and Kistler, W. K. (2002) *Spiking Neuron Models: Single Neurons, Populations, Plasticity*. Cambridge University Press, Cambridge.

Gerstner, W. and van Hemmen, J. L. (1992) Associative memory in a network of 'spiking' neurons. *Network*, **3**:139–164.

Gerstner, W. and van Hemmen, J. L. (1993) Coherence and incoherence in a globally coupled ensemble of pulse emitting units. *Phys. Rev. Lett.*, **71**(3):312–315.

Gerstner, W., Ritz, R., and van Hemmen, J. L. (1993) Why spikes? Hebbian learning and retrieval of time–resolved excitation patterns. *Biol. Cybern.*, **69**:503–515.

Gerstner, W., Kempter, R., van Hemmen, J., and Wagner, H. (1996a) A neuronal learning rule for sub-millisecond temporal coding. *Nature*, **383**(6595):76–78.

Gerstner, W., van Hemmen, J. L., and Cowan, J. D. (1996b) What matters in neuronal locking. *Neural Comput.*, **8**:1653–1676.

Gigante, G., Mattia, M., and Del Giudice, P. (2007) Diverse population-bursting modes of adapting spiking neurons. *Phys. Rev. Lett.*, **98**:148101.

Gilson, M., Burkitt, A., Grayden, D., Thomas, D., and van Hemmen, J. L. (2009) Emergence of network structure due to spike-timing-dependent plasticity in recurrent neuronal networks IV: Structuring synaptic pathways among recurrent connections. *Biol. Cybern.*, **27**:427–444.

Giorno, V., Nobile, A. G., and Ricciardi, L. M. (1992) Instantaneous return processes and neuronal firings. In Trappl, R., ed., *Cybernetics and Systems Research*, Vol. 1, pp. 829–236. World Scientific Press, Hackensack, NJ.

Glimcher, P., Fehr, E., Camerer, C., and Poldrack, R. (2008) *Neuroeconomics*. Academic Press, Salt Lake City, UT.

Gluss, B. (1967) A model of neuron firing with exponential decay of potential resulting in diffusion equations for the probability density. *Bull. Math. Biophys.*, **29**:233–243.

Gold, J. and Shadlen, M. (2007) The neural basis of decision making. *Ann. Rev. Neurosci.*, **30**:535–547.

Goldberg, J., Adrian, H., and Smith, F. (1964) Response of neurons of the superior olivary complex of the cat to acoustic stimuli of long duration. *J. Neurophys.*, **27**:706–749.

Golding, N., Mickus, T. J., Katz, Y., Kath, W. L., and Spruston, N. (2005) Factors mediating powerful voltage attenuation along CA1 pyramidal neuron dendrites. *J. Physiol.*, **568**:69–82.

Gollisch, T. and Meister, M. (2008) Rapid neural coding in the retina with relative spike latencies. *Science*, **319**:1108–1111.

Golomb, D., Hansel, D., Shraiman, B., and Sompolinsky, H. (1992) Clustering in globally coupled phase oscillators. *Phys. Rev. A*, **45**:3516–3530.

Golomb, D. and Rinzel, J. (1994) Clustering in globally coupled inhibitory neurons. *Physica D*, **72**:259–282.

Gray, C. M. and Singer, W. (1989) Stimulus-specific neuronal oscillations in orientation columns of cat visual cortex. *Proc. Natl. Acad. Sci. USA*, **86**:1698–1702.

Grossberg, S. (1969) On learning, information, lateral inhibition, and transmitters. *Math. Biosci.*, **4**:255–310.

Grossberg, S. (1973) Contour enhancement, short term memory and constancies in reverberating neural networks. *Stud. Appl. Math.*, **52**:217–257.

Grossberg, S. (1976) Adaptive pattern classification and universal recoding I: Parallel development and coding of neuronal feature detectors. *Biol. Cybern.*, **23**:121–134.

Gütig, R., Aharonov, S., Rotter, S., and Sompolinsky, H. (2003) Learning input correlations through nonlinear temporally asymmetric Hebbian plasticity. *J. Neurosci.*, **23**(9):3697–3714.

Gutkin, B. S., Ermentrout, G. B., and Reyes, A. D. (2005) Phase-response curves give the responses of neurons to transient inputs. *J. Neurophysiol.*, **94**:1623–1635.

Haggard, P. (2008) Human volition: towards a neuroscience of will. *Nat. Rev. Neurosci.*, **9**:934–946.

Hale, J. K. and Koçac, H. (1991) *Dynamics and Bifurcations*. Text in Applied Mathematics 3. Springer, Berlin.

Hamill, O. P., Huguenard, J. R., and Prince, D. A. (1991) Patch-clamp studies of voltage-gated currents in identified neurons of the rat cerebral cortex. *Cerebral Cortex*, **1**(1):48–61.

Hansel, D. and Mato, G. (2001) Existence and stability of persistent states in large neuronal networks. *Phys. Rev. Lett.*, **86**:4175–4178.

Hansel, D. and Sompolinsky, H. (1998) Modeling feature selectivity in local cortical circuits. In Koch, C. and Segev, I., eds, *Methods in Neuronal Modeling*. MIT Press, Cambridge, MA.

Hay, E., Hill, S., Schürmann, F., Markram, H., and Segev, I. (2011) Models of neocortical layer 5b pyramidal cells capturing awide range of dendritic and perisomatic active properties. *PLoS Comput. Biol.*, **7**(7):e1002107.

Haykin, S. (1994) *Neural Networks*. Prentice Hall, Upper Saddle River, NJ.

Hebb, D. O. (1949) *The Organization of Behavior*. Wiley, New York.

Helmchen, F., Konnerth, A., and Yuste, R. (2011) *Imaging in Neuroscience: A Laboratory Manual*. Cold Spring Harbor Laboratory Press.

Hennequin, G. (2013) Amplification and stability in cortical circuits. Thesis, Ecole Polytechnique Fédérale de Lausanne.

Hennequin, G., Vogels, T., and Gerstner, W. (2014) Optimal control of transient dynamics in balanced networks supports generation of complex movements. *Neuron*, to appear.

Herrmann, A. and Gerstner, W. (2001) Noise and the PSTH response to current transients: I. General theory and application to the integrate-and-fire neuron. *J. Comput. Neurosci.*, **11**:135–151.

Hertz, J., Krogh, A., and Palmer, R. G. (1991) *Introduction to the Theory of Neural Computation*. Addison-Wesley, Redwood City, CA.

Herz, A. V. M., Sulzer, B., Kühn, R., and van Hemmen, J. L. (1988) The Hebb rule: Representation of static and dynamic objects in neural nets. *Europhys. Lett.*, **7**: 663–669.

Herz, A. V. M., Sulzer, B., Kühn, R., and van Hemmen, J. L. (1989) Hebbian learning reconsidered: Representation of static and dynamic objects in associative neural nets. *Biol. Cybern.*, **60**:457–467.

Hessler, N. A., Shirke, A. M., and Malinow, R. (1993) The probability of transmitter release at a mammalian central synapse. *Nature*, **366**:569–572.

Hill, A. (1936) Excitation and accommodation in nerve. *Proc. R. Soc. Lond. B*, **119**:305–355.

Hille, B. (1992) *Ionic Channels of Excitable Membranes*. Sinauer, Sunderland.

Hille, B. (2001) *Ion Channels of Excitable Membranes*, 3rd edn. Sinauer, Sunderland.

Hodgkin, A. L. (1948) The local electric changes associated with repetitive action in a non-medullated axon. *J. Physiol. (Lond.)*, **107**:165–181.

Hodgkin, A. L. and Huxley, A. F. (1952) A quantitative description of membrane current and its application to conduction and excitation in nerve. *J. Physiol*, **117**(4):500–544.

Hoehn, K., Watson, T. W., and MacVicar, B. A. (1993) A novel tetrodotoxin-insensitive, slow sodium current in striatal and hippocampal beurons. *Neuron*, **10**(3):543 – 552.

Hoerzer, G., Legenstein, R., and Maass, W. (2012) Emergence of complex computational structures from chaotic neural networks through reward-modulated Hebbian learning. *Cerebral Cortex*, xx:doi:10.1093/cercor/bhs348.

Hopfield, J. J. (1982) Neural networks and physical systems with emergent collective computational abilities. *Proc. Natl. Acad. Sci. USA*, **79**:2554–2558.

Hopfield, J. J. (1984) Neurons with graded response have computational properties like those of two-state neurons. *Proc. Natl. Acad. Sci. USA*, **81**:3088–3092.

Hoppensteadt, F. C. and Izhikevich, E. M. (1997) *Weakly Connected Neural Networks*. Springer, Berlin.

Horn, R. A. and Johnson, C. R. (1985) *Matrix Analysis*. Cambridge University Press, Cambridge.

Hubel, D. H. (1988) *Eye, Brain, and Vision*. W. H. Freeman, New York.

Hubel, D. and Wiesel, T. (1968) Receptive fields and functional architecture of monkey striate cortex. *J. Physiol.*, **195**:215–243.

Hubel, D. H. and Wiesel, T. N. (1962) Receptive fields, binocular interaction and functional architecture in the cat's visual cortex. *J. Physiol. (Lond.)*, **160**:106–154.

Huguenard, J. R., Hamill, O. P., and Prince, D. A. (1988) Developmental changes in Na+ conductances in rat neocortical neurons: appearance of a slowly inactivating component. *J. Neurophysiol.*, **59**(3):778–795.

Hunter, J. D. and Milton, J. G. (2003) Amplitude and frequency dependence of spike timing: implications for dynamic regulation. *J. Neurophysiol.*, **90**(1):387–94.

Huys, Q. J. M., Ahrens, M. B., and Paninski, L. (2006) Efficient estimation of detailed single-neuron models. *J. Neurophysiol.*, **96**(2):872–890.

Itti, L., Koch, C., and Niebur, E. (1998) A model of saliency-based visual attention for rapid scene analysis. *IEEE Trans. Patt. Anal. Mach. Intell.*, **20**:1254–1259.

Izhikevich, E. M. (2003) Simple model of spiking neurons. *IEEE Trans. Neural Networks*, **14**(6):1569–1572.

Izhikevich, E. (2007a) Solving the distal reward problem through linkage of STDP and dopamine signaling. *Cerebral Cortex*, **17**:2443–2452.

Izhikevich, E. M. (2007b) *Dynamical Systems in Neuroscience: The Geometry of Excitability and Bursting.* MIT Press, Cambridge, MA.

Jackson, J. (1962) *Classical Electrodynamics.* Wiley, New York.

Jaeger, H. and Haas, H. (2004) Harnessing nonlinearity: Predicting chaotic systems and saving energy in wireless communication. *Science*, **304**:78–80.

James, W. (1890) *Psychology (Briefer Course)*, Ch. 16. Holt, New York.

Johannesma, P. I. M. (1968) Diffusion models for the stochastic acticity of neurons. In Caianiello, E. R., ed., *Neural Networks*, pp. 116–144. Springer, Berlin.

Johansson, R. and Birznieks, I. (2004) First spikes in ensembles of human tactile afferents code complex spatial fingertip events. *Nature Neurosci.*, **7**:170–177.

Jolivet, R., Lewis, T., and Gerstner, W. (2004) Generalized integrate-and-fire models of neuronal activity approximate spike trains of a detailed model to a high degree of accuracy. *J. Neurophysiol.*, **92**:959–976.

Jolivet, R., Rauch, A., Lüscher, H.-R., and Gerstner, W. (2006) Predicting spike timing of neocortical pyramidal neurons by simple threshold models. *J. Comput. Neurosci.*, **21**:35–49.

Jolivet, R., Kobayashi, R., Rauch, A., Shinomoto, S., and Gerstner, W. (2008a) A benchmark test for a quantitative assessment of simple neuron models. *J. Neurosci. Methods*, **169**:417–424.

Jolivet, R., Schurmann, F., Berger, T., Naud, R., Gerstner, W., and Roth, A. (2008b) The quantitative single-neuron modeling competition. *Biol. Cybern.*, **99**:417–426.

Kandel, E. C., Schwartz, J. H., and Jessell, T. (2000) *Principles of Neural Science*, 4th edn. Elsevier, New York.

Kaschube, M., Schnabel, M., Lowel, S., Coppola, D., White, L., and Wolf, F. (2010) Universality in the evolution of orientation columns in the visual cortex. *Science*, **330**:1113–1116.

Kass, R. and Raftery, A. (1995) Bayes factors. *J. Am. Stat. Assoc.*, **90**:773–795.

Kass, R. E. and Ventura, V. (2001) A spike-train probability model. *Neural Comput.*, **13**:1713–1720.

Keat, J., Reinagel, P., Reid, R., and Meister, M. (2001) Predicting every spike: A model for the responses of visual neurons. *Neuron*, **30**:803–817.

Kempter, R., Gerstner, W., van Hemmen, J. L., and Wagner, H. (1998) Extracting oscillations: Neuronal coincidence detection with noisy periodic spike input. *Neural Comput.*, **10**:1987–2017.

Kempter, R., Gerstner, W., and van Hemmen, J. L. (1999a) Hebbian learning and spiking neurons. *Phys. Rev. E*, **59**:4498–4514.

Kempter, R., Gerstner, W., van Hemmen, J. L., and Wagner, H. (1999b) The quality of coincidence detection and ITD-tuning: a theoretical framework. In Dau, T., Hohmann,

V., and Kollmeier, B., eds, *Psychophysics, Physiology and Models of Hearing*, pp. 185–192. World Scientific, Singapore.

Kempter, R., Gerstner, W., and van Hemmen, J. L. (2001) Intrinsic stabilization of output rates by spike-based Hebbian learning. *Neural Comput.*, **13**:2709–2741.

Kepler, T. B., Abbott, L. F., and Marder, E. (1992) Reduction of conductance-based neuron models. *Biol. Cybern.*, **66**:381–387.

Kistler, W. M. and De Zeeuw, C. I. (2002) Dynamical working memory and timed responses: The role of reverberating loops in the olivo-cerebellar system. *Neural Comput.*, **14**(11):2597–2626.

Kistler, W. M. and van Hemmen, J. L. (2000) Modeling synaptic plasticity in conjunction with the timing of pre- and postsynaptic potentials. *Neural Comput.*, **12**:385–405.

Kistler, W. M., Gerstner, W., and van Hemmen, J. L. (1997) Reduction of Hodgkin-Huxley equations to a single-variable threshold model. *Neural Comput.*, **9**:1015–1045.

Klausberger, T. and Somogyi, P. (2008) Neuronal diversity and temporal dynamics: The unity of hippocampal circuit operations. *Science*, **321**:53–57.

Knight, B. W. (1972) Dynamics of encoding in a population of neurons. *J. Gen. Physiol.*, **59**:734–766.

Knight, B. W. (2000) Dynamics of encoding in neuron populations: some general mathematical features. *Neural Comput.*, **12**:473–518.

Kobayashi, R. and Shinomoto, S. (2007) State space method for predicting the spike times of a neuron. *Phys. Rev. E*, **75**(1):011925.

Kobayashi, R., Tsubo, Y., and Shinomoto, S. (2009) Made-to-order spiking neuron model equipped with a multi-timescale adaptive threshold. *Front. Comput. Neurosci.*, **3**:9.

Koch, C. (1999) *Biophysics of Computation*. Oxford University Press, Oxford.

Koch, C., Bernander, Ö., and Douglas, R. (1995) Do neurons have a voltage or a current threshold for action potential initiation? *J. Comput. Neurosci.*, **2**:63–82.

Kohonen, T. (1972) Correlation matrix memories. *IEEE Trans. Comp.*, **C-21**:353–359.

Kohonen, T. (1984) *Self-Organization and Associative Memory*. Springer-Verlag, Berlin.

Kole, M. H. P., Hallermann, S., and Stuart, G. J. (2006) Single Ih channels in pyramidal neuron dendrites: properties, distribution, and impact on action potential output. *J. Neurosci.*, **26**(6):1677–1687.

König, P., Engel, A. K., and Singer, W. (1996) Integrator or coincidence detector? The role of the cortical neuron revisited. *Trends Neurosci.*, **19**(4):130–137.

Konishi, M. (1993) Listening with two ears. *Scientific American*, **268**:34–41.

Kopell, N. (1986) Symmetry and phase locking in chains of weakly coupled oscillators. *Comm. Pure Appl. Math.*, **39**:623–660.

Korngreen, A. and Sakmann, B. (2000) Voltage-gated K+ channels in layer 5 neocortical pyramidal neurones from young rats: subtypes and gradients. *J. Physiol.*, **525**(3): 621–639.

Koyama, S., Castellanos Pérez-Bolde, L., Shalizi, C. R., and Kass, R. E. (2010) Approximate methods for state-space models. *J. Am. Stat. Assoc.*, **105**(489):170–180.

Kree, R. and Zippelius, A. (1991) Asymmetrically diluted neural networks. In Domany, E., van Hemmen, J., and Schulten, K., eds, *Models of Neural Networks*, pp. 193–212. Springer, Berlin.

Kreuz, T., Haas, J., Morelli, A., Abarbanel, H., and Politi, A. (2007) Measuring spike train synchrony. *J. Neurosci. Methods*, **165**(1):151–161.

Kreuz, T., Chicharro, D., Andrzejak, R. G., Haas, J. S., and Abarbanel, H. D. I. (2009) Measuring multiple spike train synchrony. *J. Neurosci. Methods*, **183**(2):287–99.

Kulkarni, J. E. and Paninski, L. (2007) Common-input models for multiple neural spike-train data. *Network: Comp. in Neural Sys.*, **18**(4):375–407.

Kuramoto, Y. (1984) *Chemical Oscillations, Waves, and Turbulence*. Springer, Berlin.

Laing, C. R. and Chow, C. C. (2001) Stationary bumps in a network of spiking neurons. *Neural Comput.*, **13**:1473–1494.

Lansky, P. (1984) On approximations of Stein's neuronal model. *J. Theor. Biol.*, **107**: 631–647.

Lansky, P. (1997) Sources of periodical force in noisy integrate-and-fire models of neuronal dynamics. *Phys. Rev. E*, **55**:2040–2043.

Lansky, P. and Lanska, V. (1987) Diffusion approximation of the neuronal model with synaptic reversal potentials. *Biol. Cybern.*, **56**:19–26.

Lapicque, L. (1907) Recherches quantitatives sur l'excitation electrique des nerfs traitée comme une polarization. *J. Physiol. Pathol. Gen.*, **9**:620–635. Cited in H. C. Tuckwell, *Introduction to Theoretic Neurobiology* (Cambridge University Press, Cambridge, 1988).

Larkum, M. and Nevian, T. (2008) Synaptic clustering by dendritic signalling mechanisms. *Curr. Opinion Neurobiol.*, **18**:321–331.

Larkum, M., Zhu, J., and Sakmann, B. (2001) Dendritic mechanisms underlying the coupling of the dendritic with the axonal action potential initiation zone of adult rat layer 5 pyramidal neurons. *J. Physiol. (Lond.)*, **533**:447–466.

Latham, P. E., Richmond, B., Nelson, P., and Nirenberg, S. (2000) Intrinsic dynamics in neuronal networks. I. Theory. *J. Neurophysiol.*, **83**:808–827.

Laurent, G. (1996) Dynamical representation of odors by oscillating and evolving neural assemblies. *Trends Neurosci.*, **19**:489–496.

Lefort, S., Tomm, C., Sarria, J., and Petersen, C. (2009) The excitatory neuronal network of the C2 barrel column in mouse primary somatosensory cortex. *Neuron*, **61**:301–316.

Legenstein, R., Pecevski, D., and Maass, W. (2008) A learning theory for reward-modulated spike-timing-dependent plasticity with application to biofeedback. *PLOS Comput. Biol.*, **4**:e1000180.

Levy, W. B. and Stewart, D. (1983) Temporal contiguity requirements for long-term associative potentiation/depression in hippocampus. *Neurosci.*, **8**:791–797.

Lewi, J., Butera, R., and Paninski, L. (2009) Sequential optimal design of neurophysiology experiments. *Neural Comput.*, **21**:619–687.

Libet, B. (1985) Unconscious cerebral initiative and the role of conscious will in voluntary action. *Behav. Brain Sci.*, **8**:529–566.

Lindner, B. and Schimansky-Geier, L. (2001) Transmission of noise coded versus additive signals through a neuronal ensemble. *Phys. Rev. Lett.*, **86**:2934–2937.

Lindner, B., Doiron, B., and Longtin, A. (2005) Theory of oscillatory firing induced by spatially correlated noise and delayed inhibitory feedback. *Phys. Rev. E*, **72**(6):061919.

Linsker, R. (1986) From basic network principles to neural architecture: emergence of spatial-opponent cells. *Proc. Natl. Acad. Sci. USA*, **83**:7508–7512.

Linz, P. (1985) *Analytical and Numerical Methods for Volterra Equations*, Vol. 7. SIAM, Philadelphia, PA.

Lisman, J. (2003) Long-term potentiation: outstanding questions and attempted synthesis. *Phil. Trans. R. Soc. Lond. B*, **358**:829–842.

Lisman, J., Schulman, H., and Cline, H. (2002) The molecular basis of CaMKII function in synaptic and behavioural memory. *Nat. Rev. Neurosci.*, **3**:175–190.

Little, W. A. (1974) The existence of persistent states in the brain. *Math. Biosc.*, **19**: 101–120.

Liu, Y.-H. and Wang, X.-J. (2001) Spike-frequency adaptation of a generalized leaky integrate-and-fire model neuron. *J. Comput. Neurosci.*, **10**:25–45.

Loewenstein, Y. (2008) Robustness of learning that is based on covariance-driven synaptic plasticity. *PLOS Comput. Biol.*, **4**:e1000007.

Loewenstein, Y. and Seung, H. (2006) Operant matching is a generic outcome of synaptic plasticity based on the covariance between reward and neural activity. *Proc. Natl. Acad. Sci. USA*, **103**:15224–15229.

Longtin, A. (1993) Stochastic resonance in neuron models. *J. Stat. Phys.*, **70**:309–327.

Lubenov, E. and Siapas, A. G. (2008) Decoupling through synchrony in neuronal circuits with propagation delays. *Neuron*, **58**:118–131.

Lund, J., Angelucci, A., and Bressloff, P. (2003) Anatomical substrates for functional columns in macaque monkey primary visual cortex. *Cerebral Cortex*, **12**:15–24.

Lundstrom, B., Higgs, M., Spain, W., and Fairhall, A. (2008) Fractional differentiation by neocortical pyramidal neurons. *Nature Neurosci.*, **11**:1335–1342.

Maass, W., Joshi, P., and Sontag, E. (2007) Computational aspects of feedback in neural circuits. *PLOS Comput. Biol.*, **3**:e165.

Maass, W., Natschläger, T., and Markram, H. (2002) Real-time computing without stable states: a new framework for neural computation based on perturbations. *Neural Comput.*, **14**:2531–2560.

Mach, E. (1865) Über die Wirkung der räumlichen Verteilung des Lichtreizes auf die Netzhaut. *Sitz. -Ber. Akad. Wiss. Wien*, **52**:303–322.

Mach, E. (1906) *Die Analyse der Empfindungen*, 5th edn, Chapter X. Gustav Fischer, Jena, www.uni-leipzig.de/ psycho/wundt/opera/mach/empfndng/AlysEmIn.htm.

Machens, C. (2002) Adaptive sampling by information maximization. *Phys. Rev. Lett.*, **88**:228104–228107.

Machens, C., Romo, R., and Brody, C. (2005) Flexible control of mutual inhibition: a neuron model of two-interval discrimination. *Science*, **307**:1121–1124.

Mackay, D. (1992) Information-based objective functions for active data selection. *Neural Comput.*, **4**:589–603.

MacKay, D. J. C. and Miller, K. D. (1990) Analysis of Linsker's application of Hebbian rules to linear networks. *Network*, **1**:257–297.

MacPherson, J. M. and Aldridge, J. W. (1979) A quantitative method of computer analysis of spike train data collected from behaving animals. *Brain Res.*, **175**(1):183–7.

MacLeod, C. M. (1991) Half a century of research on the Stroop effect: An integrative review. *Psych. Bull.*, **109**:163–203.

Magee, J. C. (1998) Dendritic hyperpolarization-activated currents modify the integrative properties of hippocampal CA1 pyramidal neurons. *J. Neurosci.*, **18**(19):7613–7624.

Mainen, Z. F., Joerges, J., Huguenard, J. R., and Sejnowski, T. J. (1995) A model of spike initiation in neocortical pyramidal neurons. *Neuron*, **15**(6):1427–1439.

Mainen, Z. F. and Sejnowski, T. J. (1995) Reliability of spike timing in neocortical neurons. *Science*, **268**:1503–1506.

Mainen, Z. F. and Sejnowski, T. J. (1996) Influence of dendritic structure on firing pattern in model neocortical neurons. *Nature*, **382**:363–366.

Makram, H., Sjostrom, J., and Gerstner, W. (2011) A history of spike-timing dependent plasticity. *Front. Syn. Neurosci.*, **3**:4.

Manwani, A. and Koch, C. (1999) Detecting and estimating signals in noisy cable structures, I: Neuronal noise sources. *Neural Comput.*, **11**:1797–1829.

Markram, H. and Tsodyks, M. (1996) Redistribution of synaptic efficacy between neocortical pyramidal neurons. *Nature*, **382**:807–810.

Markram, H., Lübke, J., Frotscher, M., and Sakmann, B. (1997) Regulation of synaptic efficacy by coincidence of postysnaptic AP and EPSP. *Science*, **275**:213–215.

Markram, H., Toledo-Rodriguez, M., Wang, Y., Gupta, A., Silberberg, G., and Wu, C. (2004) Interneurons of the neocortical inhibitory system. *Nature Rev. Neurosci.*, **5**:793–807.

Marsalek, P., Koch, C., and Maunsell, J. (1997) On the relationship between synaptic input and spike output jitter in individual neurons. *Proc. Natl. Acad. Sci. USA*, **94**:735–740.

Mascaro, M. and Amit, D. J. (1999) Effective neural response function for collective population states. *Network*, **10**:351–373.

Mauro, A., Conti, F., Dodge, F., and Schor, R. (1970) Subthreshold behavior and phenomenological impedance of the squid giant axon. *J. Gen. Physiol.*, **55**(4):497–523.

McCormick, D. A., Wang, Z., and Huguenard, J. (1993) Neurotransmitter control of neocortical neuronal activity and excitability. *Cereb. Cortex*, **3**(5):387–398.

McCulloch, W. S. and Pitts, W. (1943) A logical calculus of ideas immanent in nervous activity. *Bull. Math. Biophys.*, **5**:115–133.

McNamara, B. and Wiesenfeld, K. (1989) Theory of stochastic resonance. *Phys. Rev. A*, **39**:4854–4869.

Mel, B. W. (1994) Information processing in dendritic trees. *Neural Comput.*, **6**:1031–1085.

Mensi, S., Naud, R., and Gerstner, W. (2011) From stochastic nonlinear integrate-and-fire to generalized linear models. In Shawe-Taylor, J., Zemel, R., Bartlett, P., Pereira, F., and Weinberger, K., eds, *Advances in Neural Information Processing System* 24, p. **0794**.

Mensi, S., Naud, R., Avermann, M., Petersen, C. C. H., and Gerstner, W. (2012) Parameter extraction and classification of three neuron types reveals two different adaptation mechanisms. *J. Neurophys.*, **107**:1756–1775.

Mensi, S., Pozzorini, C., Hagens, O., and Gerstner, W. (2013) Evidence for a nonlinear coupling between firing threshold and subthreshold membrane potential. *Cosyne Abstracts*, Salt Lake City, UT.

Meyer, C. and van Vreeswijk, C. (2002) Temporal correlations in stochastic networks of spiking neurons. *Neural Comput.*, **14**:369–404.

Miller, E. and Cohen, J. (2001) An integrative theory of prefrontal cortex function. *Ann. Rev. Neurosci.*, **24**:167–202.

Miller, K. and Fumarola, F. (2012) Mathematical equivalence of two common forms of firing rate models of neural networks. *Neural Comput.*, **24**:25–31.

Miller, K., Keller, J. B., and Stryker, M. P. (1989) Ocular dominance column development: analysis and simulation. *Science*, **245**:605–615.

Miller, K. D. (1994) A model for the development of simple cell receptive fields and the ordered arrangement of orientation columns through activity dependent competition between ON- and OFF-center inputs. *J. Neurosci.*, **14**:409–441.

Miller, K. D. and MacKay, D. J. C. (1994) The role of constraints in Hebbian learning. *Neural Comput.*, **6**:100–126.

Miller, M. I. and Mark, K. (1992) A statistical study of cochlear nerve discharge patterns in reponse to complex speech stimuli. *J. Acoust. Soc. Am.*, **92**:202–209.

Mirollo, R. E. and Strogatz, S. H. (1990) Synchronization of pulse coupled biological oscillators. *SIAM J. Appl. Math.*, **50**:1645–1662.

Miyashita, Y. (1988a) Neuronal correlate of visual associative long-term memory in the primate temporal cortex. *Nature*, **335**:817–820.

Miyashita, Y. (1988b) Neuronal correlate of visual associative long-term memory in the primate temporal cortex. *Nature*, **335**(6193):817–820.

Mongillo, G., Barak, O., and Tsodyks, M. (2008) Synaptic theory of working memory. *Science*, **319**:1543–1546.

Moreno-Bote, R. and Parga, N. (2004) Role of synaptic filtering on the firing response of simple model neurons. *Phys. Rev. Lett.*, **92**:28102.

Morris, C. and Lecar, H. (1981) Voltage oscillations in the barnacle giant muscle fiber. *Biophys. J.*, **35**:193–213.

Morrison, A., Diesmann, M., and Gerstner, W. (2008) Phenomenological models of synaptic plasticity based on spike timing. *Biol. Cybern.*, **98**:459–478.

Mountcastle, V. B. (1957) Modality and topographic properties of single neurons of cat's somatosensory cortex. *J. Neurophysiol.*, **20**:408–434.

Murray, J. D. (1993) *Mathematical Biology*, 2nd edn. Biomathematics Texts 19. Springer–Verlag, Berlin.

Nagumo, J., Arimoto, S., and Yoshizawa, S. (1962) An active pulse transmission line simulating nerve axon. *Proc. IRE*, **50**:2061–2070.

Naud, R. and Gerstner, W. (2012a) Coding and decoding in adapting neurons: A population approach to the peri-stimulus time histogram. *PLoS Comput. Biol.*, **8**:e1002711.

Naud, R. and Gerstner, W. (2012b) The performance (and limits) of simple neuron models: Generalizations of the leaky integrate-and-fire model. In Le Novère, N. L., ed., *Computational Systems Neurobiology*. Springer, Berlin.

Naud, R., Marcille, N., Clopath, C., and Gerstner, W. (2008) Firing patterns in the adaptive exponential integrate-and-fire model. *Biol. Cybernetics*, **99**:335–347.

Naud, R., Gerhard, F., Mensi, S., and Gerstner, W. (2011) Improved similarity measures for small sets of spike trains. *Neural Comput.*, **23**:3016–3069.

Nelder, J. and Wederburn, R. (1972) Generalized linear models. *J. R. Stat. Soc. A*, **135**:370–384.

Nelken, I., Prut, Y., Vaadia, E., and Abeles, M. (1994) In search of the best stimulus: an optimization procedure for finding efficient stimuli in the cat auditory cortex. *Hearing Res.*, **72**:237–253.

Nelson, M. and Rinzel, J. (1995) The Hodgkin-Huxley model. In Bower, J. M. and Beeman, D., ed, *The Book of Genesis*, Chapter 4, pp. 27–51. Springer, New York.

Newsome, W., Britten, K., and Movshon, J. (1989) Neuronal correlates of a perceptual decision. *Nature*, **341**:52–54.

Ngezahayo, A., Schachner, M., and Artola, A. (2000) Synaptic activation modulates the induction of bidirectional synaptic changes in adult mouse hippocampus. *J. Neurosci.*, **20**:2451–2458.

Nini, A., Feingold, A., Slovin, H., and Bergman, H. (1995) Neurons in the globus pallidus do not show correlated activity in the normal monkey, but phase-locked oscillations appear in the MPTP model of parkinsonism. *J. Neurophysiol.*, **74**:1800–1805.

Nützel, K. (1991) The length of attractors in asymmetric random neural networks with deterministic dynamics. *J. Phys. A.*, **24**:L151–L157.

Nykamp, D. and Tranchina, D. (2000) A population density approach that facilitates large-scale modeling of neural networks: Analysis and application to orientation tuning. *J. Comput. Neurosci.*, **8**:19–50.

Oja, E. (1982) A simplified neuron model as a principal component analyzer. *J. Math. Biol.*, **15**:267–273.

O'Keefe, J. and Recce, M. (1993) Phase relationship between hippocampal place units and the hippocampal theta rhythm. *Hippocampus*, **3**:317–330.

Okun, M. and Lampl, I. (2008) Instantaneous correlation of excitation and inhibition during ongoing and sensory-evoked activities. *Nat. Neurosci.*, **11**:535–537.

Omurtag, A., Knight, B., and Sirovich, L. (2000) On the simulation of a large population of neurons. *J. Comput. Neurosci.*, **8**:51–63.

Optican, L. M. and Richmond, B. J. (1987) Temporal encoding of two-dimensional patterns by single units in primate inferior temporal cortex. 3. Information theoretic analysis. *J. Neurophysiol.*, **57**:162–178.

Ostojic, S. and Brunel, N. (2011) From spiking neuron models to linear-nonlinear models. *PLOS Comput. Biol.*, **7**:e1001056.

Ozeki, H., Finn, I., Schaffer, E., Miller, K., and Ferstner, D. (2009) Inhibitory stabilization of the cortical network underlies visual surround suppression. *Neuron*, **62**:587–592.

Paiva, A. R. C., Park, I., and Príncipe, J. (2009a) A comparison of binless spike train measures. *Neural Comp. Appl.*, **19**(3):1–15.

Paiva, A. R. C., Park, I., and Príncipe, J. (2009b) A reproducing kernel hilbert space framework for spike train signal processing. *Neural Comput.*, **21**(2):424–449.

Paiva, A. R. C., Park, I., and Príncipe, J. (2010) Inner products for representation and learning in the spike train domain. In Oweiss, K. G., ed., *Statistical Signal Processing for Neuroscience and Neurotechnology*. Academic Press, New York.

Paninski, L. (2003) Convergence properties of three spike-triggered analysis techniques. *Network*, **14**:437–464.

Paninski, L. (2004) Maximum likelihood estimation of cascade point-process neural encoding models. *Network*, **15**:243–262.

Paninski, L. (2005) Asymptotic theory of information-theoretic experimental design. *Neural Comput.*, **17**:1480–1507.

Paninski, L., Fellows, M., Shoham, S., Hatsopoulos, N., and Donoghue, J. (2004) Superlinear population encoding of dynamic hand trajectory in primary motor cortex. *J. Neurosci.*, **24**:8551–8561.

Paninski, L., Pillow, J., and Lewi, J. (2007) Statistical models for neural encoding, decoding, and optimal stimulus design. In Cisek, P., Drew, T., and Kalaska, J., eds, *Computational Neuroscience: Theoretical Insights into Brain Function*, Progress in Brain Research, 165, pp. 493–508. Elsevier Science, Amsterdam.

Paninski, L., Ahmadian, Y., Ferreira, D. G., Koyama, S., Rad, K. R., Vidne, M., Vogelstein, J., and Wu, W. (2010) A new look at state-space models for neural data. *J. Comput. Neurosci.*, **29**(1–2):107–126.

Paninski, L., Pillow, J., and Simoncelli, E. (2005) Comparing integrate-and-fire-like models estimated using intracellular and extracellular data. *Neurocomputing*, **65**:379–385.

Papoulis, A. (1991) *Probability, Random Variables, and Stochastic Processes*. McGraw-Hill, New York.

Pare, D., Curro'Dossi, R., and Steriade, M. (1990) Neuronal basis of the parkinsonian resting tremor: A hypothesis and its implications for treatment. *Neurosci.*, **35**: 217–226.

Park, I., Seth, S., Rao, M., and Principe, J. (2012) Strictly positive-definite spike train kernels for point-process divergences. *Neural Comput.*, **24**(8):2223–2250.

Patlak, J. and Ortiz, M. (1985) Slow currents through single sodium channels of the adult rat heart. *J. Gen. Phys.*, **86**(1):89–104.

Pawlak, V. and Kerr, J. (2008) Dopamine receptor activation is required for corticostriatal spike-timing-dependent plasticity. *J. Neurosci.*, **28**:2435–2446.

Pawlak, V., Wickens, J., Kirkwood, A., and Kerr, J. (2010) Timing is not everything: neuromodulation opens the STDP gate. *Front. Synaptic Neurosci.*, **2**:146.

Perkel, D. H., Gerstein, G. L., and Moore, G. P. (1967a) Neuronal spike trains and stochastic point processes I. The single spike train. *Biophys. J.*, **7**:391–418.

Perkel, D. H., Gerstein, G. L., and Moore, G. P. (1967b) Neuronal spike trains and stochastic point processes II. Simultaneous spike trains. *Biophys. J.*, **7**:419–440.

Pfister, J.-P. and Gerstner, W. (2006) Triplets of spikes in a model of spike timing-dependent plasticity. *J. Neurosci.*, **26**:9673–9682.

Pfister, J.-P. and Tass, P. (2010) STDP in oscillatory recurrent networks: Theoretical conditions for desynchronization and applications to deep brain stimulation. *Front. Comput. Neurosci.*, **4**:22.

Pfister, J.-P., Toyoizumi, T., Barber, D., and Gerstner, W. (2006) Optimal spike-timing dependent plasticity for precise action potential firing in supervised learning. *Neural Comput.*, **18**:1318–1348.

Pikovsky, A. and Rosenblum, M. (2007) Synchronization. *Scholarpedia*, **2**:1459.

Pillow, J., Paninski, L., Uzzell, V., Simoncelli, E., and E. J. Chichilnisky (2005) Prediction and decoding of retinal ganglion cell responses with a probabilistic spiking model. *J. Neurosci.*, **25**:11003–11023.

Pillow, J., Shlens, J., Paninski, L., Sher, A., Litke, A. M., Chichilnisky, E. J., and Simoncelli, E. (2008) Spatio-temporal correlations and visual signalling in a complete neuronal population. *Nature*, **454**:995–999.

Pillow, J. W., Ahmadian, Y., and Paninski, L. (2011) Model-based decoding, information estimation, and change-point detection techniques for multineuron spike trains. *Neural Comput.*, **23**(1):1–45.

Platt, M. and Huettel, S. (2008) Risky business: the neuroeconomics of decision making under uncertainty. *Nat. Neurosci.*, **11**:398–403.

Plesser, H. (1999) *Aspects of Signal Processing in Noisy Neurons*. PhD thesis, Georg-August-Universität, Göttingen.

Plesser, H. E. (2000) The ModUhl software collection. Technical report, MPI für Strömungsforschung, Göttingen. www.chaos.gwgd.de/plesser/ModUhl.htm.

Plesser, H. E. and Gerstner, W. (2000) Noise in integrate-and-fire models: from stochastic input to escape rates. *Neural Comput.*, **12**:367–384.

Plesser, H. E. and Tanaka, S. (1997) Stochastic resonance in a model neuron with reset. *Phys. Lett. A*, **225**:228–234.

Pozzorini, C., Naud, R., Mensi, S., and Gerstner, W. (2013) Temporal whitening by power-law adaptation in neocortical neurons. *Nature Neurosci.*, **16**:942–948.

Prinz, W. (2004) Der Mensch ist nicht frei. Ein Gespräch. In Geyer, C., ed., *Hirnforschung und Willensfreiheit*. Suhrkamp, Frankfurt.

Purves, D., Augustine, G. J., Fitzpatrick, D., Hall, W. C., LaMantia, A.-S., and White, L. E. (2008) *Neuroscience*, 4th edn. Sinauer, Sunderland, MA.

Quiroga, R. Q., Kreuz, T., and Grassberger, P. (2002) Event synchronization: A simple and fast method to measure synchronicity and time delay patterns. *Phys. Rev. E*, **66**(4):041904.

Quiroga, R. Q., Reddy, L., Kreiman, G., Koch, C., and Fried, I. (2005) Invariant visual representation by single neurons in the human brain. *Nature*, **435**:1102–1107.

Rainer, G. and Miller, E. (2002) Timecourse of object-related neural activity in the primate prefrontal cortex during a short-term memory task. *Europ. J. Neurosci.*, **15**: 1244–1254.

Rajan, K. and Abbott, L. (2006) Eigenvalue spectra of random matrices for neural networks. *Phys. Rev. Lett.*, **97**:188104.

Rall, W. (1989) Cable theory for dendritic neurons. In Koch, C. and Segev, I., eds., *Methods in Neuronal Modeling*, pp. 9–62. MIT Press, Cambridge, MA.

Ramirez, A. D., Ahmadian, Y., Schumacher, J., Schneider, D., Woolley, S. M. N., and Paninski, L. (2011) Incorporating naturalistic correlation structure improves spectrogram reconstruction from neuronal activity in the songbird auditory midbrain. *J. Neurosci.*, **31**(10):3828–3842.

Ramòn y Cajal, S. (1909) *Histologie du système nerveux de l'homme et des vertébré*. A. Maloine, Paris.

Randall, A. D. and Tsien, R. W. (1997) Contrasting biophysical and pharmacological properties of T-type and R-type calcium channels. *Neuropharmacology*, **36**(7):879–93.

Rangel, A., Camerer, C., and Montague, P. (2008) A framework for studying the neurobiology of value-based decision making. *Nat. Rev. Neurosci.*, **9**:545–556.

Ranjan, R., Khazen, G., Gambazzi, L., Ramaswamy, S., Hill, S. L., Schürmann, F., and Markram, H. (2011) Channelpedia: an integrative and interactive database for ion channels. *Front. Neuroinform.*, **5**:36.

Rapp, M., Yarom, Y., and Segev, I. (1994) Physiology, morphology and detailed passive models of guinea-pig cerebellar Purkinje cells. *J. Physiol.*, **474**:101–118.

Ratcliff, R. and McKoon, G. (2008) The diffusion decision model: theory and data for two-choice decision tasks. *Neural Comput.*, **20**:873–922.

Ratcliff, R. and Rouder, J. (1998) Modeling response times for two-choice decisions. *Psychol. Sci.*, **9**:347–356.

Ratnam, R. and Nelson, M. (2000) Nonrenewal statistics of electrosensory afferent spike trains: Implications for the detection of weak sensory signals. *J. Neurosci*, **10**: 6672–6683.

Redish, A., Elga, A., and Touretzky, D. (1996) A coupled attractor model of the rodent head direction system. *Network*, **7**:671–685.

Reich, D., Victor, J., and Knight, B. (1998) The power ratio and the interval map: spiking models and extracellular recordings. *J. Neurosci.*, **18**(23):10090–10104.

Renart, A., de la Rocha, J., Hollender, L., Parta, N., Reyes, A., and Harris, K. (2010) The asynchronous state in cortical circuits. *Science*, **327**:587–590.

Rettig, J., Wunder, F., Stocker, M., *et al.* (1992) Characterization of a shaw-related potassium channel family in rat brain. *EMBO J*, **11**(7):2473–86.

Reuveni, I., Friedman, A., Amitai, Y., and Gutnick, M. (1993) Stepwise repolarization from Ca^{2+} plateaus in neocortical pyramidal cells: evidence for nonhomogeneous distribution of HVA Ca^{2+} channels in dendrites. *J. Neurosci.*, **13**(11):4609–4621.

Reynolds, J. and Wickens, J. (2002) Dopamine-dependent plasticity of corticostriatal synapses. *Neural Networks*, **15**:507–521.

Ricciardi, L. (1976) Diffusion approximation for a multi-input neuron model. *Biol. Cybern.*, **24**:237–240.

Richardson, M. (2004) The effects of synaptic conductance on the voltage distribution and firing rate of spiking neurons. *Phys. Rev. E*, **69**:51918.

Richardson, M. (2007) Firing-rate response of linear and nonlinear integrate-and-fire neurons to modulated current-based and conductance-based synaptic drive. *Phys. Rev. E*, **76**:021919.

Richardson, M. (2009) Dynamics of populations and networks of neurons with voltage-activated and calcium-activated currents. *Phys. Rev. E*, **80**:021928.

Richardson, M. and Gerstner, W. (2005) Synaptic shot noise and conductance fluctuations affect the membrane voltage with equal significance. *Neural Comput.*, **17**:923–947.

Richardson, M., Brunel, N., and Hakim, V. (2003) From subthreshold to firing-rate resonance. *J. Neurophysiol.*, **89**(5):2538–2554.

Rieke, F., Warland, D., de Ruyter van Steveninck, R., and Bialek, W. (1997) *Spikes: Exploring the Neural Code*. MIT Press, Cambridge, MA.

Rinzel, J. (1985) Excitation dynamics: insights from simplified membrane models. *Theor. Trends Neurosci.*, **44**(15):2944–2946.

Rinzel, J. and Ermentrout, G. B. (1998) Analysis of neural excitability and oscillations. In Koch, C. and Segev, I., eds, *Methods in Neuronal Modeling*, 2nd edn, pp. 251–291. MIT Press, Cambridge, MA.

Risken, H. (1984) *The Fokker Planck Equation: Methods of Solution and Applications*. Springer-Verlag, Berlin.

Ritz, R. and Sejnowski, T. (1997) Synchronous oscillatory activity in sensory systems: new vistas on mechanisms. *Current Opinion Neurobiol.*, **7**:536–546.

Roberts, P. and Bell, C. (2000) Computational consequences of temporally asymmetric learning rules: II. Sensory image cancellation. *Comput. Neurosci.*, **9**:67–83.

Roitman, J. and Shadlen, M. (2002) Response of neurons in the lateral intraparietal area during a combined visual discrimination reaction time task. *J. Neurosci.*, **22**: 9475–9489.

Romo, R. and Salinas, E. (2003) Flutter discrimination: neural codes, perception, memory and decision making. *Nat. Rev. Neurosci.*, **4**:203–218.

Rosin, B., Slovik, M., Mitelman, R., *et al.* (2011) Closed-loop deep brain stimulation is superior in ameliorating parkinsonism. *Neuron*, **72**:370–384.

Rospars, J. P. and Lansky, P. (1993) Stochastic model neuron without resetting of dendritic potential: application to the olfactory system. *Biol. Cybern.*, **69**:283–294.

Roxin, A. and Ledberg, A. (2008) Neurobiological models of two-choice decision making can be reduced to a one-dimensional nonlinear diffusion equation. *PLOS Comput. Biol.*, **4**:e1000046.

Rubin, J., Lee, D. D., and Sompolinsky, H. (2001) Equilibrium properties of temporally asymmetric Hebbian plasticity. *Phys. Rev. Lett.*, **86**:364–367.

Rubin, J. and Terman, D. (2004) High frequency stimulation of the subthalamic nucleus eliminates pathological thalamic rhythmicity in a computational model. *J. Comput. Neurosci.*, **16**:211–235.

Rust, N., Mante, V., Simoncelli, E., and Movshon, J. (2006) How MT cells analyze the motion of visual patterns. *Nature Neurosci.*, **11**:1421–1431.

Sabah, N. H. and Leibovic, K. N. (1969) Subthreshold oscillatory responses of the Hodgkin-Huxley cable model for the squid giant axon. *Biophys. J.*, **9**(10):1206–1222.

Sahani, M. and Linden, J. (2003) Evidence optimization techniques for estimating stimulus-response functions. In *Advances in Neural Information Processing Systems* 15, pp. 301–308. MIT Press, Cambridge, MA.

Sakata, S. and Harris, K. (2009) Laminar structure of spontaneous and sensory-evoked population activity in auditory cortex. *Neuron*, **64**:298–300.

Salzman, C., Britten, K., and Newsome, W. (1990) Cortical microstimulation influences perceptual judgements of motion directions. *Nature*, **346**:174–177.

Sanfey, A. and Chang, L. (2008) Multiple systems in decision making. *Ann. NY. Acad. Sci*, **1128**:53–62.

Schneidman, E., Freedman, B., and Segev, I. (1998) Ion channel stochasticity may be critical in determining the reliability and precision of spike timing. *Neural Comput.*, **10**:1679–1703.

Schrauwen, B. and Campenhout, J. (2007) Linking non-binned spike train kernels to several existing spike train metrics. *Neurocomputing*, **70**(7-9):1247–1253.

Schreiber, S., Fellous, J., Whitmer, D., Tiesinga, P., and Sejnowski, T. J. (2003) A new correlation-based measure of spike timing reliability. *Neurocomputing*, **52**(54): 925–931.

Schrödinger, E. (1915) Zur Theorie der Fall- und Steigversuche and Teilchen mit Brownscher Bewegung. *Phys. Zeitschrift*, **16**:289–295.

Schultz, W. (2007) Behavioral dopamine signals. *Trends Neurosci.*, **30**(5):203–210.

Schultz, W. (2010) Dopamine signals for reward value and risk: basic and recent data. *Behav. Brain Funct.*, **6**:24.

Schultz, W., Dayan, P., and Montague, R. (1997) A neural substrate for prediction and reward. *Science*, **275**:1593–1599.

Schwalger, T., Fisch, K., Benda, J., and Lindner, B. (2010) How noisy adaptation in neurons shapes interspike interval histograms and correlations. *PLOS Comput. Biol.*, **6**:e1001026.

Segev, I., Rinzel, J., and Shepherd, G. M. (1994) *The Theoretical Foundation of Dendritic Function*. MIT Press, Cambridge, MA.

Sejnowski, T. (1977) Storing covariance with nonlinearly interacting neurons. *J. Math. Biol.*, **4**:303–321.

Sejnowski, T. J. (1999) The book of Hebb. *Neuron*, **24**:773–776.

Sejnowski, T. J. and Tesauro, G. (1989) The Hebb rule for synaptic plasticity: algorithms and implementations. In Byrne, J. H. and Berry, W. O., eds., *Neural Models of Plasticity*, Ch. 6, pp. 94–103. Academic Press, Salt Lake City, UT.

Senn, W. (2002) Beyond spike timing: the role of non-linear plasticity and unreliable synapses. *Biol. Cyber.*, **87**:344–355.

Senn, W., Tsodyks, M., and Markram, H. (2001) An algorithm for modifying neurotransmitter release probability based on pre- and postsynaptic spike timing. *Neural Comput.*, **13**:35–67.

Shadlen, M. N. and Newsome, W. T. (1994) Noise, neural codes and cortical organization. *Current Opinion Neurobiol.*, **4**:569–579.

Shatz, C. (1992) The developing brain. *Sci. Am.*, **267**:60–67.

Shenoy, K., Kaufman, M., Sahani, M., and Churchland, M. (2011) A dynamical systems view of motor preparation: implications for neural prosthetic system design. *Progr. Brain Res.*, **192**:33–58.

Shoham, S. (2001) Advances towards an implantable motor cortical interface. PhD thesis, University of Utah.

Shriki, O., Hansel, D., and Sompolinsky, H. (2003) Rate models for conductance-based cortical neuronal networks. *Neural Comput.*, **15**:1809–1841.

Siebert, W. M. and Gray, P. R. (1963) Random process model for the firing pattern of single auditory nerve fibers. Quarterly Progress Report No. 71, Research Laboratory of Electronics, MIT, pp. 241–245.

Siegert, A. (1951) On the first passage time probability problem. *Phys. Rev.*, **81**:617–623.

Silberberg, G., Bethge, M., Markram, H., Pawelzik, K., and Tsodyks, M. (2004) Dynamics of population rate codes in ensembles of neocortical neurons. *J. Neurophysiol.*, **91**:704–709.

Simoncelli, E., Paninski, L., Pillow, J., and Schwarz, O. (2004) Characterization of neural responses with stochastic stimuli. In Gazzaninga, M., ed., *The Cognitive Neurosciences*, 3rd edn. MIT Press, Cambridge, MA.

Singer, W. (1993) Synchronization of cortical activity and its putative role in information processing and learning. *Ann. Rev. Physiol.*, **55**:349–374.

Singer, W. (2007) Binding by synchrony. *Scholarpedia*, **2**:1657.

Sirovich, L. and Knight, B. W. (1977) On subthreshold solutions of the Hodgkin-Huxley equations. *Proc. Nat. Acad. Sci.*, **74**(12):5199–5202.

Sjöström, J. and Gerstner, W. (2010) Spike-timing dependent plasticity. *Scholarpedia*, **5**:1362.

Sjöström, P., Turrigiano, G., and Nelson, S. (2001) Rate, timing, and cooperativity jointly determine cortical synaptic plasticity. *Neuron*, **32**:1149–1164.

Smith, A. and Brown, E. (2003) Estimating a state-space model from point process observations. *Neural Comput.*, **15**:965–991.

Smyth, D., Willmore, B., Baker, G. E., Thompson, I. D., and Tolhurst, D. J. (2003) The receptive-field organization of simple cells in primary visual cortex of ferrets under natural scene stimulation. *J. Neurosci.*, **23**(11):4746–4759.

Softky, W. R. (1995) Simple codes versus efficient codes. *Current Opinion Neurobiol.*, **5**:239–247.

Softky, W. R. and Koch C. (1993) The highly irregular firing pattern of cortical cells is inconsistent with temporal integration of random EPSPs. *J. Neurosci.*, **13**:334–350.

Sompolinsky, H. and Kanter, I. (1986) Temporal association in asymmetric neural networks. *Phys. Rev. Lett.*, **57**:2861–2864.

Sompolinksy, H., Crisanti, A., and Sommers, H. (1988) Chaos in random neural networks. *Phys. Rev. Lett.*, **61**:259–262.

Song, S., Miller, K., and Abbott, L. (2000) Competitive Hebbian learning through spike-time-dependent synaptic plasticity. *Nature Neurosci.*, **3**:919–926.

Soon, C., Brass, M., Heinze, H., and Haynes, J. (2008) Unconscious determinants of free decisions in the human brain. *Nat. Neurosci.*, **11**:543–545.

Spiridon, M. and Gerstner, W. (2001) Effect of lateral connections on the accuracy of the population code for a network of spiking neurons. *Network*, **12**(4):409–421.

Spiridon, M., Chow, C., and Gerstner, W. (1998) Frequency spectrum of coupled stochastic neurons with refractoriness. In Niklasson, L., Bodén, M., and Ziemke, T., eds, *ICANN 98*, pp. 337–342. Springer, Berlin.

Srinivasan, L. and Brown, E. N. (2007) A state-space framework for movement control to dynamic goals through brain-driven interfaces. *IEEE Trans. Biomed. Engng.*, **54**(3):526–535.

Stein, R. B. (1965) A theoretical analysis of neuronal variability. *Biophys. J.*, **5**:173–194.

Stein, R. B. (1967a) The information capacity of nerve cells using a frequency code. *Biophys. J.*, **7**:797–826.

Stein, R. B. (1967b) Some models of neuronal variability. *Biophys. J.*, **7**:37–68.

Steinmetz, P. N., Roy, A., Fitzgerald, P. J., Hsiao, S. S., Johnson, K., and Niebur, E. (2000) Attention modulates synchronized neuronal firing in primate somatosensory cortex. *Nature*, **404**:187–190.

Stevens, C. F. and Zador, A. M. (1998) Novel integrate-and-fire like model of repetitive firing in cortical neurons. In *Proceedings of the 5th Joint Symposium on Neural Computation*. Available at: http://cnl.salk.edu/zador/PDF/increpfire.pdf.

Strogatz, S. H. (1994) *Nonlinear Dynamical Systems and Chaos*. Addison Wesley, Reading, MA.

Stroop, J. (1935) Studies of interference in serial verbal reactions. *J. Exp. Psychol.*, **18**:643–662.

Stuart, G., Spruston, N., and Häusser, M. (2007) *Dendrites*, 2nd edn. Oxford University Press, Oxford.

Sussillo, D. and Abbott, L. (2009) Generating coherent patterns of activity from chaotic neural networks. *Neuron*, **63**: 544–447.

Sussillo, D. and Barak, O. (2013) Opening the black box: Low-dimensional dynamics in high-dimensional recurrent neural networks. *Neural Comput.*, **25**:626–649.

Tass, P. (2003) A model of desynchronizing deep brain stimulation with a demand-controlled coordinated reset of neural subpopulations. *Biol. Cybern.*, **89**:81–88.

Tass, P., Adamchic, I., Freund, H.-J., von Stackelberg, T., and Hauptmann, C. (2012a) Counteracting tinnitus by acoustic coordinated reset neuromodulation. *Restor. Neurol. Neurosci,*, **30**:137–159.

Tass, P., Qin, L., *et al.* (2012b) Coordinated reset has sustained aftereffects in parkinsonian monkeys. *Ann. Neurol.*, **72**:816–820.

Tass, P., Smirnov, D., *et al.* (2010) The causal relationship between subcortical local field potential oscillations and parkinsonian resting tremor. *J. Neur. Eng.*, **7**:016009.

Taube, J. S. and Muller, R. U. (1998) Comparisons of head direction cell activity in the postsubiculum and anterior thalamus of freely moving rats. *Hippocampus*, **8**:87–108.

Tchumatchenko, T., Malyshev, A., Wolf, F., and Volgushev, M. (2011) Ultrafast population encoding by cortical neurons. *J. Neurosci.*, **31**:12171–12179.

Theunissen, F. and Miller, J. (1995) Temporal encoding in nervous systems: a rigorous definition. *J. Comput. Neurosci,*, **2**:149–162.

Thompson, R. F. (1993) *The Brain*, 2nd edn. W. H. Freeman, New York.

Thorpe, S., Fize, D., and Marlot, C. (1996) Speed of processing in the human visual system. *Nature*, **381**:520–522.

Tiesinga, P. H. E. (2004) Chaos-induced modulation of reliability boosts output firing rate in downstream cortical areas. *Phys. Rev. E*, **69**(3 Pt 1):031912.

Toledo-Rodriguez, M., Blumenfeld, B., Wu, C., Luo, J., Attali, B., Goodman, P., and Markram, H. (2004) Correlation maps allow neuronal electrical properties to be predicted from single-cell gene expression profiles in rat neocortex. *Cerebral Cortex*, **14**:1310–1327.

Touboul, J. (2009) Importance of the cutoff value in the quadratic adaptive integrate-and-fire model. *Neural Comput.*, **21**:2114–2122.

Touboul, J. and Brette, R. (2008) Dynamics and bifurcations of the adaptive exponential integrate-and-fire model. *Biol. Cybernetics*, **99**:319–334.

Tovee, M. J. and Rolls, E. T. (1995) Information encoding in short firing rate epochs by single neurons in the primate temporal visual cortex. *Visual Cogn.*, **2**(1):35–58.

Traub, R. (2006) Fast oscillations. *Scholarpedia*, **1**:1764.

Treves, A. (1993) Mean-field analysis of neuronal spike dynamics. *Network*, **4**:259–284.

Troyer, T. W. and Miller, K. (1997) Physiological gain leads to high ISI variability in a simple model of a cortical regular spiking cell. *Neural Comput.*, **9**:971–983.

Truccolo, W., Eden, U. T., Fellows, M. R., Donoghue, J. P., and Brown, E. N. (2005) A point process framework for relating neural spiking activity to spiking history, neural ensemble, and extrinsic covariate effects. *J. Neurophysiol.*, **93**(2):1074–1089.

Tsodyks, M. and Feigelman, M. (1986) The enhanced storage capacity in neural networks with low activity level. *Europhys. Lett.*, **6**:101–105.

Tsodyks, M., Mitkov, I., and Sompolinsky, H. (1993) Patterns of synchrony in inhomogeneous networks of oscillators with pulse interaction. *Phys. Rev. Lett.*, **71**:1281–1283.

Tsodyks, M., Skaggs, W., Sejnowski, T., and McNaughton, B. (1997) Paradoxical effects of external modulation of inhibitory interneurons. *J. Neurosci.*, **17**:4382–4388.

Tuckwell, H. C. (1988) *Introduction to Theoretic Neurobiology*. Cambridge University Press, Cambridge.

Tuckwell, H. C. (1989) *Stochastic Processes in the Neurosciences*. SIAM, Philadelphia, PA.

Uhlenbeck, G. E. and Ornstein, L. S. (1930) On the theory of the Brownian motion. *Phys. Rev*, **36**:823–841.

Uzzell, V. and Chichilnisky, E. (2004) Precision of spike trains in primate retinal ganglion cells. *J. Neurophysiol.*, **92**:780–789.

van Kampen, N. G. (1992) *Stochastic Processes in Physics and Chemistry*, 2nd edn. North-Holland, Amsterdam.

van Rossum, M. C. W. (2001) A novel spike distance. *Neural Comput.*, **13**:751–763.

van Rossum, M. C. W., Bi, G. Q., and Turrigiano, G. G. (2000) Stable Hebbian learning from spike timing-dependent plasticity. *J. Neurosci.*, **20**:8812–8821.

van Vreeswijk, C. and Sompolinsky, H. (1996) Chaos in neuronal networks with balanced excitatory and inhibitory activity. *Science*, **274**:1724–1726.

van Vreeswijk, C. and Sompolinsky, H. (1998) Chaotic balanced state in a model of cortical circuits. *Neural Comput.*, **10**:1321–1371.

Victor, J. D. and Purpura, K. (1996) Nature and precision of temporal coding in visual cortex: a metric-space analysis. *J. Neurophysiol.*, **76**(2):1310–1326.

Victor, J. and Purpura, K. (1997) Metric-space analysis of spike trains: theory, algorithms and application. *Network*, **8**:127–164.

Vidne, M., Ahmadian, Y., Shlens, J. *et al.* (2012) Modeling the impact of common noise inputs on the network activity of retinal ganglion cells. *J. Comput. Neurosci.*, **33**(1):97–121.

Vogels, T. P. and Abbott, L. (2005) Signal propagation and logic gating in networks of integrate-and-fire neurons. *J. Neurosci.*, **25**:10786–10795.

Vogels, T. P. and Abbott, L. (2009) Gating multiple signals through detailed balance of excitation and inhibition in spiking networks. *Nature Neurosci.*, **12**:438–491.

Vogels, T., Sprekeler, H., Zenke, F., Clopath, C., and Gerstner, W. (2011) Inhibitory plasticity balances excitation and inhibition in sensory pathways and memory networks. *Science*, **334**:1569–1573.

von der Malsburg, C. (1973) Self-organization of orientation selective cells in the striate cortex. *Kybernetik*, **14**:85–100.

von der Malsburg, C. (1981) The correlation theory of brain function. Internal Report 81-2, MPI für Biophysikalische Chemie, Göttingen. Reprinted in *Models of Neural Networks II*, Domany *et al.* (eds.), Springer, Berlin, 1994, pp. 95–119.

Wang, H.-X., Gerkin, R., Nauen, D., and Wang, G.-Q. (2005) Coactivation and timing-dependent integration of synaptic potentiation and depression. *Nature Neurosci.*, **8**:187–193.

Wang, X.-J. (2002) Probabilistic decision making by slow reverberation in cortical circuits. *Neuron*, **36**:955–968.

Wang, Y., Gupta, A., Toledo-Rodriguez, M., Wu, C., and Markram, H. (2002) Anatomical, physiological, molecular and circuit properties of nest basket cells in the developing somatosensory cortex. *Cerebral Cortex*, **12**:395–410.

Waxman, S. G. (1980) Determinants of conduction velocity in myelinated nerve fibers. *Musc. Nerve*, **3**(2):141–150.

Wehmeier, U., Dong, D., Koch, C., and van Essen, D. (1989) Modeling the mammalian visual system. In Segev, I., ed., *Methods in Neuronal Modeling*, pp. 335–359. MIT Press, Cambridge, MA.

Weiss, T. (1966) A model of the peripheral auditory system. *Kybernetik*, **3**:153–175.

Welsh, J., Lang, E., and Llinas, I. S. (1995) Dynamic organization of motor control within the olivocerebellar system. *Nature*, **374**:453–457.

Willshaw, D. J., Bunemann, O. P., and Longuet-Higgins, H. C. (1969) Non-holographic associative memory. *Nature*, **222**:960–962.

Willshaw, D. J. and von der Malsburg, C. (1976) How patterned neuronal connections can be set up by self-organization. *Proc. R. Soc. Lond. B*, **194**:431–445.

Wilson, C., Beverlin, B., and Netoff, T. (2011) Chaotic desynchronization as the therapeutic mechanism of deep brain stimulation. *Front. Syst. Neurosci.*, **5**:50.

Wilson, H. R. and Cowan, J. D. (1972) Excitatory and inhibitory interactions in localized populations of model neurons. *Biophys. J.*, **12**:1–24.

Wilson, H. R. and Cowan, J. D. (1973) A mathematical theory of the functional dynamics of cortical and thalamic nervous tissue. *Kybernetik*, **13**:55–80.

Wilson, M. A. and McNaughton, B. L. (1993) Dynamics of the hippocampal ensemble code for space. *Science*, **261**:1055–1058.

Winfree, A. T. (1980) *The Geometry of Biological Time*. Springer-Verlag, Berlin.

Wiskott, L. and Sejnowski, T. (1998) Constraint optimization for neural map formation: a unifying framework for weight growth and normalization. *Neural Comput.*, **10**: 671–716.

Wolff, L. and Lindner, B. (2011) Mean, variance, and autocorrelation of subthreshold potential fluctuations driven by filtered conductance shot noise. *Neural Comput.*, **22**:94–120.

Wong, K. and Wang, X. (2006) A recurrent network mechanism of time integration in perceptual decisions. *J. Neurosci.*, **26**:1314–1328.

Woosley, T. A. and Van der Loos, H. (1970) The structural organization of layer IV in the somatosensory region (SI) of mouse cerebral cortex: The description of a cortical field composed of discrete cytoarchitectonic units. *Brain Res.*, **17**:205–242.

Wu, M., David, S., and Gallant, J. (2006) Complete functional characterization of sensory neurons by system identification. *Ann. Rev. Neurosci.*, **29**(1):477–505.

Wu, W. and Srivastava, A. (2012) Estimating summary statistics in the spike-train space. *J. Comput. Neurosci.*, **34**(3):391–410.

Yamada, W. M., Koch, C., and Adams, P. R. (1989) Multiple channels and calcium dynamics. In Koch, C. and Segev, I., eds, *Methods in Neuronal Modeling*. MIT Press, Cambridge, MA.

Yu, B. M., Cunningham, J. P., Santhanam, G., Ryu, S. I., Shenoy, K. V., and Sahani, M. (2009) Gaussian-process factor analysis for low-dimensional single-trial analysis of neural population activity. *J. Neurophysiol.*, **102**:614–635.

Zeldovich, Y. B. and Frank-Kamenetskii, D. (1938) Thermal theory of flame propagation. *Zh. Fiz. Khim*, **12**(1):100–105.

Zhang, J.-C., Lau, P.-M., and Bi, G.-Q. (2009) Gain in sensitivity and loss in temporal contrast of STDP by dopaminergic modulation at hippocampal synapses. *Proc. Natl. Acad. Sci. USA*, **106**:13–28–13033.

Zhang, K. (1996) Representaton of spatial orientation by the intrinsic dynamics of the head-direction ensemble: a theory. *J. Neurosci.*, **16**:2112–2126.

Zhang, L., Tao, H., Holt, C., W. A. Harris, and Poo, M.-M. (1998) A critical window for cooperation and competition among developing retinotectal synapses. *Nature*, **395**:37–44.

Zugaro, M., Arleo, A., Berthoz, A., and Wiener, S. I. (2003) Rapid spatial reorientation and head direction cells. *J. Neurosci.*, **23**(8):3478–3482.

Index

Printed in the United States
By Bookmasters